Comparative Blended Learning Practices and Environments

Eugenia M. W. Ng
Hong Kong Institute of Education, Hong Kong

Information Science REFERENCE
INFORMATION SCIENCE REFERENCE
Hershey · New York

Director of Editorial Content:	Kristin Klinger
Senior Managing Editor:	Jamie Snavely
Assistant Managing Editor:	Michael Brehm
Publishing Assistant:	Sean Woznicki
Typesetter:	Michael Brehm, Kurt Smith
Cover Design:	Lisa Tosheff
Printed at:	Yurchak Printing Inc.

Published in the United States of America by
Information Science Reference (an imprint of IGI Global)
701 E. Chocolate Avenue
Hershey PA 17033
Tel: 717-533-8845
Fax: 717-533-8661
E-mail: cust@igi-global.com
Web site: http://www.igi-global.com/reference

Library of Congress Cataloging-in-Publication Data

Comparative blended learning practices and environments / Eugenia M.W. Ng, editor.
p. cm.
Includes bibliographical references and index.
Summary: "This book offers in-depth analysis of new technologies in blended learning that promote creativity, critical thinking, and meaningful learning"--Provided by publisher.
ISBN 978-1-60566-852-9 (hardcover) -- ISBN 978-1-60566-853-6 (ebook) 1. Blended learning--Cross-cultural studies. 2. Educational technology--Cross-cultural studies. 3. Comparative education. I. Ng, Eugenia M. W., 1959-
LB1028.5.C5274 2010
371.3--dc22

2009035427

British Cataloguing in Publication Data
A Cataloguing in Publication record for this book is available from the British Library.

Table of Contents

Foreword ... xvii

Preface ... xix

Acknowledgment ... xxv

Section 1
Blended Learning Environments

Chapter 1
Beyond Control: Will Blended Learning Subvert National Curricula? ... 1
Peter Williams, University of Hull, UK

Chapter 2
Perspectives on Blended Open Distance Education Learning and Teaching in a South African Context ... 20
Shawren Singh, University of South Africa, South Africa
Hsuan Lorraine Liang, University of South Africa, South Africa

Chapter 3
Enhancing Student Learning through Blending Varied Learning and Assessment Experiences ... 50
Paula Hodgson, University of Hong Kong, Hong Kong

Chapter 4
Implementing and Promoting Blended Learning in Higher Education Institutions: Comparing Different Approaches ... 70
Lixun Wang, The Hong Kong Institute of Education, Hong Kong

Section 2
Blended Learning Practices

Chapter 5
Student Profile and Its Effects on Online and Hybrid Courses 89
Seta Boghikian-Whitby, University of La Verne, California, USA
Yehia Mortagy, University of La Verne, California, USA

Chapter 6
Using Action Research to Assess Student Performance in Traditional vs. E-Learning Formats 112
Retta Guy, Tennessee State University, USA
Craig Wishart, Fayetteville State University, USA

Chapter 7
Examining Individual Students' Perceptions of Curiosity Utilizing a Blend of Online
and Face-to-Face Discussions: A Case Study 125
Ronnie H. Shroff, The Hong Kong Institute of Education, Hong Kong

Chapter 8
Online Discussion and E-Mentoring Strategies in Blended Continuing Education Courses 146
Lung-Hsiang Wong, National Institute of Education, Singapore
Chee-Kit Looi, National Institute of Education, Singapore

Chapter 9
A Case Study of Infusing Web 2.0 Tools for Blended Learning: Virtual Presentations
as an Alternative Means of Assessment 170
Yiu Chi Lai, The Hong Kong Institute of Education, Hong Kong
Eugenia M. W. Ng, The Hong Kong Institute of Education, Hong Kong

Chapter 10
Reflective Practice, Professional Learning, and Educational Partnerships:
Effecting Change in Classroom Settings 188
Chris Brook, Curtin University of Technology, Australia
Graeme Lock, Edith Cowan University, Australia

Chapter 11
Allegheny Women's Biotechnology Workforce Collaborative: Investing
in Disadvantaged Populations with Technology 204
Michelle Zuckerman-Parker, Allegheny-Singer Research Institute, USA
Christine Compliment, Allegheny-Singer Research Institute, USA
Megan Rodella, Allegheny-Singer Research Institute, USA
Garth Ehrlich, Allegheny-Singer Research Institute, USA
J. Christopher Post, Allegheny-Singer Research Institute, USA
Allysen Todd, Community College of Allegheny County, USA
James Schreiber, Duquesne University, USA

Chapter 12
Blending Classroom Activities with Multi-User Virtual Environment for At-Risk Primary School Students in an After-School Program: A Case Study 231
Lee Yong Tay, Beacon Primary School, Singapore
Cher Ping Lim, Edith Cowan University, Australia

Chapter 13
Comparing Face-to-Face with Blended Learning in the Context of Foreign Language Education 250
Kosmas Vlachos, Hellenic Open University, Greece

Section 3
Cultural Differences Studies

Chapter 14
When Cultures Meet in Blended Learning: What Literature Tells Us 278
Chun Hu, University of Sydney, Australia

Chapter 15
Online Literacy among Students and Faculty: A Comparative Study between the United States and Eastern European Countries 301
Plamen Miltenoff, St. Cloud State University, USA
John H. Hoover, St. Cloud State University, USA
Galin Tzokov, Paisii Khilendarski University, Bulgaria

Chapter 16
The Efficacy of Security Awareness Programs from a Cross-Cultural Perspective 323
B. Dawn Medlin, Appalachian State University, USA
Charlie C. Chen, Appalachian State University, USA

Section 4
Cross-Disciplinary Studies

Chapter 17
Cross Disciplinary Learning in Distance Higher Education: Empowerment for Sustainable Research Prowess among Professionals in the African Sub-Region 345
Jonathan O. Osiki, National University of Lesotho, Southern Africa

Chapter 18
Comparing IT and Non-IT Faculty and Students' Perceptions on Blended Learning 365
Eugenia M. W. Ng, Hong Kong Institute of Education, Hong Kong

Compilation of References 389

About the Contributors 425

Index 433

Detailed Table of Contents

Foreword xvii

Preface xix

Acknowledgment xxv

Section 1
Blended Learning Environments

Commercial, or tailored made learning management systems, are widely used as a learning portal to allow students to learn at anytime and anyplace, as long as they have access to an Internet connection. This section contains different issues and examples related to using different learning environments to enhance blended learning.

Chapter 1
Beyond Control: Will Blended Learning Subvert National Curricula? 1
Peter Williams, University of Hull, UK

Williams discusses blended learning by examining key issues of educational policy and the creation and implementation of policy at national levels. The nature and significance of Web 2.0 applications and open educational resources are also discussed with examples to illustrate the growing gap between traditional educational systems and the current digital cultures. Whether cultural threats can be turned to advantage depends crucially upon how national policies are formulated and how they are implemented at all levels.

Chapter 2
Perspectives on Blended Open Distance Education Learning and Teaching in a South African Context 20
Shawren Singh, University of South Africa, South Africa
Hsuan Lorraine Liang, University of South Africa, South Africa

Singh and Liang present a micro-comparison of two different learning platforms, which facilitate open and distance learning at the University of South Africa. The authors had described myUnisa, the self-created learning platform, and Osprey, which is the custom-made Web site at the School of Computing at the University of South Africa. They also discussed the future trends of the use of blended approaches in the context of open distance education and learning, which is informative for those who would like to adopt e-learning in developing countries.

Chapter 3
Enhancing Student Learning through Blending Varied Learning
and Assessment Experiences.. 50
Paula Hodgson, University of Hong Kong, Hong Kong

Hodgson gives a very good review and comparison between traditional learning, teaching, and assessment vs. online methods, which gives readers a good understanding of blended learning. Theories and good practices were shown clearly so that readers can select appropriate approaches for their undergraduate students. In particular, e-portfolio systems are neither well adopted nor documented, but the collected students' competences should be able to portray a comprehensive university experience.

Chapter 4
Implementing and Promoting Blended Learning in Higher Education Institutions:
Comparing Different Approaches 70
Lixun Wang, The Hong Kong Institute of Education, Hong Kong

Wang compares various forms and expressions of blended learning adopted by different parts of the world. The limitations of commercial LMS were discussed and the constraints lead to his discussion on subject-specific Web sites to supplement a commercial LMS to facilitate blended learning. How and what to use Wikibook projects to foster academic reading and writing in English for non-English native speakers were described in greater detail. Student teachers worked in groups to write an academic textbook collaboratively online and evidence showed that these projects were highly effective and the wiki technology also made peer editing much more efficient and effective.

Section 2
Blended Learning Practices

There are numerous face-to-face learning and teaching methods and technology is only one of the factors that affect blended learning. From the different practices illustrated in this book (Chapter 7 to 13), I argue that pedagogy is the most important variables for quality blended learning, even though findings from Chapter 6 illustrate that the grades that students scored had no relationship to pedagogy. Perhaps the authors had not fully designed and created appropriate digital materials nor took full use of different features of learning platforms.

Chapter 5
Student Profile and Its Effects on Online and Hybrid Courses.. 89
Seta Boghikian-Whitby, University of La Verne, California, USA
Yehia Mortagy, University of La Verne, California, USA

Boghikian-Whitby and Mortagy took the effort to analyze the profile of students who were enrolled in a face-to-face and an online course of management information systems over 15 semesters at an American university. It was found that most online students were adult students who were of African American and Hispanic descent. Forty percent of the students enrolled in online delivery modality were of extravert type. It was recommended that short modules and using different exercises would be able to accommodate various learning styles.

Chapter 6
Using Action Research to Assess Student Performance in Traditional vs. E-Learning Formats........ 112
Retta Guy, Tennessee State University, USA
Craig Wishart, Fayetteville State University, USA

Action research is commonly used by many academics to reflect and to refine their teaching approaches. Guy and Wishart adopted different teaching approaches to students who took online courses in the United States who were mainly blacks. They changed the teaching strategy for e-learning class from student-centered to instructor-centered to even more instructor-centered for the three years. Students' grades of face-to-face and online courses were compared, but it was found that neither the strategy nor the delivery method had any impact on student performances.

Chapter 7
Examining Individual Students' Perceptions of Curiosity Utilizing a Blend of Online and Face-to-Face Discussions: A Case Study 125
Ronnie H. Shroff, The Hong Kong Institute of Education, Hong Kong

Shroff created a blended learning platform that allowed students to interact and collaborate in both online and face-to-face settings. Data were obtained through in-depth, semi-structured interviews with information systems undergraduate students. The interviewees appeared to derive pleasure from the online discussions, which also provided them with a level of surprise, conflicting discrepancy, and novelty. Results from the qualitative study showed that individuals' perceptions of curiosity were strongly supported.

Chapter 8
Online Discussion and E-Mentoring Strategies in Blended Continuing Education Courses 146
Lung-Hsiang Wong, National Institute of Education, Singapore
Chee-Kit Looi, National Institute of Education, Singapore

Wang and Looi analysed online discussions in a course portal that supplemented class discussion in three continuing master education courses in Singapore. The courses combined face-to-face and online approaches to instruction. Henri's model was adopted to quantitatively and qualitatively analyse the online discussion. This chapter emphasizes the role of the e-mentors in promoting and mediating the discussions. Transcript content analyses showed that students' messages were on-task, thoughtful, and indicative of student-initiated learning and a good amount of peer help.

Chapter 9
A Case Study of Infusing Web 2.0 Tools for Blended Learning: Virtual Presentations as an Alternative Means of Assessment 170
Yiu Chi Lai, The Hong Kong Institute of Education, Hong Kong
Eugenia M. W. Ng, The Hong Kong Institute of Education, Hong Kong

Lai and Ng describe an innovative practice of infusing Web 2.0 in assessment in Hong Kong. The participants were two groups of student teachers who created virtual presentations, which could either be videos or other digital formats for each group to learn from each other. Quantitative and qualitative data were collected, analyzed, and compared. It was found that most of the participants were positive about this new presentation approach and ready to accept it as a part in assessments but they gave more feedback to their class rather than the other class.

Chapter 10
Reflective Practice, Professional Learning, and Educational Partnerships: Effecting Change in Classroom Settings 188
Chris Brook, Curtin University of Technology, Australia
Graeme Lock, Edith Cowan University, Australia

Brook and Lock presented a model of professional learning that incorporated blended learning, reflective practice, performance management processes, authentic experiences, and tertiary learning to encourage change in classroom settings for practicing teachers. Teachers in this study found that a blended learning setting connect between theory and practice and collaborative learning provided a strong learning experience that translated to change in classroom practice. In particular, the use of video recording of their classroom teaching was seen by the participants as a powerful tool in reflecting on their teaching.

Chapter 11
Allegheny Women's Biotechnology Workforce Collaborative: Investing in Disadvantaged Populations with Technology 204
Michelle Zuckerman-Parker, Allegheny-Singer Research Institute, USA
Christine Compliment, Allegheny-Singer Research Institute, USA
Megan Rodella, Allegheny-Singer Research Institute, USA
Garth Ehrlich, Allegheny-Singer Research Institute, USA
J. Christopher Post, Allegheny-Singer Research Institute, USA
Allysen Todd, Community College of Allegheny County, USA
James Schreiber, Duquesne University, USA

Zuckerman-Parker, Compliment, Hall-Stoutly, Rosella, Ehrlich, Post, and Todd describe a research based educational intervention designed to support participants in Pennsylvania with "lifelines" using blended learning so that they further their education and enter the biotechnology workforce. This holistic educational approach focuses on individualized learning using technology to foster personal skill development and mentoring from industry professionals. Quantitative data and qualitative data showed that those participants who had been using the technology to learn and to reflect were better than those who did not use the technology.

Chapter 12
Blending Classroom Activities with Multi-User Virtual Environment for At-Risk Primary School Students in an After-School Program: A Case Study 231
Lee Yong Tay, Beacon Primary School, Singapore
Cher Ping Lim, Edith Cowan University, Australia

Tay and Lim explored an uncommon way to adopt blended learning for primary education. A group of 14 academically low Primary 5 students were engaged in academic related tasks in an after-school program mediated by a game-like 3 dimensional multi-user virtual environment. Qualitative findings from the observation notes, interviews with the students, and students' activities showed that the students were engaged with 'play and fun' and 'recognition and affirmation of performance.' The game played a significant role in attracting the students to attend the after-school program, as they were allowed to explore, discover, and satisfy their sense of curiosity, but non-ICT activities were also necessary to further enhance their learning.

Chapter 13
Comparing Face-to-Face with Blended Learning in the Context of Foreign Language Education 250
Kosmas Vlachos, Hellenic Open University, Greece

Vlachos also investigated the usefulness of blended learning for primary school children, but the study involved three classes from Finland, Spain, and Greece. He collated and explored the blended learning modes related to a number of critical language learning issues. Asynchronous online collaboration was regularly and systematically integrated into learning English as a foreign language. Findings showed that the blended learning group scored slightly higher than the face-to-face group even though the former scored lower than the latter before they conducted the experiment.

Section 3
Cultural Differences Studies

Different cultures have different believes, norms, and practices which could affect pedagogy, technology adoption, and access. Many research studies reported the benefits of using the technology to connect learners from diverse backgrounds and countries so as to enrich their learning experiences. Chapters 15 and 16 show that there are cultural differences regarding technology access and security awareness.

Chapter 14
When Cultures Meet in Blended Learning: What Literature Tells Us 278
Chun Hu, University of Sydney, Australia

Hu presents a summary of relevant research studies, their underpinning theoretical frameworks, methodologies used, and examples of the projects involving learners and teachers from culturally diverse backgrounds. The chapter specifically addresses the feasibility of cross-cultural blended learning and learner differences. It appears that successful cross-cultural blended learning programs require more than technology. It was found that the committed teaching teams could make right decisions on curriculum choices, learning tasks and assessments, and types of technology.

Chapter 15
Online Literacy among Students and Faculty: A Comparative Study between
the United States and Eastern European Countries...301
Plamen Miltenoff, St. Cloud State University, USA
John H. Hoover, St. Cloud State University, USA
Galin Tzokov, Paisii Khilendarski University, Bulgaria

Miltenoff, Hoover, and Tzokov conducted a survey to faculty members and students from the Midwest of the U.S. and three Eastern European countries. The results confirm findings from the literature about the existence of a digital divide between developed and emerging nations. The digital divide may be caused by rigid administration in Eastern countries as they had less access to computer labs due to fewer and less flexible hours. However, Eastern European students were satisfied and comfortable with technology.

Chapter 16
The Efficacy of Security Awareness Programs from a Cross-Cultural Perspective 323
B. Dawn Medlin, Appalachian State University, USA
Charlie C. Chen, Appalachian State University, USA

Medlin and Chen argue that different cultures have different technological capabilities and perhaps face different security challenges. They conducted an intercultural study to investigate if users from the U.S. and Taiwan engaged in the same situational awareness learning would have different performance in security awareness outcomes or not. Pre- and post-tests were conducted to assess both cultures' receptivity to the use of technology-driven security awareness programs. It was found that that security awareness was not universal, that is, high individualists have a higher level of security awareness than low individualists after receiving situational training.

Section 4
Cross-Disciplinary Studies

It is logical and natural for IT professionals to take the lead to integrate IT in teaching and learning and the majority of the blended or e-learning studies are related students who took information technology or related courses. However, learning is no longer confined to a single discipline to cope with the real world situation. It was found that cross-disciplinary collaboration between authors, co-classification analysis, interdisciplinary nature of publication journals, and cross-disciplinary references are the most useful approaches to enhance learning.

Chapter 17
Cross Disciplinary Learning in Distance Higher Education: Empowerment
for Sustainable Research Prowess among Professionals in the African Sub-Region 345
Jonathan O. Osiki, National University of Lesotho, Southern Africa

Osiki argues the benefits of inter-disciplinarily can enhance learning, especially when their emotions are understood. The author investigates the relative and differential effectiveness of three behavioural techniques in relieving learners' emotional tension when they took research writing module. The distance students took part in a pre-test, post-test, control quasi-experimental research design. It was found that that the participants' research capacity had improved tremendously.

Chapter 18
Comparing IT and Non-IT Faculty and Students' Perceptions on Blended Learning 365
Eugenia M. W. Ng, Hong Kong Institute of Education, Hong Kong

Ng conducted interviews and focus group meetings with both IT and non-IT academics in order to find out if there were any differences between their perceptions on e-learning. Their findings were also cross referenced with findings from students who participated in a questionnaire survey. These two groups of students also gave high ratings on most of the questionnaire items even though there were some minor differences between them.

Compilation of References 389

About the Contributors 425

Index 433

Foreword

It is a pleasure to provide a foreword for this volume of collected contributions from global scholars. Blended learning is especially relevant and practical in today's contexts. However, it poses threats and challenges in addition to opening opportunities. This book helps to explore concepts and remove uncertainties in this important area. A wide range of international recognized authors, global institutions and perspectives are represented with a heavy Asian influence, especially Hong Kong. The book brings to the fore a wide range of relevant topics that are contemporary and important in the context of blended learning.

Section 1 focuses on blended learning environments with chapters supporting key issues that are beyond control: will blended learning subvert national curricula?, perspectives on blended open distance education learning and teaching in a South African context, enhancing student learning through blending varied learning and assessment experiences, and implementing and promoting blended learning in higher education institutions: comparing different approaches.

Section 2 focuses on blended learning practices with chapters supporting key issues, such as student profile and its effects on online and hybrid courses, using action research to assess student performance in traditional versus e-learning formats, examining individual students' perceptions of curiosity utilizing a blend of online and face-to-face discussions: a qualitative study, online discussion and e-mentoring strategies in blended continuing education courses, infusing Web 2.0 tools for blended learning: virtual presentations as an alternative means of assessment, reflective practice, professional learning and educational partnerships: effecting change in classroom settings, Allegheny Women's Biotechnology Workforce Collaborative: investing in disadvantaged populations with technology, blending classroom activities with multi-user virtual environment for at-risk primary school students in an after-school program, and comparing face-to-face with blended learning in the context of foreign language education and cross cultural communication.

Section 3 focuses on cultural differences studies with chapters supporting key issues, such as when cultures meet in blended learning–what literature tells us?, online literacy among students and faculty: a comparative study between the United States and Eastern European countries and the efficacy of security awareness programs from a cross-cultural perspective.

Section 4 focuses on cross disciplinary studies with chapters supporting key issues, such as cross disciplinary learning in distance higher education: empowerment for sustainable research prowess among professionals in the African sub-region, as well as comparing IT and non-IT faculty and students' perceptions on blended learning.

If properly designed and implemented, blended learning is a win-win-win for students, instructors, and institutions. It can boost students' cognitive, metacognitive, and social strategies, as well as their critical thinking skills. However, the role of e-mentors is critical. Blended learning demands a committed teacher team who make important decisions on curriculum choice, learning task and assessment, and choice of appropriate technology. In many ways, it is a sustaining innovation for students, but a disruptive innovation for faculty. More flexibility and variety are required than historically encountered and there is a definite impact on institutional strategy and national policy.

Knowing what to apply (and how) with respect to blended learning is the key to success. From a technological perspective, there is a role for learning management systems and varied forms of technology support, for example wikis, blogs, Facebook, and SecondLife. Blended learning brings to the fore the best of old and new but not without challenges as noted. Teacher education is especially important. Further, inducing research competencies with an interdisciplinary need and focus is crucial. Student population learning style and motivation is also an important consideration. Disadvantaged populations pose special challenges, as well as opportunities. Much remains to be learned and applied. This book is an important step in that direction. The future for blended learning is challenging but bright.

Doug Vogel
Chair Professor of Information Systems
City University of Hong Kong

Douglas R. Vogel *is Professor (Chair) of Information Systems at City University of Hong Kong. He has been involved with computers and computer systems in various capacities for over 35 years. He received his M.S. in Computer Science from U.C.L.A. in 1972 and his Ph.D in Business from University of Minnesota in 1986. Professor Vogel's research interests bridge the business and academic communities in addressing questions of the impact of management information systems on aspects of interpersonal communication, group problem solving, cooperative learning and multi-cultural team productivity. He has published widely and directed extensive research on group support systems and technology support for education. He has been ranked 3rd in a journal report of top researchers in Group Support Systems and ranked 10th in a worldwide list of top researchers in MIS as well as 4th in the list of most collaborative information systems researchers.*

Preface

This edited book is about blended learning, which means using a combination of face-to-face and online teaching methods to facilitate learning even though there is no agreed definition. Blended learning offers unlimited ways to offer courses that facilitate creativity, critical thinking, higher order thinking, and meaningful learning. Some use information technology (IT) as an add-on tool; some use the online platforms as resource repertoires, whilst some use electronic resources as electronic books. However, it is well understood that most academics and teachers did not have the experiences of using blended approach to learn when they pursued their own educations and, obviously, there is a lack of best practices to follow suit.

This book offers insightful perspectives related to blended learning, as there are chapters which overview practices, analyse pertinent literature, discuss issues, and compare practices. It is more than showcasing the good practices of pedagogy, research, and practices of using blended learning, as this book contains an added element of comparative studies, which is distinctive from other blended learning books. The comparative discussions facilitate readers to analyze and compare ideas and practices easily and come up with a creative use of the dual delivery modes. Indeed, this edited book is about rethinking and redesigning the learning and teaching activities to maximize learning effectiveness regardless of the learners' background and experiences.

This book informs academics, administrators, and researchers with the contemporary knowledge and best practices so that they can avoid any unnecessary frustrations and pitfalls and yet to be inspired by quality practices and research in blended learning. It is contributed by 34 authors and co-authors from 8 countries (namely, Australia, Bulgaria, Greece, Hong Kong SAR, Singapore, South Africa, the United Kingdom, and the United States of America). There are 18 chapters which have been organized into four sections, namely: blended learning environments (4 Chapters); blended learning practices (9 chapters); culture differences studies (3 chapters); and cross disciplinary studies (2 chapters). Each section has its unique theme. Exemplary practices were drawn from primary school children, information technology undergraduate students, student teachers, and practicing teachers from developed and developing countries.

OVERVIEW OF CONTENTS

This book is useful to teachers, academics, administrators, and researchers regardless of their background and blended learning experiences. For example, Chapter 1 is useful to policy-makers and educational practitioners around the globe to ponder, especially to seriously answer the four key questions that are related to blended learning. Chapter 3 gives lots of ideas to academics and teachers who are interested to mix and match different face-to-face and online activities. Chapter 8 is not only appealing to those academics who are keen to facilitate discussion via e-mentoring, but also to researchers who would like to analyze online discussion. Chapter 11 and Chapter 12 shed light on how to use blended learning as an alternative mode of motivating problematic learners. Chapter 14 is useful to researchers who are keen to know more about the role of culture plays in blended learning and the content of relevant literature. Chapter 16 suggests there is a cultural difference between users from different countries. Finally, Chapter 18 provides a holistic view of IT and non-IT academics and students on blended learning, which serves as an invaluable source for administrators and researchers. The following paragraphs will highlight the essence of the chapters.

Section 1: Blended Learning Environments

Commercial, or tailored made learning management systems (LMS), are commonly adopted to facilitate blended learning. There are different ways to term LMS and the term "learning platform" is more commonly known than LMS. Learning platforms are widely used as a learning portal to allow students to learn at anytime and anyplace as long as they have access to an Internet connection (Boggs & Shore, 2004; Freeman, 1997; Palloff & Pratt, 2001). LMS contain the unique functionalities of the Internet and learning resources, online assessment, and course statistics.

Chapter 1: "Beyond Control: Will Blended Learning Subvert National Curricula?"—Williams discusses blended learning by examining key issues of educational policy and the creation and implementation of policy at national levels. The nature and significance of Web 2.0 applications and open educational resources are also discussed with examples to illustrate the growing gap between traditional educational systems and the current digital cultures. Although blended learning poses cultural threats, it also opens new opportunities. Whether these threats can be turned to advantage depends crucially upon how national policies are formulated and how they are implemented at all levels.

Chapter 2: "Perspectives on Blended Open Distance Education Learning and Teaching in a South African Context"—Singh and Liang present a micro-comparison of two different learning platforms which facilitate open and distance learning at the University of South Africa. The authors had described myUnisa, the self-created learning platform, and Osprey, which is the custom-made Web site at the School of Computing at the University of South Africa. They also discussed the future trends of the use of blended approaches in the context of open distance education and learning, which is informative for those who would like to adopt e-learning in developing countries.

Chapter 3: "Enhancing Student Learning through Blending Varied Learning and Assessment Experiences"—Hodgson gives a very good review and comparison between traditional learning, teaching, and assessment vs. online methods, which gives readers a good understanding of blended learning. Theories and good practices were shown clearly so that readers could select appropriate approaches for their undergraduate students. In particular, e-portfolio systems are neither well adopted nor documented, but the collected students' competences should be able to portray a comprehensive university experience.

Chapter 4: "Implementing and Promoting Blended Learning in Higher Education Institutions: Comparing Different Approaches"—Wang compares various forms and expressions of blended learning adopted by different parts of the world. The limitations of commercial LMS were discussed and the constraints led to his discussion on subject-specific Web sites to supplement a commercial LMS to facilitate blended learning. How and what to use Wikibook projects to foster academic reading and writing in English for non-English native speakers were described in greater details. Student teachers worked in groups to write an academic textbook collaboratively online and evidences showed that these projects were highly effective and the wiki technology also made peer editing much more efficient and effective.

Section 2: Blended Learning Practices

There are numerous face-to-face learning and teaching methods and technology is only one of the factors that affects blended learning. Benbunan-Fich, Hiltz, and Harasim (2005) designed a research framework, an input-process-output model, which is very wide-ranging and comprehensive in its scope. The input factors in this framework include technology, course, instructor, and student characteristics; the intervening factor is the learning process; and the outcomes include access, faculty satisfaction, student learning, student satisfaction, and cost effectiveness. From the different practices illustrated in this book (Chapter 7 to 13), I argue that pedagogy is the most important variable for conducting blended learning, even though findings from Chapter 6 illustrate that the grades that students scored had no relationship to pedagogy. Perhaps the authors had not fully designed and created appropriate digital materials, nor took full use of different features of and learning platforms. They have not mentioned using the discussion forum, which is rated as the most important element of e-learning (Alexander, 2001; Fredericksen, Pickett, & Shea, 2000; Sims, 2003).

Chapter 5: "Student Profile and Its Effects on Online and Hybrid Courses"—It is imperative to know our students when offering blended courses to meet their needs and expectations. Boghikian-Whitby and Mortagy took the effort to analyze the profile of students who were enrolled in a face-to-face and an online course of management information systems over 15 semesters at an American university. It was found that most online students were adult students who were of African American and Hispanic background. Forty percent of the students enrolled in online delivery modality were of extravert type. It was recommended that short modules and using different exercises would be able to accommodate various learning styles.

Chapter 6: "Using Action Research to Assess Student Performance in Traditional vs. E-Learning Formats"—Action research is commonly used by many academics to reflect and to refine their teaching approaches. Guy and Wishart adopted different teaching approaches to students who took online courses in the United States who were mainly blacks. They changed the teaching strategy for e-learning class from student-centred to instructor-centred to even more instructor-centred for the three years. Students' grades of face-to-face and online courses were compared but it was found that neither the strategy nor the delivery method had any impact on student performances. The amazing results are rather different from other research findings in this book.

Chapter 7: "Examining Individual Students' Perceptions of Curiosity Utilizing a Blend of Online and Face-to-Face Discussions: A Qualitative Study"—Little is known about the impact of a blended learning approach on individual student curiosity and whether combinations of online and face-to-face learning activities significantly enhance student exploratory behavior. Shroff created a blended learning platform that allowed students to interact and collaborate in both online and face-to-face settings. Data were obtained through in-depth, semi-structured interviews with information systems undergraduate students. The interviewees appeared to derive pleasure from the online discussions, which also provided them with a level of surprise, conflicting discrepancy, and novelty. Results from the qualitative study showed that individuals' perceptions of curiosity were strongly supported.

Chapter 8: "Online Discussion and E-Mentoring Strategies in Blended Continuing Education Courses"—Wang and Looi analysed online discussions in a course portal that supplemented class discussion in three continuing master education courses in Singapore. The courses combined face-to-face and online approaches to instruction. The participants were full-time professionals who studied on a part-time basis. Henri's model was adopted to quantitatively and qualitatively analyse the online discussion. This chapter emphasizes the role of the e-mentors in promoting and mediating the discussions. Factors that contributed to the effective e-mentoring strategies were also discussed in detail. Transcript content analyses showed that students' messages were on-task, thoughtful, and indicative of student-initiated learning and a good amount of peer help.

Chapter 9: "Infusing Web 2.0 Tools for Blended Learning: Virtual Presentations as an Alternative Means of Assessment"—Academic's lead in discussion forum is invaluable to foster learning but it is equally important for student teachers to master different strategies and skills to integrate learning, teaching, and assessment. Lai and Ng describe an innovative practice of infusing Web 2.0 in assessment in Hong Kong. The participants were two groups of student teachers who created virtual presentations, which could either be videos or other digital formats for each group to learn from each other. Quantitative and qualitative data were collected, analyzed, and compared. It was found that most of the participants were positive about this new presentation approach and ready to accept it as a part in assessments but they gave more feedback to their class rather than the other class. Furthermore, their attitudes were influenced by the tutors' participation and this finding echo the importance of e-mentoring strategies (Chapter 6).

Chapter 10: "Reflective Practice, Professional Learning, and Educational Partnerships: Effecting Change in Classroom Settings"—Discussion forums were not only useful to student teachers, but also useful for professional development for teachers. Brook and Lock presented a model of professional learning that incorporated blended learning, reflective practice, performance management processes, authentic experiences, and tertiary learning to encourage change in classroom settings for practicing teachers. Teachers in this study found that a blended learning setting connect between theory and practice and collaborative learning provided a strong learning experience that translated to change in classroom practice. In particular, the use of video recording of their classroom teaching was seen by the participants as a powerful tool in reflecting on their teaching.

Chapter 11: "Allegheny Women's Biotechnology Workforce Collaborative: Investing in Disadvantaged Populations with Technology"—This chapter sheds light on how blended learning assists underprivileged learners. Zuckerman-Parker, Compliment, Rosella, Ehrlich, Post, Todd, and Schreiber describe a research-based educational intervention designed to support participants at Pennsylvania with "lifelines" using blended learning so that they further their education and enter the biotechnology workforce. This holistic educational approach focuses on individualized learning using technology to foster personal skill development and mentoring from industry professionals. Quantitative data and qualitative data showed that those participants who had been using the technology to learn and to reflect were better than those who did not use the technology. Technology also provided a safe haven for participants to express themselves, a medium to reduce and mediate the stress. Interesting background of the participants and their text exchanges were also included in this chapter, which warm our hearts.

Chapter 12: "Blending Classroom Activities with Multi-User Virtual Environment for At-Risk Primary School Students in an After-School Program: A Case Study"—Tay and Lim explored an uncommon way to adopt blended learning for primary education. A group of 14 academically low Primary 5 students were engaged in academic related tasks in an after-school program mediated by a game-like 3 dimensional multi user virtual environment. Qualitative findings from the observation notes, interviews with the students, and students' activities showed that the students were engaged with 'play and fun' and 'recognition and affirmation of performance.' The game played a significant role in attracting the students to attend the after-school program, as they were allowed to explore, discover, and satisfy their sense of curiosity, but non-ICT activities were also necessary to further enhance their learning.

Chapter 13: "Comparing Face-to-Face with Blended Learning in the Context of Foreign Language Education and Cross Cultural Communication"—Vlachos also investigated about the usefulness of blended learning for primary school children but the study involved three classes from Finland, Spain, and Greece. He collated and explored the blended learning modes related to a number of critical to language learning issues. Asynchronous online collaboration was regularly and systematically integrated into learning English as a foreign language. Findings showed that the blended learning group scored slightly higher than the face-to-face group, even though the former scored lower than the latter before they conducted the experiment. Furthermore, almost all blended learning students acknowledged the online communication and blended learning enrich their intercultural knowledge and experiences even though the face-to-face appeared enjoying cooperating and working in groups more.

Section 3: Cultural Differences Studies

Different cultures have different beliefs, norms, and practices, which could affect pedagogy, technology adoption, and access. Hofstede (2001) defines culture as "the collective programming of the mind that distinguishes the members of one group or category of people from another" (p. 9). This collective programming of the mind consists of a patterned way of people thinking, feeling, and reacting, acquired and transmitted mainly by symbols, which are based on their traditional ideas and values. Many research studies reported the benefits of using the technology to connect learners from diverse background and countries so as to enrich their learning experiences. Chapter 15 and 16 show that there are cultural differences regarding technology access and security awareness.

Chapter 14: "When Cultures Meet in Blended Learning: What Literature Tells Us"—Hu presents a summary of relevant research studies; their underpinning theoretical frameworks, methodologies used, and examples of the projects involving learners and teachers from culturally diverse backgrounds. The chapter specifically addresses the feasibility of cross-cultural blended learning and leaner differences. It appears that successful cross-cultural blended learning programs requires more than technology. It was found that the committed teaching teams could make better decisions on curriculum choices, learning tasks and assessments, and types of technology.

Chapter 15: "Online Literacy among Students and Faculty: A Comparative Study between the United States and Eastern European Countries"—Miltenoff, Hoover, and Tzokov conducted a survey to faculty members and students from the Midwest of the U.S. and three Eastern European countries. The results confirm findings from the literature about the existence of a digital divide between developed and emerging nations. The digital divide may be caused by rigid administration in Eastern countries as they had less access to computer labs due to fewer and less flexible hours. However, Eastern European students were satisfied and comfortable with technology. Perhaps, Eastern European students and faculty members tended to compensate the deficiency by using alternative access sites such as Internet Café and home.

Chapter 16: "The Efficacy of Security Awareness Programs from a Cross-Cultural Perspective"—Medlin and Chen argue that different cultures have different technological capabilities and perhaps face different security challenges. They conducted an intercultural study to investigate if users from the U.S. and Taiwan engaged in the same situational awareness learning would have different performance in security awareness outcomes or not. Pre- and post-tests were conducted to assess both cultures' receptivity to the use of technology-driven security awareness programs. It was found that that security awareness was not universal, that is, high individualists had a higher level of security awareness than low individualists after receiving situational training. Since security awareness is an important issue for all Internet users, it is imperative to have different learning approaches to cater to users around the globe.

Section 4: Cross-Disciplinary Studies

It is logical and natural for IT professionals to take the lead to integrate IT in teaching and learning and majority of the blended or e-learning studies are related students who took information technology or related courses. However, learning is no longer confined to a single discipline to cope with the real world situation. Bordons, Morillos, and Gomez (2005) found that cross-disciplinary collaboration between authors, coclassification analysis, interdisciplinary nature of publication journals, and cross-disciplinary references are the most useful approaches to enhance learning.

Chapter 17: "Cross Disciplinary Learning in Distance Higher Education: Empowerment for Sustainable Research Prowess among Professionals in the African Sub-Region"—Osiki argues the benefits of interdisciplinarily can enhance learning especially when their emotions are understood. The author investigated the relative and differential effectiveness of three behavioural techniques in relieving learners' emotional tension when they took research writing module. The distance students took part in a pre-test, post-test, control quasi-experimental research design. It was found that that the participants' research capacity had improved tremendously.

Chapter 18: "Comparing IT and Non-IT Faculty and Students' Perceptions on Blended Learning"—Many blended research findings were related with IT or related disciplines, but there are not many studies related to non-IT disciplines. Ng conducted interviews and focus group meetings with both IT and non-IT academics in order to find out if there were any differences between their perceptions on e-learning. Their findings were also cross referenced with findings from students who participated in a questionnaire survey. These two groups of students also gave high ratings on most of the questionnaire items even though there were some minor differences between them.

REFERENCES

Alexander, S. (2001). E-learning developments and experiences. *Education & Training, 4/5*(43), 240-248.

Benbunan-Fich, R., Hiltz, S. R., & Harasim, L. (Eds.). (2005). *The online interaction learning model: An integrated theoretical framework for learning networks*. NJ: Lawrence Erlbaum Associates Publishers.

Boggs, S., & Shore, M. (2004). Using e-learning platforms for mastery learning in developmental mathematics courses. *Mathematics and Computer Education, 38*(2), 213-220.

Bordons, M., Morillo, F., & Gómez, I. (2005). Analysis of cross-disciplinary research through bibliometric tools. In H. F. Moed, W. Glänzel & U. Schmoch (Eds.), *Handbook of quantitative science and technology research* (pp. 437-456). The Netherlands: Springer.

Fredericksen, E., Pickett, A., & Shea, P. (2000). Student satisfaction and perceived learning with online courses: Principles and examples from the SUNY learning network. *Jouranl of Asynchronous Learning Networks, 4*(2).

Freeman, M. (1997). Flexibility in access, interaction, and assessment: The case for Web-based teaching programs. *Australian Journal for Educational Technology, 13*(1), 23-39.

Hofstede, G. (2001). *Cultures consequences: Comparing values, behaviors, institutions, and organisations across nations.* Thousand Oaks, London, New Delhi: Sage Publications.

Palloff, R., & Pratt, K. (2001). *Lessons from the cyberspace classroom: The realities of online teaching.* San Francisco: Jossey-Boss.

Sims, R. (2003). Promises of interactivity: Aligning learner perceptions and expectations with strategies for flexible and online learning. *Distance Education, 24*(1), 85-103.

Acknowledgment

This is my first time to edit a book and I did not know how much time and effort I needed to spend on it throughout the whole process. I have been extremely lucky to have dedicated reviewers who were not only serious in reviewing, but also adhere to deadlines. The reviewers' detailed and constructive comments helped authors improve the quality of their chapters greatly. I appreciate those authors who also serve as reviewers, so that they contribute to the book in dual roles. Reviewers' information is listed in the reviewers' list and Katy Campbell, Larbi Esmahi, Jan Frick, George Ghinea, Ikuo Kitagaki, and Sergio Lujan Mora also serve as editorial advisory board members.

It has been a frustrating and yet rewarding experience working with authors, in particular those who needed extra support. Sincere thanks go to my husband who encouraged me to take this challenge. I would like to acknowledge the support from IGI Global. Last but not least, my research assistant, Wilson Chung, who has helped me in many tedious logistic work.

Eugenia M. W. Ng
Hong Kong Institute of Education, Hong Kong

Section 1
Blended Learning Environments

Chapter 1
Beyond Control:
Will Blended Learning Subvert National Curricula?

Peter Williams
University of Hull, UK

ABSTRACT

Blended learning seems to entail a relatively innocuous set of techniques, but closer examination reveals some of these carry implicit assumptions–of constructivist philosophy, peer collaboration, and situative learning–which may make their export to other countries and national cultures problematic. They also provide a route to the Internet: a storehouse of Westernised, unauthorized, and anarchic content. So will blended learning subvert national curricula? This chapter contributes to the debate by examining the milieu of national educational policy, relating it to forms of knowledge. Web 2.0 applications and open educational resources are discussed in relation to the growing gap between traditional curricula and the digitally-enabled communities of mass collectivism and direct action. Blended learning is shown to pose cultural threats, but also open opportunities, and whether these threats can be turned to advantage depends crucially upon how national policies are formulated and implemented. The conclusion poses key questions for policy-makers and practitioners.

INTRODUCTION

A significant expression of the national identity of a country is the way in which it orients its educational system. *National curricula* – used here to include those statutory declarations of the aims and content of schooling and higher education of a country, as well as the nationally distinctive features of its educational institutions – embody particular, and in some cases unique, views of the world, reflecting that country's shared national values and history as well as its social, economic and technological priorities.

DOI: 10.4018/978-1-60566-852-9.ch001

Generally speaking, national curricula and the educational institutions which transmit their values, are relatively static and have not kept pace with the changing practices and needs of an emerging 21st Century knowledge economy. By some analyses it is in procedural know-how rather than formal propositional knowledge that economic competitiveness increasingly lies. There is perhaps a greater mismatch between these two facets of knowledge in Developing Countries, where new technologies and knowledge-intensive occupations are less established; but in most countries strong associations exist between new technologies, aspirations of modernity, and perceived wealth. It is for these reasons that students may be tempted to look beyond the confines of national curricula for more relevant vocational preparation.

Open Educational Resources is a term given to educational content and materials which are made available at little or no cost, generally for use in not-for-profit education. Where in the past there were physical and financial constraints on the distribution of educational resources in printed form, the arrival of the World Wide Web has removed almost all barriers to dissemination. The quantity and variety – and latterly quality – of Open Educational Resources has grown rapidly; however, it is currently dominated by English-language materials from the USA and UK, and so reflects the national and socio-cultural orientations of these countries.

The World Wide Web has developed substantially over the last two decades, but in the early days adopted a 'broadcast' metaphor whereby information was typically presented by an organisation or authority for access by the individual. The last few years have seen explosive growth in a far more interactive and symmetric use of this technology, in what has come to be known as *Web 2.0*. Principally used for social networking, Web 2.0 also enables informal and peer-to-peer interaction and learning unconstrained by the limitations of time and space. It is similarly not culture-neutral but embodies ideas of individualistic expression, democratic and active learner engagement, pluralism and the acceptance of multiple representations of 'truth', which are identified with Western countries.

To this digital divide can be added a generational component; for the young people who have grown up with digital technologies, there is impatience with print-bound media and the ethos and approach of traditional educational institutions. What these students regard as a reluctant adoption of new technologies by their teachers may reinforce a desire to reject their national system in favour of what they see as more relevant digital materials and practices. These views are further advanced when there is an identification of the latter with progress, prosperity and vocational opportunity.

It can be seen that the greater employment of Blended Learning – incorporating elements of traditional methods alongside eLearning – within national educational systems across the world will inevitably promote online access to Web-based educational resources. The danger for national curricula is that learners, perhaps impelled by vocational ambitions or simply a desire for social engagement, will go beyond state-prescribed requirements to explore Open Educational Resources and Web 2.0 applications. This access to unsanctioned content is likely to present challenges to the authority and relevance of all national educational systems, but in non-Western countries may present challenges also to their social and cultural values.

The debate around Blended Learning has so far focused on the immediate practicalities of educational technology and pedagogical practice; but the important dimension of socio-cultural and policy issues must also be confronted. There appear to be two distinct sets of issues: pertaining firstly to Open Educational Resources and secondly to Web 2.0. The first concerns relatively minor questions of whether the importation of 'foreign' resources is always a bad thing, and to what extent the dangers of Western bias might be offset by the utility of high quality and vocationally relevant materials. The second set of issues is more worrying however, as a change of learner focus, from meeting statutory and institutional requirements to the pursuit of individual and social educational goals, could signal a rejection of some of the values underpinning national curricula. Thus, radical, transformative and unexpected outcomes could result through adoption of what seems the relatively innocuous practice of Blended Learning.

This chapter aims to contribute to the Blended Learning debate by examining key issues of educational policy, and the creation and implementation of policy at national levels. It will begin by discussing the context within which national curricula operate, and related to this it will contrast forms of knowledge and their educational implications. The nature and significance of Web 2.0 applications and Open Educational Resources will be discussed with reference to examples and in relation to the growing gap between traditional educational systems and the digital cultures of mass collectivism and direct action. Following an analysis of the nature of Blended Learning, its cultural concomitants will be shown to pose significant threats to national curricula – while at the same time presenting many opportunities. Whether the threats of these powerful pedagogic, socio-cultural and economic forces can be turned to advantage within national systems depends crucially upon what educational policies are formulated and how they are implemented at all levels. In conclusion, four key questions will be posed for policy-makers and educational practitioners.

EDUCATING FOR THE FUTURE

The most important pragmatic concern of a national education system is to enable that country to promote its economic competitiveness. In the industrial age wealth was derived from the exploitation of natural resources, so the education of the majority of its citizens – destined for low-skilled occupations in fields and factories – need not advance beyond an elementary level. In the post-industrial age, Western countries and many of those in the Developing World see economic competition in the new knowledge-based occupations as key (Reich, 1991), and education as the way to achieve this (Castells, 1997; Scott, 2002). In the place of low-skilled standardisation and conformity, the qualities of originality, creativity and problem solving must be nurtured (Gibbons et al., 1994), and national curricula must become more flexible and responsive to change. Rapid growth in the use of information and communications technologies (ICT) has enabled a move towards globalisation which some commentators would argue holds more implications than merely economic (Micklethwait & Wooldridge, 2000; Castells, 2001). For example, for the European Union, ICT offers the vision of an Information Society supporting inclusion, better public services and quality of life (Magalhães & Stoer, 2003; EC, 2008).

There is a mismatch between the anticipation of a knowledge-based future and the adaptability of national curricula and educational institutions. Some countries in the Developing World are still coping with the legacy of imposed colonial systems unsympathetic to their religious and cultural traditions – in Bangladesh, for example (Barua, 2007), and in Mexico (Norget, 2007). In a major international study, Coulby & Zambeta (2005) found some national systems structured in such a way as to be in effect antagonistic to change. On the other hand, curricula may be conceived as agents of change in different ways, and Marshall & Arnot (2008) contrast three potential purposes: 'curriculum as opportunity', 'curriculum as reform' and 'curriculum as a democratic tool'. In this latter regard Mukhamedyarova & Cotter (2005) describe the adoption of interactive methods of teaching in Kazakhstan as a way to foster ideas of citizenship and democratic engagement.

Many national curricula are infrequently revised, and there may be a lack of coherence and agreement between the various bodies and authorities in charge of subject content, assessment and quality monitoring. In England the last revisions to the national secondary school curriculum were made in 2000 and 2007, with in each case almost two years from announcement to rollout. The national school curriculum in South Korea has a comparable revision cycle of between 5-10 years, and regional subject curricula in Germany can take up to five years to update (INCA, 2008). At higher education level the pattern is even more heterogeneous, with varying degrees of state influence over what can in some cases be largely autonomous universities focused on competing imperatives and missions (Scott, 1998). The complexity and number of stakeholders involved in curriculum revision inevitably hinders the responsiveness of national systems to changing needs.

While some elements of curriculum content may be generic across different countries, others are not. For example, Finland and South Korea are the two most successful school systems, as rated by the International Student Assessment Index (PISAPISAPISA: OECD, 2006), yet they are very different in nature. Finland's schools are egalitarian and comprehensive, whereas private academies and competitive selection characterise the Korean system (Opetusministeriö, 2008; MEST, 2008). Interestingly, these two countries are in the top five for average time spent by World Wide Web users, almost doubling that of the USA.

Many commentators see the nation state as being in long-term decline against burgeoning multinational corporations and international trade alliances (Ohmae, 1995; Strange, 1996; Annan, 2002). Even in the rich West this is a challenge, and the European Higher Education Area being developed through the Bologna Process requires member countries to make their national systems compliant in an overarching qualifications framework (EU, 2008). In the Developing World the problem is much more acute, and, as discussed earlier, some countries beset by more immediate problems have yet to address the issues of taking their curricula beyond post-colonial legacies. In a UNESCO study, Benavot (2006) reports that although secondary school enrolment continues to grow worldwide, many school systems are still in the early stages of effecting transition from an academic focus and elite, selective provision towards a more vocational orientation with inclusive access.

FORMS OF KNOWLEDGE

One characteristic feature of the knowledge economy is the timely application of *procedural knowledge* in the solution of work-based problems. In the past the professional status of workers was due in part to their mastery of a specialist body of knowledge, in a form that Schön (1983) called *propositional*. This knowledge is codified and relatively static, taught on a *just-in-case* basis (Moe et al., 1999) in an intensive period of learning at the start of a professional career. This is contrasted with Schön's (1983) procedural knowledge – or 'know-how', as distinct from 'know-what' – acquired rather than taught, and frequently *just-in-time* (Moe et al., 1999) at many points throughout a career. Nguyen (2004) argues that in order to meet the needs of the new economy, *knowledge workers* (Reich, 1991) must adopt appropriate systems and procedures on a just-in-time basis to access the procedural knowledge which constitutes the organisation's collective memory and which contributes to its market position. Another feature of knowledge working is the greater frequency and extent of communication and team collaboration. Problem resolution by project teams enabled by ICT is a critical success factor, and effective collaboration requires both the cognitive abilities fostered by formal education and a range of general and interpersonal abilities (Ducatel, 1998).

The application of procedural knowledge and collaborative working in novel situations results in knowledge generation and contributes to an organisation's knowledge base. Unlike the relatively one-way delivery of just-in-case learning, this is more of a two-way process of sharing and interaction, and one which is mirrored in the way the World Wide Web is increasingly being used. Scott (2002, p.66) speculates

Maybe we are moving beyond the idea of reliable knowledge, derived from objective empirical scientific research, to a more diffuse (but also powerful) idea of socially robust knowledge, knowledge which is embedded in specific contexts rather than simply being subsequently applied within these contexts.

The other side of this coin is the future of traditional propositional knowledge as the definitive articulation of truth. A key trend in higher education identified in the Horizon Report is that "academic review and faculty rewards are increasingly out of sync with new forms of scholarship" (NMC/EDUCAUSE, 2007, p. 4) and it is observed that the growth of digitally-published interdisciplinary and collaborative activities "continue to move away from the standards of traditional peer-reviewed paper publication" (ibid.). However, the position taken in this paper is not that propositional knowledge is no longer relevant, as an inadequate understanding of formal knowledge can hinder the acquisition of procedural know-how (e.g. Broers, 2002). Instead, it is that propositional knowledge can no longer be the sole source of 'valid knowledge' (Williams, 2007) in national education systems.

The issue of what formal knowledge, procedural know-how and skills should be regarded as essential in a curriculum raises the question of what should be assessed, and by what methods. Williams (2008a) argues that the considerable problems posed by *authentic assessment* – the assessment of learning in realistic contexts for its use – must be confronted, as continued reliance upon timed, handwritten examinations seems an increasingly inappropriate way to gauge students' preparedness for employment in the new occupations of the knowledge-based economy. It is possible that the affordances of Blended Learning may provide opportunities for the greater adoption of Context Based Learning (ibid.), and the potential use of *learning objects* for this purpose is discussed below.

WEB 2.0 AND OPEN EDUCATIONAL CONTENT

Web 2.0 is an umbrella term coined in 2004 (O'Reilly, 2005) for a range of Web-based services including social networking, wikis, social bookmarking and collaborative tools. Where the 'Web 1.0' metaphor was the *Encyclopedia Britannica Online* – a subscription service – Web 2.0's flagship is *Wikipedia*, a free content encyclopedia project developed collaboratively by volunteers from around the world (Wikipedia, 2008). Web 2.0 is symmetric and interactive, as distinct from the one-way information source of television. As even basic computers – including the Simputer (PicoPeta, 2008) designed for Developing countries – now possess multimedia capabilities, this greater two-way exchange has become widely realisable. The effect is to shift from a television/broadcast model to peer-to-peer interaction. Anderson (2007) identifies six "big ideas" of Web 2.0. The first of these is the explosive growth of *user-generated content*, evidenced by social networking sites such as You Tube (2008) which according to Digital Ethnography (2008) hosts over 80 million amateur videos and in three years has become one of the largest websites on the Internet. The second idea is that of the *wisdom of crowds* in collaborative problem solving and decision making over the Internet, and Anderson describes *folksonomies* as shared taxonomies (e.g. del.icio.us, 2008) for the communal tagging of information. The third idea is *data on an epic scale*, whereby the immense database systems of corporations such as Google have been designed to aggregate, manage and supply information in response to billions of selections made by their individual users. Related to this is the fourth big idea, described as an *architecture of participation*.

Web 2.0 services are designed to be adaptive to the requests of their users, so that they become more efficient and targeted the more they are used. This links in turn to the fifth big idea, concerning the *network effects* of mass usage. Hence, social networking sites such as Facebook (2008) become more useful as they attract more users, and there is a mathematical power law to model this relationship. Like all exponential functions, it has a *long tail* of slowly declining popularity, but the sheer scale of use means that even this area of usage is substantial, enabling Web-based vendors such as Amazon.com (2008) to maintain turnover and profitability even for low-demand products. The long tail also has social and educational significance, as it is the region in which minority and emerging ideas can find expression. In smaller-scale environments such as communities and nations such esoteric views might be shared by only very small numbers, but the aggregation potential of the Web supports extended communities of discourse and what Anderson (p. 24) calls "the sociology of new content creation", and abundant examples can be found in the proliferation of blogs and single-issue campaign websites. The Horizon Report calls this "collective intelligence and mass amateurization" (NMC/EDUCAUSE, 2007), and Scott (2002) uses the phrase a "democratisation of expertise". This viewpoint is shared by Benkler, who examines far-reaching social, economic and political implications, contending that the most significant effect will lie in a changing power balance between the citizen and the state.

This new freedom holds great practical promise: as a dimension of individual freedom; as a platform for better democratic participation; as a medium to foster a more critical and self-reflective culture; and, in an increasingly information-dependent global economy, as a mechanism to achieve improvements in human development everywhere. (Benkler, 2006, p. 2)

From a Postmodernist perspective, such developments reflect wider changes in relationships between the individual and authority in Western societies, which have been the focus of writers such as Baudrillard (1983) and Lyotard (1984). The last big idea outlined by Anderson is that of *openness* and the growth of the open source movement, and these matters are now discussed in relation to Education.

The last few years have seen the emergence of Open Educational Resources alongside the free service of *Wikipedia*. The provision of free resources drawn from existing proprietary content was pioneered by the Massachusetts Institute of Technology (OCW, 2008) and has been followed by other leading universities and supported by not-for-profit trusts (e.g. Creative Commons, 2008; OER Commons, 2008), making available free resources for primary (elementary) and secondary schools through to higher education. The OpenLearn initiative by the UK Open University (UKOU, 2008) develops this idea into a wiki by inviting users to download, adapt and upload back revised resources. The attraction of online Western materials for developing countries is amply evidenced by SCHOLAR (2008), the world's largest distance education programme. Run by Heriot-Watt University in Edinburgh, this (for-profit) service provides curriculum materials to enable thousands of students in India and other countries annually to gain Scottish school qualifications. The quantity and variety – and latterly quality – of Open Educational Resources has grown rapidly; however, as observed earlier, the predominance of English-language materials introduces bias. For example, Crystal (2003, ch. 1) identifies some possible effects of English becoming the *lingua franca* of the Internet: as a decline in minority languages, a reluctance to learn other languages, and a status gap between native English speakers and others. Dunbar (1991) asserts that the problem runs deeper: in a culture-specificity of the physical design, attributes and usability of computer hardware and software. While such effects could be reduced through careful redesign of learning resources, the difficulties of achieving this are considerable. McAndrew (2005, p. 18) suggests,

... we need to capture the essence of good designs in a way that allows as much as possible of the learning experience to be transferred to the students' control while at the same time limiting dependence on particular aspects of culture. One possible way to achieve this involves separation of the resources (as learning objects), the design structure (as learning design), and the design rationale (as a pattern) within a framework that recognises the need for people support and the value of global collaboration. Such an approach will not be a solution for all cases but rather for those where part of the intention is to share views and allow diversity.

The flexible deployment of reusable learning objects, otherwise known as *shareable content objects* (SCOs) as the units of content within Blended Learning courses holds considerable potential for the future, not least in the provision of more authentic assessment of learning in context. In order to enable interoperability with other learning objects, SCOs must be designed to a common set of specifications known as the Shareable Content Object Reference Model (CETIS, 2005). Complex descriptors of each SCO are contained within a Learning Object Metadata (LOM) model. Educational criteria in the LOM include language, interactivity type and level, end user role and age range, difficulty level and semantic density. Given a sufficiently detailed LOM profile of each of the SCOs in a global 'learning object economy', it is theoretically possible that learning objects with low culture-specificity could be selected to match the needs of learners in a wide variety of national milieu. As discussed earlier, the assessment activities which are an integral part of many SCOs provide immediate feedback to learners, but can also be used to track their progress. However, overcoming human as well as technical obstacles has delayed the appearance of SCOs at the scale predicted, and the idea has its critics. Malcolm (2005) questions whether a learning object economy will be able to meet the quality as well as efficiency needs of higher education, and Metrios (2005) comments on the practical problems which have resulted in the much slower than anticipated widespread availability and adoption of learning objects in education and training.

GENERATION GAPS

How British secondary school students employ Web 2.0 applications is the focus of the Demos report *Their Space* (Green & Hannon, 2007). As the report's title suggests, social networking is heavily colonised by the young, but the main finding of the project is articulated in the prefacing observation "Young people are spending their time in a space which adults find difficult to supervise or understand". The project collected data from academics, commentators, school leaders, secondary school students and their parents. The intensive home use of ICT was found to be commonplace, with four types of student users identified:

- Digital pioneers were blogging before the phrase had been coined
- Creative producers are building websites, posting movies, photos and music to share with friends, family and beyond
- Everyday communicators are making their lives easier through texting and MSN
- Information gatherers are Google and Wikipedia addicts, 'cutting and pasting' as a way of life. (Green & Hannon, 2007, p. 11)

Overall, the report concluded that students were completely confident with the Web, using it recreationally and productively to create, maintain friendship networks, and to assist with their school studies. However, it does comment upon a gulf which is growing between this emerging digital youth culture and the institutional culture of schools.

The idea of a generational culture gap between young ICT users and their elders is well documented. Tulgan & Martin (2001) describe the globalised lifestyles of a digitally-enabled *Generation Y*, born in the late 1970s and early 80s. Prensky (2001) dubs them *digital natives*, arguing that their neurological development, shaped by their early experiences, leads them to think in different ways to their *digital immigrant* parents. Oblinger & Oblinger (2005) in their book *Educating the Net Generation* report a similar facility with ICT among 'Net Gen' university students in the USA, and identify a gap between students' learning orientation and that of their teachers. A large-scale study by Roberts et al. (2005) concluded that young people are comfortable with the simultaneous use of multiple media inputs to an extent which their parents would find intolerable. Digital immigrant parents grew up in a print-dominated world of one-thing-at-a-time linear narratives, so by this account are less ready to cope with situations involving multiple and fast-moving sensory inputs. They are, however more oriented to didactic teaching methods which their children would find unappealing. In the view of Charron et al. (2006), it is the ease of communication and 'perpetual contact' (Katz & Aakhus, 2002) made possible by handheld technology that has fostered a reorientation of trust in digitally-enabled communities, from traditional authority to the peer group:

Easy connections brought about by cheap devices, modular content, and shared computing resources are having a profound impact on our global economy and social structure. Individuals increasingly take cues from one another rather than from institutional sources like corporations, media outlets, religions, and political bodies. (Charron et al., 2006 [unpaginated])

A further gap between what might be called digital youth groups and the education establishment is an organisational one. The establishment, including curriculum experts, educational institutions and teachers, is hierarchically structured in what Brafman & Beckstrom (2006) call a *spider organisation*. Contrasting this is the *starfish organisation*: decentralised and essentially leaderless. As examples, the authors describe the rapid capitulation of the hierarchical Aztec empire to the Spanish *conquistadores* in the 16th Century CE, and compare this to the successful defence of their territory made by the Native American Apache tribe. For over two centuries the Apaches proved easily able to defeat Spanish invading troops by their use of guerrilla tactics. As a starfish organisation and unlike the Aztecs, they had no 'head' to be captured and no command structure to be disrupted. Apache society was by tradition decentralised; in the place of formal chiefs with statutory powers were *Nant'ans* – spiritual and community leaders who led by example rather than by coercion. Social networks, in the context described earlier, are similarly leaderless organisations; the relationships are peer-to-peer and membership is entirely voluntary, mirroring the decentralised, multiply-redundant, interconnected web structure of the Internet. In Green & Hannon's *Their Space* account the Nant'ans are the digital pioneers; talented and driven by curiosity, they lead by example in exploring new applications and interconnections.

Leadbeater (2008) provides many examples of how mass – but decentralised – decision-making via Internet collaboration has proved highly effective (resulting in Scott's 'democratisation of expertise' discussed earlier), citing the Samaritans charity, Linux 'open source' computer software and the Human Genome Project as examples of collective voluntary effort outwith the control of governments and corporations. The Internet, especially in its Web 2.0 manifestation, seems a powerful enabler of starfish organisation, making this way of achieving social goals a viable alternative to hierarchical command-and-control in the conventional capitalist market model of what Ritzer (2000) tellingly describes as *McDonaldization*.

So far, this chapter has identified important factors contextualising the employment of national curricula within current institutional systems. The following two sections examine firstly, how Blended Learning will prove a threat to traditional practice and secondly, how Blended Learning might provide opportunities for creative engagement between policymakers, teachers and students in the development of more flexible and adaptive curricula to meet emerging needs.

BLENDED LEARNING: THE UK EXPERIENCE

Blended Learning is described by many commentators as having the potential to transform educational delivery and content. In the view of Littlejohn & Pegler (2007) it fosters flexibility in time, enabling asynchronous working, and in space, allowing students to learn outside campus and classroom. The wider range of media employed make it possible for students to create and share their own resource collections, and the authors observe that "this brings into question some of the traditional values of education, such as who owns, creates and controls resources and knowledge" (ibid., p. 3). Garrison & Kanuka (2004, p. 97) describe Blended Learning as representing "a fundamental reconceptualization and reorganization of the teaching and learning dynamic" and identify that "what makes blended learning particularly effective is its ability to facilitate a community of inquiry." Recognising that such radical departures are uncharacteristic of conventional university teaching yet increasingly relevant to the 'information age', they argue:

... it is becoming clear that it is essential we do better at facilitating critical, creative, and complex thinking skills. Blended learning offers possibilities to create transformative environments that can effectively facilitate these skills. (ibid., p. 99)

These views are echoed elsewhere by Otte & Benke (2006) in the USA, and by Sharpe et al. (2006) in the UK. This latter review of the undergraduate experience of 'blended e-learning' followed an examination of over 300 research studies with visits to seven universities to evaluate practice. The review found three ways in which Blended Learning was being used:

Currently the most common type of blended learning is the provision of supplementary resources for courses that are conducted predominantly along traditional lines through an institutionally supported virtual learning environment. Second, we found some, but far fewer, impressive examples of transformative course level practices underpinned by radical course designs. These often make use of technology to facilitate interaction and communication and replace other modes of teaching and learning. Third, we are aware of students taking a holistic view of the interaction of technology and their learning, including the use of their own technologies... (ibid., p. 2)

The first of these ways seems to pose no threat to the status quo, but the others do. In the second way, staff felt empowered to radically transform courses, replacing traditional didactic methods with technology-enhanced techniques and negotiated curricula to engage students in active participation and dialogue. In some cases, existing course content was replaced with enquiry-based learning approaches which situated problems in realistic contexts. In these situations there seems to have been a rejection of traditional content and methods as the initiative has been seized by practitioners. The third way can also be seen as empowerment, where students, drawn into a more active role and enabled by ICT, have become less the passive recipients of just-in-case content and more the shapers of their own learning. Indeed, this may be one reason why the response of students to their Blended Learning experiences was reported to be "overwhelmingly positive". The review draws upon the work of Mayes and de Freitas (2004), in their categorisation of learning theories that have impacted on e-learning, into three broad groupings: *associative*, *constructivist* and *situative*, and examples are identified of Blended Learning practice falling into these groups. The constructivist orientation, shared by Garrison & Kanuka (2004), underpins their emphasis on the active engagement of students and teachers in knowledge communities which seek to encourage and respect a diversity of opinions and viewpoints. The situative orientation underpins the moves discussed earlier, away from a sole concern with the delivery of propositional knowledge and its abstract conceptualisation, towards procedural understandings of knowledge in realistic contexts and in application.

In the UK university environment within which the review had been conducted, these findings are encouraging rather than threatening, and exemplify existing notions of the transformative potential of eLearning (Garrison & Anderson, 2003). There is a general acceptance of constructivist approaches and an active encouragement of students to form individual opinions at variance with accepted orthodoxy. The (relative) academic freedom enjoyed by academic staff to adapt content and practice is also regarded as normative rather than subversive. It is, however, when attempts are made to 'export' the approaches of Blended Learning developed in the West to the educational systems of other countries that dissonances might result.

BLENDED LEARNING: CULTURAL COMPLICATIONS

The cultural complications of transplanting one country's educational practices to another have been discussed earlier in the context of the post-colonial legacies which continue to hamper the establishment of more appropriate structures and systems within Developing countries. In this respect the widespread adoption of Blended Learning can be seen as a second wave of this phenomenon, as the expectations and relative freedom of action of Western educators and their students is part of the values baggage accompanying the arrival of what appears to be culturally neutral. In place of the relaxed acceptance of change in the UK reported in the previous section, other national cultures have traditionally maintained greater distance between teachers and taught. Al-Hunaiyyan et al. (2008, p. 23) comment:

Originating from the respect for authority and harmony, Asian people generally prefer formality and indirectness in requesting and criticizing, especially when the authority [is] in presence. The pattern can be found in some small things such as, addressing people by family name with title, to general communication patterns.

As Mason (1998) observes, economic globalisation has proceeded at a far faster pace than educational globalisation, and the national curricula of many countries have been slow to reflect changing economic circumstances. As has been discussed earlier, their content is likely to be embodied in formal, propositional knowledge constructed on the just-in-case assumption that it may be needed in the (relatively predictable) future. There may be less in the way of developing process skills through direct experience in authentic contexts, and more in the way of teaching a defined corpus of knowledge for (perhaps) later application. Didactic methods in the one-size-fits-all environment of the traditional classroom are likely to predominate, and students may be discouraged from collaborating in the pursuit of new understandings. Similarly, teachers may be expected to 'deliver' the curriculum in a standardised fashion, rather than to innovate and – by implication – challenge the wisdom of authority.

Although the bulk of research studies are testament to the effectiveness of Blended Learning, it may be naïve to think of the process as a culture-neutral solution for indiscriminate extension to fit all educational situations. Mason (1998) identifies a whole complex of factors involved: including relations between teachers, schools and curriculum authority; between the status of students, their teachers and the expectations of parents; and between an emphasis on the maintenance of national cultures and cherished traditions, and the preparedness to embrace new ideas and practices. Even the design of computer interfaces carries cultural connotations. In a fascinating study, Marcus & Gould (2000) applied the ideas of cultural anthropologist Geert Hofstede in rating a collection of websites according to five cultural dimensions, including power-distance, collectivism vs. individualism, and femininity vs. masculinity. Their comparison of the homepages of a Malaysian and a Dutch university revealed considerable implicit differences in attitudes to authority and in the role of the individual.

But it is not just in the Western interfaces and (potentially transformative) educational practices of Blended Learning that threats are posed to traditional cultures. Blended Learning inevitably provides some degree of access to Web content. On the one hand, is the availability of Open Educational Resources, and the point has already been made that these materials, largely created in the English-speaking West, may carry unconscious messages. For example, Coulby & Zambeta (2005) discuss effects of the 'narrative of civilization' based on classical Greece, imbuing Western perspectives, which ignores the achievements of other cultures. To non-Western students the content and presentation of Open Educational Resources materials may prove particularly attractive, redolent with perceptions of technological progress and prosperity, but reinforcing a negative view of their own country. For example, Pyvis & Chapman's study (2007) found two types of motivation behind Malaysian students' selection of an Australian offshore campus in preference to a Malaysian university: these were a perception of the Australian degree as a better qualification for employment, and a desire for personal transformation (Westernisation?) through exposure to international ideas and expectations. A similar phenomenon, reported by Van Deven (2008), was the widespread protest in Hong Kong after the 1997 Handover, following a decision by the new government to make Chinese the language of instruction in the majority of its schools. Parents, teachers and businesses objected, seeing English as the language of advancement for their children. On the other hand, there lies a potentially greater threat, through access to Web 2.0 applications, their subversive transnational ideas and communities, and the brash individualism underpinning user-generated content. This trend towards what Lanier (2006) dubs *Digital Maoism* can result in the rapid formation of groups taking direct action against authority. Rheingold (2002) calls these *smart mobs* and describes many examples of how email and SMS text messaging have been used to dynamically orchestrate protest by digitally-enabled members of what Brafman & Beckstrom would call starfish organisations. Such exposure to Western individualism, informality and egalitarianism may contrast sharply with the practices of traditional societies, and may lead to antipathy and rejection.

A development of this view is to regard the complex of educational assumptions and pedagogical practices of Blended Learning as a set of *memes*: described by Dawkins (1976) as powerful ideas with the dynamic of virus-like propagation through societies. This paper identifies six powerful ideas as memes and the conceptual model of their interrelationships is presented in Figure 1.

The *Internet medium* set is seen here as a 'transport layer' enabling open knowledge access and communications. The *Globalisation* set is a complex of socio-cultural, economic and educational practices. In the intersection of these sets lies Blended Learning. The six memes which have been located within these sets are as follows.

Figure 1. Conceptual model of memes associated with blended learning

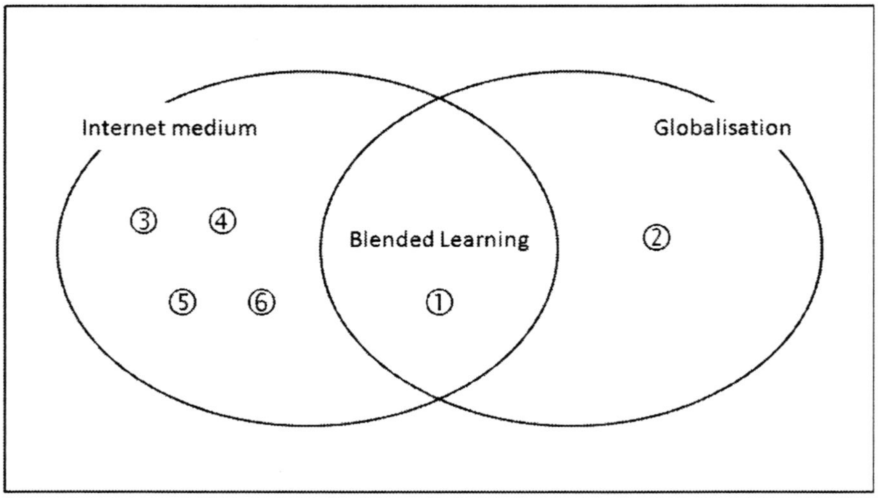

1. A complex of pedagogical practices characteristic of transformative Blended Learning, emphasising constructivist student engagement and empowerment and employing negotiated and situative curricula.
2. 'Westernism': the economic dividend of globalisation, encompassing knowledge economy practices, highly-paid employment, and the perception of prosperity and consumerism.
3. 'Unofficial' use of the Internet medium in the form of Web 2.0 applications for social networking, effectively empowering its young users irrespective of national origin.
4. The mass, decentralised decision-making which is the product of Internet collaboration, leading sometimes into Digital Maoism and the direct action of smart mobs.
5. The growth of the open source movement to bypass proprietary for-profit products and conventional capitalism, and to provide free Open Educational Resources and services.
6. The growing status of procedural know-how against formal, codified propositional knowledge, leading to concerns about the flexibility and relevance of national curricula.

This view of Blended Learning as a set of practices associated with powerful memes makes its adoption much more significant than merely the introduction of new pedagogical techniques. Commentators on memes, such as Kelly (1994), see their power as deriving from the dynamic interplay of economic and socio-cultural forces, and observe that successful memes replicate themselves irrespective of the fortunes – and sometimes to the detriment – of their often unwilling hosts.

BLENDED LEARNING AND NATIONAL CURRICULA: OPPORTUNITIES

Optimistic tacticians know that there are no problems, there are only opportunities; and if the threats discussed above can be recognised and addressed then solutions may be found which can be, in Mason's phrase "globalising without colonising" (1998, p.156). Although many countries have attempted to control the Internet access of their citizens, all have failed to some degree, as the interconnectedness of the Web provides so many alternative routes (Deibert et al., 2008). The attractions of Blended Learning as an effective educational approach are also too great to be ignored. What is needed is an engagement with new techniques and wider perspectives. It must be accepted that the 'genie is out of the bottle' and can never be replaced, and that the tide of powerful memes is unstoppable.

If a proactive stance is taken, the opportunities for knowledge content and pedagogy are significant, and four are considered here. Firstly, there are the scalable cost benefits offered by the online component of Blended Learning once the fixed costs of ICT infrastructure have been met, and the opportunity costs of this need to be laid against the recurrent costs of conventional institution-based educational delivery. Secondly, the adoption of Blended Learning can be a liberating influence upon both the curriculum content and the pedagogical practices of national systems, bringing fresh ideas and approaches into the rather static, introspective and restrictive knowledge bases of some curricula. Coulby & Zambeta (2005) argue that globalisation and nationalism are not necessarily opposing forces, and cite a number of countries which are experiencing a resurgence of national identity, in part as a reaction to greater global awareness. This process seems similar to the notion of *glocalization* popularised by Robertson (1995), in which there can exist contemporaneously a global/virtual as well as a local/community-focus. Thirdly, the employment of ICT opens opportunities for productive collaboration between national systems. Blight et al. (1999) contend that educational partnerships forged at various levels across national borders can result in distinctiveness and variety rather than the inevitability of global homogenisation.

In contrast with globalisation, internationalisation of higher education recognises nations and describes a process of interchange of higher education between nations. It involves partnerships, between nations, between national systems, between accreditation systems, between institutions. (ibid., p. 28)

Fourthly, Blended Learning might help to address the various gaps discussed earlier, so that the educational establishment is seen to be adopting some of the methods and technologies of the knowledge economy, and beginning a process of dialogue and engagement with the leaderless, starfish-structured organisations of mass collectivism.

QUESTIONS FOR NATIONAL POLICY AND PRACTICE

This chapter has examined various types of evidence pointing to the conclusion that Blended Learning and its associated memes will make significant impacts upon the national curricula of many, if not all, countries around the world. Whether these impacts will be beneficial or destabilising to a country will depend crucially upon the policy stances adopted by its educational establishment and how these are implemented at all levels. The chapter concludes with four key questions for educational policy-makers and practitioners in national systems.

1) To what extent have the wider implications of Open Educational Resources and informal, collaborative learning through Web 2.0 been recognised: at national and institutional levels?

This first and most important question concerns what level of awareness politicians and education professionals have of the socio-cultural and pedagogical fall-out of Blended Learning.

The last thirty years have seen the rise of managerialism in Western countries, and in the USA and UK in particular a corresponding decline in the power of education professionals (Clarke & Newman, 1997; Bottery, 2000; Williams, 2005). Here, increasingly prescriptive policy frameworks have been established by governments motivated by factors other than purely educational (Shuayb & O'Donnell, 2008). It is therefore vital for educators in all countries to debate these issues and to raise them in the public consciousness.

2) What strategies might be employed at national level to address the implications of Blended Learning which have been discussed in this chapter?

This second question for national systems, especially in non-Western countries, concerns the choice of an appropriate and proactive policy response. Some potential benefits of Blended Learning as well as threats have been identified, so the aim should be to craft educational policies which maximise the former while simultaneously offsetting the latter.

3) How might curricula be made more flexible and adaptive, while retaining their national distinctiveness?

The third question is related to the previous, but concerns pedagogical rather than wider issues. Again, the opportunities presented by Blended Learning are considerable, but careful and sensitive introduction strategies are necessary in order to manage the pedagogic transition in a way that preserves characteristic national values.

4) How might schools and universities embrace these unfamiliar practices in socially and culturally as well as educationally blended learning?

This final question is not so much for policy-makers as for educational practitioners. The central contention of this chapter has been that for non-Western countries the adoption of Blended Learning entails more than changes in pedagogic practice. This implies a broader interpretation of Blended Learning: as a social and cultural as well as pedagogic blend, sensitive to wider national considerations as well as recognising and negotiating the different perceptions and organisational dynamics of 'digital native' students. As Williams (2008b) argues, to achieve this goal will require considerable preparedness on the part of educational practitioners to extend their personal ICT skills, to develop their professional practice in the employment of educationally effective blending, and to share and delegate some of their traditional authority in forging new, more interactive and democratic patterns of engagement with students and their communities.

REFERENCES

Al-Hunaiyyan, A., Al-Huwail, N., & Al-Sharhan, S. (2008). Blended e-learning design: Discussion of cultural issues. *International Journal of Cyber Society and Education, 1*(1), 17-32. Retrieved on December 1, 2008, from http://www.academic-journals.org/ojs2/index.php/IJCSE/article/viewFile/401/3

Amazon.com. (2008). *Amazon Web site*. Retrieved on September 1, 2008, from http://www.amazon.com

Anderson, P. (2007). *What is Web 2.0? Ideas, technologies, and implications for education*. JISC Technology and Standards Watch. London: Joint Information Systems Committee. Retrieved on September 1, 2008, from http://www.jisc.ac.uk/media/documents/techwatch/tsw0701b.pdf

Annan, K. (2002). *The role of the state in the age of globalisation, keynote address to conference on globalisation and international relations in the 21st century*. New York: United Nations Publications.

Barua, B. (2007). Colonialism, education, and rural Buddhist communities in Bangladesh. *International Education, 37*(1), 60–77.

Baudrillard, J. (1983). *Simulations*. New York: Semiotexte.

Benavot, A. (2006). *The diversification of secondary education: School curricula in comparative perspective*. Working Papers on Curriculum Issues N° 6, International Bureau of Education. Paris: UNESCO.

Benkler, Y. (2006). *The wealth of networks: How social production transforms markets and freedom*. New Haven: Yale University Press.

Blight, D., Davis, D., & Olsen, A. (1999). The internationalisation of higher education. In K. Harry (Ed.), *Higher education through open and distance learning, world review of distance education and open learning* (Vol. 1, pp. 15-31). London: RoutledgeFalmer.

Bottery, M. (2000). *Education, policy, and ethics*. London: Continuum.

Brafman, O., & Beckstrom, R. (2006). *The starfish and the spider: The unstoppable power of leaderless organisations*. New York: Portfolio.

Broers, N. (2002). Selection and use of propositional knowledge in statistical problem solving. *Learning and Instruction, 12*(3), 323–344. doi:10.1016/S0959-4752(01)00025-1

Castells, M. (1997). *End of millennium, volume three of the information age: Economy, society, and culture*. Oxford: Blackwell.

Castells, M. (2001). *The Internet galaxy: Reflections on the Internet, business, and society*. Oxford: Oxford University Press.

CETIS. (2005). *What is ADL SCORM?* Standards Briefings Series, Centre For Educational Technology Interoperability Standards, UK Joint Information Systems Committee. Retrieved on December 1, 2008, from http://www.icodeon.com/pdf/WhatIsScorm2_web.pdf

Charron, C., et al. (2006). *Social computing: How networks erode institutional power, and what to do about it*. Forrester Research. Retrieved on September 1, 2008, from http://www.forrester.com/Research/Document/Excerpt/0,7211,38772,00.html

Clarke, J., & Newman, J. (1997). *The managerial state*. London: Sage.

Commons, O. E. R. (2008). *OER Commons Web site*. Retrieved on September 1, 2008, from http://www.oercommons.org

Coulby, D., & Zambeta, E. (Eds.). (2005). *Globalization and nationalism in education*. London: RoutledgeFalmer.

Creative Commons. (2008). *Creative commons*. Retrieved on September 1, 2008, from http://creativecommons.org

Crystal, D. (2003). *English as a global language* (second edition). Cambridge: Cambridge University Press.

Dawkins, R. (1976). *The selfish gene*. Oxford: Oxford University Press.

Deibert, R., Palfrey, J., Rohozinski, R., & Zittrain, J. (2008). *Access denied: The practice and policy of global Internet filtering*. Massachusetts: MIT Press. del.icio.us. (2008). *Delicious Web site*. Retrieved on September 1, 2008, from http://del.icio.us

Digital Ethnography. (2008). *You Tube usage statistics, digital ethnography Web site*. Retrieved on December 1, 2008, from http://ksudigg.wetpaint.com/page/YouTube+Statistics?t=anon

Ducatel, K. (1998). *Learning and skills in the knowledge economy*. DRUID Working Paper No 98-2, Danish Research Institute for Industrial Dynamics, Aalborg University. Retrieved on September 1, 2008, from http://www.druid.dk/wp/pdf_files/98-2.pdf

Dunbar, R. (1991). Adapting distance education for Indonesians: Problems with learner heteronomy and a strong oral tradition. *Distance Education, 12*(2), 163–174. doi:10.1080/0158791910120203

EC. (2008). *i2010-a European information society for growth and employment*. Brussels: European Commission. Retrieved on September 1, 2008, from http://ec.europa.eu/information_society/eeurope/i2010/strategy/index_en.htm

EU. (2008). Bologna process Web site. Brussels: Benelux Bologna Secretariat. Retrieved on September 1, 2008, from http://www.ond.vlaanderen.be/hogeronderwijs/bologna

Facebook. (2008). *Facebook Web site*. Retrieved on September 1, 2008, from http://www.facebook.com

Garrison, D., & Anderson, T. (2003). *E-learning in the 21st century: A framework for research and practice*. London: RoutledgeFalmer.

Garrison, D., & Kanuka, H. (2004). Blended learning: Uncovering its transformative potential in higher education. *The Internet and Higher Education*, *7*(2), 95–105. doi:10.1016/j.iheduc.2004.02.001

Gibbons, M., Limoges, C., Nowotny, H., Scott, P., Schwartzman, S., & Trow, M. (1994). *The new production of knowledge–the dynamics of science and research in contemporary societies*. London: Sage Publications.

Green, H., & Hannon, C. (2007). *Their space: Education for a digital generation*. London: Demos.

Harry, K. (Ed.). (n.d.). *Higher education through open and distance learning, world review of distance education and open learning* (Vol. 1, pp. 15-31). London: RoutledgeFalmer.

INCA. (2008). *International review of curriculum and assessment frameworks Internet archive*. Retrieved on September 1, 2008, from http://www.inca.org.uk

Katz, J., & Aakhus, M. (Eds.). (2002). *Perpetual contact: Mobile communication, private talk, public performance*. Cambridge: Cambridge University Press.

Kelly, K. (1994). *Out of control: The new biology of machines, social systems, and the economic world*. Boston: Addison-Wesley.

Lanier, J. (2006). *Digital Maoism: The hazards of the new online collectivism. Edge: The third culture*. Edge Foundation, Inc. Retrieved on September 1, 2008, from http://www.edge.org/3rd_culture/lanier06/lanier06_index.html

Leadbeater, C. (2008). *We-think*. London: Profile Books.

Littlejohn, A., & Pegler, C. (2007). *Preparing for blended e-learning*. Abingdon: Routledge.

Lyotard, J.-F. (1984). *The postmodern condition: A report on knowledge*. Manchester: Manchester University Press.

Magalhães, A., & Stoer, S. (2003). Performance, citizenship, and the knowledge society: A new mandate for European education policy. *Globalisation, Societies and Education*, *1*(1), 41–66. doi:10.1080/1476772032000061815

Malcolm, M. (2005). The exercise of the object: Issues in resource reusability and reuse. *British Journal of Educational Technology*, *36*(1), 33–41. doi:10.1111/j.1467-8535.2005.00436.x

Marcus, A., & Gould, E. W. (2000). Cultural dimensions and global Web user-interface design: What? So what? Now what? *Interactions (New York, N.Y.)*, *7*(4), 32–46. doi:10.1145/345190.345238

Marshall, H., & Arnot, M. (2008). *Globalising the school curriculum: Gender, EFA, and global citizenship education*. Working Paper No. 17, Research Consortium on Educational Outcomes and Poverty (RECOUP). Cambridge: University of Cambridge.

Mason, R. (1998). *Globalising education: Trends and applications*. London: Routledge.

Mayes, T., & de Freitas, S. (2004). *Review of e-learning theories, frameworks, and models. Stage 2 of the e-learning models desk study*. Joint Information Systems Committee (JISC). Retrieved on September 1, 2008, from http://www.jisc.ac.uk/uploaded_documents/Stage%202%20Learning%20Models%20(Version%201).pdf

McAndrew, P. (2005). *What is needed for global e-learning?* Document ID KN6779, OU Knowledge Network. Retrieved on December 1, 2008, from http://kn.open.ac.uk/public/document.cfm?docid=6779

MEST. (2008). *Ministry of Education, Science and Technology.* South Korea. Retrieved on September 1, 2008, from http://english.mest.go.kr

Metrios, S. (2005). Learning objects: A rose by any other name... *Educause Review, 40*(4), 12–13. Retrieved on December 1, 2008, from http://connect.educause.edu/Library/EDUCAUSE+Review/LearningObjectsARosebyAny/40559

Micklethwait, J., & Wooldridge, A. (2000). *A future perfect: The essentials of globalization.* New York: Crown Business.

Moe, M., Bailey, K., & Lau, R. (1999). *The book of knowledge: Investing in the growing education and training industry.* Global Securities Research and Economic Group and Global Fundamental Equity Research Department. San Francisco: Merrill Lynch and Co.

Mukhamedyarova, Z., & Cotter, M. (2005). Interactive methods of teaching as a condition for developing students' independent learning skills in Kazakhstan and the U.S. *International Education, 34*(2), 62–72.

Nguyen, F. (2004). *Killing two birds with one stone: Creating EPSS through e-learning.* Arizona State University/Intel Corporation, reproduced on the American Society for Training & Development Web site. Retrieved on September 1, 2008, from http://www.astd.org/NR/rdonlyres/8F40492E-4850-4F5AB74B0D-3C25C4BF61/5840/W206forWeb.pdf

NMC/EDUCAUSE. (2007). *2007 horizon report.* Joint publication of the New Media Consortium (NMC) and EDUCAUSE. Retrieved on September 1, 2008, from http://www.nmc.org/horizon

Norget, K. (2007). Decolonization and the politics of syncretism: The Catholic Church, indigenous theology, and cultural autonomy in Oaxaca, Mexico. *International Education, 37*(1), 78–97.

O'Reilly. (2005). *What is Web 2.0: Design patterns and business models for the next generation of software.* O'Reilly Media. Retrieved on September 1, 2008, from http://www.oreillynet.com/pub/a/oreilly/tim/news/2005/09/30/what-is-web-20.html

Oblinger, D., & Oblinger, J. (2005). Is it age or IT: First steps toward understanding the Net generation. In D. Oblinger & J. Oblinger (Eds.), *Educating the Net generation.* Educause (pp. 2.1-2.19). Retrieved on September 1, 2008, from http://www.educause.edu/educatingthenetgen

OCW. (2008). MIT OpenCourseWare. Massachusetts Institute of Technology. Retrieved on September 1, 2008, from http://ocw.mit.edu

OECD. (2006). Programme for international student assessment. Paris: Organisation for Economic Cooperation and Development. Retrieved on September 1, 2008, from http://www.pisa.oecd.org/pages/0,2987,en_32252351_32235731_1_1_1_1_1,00.html

Ohmae, K. (1995). *The end of the nation state: The rise of regional economies.* New York: The Free Press.

Opetusministeriö. (2008). Finland: Ministry of Education. Retrieved on September 1, 2008, from http://www.minedu.fi/OPM/Koulutus/koulutusjaerjestelmae/?lang=en

Otte, G., & Benke, M. (2006). Online learning: New models for leadership and organization in higher education. *Journal of Asynchronous Learning Networks, 10*(2).

PicoPeta. (2008). PicoPeta Simputers Pvt. Ltd. Retrieved on September 1, 2008, from http://www.picopeta.com

Prensky, M. (2001). Digital natives, digital immigrants. *On the Horizon, 9*(5). NCB University Press.

Pyvis, D., & Chapman, A. (2007). Why university students choose an international education: A case study in Malaysia. *International Journal of Educational Development, 27*, 235–246. doi:10.1016/j.ijedudev.2006.07.008

Reich, R. (1991). *The work of nations*. New York: Vintage Books.

Rheingold, H. (2002). *Smart mobs: The next social revolution*. Cambridge, MT: Basic Books.

Ritzer, G. (2000). *The McDonaldization of society*. Thousand Oaks, CA: Pine Forge Press.

Roberts, D., Foehr, U., & Rideout, V. (2005). *Generation M: Media in the lives of 8-18 year-olds*. Menlo Park, CA: Kaiser Family Foundation. Retrieved on September 1, 2008, from http://www.kff.org/entmedia/upload/Generation-M-Media-in-the-Lives-of-8-18-Year-olds-Report.pdf

Robertson, R. (1995). Glocalization. In M. Featherstone, et al. (Eds.), *Global modernities*. London: Sage.

SCHOLAR. (2008). *The SCHOLAR programme Web site*. Heriot-Watt University, Edinburgh. Retrieved on September 1, 2008, from http://scholar.hw.ac.uk/

Schön, D. (1983). *The reflective practitioner: How professionals think in action*. New York: Basic Books.

Scott, P. (1998). Massification, internationalization, and globalization. In P. Scott (Ed.), *The globalization of higher education* (pp. 108-129). Buckingham: The Society for Research into Higher Education & Open University Press.

Scott, P. (2002). The future of general education in mass higher education systems. *Higher Education Policy, 15*, 61–75. doi:10.1016/S0952-8733(01)00036-8

Sharpe, R., Benfield, G., Roberts, G., & Francis, R. (2006). *The undergraduate experience of blended e-learning: A review of UK literature and practice*. York: The Higher Education Academy.

Shuayb, M., & O'Donnell, S. (2008). *Aims and values in primary education: England and other countries*. The Primary Review, Research Survey 1/2, National Foundation for Educational Research. Cambridge: University of Cambridge.

Strange, S. (1996). *The retreat of the state: The diffusion of power in the world economy*. Cambridge: Cambridge University Press.

Tulgan, B., & Martin, C. (2001). *Managing generation Y: Global citizens born in the late seventies and early eighties*. Amherst, MA: Human Resource Development Press.

UKOU. (2008). *LabSpace*. UK: The Open University. Retrieved on September 1, 2008, from http://labspace.open.ac.uk

Van Deven, T. (2008). Access denied: A story of resistance. In J. Zajda, L. Davies & S. Majhanovich (Eds.), *Globalisation, comparative, and global Pedagogies* (Vol. 2, pp. 71-86). The Netherlands: Springer.

Wikipedia. (2008). *Wikipedia: The free encyclopedia*. Retrieved on September 1, 2008, from http://en.wikipedia.org

Williams, P. (2005). Lessons from the future: ICT scenarios and the education of teachers. *Journal of Education for Teaching, 31*(4), 319–339. doi:10.1080/02607470500280209

Williams, P. (2007). Valid knowledge: The economy and the academy. *Higher Education, 54*(4), 511–523. doi:10.1007/s10734-007-9051-y

Williams, P. (2008a). Assessing context based learning: Not only rigorous but also relevant. *Assessment & Evaluation in Higher Education, 33*(4), 395–408. doi:10.1080/02602930701562890

Williams, P. (2008b). Leading schools in the digital age: A clash of cultures. *School Leadership & Management*, *28*(3), 213–228. doi:10.1080/13632430802145779

You Tube. (2008). Retrieved on September 1, 2008, from http://www.youtube.com

Chapter 2
Perspectives on Blended Open Distance Education Learning and Teaching in a South African Context

Shawren Singh
University of South Africa, South Africa

Hsuan Lorraine Liang
University of South Africa, South Africa

ABSTRACT

In this chapter, we will discuss the blended learning approach that has been adopted by the University of South Africa (an open and distance learning tertiary education institute). We will discuss our perspectives on using these blended learning approaches and tools in order to facilitate our teaching. We will then provide a comparison on the advantages and disadvantages of some of the blended approaches we have used. We will also discuss the future trends of the use of blended approaches in the context of open distance education and learning. Lastly, we will conclude this chapter by providing our perspectives on the blended learning and teaching approaches adopted by the University of South Africa.

INTRODUCTION

In this chapter, we will discuss the blended learning approaches that have been adopted by the University of South Africa (Unisa). Unisa combines distance education and open learning in order to form its unique open-distance-learning model. Open Distance Learning (ODL) is seen as a multi-dimensional system aimed at bridging the time, geographical and transactional distance between students, lecturers, tutors, courseware, and the university.

Various approaches and models exist to blended learning (Ginns & Ellis, 2007; Khine & Lourdusamy, 2003; Valiathan, 2002). Each has its own advantages and disadvantages. At this university being an ODL university, we use a blended approach taking into account the limited resources and students who have diverse needs and who are geographically spread around the world. We do not echo the technologies used in developed countries.

DOI: 10.4018/978-1-60566-852-9.ch002

First and foremost, we will provide the background and explain the nature of Unisa and its blended learning and teaching approaches. The purpose of this chapter is to provide other institutions of higher education, particularly those in developing countries, adequate knowledge and insights into the problems experienced by Unisa through our experiences and perspectives. We will discuss the challenges and issues of embarking on blended open distance education learning and teaching in a developing country, specifically South Africa. We write a personal account of our experiences using these blended learning approaches and tools in order to facilitate our teaching. We will then provide a comparison on the advantages and disadvantages of some of the blended approaches we have used. We will also discuss the future trends of the use of blended approaches in the context of open distance education and learning. Finally, we will conclude this chapter by providing our perspectives on the blended learning and teaching approaches adopted by Unisa.

BACKGROUND

Unisa – a Mega University

The vision of Unisa is to become Africa's premier distance education provider, serving every country on the continent and around the world and transcending language, cultural and political barriers.

Unisa is an ODL university that offers degrees in agriculture and environmental sciences, economic and management sciences, human sciences, law, and science, engineering and technologies. The South African Department of Education has mandated Unisa to produce high quality gradu-

Table 1. Brief history of Unisa (University of South Africa, 2008)

Year	Key Events	Comments
1873	Establishment of the University of the Cape of Good Hope in Cape Town.	
1877	The University of the Cape of Good Hope received a Royal Charter from Queen Victoria.	
1877 to 1916	The University of the Cape of Good Hope served as an examining body for Victoria College, Stellenbosch and the University of Cape Town.	
1916	Act 12 of 1916 decreed that the University of the Cape of Good Hope is to be incorporated into the federal University of South Africa on 2 April 1918.	The structure of the university was radically amended. Control was vested in a council and senate, upon which seven constituent colleges were represented. These colleges later became various independent universities.
1918	The university moved to Pretoria.	The federal university did not teach private students; it merely examined them. Other correspondence colleges existed.
1945	More than 20 institutions were teaching private students and Unisa's Council appointed a Director of External Studies.	
	The Higher Education Amendment Act of 1946 enables the university to undertake tuition and guidance of students for its examinations.	
1946	Unisa became the first public university in the world to teach exclusively by means of correspondence.	The university started progressing through different generations of distance education models: A correspondence institution, the incorporation of multimedia (radio, tapes, videos and videoconferencing), the use of tutors, and the use of the Internet.
2004	There was a merger of Unisa, Technikon South Africa and the distance education unit of Vista University.	This was a Department of Education initiative.

ates who are both nationally and internationally marketable. We provided a brief history of Unisa in Table 1.

Unisa has become the only dedicated, public, distance education institution in South African when it merged with Technikon South Africa and Vista University in 2004. The merger took place as a result of the vision for a transformed higher education landscape envisaged in the South African National Plan for Higher Education (NPHE2001). Unisa was accredited by the Distance Education and Training Council (DETC) in Washington DC, in the United States.

Prior to the merger, Unisa progressed through different methods of distance education: a correspondence institution; the incorporation of multimedia; the introduction of a tutor system; and the use of Student OnLine (SOL) portal where students can perform administrative tasks such as checking assignment/examination results, modifying personal details, submitting assignments, accessing study material, and interacting with fellow students through the online forum.

The merger has presented various opportunities. They are an integration of academic offerings, administrative functions, understanding tuition models, different pedagogical stances, meeting strategic needs of the South Africa, providing a transparent merger, and integrating different academic profiles and cultures, to name a few (Singh & De Ridder, 2005).

For the academics of the university to efficiently and effectively carry out the mandate of the South African Department of Education, Unisa employs a blended approach to teach its increasing number of students. In line with the goals of the Department of Education, Unisa is aiming to be one of the first South African paperless campuses.

As mentioned earlier, various approaches and models exist to blended learning (Ginns & Ellis, 2007; Khine & Lourdusamy, 2003; Valiathan, 2002). Unisa being an ODL university uses a blended approach taking into account the limited resources (i.e. human resource) and students who have diverse needs and who are geographically spread around the world. The study conducted by Singh & Kotze (2003) focused on the divides and attempts to find common grounds amongst a culturally diverse population in their uses of technology. The study indicated that cultural differences for the so-called "net-generation" target audience do not affect their activities on the Web (Singh & Kotze, 2003).

According to the studies conducted by Singh & Engelbrecht (2004), the major factors that influence Unisa and its students are social political issues (such as economic forces, political factors, primary and secondary schooling, university policy, and cultural forces); support structures (such as technology, country's infrastructure, university policies, and schooling systems); and social clustering (such as geography and local/international resident). Each of these factors contributes to the degree of involvement of technology in the teaching and learning model of Unisa. All of the mentioned factors together with the students' backgrounds in turn influence the teaching approaches adopted by this ODL university.

One crucial hindrance is that although Internet access (and telecommunication networks in general) in South Africa has continued to grow each year, it has been a very slow growth and the growth has slowed down significantly (Singh, 2006). This is due to high usage costs (the telecommunication company's monopoly) and poor access (infrastructures needs to be expanded over large geographic areas). We will support this claim later in this chapter.

One of the biggest challenges for distance education, particularly in the context of South Africa as a developing country, is achieving effective and efficient communication between all relevant parties, namely students, the university, and academic staff. Blended learning is one of the proposed solutions for achieving sustained communication, building on existing good practices, and introducing change plans where needed.

Unisa has combined several delivery methods to facilitate flexibility, encourage student's access to and participation in higher education (e.g. the use of *my*Unisa and Osprey which we will discuss in detail in the subsequent sections), and improve the engagement and autonomy of the students.

The Birth of *my*Unisa

According to University of South Africa (2008), the needs of developing countries in Africa are rather different from those of developed countries. For this reason, the South African Sakai community has consolidated to form a united voice for the African continent and its unique needs. The first version of *my*Unisa built on Sakai went live in January 2006. After the roll out of *my*Unisa, an extensive training and documentation was launched (it is the opinion of the authors, from a software engineering perspective, key stakeholders participation should have been considered and included earlier. Here key stakeholders are referring to the university (the lecturers in particular), students, and *my*Unisa support staff.).

- Integrating academic offerings
- Integrating administrative functions
- Understanding tuition models
- Different pedagogical stances
- Meeting strategic needs of South Africa
- Providing a transparent assessment approach
- Integrating different academic profiles and cultures

*my*Unisa has the functionalities of a commercial software. However, a decision was taken that many features were deactivated when *my*Unisa was first launched. One reason for this decision was that of the immaturity of the online tuition abilities of most of Unisa's academic staff (it is the opinion of the authors that this would not be the case if the academics were involved in the process and concurrently trained). For example, we experimented with Skype (and vSkype) as a 'cheap' and alternative communication tools for our students. Out of our own funds, we purchased the microphones and webcams. The consequences of this experiment lead to the increase of our Internet usage for which we were disciplined. It was costly to the university, which is probably the reason why most features of *my*Unisa may have been deactivated. It must be noted from a technical support staff perspective that the *my*Unisa's support team is severely understaffed at this stage (University of South Africa, 2008).

Adoption of *my*Unisa by Unisa's students is on the increase. By the end of 2006, the total number of registered students at Unisa were 284 783 and 120 765 were registered as *my*Unisa users. This is 42.4% of the student population. The number of students that joined *my*Unisa at the end of 2007 were 159 538 out of a total of 265 912 registered students. This accounts for 60% of the student population at Unisa and this is an 18% increase in usage. During 2007, 77 154 additional students joined *my*Unisa. 161 655 students who were registered for the 2007 academic year used *my*Unisa. A total of 327 040 students registered on the Unisa central system in 2007 and of these, 313 297 had cellular phone numbers, 212 415 had e-mail addresses, and 206 903 had both. It is estimated by the university that it will reach 100% adoption rate by Unisa's students at the end of 2009.

Although *my*Unisa is slowly being accepted and adopted as a teaching tool, there are several areas that pose challenges (University of South Africa, 2008):

- The adoption rate is low amongst academics.
- The general feeling from several academic staff members is that it incurs additional work because not all students are online as it is optional.
- Access to technology is still a challenge for students.

- The core development team is understaffed.
- *my*Unisa's team members also support and maintain the information systems of other universities.
- Collaboration among ICT staff is strained.
- Difficulty is experienced in delivering a truly 24/7 service.
- High usage during assignment submission deadlines places a severe strain on the general Unisa infrastructure.

In the following section, we will write a personal account of our experiences using blended learning and blended learning tools in our modules. We will discuss our experiences from the perspectives of the usage of the tools.

BLENDED LEARNING TOOLS ADOPTED

One of the objectives of Unisa is to establish service-oriented technology-enhanced learner support to address the needs of a diverse learner profile by offering relevant learner support facilitated by appropriate information and communication technologies. Blended learning is a solution that combines a number of different delivery methods and various event-based activities. The nature of a blended learning tool can either be active or passive. In this section, we will discuss how we use a blend of active and passive tools to facilitate the learning process. Figure 1 illustrates the approaches that have been adopted by Unisa. On a more context-specific level, we will discuss

Figure 1. Blended tools used

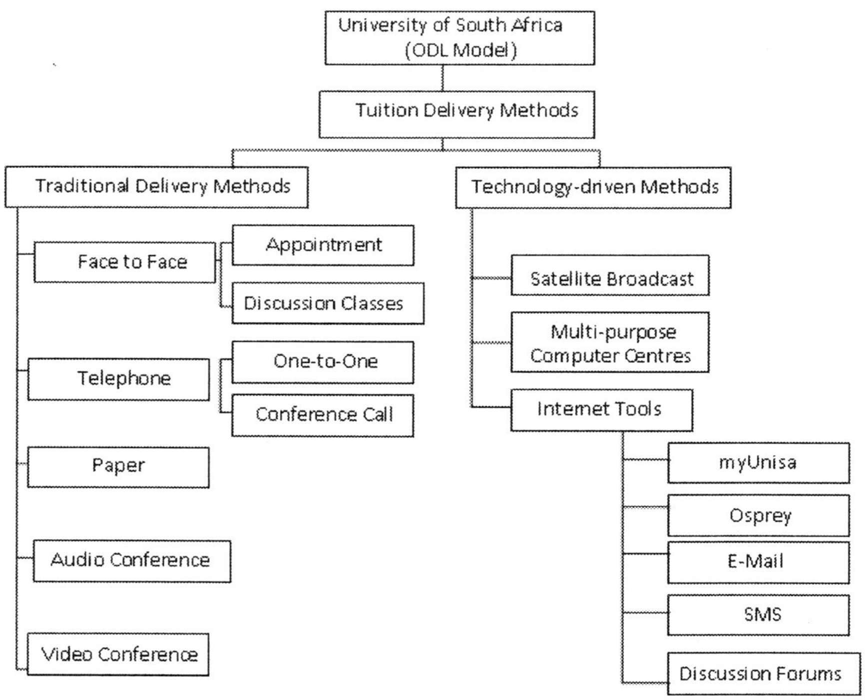

the barriers to blended learning that affect the Unisa students.

Active Tools

The active blended learning tools adopted by Unisa are:

- ***my*Unisa** is a generic Web-based tool offered campus-wide to all faculties by the university. *my*Unisa supports assignment uploads, examination administration, graduation information, library information and services, peer collaborative learning, study information and registration, and tutorial services amongst others. The development of this student portal is an ongoing activity by the ICT department at Unisa. It has undergone many generations of transformation.
- **Osprey** is a customised Web-based tool used exclusively by the School of Computing to facilitate communication with their students. Osprey supports dynamic availability of academics in the School and the College of Science, Engineering and Technologies, peer collaborative learning, tutorial matter downloads, and tutorial services. On Osprey, the module facilitators have more control and management over the tool.
- **E-mail** is becoming a common tool of virtual collaboration between academics and students. We have two methods of e-mailing communication, namely individual e-mails and generic bulk e-mails.
- **Telephone service** is still a key communication tool between academics and students. Students still prefer the human resource aspect.
- **Face-to-face** is no doubt still an essential method of interaction between lecturers and students. Limited availability of lecturers dictates that face-to-face discussion classes, workshops and one-on-one consultation are kept to the bare minimum.
- **Discussion forums**: Online discussion forums/bulletin boards/newsgroups serve as a powerful means of enhancing learning in distance education. Discussion forums can serve a simple socialising function, i.e. a medium for students to informally communicate with other fellow students or express emotions concerning their studies (what we refer to as "effective issues"). Students also use them to attempt to resolve administrative and technical problems. More importantly, discussion forums provide a means for students to express content-related problems that they are experiencing. Lecturer/tutor involvement in discussion forums provides a means of helping a number of students simultaneously, as opposed to telephone or email communication which can provide help to one student at a time. Many students participate in the forums and help others - a proven means of enhancing their own learning - whereas other students simply "lurk", benefiting from the interaction of active participants.

Discussion forums represent a low cost and powerful means of addressing a number of problems particular to students learning at a distance. They provide a means of helping a large number of students with their studies, whether they have questions relating to module content or technical and administrative problems. They can also serve as a place for socialising and for building a learning community. Lecturers' involvement appears to be important, particularly in the earlier stages, for the discussion forums to gain momentum. Lecturers' intervention is seldom required as it can stifle further discussion between students and a learning opportunity. By participating, students have to reflect on their problems to be able to express them in words. They learn by helping others. Finally, discussion forums provide an opportunity for students to learn by simply observing the discussion and interaction of others (Matyila & Halland, 2004).

Other than the above-mentioned blended learning tools, Unisa also provides digital learner support in the forms of telemetric technologies. They include the following:

- **Satellite broadcasting**: This tool has mainly been used for live or pre-recorded presentations of lectures, tutorials, scientific experiments, and training programmers' to students at remote venues via a television screen. This is a fairly new service delivery option offered by Unisa.
- **Audio conferencing and videoconferencing**: These tools can be easily integrated into the ODL program with minimal adaptation to the module design. They support two-way audio and video communication between students and lecturers, students and tutors, or peer students at decentralized locations.
- **Multi-purpose computer centers**: This tool bridges the digital divide among students, especially those who locate in remote rural and disadvantaged communities. It enables access to technology.

In the following section, we will discuss how we use these active tools to facilitate the learning process.

THE USAGE OF THE ACTIVE TOOLS

In this subsection, we will discuss how the tools described earlier are adopted to facilitate the learning and teaching process in the context of Unisa. We will describe *my*Unisa and Osprey separately. Notice that *my*Unisa and Osprey are both described in great details in order to illustrate the levels of difficulty for using each of the tools without any prior training. We explain how the tools work and also highlight how the lecturer can set up and use the tools without any prior training and why there is initial resistance from academics.

*my*Unisa

*my*Unisa is the official university website for Unisa. It is a secure student portal where only students and staff members can log onto by using the URL: http://my.unisa.ac.za. The ICT department has adopted the ISO9001/2000, ITIL and CoBit standards (Official ITIL Website, 2008) as its quality assurance and governance frameworks. Here we provide an overview of the interaction of various tools on this service portal.

The welcome page for the *my*Unisa portal is shown in Figure 6 (see Appendix). This is where general information concerning the university is provided and where students and/or staff members can log on to access their personal accounts.

Figure 2 represents the tools provided on the *my*Unisa portal from both the lecturer's and the student's views. It is an overview of how different tools are integrated by the portal. The diagram is divided into four quadrants and each of which is indicated in Figures 7 to 17 (see Appendix).

Quadrant 1

The lecturer's view for the *my*Unisa portal is shown in Figure 7. This is where the lecturers can obtain tools to assist them to manage general administrative and student-related issues. This can be broadly divided into: course administration, communication and assessment.

Quadrant 2

Figure 8 provides lecturers with tools for module-specific management. This can be simply describes as the nuts and bolts of a particular module.

Figure 2. myUnisa Portal

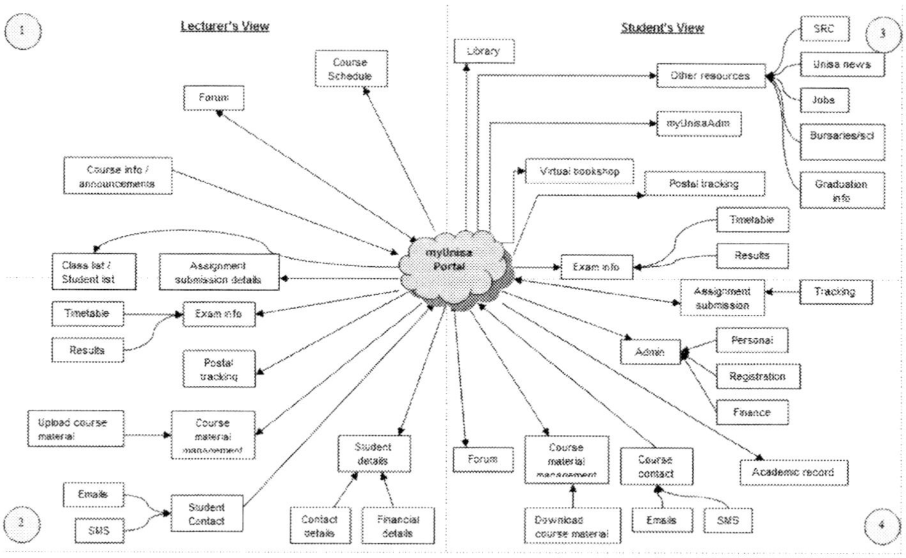

Quadrant 3

The student's view for the *my*Unisa portal is shown in Figure 9. This is a personalised space where the student obtains both administrative information and is a portal that leads to module-specific information.

Some of the features that the student has access to are the:

- Library
- Virtual bookshop
- Examination information
- Administrative tools (to update personal data, change examination centre)
- Postal tracking: This is an important feature as students can track their study material. Unisa is currently still a paper-based university.

Quadrant 4

Figure 10 is where the student obtains module-specific information. This is the core area where the student is involved in various academic activities. Some of the key features are:

- Assignment submission
- Download tutorial material
- Discussion forums

*my*Unisa Online Discussion Forum

The discussion forum on *my*Unisa works and behaves like any other generic discussion forum. Some instructors encourage their students to use the discussion forum by awarding the most active participant with a prize. Students using the discussion forum can use any language of choice; the rule of thumb, however, is for students to use English. A simple pictorial explanation of the forum can be found in Figures 11 to 20 (see Appendix).

Initial view of a course discussion forum (Default setting/Initial view) is shown in Figure 11. Figure 12 provides the view of a course discussion forum after the user clicked on the Forum Name displayed on the previous screen (we have now gone one level deeper into the hierarchy of the discussion forum). Figure 13 shows how one can add new messages or reply to a message. Figure 15 shows how one can create a new forum topic. Figure 17 provides the view of the forum "General Subject Related Discussions" which has two topics. Figure 18 shows how one can create new forum categories (for lecturers only). Figure 19 is available for the user to enter a new forum title or name and a brief description of the purpose of the forum. Figure 20 shows what the Discussion Forum for MEL8246-07-S1 looks like when there are two forum titles.

Note that some usability considerations were taken into account in the design of this forum. Furthermore, it is to emphasise the fact that this is the only channel that students, who are geographically dispersed, can communicate with each other and as well with their lecturers. In the School of Computing at Unisa, the lecturers strongly encourage our students to make use of the forum.

Student List Tool

The Student List tool allows lecturers to generate a customised list of students registered for a specific module or a selection of modules. The Class List on the other hand, will only display the contact information of those students who indicated on their registration form that their information may be displayed on *my*Unisa. It is advisable not to use the Student List to send bulk e-mails to students, instead use the Mailing List. An e-mail is considered spam in the Unisa context when it contains superfluous information not directly linked to the teaching and learning of the subjects. Therefore, research questionnaires, marketing of commercial products, etc. are considered as spam. Figure 21 (see Appendix) shows the customising options for a student list.

Mailing List Tool

The Mailing List tool allows lecturers to send urgent, short messages to students in one or more of the modules for which the lecturers are responsible. This tool allows the lecturers to confine the list of e-mail addresses to which they wish to send the message by searching for specific groups such as gender and/or race. Note that it will only send messages to registered student who are also registered on *my*Unisa with valid and verified e-mail addresses.

Tutorial on the *my*Unisa Materials Tool

*my*Unisa provides a Materials tool which has become the most widely used feature for sharing information. In the Materials tool, the lecturers or the administrator can make many types of files available online. Notice that the Materials tool consists of a folder called **Official Study Material** which is automatically created and one may create as many folders as one wishes. Sharing of information with the students is easy and controllable. Simply create any necessary folders in each module site and upload materials for the students of that particular module. The **Official Study Material** folder only contains files uploaded via the File Manager (PDF process). Any files or sub-folders created will be deleted. Additional files and folders in the Materials tool are not automatically printed and mailed to students. It acts as a valuable source of module information for diligent students. Additional materials that were not distributed to all students may not be examined. Additional materials are considered in the same category as the "in office" discussions with students which provide students with an edge without taking away or disadvantaging those who never visit or choose to ignore any additional and recommended materials. It is also possible to set additional materials active or inactive based on the dates stipulated on the system.

Discussion Forums in the Unisa Context

Lecturers should clearly explain the aim and the usage of the discussion forums. In addition, lecturers need to inform students what they can expect from the lecturers. It is important that students feel the "presence" of the lecturers in the forums.

- For example, if there are 13 000 students in one module, the lecturer must make it clear that not all questions will be answered in the discussion forum. One may wish to merely give general comments periodically.
- On the other hand, if there are a small number of students in a postgraduate module, the lecturer may want to participate more actively in the discussion forum.

Categories and topics can be set up early in the year or one can create new categories and topics during the course of the academic year as needed.

OSPREY

Osprey is the custom-made website for the School of Computing at Unisa. Osprey makes use of panels (see Figures 22 and 23 in the Appendix), which are nothing more than different "sections" offering information on all aspects of modules (all presented on one page). Students start with personalising the page (shown in Figures 22 and 23 in the Appendix) and then they may customise it. This customisation process requires the use of cookies. The student's chosen modules with their corresponding information will appear in the lower-centre panel, the news groups will appear in the bottom-left panel, the available downloads in the bottom-right panel, news concerning new downloads (and new module news) will appear in the top-right panel. Other panels contain information such as staff availability and departmental news, which can be turned off or hidden.

Osprey provides a "desktop" environment. The principle is that while one is working, the desktop always remains open in the background and serves as a launching pad for information. Following a link from this desktop opens information in a new window, which can be closed quickly using the links provided on such a page. One can then navigate freely within the new window. It is far quicker to open windows from the desktop and close them than having to navigate hence and forth.

Explanation of the Osprey Web Page

We will briefly discuss each aspect of the Osprey Web page (see Figures 22 and 23 in the Appendix):

1. Panel 1 is the navigation panel. Students can contact the School or navigate to other areas on the Schools website.
2. Panel 2 allows for resizing of text for visually impaired persons and there is also a search tool.
3. Panel 3 provides information on how to use this Web page.
4. Panel 4 is a notice board. This board occupies a significant part of screen real estate. Since Unisa is a distance education university, this notice board is a key tool for communication with our students.
5. Panel 5 shows the availability of lecturer(s) on a particular module. Students can click on a lecture's name to send an e-mail or see his/her direct telephone extension.
6. Panel 6 shows the academic and social forums.
7. Panel 7 provides the general information about the student's registered modules.
8. Panel 8 is the download section of the Web page. Students can download module materials and related software.
9. Panel 9 is a module-specific new.

All of the above-mentioned functions can be seen at a glance.

COMPARISON BETWEEN MYUNISA AND OSPREY

There is no information hiding on the Osprey Web page. This is a one-stop shop where prospective, registered and certificate students and prospective and current employees can visit this page and find the information that they are looking for. For registered students, this is of particular importance. At a glance, they can see what is happening with their modules. The *my*Unisa Web page may be perceived by students to be slightly more challenging to first-time users.

For the Osprey Web page, the School of Computing staff members play a greater role in the development of the page. There has been much short iteration during the development of the Osprey Web page. The *my*Unisa portal, on the other hand, has a more complicated systems lifecycle - to crudely state it 'there are many gods to satisfy.'

The Osprey Web tool is designed for a specific set of users, whereas the *my*Unisa portal is designed for a generic set of users. The Osprey Web page has been optimised for mobile devices, whereas the mobile device compatibility is still in the planning phase for *my*Unisa. In Table 2 we provide a comparison for the *my*Unisa Web portal and the Osprey Web tool.

PASSIVE TOOLS

The passive blended learning tools adopted by Unisa are as follows:

- **Tutorial matters** entail paper-based communication material. Currently at Unisa, paper-based communication with students is the predominant medium. Unisa has a well-defined series of tutorial matters that have evolved over the years to facilitate the distance education learning approach. We will now briefly describe each type of tutorial letter issued by Unisa (University of South Africa, 2007).
  - The 000 series: Tutorial letters in this series are issued to students by lecturers and not by the Department of Despatch. Not all students receive tutorial letters in this series.
  - The 100 series: Tutorial letters in this series normally deal with assignments, deadlines and information such as prescribed books and admission requirements for the examinations that are applicable to a specific module.
  - The 200 series: Tutorial letters in this series should not be issued before a specific date (e.g. not before the deadline of an assignment), letters of information aimed at a particular language group only, or tutorial letters for students who reside in a specific geographical area.
  - The 300 series: Tutorial letters in this series are mostly of a general nature.
  - The 500 series: The tutorial letters in this series serve as study guides or study manuals in most cases.
- **DVD** has been used to replace or assist the use of paper-based tutorial matters. In order to make a faceless environment of distance education friendlier to students, Unisa, for example, sends every registered student a comprehensive DVD which provides general information on its colleges and services. The instrument covers a collection of life skills and helpful information that will assist students to successfully navigate the Unisa environment and achieve their life and career goals.

Table 2. Comparison for myUnisa and Osprey

*my*Unisa	Osprey	Comment
Official student and lectures portal for the university	In-house tool specifically designed for the staff and students of the School of Computing.	Osprey was designed keeping in mind the inputs from the lecturers. *my*Unisa was designed and launched without involving any inputs from the key stakeholders.
Generic tool	Specific tool	*my*Unisa treats all academic modules from different faculties the same. Osprey only caters for School of Computing modules.
Interactive components	Static page	A large number of the interactive components on *my*Unisa are inactive. Two possible reasons are the financial impact to the university and high cost of technology for the students.
Lecturer availability does not reflect on the system.	Lecturer availability reflects on the system.	Osprey allows the lecturer to indicate his or her availability online in real time, e.g. a lecturer may be at the university, but may be attending a meeting and is unavailable to see students and other staff. The lecturer may put a note on the Osprey system for notification.
Aggressively marketed	Marketed in the School of Computing	
Call centre facility for help	No helpline facility	Osprey has a limited set of functions and the students who use the tools are more technology oriented. Thus, it does not require a helpline facility.
Free e-mail addresses for students	No free e-mail addresses for students	
Requires a four-step registration process	No registration required	For the Osprey system, all students registered in the School of Computing automatically receive a tutorial letter containing the login information.
Free to all registered students in the university	Free to all registered students in the School of Computing	On Osprey, lecturers can collaborate and share materials with other non-registered parties.
One-stop portal for students	Limited features	*my*Unisa provides a set of more completed functions for students in the university, e.g. update personal details, look at student record, and track postal material. Osprey mainly enables download material and forum interaction for students.
Provide Short Messaging Service to mobile devices	Does not support Short Messaging Service to mobile devices	
Not optimised for mobile devices	Optimised for mobile devices	
Students can submit their assignments online	Students cannot submit their assignments online	

BARRIERS TO BLENDED LEARNING

In this section, we will discuss the barriers or challenges of blended learning that affect the Unisa students on a more context-specific level.

South Africa is a multi-lingual and multicultural country. The population is approximately 48.8 million people. There are 11 official languages in South Africa (Singh, 2006). As mentioned in the background section, South Africa is a country of great contrasts socially, economically and geographically (Singh & Engelbrecht, 2004). A student's background greatly influences the teaching approaches adopted by this ODL university.

Unisa students can be divided into two categories: traditional and adoptive. Traditional students are ones who have never used computers or Internet prior to studying at Unisa and they are resistant towards the use of technology due to their fear of the unknown. Adoptive students, on the other hand, are ones who may have or may not have used computers or Internet prior to studying at

Unisa, but they are enthusiastic in making use of technology.

From our experience, there exist two types of attitudes amongst the academics in regard to the use of technology. They are resisting or adopting. These attitudes are often based on social acceptance.

There exist three transition steps amongst those who are resistant towards the adoption of technology usage. Some of the academic members of staff were initially resisting the use of technology (more specifically *my*Unisa) in their teaching. One of the reasons for this was fear of the unknown. The other reason is because a lecturer's workload has become much more dynamic whilst students number is increasing drastically. The dynamic workload is the cause of lack of time for the lecturer to attend official training offered by *my*Unisa support staff. This calls for a need for a well-documented approach for *my*Unisa in order to help the lecturer navigating the tool on his/her own. The second step is reluctantly accepting due to the enforcement of the university. The last step is adopting the use of technology and making it a part of their teaching.

Adoption of Internet Usage

From a communication perspective, South Africa has 4.642 million landlines in use, 42.3 cellular phones in use, and 5.1 million Internet users (Central Intelligence Agency, 2008). The Internet usage in South Africa is growing but at a very slow rate. From the year 2000 to 2006, we saw proportionally the slow growth of Internet usage (Goldstuck, 2002; Goldstuck, Whitford & Super, 2006). The reasons for the slow growth of Internet usage are insufficient infrastructure for the Internet, costs of computer technology, and high costs and poor qualities of service providers.

In addition, Guomundsdottir (2005) suggested that there are several factors that challenge the growth of the Internet in South Africa. Before these challenges are tackled, he aptly suggested that fulfilling the basic needs of the greater population has to become a prerequisite to bridging the digital divide (Table 3). Guomundsdottir (2005) proposed the following model:

When we consider the complexity that the Internet adds to the development of an interactive application, our research revealed that the application designers need to look further and should consider, for example, the following:

- How does culture affect the project?
- How do social aspects affect the project?
- Is the right 'fit' of technology being used?
- What change of management issue is involved?
- Are there the right subject matter experts on the project? Such experts could be:
    - Computer networking experts: Can the country's telecommunication

Table 3. Models of digital divides

	Type of Needs	The Type of Divide	Comments
1	Basic needs	The real divide	This includes access to clean water, electricity, social justice, and democracy.
2	Hardware - software	Material divide	This includes poor access or costly technology and/or telecommunication.
3	Mentality - content	Mentality/opportunity divide	How will the Internet really help me?
4	Skills – knowledge – support	Utilisation divide	Lack of basic computer skills and user support
5	Culture – language / social diversity	Suitability divide	The alien-ness of the Internet; it is modeled more on a Western cultural background.

infrastructure handle the Web page content and is it stable?
    - Computer security experts
    - Distributed database experts: A well-optimised database may improve response time of a Web transaction.
    - Hardware experts: Does the appropriate, high quality hardware with the relevant support infrastructure exist?
    - Linguistic experts: Does the displayed Web page convey an unambiguous message to the users?
    - Legal experts
    - Information technology auditors: Are there qualified, independent information technology auditors available to audit the electronic commerce application?

Challenges Facing Unisa with the Electronic Delivery of Material

Some of the major issues associated with the use of Internet course-delivery method are:

- Computer networks are costly to develop. Although individual computers are relatively inexpensive and the computer hardware and software market is very competitive, it is still costly to develop instructional networks and purchase the software to run them (Willis, 1996).
- Technology is changing rapidly. Computer technology evolves so quickly that distance educators focused solely on innovation. "Not meeting tangible needs" will constantly replace equipment and software in an effort to keep pace with the "latest" technical advancements (Willis, 1996).
- Computer illiteracy still exists. While computers have been widely used since the 1960's, there are many people who still do not have access to a computer or a computer network (Willis, 1996). This is especially true in developing countries.
- The Internet has not solved the problem of finding a substitute for the 'good teacher'. While it can deliver teaching material to students regardless of geography, it cannot yet provide spontaneous and adaptive teaching for diverse student populations (Carswell, 1998).
- Restrictive network bandwidth in developing countries impeded synchronous communication (Wade & Power, 1997).
- Students dislike reading from the screen for long periods, having been conditioned to read printed material (Wade & Power, 1997).
- Maddux and Johnson (1997) identified the scarcity of design guidelines as being partly responsible for the great diversity in Web-based instructional material.
- Students who lack discipline or time management skills may become disenfranchised (Sherry, 1996).

Furthermore, we will discuss this from two perspectives, that of the lecturer and that of the student. From a lecturer's perspective, the lecturer has become a jack of several trades. The lecturer has to master/or at least vaguely understand typography, be able to edit documents and produce documents in a timely fashion. Apart from the administrative aspects of the module, the lecturer has to creatively build in a pedagogical framework into study material, for example, at Unisa a study plan is built into the tutorial letter for students. The study plan is reinforced by summative and formative tasks.

From a student's perspective, there exist several challenges; the most persistent at Unisa is the online delivery of assignments. When it comes to assignment deadlines, the trend is for most students to apply the 'last minute crunch' approach. This is to say students leave it to the very last minute to upload their assignments onto the *my*Unisa server. This sudden increase of network activity has in the past caused technical problems with the *my*Unisa server. Now assuming that the students have successfully uploaded their assignments, these assignments are printed and sent to the respective lecturers for marking. The printing of the assignments are faced with several problems such as if the student did not follow the procedures stated in the *Unisa: Services and Procedures* manual (this document is given to every student at registration at Unisa), the printer would print garbled characters. As of 2009, the School of Computing is standardising the submission process by requiring students to submit their assignments in the PDF format to avoid this particular problem.

From a technology perspective, making use of technologies is still very expensive for the average students. Expenses aside, technology is still notoriously unreliable and unpredictable. For example, in 2008, Unisa upgraded all hardware and software on all the campuses. As part of the upgrade process, the previously used e-mail client and server, Novel, was replaced by MS Outlook. Some time later, the entire Unisa network was out of commission for three weeks. This was attributed to a worm that may have slipped in through the e-mail system.

Figure 3 depicts the registration methods used by Unisa students (both formal and non-formal students are included). It also includes all registered, temporary, and cancelled-registration student status. It is clear that to this date Unisa students still prefer counter registration. Very few students are using the Internet to register. This leads us to assume that many students have not adopted using *my*Unisa as a tool for their learning.

Figure 4 depicts the breakdown of formally registered students by age groups. The vast majority of students fall in the 20-29 age group. These students are young and inexperienced but should feel comfortable in embracing technologies.

Figure 5 shows that there has been a steady growth in student numbers at Unisa over the years. This increase in student numbers and the shortage of resources are an indication that using *my*Unisa to manage these student numbers is a prudent strategy.

However, the development of Unisa attracts learners from a diverse range of socio-political-economic-cultural backgrounds. Student Talk (an in-house student news-letter), issue 2, 2003 documented the achievements of various students. We will briefly summarise a few:

Figure 3. Registrations by registration methods, 2004 - 2007

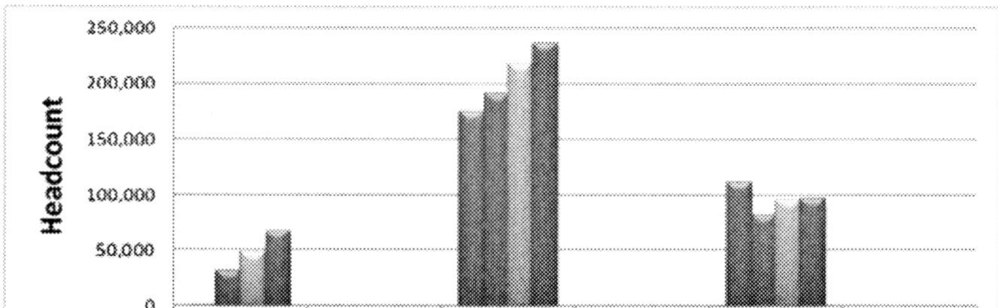

	Internet	%	Counter	%	Postal	%
2004	994	0.3%	174,931	61.0%	110,833	38.7%
2005	31,608	10.4%	191,874	62.8%	81,865	26.8%
2006	49,301	13.6%	217,284	60.1%	94,894	26.3%
2007	66,953	16.7%	236,793	59.0%	97,396	24.3%

Figure 4. Registrations by Age Groups, 2004 – 2007

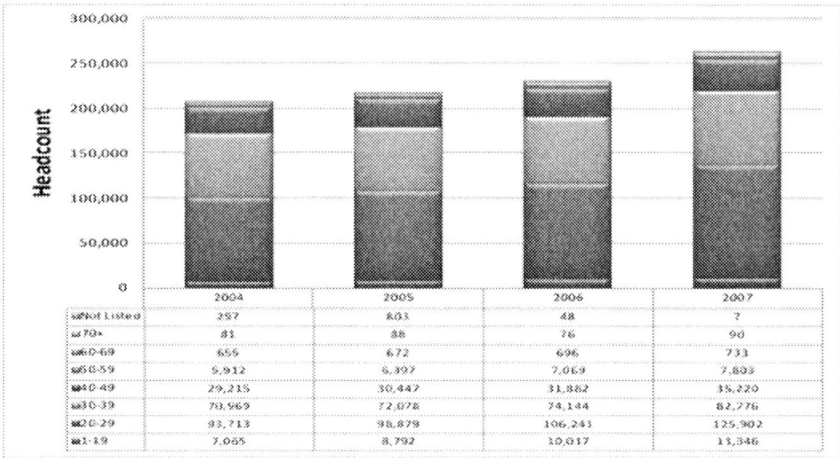

	2004	2005	2006	2007
Not Listed	297	803	48	7
70+	81	88	76	90
60-69	655	672	696	733
50-59	5,912	6,397	7,069	7,803
40-49	29,215	30,447	31,882	35,220
30-39	70,969	72,078	74,144	82,776
20-29	93,713	98,879	106,241	125,902
1-19	7,065	8,792	10,017	11,346

Figure 5. Registrations by Regional Offices, 2004 - 2007

	2004	2005		2006		2007	
Hub / Regional Office	Headcount	Headcount	% Growth	Headcount	% Growth	Headcount	% Growth
CAPE COASTAL	**20,881**	**21,301**	**2.0%**	**21,761**	**2.2%**	**25,898**	**19.0%**
East London	2,649	2,758	4.1%	2,376	-13.9%	3,341	40.6%
George	561	772	37.6%	759	-1.7%	1,189	56.7%
Parow	14,677	14,358	-2.2%	14,093	-1.8%	15,191	7.8%
Port Elizabeth	1,392	1,578	13.4%	1,693	7.3%	2,344	38.5%
Umtata	1,602	1,835	14.5%	2,840	54.8%	3,833	35.0%
GAUTENG	**121,386**	**124,531**	**2.6%**	**143,020**	**14.8%**	**161,331**	**12.8%**
Benoni	632	539	-14.7%	340	-36.9%	2,185	542.6%
Florida	3,511	3,775	7.5%	20,315	438.1%	24,834	22.2%
Johannesburg	1,248	1,180	-5.4%	922	-21.9%	5,286	473.3%
Pretoria	115,995	119,037	2.6%	121,443	2.0%	129,026	6.2%
KWAZULU NATAL	**29,826**	**31,756**	**6.5%**	**35,678**	**12.4%**	**39,972**	**12.0%**
Durban	24,409	25,929	6.2%	29,861	15.2%	31,780	6.4%
Newcastle	975	988	1.3%	995	0.7%	1,937	94.7%
Pietermaritzburg	4,442	4,839	8.9%	4,822	-0.4%	6,255	29.7%

	2004	2005		2006		2007	
Hub / Regional Office	Headcount	Headcount	% Growth	Headcount	% Growth	Headcount	% Growth
MIDLANDS	**17,825**	**19,575**	**9.8%**	**7,749**	**-60.4%**	**10,616**	**37.0%**
Bloemfontein	2,925	2,876	-1.7%	2,654	-7.7%	3,559	34.1%
Kimberley	3,131	3,045	-2.7%	1,966	-35.4%	2,246	14.2%
Kroonstad	7,494	9,068	21.0%	555	-93.9%	870	56.8%
Mafikeng	1,205	1,243	3.2%	992	-20.2%	1,384	39.5%
Potchefstroom	2,293	2,225	-3.0%	690	-69.0%	1,191	72.6%
Rustenburg	777	1,118	43.9%	892	-20.2%	1,366	53.1%
NORTH EASTERN	**13,599**	**13,966**	**2.7%**	**18,051**	**29.2%**	**21,892**	**21.3%**
Giyani	404	392	-3.0%	509	29.8%	959	88.4%
Makhado	788	774	-1.8%	1,109	43.3%	1,720	55.1%
Middelburg (Mpuma	1,901	2,088	9.8%	1,758	-15.8%	2,487	41.5%
Nelspruit	3,797	3,617	-4.7%	3,669	1.4%	4,493	22.5%
Polokwane	6,709	7,095	5.8%	11,006	55.1%	12,233	11.1%
(blank)	**4,390**	**7,027**	**60.1%**	**3,914**	**-44.3%**	**4,168**	**6.5%**
CBM						61	
CTD	2,099	2,436	16.1%		-100.0%		
IOB	798	724	-9.3%		-100.0%		
Wellington	1,328	1,988	49.7%	3,549	78.5%	3,731	5.1%
Wildcoast						369	
(blank)	165	1,879	1038.8%	365	-80.6%	7	-98.1%

- Ms Johanna Baloyi a former domestic worker graduated with a BA in Communication and is now communication intern at the Department of Minerals in South Africa,
- Queen Lamatsebula of Swaziland graduated with a BA degree,
- Zwi Sacho was named as one of the world's top 30 accounting graduates.
- To Ms Trish Zweid a waitress, who at the age of 41, graduated with distinctions.

It is compulsory for the students at the School of Computing at Unisa to make use of technology as part of their learning tools. The School strongly encourages students to use discussion forums and module e-mails for interaction between students and lecturers and amongst their peer students. The School, for example, has a policy that all e-mails will be answered within 24 hours upon receipt. Only word-processed assignments from students will be accepted, unless students make other arrangements with the responsible lecturers. However, students and some academics still prefer the traditional approach to distance education. In addition, students who have modules from different faculties (e.g. one module from the School of Computing and one module from Philosophy) find it a major drawback having to deal with two different Web tools, namely Osprey and *my*Unisa, at the same time. There is no seamless solution between the usages of the two Web tools.

Unisa encourages lecturers making use of *my*Unisa as one of the main technological tools for tuition. The use of *my*Unisa has been made part of the assessment criteria for recognising excellence in tuition for lecturers in Unisa's policy.

FUTURE TRENDS

It is rumored that there are more cellular phone owners in South African than there are taxpayers. Involving mobile technology to assist students in the learning process is a possible future plan.

MXit, a free instant messaging programme for mobile devices, is planned to be used on *my*Unisa. The creation of a social network infrastructure for students using Microsoft's Live@edu is also planned for *my*Unisa. All of these will not cost Unisa a cent.

South Africa has been described as a melting pot of different cultures. These cultures add to the rich South African heritage. We are one of very few countries to boast eleven official languages. However, the cultural diversity poses a unique challenge for designers of software packages, especially when one has to design educational software tools.

*my*Unisa is still young and evolving. It would be of interest to obtain students' perspectives on their learning experience through the ODL model via surveys or interviews once *my*Unisa has become more mature. The results can serve as an indication to how ODL is evolving in a developing country.

The target audience of the majority of learning tools is people who are familiar with technology and often the younger generation of the population. There has been little research on design for older people in general, see (Howthorn, 2000; Rodgers, 1997) for a collection of relevant research. There is even less research conducted on interface design for older computer users. We can expect older people to have slower reaction time, have some problems with their eyesight, and show some decline in cognitive ability. It would be of interest to investigate more on the design of learning tools for more matured Unisa students.

CONCLUSION

Just like during the Gold Rush in the 19th century, the Internet has attracted many people who believe they can make money for nothing. While people in the 19th century died in the cold, today's adventurers only lose their money. The Internet has revolutionised the way we work and study (Amor,

2001). If technology is well suited to the job it is intended for, it can be a great enabler. There are many instances of successful deployment of technologies. There are also examples where it did not work. Suffice to say that the common cause in these examples was not the technology per se, but the way in which it was handled. In other words, the organisation was not appropriately operated - they were following a false God (Norris, West & Gaughan, 2000). The consequences of the fact that precious resources are wasted which has an adverse effect on the community that the organisation operates in.

It is possible to summarise and identify some critical factors influencing Unisa as follows:

1. *Social political issues:* economical forces, political factors, primary and secondary schooling, university policy, and cultural forces.
2. *Support structure:* technology, countries infrastructure, university policies, and schooling system.
3. *Social clustering:* geography and local-international forces.

The factors presented above are by no means a definitive list and it is beyond the scope of this chapter to fully analyse the identified factors.

Gaps in user knowledge address bridging the gap between what users know and what they need to know (Shneiderman, 2000) - a further challenge to course development is to bridge the gap between what students know and what they need to know. Many students do not know where to begin, what to choose in a dialogue box, how to handle system crashes, or what to do about viruses.

When it comes to students accurately completing official university forms, in some instances, students perform a screening process by omitting data intentionally since they perceive the only possible use of that data element to be intrusive or in violation of their privacy, e.g. home telephone numbers. In other instances, they perceive the standard of their position regarding a certain data element not to be sufficient, e.g. they are not personally available at a telephone number during office hours.

In many instances, students neglect to update their personal information as they consider the processes too cumbersome. In addition, they do not perceive this action as either a priority or urgent in terms of their studies.

Academics who rely on institutional student databases should be aware that the data could contain a degree of inaccuracy due to some of the reasons mentioned previously. They should also be aware that the general student profile, especially in a distance education environment, will exhibit change during the academic year.

Academics who do not take cognisance of student attitudes towards personal data and data anomalies may end up with a fuzzy picture. In a face-to-face environment, the danger is that the mental picture of the academics will be based only on the "visible students". In a distance education environment, the student may thus remain an unknown quantity, whereas in a residential university setup, the student will be "judged by her cover". In our experience, many changes to study objects are driven by results rather than by the student profile. The danger that lurks in this approach is that academics fall into a reactive mode of behaviour. The "unsatisfactory results" are also viewed as one problem and seldom analysed in terms of the examination paper and the marking process on the one hand and the student performance and expected student performance on the other.

The design of a course is no longer the domain of a single person. It has become a combination of various experts from different disciplines to design Internet modules.

There is an exponential increase in student numbers, there is a poor lecturer-student ratio, there is no recognition for hard work, and there are deteriorating working conditions and a number of related challenges. The use of technology can either compound the problem or alleviate it. What is required is a creative team approach to solve these problems. In the Unisa context *my*Unisa and Osprey both enable lecturers to involve the students and let them feel part of a bigger group, which is a great contributor to student motivation and involvement. It can be very lonely when one studies in a distance education environment.

The South African context of multi-cultural and multi-lingual groups is seen as a major obstacle to the dissemination of an effective Web-based courseware. Interface design in South Africa is particularly difficult for such a disparate audience. It is rather encouraging considering much work has been involved in assisting lecturers to become innovative in their teaching in a developing country. There is a great potential for Unisa to provide better support to students when the technical infrastructure is matching with the technology advancement.

Finally, we noticed that technology is not the 'silver bullet' for the design of successful, relevant and appropriate courses. There are other factors that need to be considered and incorporated into the design of a Web-based course. A holistic socio-technical approach should be adopted in the design of such courses.

REFERENCES

Amor, D. (2001). The industrialisation of the Internet gold rush. *Journal of Information Technology Theory and Application, 3*(4), 20–22.

Carswell, L. (1998). The 'virtual university': Toward an Internet paradigm. *SIGCSE Bulletin, 30*(3), 46–50. doi:10.1145/290320.283017

Central Intelligence Agency. (2008). *The world factbook 2008*. Retrieved on January 12, 2009, from https://www.cia.gov/library/publications/the-world-factbook/geos/sf.html

Ginns, P., & Ellis, R. (2007). Quality in blended learning: Exploring the relations between online and face-to-face teaching and learning. *The Internet and Higher Education, 10*, 53–64. doi:10.1016/j.iheduc.2006.10.003

Goldstuck, A. (2002). *The goldstuck report: Internet access in South Africa, 2002*. Johannesburg: World Wide Worx (Pty) Ltd.

Goldstuck, A., Whitford, S., & Super, R. (2007). *The goldstuck report: Online retail in South Africa, 2006*. Johannesburg: World Wide Worx (Pty) Ltd.

Guomundsdottir, G. B. (2005, December). *Approaching the digital divide in South Africa*. Paper presented at the NETREED Conference, Beitostlølen, Norway.

Hawthorn, D. (2000). *Designing for older users: Display quality versus task complexity*. Paper presented at the OzChi 2000: Interfacing Reality in the New Millennium, The University of Technology, Sydney, Australia.

Khine, M. S., & Lourdusamy, A. (2003). Blended learning approach in teacher education: Combining face-to-face instruction, multimedia viewing, and online discussion. *British Journal of Educational Technology, 34*(5), 671–675. doi:10.1046/j.0007-1013.2003.00360.x

Maddux, C. D., & Johnson, D. L. (1997). The World Wide Web: History, cultural context, and a manual for developers of educational information-based Web sites. *Educational Technology, 37*(5), 5–12.

Matyila, M., & Halland, K. (2004, June). *Using discussion forums in distance education*. Paper presented at the 34th Annual SACLA Conference, Durban, South Africa.

Norris, M., West, S., & Gaughan, K. (2000). E-business essentials: Technology and network requirements for the electronic marketplace. Chicester: John Wiley & Sons Ltd.

Official ITIL Web site. (2008). *ITIL*. Retrieved on October 15, 2008, from http://www.itil-officialsite.com/home/home.asp

Rodgers, W. A. (Ed.). (1997). *Designing for an aging population*. Santa Monica, CA: Human Factors and Ergonomics Society.

Sherry, L. (1996). Issues in distance learning. *International Journal of Educational Telecommunications, 1*(4), 337–365.

Shneiderman, B. (2000). Universal usability. *Communications of the ACM, 43*(5), 84–91. doi:10.1145/332833.332843

Singh, S. (2006). HCI in South Africa. In C. Ghaoui (Ed.), *Encyclopedia of human computer interaction* (pp. 261-265). UK: Liverpool John Moores University, Idea Group Reference.

Singh, S., & De Ridder, C. (2005, June). *My marriage to cousin Lily*. Paper presented at the 35th Annual SACLA Conference, Kasane, Botswana.

Singh, S., & Engelbrecht, K. (2004, June). *Profiling the learner*. Paper presented at the 34th Annual SACLA Conference, Durban, South Africa.

Singh, S., & Kotze, P. (2003). The socio-political culture of users. In M. Rauterberg, et al. (Eds.), *Human-computer interaction–INTERACT '03* (pp. 900-903). IOS Press.

University of South Africa. (2007). *Services and procedures 2007*. Pretoria: University of South Africa.

University of South Africa. (2008). *Self-evaluation portfolio for the HECQ institutional audit 2008*. Pretoria: University of South Africa.

Valiathan, P. (2002). *Blended learning models*. Retrieved on May 26, 2008, from http://www.learningcircuits.com/2002/aug2002/valiathan.html

Wade, V. P., & Power, C. (1997). Evaluating the design and delivery of WWW based educational environment and courseware. *SIGCSE Bulletin, 30*(3), 243–248. doi:10.1145/290320.283556

Willis, B. (1996). Distance education at a glance series from University of Idaho. Retrieved on July 20, 1998, from http://www.uidaho.edu/evo/distglan.html

KEY TERMS AND DEFINITIONS

University of South Africa (Unisa): The University of South Africa (UNISA) is a distance education university with headquarters in Pretoria, South Africa. With approximately 220 000 enrolled students, it qualifies as one of the World's mega universities.

Open Distance Education: Open distance learning represents an approach or philosophy which combines the principles of learner centredness, lifelong learning, flexibility of learning facilitation provisioning, removal of barriers to access, recognition of prior learning, provision of relevant learner support, and construction of learning programmes in the expectation that learners will succeed; and the maintenance of rigorous quality assurance over the design of learning materials and support services. In terms of distance education, teachers and learners are separated. Learning involves the use of various techniques such as integrated and mixed media, and courseware with various modalities for learning development, facilitation and support. UNISA, as an open distance education institution, determines its own admission requirements, grants access to traditionally disadvantaged students, recognises prior experiential learning and promotes flexible learning in terms of its interactive learning material.

Digital Divide: The term digital divide refers to the gap between people with effective access to digital and information technology and those with very limited or no access at all. It includes the imbalances in physical access to technology as well as the imbalances in resources and skills needed to effectively participate as a digital citizen.

***my*Unisa:** *my*Unisa is a Web-based system for academic collaboration and study related interaction. This system has been developed to supplement and enhance academic interaction and improve communication between Unisa and its students as well as provide opportunity for engagement among students.

APPENDIX

Figure 6. myUnisa - Welcome Page. ©2009 Shawren Singh and Hsuan Lorraine Liang. Used with permission.

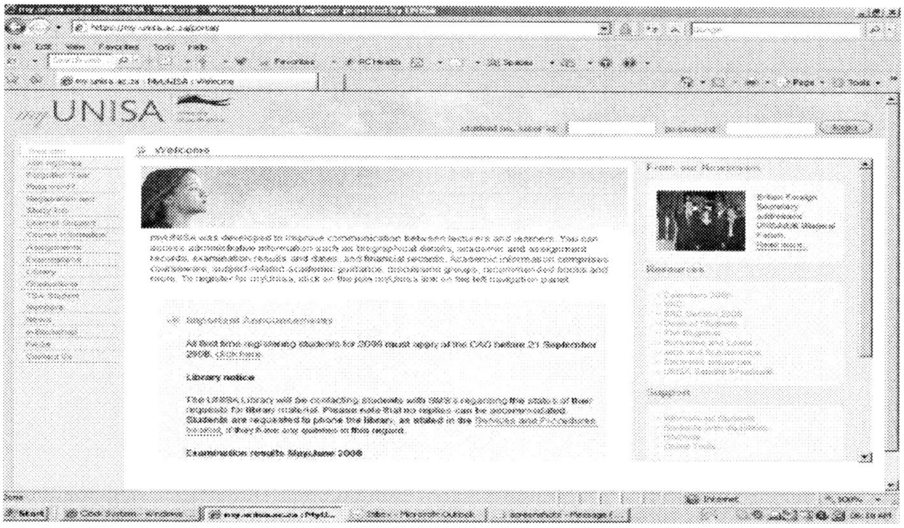

Figure 7. myUnisa – Lecturer's View 1. ©2009 Shawren Singh and Hsuan Lorraine Liang. Used with permission.

Figure 8. myUnisa – Lecturer's View 2. ©2009 Shawren Singh and Hsuan Lorraine Liang. Used with permission.

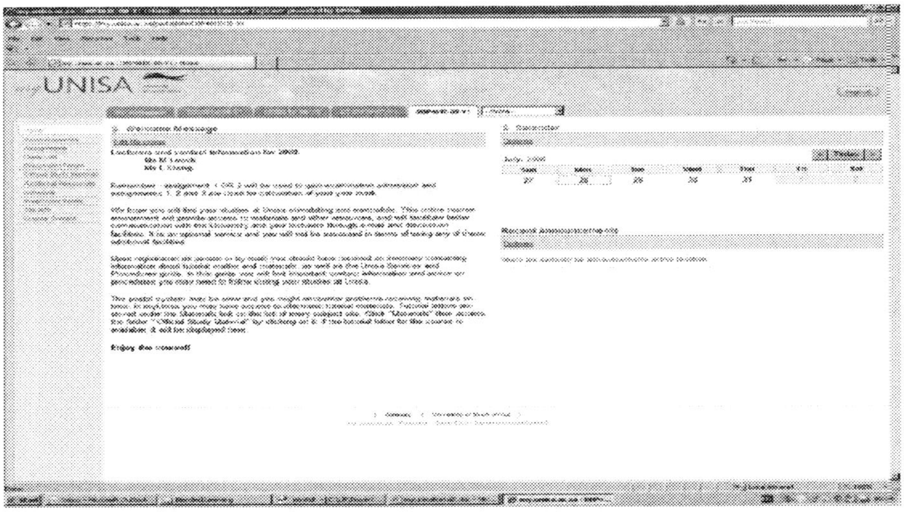

Figure 9. myUnisa – Student's View 1. ©2009 Shawren Singh and Hsuan Lorraine Liang. Used with permission.

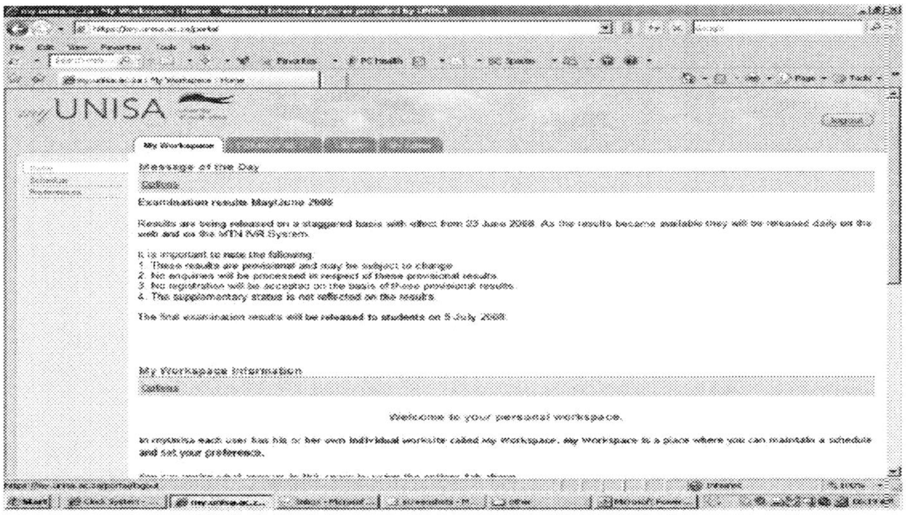

Figure 10. myUnisa – Student's View 2. ©2009 Shawren Singh and Hsuan Lorraine Liang. Used with permission.

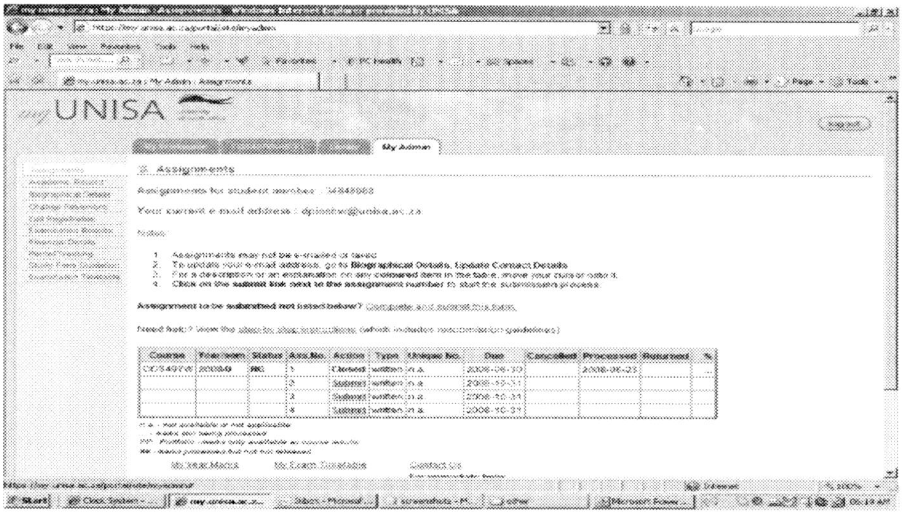

Figure 11. myUnisa – Discussion Forum (Part 1). ©2009 Shawren Singh and Hsuan Lorraine Liang. Used with permission.

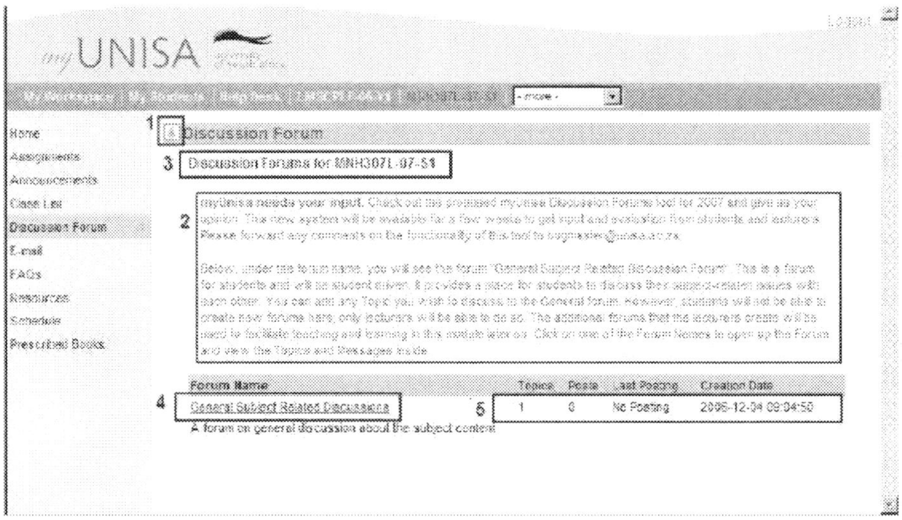

Figure 12. myUnisa – Discussion Forum (Part 2). ©2009 Shawren Singh and Hsuan Lorraine Liang. Used with permission.

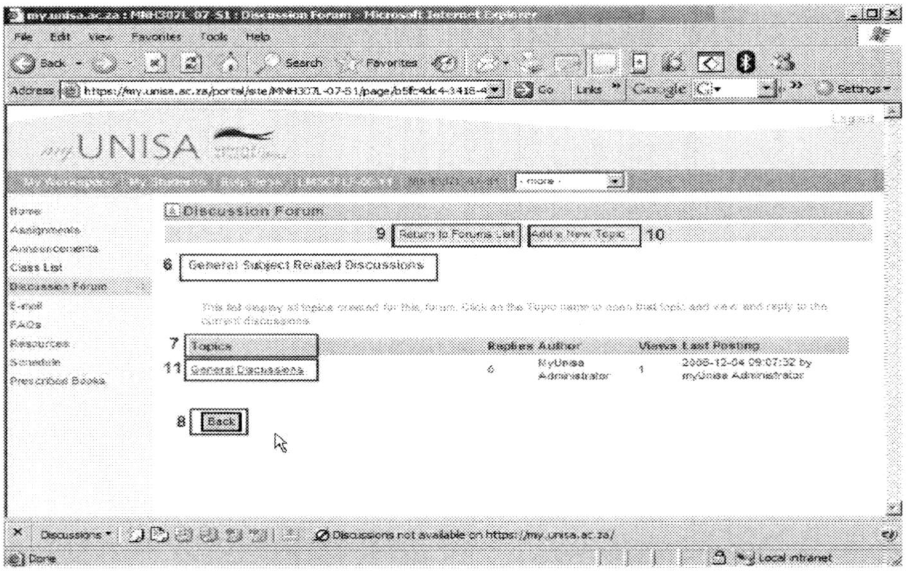

Figure 13. myUnisa – Discussion Forum (Part 3). ©2009 Shawren Singh and Hsuan Lorraine Liang. Used with permission.

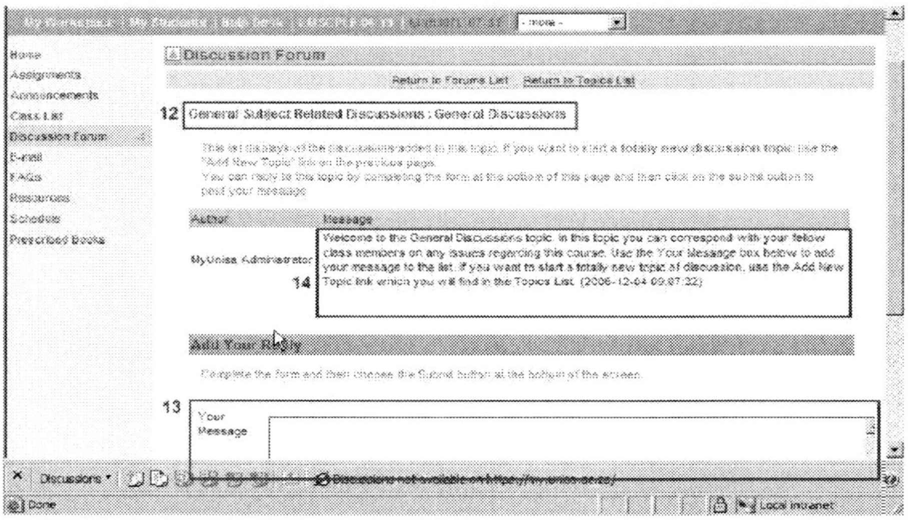

Figure 14. myUnisa – Discussion Forum (Part 4). ©2009 Shawren Singh and Hsuan Lorraine Liang. Used with permission.

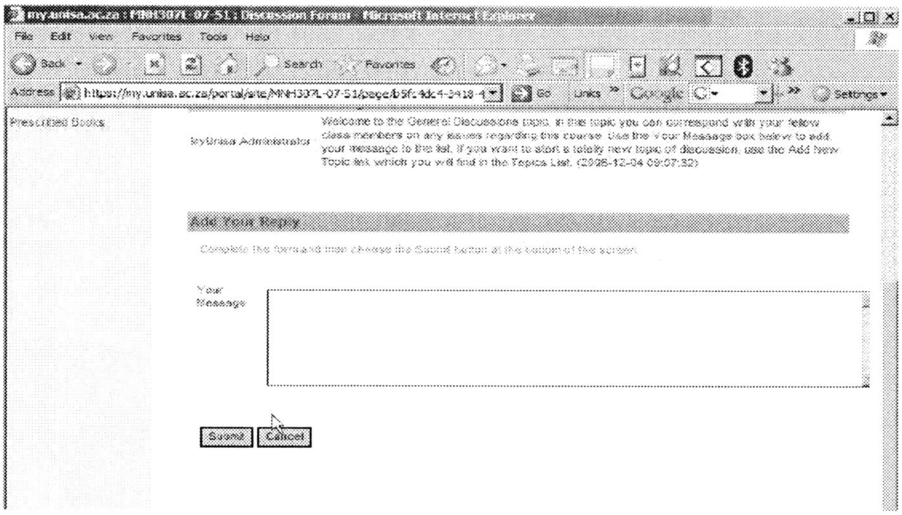

Figure 15. myUnisa – Discussion Forum (Part 5). ©2009 Shawren Singh and Hsuan Lorraine Liang. Used with permission.

Figure 16. myUnisa – Discussion Forum (Part 6). ©2009 Shawren Singh and Hsuan Lorraine Liang. Used with permission.

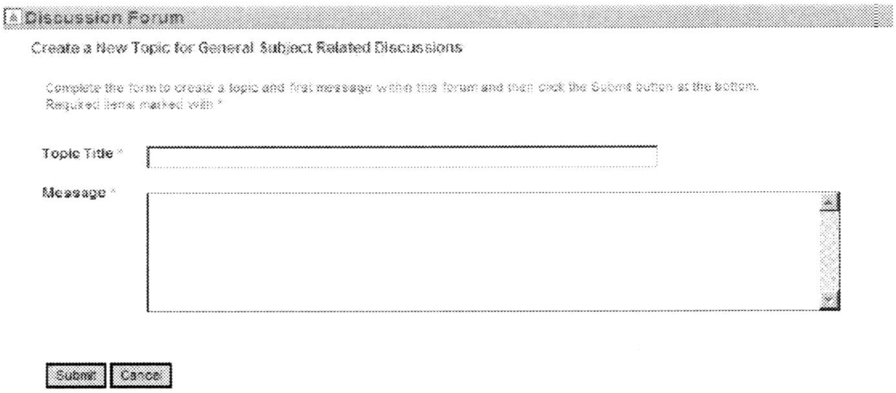

Figure 17. myUnisa – Discussion Forum (Part 7). ©2009 Shawren Singh and Hsuan Lorraine Liang. Used with permission.

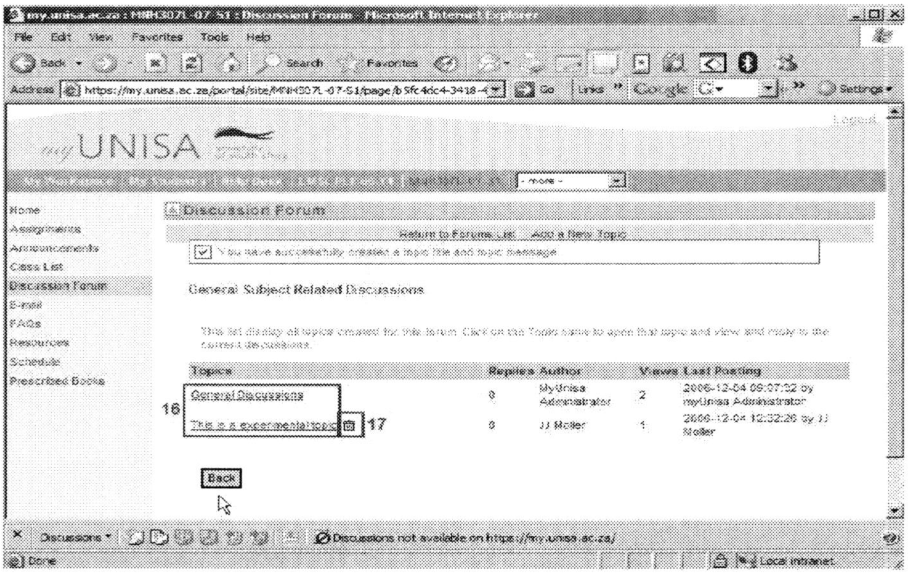

Figure 18. myUnisa – Discussion Forum (Part 8). ©2009 Shawren Singh and Hsuan Lorraine Liang. Used with permission.

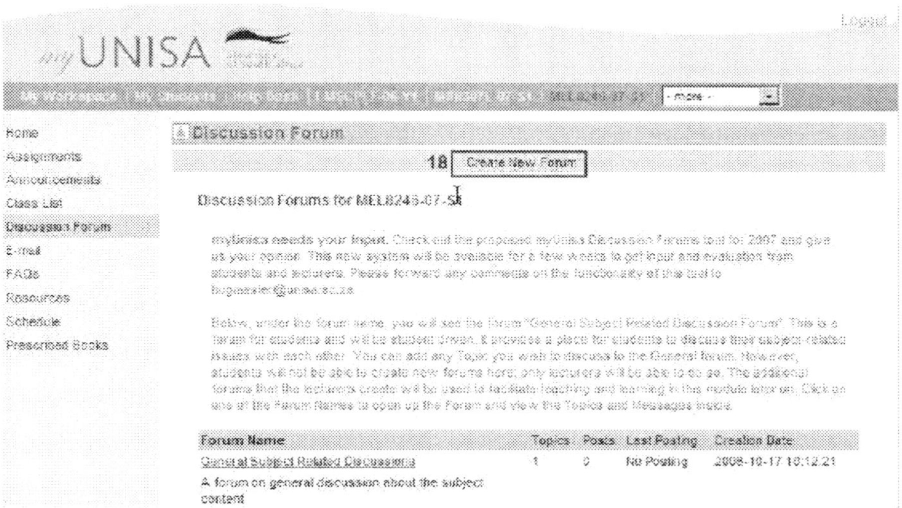

Figure 19. myUnisa – Discussion Forum (Part 9). ©2009 Shawren Singh and Hsuan Lorraine Liang. Used with permission.

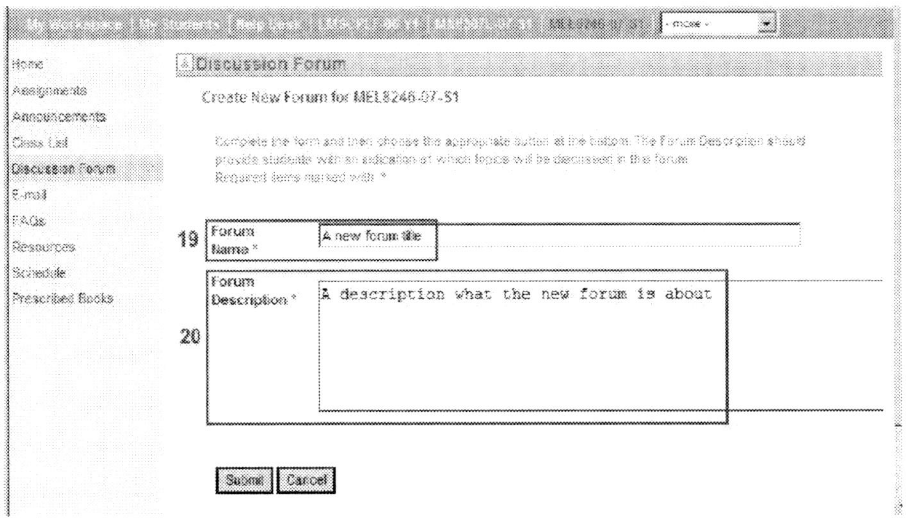

Figure 20. myUnisa – Discussion Forum (Part 10). ©2009 Shawren Singh and Hsuan Lorraine Liang. Used with permission.

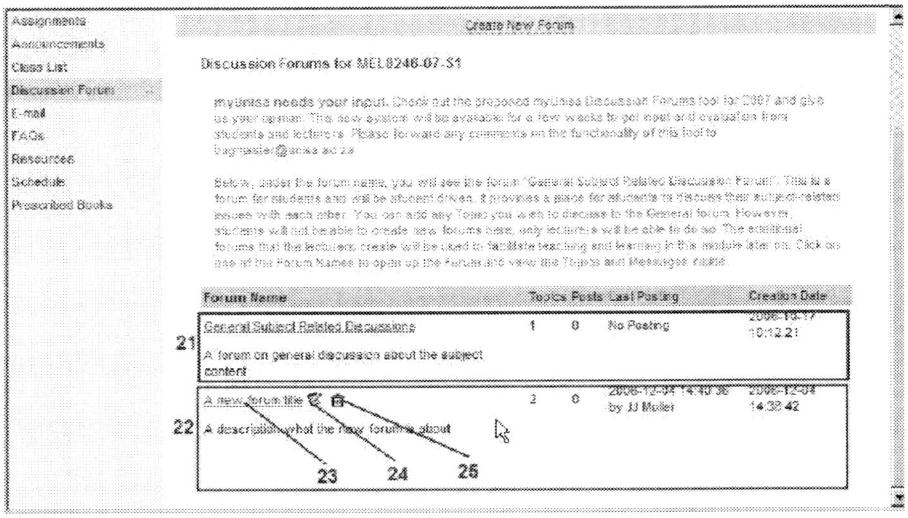

Figure 21. myUnisa – Student Link Tool. ©2009 Shawren Singh and Hsuan Lorraine Liang. Used with permission.

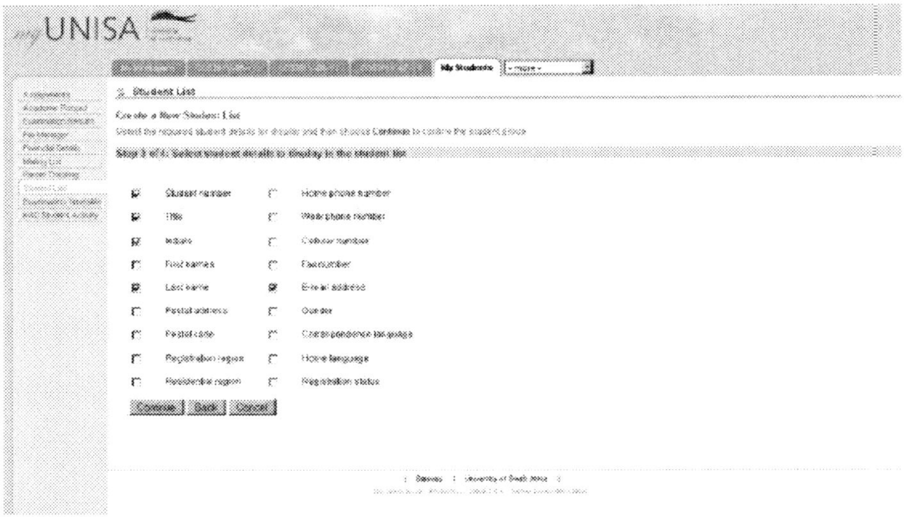

Figure 22. Osprey Web Page (Part 1). ©2009 Shawren Singh and Hsuan Lorraine Liang. Used with permission.

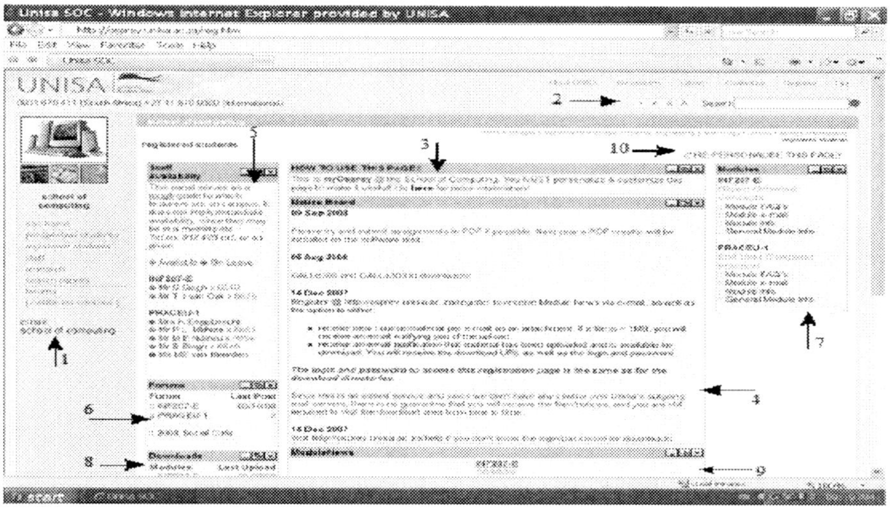

Figure 23. Osprey Web Page (Part 2). ©2009 Shawren Singh and Hsuan Lorraine Liang. Used with permission.

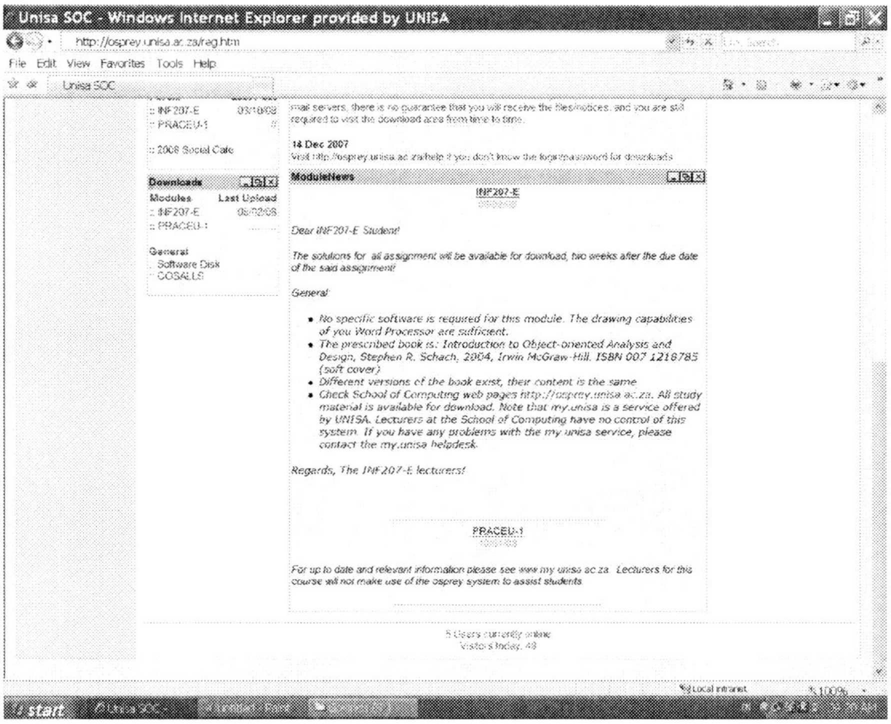

Chapter 3
Enhancing Student Learning through Blending Varied Learning and Assessment Experiences

Paula Hodgson
University of Hong Kong, Hong Kong

ABSTRACT

The purpose of this chapter is to compare the learning opportunities that are available in conventional and the current Web-mediated learning environment in Hong Kong in relation to some of the applications that are available in Web 2.0 and practice-based simulation. Some of these applications can provide faster access to subject-related resources, offer greater connectivity and wider interactions with stakeholders, such as students and professionals locally and overseas, and keep track of students' learning experiences across their years of university study. Furthermore, Web-mediated assessment can provide faster feedback than conventional paper-based methods, which can streamline the process of reporting and the provision of peer feedback. The potential of and future trends in web-mediated assessment are also discussed.

INTRODUCTION

Although e-learning has been advocated in universities in Hong Kong for over a decade, most university students there experience learning through attending mass lectures and participating in face-to-face group tutorials as part of full-time campus-based programs. In the university where I worked, the implementation of e-learning in traditional teaching evolved slowly. The most common e-learning experience described by the majority of students was accessing teaching notes via a university-wide supported learning management system (LMS). However, some may have been asked to do online quizzes, hold discussions in an online forum, submit assignments through the LMS, or search for information from the Web. The LMS can be a platform for students to access information, communicate between educators and fellow students and do assessment tasks. Generally, students welcome online quizzes because they can obtain immediate feedback on their performance. In contrast, there are limited opportunities for stu-

DOI: 10.4018/978-1-60566-852-9.ch003

dents to be actively engaged in lectures, and the LMS may not allow learners to reflect on their learning experiences across subjects or years of university study. The aim of this chapter is to compare the various learning opportunities with some of the applications available in Web 2.0 and practice-based simulation, and to discuss the potential for enhancing the learning experience from the perspective of learning, assessment and building a portfolio of competence. Examples will be shown to illustrate some innovative practices in the university.

LEARNING: TRADITION VERSUS INNOVATION

When educators plan a curriculum, they are required to design what to teach and how to teach it in order to bring about desired changes in knowledge and skills. They can deploy a variety of learning challenges in their teaching in order to help students to develop professional skills and to become all-round graduates. Consequently, they need to (1) identify course aims and objectives; (2) define students' learning needs, which include their current level of understanding of a subject and where this needs to be; and (3) to design learning activities, learning actions required and feedback provided through technologies (Laurillard, 2002). To align the assessment activities with the intended learning outcome, Biggs (2007) stresses the need to provide purposeful assessment activities when planning the curriculum.

Through face-to-face lectures and tutorials, students can interact with teachers and their peers in an environment where facial expression, tone of voice and gestures all contribute to enriched meaning in the process of communication (Tolmie and Boyle, 2000). To transfer abstract theoretical concepts, however, educators need to encourage students to engage in learning tasks that are both relevant and in context, thus allowing them to experience the dynamics of a rapidly changing modern world (Herrington and Herrington, 2006). In order to transform conceptual knowledge into practice, they are offered learning opportunities through the incorporation of a practical component in the curriculum: practising skills in a laboratory, consolidating concepts through projects, and experiencing the real working environment in local or overseas work placements. These blended learning activities aim to assist students to practise, rehearse and reflect on their actions when interacting with their peers and with professionals in the field so as to develop both professional and generic competence.

'Blended learning' was redefined when the World Wide Web (WWW) was found to be useful by educational communities and is now commonly referred to as mixing the face-to-face and the virtual learning environments (Alonso, López, Manrique and Vines, 2005; Garrison and (Kanuka, 2004; Hughes, 2007; Osguthorpe and Graham, 2003). Educators can now incorporate different instructional methods into traditional university programs. They can lecture on key disciplinary knowledge, while students can be involved in discussions or group debates in the web environment after class. Teachers can evaluate students' prior knowledge of the topic, and students can be asked to do web-based quizzes before attending lectures. However, 'blended learning' may also refer to a combination of different modalities or delivery media (Graham, Allen and Ure, 2003; Harden and Hart, 2002). For instance, students can be instructed to conduct audio interviews and prepare a brief written or oral report of their findings in an online forum so that peer groups can share their experiences. Besides, a blended approach can provide options to meet the needs of students with a variety of learning styles, as described by Felder and Silverman (1988), who define the five dimensions of learning style as processing (active/reflective), perception (sensing/intuitive), input (visual/verbal), understanding (sequential/global) and organization (inductive/deductive). However, Oliver and Trigwell (2005) argue that this refers not merely to the mode of teaching or the instructional strategies with different media but also to the variations in learning experiences that trigger learning moments.

Conventional classroom teaching is often teacher-directed, and students can make only limited contributions in class time, particularly if the class is large. However, the web environment allows students greater opportunities to participate in and a wider space to demonstrate their learning experiences as they achieve both intended and unintended learning outcomes. Consequently, the application of an electronic mode of learning (e-learning) has become more and more important in universities around the world, and the traditional face-to-face mode of teaching in higher education can benefit from being integrated with the interactive networked environment that is the WWW. Educators can promote innovative practice via an LMS such as WebCT (now Blackboard, www.blackboard.com), FirstClass (www.firstclass.com) or Moodle (www.moodle.org). A continuous wave of innovative practice is now evolving as emerging Web 2.0 applications such as weblogs (blogs) and wikis are adopted by innovative teachers. A blog is a website that allows individual authors to publish their latest written work, which can be enriched with images or videos, and invite their audience to provide comments, which are presented in reverse order of posting. Figure 1 shows an example of a language teacher getting her students to practise news writing in the central column of the course-based blog, while current news from the BBC can be provided by Real Simple Syndicate (RSS) feeds and read by students in the right-hand column of the block. Student work can be archived, subscribed to by other blog authors and linked to web resources.

Group tasks are often assigned as part of course work, and students often produce written project reports to demonstrate their understanding of declarative and procedural knowledge. Nowadays, this can be set in stages to allow students to collate, revise and reflect on both the process and the product of group work. Figure 2 shows an example of a business teacher asking his students to do a group project in a wiki, which is a website that allows members with common interests to create web content, possibly enriched with multimedia, that can be edited easily by fellow members. Participating students can take turns to add new information and revise the report, and they are then able to view the latest version of the project. Students can instantly publish their work through blogs and wikis, and both the process and the deliverable of student performance can easily be captured with little technical barrier (Hodgson, 2008). Given these features, there are a variety of different ways to integrate the new web applications with the LMS into traditional classroom teaching. Students can be assigned in groups to collect raw data for their project and share only between group members. They may formulate drafts when they have processed the raw data, and these drafts can be revised by group members. This version can be released to all students in the cohort for further comments before final revision and submission. Alternatively, a wiki can be used by individual students to document versions of their academic writing, particularly when they need to work extensively and intensively on their final-year projects.

Learning Resources: Push and Pull

Learning resources are no longer limited to print-based media but can be in a digital format with multimedia enrichment. Bates and Poole (2003, p. 60) define the term 'multimedia' to include 'the combination of text, still graphics, animations, audio and video within a single technology, such as a computer or television', and it is used to represent concepts/information in a range of presentations. Type(s) of media should be selected after a thorough analysis and understanding of the added value of that technology to enhance learning. Experimenting with simulation activities on the Web or simulated scenarios through CD-ROMs

Figure 1. Students practise news writing in a blog

Figure 2. Students can edit peer work for a group project in a wiki

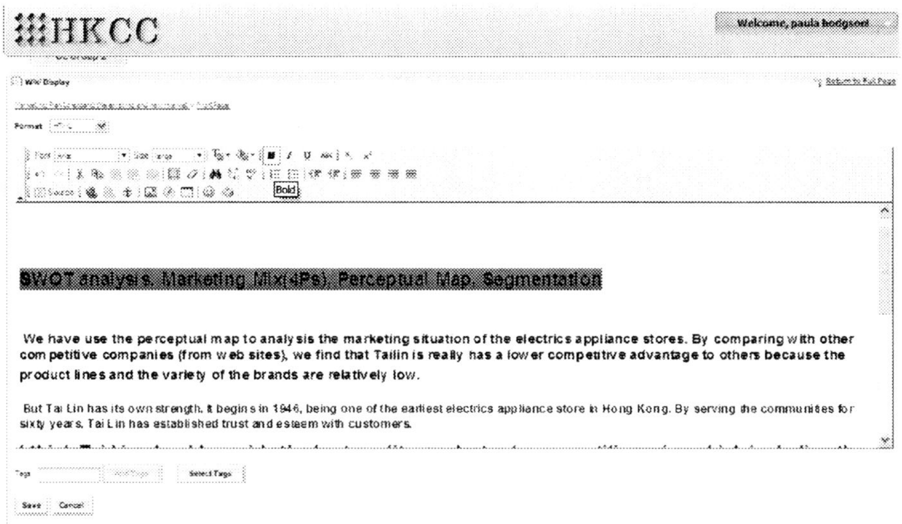

promotes the development of analytical skills because learners are able to test their assumptions and hypotheses. Students can also review the processes and procedures again in their own time, even if they have seen a live demonstration by the lecturer (Hardy, Ashcroft and Abbiatti, 1996). The availability of a range of technologies has opened up more options to enhance the learning process.

Having prepared their learning resources, educators commonly upload teaching materials and a list of web links to the LMS so that students can access them easily in order to prepare before attending lectures or tutorials. Other learning resources are provided through university libraries, some of which have collected subject-specific web resources, which are updated annually. Apart from receiving prescribed teaching materials from educators and librarians, students can also access additional interactive web-based resources provided by publishers. Although traditional printed textbooks are still on the list of prescribed reading in many programs, students can also browse through chapters in a web version using their own computers in addition to borrowing a hard copy from the library. The e-copy becomes a viable solution to growing class sizes in many universities, bearing in mind that while some students prefer to read a printed version, others are equally satisfied with the electronic version.

High-quality resources can be provided by educators or via subscription by their university. However, students may also need to search the electronic databases that are subscribed to by their university library – many regularly use Google search to find relevant web resources when they prepare for project or essay writing, but they need evaluative skills if they are to select sources that are both relevant and reliable when searching the Web. They often need to spend a lot of time scrutinizing information that takes a fraction of second to collect through whichever search engine they happen to be using.

However, there is a need to provide students with current resources and avoid those that may be out of date. One answer is RSS feeds, which are a key feature of Web 2.0 technologies and are an automated syndication of content. Students can subscribe to current information from one or more source, and the contents can be aggregated for reading in one convenient and coherent view using an RSS reader (Martindale and Wiley, 2005). Figure 1 shows this feature, which allows students to receive daily news from BBC Asia-Pacific and updates of subject-related content for students learning to write news articles in a course titled 'English for the Media' (Hodgson and Wong, 2008). Students can also read current articles from different online journals without going through the steps needed to access the electronic database subscribed to by the university library. Students may therefore spend less time searching once having subscribed to useful resources. As a result, they are encouraged to read more because new information is constantly streaming in (Huffaker, 2004).

Easy access to information does not imply that students experience high-quality learning. They may merely browse electronic pages or practise some mechanical drills that require factual recall of information with little demand on thinking. This is a problem if they are expected to become critical in what they read and learn how to apply theories and concepts in practice. Phipps and Merisotis (2000) argue that learning technologies should be designed to engage students in active learning and to develop skills in analysis, synthesis and evaluation as part of their course and program requirements. This means that streamed resources need to be analysed critically and used selectively when students engage in topical discussions, individual assignments or group projects.

Cognitive Apprentice: Class, Web and Laboratory

Reading and discussion can assist students to clarify declarative knowledge. They may learn about good professional practice from senior students or practitioners already in the field. Nevertheless, they need to practise and rehearse performance skills in order to develop functional knowledge and become professionals themselves. Consequently, practically based authentic learning experience is an essential component of a university program to prepare future professionals in such fields as medicine, nursing, rehabilitation sciences and occupational sciences, because they are required to develop clinical skills before they attend placements, through which they have a valuable opportunity to synthesize theory, research and practice.

While they are introduced to the needed professional skills in lectures, students may observe live demonstrations or view video clips. They can subsequently review the procedures if the clips are uploaded to the LMS. However, they need to practise in order to acquire an acceptable level of professional competence. Typically, students carry out tests and experiments in a laboratory individually, but in order to develop a broad base of competence, they can also examine cases with different levels of complexity in the web environment (see Figures 3 and 4), which can reinforce knowledge and supplement experiential learning (Hodgson, So and Hung, 2008; Tong and Hodgson, 2007). Figure 3 shows an example of a nursing educator designing web-based cases with stages whereby students were required to carry out clinical analysis for each stage of development of a case in the online forum. Figure 4 shows an example of one such web-based exercise: handling mercury spillage (students are required to learn the relevant safety precautions before practising laboratory work). The networked environment provides an alternative learning experience: instead of working independently to examine a case, they can now arrange to work collaboratively. As students are new to a given case, which can be complex and hard to resolve, exploring that case in a group setting can help them to co-construct their professional knowledge (Herrington and Herrington 2006). They can use non-class time to study cases, which means that they can start thinking about the issues related to a case and commence independent disciplined inquiry. They can search related resources through the facilities provided by the library and hold discussions with their peers through the online forum (Tong and Hodgson, 2007). Educators can reinforce this with feedback given to students in class, because they can elaborate or offer further clarification based on what and how students perform in the online discussion. The enriched opportunities in the blended mode of learning can contribute to 'real-world authenticity' (Jones, 2006, p. 172). Students may obtain some form of automated suggested solution generated by computer. Figure 5 shows an example of a student practising an eye examination with a virtual retinoscope; the student optometrist needs to adjust the virtual angle of the beam and lenses of different focal lengths for each eye, and the level of accuracy is then tested against the computer program. While students work on cases or programmed simulations, they may consolidate or clarify concepts before they start practising, but there is still a gap between conceptual understanding in university study and real-world practice.

In fields such as medicine, e-learning practice must be complemented by authentic laboratory practice in which groups of students execute procedural steps to minimize any critical medical complications. However, although students can practise using clinical equipment with their peers in the laboratory, to synthesize theories, they may need to practise with human patient simulation in a simulated ward. By doing so, they can work through the clinical steps with no risk of making errors with real patients Hogan, Pace, Hapgood and Boone, 2006; Wright *et al.*, 2005). Unlike working on cases in the web environment or practising with peers, students need to react in real time because the condition of the simulated patient can change by the second. They also need to consider how they communicate with other clinical professionals and how they make decisions if the condition of the patient changes. Because students will undergo a debriefing session after simulated practice, they can receive just-in-time feedback when the memory of their actions and decisions remains fresh. Having experienced practice through human patient simulation, many students develop great confidence and have high

Figure 3. Online clinical case

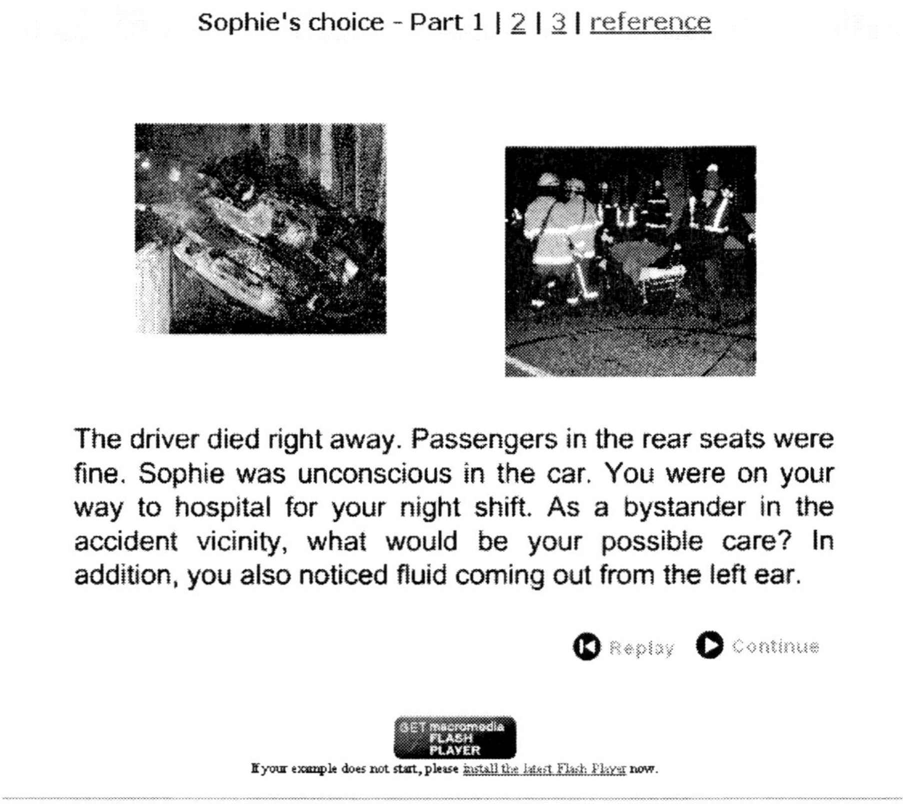

Figure 4. eLaboratory safety orientation: handling mercury spillage

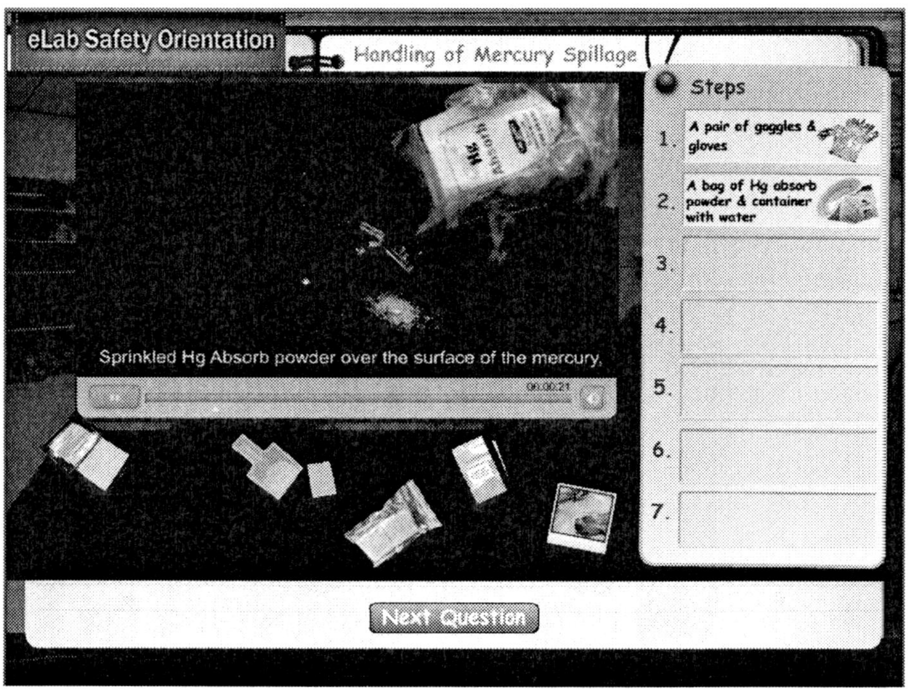

Figure 5. Computerized feedback on an eye assessment with a web-based retinoscope

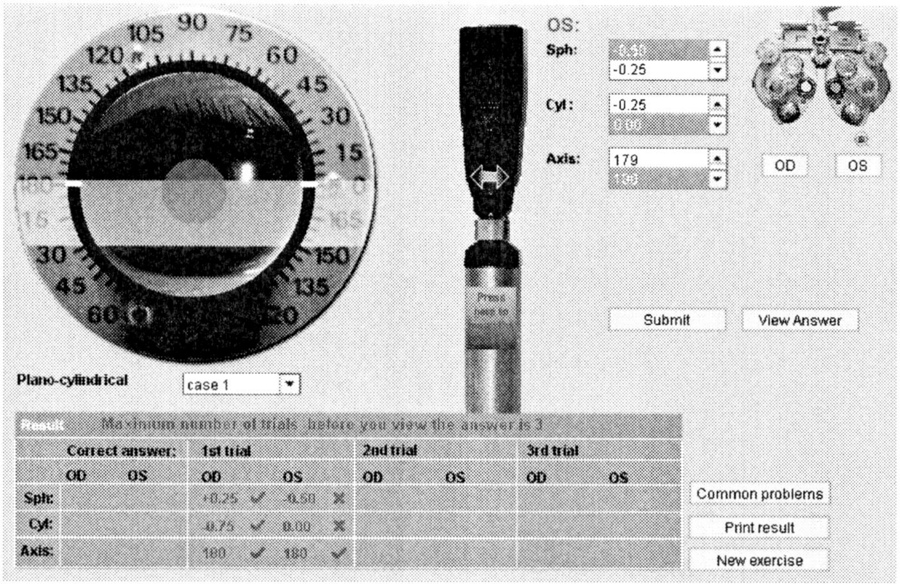

satisfaction in the experience (Foster, Sheriff and Cheney, 2008).

Interactions: Peers, Educators and Professionals

Students may be asked to hold small group discussions so that they can articulate ideas and build a deeper understanding of what they have learned from lectures and reading. Underwood and Underwood (1999) claim that interactions between peers have a significant impact on the learning experience. In classroom teaching, student contributions have been found to constitute only 5 percent of class time across all disciplines (Bonwell and Eison, 1991). Interactions between students are often very limited, and opportunities for participation by individuals are greatly reduced in large classes. However, although students can interact spontaneously, which may generate a wide variety of ideas in a short time, a democratic system of participation is only possible if this has been facilitated by the teacher. Because there is little time for such interactions between teacher and students, and among students, educators may consider integrating the asynchronous and synchronous modes of communication provided by the LMS. Many studies have been conducted on the impact of asynchronous communication on student learning. Compared with face-to-face interactions, the asynchronous mode of communication through the online environment promotes equality between participants (Abrams, 2001; Harasim, 1989; Steeples *et al.*, 1996); encourages greater participation by less vocal students (Downing and Chim, 2004; Sproull and Kiesler, 1991); and allows more time to compose ideas and for reflection before responding, which leads to more thoughtful and better-quality discussions (Benhunan-Fich and Hiltz, 1999). It is particularly useful for students whose first language is not English, because they have more time to organize their thoughts and present them in a coherent manner (Maier and Warren, 2000; Steeples *et al.*, 1996).

The LMS provides a channel through which to develop a learning conversation between peers in which learners can receive individualized feedback and develop different perspectives through interactions (Laurillard, 2000). Two-way technology applications such as email and electronic bulletin boards enable students to continue their learning dialogue and construct knowledge beyond the classroom interactions and thus extend social support from peers (Bates, 1995). Furthermore, interactions can be extended to include learners from separate campuses or students studying overseas through audio- and video-conferencing. Interacting with overseas students can also raise inter-cultural awareness and widen perspectives when discussing practice in other countries; this can be achieved easily through technology with no physical barriers.

However, it is not uncommon to find that learners may respond to peer comments on a regular basis in asynchronous mode (Martindale and Wiley, 2005). Generally, students are strategic in how they spend their time and allocate efforts to such interactions. Many students participate regularly or respond to one another if their contributions are tied to some component of assessment (Dickey, 2004; West, Wright, Gabbitas and Graham, 2006). According to the study conducted by Tong and Hodgson (2007), students had problem-based face-to-face learning sessions on the course 'Nursing Therapeutics', and their contribution to discussing clinical cases in the online forum was high when they were awarded marks. The blended mode of learning has a definite advantage over the single mode of face-to-face interaction because students who had no clinical experience were given time to read and study relevant articles from journals and online resources to substantiate their arguments when they analysed clinical actions. The majority of the student commitment to online activities was consistently high across the few years of implementation (*ibid.*). Furthermore, students pay close attention to comments from peers on individual or group work, because this allows them to learn to broaden their perspective and be more critical when commenting and receiving feedback during the peer review process, as indicated in the student survey (Hodgson and Wong, 2008).

Interactions through the LMS are primarily between students and teacher and among students on a course, but it would be of great value if students could interact with members of earlier cohorts, graduates and professionals in their field. While educators can arrange real-time conferencing, they also have the option of allowing non-participants on a course access through subscription or by invitation to blogs or wikis (Tryon, 2006). Students, who are still serving their apprenticeships, highly value comments and experiences provided by senior cohorts and professionals.

To sum up, students may encounter various learning experiences in universities nowadays. Apart from the conventional mode of lectures and seminars, they can access print-based and web-based prescribed and subscribed resources. To practise professional and generic knowledge and skills, students can model the process by tackling web-based cases and human patient simulation. Students can interact intuitively with educators and peers in class, engage with the asynchronous mode of communication in an online forum or via email, and communicate with a non-course audience through audio- and video-conferencing, or through invitation to blogs and wikis. However, despite the various learning opportunities discussed earlier, students may or may not be engaged. Educators often notice that the majority of students pay close attention if learning activities contribute to a grade or mark in assessment. The next section will discuss how assessment can be redesigned to promote an enriched learning experience.

ASSESSMENT FOR LEARNING

Written examinations, which are still the most common form of assessment, typically allow students to demonstrate their understanding of theoretical concepts. Assessment of learning is conducted conventionally in paper and pen format in several ways, either singly or in combination. It can include activities such as multiple-choice tests, research and analysis, a dissertation or thesis, a project, a portfolio of work, clinical fieldwork, laboratory work, independent and self-directed study, an oral presentation, and original writing (Glasner, 2000; Knight, 2002). Students may receive a grade, sometimes with comments indicating the level of performance, by the end of the semester. However, they often overlook comments (Crisp, 2007), and grades may not be effective in helping students to improve and accelerate their learning (Sadler, 1998). While summative assessment has become the most common means of measuring student performance, educators can consider alternative methods that may provide much better opportunities for student learning.

Computer-generated assessment can provide immediate feedback for tasks such as multiple-choice questions (MCQs), true-or-false questions, drag and drop, and fill-in-the-blanks types of activity. Many academics choose to assess students on their understanding of course content objectively through closed-ended MCQ tests or examinations. In this way, students can be assessed on their recall of factual information or on their ability to apply theories or principles to solve problems. An advantage of this type of computer-generated assessment is that it can provide immediate feedback to students with the option of model answers from automated comment banks, so students are encouraged to review their conceptual understanding (Freeman and Lewis, 1998).

Although this type of assessment activity can assess students efficiently and objectively on knowledge of subject matter, common forms of MCQ testing cannot assess capability in analysing, evaluating and synthesizing knowledge or in the broad range of professional skills that may be required. These skills are better assessed through other methods, such as computerized adaptive tests. Some teachers use commercially produced computerized simulations for assessment, integrating these programs to address the theories that are being taught. Some parameters in programs can be modified, allowing teachers to make responsive changes to reflect current real-world events or issues. Scores can be generated automatically from complex responses in this type of program so that results reflect professional actions or judgement. It was observed by the teacher of business studies, who shared his experience in an educational development seminar, that students participating in the game-based simulation 'Marketplace' spent over six hours per week, and they had to apply knowledge in marketing, strategic management, operational management, accounting, finance, human resource management, economics and organizational behaviour when solving problems in the simulation. Students received feedback through the computerized system and were debriefed by the lecturer in class.

However, students cannot experience tacit knowledge through working in computer-based assessment activities, so educators may consider having students conduct subject-specific projects, produce a portfolio of work, or take part in clinical fieldwork. Students may be involved in interacting with stakeholders in the field and with peers if this is a group task. While students may apply some theories and test them by working in a realistic situation, they also have the opportunity to gain insights and feedback by interacting with stakeholders. As an assessment task, students are commonly required to submit a written report (individually or as a group) on their learning experiences for grading. To allow students to reflect on their actions in the learning process, they can compile a learning log documenting their learning experience in a blog and extract individual work to be compiled into a wiki when they prepare the report; this is particularly valued by students when working in groups because they can share resources, work flexibly and be able to retrieve key artifacts from their blogs when they work on different parts of a report (Hodgson, 2008).

Although students working in groups may allocate different roles and responsibilities based on individual strengths, this does not often happen. The most negative comment about group work concerns the unfairness of mark distribution within a group, because not all group members contribute equally to the final deliverable (Miller, Imrie and Cox, 1998). Therefore, peer participation in peer assessment may allow a fairer mark for individuals based on their contributions to the group. However, Elliott and Higgins (2005) argue that assessment in this context works counter to the concept of collaboration when assessing peer learning, although there are studies that show positive effects of peer assessment. Students are more satisfied with the mark given, because there is increased transparency in the marking process; they have improved confidence in preparing assignments autonomously, and the process of peer assessment motivates students to impress one another (Hanrahan and Isaacs, 2001; McLaughlin and Simpson, 2004; Smith, Cooper and Lancaster, 2002). In addition, students have a better understanding of the marking criteria and know how the feedback is derived (Bloxhan and West, 2004; Morris, 2001; Sluijsmans and Prins, 2006). They also benefit from acquiring evaluative skills through critically reflecting on the criteria. Furthermore, reviewing feedback from peer assessment helps students to build their satisfaction, self-confidence and academic standards (Nesbit and Burton, 2006). However, some students may feel uncomfortable providing peer feedback because of social pressure, although the process of peer assessment can be streamlined in the web environment because the facility to post anonymous reviews can easily be set up so that students can provide objective and fair comments and grades (Freeman and McKenzie, 2002).

As already discussed, computer-mediated assessment activities create more opportunities for providing prompt and useful feedback to students, consolidate concepts, bring multiple perspectives to the learning process, and demonstrate skills and knowledge with applied theories (Lam, Hodgson and Csete, 2007). Although assessment serves primarily for classification and selection, the alternative assessment methods that have emerged allow students to document their learning history, which may then be used as part of their career portfolio, and to develop a deeper understanding of the subject. They can also provide further evidence of students' achievements beyond that which can be collected by traditional summative assessment methods.

PORTFOLIO OF COMPETENCE: PROFESSIONAL VERSUS PERSONAL

A transcript of university study may summarize the overall performance on a course, but this provides limited information of the competence that students may have developed over the years. To counter this and prepare for their careers, students can start to develop a professional profile that captures evidence of professional performance and generic competence. A personal portfolio, when presented through the Web, can progress from the e-portfolio as a scrapbook to a web-based and hyperlinked collection of authentic evidence for assessment, evaluation and reporting, and reflections on curricular and co-curricular activities (see Figures 6 and 7). A professional portfolio can be in the form of a collection of student performances, including academic results, artifacts of their academic work, reflections on placements across contexts, feedback on placements by professionals, and their *curriculum vitae* during the years of university study.

Compiling evidence of initial ideas, lines of thought developed and the final product is common in some subjects, notably art and design and architecture. Apart from documenting the process of idea development, portfolios can be used in other disciplines to present exemplary work that best illustrates a student's ability (Brown, 1999;

Cole, 2000; Gibbs, 1995). Students with diverse talents can use alternative ways to demonstrate their competence: they can create a combination of digitized images and video clips to show the development of the design and development of a prototype of a project and hyperlink these artifacts to reflections. This enables students to reassess their own work and rethink what they have achieved before they organize and present their work in a portfolio. 'A quality portfolio evidences complex thinking and problem solving and invokes authentic applications that represent significant learning' (Montgomery and Wiley, 2004, p. 8).

In general, e-portfolios can serve to promote authentic inquiry when students start reflecting on their apprenticeships. Students can focus on how to transfer academic knowledge and skills and how to apply them when they have realistic learning activities. To reflect on their actions, students can start open discussions with practitioners in a blog. Concerning the development of best professional practice, academic mentors can provide feedback on theoretical and conceptual analyses and thus nurture reflective learning (Graham and Megarry, 2005). However, comments from practitioners are often from different perspectives: for example, they may benchmark industrial protocols, expectations and standards (Costley and Armsby, 2007). Nevertheless, self-reflective learning with input and feedback from academics and practitioners is a crucial factor for future graduates to transfer learning between university study and the real world (Crebert, Bates, Bell, Patrick and Cragnolini, 2004). Therefore, students need to reflect on any feedback provided by practitioners, even if they focus on different perspectives. This can then become a 'foundation for career-long self-

Figure 6. Reflection on learning experiences in a student blog

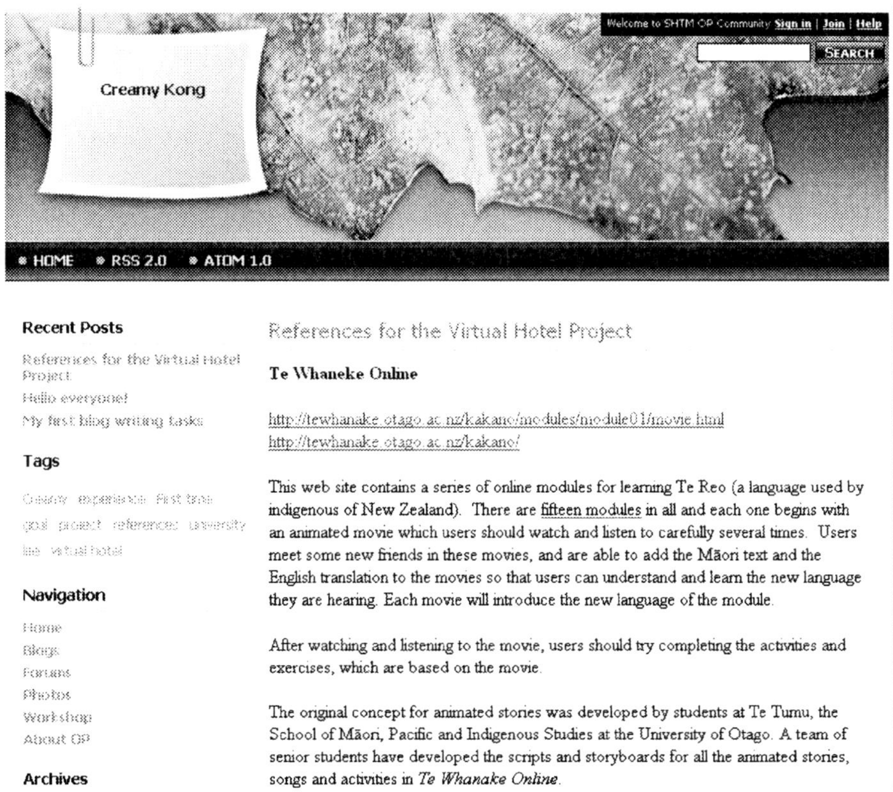

Figure 7. Personal portfolio

evaluation' so that students can identify possible areas for further development of professional and generic competence (Winsor, Butt and Reeves, 1999, p. 21).

Apart from reviewing feedback from academics and practitioners, students may find some trusted peers with whom they can discuss and debate underlying assumptions and personal values in full confidentiality. E-portfolios allow students to reflect critically and self-assess the overall learning progress of their university programs. This implies that they may document new insights into learning experiences, changes in behaviour, and any evidence of readiness to apply learning for improved professional practice (Graham and Megarry, 2005). Students can also include the process of idea development, methods for tackling problems that they may have encountered, and a review of actions taken (Cole, 2000). These can help to develop a deeper understanding of professional practice. However, this is not a fast and direct process for students to establish full confidence, although they can observe personal growth when the learning portfolio is unfolded. As the writing process in portfolios stimulates students to make conscious thoughts, this serves as a vehicle for learning (Winsor *et al.*, 1999). Over time, the process may allow students to grow in confidence and develop their own independent intellectual thinking (Harland, 2005).

FUTURE TRENDS

Curricula vs. Technology

University curricula may change over time, but technology never stops evolving. This provides much food for thought for educators in Hong Kong on how to improve learning, teaching and assessment by using existing technologies to provide meaningful experiences for students. Technology can also affect the way how educators teach (Wilson and Jennings, 2000). For conventional programs, many universities therefore adopted a university-wide LMS in the 1990s.

Educators can make use of the LMS to upload learning resources, communicate with students and manage assessment activities. A web-based master program was first introduced by the Hong Kong Polytechnic University in 2000 (http://www.hkcyberu.com). However, learning environments become more dynamic when Web 2.0 technologies such as blogs and wikis are embedded for educational use. The blended mode can provide wider opportunities for students to interact beyond the tradition face-to-face and distance learning, and communications between students through the new applications are also better (Hiltz and Turoff, 2005). They provide a learning space in which students, individually and in groups, can share additional learning resources with peers and chart the progress of their learning. Besides, learning opportunities are blended with face-to-face and web-based interactions, and students have greater opportunities to communicate and interact with stakeholders: teachers, peers, and local and overseas professionals. It therefore becomes more possible to organize international collaborations, which would make future graduates more ready to master professional practice with local knowledge but a global perspective.

Traditional vs. Innovative Assessment Techniques

Traditional paper-based assessment still predominates in practice, although there is good potential for considering alternative assessment methods. Educators can consider taking innovative steps in assessment progressively. As discussed earlier, computer-mediated assessment activities may offer the possibility of (1) providing faster feedback, (2) encouraging students to become engaged in the process and outcomes of assessment activities, and (3) developing evaluative skills and building trusting relationship when they are involved in the process of peer assessment. There is growing use of web-based MCQ testing as formative and summative assessment (Grabe and Sigler, 2002; Nicol, 2007; Palmer and Devitt, 2007). The automated scoring system allows educators to have instant feedback on student performance. Furthermore, the constraints of using a pen and paper-based method can be circumvented by the use of a web-based evaluative self- and peer-assessment system (Sung, Chang, Chiou and Hou, 2005). Tension between students can be minimized when the online review process is made anonymous. More educators may involve students in evaluation as part of the assessment process. Furthermore, to evaluate the declarative and procedural knowledge expected in a profession, students can be assessed on how they analyse cases, problems or scenarios (Hodgson and Csete, 2007). Educators may introduce web-based self-assessment tasks with multimedia-enriched or flash-animated cases (Allen, 1998). However, it can be very time-consuming to create resources for assessment activities such as web-based cases or computerized adaptive tests. Consequently, to redesign assessment activities so that less effort is required, they may consider creating and sharing a database of web-based cases that can be reused by other disciplines and between institutions.

Use of e-Portfolios

Although a policy of adopting a reflective culture by embracing e-portfolios for learning is not universal in Hong Kong universities, students studying some disciplines, such as architecture and design, are required to create a portfolio. When developing a comprehensive profile to demonstrate collective evidence of professional competence for students across courses of university study, there are some concerns concerning implementation. Technological barriers are perceived as less of a challenge to students, but they are often concerned about the scope and scale of the final deliverable. It is not possible to differentiate a team project from individual efforts or contributions when it is presented in a personal portfolio. Students may not commit to developing a portfolio if they do not see its value, unless it is aligned with their university culture and philosophy, the criteria for pursuing further education, and expectations from future employers (Wright, Knight and Pomerleau, 1999). It is important for educators to provide guidelines that demystify any concerns that students may have about feedback from practitioners, whether the portfolio serves for personal development or as a tool to assess performance (Smith and Tillema, 2003).

Other Future Trends

University students in Hong Kong are generally technically competent to retrieve a variety of web-based information, create their own personal diaries in blogs with digital images or videos, and communicate with friends through mobile phones and social networking websites. Students' learning experience should therefore be expanded beyond scheduled face-to-face lectures and tutorials. Over the past decade, although there were few early adopters of the new technologies, these pioneers replaced regular lectures with web-based narrated teaching resources, had students actively participating in forum discussions and paid extra attention to facilitating discussions in interactive face-to-face tutorials. It was observed that students were better prepared for tutorials as a result (Hodgson, Chan and Liu, 2007; Tong and Hodgson, 2007). These students were positive about their learning experience, having acquired self-managed learning skills and developed a proactive, self-directed learning attitude (Kwok and Hodgson, 2004). Besides, there were more international interactions between students through the use of video-conferencing in different programs (O'Dowd, 2007). This can certainly broaden awareness of cross-cultural diversity and variations in international practice. The outcome would be that future graduates are better prepared beyond the prescribed curriculum.

CONCLUSION

Traditional classroom teaching provides direct interaction between educators and students, but students are exposed to limited learning opportunities and experience. Conventional end-of-term paper-based assessment activities provide a uniform assessment protocol but cannot allow students to demonstrate fully what they have learned. With the integration of technologies into teaching, learning and assessment, learners will be open to more learning opportunities and will be able to extend their horizons internationally. However, the quality of the learning experience depends not on the variety of technologies employed but on learners' commitment to and engagement with the learning process. Educators can deploy different teaching strategies, either face-to-face or online, synchronous or asynchronous, or setting up connections either locally or overseas. Learners with different learning styles can develop both professional and generic competence when they are provided with a range of learning opportunities: in class, via the Web, in the laboratory or through work placement. Blogs and wikis provide a space in which students can easily maintain a record of learning experiences. They should take the opportunity to build a profile illustrating enriched experiences so that they can thereby illustrate their competence for their future careers over and above the piece of paper that certifies they 'passed' the course.

ACKNOWLEDGMENT

This is to acknowledge that the images captured are from the educational projects supported from e3Learning Project which was funded by the University Grants Committee in Hong Kong and the eLearning Development & Support Section of Educational Development Centre, the Hong Kong Polytechnic University.

REFERENCES

Abrams, Z. I. (2001). Computer-mediated communication and group journals: Expanding the repertoire of participant roles. *System, 29*(4), 489–503. doi:10.1016/S0346-251X(01)00041-0

Allen, R. (1998). The Web: Interactive and multimedia education. *Computer Networks and ISDN Systems, 30*(16–18), 1717–1727. doi:10.1016/S0169-7552(98)00200-1

Alonso, F., López, G., Manrique, D., & Vines, J. M. (2005). An instructional model for Web-based e-learning education with a blended learning process approach. *British Journal of Educational Technology, 36*(2), 217–235. doi:10.1111/j.1467-8535.2005.00454.x

Bates, T. (1995). *Technology, open learning, and distance education*. London & New York: Routledge.

Bates, T., & Poole, G. (2003). *Effective teaching with technology in higher education: Foundations for success*. San Francisco: Jossey-Bass.

Benhunan-Fich, R., & Hiltz, S. R. (1999). Educational applications of cmcs: Solving case studies through asynchronous learning networks. *Journal of Computer-Mediated Communication, 4*(3).

Biggs, J. B., & Tang, C. (2007). *Teaching for quality learning at university: What the student does*, 3rd ed. Philadelphia: Society for Research into Higher Education and Open University Press.

Bloxhan, S., & West, A. (2004). Understanding the rules of the game: Marking peer assessment as a medium for developing students' conceptions of assessment. *Assessment & Evaluation in Higher Education, 29*(6), 721–733. doi:10.1080/0260293042000227254

Bonwell, C. C., & Eison, J. A. (1991). *Active learning: Creating excitement in the classroom*. Washington: George Washington University Press.

Brown, S. A. (1999). Assessing practice. In S.A. Brown & A. Glasner (Eds.), *Assessment matters in higher education: Choosing and using diverse approaches*. Buckingham, UK & Philadelphia: Open University Press and Society for Research into Higher Education.

Cole, D. J. (2000). *Portfolios across the curriculum and beyond*, 2nd ed. Thousand Oaks, CA: Corwin Press.

Costley, C., & Armsby, P. (2007). Work-based learning assessed as a field or a mode of study. *Assessment & Evaluation in Higher Education, 32*(1), 21–33. doi:10.1080/02602930600848267

Crebert, G., Bates, M., Bell, B., Patrick, C.-J., & Cragnolini, V. (2004). Ivory tower to concrete jungle revisited. *Journal of Education and Work, 17*(1), 47–70. doi:10.1080/1363908042000174192

Crisp, B. R. (2007). Is it worth the effort? How feedback influences students' subsequent submission of assessable work. *Assessment & Evaluation in Higher Education, 32*(5), 571–581. doi:10.1080/02602930601116912

Dickey, M. (2004). The impact of Web-logs (blogs) on student perceptions of isolation and alienation in a Web-based distance-learning environment. *Open Learning, 19*(3), 279–291. doi:10.1080/0268051042000280138

Downing, K., & Chim, T. M. (2004). Reflectors as online extroverts? *Educational Studies, 30*(3), 265–276. doi:10.1080/0305569042000224215

Elliott, N., & Higgins, A. (2005). Self and peer assessment–does it make a difference to student group work? *Nurse Education in Practice, 5*(1), 40–48. doi:10.1016/j.nepr.2004.03.004

Felder, R. M., & Silverman, L. K. (1988). Learning and teaching styles in engineering education. *English Education, 78*(7), 674–681.

Foster, J. G., Sheriff, S., & Cheney, S. (2008). Using nonfaculty registered nurses to facilitate high-fidelity human patient simulation activities. *Nurse Educator, 33*(3), 137–141. doi:10.1097/01.NNE.0000312186.20895.50

Freeman, M., & McKenzie, J. (2002). Spark, a confidential Web-based template for self and peer assessment of student teamwork: Benefits of evaluating across different subjects. *British Journal of Educational Technology, 33*(5), 551–569. doi:10.1111/1467-8535.00291

Freeman, R., & Lewis, R. (1998). *Planning and implementing assessment*. London: Kogan Page.

Garrison, D. R., & Kanuka, H. (2004). Blended learning: Uncovering its transformative potential in higher education. *The Internet and Higher Education, 7*(2), 95–105. doi:10.1016/j.iheduc.2004.02.001

Gibbs, G. (1995). *Assessing student centred courses*. Oxford: Oxford Centre for Staff Development.

Glasner, A. (2000). Innovations in student assessment: A system-wide perspective. In S. A. Brown & A. Glasner (Eds.), *Assessment matters in higher education: Choosing and using diverse approaches*. Buckingham, UK & Philadelphia: Open University Press and Society for Research into Higher Education.

Grabe, M., & Sigler, E. (2002). Studying online: Evaluation of an online study environment. *Computers & Education, 38*(4), 375–383. doi:10.1016/S0360-1315(02)00020-9

Graham, C. R., Allen, S., & Ure, D. (2003). *Blended learning environments: A review of the research literature*. Unpublished manuscript, Provo, UT.

Graham, G., & Megarry, B. (2005). The social care work portfolio: An aid to integrated learning and reflection in social care training. *Social Work Education, 24*(7), 769–780. doi:10.1080/02615470500238686

Hanrahan, S. J., & Isaacs, G. (2001). Assessing self- and peer-assessment: The students' views. *Higher Education Research & Development, 20*(1), 53–70. doi:10.1080/07294360123776

Harasim, L. M. (1989). Online education: A new domain. In R. Mason & A. Kaye (Eds.), *Mindweave: Communication, computers, and distance education*. Oxford & New York: Pergamon Press.

Harden, R. M., & Hart, I. R. (2002). An international virtual medical school (ivimeds): The future for medical education? *Medical Teacher, 24*(3), 261–267. doi:10.1080/01421590220141008

Hardy, D. W., Ashcroft, J. C., & Abbiatti, M. D. (1996). The motion curricula concept: Technology selection in distance education. Paper presented at the Proceedings of the 12th Distance Teaching and Learning Conference, University of Wisconsin at Madison.

Harland, T. (2005). Developing a portfolio to promote authentic enquiry in teacher education. *Teaching in Higher Education, 10*(3), 327–337. doi:10.1080/13562510500122180

Herrington, T., & Herrington, J. (2006). What is an authentic learning environment? In T. Herrington & J. Herrington (Eds.), *Authentic learning environments in higher education*. Hershey, PA: Information Science Publishers.

Hiltz, S. R., & Turoff, M. (2005). Education goes digital: The evolution of online learning and the revolution in higher education. *Communications of the ACM, 48*(10), 59–64. doi:10.1145/1089107.1089139

Hodgson, P. (2008). *Building a community of practice through liferay*. Paper presented at the 2008 International Conference on ICT in Teaching and Learning, Hong Kong.

Hodgson, P., Chan, K., & Liu, Y. W. J. (2007). *Learning through e-situated challenges.* Paper presented at the 2007 International Conference on ICT in Teaching and Learning, Hong Kong.

Hodgson, P., & Csete, J. (2007). Creating new learning challenges through ecases [electronic version]. *The Information, Technology, and Educational Change (ITEC) Journal*. Retrieved from http://ejournal.cite.hku.hk/articles/volume2issue2/Hodgson_Csete/Hodgson_Csete.htm

Hodgson, P., & Wong, D. (2008). *Motivation, engagement, and quality of writing through blogs.* Paper presented at the 2008 International Conference on ICT in Teaching and Learning, Hong Kong.

Hogan, M. P., Pace, D. E., Hapgood, J., & Boone, D. C. (2006). Use of human patient simulation and the situation awareness global assessment technique in practical trauma skills assessment. *The Journal of Trauma, 61*(5), 1047–1052. doi:10.1097/01.ta.0000238687.23622.89

Huffaker, D. (2004). The educated blogger: Using Weblogs to promote literacy in the classroom [electronic version]. *First Monday*. Retrieved on April 8, 2008, from http://www.firstmonday.org/issues/issue9_6/huffaker/#author

Hughes, G. (2007). Using blended learning to increase learner support and improve retention. *Teaching in Higher Education, 12*(3), 349–363. doi:10.1080/13562510701278690

Jones, S. (2006). Using IT to augment authentic learning environments. In T. Herrington & J. Herrington (Eds.), *Authentic learning environments in higher education.* Hershey, PA: Information Science Publishers.

Knight, P. T. (2002). *Being a teacher in higher education.* Buckingham, UK & Philadelphia: Open University Press and Society for Research into Higher Education.

Kwok, P. M. H., & Hodgson, P. (2004). *Tea or tears with SARS?* Paper presented at the 38th Academy of Marketing Conference, July 5–7, Cheltenham, England.

Lam, P., Hodgson, P., & Csete, J. (2007). Enrichment of interaction in online assessments. In S. Frankland (Ed.), *Enhancing teaching and learning through assessment: Deriving an appropriate model*. The Netherlands: Springer.

Laurillard, D. (2000). New technologies, students, and the curriculum: The impact of communications and information technology on higher education. In P. Scott (Ed.), *Higher education reformed.* London & New York: Falmer Press.

Laurillard, D. (2002). *Rethinking university teaching: A conversational framework for the effective use of learning technologies*, 2nd ed. London & New York: RoutledgeFalmer.

Maier, P., & Warren, A. (2000). *Integrating technology in learning & teaching: A practical guide to educators*. London: Kogan Page.

Martindale, T., & Wiley, D. A. (2005). Using Weblogs in scholarship and teaching. *TechTrends: Linking Research & Practice to Improve Learning, 49*(2), 55–61.

McLaughlin, P., & Simpson, N. (2004). Peer assessment in first year university: How the students feel. *Studies in Educational Evaluation, 30*(2), 135–149. doi:10.1016/j.stueduc.2004.06.003

Miller, A. H., Imrie, B. W., & Cox, K. (1998). *Student assessment in higher education: A handbook for assessing performance*. London: Kogan Page.

Montgomery, K., & Wiley, D. A. (2004). *Creating e-portfolios using powerpoint: A guide for educators*. Thousand Oaks, CA: Sage Publications.

Morris, J. (2001). Peer assessment: A missing link between teaching and learning? A review of the literature. *Nurse Education Today*, *21*(7), 507–515. doi:10.1054/nedt.2001.0661

Nesbit, P. L., & Burton, S. (2006). Student justice perceptions following assignment feedback. *Assessment & Evaluation in Higher Education*, *31*(6), 655–670. doi:10.1080/02602930600760868

Nicol, D. (2007). E-assessment by design: Using multiple-choice tests to good effect. *Journal of Further and Higher Education*, *31*(1), 53–64. doi:10.1080/03098770601167922

O'Dowd, R. (2007). Evaluating the outcomes of online intercultural exchange. *ELT Journal: English Language Teachers Journal*, *61*(2), 144–152.

Oliver, M., & Trigwell, K. (2005). Can 'blended learning' be redeemed? *E-learning*, *2*(1), 17–26.

Osguthorpe, R. T., & Graham, C. R. (2003). Blended learning environments: Definitions and directions. *The Quarterly Review of Distance Education*, *4*(3), 227–233.

Palmer, E., & Devitt, P. (2007). Assessment of higher order cognitive skills in undergraduate education: Modified essay or multiple choice questions? Research paper. *BMC Medical Education*, *7*(1), 49–55. doi:10.1186/1472-6920-7-49

Phipps, R., & Merisotis, J. (2000). *Quality on the line: Benchmarks for success in Internet-based distance education*. Washington: Institute for Higher Education Policy.

Sadler, D. R. (1998). Formative assessment: Revisiting the territory. *Assessment in Education: Principles . Policy & Practice*, *5*(1), 77–84.

Sluijsmans, D., & Prins, F. (2006). A conceptual framework for integrating peer assessment in teacher education. *Studies in Educational Evaluation*, *32*(1), 6–22. doi:10.1016/j.stueduc.2006.01.005

Smith, H., Cooper, A., & Lancaster, L. (2002). Improving the quality of undergraduate peer assessment: A case for student and staff development. *Innovations in Education and Teaching International*, *39*(1), 71–81. doi:10.1080/13558000110102904

Smith, K., & Tillema, H. (2003). Clarifying different types of portfolio use. *Assessment & Evaluation in Higher Education*, *28*(6), 625. doi:10.1080/0260293032000130252

Sproull, L., & Kiesler, S. B. (1991). *Connections: New ways of working in the networked organization*. Cambridge, MA: MIT Press.

Steeples, C., Unsworth, C., Bryson, M., Goodyear, P., Riding, P., & Fowell, S. (1996). Technological support for teaching and learning: Computer-mediated communications in higher education. *Computers & Education*, *26*(1–3), 71–80. doi:10.1016/0360-1315(95)00082-8

Sung, Y.-T., Chang, K.-E., Chiou, S.-K., & Hou, H.-T. (2005). The design and application of a Web-based self- and peer-assessment system. *Computers & Education*, *45*(2), 187–202. doi:10.1016/j.compedu.2004.07.002

Tolmie, A., & Boyle, J. (2000). Factors influencing the success of computer mediated communication (CMC) environments in university teaching: A review and case study. *Computers & Education*, *34*(2), 119–140. doi:10.1016/S0360-1315(00)00008-7

Tong, E. T. F., & Hodgson, P. (2007). *Developing higher-order thinking through blended problem-based learning*. Paper presented at the 2007 International Conference on ICT in Teaching and Learning, Hong Kong.

Tryon, C. (2006). Writing and citizenship: Using blogs to teach first-year composition. *Pedagogy*, *6*(1), 128–132.

Underwood, J., & Underwood, G. (1999). Task effects on cooperative and collaborative learning with computers. In K. Littleton & P. Light (Eds.), *Learning with computers: Analysing productive interactions*. London: Routledge.

West, R., Wright, G., Gabbitas, B., & Graham, C. (2006). Reflections from the introduction of blogs and RSS feeds into a preservice instructional technology course. *TechTrends: Linking Research & Practice to Improve Learning*, *50*(4), 54–60.

Wilson, J. M., & Jennings, W. C. (2000). Studio courses: How information technology is changing the way we teach, on campus and off. *Proceedings of the IEEE, 8*8(1), 72–79.

Winsor, P. J. T., Butt, R. L., & Reeves, H. (1999). Portraying professional development in preservice teacher education: Can portfolios do the job? *Teachers and Teaching*, *5*(1), 9. doi:10.1080/1354060990050102

Wright, M. C., Taekman, J. M., Barber, L., Hobbs, G., Newman, M. F., & Stafford-Smith, M. (2005). The use of high-fidelity human patient simulation as an evaluative tool in the development of clinical research protocols and procedures. *Contemporary Clinical Trials*, *26*(6), 646–659. doi:10.1016/j.cct.2005.09.004

Wright, W. A., Knight, P. T., & Pomerleau, N. (1999). Portfolio people: Teaching and learning dossiers and innovation in higher education. *Innovative Higher Education*, *24*(2), 89–103. doi:10.1023/B:IHIE.0000008148.71650.e6

Chapter 4
Implementing and Promoting Blended Learning in Higher Education Institutions:
Comparing Different Approaches

Lixun Wang
The Hong Kong Institute of Education, Hong Kong

ABSTRACT

With the rapid development of the Internet, blended learning (online learning plus face-to-face learning) has become a model that more and more higher education institutions are intending to adopt. This chapter first compares various forms and expressions of blended learning adopted by different institutions around the world, and then reports on how blended learning has been implemented and promoted in the English Department at the Hong Kong Institute of Education (HKIEd) using a variety of approaches. Here, a number of projects have been carried out over the past seven years, focusing on the conversion of traditional face-to-face modules into partly face-to-face, partly online modules. In addressing these developments, the Blackboard online learning management system, which has been adopted as the main platform for the delivery of blended learning at HKIEd, is first examined. Then the design of a series of subject-specific Web sites to supplement the Blackboard system and facilitate blended learning is introduced. Finally, the implementation of innovative Wikibook projects is illustrated and discussed. Such Wikibook projects, where students are required to work in groups to write an academic textbook collaboratively online, are highly effective in promoting not only autonomous yet collaborative online academic reading and writing, but also online peer editing. This adds a new dimension to blended learning. Feedback from students shows that they greatly enjoyed the experience of collaborative academic writing through the Wikibook projects, and found that the wiki technology made peer editing much more efficient and effective. All the evidence suggests that blended learning has great potential as a vehicle for teaching and learning and is a notable current trend in higher education.

DOI: 10.4018/978-1-60566-852-9.ch004

GENERATIONS OF EDUCATIONAL DELIVERY MODES

Educational delivery modes have evolved through three generations: the first generation being the face-to-face and print-based mode; the second generation involving the frequent use of Radio (audio), Television (audio-visual), and Computer (data and image manipulation) technologies; and the third generation, the current one, requiring the incorporation of all the above features into a blended learning environment (face-to-face plus online) where interactivity is highly emphasized. This mode of learning can be termed Distributed Learning. Distributed learning is "part of a trend to use a mix of delivery modes to complement face-to-face classroom learning opportunities. Part of this mix usually includes the use of multimedia learning opportunities and participation in online activities, as well as working with print-based sources" (White, 2003, p.31). The blended learning delivery mode, which has been frequently discussed in the literature in recent years (Larson & Keiper, 2002; Pearson, 2006; Ng, Yeung & Hon, 2006; Xie, DeBacker, & Ferguson, 2006; Condie & Livingston, 2007; Smith & Kurthen, 2007), is the focus of this chapter, and is explored in detail in the sections that follow.

COMPARING DIFFERENT APPROACHES TO BLENDED LEARNING

In different parts of the world, blended learning has been implemented in various formats in schools and higher education institutions. To obtain an overview of current practices in blended learning, a number of sample cases are discussed below.

Sample Case in South Africa

At the University of the Witwatersrand in South Africa, two undergraduate psychology modules adopted a blended learning approach (Thatcher, 2007). In the first initiative, a course website entitled 'Cognitive Ergonomics' was developed. The earlier versions of the site contained only "background construct definitions, links to related websites, course outlines, assignment details, a notice-board, and a questions and answers section" (Thatcher, 2007, p.349). Later versions refined the notice-board to lecture-by-lecture notes and also introduced example questions and model answers to tests and assignments, and posted student assignment marks (Thatcher, 2007). As for the second initiative, both a website entitled 'Cognition' and a blog were used. The reason for using the blog was that blogging was becoming a popular means for people to post ideas, thoughts, or articles on the Web and to receive feedback on these postings. As Thatcher (2007, p.350) puts it, "a blog is a cross between a website and a discussion forum (if the feedback facility is activated)."

A formal website evaluation undertaken in 2006 revealed that students found the question and answer section, the notice board, and the past test and examination papers to be most useful. They also appreciated that they were able to communicate with the lecturer outside scheduled consultation times. The lecturers gave the impression that they were available 24 hours a day to deal with students' queries, and the students valued the fact that vital course information could be communicated immediately to a geographically dispersed class. They found that the online medium was particularly useful in conveying unambiguous content (Thatcher, 2007).

Sample Case in Singapore

A polytechnic in Singapore applied blended learning in a program called "the Speaker's Program" (Fang, 2007). In this program, the face-to-face sessions comprised a two-hour session once a week, followed by a three-hour project presentation session at the end of the program. The online sessions, which were managed through the

Blackboard (Blackboard Inc., n. d.) online learning management system, ran parallel to the face-to-face sessions. The participants were required to learn online, and respond to "the content, the trainer, the senior Student Ambassadors (who acted as online coaches or chat leaders), and each other" (Fang, 2007, p.244).

The participants found this blended learning experience beneficial, as they appreciated the chance to learn at their own pace, reflect and recapitulate what was taught in class, connect socially with other participants, and learn useful computer skills which could benefit their future studies. They enjoyed this new learning experience, and found it less stressful, as it allowed them to complete their work at any time, so that those who fell behind in their online submissions could eventually catch up (Fang, 2007).

Sample Case in the United States

At the University of California in the US, a Spanish language course titled Spanish Without Walls (SWW) was offered in both blended and distance-learning (DL) format (Blake, Wilson, Cetto & Pardo-Ballester, 2008). The course combines multimedia language materials including: CDs/ DVD named "Tesoros" serving as the course textbook, a SWW website for "Content-based web readings and Flash activities", a "collaborative CMC tool running on the Flash communications server that allows for both asynchronous and synchronous textual communication (both controlled character-by-character and by carriage return) in addition to Voice-over Internet protocol (VoIP) sound exchange" (Blake, Wilson, Cetto & Pardo-Ballester, 2008, p.117). The course management system Moodle (Moodle.org, n.d.) was used to manage the course materials to "teach first-year Spanish grammar and vocabulary, provide exercises, conduct testing, present authentic Spanish-language readings, and enable oral communication with teachers and peers" (Blake, Wilson, Cetto & Pardo-Ballester, 2008, p.117). The blended learning environment differs from the classroom courses principally in terms of the nature of the chat activities, the amount of individual attention received from instructors during chat sessions, and the amount of out-of-class study time. The required synchronous chat sessions (both text and audio exchanges) for the blended learning students make a major contribution to the level of individual practice and the extent of instructor attention, which might even exceed what can be found in traditional classrooms, where the lecturer has to face 25 to 30 students in a 50-minute period (Blake, Wilson, Cetto & Pardo-Ballester, 2008). The SWW project and its blended derivatives proved to be a successful experiment, as the students were not disadvantaged by taking Spanish in a non-traditional format (Blake, Wilson, Cetto & Pardo-Ballester, 2008).

Sample Case in Northern Ireland

In the Northern Ireland Centre for Entrepreneurship (NICENT), a partnership led by the University of Ulster and including Queen's University Belfast and the College of Agriculture, Food and Rural Enterprise, adopted a blended learning approach to their Entrepreneurship e-learning modules (Hegarty, 2006). The modules were placed in a WebCT (now merged with Blackboard (Blackboard Inc., n.d.)) learning environment and were designed for self-directed learning, and supported by two to three workshops; even assessments could be submitted online.

The challenge that the educators faced was their lack of experience in using WebCT: those who were interested in the possibility of delivering an e-learning module were therefore given an introductory demonstration and access. During the initial period they used the NICENT e-learning module as a support-teaching tool. Most of them were overwhelmed by the sheer volume of the content in the online module and expressed concern about how students would be able to interpret this. Later, they realized that the content could be automatically released on a weekly basis and customised to suit the educational needs of the individual learners (Hegarty, 2006). Although students sensed that their e-tutors did not possess much experience of using WebCT, they still gave extremely positive feedback, and reported that they had enjoyed various aspects of the blended learning mode, such as the ability to learn at their own pace independently. They found online learning more inclusive since it provided a flexible approach for people with learning difficulties. Also, the competitiveness of the classroom situation was removed, and the learners occupied a more comfortable learning zone. In addition, students enjoyed the interactive computer simulations and seeing and hearing the evidence from the "entrepreneur's mouth" through video clips (Hegarty, 2006, p.332). In the end, both educators and students were able to fully embrace WebCT as a learning environment.

Sample Case in Scotland

In Scotland, blended learning was implemented through the use of an online learning programme called SCHOLAR. The programme was initially designed to "support pupils in the post-compulsory years of schooling in Scotland studying for national examinations (Higher and Advanced Higher) in the key areas of science, mathematics and computing studies (Condie, & Livingston, 2007, p.340)." It consists of text booklets complemented by online resources, including electronic versions of the texts with additional animations and simulations, revision materials, short assessment exercises, a notice board and a discussion forum. All 32 local authorities in Scotland had registered with the programme and made it available to schools (Condie, & Livingston, 2007).

Although this programme was strongly promoted by the local authorities, it met resistance from teachers. They felt that online learning programmes and independent study are not appropriate for students of all abilities, and some suggested that students need to be particularly mature and self-motivated. They also stated that the blending of online learning with traditional approaches would require the acquisition of new pedagogic skills in order for the learner to gain significantly from online programmes such as SCHOLAR. Indeed, the evaluation of SCHOLAR revealed some possible barriers to developing such new skills and approaches: some teachers may be reluctant to engage with new technology while others "remain fearful of trying new approaches which they perceive might have a negative impact on exam results (Condie, & Livingston, 2007, p.346)."

Sample Case in Australia

The University of Australia offered distance education program for the Bachelor of Computing course which included a unit called "Computer Ethics" (Lanham & Zhou, 2003). This unit uses a combination of two online platforms, WebCT and FirstClass (Open Text Corporation, n.d.). The WebCT site was the resource page, where students could access unit-related information. The FirstClass platform was used as a discussion center, where students interacted with one another. This featured a message board for instructors to update daily information, a storage area where students could post their response and store their work, a resume section containing self-entered student information, a facility for conducting synchronous (real-time) communication, and a social club where students can freely address any topic. Students were also required to submit assignments through the FirstClass platform. According to Lanham & Zhou (2003), the complexity of having two online platforms running in parallel did not assist students with problems encountered when learning online, but rather "adds to the confusion and uncertainty encountered (p.277)." The unit was intended to run completely online. However, it was acknowledged that the simple transfer of text-based information to online courses was not the answer, and that the materials needed to be adapted to fit the online environment. As different students responded to the online environment with varying degrees of acceptance, it was consequently decided that a blended learning environment would represent a better choice, as it caters for various learning styles and learning needs (Lanham & Zhou, 2003).

Sample Case in Egypt

In Egypt, a study was carried out on a pre-service teaching programme in the School of Education at a small urban governmental university, namely Suez Canal University, to examine the effectiveness of a blended e-learning cooperative approach to deliver a science teaching methods course in comparison to delivering the same course content by the same tutor in the form of face-to-face (F2F) lectures (EL-Deghaidy & Nouby, 2008). According to EL-Deghaidy & Nouby (2008, p.989) "the blend could be between any form of instructional technology (videotape, CD-ROM, Web-based training, films) with F2F instructor-led training." Therefore, in this particular blended e-learning environment, no Web-based learning management system was used.

The study involved building the software of the e-learning process. Software applications used include 'FrontPage' that can take onboard text, images and video clips. Pre and post-test were developed using 'AuthorWare' that allows student interaction and immediate feedback (EL-Deghaidy & Nouby, 2008). Then the electronic version of the course was loaded on students' computers in a lab established on-campus during the execution phase.

The feedback received on the use of BeLCA (blended e-learning cooperative approach) to deliver the science teaching methods course was mainly positive and encouraging (EL-Deghaidy & Nouby, 2008). PSTs (Pre-Service Teachers) generally favoured the design and delivery of the course, but some suggested the inclusion of an online component for off-campus access (EL-Deghaidy & Nouby, 2008). It seems that the constraint of having to study the course content in the computer lab seriously limited students' freedom, and made learning less flexible and accessible than it might have been.

What has been discussed above are a few examples of various forms and expressions of blended learning. Having studied the sample cases closely, it appears that these various forms share some common features, as seen in table 1:

From Table 1 we can see that typically people adopt the F2F plus online mode in blended learning, and an online learning management system (LMS) is used to facilitate online learning. In fact, a vast number of online learning management systems have been developed over the past decade. The following are some of the major online learning management systems available either commercially or as an open source for free download (Wikipedia: Learning Management System, n.d.).

Commercial LMS:

- ANGEL_Learning (http://angellearning.com):
- Blackboard (http://www.blackboard.com)
- Desire2Learn (http://www.desire2learn.com)
- eCollege (http://www.ecollege.com)
- it's learning (http://www.itslearning.com)
- Learn.com (http://www.learn.com)
- Meridian KSI (http://www.meridianksi.com)
- WebCT (now merged with Blackboard, will be phased out by 2011)

Open source LMS (free download):

- ATutor (http://www.atutor.ca)
- Claroline (http://www.claroline.net)
- Dokeos (http://www.dokeos.com)
- eFront (http://www.efrontlearning.net)
- ILIAS (http://www.ilias.de)

Table 1. Common features of blended learning environments

Feature Sample Case	F2F + online sessions	Online learning management system	Independent course website	Course materials on CD/DVD	Synchro-nous online interaction	Asynchro-nous online interaction	Online interactive assessment exercises
South Africa	✓	×	✓ (Cognition)	×	×	✓ (Blog, online Q&A)	×
Singapore	✓	✓ (Black-board)	×	×	✓ (Chat)	✓ (Email, Discussion board)	×
USA	✓	✓ (Moodle)	✓ (SWW)	✓	✓ (Chat)	✓ (Email, Discussion board)	✓
Northern Ireland	✓	✓ (WebCT)	×	×	✓(Chat)	✓ (Email, Discussion board)	✓
Scotland	✓	✓ (SCHOL-AR)	×	×	×	✓ (Discussion board)	✓
Australia	Started as fully online	✓ (WebCT, FirstClass)	×	×	✓(Chat)	✓ (Email, Discussion board)	×
Egypt	F2F + computer lab sessions	×	×	✓	Interacting with computer	×	Interactive exercises on computer

- Moodle (http://moodle.org)
- OLAT (http://www.olat.org/website/en/html/index.html)
- Sakai Project (http://www.sakaiproject.org/portal)

Other than making use of online learning management systems, in some blended learning environments independent course websites are developed to further facilitate the sharing of resources online. Also, some institutions prefer to have the course materials available on CDs/DVDs, so that students can get access to them even without having Web access. Another common feature of blended learning environment is that both the synchronous and asynchronous online interaction are emphasized. Last but not the least, in many blended learning environments, online assessment exercises are provided.

Within this context, a particular case of blended learning at the HKIEd (Hong Kong Institute of Education) is now presented in order to further illustrate how blended learning could be designed and implemented. Some innovative ideas will be introduced, and based on a discussion of the overall findings, a number of recommendations will be given for the future implementation of blended learning in higher education.

BLENDED LEARNING IN THE ENGLISH DEPARTMENT AT HKIED

Since 2002, The Department of English at the HKIEd has been exploring various ways of delivering some of its traditional academic modules partly online. One of the initial purposes was to enable in-service teachers to engage in in-service training opportunities without the burden of long commutes from remote locations, so alleviating job-related time constraints. Another aim was to provide structured reading online in some undergraduate modules so freeing up some teaching contact time for small group work around that reading. At the same time, as students and staff became increasingly aware of the values of ICT in education, more and more participants in the educational process became anxious to take full advantage of it. Based on such demands, the department started the blended learning initiative, looking for ways to facilitate teaching and learning through the creation of blended learning environments. The pedagogical benefits of blended learning are well established in terms of providing alternative learning space and increased use of written feedback from students and staff (Warschauer & Kern, 2000; Kwan & Fong, 2005; Juwah, 2006; Gommlich & Minick, 2007). Over the past 7 years, the department has carried out a series of experiments that seek to maximize the effectiveness of blended learning.

The Blackboard Online Learning Platform

As the literature review indicates, one of the common features of blended learning is the adoption of an online learning management system. Since 2002, the HKIEd has employed the popular Blackboard online learning platform for online delivery. Blackboard is a leading provider of e-Education enterprise software applications and services, and has been widely adopted by tertiary institutions worldwide (Blackboard Inc., 2008).

Typically, when using the Blackboard online learning platform, colleagues would set up a module account on the Blackboard system, and only students studying that module and staff teaching that module would have access to it. This arrangement serves to protect the privacy of the students and staff, and also offers a secure learning environment, in which students can exchange files, submit assignments, post messages, access and download online materials safely without worrying that the data may be lost or be viewed by unauthorized parties. The standard components of a Blackboard module website include Announcements, Course Information, Staff Information, Course Materials, Assignments, Communication, Discussion Board, External Links, Tools and Books (Blackboard Inc., 2008).

A survey conducted in the 2003-04 academic year indicated that only 20% of staff in the English Department used Blackboard in their module teaching. This figure rose to 46% in 2004-05, and then jumped sharply to 91% in 2006-07, a strong indication that the blended learning mode has gradually gained acceptance by a majority of colleagues.

Drawbacks of Blackboard

Although Blackboard is an efficient and effective system for managing learning activities, such as uploading course materials, organizing online discussions, sharing files, and submitting assignments online, many lecturers found that the temporary and private nature of the module website account means that for each semester and for each individual module they have to set the online materials up repeatedly and are unable to spread resources across modules. As Ng (2008, p. 22) pointed out, 'many popular Web-based learning platforms have limitations such as the lack of facilities for the reuse of teaching material.' In addition, resources published on the Blackboard module website cannot be shared by other colleagues and students who do not have access rights. Blackboard was also reported to have some technical limitations in respect of managing hyperlinks between and within documents (Ng, 2008), thus limiting the potential of the medium and tying it more closely to a print-based formula.

Standalone Subject-Specific Websites

In order to solve such problems which militate against the efficient use of staff, a project was carried out in 2006-08 to develop a series of stand-

Figure 1. Screenshot of the English Department Resources homepage. ©2008 Wang Lixun. Used with permission.

alone subject-specific or module-specific websites to support the online delivery of modules offered in the Department of English. This is, as noted, a common practice in blended learning (Lanham, & Zhou, 2003; Thatcher, 2007; Blake, Wilson, Cetto & Pardo-Ballester, 2008). A group of colleagues with expertise in different subject areas formed the project team, and were responsible for developing various websites (Introduction to Linguistics, Literature Studies, Assessment for Learning, Vocabulary Studies, Grammar, English in the Global Context, Sociolinguistics, Language Arts, etc.). All the websites adopted a standardized user-friendly interface for easy recognition and operation by students. Standard components of these websites include E-lectures, Online Readings, Multimedia Resources, Tasks, Online Quizzes, Exemplars, and Bibliography, although there might be slight variations depending on the nature of the subject area or module. These websites serve as a standalone home for reusable module resources and were combined with the Blackboard system to support module learning for both part-time and full-time students.

Through developing and publicizing these subject-specific websites, colleagues in the English Department managed to enhance their academic profile and to some extent gain local and international recognition in specific subject areas. It also increased opportunities for international academic exchanges as some scholars from outside the Institute, who had accessed the websites, offered future collaboration in different ways. These websites have become a crucial component in the blended learning environment, as easy online access to the course materials is essential for ensuring the flexibility and accessibility of the online learning environment (Hegarty,

2006; Fang, 2007; Vaughan, 2007). The sites can be accessed through the English Department Resources homepage: http://engres.ied.edu.hk (see Figure 1).

Sample Mini-Website: Introduction to Linguistics

To give a clearer picture of the design of these subject-specific websites, the structure of the Introduction to Linguistics mini-website (http://engres.ied.edu.hk/linguistics/linguistics.html) is illustrated by way of example. The Introduction section offers users an oversight of the website's various features and functions. In the E-lectures section, a series of E-lecture notes used in the relevant module are made accessible online. In the Multimedia Resources section, various online multimedia resources (sound and video clips, pictures, animations, etc.) related to different topics covered in the relevant module are provided. In the Online Readings section, links to various online academic articles related to the pertinent academic topics are listed. In the Tasks section, different tasks for student completion in the relevant module are described. As for the Online Quizzes section, it merits particular attention.

Online Quizzes: Self Assessment for Learning

In this section, online quizzes based on lecture notes, online readings and other forms of readings are created using a self-developed quiz building program and these in turn are made available periodically (students are required to complete a certain quiz within a given but limited period of time). Figure 2 shows a screenshot of a quiz page. These quizzes offer students opportunities to self-assess their comprehension of the academic readings. Linking assignments with online quizzes is an effective way to introduce homework into large lecture courses without burdening instructors with excessive grading (Cooper, Tyser & Sandheinrich, 2007).

Figure 2. Screenshot of the Online Quizzes page of the Introduction to Linguistics website. ©2008 Wang Lixun. Used with permission.

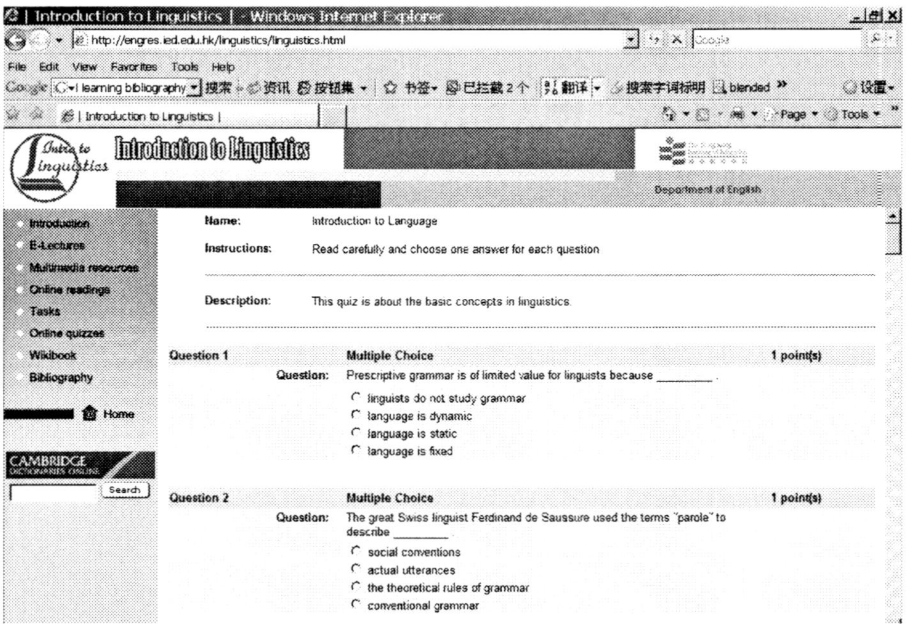

A unique feature of the self-developed quiz program is that, every time a student starts a quiz, even if s/he does the same quiz several times, 10 items are randomly generated from a database, which means that each time a quiz appears on the screen is a different quiz, even if a few of the items have been re-cycled. This obviates the danger of students copying each other's answers, as each person is engaged with a different quiz. After students submit a quiz online, they receive immediate feedback on their answers and how many points they have scored. Students are also allowed to take the quiz repeatedly within the specified time limit (3 days), and only the highest score is formally recorded. Since the 10 weekly online quizzes are part of the formal assessment of the relevant module (10% of the overall grade), most students are willing to do the quiz as many times as necessary in order to achieve the highest possible score. However, they cannot simply remember the answers and repeat the same quiz since each time the programme generates a different set of questions on the screen. The quiz program records all the attempts of the students, and statistics already obtained indicate that a student is likely to take a quiz 5-8 times on average in order to obtain a high score. As shown in Figure 3, Student A did Quiz_1_IL five times, and scored 10 out of 10 in one of the five randomly generated quizzes (those numbers in brackets indicate different items taken out of a database). This very much promotes self-assessment for learning (McNamara & Deane, 1995; Black, Harrison, Lee, Marshall, & Wiliam, 2003; Carless, 2005), as every time students submit their answers, the quiz program provides instant written feedback explaining the correct solution, so that students can learn without actually having a tutor explain to them why a particular answer is right or wrong. Feedback from students regarding the online quizzes has so far been extremely positive, since they find that the quizzes foster self motivation, and promote successful and truly autonomous learning. At the same time students do not experience the pressure they would normally feel when taking a test in a formal classroom situation. They all agree that

Figure 3. Screenshot of student scores for quiz page. ©2008 Wang Lixun. Used with permission.

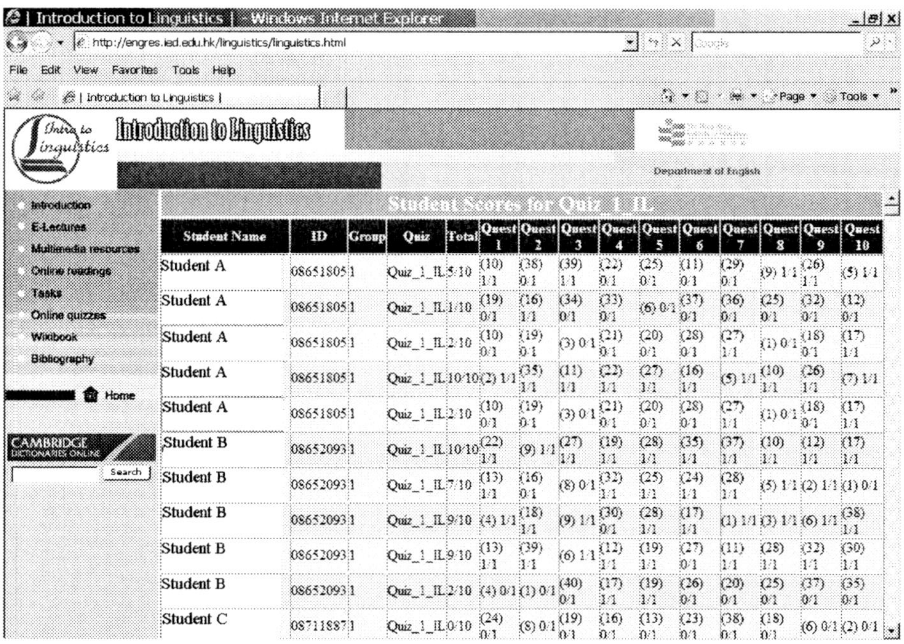

Student Scores for Quiz_1_IL

Student Name	ID	Group	Quiz	Total	Quest 1	Quest 2	Quest 3	Quest 4	Quest 5	Quest 6	Quest 7	Quest 8	Quest 9	Quest 10
Student A	08651805	1	Quiz_1_IL	5/10	(10) 1/1	(38) 0/1	(39) 1/1	(22) 0/1	(25) 0/1	(11) 0/1	(29) 0/1	(9) 1/1	(26) 1/1	(5) 1/1
Student A	08651805	1	Quiz_1_IL	1/10	(19) 0/1	(16) 1/1	(34) 0/1	(33) 0/1	(6) 0/1	(37) 0/1	(36) 0/1	(25) 0/1	(32) 0/1	(12) 0/1
Student A	08651805	1	Quiz_1_IL	2/10	(10) 0/1	(19) 0/1	(3) 0/1	(21) 0/1	(20) 0/1	(28) 0/1	(27) 1/1	(1) 0/1	(18) 0/1	(17) 1/1
Student A	08651805	1	Quiz_1_IL	10/10	(2) 1/1	(35) 1/1	(11) 1/1	(22) 1/1	(27) 1/1	(16) 1/1	(5) 1/1	(10) 1/1	(26) 1/1	(7) 1/1
Student A	08651805	1	Quiz_1_IL	2/10	(10) 0/1	(19) 0/1	(3) 0/1	(21) 0/1	(20) 0/1	(28) 0/1	(27) 1/1	(1) 0/1	(18) 0/1	(17) 1/1
Student B	08652093	1	Quiz_1_IL	10/10	(22) 1/1	(9) 1/1	(27) 1/1	(19) 1/1	(28) 1/1	(35) 1/1	(37) 1/1	(10) 1/1	(12) 1/1	(17) 1/1
Student B	08652093	1	Quiz_1_IL	7/10	(13) 1/1	(16) 0/1	(8) 0/1	(32) 1/1	(25) 1/1	(24) 1/1	(28) 1/1	(5) 1/1	(2) 1/1	(1) 0/1
Student B	08652093	1	Quiz_1_IL	9/10	(4) 1/1	(18) 1/1	(9) 1/1	(30) 0/1	(28) 1/1	(17) 1/1	(1) 1/1	(3) 1/1	(6) 1/1	(38) 1/1
Student B	08652093	1	Quiz_1_IL	9/10	(13) 1/1	(39) 1/1	(6) 1/1	(12) 1/1	(19) 1/1	(27) 0/1	(11) 1/1	(28) 1/1	(32) 1/1	(30) 1/1
Student B	08652093	1	Quiz_1_IL	2/10	(4) 0/1	(1) 0/1	(40) 0/1	(17) 1/1	(19) 1/1	(26) 0/1	(20) 0/1	(25) 0/1	(37) 0/1	(35) 0/1
Student C	08711887	1	Quiz_1_IL	0/10	(24) 0/1	(8) 0/1	(19) 0/1	(16) 0/1	(13) 0/1	(23) 0/1	(38) 0/1	(18) 0/1	(6) 0/1	(2) 0/1

these online quizzes are far more effective for learning than traditional paper-based tests.

Other than the above mentioned sections, there are two further important components of this module website: the Wikibook Project section and the Bibliography section. In the Bibliography section, a detailed bibliography is provided for the relevant subject area. The Wikibook Project, being a major innovation in this study, is discussed separately in detail in the following section.

Promoting Online Academic Reading and Writing through Wikibook Projects

Academic reading and writing skills are extremely important in tertiary education. However, students who have just graduated from secondary schools and entered university may lack such formal skills. At the same time, the assessment formats have shifted from traditional paper-based examinations in secondary schools to multiple and multi-mode assessment tasks (academic writing being a major element) in the tertiary institutions. Being unfamiliar with the necessary academic text types can create a sense of trepidation among students, and as a result, lecturers have often found the promotion of academic reading and writing among first-year university students to be a major challenge. Since it is logistically impractical for lecturers to spend unlimited hours editing students' academic writing, many students discover they desperately need more support.

In order to address this problem, a team of colleagues in the English Department implemented student-authored online Wikibook projects to promote academic reading and writing among first-year English majors at HKIEd in 2007 and 2008. A wiki is 'a page or collection of Web pages designed to enable anyone who accesses it to contribute or modify content, using a simplified markup language (Wiki - Wikipedia, n.d.).' It is a technology that has emerged in recent years, and has attracted more and more attention in the education field (Lund, Pierroux, Rasmussen, Smørdal & Blevis, 2007).

The Sample Students and the Module

In 2007, a total of 169 first-year Bachelor of Education (English Language) students at HKIEd participated in the Wikibook project. In 2008, the number was 139. The module taught was 'Introduction to Language Studies', which is an introductory module to linguistic systems and other language topics. The students were divided into five tutorial classes (around 27-34 in each class).

Assessment Task: Student-Authored Wikibook Project

Herron and Wright (2006) point out that assessment should be allowed to play a major role in the design of a blended mode course. Powers and Dallas (2006) further suggest that problem-based learning (PBL) is an excellent tool for authentic assessment in an online environment. PBL is 'a way of constructing and teaching courses using problems as the stimulus and focus for student activity' (Boud & Feletti, 1991, p.14). When investigating problems, students work co-operatively in a small group, usually with the assistance of a tutor and with access to other resources to: (a) clarify the problem; (b) identify learning needs to address the problem; (c) undertake individual read/study; and, (d) apply newly acquired insights and understandings to re-address the problem (Boud & Feletti, 1991). As a problem-based learning task, the Wikibook project requires students to undertake academic read/study in small groups to complete the joint authoring of an academic book .

Students work in groups of 3 or 4, and each group member contributes 1000 words to a chapter of a student-authored academic book entitled 'Introduction to Language Studies' based on the topics introduced in the module. Each chapter must also include 10 multiple-choice comprehension questions based on the content of the chapter. Group members are required to peer-edit each other's sections in the corresponding chapter of the book. A draft of the group chapter must be posted on the Wetpaint Wikibook website online according to a prescribed schedule. Chapter drafts are due periodically throughout the semester, according to the order in which the topics are introduced in class. Meeting the draft posting deadline is essential to allow ample opportunities for tutor feedback and peer editing. Members in the same group receive the same group grade.

Why Wikibook?

Wikibook is an open-content online textbook that anyone can edit by clicking on the "edit this page" link that appears near the top of each Wikibook module. Contributors maintain the proprietary rights to their contributions, while the GNU Free Documentation License makes sure that the submitted version and its derivative works will always remain freely distributable and reproducible (Wikibooks:About, n.d.). Doolan (2007) points out that Wikis help to create a'Group Work Scenario': they are best used for student group work in the context of learning groups and of grouping for assessment. This can help to build online learning communities, and complement traditional face-to-face practice in higher education. It also helps to enhance the communicative and collaborative components of a blended learning environment. According to a study carried out by Pae (2007), wiki-based English writing classes positively affect the students' English writing proficiency, and are beneficial for collaborative writing. Furthermore, students find that wikis are fun for practicing English composition.

The Wetpaint Wikibook Project

For the Wikibook project, the Wetpaint website provides free Wikibook hosting: http://www.wetpaint.com/. Five independent Wikibooks were created by five classes of students. Each book has

Figure 4. Screenshot of one of the Wikibook websites. ©2008 Wang Lixun. Used with permission.

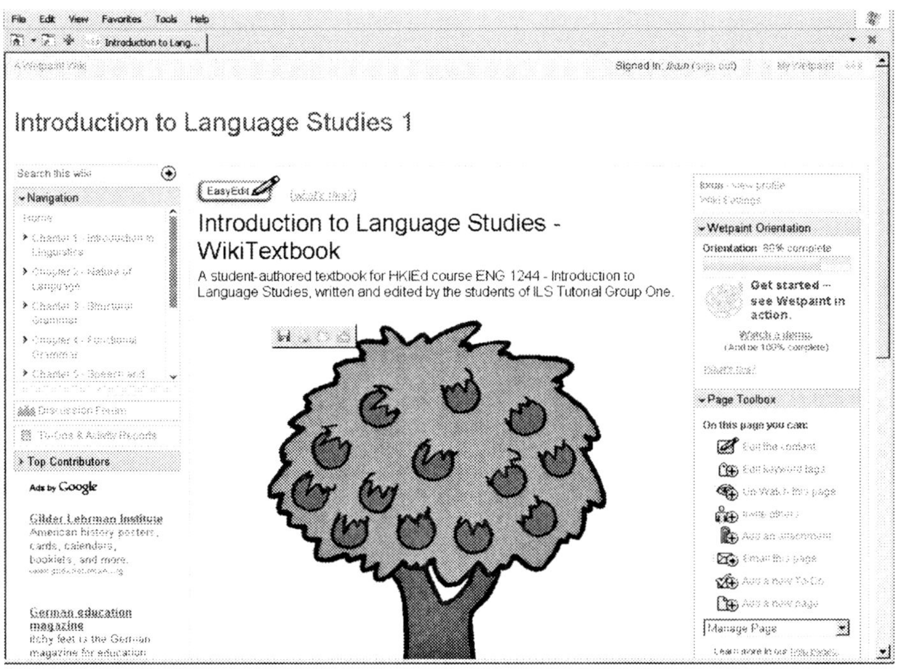

9-10 chapters. Students study the module content through a mixture of face-to-face instruction and online learning, and they work collaboratively online to complete the chapters in groups. In order to enable students to help each other with their academic writing, peer-editing was required in the module. Figure 4 shows a screenshot of one of the Wikibook websites.

Peer Editing Online

Group members are required to peer-edit each other's sections of the relevant chapter of the book to ensure that: each section includes sufficiently detailed content; the writing is polished (academic style, appropriate referencing, etc.); and the whole chapter is coherent.

Jones, Garralda, Li and Lock (2006) discussed the interactional dynamics in on-line and face-to-face peer-tutoring sessions for second language writers. They found that face-to-face interactions involved more hierarchal encounters in which tutors took control of the discourse, whereas on-line interactions were more egalitarian, with clients controlling the discourse to a greater extent. Such egalitarian relationships between tutors and clients help to achieve good tutoring sessions, which are seen to be collaborative (Blau, Hall & Strauss, 1998), and the goal of such sessions is to enable the writers to take charge of the writing process (Fletcher, 1993). These concepts provided the rationale for building the element of peer editing into the Wikibook project.

In order to discover how effectively students were able to help each other online with their academic writing, the peer editing comments posted online were analysed. We found four major categories of comments: Praising peers' work; Making suggestions for improving the draft; Discussing teamwork / requesting help; Providing new information on content. These comments are highly constructive and the students considered them extremely helpful. Since students can post comments freely online, they are more willing to offer each other comments and opinions. At the same time, since the whole group will get the same group grade, students in each group are greatly concerned to monitor and improve the various sections in their Chapter. This assessment aspect provided considerable impetus for mutual support and collaboration.

Survey on the Wikibook Project

To discover whether the Wikibook project was effective or not, we carried out an end-of-module survey and also conducted a number of individual interviews. Table 2 shows the results of statistical analysis of the survey carried out in 2007.

The overall findings indicate that most students found the blended learning experience very rewarding, and believed they had improved their academic reading and writing skills more through participation in the Wikibook project. The Problem-based Learning approach was effectively adopted in the project, as the criteria for a successful model of PBL in a blended learning environment, as described by Pearson (2006), were met, namely: an explicit PBL strategy was followed when topics were investigated; an academic discourse developed as these topics were analyzed, researched and discussed; 'new' knowledge was evident in relation to issues, concerns and solutions about perceived 'problems'; the role adopted by the tutor facilitated group participation and outcomes; and the online learning context was consistent with features of the students' 'preferred' learning environment. Nevertheless, through a number of individual interviews, we found that there are some areas of concern, for example: originality vs. referencing and the danger of plagiarism; different writing styles (Intra/Inter-chapter cohesion and coherence); level of difficulty (for Year One students); reliance on others; technical issues; lack of group communication, etc. Despite all these limitations, the Wikibook project may still be pronounced a resounding success, as most students greatly enjoyed the experience of col-

Table 2. Survey results

Item 1. My academic reading skills were developed and improved more through the Wetpaint Wikibook assignment than through other assignments.		
Agreed/Strongly agreed	Not sure	Disagreed/Strongly disagree
85 (64.9%)	39 (29.8%)	7 (5.4%)
Item 2. My academic writing skills were developed and improved more through the Wetpaint Wikibook assignment than through other assignments.		
Agreed/Strongly agreed	Not sure	Disagreed/Strongly disagree
82 (62.6%)	36 (27.5%)	13 (10%)
Item 3. The Wetpaint Project assignment caused me to become actively involved in the course learning.		
Agreed/Strongly agreed	Not sure	Disagreed/Strongly disagree
90 (68.7%)	36 (27.5%)	5 (3.9%)
Item 4. My peer-editing skills were developed and improved more through the Wetpaint assignment.		
Agreed/Strongly agreed	Not sure	Disagreed/Strongly disagree
87 (66.4%)	39 (29.8%)	5 (3.9%)
Item 5. The skills that I have learned in the Wetpaint assignment will be useful to me in my future as a teacher.		
Agreed/Strongly agreed	Not sure	Disagreed/Strongly disagree
81 (61.9%)	44 (33.6%)	6 (4.6%)
Item 6. I would enjoy using Wetpaint or Wikibook in other modules.		
Agreed/Strongly agreed	Not sure	Disagreed/Strongly disagree
86 (65.6%)	28 (21.4%)	17 (13.0%)
Item 7. The tutors were able to help me with any questions or concerns I had about the Wetpaint assignment.		
Agreed/Strongly agreed	Not sure	Disagreed/Strongly disagree
110 (83.9%)	16 (12.2%)	5 (3.9%)
Item 8. Overall, I enjoyed the Wetpaint assignment.		
Agreed/Strongly agreed	Not sure	Disagreed/Strongy disagree
91 (69.4%)	29 (22.1%)	11 (8.4%)

Table 3. Features of blended learning environments: the case of HKIEd

Feature Sample Case	**F2F + online sessions**	**Online learning management system**	**Independent course website**	**Course materials on CD/ DVD**	**Synchro-nous online interaction**	**Asynchro-nous online interaction**	**Online interactive assessment exercises**	**Wikibook project**
HKIEd	✓	✓ (Black-board)	✓ (Intro-duction to Linguistics)	×	✓ (Chat)	✓ (Email, Discussion Board)	✓ (ran-domly gener-ated online quizzes with instant feed-back)	✓ (online academic reading and writ-ing, peer-editing)

laborative academic writing through the project. The wiki technology made peer editing much more efficient and effective. Indeed, the collaborative Wikibook project was particularly effective in promoting academic reading among students and also enhanced students' academic writing skills significantly. The online learning community, that students built together, enabled them to bond well and learn more from each other.

Having studied the details of the blended learning environment in the English Department at HKIEd, if we compare it with the sample cases mentioned at the beginning of the chapter, we will find that they share most of the common features, but at the same time the HKIEd blended learning environment has a special feature (Wikibook), as shown in Table 3.

Based on feedback from students and staff, such an online learning environment is effective in facilitating resource sharing, online synchronous and asynchronous communication, self-assessment for learning, academic reading and writing, peer editing, and collaborative yet autonomous learning.

CONCLUSION

To conclude, through comparing different cases of blended learning, and a closer analysis of the implementation and promotion of blended learning at the HKIEd, we have found that this relatively new mode of delivery is gaining increasing popularity among both students and staff. Based on the feedback collected, it is considered that blended learning formats have rendered learning more flexible and accessible while activities such as online discussion and Wikibook projects have greatly enhanced learner autonomy and collaborative learning. The case study in the English Department at the HKIEd also shows that tertiary institutions need not rely on one single particular approach (such as using the Blackboard system) when implementing blended learning. Rather, we should keep an open mind and experiment with different approaches in order to arrive at the most promising and innovative pedagogical solutions. A properly designed blended learning environment can be catered to students with different learning styles, which makes education more inclusive. The less stressful atmosphere when studying online helps to alleviate learner anxiety, and motivates students to become more active and independent learners. Wikibook projects and other similar types of online learning activities are opening new windows for teaching and learning and the full potential of blended learning is yet to be fully realized. The blended learning mode will certainly have an increasingly significant impact when traditional higher education institutions start to recruit more part-time students, perhaps resident at distant locations or in other countries, as the online delivery of modules may then become the only option when students cannot travel to the campus regularly. In a nutshell, it is evident that blended learning represents a significant development in the delivery of tertiary education, and its adoption should be carefully considered by all higher education institutions not currently using this approach.

REFERENCES

Black, P., Harrison, C., Lee, C., Marshall, B., & Wiliam, C. (2003). *Assessment for learning: Putting it into practice*. Maidenhead: Open University Press.

Blackboard Inc. (2008) *Company overview*. Retrieved on October 22, 2008, from http://www.blackboard.com/company/

Blake, R., Wilson, N. L., Cetto, M., & Pardo-Ballester, C. (2008). Measuring oral proficiency in distance, face-to-face, and blended classrooms. *Language Learning & Technology*, *12*(3), 114–127.

Blau, S. R., Hall, J., & Strauss, T. (1998). Exploring the tutor/client conversation: A linguistic analysis. *Writing Center Journal*, *19*(1), 19–48.

Boud, D., & Feletti, G. (1991). *The challenge of problem based learning*. London: Kogan Page.

Carless, D. (2005). Prospects for the implementation of assessment for learning. *Assessment in Education, 12*(1), 39–54. doi:10.1080/0969594042000333904

Claroline. (n.d.) Retrieved on November 21, 2008, from http://www.claroline.net

Condie, R., & Livingston, K. (2007). Blending online learning with traditional approaches: Changing practices. *British Journal of Educational Technology, 38*(2), 337–348. doi:10.1111/j.1467-8535.2006.00630.x

Cooper, S. T., Tyser, R. W., & Sandheinrich, M. B. (2007). The benefits of linking assignments to online quizzes in introductory biology courses. *Journal of Online Leanring and Teaching, 3*(3). Retrieved on November 21, 2008, from http://jolt.merlot.org/vol3no3/cooper.htm

Desire2Learn. (n.d.) Retrieved on November 21, 2008, from http://www.desire2learn.com

Dokeos. (n.d.) Retrieved on November 21, 2008, from http://www.dokeos.com

Doolan, M. A. (2007). 'Group work' scenario: Using Wiki for group work in the context of learning groups and grouping for assessment. *2nd Annual Blended Learning Conference "Supporting the Net Generation Learner,"* University of Hertfordshire, Hatfield. Retrieved on February 29, 2008, from http://perseus.herts.ac.uk/uhinfo/library/w46725_13.doc

eCollege. (n.d.) Retrieved on November 21, 2008, from http://www.ecollege.com

eFront. (n.d.) Retrieved on November 21, 2008 from http://www.efrontlearning.net

EL-Deghaidy, H., & Nouby, A. (2008). Effectiveness of a blended e-learning cooperative approach in an Egyptian teacher education programme. *Computers & Education, 51*(3), 988–1006. doi:10.1016/j.compedu.2007.10.001

Fang, L. (2007). Perceiving the useful, enjoyable, and effective: A case study of the e-learning experience of tertiary students in Singapore. *Educational Media International, 44*(3), 237–253. doi:10.1080/09523980701491682

Fletcher, R. (1993). *What a writer needs*. Portsmouth, NH: Heinemann.

Gommlich, K., & Minick, T. (2007). United re-invention of an online teacher education course: From cooperation to collaboration. In E. Hanson-Smith & S. Rilling (Eds.), *Learning languages through technology* (pp. 233-244). Alexandria, VA: TESOL.

Hegarty, C. (2006). It's not an exact science: Teaching entrepreneurship in Northern Ireland. *Education + Training, 48*(5), 322-335.

Herron, F. J., & Wright, V. H. (2006). Assessment in online learning: Are students really learning? In V. H. Wright, C. Szymanski Sunal & E. K. Wilson (Eds.), *Research on enhancing the interactivity of online learning* (pp. 45-64). Greenwich, CT: Information Age.

ILIAS. (n.d.) Retrieved on November 21, 2008, from http://www.ilias.de

it's learning. (n.d.) Retrieved on November 21, 2008, from http://www.itslearning.com

Jones, R. H., Garralda, A., Li, D. C. S., & Lock, G. (2006). Interactional dynamics in online and face-to-face peer-tutoring sessions for second language writers. *Journal of Second Language Writing, 15*, 1–23. doi:10.1016/j.jslw.2005.12.001

Juwah, C. (2006). *Interactions in online education: Implications for theory and practice*. London & New York: Routledge.

Kwan, R., & Fong, J. (2005). *Web-based Learning: Technology and pedagogy*. Hong Kong: World Scientific.

Lanham, E., & Zhou, W. (2003). Cultural issues in online learning: Is blended learning a possible solution? *International Journal of Computer Processing of Oriental Languages*, *16*(4), 275–292. doi:10.1142/S0219427903000930

Larson, B., & Keiper, T. A. (2002). Classroom discussion and threaded electronic discussion: Learning in two arenas. *Contemporary Issues in Technology & Teacher Education*, *2*(1), 45–62.

Learn.com. (n.d.) Retrieved on November 21, 2008, from http://www.learn.com

Learning, A. N. G. E. L. (n.d.) Retrieved on November 21, 2008, from http://angellearning.com Atutor. (n.d.) Retrieved on November 21, 2008, from http://www.atutor.ca

Lund, A., Pierroux, P., Rasmussen, I., Smørdal, O., & Blevis, E. (2007). Pre-conference event for CSCL 2007. *Emerging issues in Wiki research: Knowledge advancement and design.* CSCL 2007. Retrieved on February 29, 2008, from http://design.informatics.indiana.edu/designii/eli/images/8/8c/C wiki_final.pdf

McNamara, M. J., & Deane, D. (1995). Self-assessment activities: Towards autonomy in language learning. *TESOL Journal*, *5*(1), 17–21.

Meridian, K. S. I. (n.d.) Retrieved on November 21, 2008, from http://www.meridianksi.com

Moodle.org. (n.d.) *Moodle.org: About.* Retrieved on November 21, 2008, from http://moodle.org/about/

Ng, C., Yeung, A. S., & Hon, R. Y. H. (2006). Does online language learning diminish interaction between student and teacher? *Educational Media International*, *43*(3), 219–232. doi:10.1080/09523980600641429

Ng, M. W. (2008). An alternative learning platform to facilitate usability and synchronization of learning resources. In A. Cartelli & M. Palma (Eds.), *Encyclopedia of information communication technology* (pp. 21-31). Hershey, PA: Information Science Reference.

OLAT. (n.d.) Retrieved on November 21, 2008, from http://www.olat.org/website/en/html/index.html

Open Text Corporation. (n. d.). *FirstClass*. Retrieved on November 21, 2008, from http://www.firstclass.com/

Pae, J. K. (2007). Wiki-based English writing: Its effect on English writing proficiency and anxiety and Korean learners' perception. *Multimedia-Assisted Language Learning*, *10*(1), 4.

Pearson, J. (2006). Investigating ICT using problem-based learning in face-to-face and online learning environments. *Computers & Education*, *47*, 56–73. doi:10.1016/j.compedu.2004.09.001

Powers, S. M., & Dallas, L. (2006). Authentic assessment through problem-based learning in the online environment. In V. H. Wright, C. Szymanski Sunal & E. K. Wilson (Eds.), *Research on enhancing the interactivity of online learning* (pp. 65-74). Greenwich, CT: Information Age.

Sakai Project. (n.d.) Retrieved on November 21, 2008, from http://www.sakaiproject.org/portal

Smith, G. G., & Kurthen, H. (2007). Front-stage and backstage in hybrid e-learning face-to-face courses. *International Journal on E-Learning*, *6*(3), 455–474.

Thatcher, A. (2007). Using the World Wide Web to support classroom lectures in a psychology course. *South African Journal of Psychology. Suid-Afrikaanse Tydskrif Vir Sielkunde*, *37*(2), 348–353.

Vaughan, N. (2007). Perspectives on blended learning in higher education. *International Journal on E-Learning, 6*(1), 81–94.

Warschauer, M., & Kern, R. (2000). *Network-based language teaching: Concepts and practice*. Cambridge: Cambridge University Press.

White, C. (2003). *Language learning in distance education*. Cambridge: Cambridge University Press.

Wiki–Wikipedia. (n.d.) Retrieved on November 21, 2008, from http://en.wikipedia.org/wiki/Wiki

Wikibooks: About. (n.d.) Retrieved on February 28, 2008, from http://en.wikibooks.org/wiki/Wikibooks:About

Wikipedia: Learning Management System. (n.d.) Retrieved on November 21, 2008, from http://en.wikipedia.org/wiki/Learning_management_system

Xie, K., DeBacker, T. K., & Ferguson, C. (2006). Extending the traditional classroom through online discussion: The role of student motivation. *Journal of Educational Computing Research, 34*(1), 67–89. doi:10.2190/7BAK-EGAH-3MH1-K7C6

Section 2
Blended Learning Practices

Chapter 5
Student Profile and Its Effects on Online and Hybrid Courses

Seta Boghikian-Whitby
University of La Verne, California, USA

Yehia Mortagy
University of La Verne, California, USA

ABSTRACT

This chapter is based on a longitudinal descriptive study that identifies the types of students enrolled in a Management Information Systems class offered in face-to-face and online delivery modalities over 15 semesters. The study used a total sample of 622 students where 296 students were enrolled in the face-to-face control section and 326 students were enrolled in the online experimental sections. The study profiles the demographics of students including: student type (traditional undergraduate or adult), age, gender, ethnicity, Myers Briggs personality profile, religion, citizenship, marital status, academic family generation, academic major, academic standing (freshman, sophomore, junior, senior), and grade point average (GPA). The study findings include: (1) adult students dominated the online delivery modality. (2) African American and Hispanic female adult students prefer taking online courses compared to face-to-face. (3) Forty percent of the students enrolled in online delivery modality were of extravert type. (4) The majority of the first generation students were enrolled in face-to-face delivery modality. Recommendations include short modules, use of different exercises in order to accommodate various learning styles. The chapter and the study results will assist administrators and faculty members to make better decisions by understanding the student population type.

DOI: 10.4018/978-1-60566-852-9.ch005

Personally, I think online classes should be limited to a manageable size and that professors should be required to analyze students' papers. If we are not guided, how will we learn? How can we expect to hold an executive position if we are not offered a professor's perspective on our thought process? How can we live up to the "MBA" standard if we are not challenged to think by our professors? So far I've learned the most from you. Every professor should be judged by the standards you have for yourself and for your students.

Graduating senior at the University of La Verne, California 2008.

INTRODUCTION

In order to meet the information age requirements, Universities implement a three prong approach (see Haag & Cummings 2008 for Run-Grow-Transform framework). They **Run** by streamlining their operational processes within tight budgets. They **Grow** by offering innovative services and courses to different segments of the student population, such as certificates in certain concentrations, and they **Transform** by changing their course delivery modality from face-to-face classroom to online and hybrid delivery modalities.

The new delivery modalities represent unanswered questions. Theoretically, the idea of moving to online and hybrid course delivery modality is a brilliant strategy because it solves the major problem of satisfying enrollment growth, it eliminates the need for classroom and parking spaces, and it gives strategic competitive advantage to universities. However, have all the critical success factors been defined to insure the success of the transformation or is this going to be another case study of the "dot-com" or "dot-bomb" failure (Rhoades-Catanach, 2003)?

One of the reasons for the dot-com industry failure is that organizations expected to succeed in e-commerce while practicing their brick and mortar business processes. Most of all, organizations did not understand and study their customers' needs before designing and launching their e-commerce sites. The question remains would higher education survive this transformation?

Did higher education study their online students? Do post-secondary educational institutions know how they are satisfying their students' needs? In a face-to-face class delivery modality faculty members often walk into the classroom and fine-tune their teaching strategies and agendas based on the students' body language. However, the body language factor is missing from online courses. Would a "one style fits all" strategy fit in online education? How could they personalize their lectures if they do not know who their students are? What are the students' mind sets? For example, there are many studies that identify first generation students on campuses (Cushman, 2006), Bishop compared the self efficacy of first generation students to that of second generation students (Bishop, 2008); yet, no one is addressing first generation students' needs in online classes.

The chapter has two objectives: first, to analyze who is enrolled in a face-to-face and an online course of Management Information Systems. The second is to make specific recommendations to administrators to make better strategic decisions and to faculty to fine tune their course development in order to satisfy the appropriate student population needs.

BACKGROUND

There is an increased demand for post-secondary education since employers started requiring college degrees as a prerequisite for job applicants. This change resulted in having junior colleges and universities overflow with adult students who are coming back to finish their degrees. Online education is very appealing to such students because of its convenience. The National Center for Educational Statistics reported a total of 3,077,000 student enrollments in all online distance learning courses at four year higher education institutions during the 2000-01 academicyear (Institute of Education Science, 2003). In California, the community colleges have experienced a 552% enrollment increase from the 1995-96 to 2005-06 academic year. In 2007, state public junior colleges reported an 18% increase in their online distance learning enrollment. Moreover, they stated that they are having a problem meeting the demand in hybrid and online distance learning courses with sufficient course offerings (Nather, 2007).

Adult (mature, generation X and baby boomer) students attending such colleges and universities have one objective. They are either seeking a career change, they cannot get the promotions they deserve because they do not possess the proper degrees and credentials, or they have a dream of earning a college degree. Therefore, their objective is to acquire a bachelor's degree with the minimum number of units possible. The students in the research identified 3 criteria for college selection: Expediency or convenience, Cost or tuition fees, and Speed or rapidity (ECS). Expediency - they value convenience because some are single parents trying to multi-task with many responsibilities. They favor Online and hybrid courses because of their convenience. Williams and Nicholas (2005) identified family and work obligations as barriers to completing courses. Cost - they choose less costly tuition because family obligations take more priority of their financial resources compared to fulfilling their dreams. They seek speed of graduation because they are eager to have that promotion or new career. Therefore, they will select the university that will accept most of their transfer units and will require the minimum number of additional courses to complete their degrees. As a result, universities face the challenge of losing students to their competition due to course requirements and acceptable transfer work.

Hence, design of online courses is a vital factor in the success of both the students and colleges. The courses must be designed to satisfy the three criteria defined in the previous paragraph. They must be convenient, in terms of meeting the time availability of adults, and also accommodate the different learning styles of students enrolled in these courses. Therefore, in order to identify the critical success factors for online courses, a study was designed that defines the type of students that register, their profile and performance. The study and its findings are included in this chapter. The next section includes the literature review and research methodology. It is divided into two subsections: subsection one presents issues and problem statements and a literature reviews, subsection two includes research design and explains the study methodology, sample and population, and data collection procedures. The next section describes data analysis and findings, and section four summarizes the findings. The final two sections present specific recommendations and outline future research trends.

LITERATURE REVIEW AND RESEARCH METHODOLOGY

Issues and Problem Statements

There are four attributes to online and hybrid education (see Figure 1): Students, Administrators, Faculty, and Course Pedagogy (Boghikian-Whitby & Mortagy, 2008).

Students

Although online distance education continues to grow, there continues to be a high attrition rate. There are no national statistics, but a recent report in the Chronicle of Higher Education found that institutions are seeing dropout rates that range from 20 to 50% for distance learners. Administrators of online courses confirm that dropout rates are

Figure 1. Attributes of online education

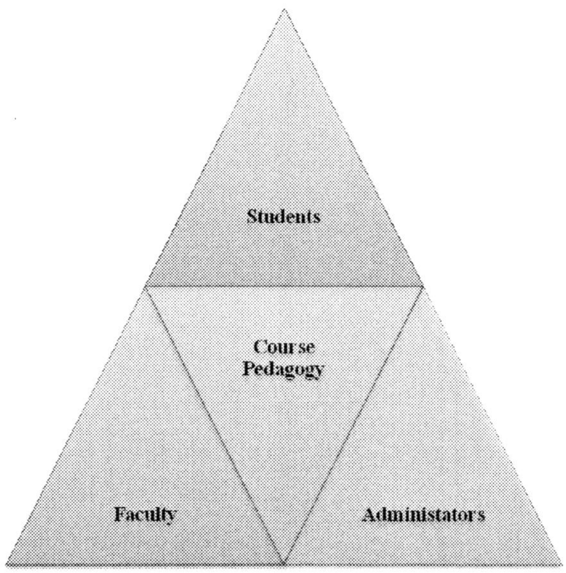

often 10 to 20% higher than in their face-to-face classes (Frankola, 2001).

Adult students look at online courses as the answer to their prayers. They consider online education as a great opportunity for them to continue their degree while working and taking care of their families. However, once they sign up for a course, some get disappointed. They start feeling isolated, they get overwhelmed with deadlines due to their lack of time management skills, they find course lecture notes unstructured and hard to follow, and most of all, they lose their motivation to complete their course. As a result, they withdraw from the course. Some even disappointedly drop out of college because they feel completing their degree in online delivery modality is an unachievable goal.

Slick (2008) researched the effectiveness of distance education by examining student grades and completion rates of online learning courses for the four learning styles as measured by the Kolb Learning Style Inventory (KSI). The four learning styles are:

1. **Concrete Experience (CE)**: (known as **Accommodator** Learning Style) those who prefer to be actively involved in a learning situation.
2. **Reflective Observation (RO)**: (known as **Diverger** Learning Style) those who watch others and develop observations based on their own experience. This group prefers exposure to different points of view.
3. **Abstract Conceptualization (AC)**: (known as **Assimilator** Learning Style) those who can create theories to explain and understand their observations.
4. **Active Experimentation (AE)**: (known as **Converger** Learning Style) those who use theories to solve problems and make decisions (Kolb & Kolb, 2005).

Slick (2008) reported that 30% of the online students are classified as Accommodator learning style, followed by 26% Converger learning style, 24% Assimilator learning style, and 20% Diverger learning style. The distribution is slightly different than Loo's (2002) meta analysis of accommodators 21.4%, Convergers with 26%, assimilators with 28.4%, and divergers with 24.1%. Moreover, Slick found that Diverger Learning Style preference had the lowest GPA and constituted 80% of the failing grades. Finally, three (Assimilator, Accommodator, Converger) Styles out of the 4 learning preference passed their courses with a "B" or better (Slick, 2008).

In this study, the researchers incorporated the learning styles of Kolb in their course design, and assessed the Myers Briggs Type Inventory (MBTI) test (Morgan & Barbour, 2008). The researchers chose MBTI because the test identifies the student's personality and not the student's learning style preference (Robey & Taggart, 2001). MBTI is designed to measure psychological preferences and how people perceive the environment, and is therefore extremely helpful in determining how to develop cases for students (Lee, Kim, Seo, & Chung, 2007). Visit http://www.myersbriggs.org/ for more details on the subject. The indicator identifies four measures, with each measure taking one of two values. Each value represents a preference of the person in a manner similar to right handed people preferring to use their right hand over their left, who are still able to use their left hand to perform tasks. MBTI measures four different types of personality -- Extravert/Introvert, Sensing/Intuitive, Thinking / Feeling, and Judging / Perceptive. The four variables are defined as follows:

1. **Extraversion** answers the question "Where, primarily, do you direct your energy?" Extraverts find energy in people. They are action oriented, "on-the-fly" thinkers, and prefer interaction with others.
2. **Introversion** answers the question "Where, primarily, do you direct your energy?" Introverts find energy in the inner world of ideas, concepts, and abstractions. They can be sociable but need quiet to recharge. They are concentrators and reflective thinkers.
3. **Sensing** answers the question "How do you prefer to process information?" Sensing people are detail oriented, want facts, and trust them. Joe Friday from the TV show Dragnet epitomizes the extreme sensing detective. All he ever wanted was "just the facts."
4. **INtuitive** answers the question "How do you prefer to process information?" Intuitive people seek out patterns and relationships among the facts they have gathered. They trust hunches and their intuition and look for the "big picture." The quintessential intuitive was Albert Einstein whose fanciful thought experiments revolutionized the 20th century. He could see patterns where others saw randomness or chaos.
5. **Thinking** answers the question "How do you prefer to make decisions?" Thinking students value fairness. Thinkers believe, what could be fairer than focusing on the situation's logic, and placing great weight on objective criteria in making a decision?
6. **Feeling** answers the question "How do you prefer to make decisions?" Feeling student's value harmony. They focus on human values and needs as they make decisions or arrive at judgments. They tend to be good at persuasion and facilitating differences among group members.
7. **Judging** answers the question "How do you prefer to organize your life?" Judging people are decisive, planning and self regimented. They focus on completing the task, only want to know the essentials, and take action quickly (perhaps too quickly). They plan their work and work their plan. Deadlines are sacred. Their motto is: "just do it!"
8. **Perception** answers the question "How do you choose to organize your life?" Perceptive people are curious, adaptable, and spontaneous. They start many tasks, want to know everything about each task, and often find it difficult to complete a task. Deadlines are meant to be stretched. Their motto is: on the other hand (Briggs Myers & Cook Briggs, 2002).

Administrators

Due to the enrollment growth in the student body, administrators in post secondary educational institutions are facing new and different challenges. For example, they attempt to operate with: budget cuts, streamline their business processes to reduce costs, attempt to resolve parking and classroom space problems, and yet, they operate in the limitation of the existing classrooms and infrastructure. Therefore, administrators started looking for different means to operate and stay competitive. They started considering possibilities to transform traditional face-to-face course delivery modality by offering online and hybrid courses. Initially administrators assumed "if we offer classes, students will enroll." They shifted their resources to an online curriculum. They gave incentives to faculty to start offering online courses. Some even paid faculty to develop the course and later hired part time faculty to teach the courses to satisfy the demand. Some universities even started offering complete programs online. Yet, even though they transformed their delivery modalities, they did not change their business practices. For example, a few years ago in state universities, students signed up for classes without knowing that they were signing up for an online class. The catalog and the course schedules did not indicate that the course was an online course (Mortagy, 2005).

Administrators soon learned that they were moving too fast without strategic planning. They noticed student attrition, persistence, and retention problems. As a result, some online programs survived, and quite a few were terminated due to student attrition and retention problems (Lynch, 2001).

Recently, administrators felt that hybrid courses would be the best practice and started encouraging faculty to teach hybrid courses. Some universities went a step further and required faculty to be certified to teach hybrid courses. Again, the catalog does not define the meaning and the expectation of a hybrid. Therefore, how can administrators expect the students to know the meaning of hybrid before enrolling in a class? What does a hybrid course entail? Is hybrid similar to a "cookie cutter mold" course? Would all student types succeed in a hybrid course? Currently, administrators seem puzzled about the withdrawal rate from hybrid and online courses. This mystery will be unveiled once they study and understand the students' behavioral profile and the students' needs.

Faculty

The qualifications for teaching in a post secondary higher education environment are a Masters Degree or a Doctorate degree. No teaching credentials are necessary. Therefore, the assumption is "Anyone with a Ph.D. can teach well enough for any college students." The problem is that faculty members use trial and error in the creation and delivery of their classes, which may or may not be tolerated by some or all enrolled students. For example, Baby Boomer students might tolerate such mistakes but will the Millennial generation students, or will they drop the course because they have zero tolerance?

Another problem faculty have is time management. They are over occupied with campus governance, research, and academic advising. They do not have the time to spare for professional development. Adding the certification before teaching hybrid and online courses might be one factor of the puzzle. The fact remains that they are not investigating the students and their needs.

Course Pedagogy

Due to the high demand and meeting deadlines, faculty often cannot design the proper course materials that a new modality course deserves. As a result, they simply put their existing lecture notes online and hope that students will be satisfied. In addition, they repeat strategies used in the face-to-face classroom environment. However, as was discovered, the two are not compatible. For example, having a 72-hour response time for e-mails is not acceptable in an online modality (Vonderwell, 2003).

Boghikian-Whitby (2003) emphasized that the success of an online and a hybrid course is in the course design and the student mindset. In a face-to-face course delivery modality, the responsibility for learning is in the control of the faculty member. The faculty orchestrates what is to be learned and how to teach it. In an online and hybrid course delivery modality, however, the responsibility for learning falls in the hands of the student. She recommends that once the student understands the mindset shift and takes responsibility of learning in his/her own hands, the student will prefer online delivery modality because he/she will understand that leaning is more fun in discovery mode as he/she moves towards lifelong learning.

To summarize, each attribute defined in online education (see figure 1) has its own problem statements and behavior that affects the overall enrollment performance. For example, students demand online courses, which encourage administrators to offer more online courses, which causes members of the faculty to develop and teach them. Faculty recognize the importance of course pedagogy for the success of the course, however, due to time constraints, they offer poorly developed courses, which disappoints some students, which causes students to withdraw, which forces administrators to make the decision of terminating programs. Hence, course design is considered the critical success factor of an online and hybrid curriculum (Boghikian-Whitby, 2003). However, faculty cannot design the proper course unless they study their student population, taking into consideration student's age, which generation they belong to, what their needs are, their learning styles, and their personalities. This study will concentrate on the student's profile and background to identify students' needs.

Research Design

This is an ongoing longitudinal research experiment that started in Fall 2001, and includes a total of 15 semesters. Each semester is fifteen weeks long. Two concurrent classes have been conducted twice a year, one face-to-face in a classroom delivery modality and the other in an online delivery modality. The average enrollment for each class was twenty-two students.

Even though there was a slight time difference in the duration of the course, students completed the same content using the same timeline. In the face-to-face modality, students had breaks such as Spring break or Thanksgiving, whereas, in the online modality there were no breaks. However, all students had exactly the same assignments and the same duration to finish their assignments.

Sample Selection

The research was implemented in a small private institution located in Southern California. The university consists of four colleges – College of Arts and Sciences, College of Business, College of Education and Organizational Leadership, and Law School. The institution serves many first generation college students, and is recognized as one of the most diverse universities in the United States. It has one main campus and several regional centers. The face-to-face courses were offered and conducted on the main campus. The online courses were offered by the regional campus for adults.

All students in this study were undergraduate students seeking a Bachelor of Science degree. The study compared two different types of students - traditional undergraduate and Campus Accelerated Program for Adults (CAPA). Traditional students were 18 – 24 years old and had started attending the university immediately after they graduated from high school. Adult (CAPA) students were over 25 years of age. Those students started working in industry right after they graduated from high school, or they started college but dropped out of college to start working in the industry. CAPA students came to the main campus and benefited from the campus environment. CAPA students had the choice of enrolling in face-to-face and online courses.

In this study, students who enrolled in the face-to-face classroom sessions were adult CAPA and traditional undergraduate students. University policy restricted traditional undergraduate students who attend the main campus from enrolling in the online Distance Learning courses. Only good standing (not on academic probation) traditional students were given permission to enroll in the online courses. However, this restriction does not apply to traditional students who matriculate in the ULV online regional campus program.

In order to investigate student background and profile, a quasi-experimental, nonequivalent separate-sample was conducted. The study used a total sample of 622 students where 296 students were enrolled in the face-to-face control section and 326 students were enrolled in the online experimental sections.

At the beginning of each semester students filled out a "Fact Sheet" survey and took a pre-test exam. At the end of the semester, the students filled out an "Assessment" survey as well as a course evaluation survey, and took a post-test exam. The assessment survey measured the following dependent variables: faculty availability, interaction, satisfaction with course activities, quality of feedback, flexibility of time, and consistency in design of human computer interface. All students including the experimental online students took the pre-test, one midterm, and post-test exams.

This paper deals with a description of the sample to demonstrate student demographic profiles. The researcher retrieved some of the data from the "Fact Sheet" survey that the students filled out at the beginning of the semester. Moreover, the researcher triangulated the data of the fact sheet for accuracy by double-checking the students' backgrounds through the students' transcripts and archival data.

DATA ANALYSIS AND FINDINGS

The experiment consisted of two independent variables: Delivery modality (face-to-face versus online) and student type (traditional undergraduate versus adult). This section presents the analysis and findings of the following variables: student type (adult or traditional undergraduate), age, gender, ethnicity, Myers Briggs personality profile, religion, citizenship, marital status, academic family generation, academic major, academic standing (freshman, sophomore, junior, senior), and Grade Point Average (GPA).

Student Type

The sample was a nonequivalent separate-sample that consisted of 622 students in total. Three hundred and twenty-eight (53%) students were adult continuing education students, also known as CAPA students, and two hundred and ninety-four (47%) students were traditional undergraduate.

In the control face-to-face section group two hundred and forty (80%) students were traditional undergraduate and fifty-six (20%) students were adult students. In the experimental online section group two hundred and seventy-two (83%) students were adult and fifty-four (17%) students were traditional undergraduate students. The control face-to-face section group consisted of two hundred and ninety-six (48%) students and the experimental online learning section group consisted of three hundred and twenty-six (52%) students (see figure 2).

The study indicates 82% of the traditional undergraduate students were enrolled in the control face-to-face section and 18% were enrolled in the experimental online section. The reverse was the case with the adult student population. 17% of the adult students were enrolled in the control face-to-face section and 83% were enrolled in the experimental online section.

Age

The total sample consisted of two hundred and ninety-four (47%) traditional undergraduate students and three hundred and twenty-eight (53%) adult students. Traditional undergraduate students were younger than twenty-five. Adult students were twenty-five years old or older. There was one student who was seventy-nine years old.

The majority of the students in the face-to-face delivery modality were traditional undergraduate students. Two hundred and forty (81%) students

Figure 2. Total number of students in face-to-face / online and student type

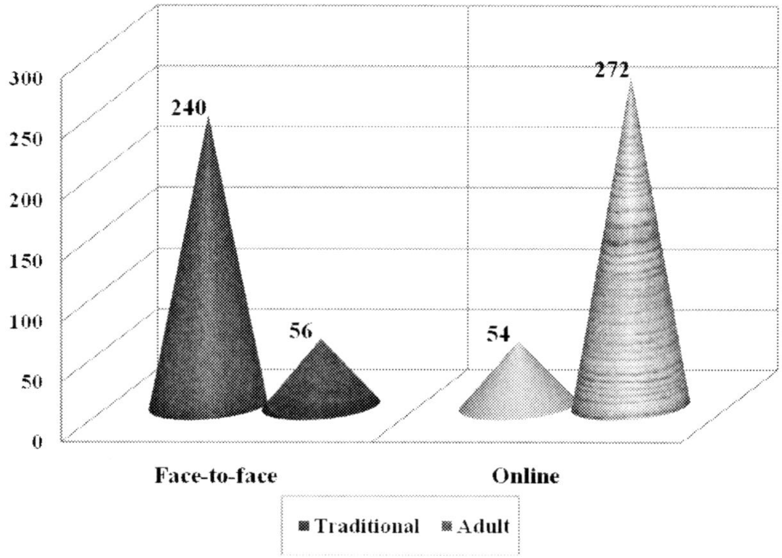

in the face-to-face control group were traditional undergraduates and fifty-six (19%) were adult CAPA students. Whereas, fifty-four (17%) students in the online learning experimental group were traditional undergraduate students and two hundred and seventy-two (83%) students were adult continuing education students (see figure 3).

The study indicates 82% of the students who were between the ages 19 – 24 were enrolled in the control face-to-face section and 18% of the students who were between the ages 25 – 79 were enrolled in the experimental online section. Moreover, 17% of the adult students were enrolled in the control face-to-face section and 83% were enrolled in the experimental online section.

Adult students had the choice of selecting online and face-to-face courses (attending class on the main campus). The data reflects that adult students prefer taking online courses compared to face-to-face. Even though their generation is known to resist change, they could see the value of online education. Traditional students did not have the same choice.

Administrators and faculty members are under the assumption that all students taking online courses are adult students over 25. The data in this study reveals otherwise. There are traditional undergraduate students enrolled in the university's regional campuses who are younger than 25. Those students are allowed to take online courses because they are not on the main campus. Yet, the same students are not allowed to sign up for a main campus face-to-face class.

Gender

The total sample was almost equally distributed between male and female. Three hundred and four (49%) students were female and three hundred and eighteen (51%) students were male.

The majority of the students in the face-to-face control group were male. One hundred and seventy-one (58%) students were male and one hundred and twenty-five (42%) students were female. The figures were reversed in the online experimental group. One hundred and seventy-nine (55%) students were female and one hundred

Figure 3. Total number of students in face-to-face / online, student type, and student age

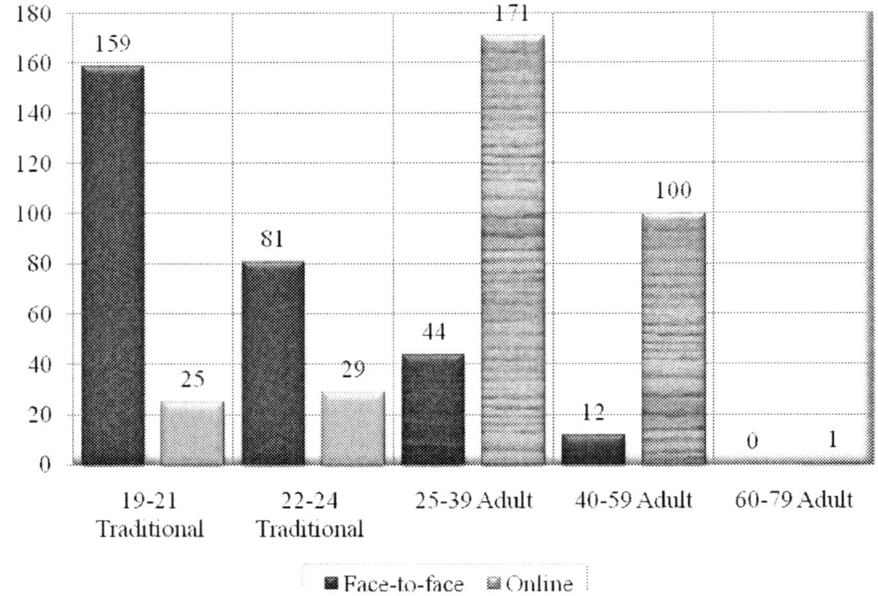

and forty-seven (45%) students were male (see Table 1).

Moreover, 41% of the female students were enrolled in the control face-to-face section and 59% were enrolled in the experimental online section. The reverse was the case with the male student population. 54% of the male students were enrolled in the control face-to-face section and 46% were enrolled in the experimental online section.

Adult Female students tend to prefer taking online courses compared face-to-face. One hundred and fifty-four (47%) of the adult female students enrolled in online compared to twenty-two (7.4%) adult female students enrolled in face-to-face.

The enrollment of female students in the online classes is more than that of male students. One hundred and seventy-nine (55%) students enrolled in online classes were female and one hundred and forty-seven (45%) students were male. Adult male students tend to prefer taking face-to-face classes compared to female students.

Twenty-nine (9%) students enrolled in online delivery modality were traditional undergraduate male students compared to twenty-five (8%) traditional undergraduate female students.

Ethnicity

The students in the study have the following ethnic backgrounds: African American, American Indian / Alaskan Native, Asian / Pacific Islander, Caucasian, Latino / Hispanic / and Multi-Ethnic / Other / unknown. Multi-Ethnic students are the students who have parents from different ethnic backgrounds. Students who came from the Middle East or Athens identified themselves as Others. Unknown identified the students who refused to answer the question (see table 2).

In the face-to-face control group, One hundred and thirty (44%) of the students in the face-to-face section were Caucasian, followed by ninety-one (31%) Hispanic, thirty (10%) Asian, twenty-eight (9%) African American, and four (1%) American-Indian. Thirteen (4%) of the students reported

Table 1. Sample distribution by gender, type, and delivery modality

Students	Face-to-face	%	Online	%	Total	%
Female						
Traditional	103	34.8%	25	7.7%	**128**	20.6%
Adult	22	7.4%	154	47.2%	**176**	28.3%
Total:	**125**	**42.2%**	**179**	**54.9%**	**304**	**48.9%**
Male						
Traditional	137	46.3%	29	8.9%	**166**	26.7%
Adult	34	11.5%	118	36.2%	**152**	24.4%
Total:	**171**	**57.8%**	**147**	**45.1%**	**318**	**51.1%**
Grnd Total:	**296**		**326**		**622**	

Table 2. Sample distribution by ethnicity

Students	Face-to-face	%	Online	%	Total	%
African American	28	9%	43	13%	**71**	11.4%
American Indian / Alaskan Native	4	1%	5	2%	**9**	1.4%
Asian / Pacific Islander	30	10%	22	7%	**52**	8.4%
Caucasian	130	44%	129	40%	**259**	41.6%
Latino / Hispanic	91	31%	86	26%	**177**	28.5%
Multi-Ethnic / Other / Unknown	13	4%	41	13%	**54**	8.7%
Total:	**296**		**326**		**622**	

Multi-Ethnic / Others / Unknown, or refused to answer.

In the online experimental group, one hundred and twenty-nine (40%) of the students in the online learning experimental group were Caucasian, followed by eighty-six (26%) Hispanic, forty-three (13%) African American, twenty-two (7%) Asian, five (2%) American-Indian. Forty-one (13%) of the students reported Multi-Ethnic / Others / Unknown, or refused to answer.

Analyzing the Data by Ethnicity

1. African American: 39% of the African American students were enrolled in the face-to-face control group and 61% were enrolled in the online experimental group.
2. American Indian / Alaskan Native: 44% of the American Indian students were enrolled in the face-to-face control group and 56% were enrolled in the online experimental group.
3. Asian / Pacific Islander: 58% of the Asian students were enrolled in the face-to-face control group and 42% were enrolled in the online experimental group.
4. Caucasian: 50% of the Caucasian students were enrolled in the face-to-face control group and online experimental group.
5. Latino / Hispanic: 51% of the Latino / Hispanic students were enrolled in the face-to-face control group and 49% were enrolled in the online experimental group.
6. Multi-Ethnic: 24% of the Multi-Ethnic / other / Unknown / refused to answer students

were enrolled in the face-to-face control group and 76% were enrolled in the online experimental group.

Having 76% of the students marking "unknown" or "refused to answer" in an online environment proves the fact that end-users like their privacy. Students like to be anonymous especially while using the Internet.

Further analysis was performed to investigate the combination of Ethnicity, Gender, and Age in face-to-face and online modalities (see table 3).

In Fall 2001, the number of students enrolled in the online class were all male students. No females were enrolled in the online course. This was not intentional. One observation is 90% of the students majoring in Computer Science at this university are male.

- African American: Adult female students prefer online delivery modality compared to male students. Traditional undergraduate male African American students enrolled in face-to-face courses more than females.
- American Indian / Alaskan Native: Male and female equally enrolled in face-to-face courses, while in the online course, more male students preferred it. However, this number is too small to generalize.

Table 3. Sample distribution by ethnicity, gender, and age

	Face-to-face		F2F Total	Online		Online Total	Grand Total
Ethnicity	**Female**	**Male**		**Female**	**Male**		
African American	**10**	**18**	**28**	**31**	**12**	**43**	**71**
Adult	2	3	**5**	28	11	**39**	**44**
Traditional	8	15	**23**	3	1	**4**	**27**
Am. Indian / Alaska N.	**2**	**2**	**4**	**1**	**4**	**5**	**9**
Adult	2	1	**3**		4	**4**	**7**
Traditional		1	**1**	1		**1**	**2**
Asian / Pacific Islander	**13**	**17**	**30**	**6**	**16**	**22**	**52**
Adult	2	5	**7**	6	11	**17**	**24**
Traditional	11	12	**23**		5	**5**	**28**
Caucasian	**48**	**82**	**130**	**65**	**64**	**129**	**259**
Adult	9	10	**19**	58	52	**110**	**129**
Traditional	39	72	**111**	7	12	**19**	**130**
Hispanic	**47**	**44**	**91**	**52**	**34**	**86**	**177**
Adult	6	14	**20**	41	27	**68**	**88**
Traditional	41	30	**71**	11	7	**18**	**89**
Other	**1**	**3**	**4**	**10**	**8**	**18**	**22**
Adult	1	1	**2**	8	5	**13**	**15**
Traditional		2	**2**	2	3	**5**	**7**
Unknown	**4**	**5**	**9**	**14**	**9**	**23**	**32**
Adult				13	8	**21**	**21**
Traditional	4	5	**9**	1	1	**2**	**11**
Grand Total	**125**	**171**	**296**	**179**	**147**	**326**	**622**

- Asian / Pacific Islander: Male Adult Asian students prefer online education compared to female Asian students. In addition they are equally enrolled in the face-to-face course.
- Caucasian: The majority of the students enrolled in online delivery modality are Caucasian. Both male and female Caucasian students equally favored online courses. In a face-to-face modality, the enrollment of the course was dominated by male Caucasian students (see figure 4).
- Hispanic: Female Hispanic students (adults and traditional) favor online courses compared to male students. In a face-to-face environment, the number of male Hispanic students was greater than female. Yet, traditional undergraduate female continues to dominate the enrollment.

Students identified as "multi-ethnic" or "unknown" when their parents were intermarried from different ethnic background. There were thirty two students who marked themselves as unknown. In addition, some European students and International students identified themselves as Other. Again, female adult students who identified themselves as other or unknown preferred online education compared to face-to-face.

Myers Briggs Type Inventory

As mentioned earlier, the Myers Briggs Type Inventory (MBTI) consists of four measurements. The first set measures attitude towards the outside (E or I). The second measure identifies the information gathering (S or N) function. The third measure identifies the decision making (Tor F) function. Finally, the fourth measure identifies "shares with outside" preferences (J or P).

Of the type P students, only 27% registered for an online class. Similarly 40% of types E and T took online classes. The remainders of the students were more or less equally divided between the two modalities (face to face and online).

Further analysis shows a more striking insight. Table 4 shows preference by the full indicator. It is clear that INFP, INFJ, INTJ and ISFJ types prefer online classes, while 0% of ISTP attended online classes. As such, course developers should

Figure 4. Total number of students in face-to-face / online, ethnicity, and gender

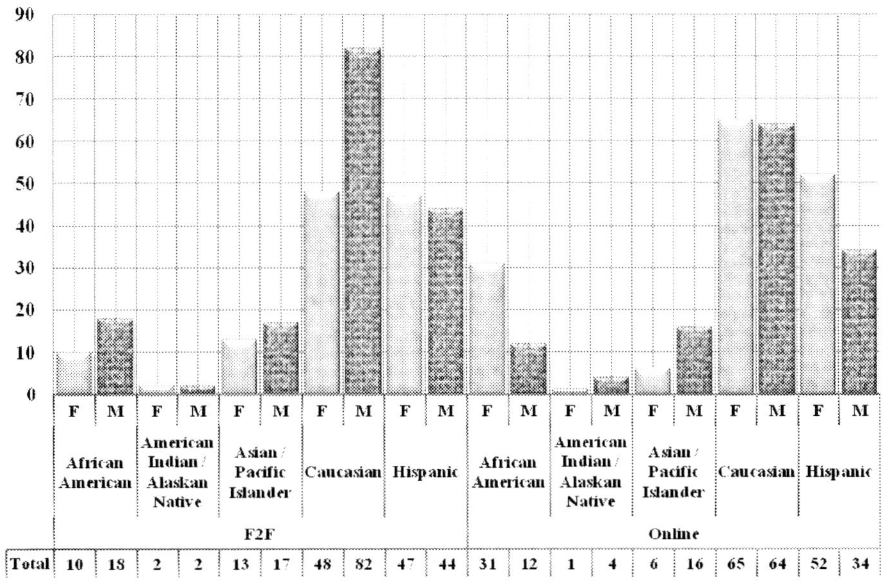

consider these types and their characteristics when developing the material for their courses.

Religion

The majority of the students were reluctant to declare their religion. One hundred and twenty-eight (43%) of the students in the face-to-face and two hundred and ninety-three (90%) of the students in the online experimental section either left the field empty or refused to answer the question.

The majority of the students enrolled in the face-to-face and online course delivery modality were Catholic and Christian (Baptist, Lutheran, and Presbyterian).

In the face-to-face control group: Eighty-three (28%) students indicated that they were Catholic, fifty-eight (19.6%) were Christian, three (1.0%) students stated Church of the Brethren, and two (0.7%) students were Mormon. Assembly of God, Buddhist, Muslim, and Jewish had one (0.3%) student each. Seventeen (5.7%) students stated no denomination, no preference, or other. One hundred and twenty-eight (43%) students were assigned unknown because they refused to answer the question.

In the online learning experimental group, fourteen (4.3%) of the students indicated that they were Catholic, thirteen (4%) were Christian. Jehovah Witness, Pentecostal, and Protestant had one (0.3%) student each. Three (0.9%) students stated no denomination, no preference, or other. Two hundred and ninety-three (90%) were assigned unknown because they refused to answer the question. These results were inconclusive due to the number of students who refused to answer the question.

To summarize, one hundred and forty-one (83%) students who were enrolled in face-to-face control group were Christians (Baptist, Catholics,

Table 4. Myers Briggs personality profile

Students	Face-to-face	%	Online	%	Total	%
ENFJ	38	17.0%	24	13.7%	**62**	15.5%
ENFP	4	1.8%	3	1.7%	**7**	1.8%
ENTJ	20	8.9%	17	9.7%	**37**	9.3%
ENTP	9	4.0%	3	1.7%	**12**	3.0%
ENXP	0	0.0%	1	0.6%	**1**	0.3%
ESFJ	21	9.4%	14	8.0%	**35**	8.8%
ESFP	5	2.2%	6	3.4%	**11**	2.8%
ESTJ	28	12.5%	30	17.1%	**58**	14.5%
ESTP	23	10.3%	3	1.7%	**26**	6.5%
INFJ	7	3.1%	15	8.6%	**22**	5.5%
INFP	1	0.4%	4	2.3%	**5**	1.3%
INTJ	12	5.4%	18	10.3%	**30**	7.5%
INTP	9	4.0%	2	1.1%	**11**	2.8%
ISFJ	10	4.5%	15	8.6%	**25**	6.3%
ISFP	4	1.8%	5	2.9%	**9**	2.3%
ISTJ	19	8.5%	15	8.6%	**34**	8.5%
ISTP	14	6.3%	0	0.0%	**14**	3.5%
Total:	**224**		**175**		**399**	

Lutheran, Presbyterian, and Protestants) and twenty-eight (17%) students who enrolled in online experimental group were Christians.

United States Citizenship

The majority of the students enrolled in the face-to-face and online course delivery modality were United States citizens. Five hundred and eighty-one students were United States citizens and forty-one (6.6%) students were non U.S. citizens.

In the face-to-face control group two hundred and sixty-eight (91%) students were U.S. citizens and twenty-eight (9%) were non U.S. citizens. Whereas in the online experimental groups, three hundred and thirteen (96%) students were U.S. citizens and thirteen (4%) were non U.S. citizens or international students.

Similarly, 46% of the U.S. citizens were enrolled in face-to-face control groups and 54% enrolled in online experimental groups. Whereas, 68% of the non U.S. citizens / international students were enrolled in the face-to-face section and 32% chose the online section.

Marital Status

The majority of the students enrolled in face-to-face and online courses are unmarried. Single parents are also categorized as unmarried. A total of three hundred and ten (50%) of the students were unmarried, followed by seventy-nine (13%) were married, and two hundred and thirty-three (37%) were unknown (see table 5).

Two hundred and twenty-two (75%) of the male and female students in the face-to-face control group were unmarried and fourteen (5%) of male and female students who were married. Sixty (20%) of the students were unknown. Whereas, eighty-eight (27%) of the male and female students in the online experimental group were unmarried followed by sixty-five (20%) of male and female students were married. One hundred and seventy-three (53%) were unknown.

Moreover, 41% of the female were enrolled in face-to-face class section. 9% of the females that were enrolled in face-to-face were married, 67% were single unmarried, and 22% were unknown. Whereas, of the 59% of the female students were enrolled in online section, 91% were married, 33% were unmarried, and 78% were unknown.

Table 5. Sample distribution by marital status and gender

Students	Face-to-face	%	Online	%	Total	%
Female						
Married	3	1.0%	32	9.8%	35	5.6%
Unmarried	93	31.4%	45	13.8%	138	22.2%
Unknown	29	9.8%	102	31.3%	131	21.1%
Total:	**125**	**42.2%**	**179**	**54.9%**	**304**	**48.9%**
Male						
Married	11	3.7%	33	10.1%	44	7.1%
Unmarried	129	43.6%	43	13.2%	172	27.7%
Unknown	31	10.5%	71	21.8%	102	16.4%
Total:	**171**	**57.8%**	**147**	**45.1%**	**318**	**51.1%**
Grand Total	**296**		**326**		**622**	

The study indicates 54% of the males were enrolled in face-to-face class section. 25% of the males in face-to-face were married, 75% were unmarried, and 30% were unknown. In the online experimental group section, 46% of the student body was male, 75% were married, 25% were unmarried, and 70% were unknown.

Academic Family Generation

Bishop defined First Generation as students whose parents did not attend or earn a degree from a four year college or university. Moreover, he defined Second Generation as a student who has had one or more parent attend college for more than one year and/or complete college (Bishop, 2008). In this study "Other" is defined as students whose parents either did not have High school degree or attended college less than one year.

The University of La Verne serves first generation students in the face-to-face control group. Male first generation student enrollment is higher than female in the face-to-face learning control group.

The total sample consisted of six hundred and twenty-two students. Two hundred and twenty-five (36%) students were categorized as first generation, thirty-two (5%) students were categorized as second generation, sixteen (3%) students were considered as Others, and three hundred and forty-nine (56%) students were unknown.

In the face-to-face control group, one hundred and ninety-two (65%) of the male and female students were First generation students, twenty-five (8%) of the male and female were Second generation students, fifteen (5%) were Other, and sixty-four (22%) were unknown. Out of two hundred and ninety-six students one hundred and twenty-five (42%) students were female and one hundred and seventy-one (57%) students were male. Eighty-three (27%) female students were First generation, nine (3%) female students were Second generation, seven (2.4%) were Others, and twenty-eight (9.5%) were unknown. One hundred and eleven (37%) male students were First generation, sixteen (5.4%) male students were Second generation, eight (3%) were Others, and thirty-six (12%) were unknown.

In the online experimental group, thirty-three (10%) of the male and female students were First generation students, seven (2%) of the male and female were Second generation students, fifteen and two hundred and eighty-five (87%) were unknown. Out of three hundred and twenty-six students one hundred and seventy-nine (55%) students were female and one hundred and forty-seven (45%) students were male. Fifteen (5%) female students were First generation, one (0.3%) female student was Second generation, and one hundred and sixty-three (50%) were unknown. Eighteen (6%) male students were First generation, six (2%) male students were Second generation, one (0.3%) was Others, and one hundred and twenty-two (37%) were unknown.

84% of First generation female students were enrolled in the face-to-face control group and 16% were enrolled in online experimental group. 90% of Second generation female students were enrolled in face-to-face control group and 10% were enrolled in online experimental group. 5% of the unknown female students were enrolled in face-to-face control group and 85% were enrolled in online experimental group. All female students who were categorized as others were enrolled in face-to-face control group.

86% of First generation male students were enrolled in face-to-face control group and 14% were enrolled in online experimental group. 73% of Second generation male students were enrolled in face-to-face control group and 27% were enrolled in online experimental group. 89% of the Other male students were enrolled in face-to-face control group and 11% were enrolled in online experimental group. 23% of the unknown male students were enrolled in face-to-face control group and 77% were enrolled in online experimental group.

Analyzing the data by student type in the face-to-face control group, out of two hundred and ninety-six students, two hundred and forty (81%) students were traditional undergraduate and fifty-six (19%) students were adults. One hundred and eighty-five (63%) of traditional undergraduates were First generation, twenty-three (8%) were Second generation. Seven (2.4%) adult students were First generation, and two (0.7%) were Second generation. The rest were others and unknown.

Analyzing the data by student type in the online experimental group, twenty-two (7%) of traditional undergraduates were First generation, and five (2%) were Second generation. Moreover, eleven (3.4%) adult students were First generation, and two (0.7%) were Second generation. The rest were others and unknown.

The study indicates 82% of traditional undergraduate students were enrolled in the face-to-face control group and only 18% of the traditional undergraduate students were enrolled in the online experimental group. 89% of First generation traditional undergraduate students were enrolled in the face-to-face control group and 11% were enrolled in the online experimental group. 82% of Second generation traditional undergraduate students were enrolled in face-to-face control group and 27% were enrolled in online experimental group.

The study reflects 48% of adult students were enrolled in face-to-face control group and 52% of the adult students were enrolled in online experimental group. 39% of First generation adult students were enrolled in face-to-face control group and 61% were enrolled in online experimental group. 50% of Second generation traditional undergraduate students were enrolled in face-to-face and online sections.

Academic Major

The total sample had two hundred and ninety-six (48%) students in the face-to-face control group and three hundred and twenty-six (52%) students in the online experimental group (see table 6). One hundred and six (17%) of the students declared their major from the Arts and Science school. The majors in the Arts & Sciences School include: Behavioral science, criminology, psychology, social science, communications / journalism, computer science and computer engineering, e-commerce, and movement and sports science. Four hundred and ninety-seven (80%) of the students declared their major in the school of Business. The majors in the Business school include: Accounting, business administration, economics, health administration, international business, marketing, organizational management, and public administration. Only two students enrolled from the Education and Organizational Leadership School. Those students were liberal studies majors. They enrolled in this course because the course satisfied their Social Science general education requirement. Seventeen (2.7%) of the students were undecided.

This Management of Information Systems course is a required course for computer science and computer engineering majors and Business majors, which reflects the high number of enrollment. In the Arts & Sciences School, eighty-one students (76%) out of one hundred and six were enrolled in the face-to-face section and twenty-five (24%) students were enrolled in the online section. In the Business School, two-hundred and one (40%) out of four hundred and ninety-seven were enrolled in face-to-face section and two hundred and ninety-six (60%) students were enrolled in the online section. The two students in the Educational and Organizational Leadership were enrolled in the face-to-face section. Out of seventeen undecided students twelve (71%) were in face-to-face section and five (29%) were in the online section.

Academic Standing

The majority of the class consisted of junior and senior students. This distribution was expected

Table 6. Sample distribution by college and major

Major	Face-to-face	Online	Total	Percent
Arts & Science School				
Behavioral Science (Criminology, Psychology, Social Sciences)	5	1	6	1.0%
Environmental Biology	1	0	1	0.2%
Communications	2	0	2	0.3%
Computer Science & Engineering	65	23	88	14.1%
e-Commerce	7	1	8	1.3%
Movement & Sports Science	1	0	1	0.2%
Total:	**81**	**25**	**106**	**17.0%**
Business School				
Accounting	21	13	34	5.5%
Business Administration	149	171	320	51.4%
Economics	5	1	6	1.1%
Health Administration	0	2	2	0.3%
International Business	3	1	4	0.6%
Marketing	11	1	12	1.9%
Organizational Management	9	93	102	16.4%
Public Administration	3	14	17	2.7%
Total:	**201**	**296**	**497**	**80.0%**
Education and Organizational Leadership				
Liberal Studies	2	0	2	0.3%
Total:	**2**	**0**	**2**	**0.3%**
Undecided	12	5	17	2.7%
Total:	**12**	**5**	**17**	**2.7%**
Grand Total:	**296**	**326**	**622**	

since the course was a 400 level course (junior or senior level). In the online regional campus, the academic advisors are staff members who are reluctant to make exceptions and allow students to sign up for courses without the proper pre-requisites. Whereas on the main campus, the academic advisors are faculty members and sometimes they over-ride pre-requisites and allow students to enroll in classes.

The total sample consisted of twenty (3%) freshman students, ninety-three (15%) sophomore students, one hundred and ninety-four (31%) junior students, and three hundred and fifteen (51%) senior students.

In the face-to-face control group, thirteen (4%) were freshmen, sixty-three (21%) were sophomores, one hundred (34%) were juniors, and one hundred and twenty (41%) were seniors. Whereas, in the online experimental group, seven (2%) were freshmen, thirty (9%) were sophomores, ninety-four (29%) were juniors, and one hundred and ninety-five (60%) were seniors.

The study indicates 65% of the students in the freshman class were enrolled in the face-to-face control group and 35% were enrolled in the online experimental group. 68% of the students in the sophomore class were enrolled in the face-to-face control group and 32% were enrolled in the online experimental group. 52% of the students in the junior class were enrolled in the face-to-face control group and 48% were enrolled in the online experimental group. 38% were enrolled in the face-to-face control group and 62% were enrolled in the online experimental group.

Grade Point Average (GPA)

The total sample consisted of nine (1%) students who had a GPA between 1.0 – 1.99, two hundred and thirty-eight (38%) students who had a GPA between 2.0 – 2.99, and three hundred and seventy-five (60%) students who had 3.0 – 4.0 GPA. In the face-to-face control group one hundred and thirty-seven (46%) had 2.0 - 2.99 GPA and one hundred and fifty (51%) had 3.0 4.0 GPA, and only nine students (3%) had 1.0 – 1.99 GPA. In the online experimental group one hundred and one (31%) of the students had 2.0 – 2.99 GPA, and two hundred and twenty-five (60%) of the students had 3.0 – 4.0 GPA.

- Forty percent of traditional undergraduate students who enrolled in this class had 3.0 GPA or better. Adult students in face-to-face courses have a better GPA compared to that of traditional students.
- In an online course delivery modality, 58% of the adult students have a GPA greater than 3.0.

SUMMARY OF FINDINGS

This longitudinal study profiles the demographics of students who were enrolled in Management of Information Systems. This is simply one snapshot of one class. Some of the interesting findings include the following:

1. **Student Type:** In this course adult students dominated the online delivery modality, whereas the opposite happened in the face-to-face delivery modality. Adult students had the choice of enrolling in face-to-face section yet they preferred the online modality for its convenience.
2. **Age:** Currently the data reveals that more adult students are enrolled in online courses. A trend indicates that recently traditional undergraduate students started enrolling in ULV online regional campus and started taking online courses.
3. **Gender:** Female adult students prefer taking online courses compared to face-to-face. traditional male and female students started enrolling in online delivery modality. The male number of students is larger than the female; however, the number is not significant.
4. **Ethnicity:** Caucasian male and female equally enrolled in face-to-face and online courses. However the same was not true in other ethnicity (see figure 4). African American and Hispanic female preferred online compared to face-to-face. Asian female students preferred face-to-face compared to online. In the multi-ethnic groups including those who refused to answer 76% preferred online (see table 2).
5. **Myers Briggs Type Inventory:** 27% of the P students enrolled in online. Similarly 40% of types E and T enrolled in online classes. Types INFP, INFJ, INTJ, and ISFJ prefer online compared to face-to-face while ISTP preferred face-to-face.
6. **Religion:** Christians including Catholic tend to favor face-to-face compared to online courses. This result is inconclusive due to unknown factor.
7. **U.S. Citizenship:** The majority of the students were U.S. citizens. International students prefer enrolling in face-to-face section compared to online. This finding implies the university should either recruit international students or they should analyze their existing resources available to international students.

8. **Marital Status:** Most of the students were unmarried, which also included single parents. The students' comments indicated that most of the students were single parents.
9. **Academic Family Generation:** there are a large number of students who did not respond to the family generation questions. Therefore further study is recommended. The majority of the First generation students were enrolled in face-to-face control group.
10. **Academic Major:** The study had a large number of students majoring in Business and Computer Science because the course is a required course for graduation. Hence, further study is required in different courses.
11. **Academic Standing:** The course is an upper division course. It is intended to be junior and senior level course. The study indicates that 35% of the freshmen students prefer face-to-face to online and gradually changing their preference as they move to senior status. 62% of seniors prefer online courses compared to face-to-face courses.
12. **Grade Point Average (GPA):** the majority of adult students register for online courses respective of their GPA. While the majority of the traditional undergraduate students register for face-to-face. As such the research cannot conclude that the GPA is a determinant factor of delivery modality.

Mature students have a tendency of resisting change to new innovative methodologies unless they recognize their value. They seem to easily adapt to online delivery modality because it is convenient. In the online experimental group the adult population is greater than traditional undergraduate students, whereas in face-to-face modality, the traditional undergraduate students dominate the enrollment compared to adult students.

RECOMMENDATIONS FOR COURSE DESIGN

1. Courses must be developed in smaller modules than an average classroom lecture. This research and other researchers identified adults as the main group of students attending online classes. One characteristic of adult learners is their inability to devote long chucks of time to study. They often devote many short time chucks instead. As such, instructors should divide each chapter into smaller lessons, with each lesson's duration of minutes (e.g. 15 to 20 minutes) instead of hours (Hubbard, 2009).
2. Courses must use more real-life current examples that would have an immediate utilization in the learner's life. Since there are different learning styles as stated both in this research and others, it is important that each lesson presents each learning style the needed tools to improve learning. For example, each lesson should include a short real life case that identifies the concepts and their implementation, a group case in order to satisfy those who prefer group activities, and a discussion of concepts to satisfy the theoretical need of other learning styles.
3. The Cases must be realistic and current, or ones that can relate to current issues. The ages of students vary (adults to traditional students) and their experience is also a variable. Case currency plays a factor in how easy it is to visualize and understand the case and concepts. An informal survey of instructors and students course evaluations in both online and face-to-face classes identified case currency as a positive attribute of classes.

4. There is a need for educational group activities that achieve two objectives. The first objective is to enforce concepts by sharing business experiences, and the second is to develop and support Maslow's needs including belonging and esteem. These needs are, in one form or another, common in educational theories (Michaelsen, Knight, & Fink, 2004).
5. Group formation in online classes is an important issue and how group members are determined is an interesting issue. In a face-to-face environment it is fairly common to ask students to form a group, which often results in friends forming a group. Another approach is for the instructor to assign students to groups. In an online environment, students often do not know who else is registered for the course and they lack the social interaction that assists them in forming groups. Additionally, there are the normal differences (the variety of the learning styles and student professional experience). One possible approach is to identify both students' background and learning styles during the first week, and then for the instructor to create groups that will improve the students class experience. This however, covers the mechanics, but does not define the criteria for successful groups (Fink, 2003).
6. Tests are important, but other activities must be included in the evaluation. Tests are important because they encourage students to read. Other activities such as assignments and group activities support the learning model shared by online students
7. It is important that educational institutions develop guidelines for online courses that differ in two areas: (1) with the subject matter being covered, (2) with the student's major. In other words, different guidelines should be developed for English courses than those developed for math and science courses. There is no one dominant learning style, and Slick (2008) stated that learners change learning styles with different courses. In addition, courses (especially general education courses that enroll students of different majors) must be designed to accommodate different learning styles. Engineering and physics students are often covergers; Math, Economics are assimilators; History and English students are divergers; and Business students are accommodators. As such, a different set of guidelines are needed for each type.
8. Instructors should be prepared for a different set of student expectations that don't deal with the course material directly. We observed that students' expectations of the instructor response time in online courses are much shorter than in face to face even if the same communication channel is utilized. For example, a 24 response time to an e-mail is acceptable in a face-to-face class. On the other hand, students expect a response in few hours in an online class. This comment may be generalized to cover other Checkering Good teaching practices.

FUTURE RESEARCH TRENDS

This research is simply a snapshot of the enrollment in one course. Future investigation in the following areas would be very interesting:

Adult population: First, looking at the starting admission status of the student (freshman, transfer, and re-admit), and second, investigating the percentage of dropouts compared to graduates. Unfortunately, the withdrawal rate could not be tabulated when a student decides to drop the class during the first week. This is simply an observation. 5% of the students signing up for the online class usually drop the class the first week, mainly after reading the syllabus. It would be interesting to find out the personality preference style of such students. Moreover, it would be fascinating to find out the personality preference style of all students enrolled in online courses and measure their success rate in the class.

Group formation is another issue that deserves further investigation. Some universities assign specific students to specific classes in order to insure that many backgrounds exist. The chapter recommends that this policy extends to the group formation in online classes. However, further research is needed in order to measure the efficacy of the recommendation.

Additional research is needed in the following areas:

- How can instructors implement Checkering's good teaching practices in an online class?
- How do some of the demographics influence course design? For example, do differences in race, religion, national origin or similar factors require differences in course design?
- What are the differences in course designs between online and hybrid courses?

REFERENCES

Bishop, E. B. (2008). *A study of differnces on the effects of parental influence on the self efficacy of first generation and second gerneation college students.* La Verne: AAT 3082008.

Boghikian-Whitby, S. (2003). *To take or not to take? The future of distance learning: A quasi-experiment comparison of the effectiveness of Internet-based distance learning versus face-to-face classroom.* La Verne: AAT 3081990.

Boghikian-Whitby, S., & Mortagy, Y. (2008). The effect of student background in virtual learning–longitudinal study. In E. B. Cohen (Ed.), *Setting knowledge free: Issues in informing science and infomation technology* (Vol. 5, p. 746). Santa Rosa, CA: Informing Science Press.

Briggs Myers, I., & Cook Briggs, K. (2002). *Myers-Briggs type indicator (MBIT)*. Association for Psychological Type.

Cushman, K. (2006). *First in the family: Advice about college from first generation students: Your college years.* Providence: Next Generation Press.

Fink, D. (2003). *Creating significant learning experiences: An integrated approach to designing college courses.* San Francisco: Jossey-Bass.

Frankola, K. (2001, October). *Workforce*. Retrieved from http://findarticles.com/p/articles/mi_m0FXS/is_10_80/ai_79352432

Haag, S., & Cummings, M. (2008). *Management information systems for the inforamtion age* (7th ed.). New York: McGraw-Hill Irwin.

Hubbard, R. (2009). Learning about e-learning. *Training Journal.*

Kolb, A. Y., & Kolb, D. A. (2005, June). Learning styles and learning spaces: Enhancing experiential learning in higher education. *Academy of Management Learning & Education*, 193–212.

Lee, C. H., Kim, K., Seo, Y. S., & Chung, C. K. (2007). The relations between personality and lanugage use. *The Journal of General Psychology, 134*(4), 405–413. doi:10.3200/GENP.134.4.405-414

Loo, R. (2002). A meta-analytic examination of Kolb's learning style preferences among business majors. *Journal of Education for Business, 5*, 77–85.

Lynch, M. (2001). *Effective student preparation for online learning*. Retrieved on October 10, 2008, from http://www.elearning.unimass.my/FeaturedSite/archives/000036.ht

Michaelsen, L., Knight, A., & Fink, D. (2004). *Team-based learning: A transformative use of small groups*. VA: Sterling.

Morgan, A., & Barbour, K. (2008). An initial study into the personality types of undergarduate business students. *Allied Academies International Conference, 13*. Cullowhee: Academy of Educational Leadership.

Mortagy, Y. (2005, June 4). *Online policies and procedures*. (S. Whitby, Interviewer)

Nather, K. (2007, July 7). *California community colleges distance education report: Fiscal years 1995-1996 through 2005-2006*. Retrieved on October 10, 2008, from http://website.cccco.edu/Portals/4/AA/Distance%20Education/7-07-DE_Report_Web.doc

Rhoades-Catanach, S. C. (2003). Dot.com or Dot.bomb? The unpleasant tax surprise of stock options in a volatile market. *Issues in Accounting Education*, *18*(4), 385. doi:10.2308/iace.2003.18.4.385

Robey, D., & Taggart, W. (2001). Measuring managers' minds: The assessment of style in human information processing. Academy of Management. *Academy of Management Review*, *6*(3), 375–383. doi:10.2307/257373

Science, I. o. (2003, July 18). *National center for educational statistic*. Retrieved on October 10, 2008, from http://nces.ed.gov/programs/coe/2008/section1/table.asp?tableID=869

Slick, T. (2008). *Do learning styles matter?* La Verne: AAT 3301965.

Vonderwell, S. (2003). An examination of asynchronous communication experiences and perspectives of students in an online course: A case study. *The Internet and Higher Education*, *6*, 77–90. doi:10.1016/S1096-7516(02)00164-1

Chapter 6
Using Action Research to Assess Student Performance in Traditional vs. E-Learning Formats

Retta Guy
Tennessee State University, USA

Craig Wishart
Fayetteville State University, USA

ABSTRACT

While the popularity and acceptance of online education is undeniable, many are concerned about measurable performance of student learning in Web-based courses. The issue of student performance dates back to the start of correspondence courses as the initial challenge to the traditional classroom (McLaren, 2004). Yet, today, it is not a question of whether we pursue this educational medium, but rather, are students in the Web-based courses performing equal to or better than their counterparts in the classroom-based courses? An action research study was conducted to assess student performance in a traditional versus e-learning format at a historically Black land-grant university located in the southern part of the United States. The population sampled included 293 declared business majors who were self enrolled in either organizational behavior or international business undergraduate courses. Both courses in both formats were conducted over a 3-year period. A chi-square test was run to determine if correlation exist between final grades and delivery method. The results revealed that the delivery method did not impact student performance; hence, concluding that there was not sufficient evidence to assert that a relationship exists between final grades and delivery method.

INTRODUCTION

The growth of the Internet and the World Wide Web are attracting the attention of educational institutions across the nation. Increasingly, the World Wide Web is viewed as an effective and inexpensive means of delivering courses in the educational sector. Professors and instructional designers are being asked to adapt courses for Internet delivery

DOI: 10.4018/978-1-60566-852-9.ch006

while students are being promised more flexible learning formats.

The move to Web-based delivery of college- and university-level programs and courses is on the rise. This trend is driven by everything from changing enrollments to increasing costs associated with maintaining school facilities. The diversity of today's student population demands that educational institutions adapt the delivery of their programs to accommodate student's concurrent commitments, including work and family.

The Internet and the World Wide Web are significantly impacting all levels of education by changing the nature of the way we teach and learn. These resources open a boundless range of new learning opportunities and experiences for the classroom. The World Wide Web provides new methods for delivering course materials, enabling distance educators to create learning communities of students and teachers that collaborate and explore subjects of interests. It has created a paradigm shift in pedagogical practices, whose potential is largely untapped.

Education via the Internet is essentially online education, which Desmond Keegan (1988) characterizes as:

- the physical disjointing of instructors and students that differentiates it from traditional classroom education;
- the use of computer networks to deliver educational content; and
- the provision of two-way communication between and among instructors and students.

There are many terms for online education, which refer to the use of electronic applications and processes to learn (e.g. e-learning, online learning, web-based learning and virtual learning, to name a few). "E-learning is here defined as interactive learning in which content is available online and provides automatic feedback to the student's learning activities" (Paulsen 2002). The term e-learning is a broader concept which encompasses the use of all available electronic media to deliver educational content, including Internet, intranets, extranets, satellite broadcast, audio/video tape, interactive TV and CD-ROM (Backroad Connections, 2003; ANTA, 2003).

While the popularity and acceptance of online education is undeniable, many are concerned about measurable performance of student learning in Web-based courses. Given the rapid pace of technological innovation, there's a subtle distinction between being on the cutting edge and the bleeding edge of change. Because our students are the one's to suffer from our mistakes, this concern for quality of learning is paramount. The issue of student performance dates back to the start of correspondence courses as the initial challenge to the traditional classroom (McLaren, 2004). Yet, today, it is not a question of whether we pursue this educational medium, but rather, are students in the Web-based courses performing equal to or better than their counterparts in the classroom-based courses. With the hopes of assuring quality instruction, numerous studies have compared the performance of distance learners to that of traditional learners. Johnson and Aragon (2003) argue that student performance is directly impacted by the quality of instructional design and recommend a conceptual framework that represents a holistic perspective when developing online courses. Rungtusanatam and colleagues (2004) suggest that educators and researchers alike should focus on how best to design instruction for diverse populations in widespread locations. Educational institutions across the nation are impacted by many diverse forces motivating institutions of higher learning to develop and deliver education via the Internet (Rungtusanatam, 2004). This chapter will provide: (1) a summary of the most notable findings from an exhaustive literature review comparing student performance in two distinct formats and (2) a detailed discussion, data analysis, and lessons learned from an action research study conducted to assess student performance in traditional and e-learning formats.

NOTABLE FINDINGS FROM THE REVIEWED LITERATURE

Experts in the field of performance assessment are actively debating whether students in Web-based courses perform equal to or better than students in traditional courses. A review of literature reports on a number of primary research studies that have provided comparable data on student performance between traditional and e-learning environments. A few notable findings (inclusive of non-significant and significant differences) are presented for your perusal.

A number of researchers have compared student performance in traditional versus e-learning courses and have found no significant difference between the two modes of instruction. The following studies add to the literature that states student learning, as measured by performance, does not appear to be different based on course delivery method. The study conducted by McFarland and Hamilton (2005) involved senior-level undergraduate MIS students who were enrolled in an E-Business course during the fall 2003 and fall 2004 semesters. Students self-selected into either the traditional section or the online section. Using Chi-Square analysis, results found no significant difference in the final course grade between the online students and the traditional students. Hoban, Neu, and Castle (2002) conducted a similar study, for two academic semesters, which compared the performance of student teacher candidates seeking state certification through the educational administration program at National University in both on-ground and online delivery modes. Data collection included student surveys, grades, and a comprehensive exit examination. The results revealed that the students academically performed comparably in on-ground and online courses and that both groups mastered established standards.

Ali and Elfessi (2004) report the findings of a study that examined student performance and attitudes towards the use of information technology in virtual and conventional settings. Participants were 47 pre-service undergraduate students enrolled in an educational media and technology course. The study consisted of two treatment groups, one group completing the course online while the other group completed the course in the conventional setting. Data collection included a survey, a likert-type attitude assessment, and a pre and posttests on student performance. Analysis of covariance (ANCOVA) revealed a non-significant difference in student performance and attitude between the two groups.

Fields and Collins (2005) compared examination scores of students enrolled in 3 self-selected, introductory statistics courses. The study consisted of three treatment groups: a face-to-face course, a hybrid course, and a fully online course. The authors found no evidence of a difference in the students' mastery of statistical concepts. Likewise, studies conducted by Hilton and Christensen (2002), Allredge and Som (2002), Zhange (2002) and Fields and Collins (2004) have consistently found no significant difference in student performance when comparing courses delivered in the traditional setting versus the e-learning format.

Buchanan and colleagues (2000) compared traditional classroom instruction with web-based equivalent courses in a graduate program in library and information science and found no significant difference in student performance. Similarly, Gagne and Shepherd (2001) analyzed the performance of students enrolled in both a face-to-face and web-based section of an introductory graduate level accounting course. A one-way fixed effect analysis of variance was used in this study and determined that the performance of students in the web-based course was similar to the performance of students in the face-to-face course.

Other notable research findings include the study conducted by Dellana, Collins and West (2000) in which they examined the effectiveness of a virtual classroom for an undergraduate course in management science. The results indicate no significant difference in student's final course score, when comparing the online option and the traditional course settings. Carey (2001) compared the outcome measures of a management information systems course offered at a small, urban, upper-division university in the two delivery modes. Data collection included a pretest/posttest to assess students' understanding of generalized knowledge of the course, final course grade, student evaluations, student satisfaction and their ability to apply course concepts. The results revealed no significant difference between the learning outcomes of students receiving the online-delivery mode and the face-to-face delivery mode. Likewise, McLaren (2004) found no significant difference in performance when comparing 7 online sections and four classroom sections of a business statistics course.

On the other hand, several notable studies have reported findings contrary to the aforesaid authors. Opposing results were reported by Ury (2004) who conducted a study in which he compared performance over time between online and traditional classroom students enrolled in a management information systems courses and an elementary programming course. Performance, as measured by final grades, indicated that the online delivery method was most effective. The results revealed that students enrolled in the online sections showed a significantly lower mean score than students enrolled in the traditional sections.

Connolly, MacArthur, Stansfield, and McLellan (2007) conducted a quasi-experimental study to investigate student performance in 3 masters-level computer courses that were developed and delivered in online and traditional formats. The study spanned 3 years and included 4,684 participants. Study results show that online students consistently performed better than face-to-face. Identical results were found by Stansfield, McLellan, and Connolly (2004) who examined the results of four modules from the Masters of Science Management of e-Business program with the purpose of comparing the overall performance of students enrolled in the modules online versus those in the face-to-face. Analysis of the results during the period 2000-2002 shows that online students in all four modules, Technologies for Global Commerce, Information Theory and Practice, International Technology Management, and Fundamentals of Database Systems, consistently performed better than the students enrolled in the face-to-face modules.

Studies conducted by Sapp and Simon (2005), Ellis, Goodyear, Prosser, and O'Hara (2006) and Carbonaro, Dawber, and Arav (2006) support the significant difference perspective when comparing student performance in a traditional setting versus the e-learning format.

ACTION RESEARCH STUDY BACKGROUND

Implicit in the term "action research assists educators in assessing needs, documenting the steps of inquiry, analyzing data, and making informed decisions that can lead to desired outcomes" through a process that is undertaken in a school setting (Watts, 1985, p. 118). The idea of using research in a natural setting is traced back to Kurt Lewin, a social psychologist and educator whose work on action research was developed during the 1940s in the United States (McFarland & Stansell, 1993). "Lewin is credited with coining the term 'action research' to describe work that did not separate the investigation from the action needed to solve the problem" (McFarland & Stansell, 1993, p. 14). Action research was introduced to the field of education by a professor at the Teachers College at Columbia University, Stephen Corey. Corey argued, "that the consequence of our own teaching is more likely to change and improve our practices than is reading about what someone else has discovered of his teaching" (Corey, 1953, p. 70). Educators and researchers alike view the practice of action research viable and of great value in the engagement of educational reform (Noffke & Stevenson, 1995; Best & Kahn, 1998).

The current study was conducted at a historically Black land-grant university located in the southern part of the United States to assess the academic performance of students in both traditional and e-learning formats. The demographics of the population sampled consisted of 73% African Americans, 18% Caucasians, 4% Hispanic, and 5% other races. Additionally, 57% were between the ages of 17-24, while 43% were reported as non-traditional students that were employed, commuting, single parents, adults with families, and/or retired military personnel. The following research question was postulated for this study: Does student performance differ based on delivery method (traditional vs. e-learning format)?

Course Design, Data Analysis and Discussion

Action research methodology was employed to examine student performance in two core senior-level undergraduate business courses that were designed for both the traditional classroom and e-learning instruction. The study included 293 declared business majors, who self selected and enrolled in Organizational Behavior and International Business courses over a 3-year period, beginning in the fall 2004 through the spring 2007. These courses were requisites for all business majors, who were required to maintain at least a 2.5 GPA in all core courses. The same instructor, who holds a Ph.D. in Organizational Behavior and has extensive international research and consulting experience, taught all the courses used in this study. Prior to developing these courses, the instructor received training in the Blackboard Learning Management System and online course design from the University's Center for Innovation in Teaching and Learning.

The traditional classroom-based sections of both courses met for 2.5 hours per week for a 16-week long semester. The pedagogical practices centered around lecture and discussion in the face-to-face courses. In addition to the chapter readings, the requirements for both courses included a variation of chapter quizzes, case analysis, formative and summative examinations and participation. Class participation was measured by the quantity and quality of oral contributions.

The e-learning courses were developed, delivered and managed with the Blackboard Learning Management System. Utilizing Blackboard's teaching and learning tools, the instructor designed the lecture notes and PowerPoint slides that were used in the Traditional classroom format. The course readings, aside from the textbook, were made available electronically as PDF files. Both the e-learning and traditional sections used Blackboard for the administration of all quizzes, examinations, and submissions of written assignments.

Because there were no face-to-face meetings of the e-learning sections, participation centered upon the discussion board, where both collaborative learning among students and open dialogue with the instructor was encouraged. The threaded discussions about the assigned readings served as a measure of participation, based upon the quantity and quality of the electronic postings of each student.

Year 1 (2004/05)

A student centered approach to teaching and learning was used in the first year in which the responsibility for managing the pace and depth of learning was left to the students. Because the chapter quizzes were primarily intended to be self-study tools, they were posted on Blackboard all semester for students to take at their own pace. The quizzes were comprised of fifteen multiple-choice and true/false questions randomly selected from a database of 120-150 questions that were timed for completion in fifteen minutes. Importantly, to enable the students to self-assess both their reading comprehension and their level of achievement, the quizzes could be taken repeatedly without limit. In an attempt to avoid the memorization and regurgitation process of examinations, case analyses were required, which served to demonstrate the students' working knowledge of the course concepts and promote analytical thinking and writing skills. Consequently, each of the two (2) case analyses was to be a minimum of ten (10) pages in length and was heavily weighted for the overall grade. The International Management courses also required fourteen (14) one-page summaries of current events in the global marketplace. As a process based strategy, the students were permitted to revise and resubmit their writing assignments repeatedly, until they achieved their desired grade. In contrast to a time centered strategy, where primacy of compliance with time limits for deliverables influences results, this strategy enables students overall effort determine their learning outcomes.

Data analysis for year 1, as represented in Table 1, show that less than twenty percent (18.8%) of the students earned grades below the required level in the traditional format. Additionally, 41.3% earned year-end grades between 91-83, 35% earned between 91-83, and 5% earned between 82-73. In the e-learning format, a significant percentage of students failed below acceptable levels (31.9%), while 29.8% earned between 100-92, 25.5% earned between 91-83, and 12.8% earned between 82-73. Descriptive statistics indicate a larger percentage of year-end grades that averaged between 100 and 73 (81.2%) in the traditional format compared to (68.1%) in the e-learning format.

During the first year, when the instructor placed minimal deadlines upon the students, he discovered that they were not taking the quizzes or responding to the discussion board assignments.

Table 1. Year 1 final grade report

Final Grades	Traditional		e-Learning	
	Count	%	Count	%
100 - 92 (A)	33	41.3	14	29.8
91 - 83 (B)	28	35.0	12	25.5
82 – 73 (C)	4	5.0	6	12.8
72 and below	15	18.8	15	31.9

Despite numerous appeals that they keep up with the readings and be prepared for class, only a few students kept up with the weekly assignments, while the majority waited until the last month and weeks of the semester to fulfill these course requirements. The students indicated that because of their work and family responsibilities, they had to prioritize the course work for their more instructor-centered classes for which there were severe penalties for failing to meet scheduled deadlines and weekly attendance.

Because the instructor actively coached the students to revise and resubmit the written assignments for evaluation, most students took advantage of the opportunity, which resulted in improved grades. Because the course quizzes and written assignments could be indefinitely revised for improvement, the students' continuous effort largely determined their final grade. In many cases, up to three and four revisions of the writing assignments and up to ten attempts at the quizzes. By the end of the semester, the instructor recognized that the time demands for both the students and he was unreasonable. He discovered that his expectations for writing exceeded most students' abilities, and the quizzes were not assessing their reading comprehension. Rather their success with these assignments reflected their persistence to re-submit papers and re-take quizzes with minimal improvements until they attained their desired results. While the dedicated students were able to achieve A's and B's, numerous students who attempted to complete the assignments at the last minute failed the class. A binomial grade curve resulted, in which the average C student either improved their grade or failed the course depending upon their self-discipline and tenacity. The disproportionate failure rate of one-third of the class leads the instructor to perceive the lack of course structure as the cause.

Year 2 (2005/06)

In response to the first year's outcomes, the instructor changed the teaching strategy for year 2, from student-centered to instructor-centered and added formative and summative evaluations. An instructor-centered approach was used to provide more structure and control over the learning process. The instructor provided more conventional guidance, disseminating the information, providing corrective feedback, and establishing timelines. While the courses chapter quizzes were similarly designed and administered, deadlines were imposed to ensure that the students didn't fall behind. These quizzes were due to be completed within two weeks of the assigned chapter readings. Unlimited revisions of the writing assignments were continually accepted, but only until the due date of each assignment. Late submissions of the written and discussion board assignments were not accepted in order to contend with pervasive procrastination. The paper's length requirement was reduced from ten to eight pages, in hopes of improving the quality of writing. And finally, to enhance the assessment of student comprehension, empirical measures were introduced in the form of four multiple-choice exams. The exams were comprised of thirty instructor-selected questions from the test bank and were administered online with a one-hour time limit.

Data analysis in year 2, as displayed in Table 2, shows 21.3% earned final averages between 100-92, 19.1% earned between 91-83, 27.7% earned between 82-73, and 31.9% fell below passing in

Table 2. Year 2 final grade report

Final Grades	Traditional		e-Learning	
	Count	%	Count	%
100 - 92 (A)	10	21.3	8	18.2
91 - 83 (B)	9	19.1	13	29.5
82 – 73 (C)	13	27.7	9	20.5
72 and below	15	31.9	14	31.8

the traditional format. Comparable percentages were reported for the e-learning courses with 18.2% earning between 100-92; 29.5% between 91-83, 20.5% between 82-73, and 31.8% with averages falling below 73%. Quite the reverse from year 1, the year-end grade averages of year 2 indicate a minute difference (.01) in the percentage of scores between 100 and 73 (68.2) in the e-learning format compared to (68.1) in the traditional format.

In year 2, the instructor imposed assignment deadlines to create more structure that would control the learning process and reduce the time commitment for evaluation. The quizzes for the assigned readings were due within two weeks, and late submissions of any assignments were not accepted. Unfortunately, many did not complete the quizzes on time. Consequently, the blackboard quizzes were made available one week prior to the exams, in hopes that they would be utilized as reviews and study tools. Upon inquiring why many of the students failed to complete the quizzes in the allocated fifteen minutes, the instructor discovered that they were using the book to look up the answers, defeating the intended purpose for self-assessment of reading comprehension.

Because the students with poor writing skills in the first year were disadvantaged, and the instructor desired to decrease cheating on the quizzes, four multiple-choice exams were introduced and the relative weight and length of the written assignments were reduced. The two writing assignments for the Organizational Behavior courses were limited to 10 pages worth 50% of their grade. Only one case analysis was required in the second year of the International Management course, in lieu of the requirement of weekly one-page summaries of current international news. Similarly, the writing assignments were weighted as 50% of the final grade in the International Management course.

Importantly, the results of the multiple-choice exams in all courses reflected the students' performance on the chapter quizzes, suggesting that they served as a reliable measure of performance. These instructor-centered changes resulted in student performance that more closely resembled a normal grading curve, yet nearly one-third of the students failed to complete the course assignments in the second year.

Year 3 (2006/07)

The third year courses incurred greater instructor-centered control over the learning process and student participation. To minimize student's open book cheating, the chapter quizzes' fifteen questions were to be completed in only ten minutes. Additionally, the quizzes had to be completed within one week of the assigned readings and could be attempted only three times. To increase quality of the eight page writing assignments, revisions were subject to one grade reduction. With hopes of improving empirical measures, while assessing analytical thinking, twenty-four review questions were assigned one week prior to the assigned exams, of which eight short answer questions were included in each of the four exams, along with sixteen instructor-selected multiple choice question. Because the required answers were comprehensive, the questions needed to be completed ahead of time. Students who failed to be fully prepared found it difficult to successfully complete the exam within the one hour allotted.

Table 3. Year 3 final grade report

Final Grades	Traditional		e-Learning	
	Count	%	Count	%
100 - 92 (A)	18	40.9	6	19.4
91 - 83 (B)	5	11.4	11	35.5
82 – 73 (C)	7	15.9	5	16.1
72 and below	14	31.8	9	29.0

Data analysis in year 3 illustrates a large percentage of students (40.9%) earned year-end averages between 100-92 in the traditional format despite 31.8% earning failing marks. This year also reported 11.4% earning scores between 91-83 and 15.9% earning between 82-73. In the e-learning format, the majority of the students earned grades between 91 and 83 (35.5%), while only 19.4% earned between 100-92, 16.1% earned between 82-73, and 29% earned grades below the acceptable average. The frequency distribution, as depicted in Table 3, show that in year 3 (reminiscent of year 2) a slightly larger percentage of year-end grades averaged between 100 and 73 (71%) in the e-learning format compared to (68.2%) in the traditional format.

In an attempt to address the failure rate, further time restrictions were imposed upon the course assignments in year 3. The chapter quizzes were due within one week of the assigned readings, in hopes that the students would keep current. To more accurately assess reading comprehension and prevent open book cheating, the fifteen question quizzes were timed for only ten minutes. As a result, the quiz scores dropped dramatically. When students who failed the quizzes achieved high scores on the first exam in the Organizational Behavior course, the instructors' investigation revealed that the students were collectively taking the online exam in the University computer lab and sharing answers. Consequently, eight short answer questions were including in all courses remaining exams for the year to more effectively prevent cheating. Due to the changes in examination methods, a disproportionate number of students withdrew or failed the Organizational Behavior courses in the third year.

FINDINGS

The performance of the 293 students enrolled in both the traditional and e-learning was measured by the final grades achieved. This data was analyzed using a Cross Tabulation to determine any significant differences between the variables, for which Statistical Package for Social Sciences (SPSS) was used with the significance level set at a = 0.05.

Data analysis in this study consisted of two phases. In Phase 1, descriptive statistics such as the mean and standard deviation were calculated (see Table 4) to measure the spread of values in the distribution of final grades. The mean and standard deviation for final grades between 92-100 were 1.31 and .467, respectively; between 83-91 were 1.46 and .502; between 73-82 were 1.45 and .504; and final grades between 72 and below were 1.46 and .502. In every instance, the final grades achieved were clustered around the mean.

Additionally, descriptive statistics provided a breakdown of final grades by delivery method. Figure 1 illustrates student performance in the e-learning format with 23% of the study population earning final grades between 92-100; 29.5% earning between 83-91; 16.4% earning between 73-82; and 31.1% earning a final grade of 72 and below.

Figure 2 depicts student performance in the traditional format with 35.7% of the study population earning a final grade between 92-100; 24.6% earning 83-91; 14% earning between 73-82; and 25.7% earning a final grade of 72 and below.

In the second phase of the data analysis, a cross tabulation of category frequencies were computed to determine if correlation exist between final grades and delivery method. A Chi-Square Test was run to obtain a measure of statistical significance with the significance level set at a=0.05. The Chi-Square Test indicates that p>.05 (.141)

Table 4. Descriptive statistics for final grades

Final Grades	N	Mean	Std. Deviation
92 – 100	89	1.31	.467
83 – 91	78	1.46	.502
73 – 82	44	1.45	.504
72 and below	82	1.46	.502
Total	293	1.42	.494

Figure 1. Student performance in e-learning format

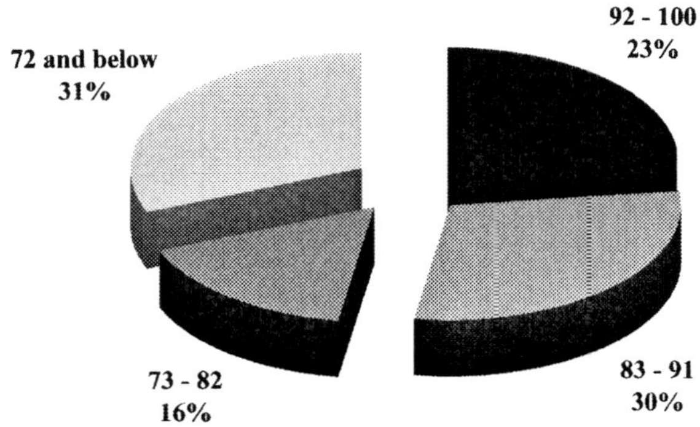

Figure 2. Student performance in traditional format

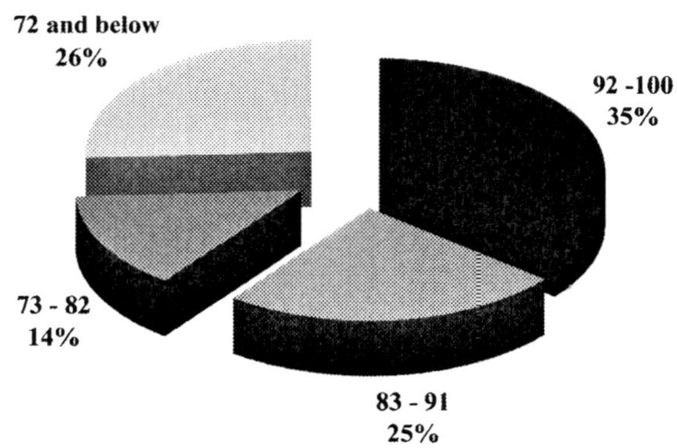

and cannot be regarded as significant (see Table 5). Accordingly, we conclude that there is not sufficient evidence to assert that a relationship exists between final grades and delivery method.

In summary, this study sought to determine whether student performance differs based on delivery method (e-learning and traditional formats). The findings revealed that the delivery method did not impact student performance. In likeness to the findings of this study, the reviewed literature reveals a predominance of non-significant differences found between the two modes of delivery.

Table 5. Delivery method chi-square test

	Value	df	Asymp. Sig.
Pearson Chi-Square	5.458[a]	3	.141
Likelihood Ratio	5.565	3	.135
Linear-by-Linear Association	3.383	1	.066
N of Valid Cases	293		

a. 0 cells (.0%) have expected count less than 5. The minimum expected count is 18.32.

STUDY LIMITATIONS

As with any research, particularly in the area of online education, there were a number of limitations that may impact this study; accordingly, caution is necessary when interpreting the findings. While this study provides research on a population that is underrepresented in the literature, it also gives way to the first limitation in focusing solely on participants attending minority-serving institutions with no comparative data from majority-serving institutions. The second limitation pertains to final grades as influenced by institutional standards, which may be at variance with the current study's articulation of final grades as a measure of the extent to which the student successfully complies with the academic requirements set forth by the university's board of regents.

The courses used for this study were business related which addresses the third limitation that frames the assumption not all disciplines have courses that are compatible with the e-learning delivery mode relative to content and subject matter. Lastly, the e-learning courses were created and delivered using Blackboard. To date, there is a significant number of management learning platforms that provide a host of online collaborative tools; therefore, caution should be exercised in generalizing the findings relative to different e-learning platforms.

LESSONS LEARNED

Academicians, researchers, and practitioners across the globe have learned valuable lessons regarding what works and what does not work for online education. As described in the discussions of this chapter, there were several challenges in the development and design of the online courses. These challenges and lessons learned can be summarized as follows:

- There is an ongoing concern regarding students dropping out of online courses. Researchers have cited poor technology skills, lack of self-discipline and motivation, and minimal interaction between and among students and faculty as reasons for the high attrition rates. As previously stated, a disproportionate number of students either withdrew or did not complete the course assignments in the e-learning format. In view of such, it is important to develop a learning community with meaningful interaction, collaboration and engagement. The use of asynchronous and synchronous communication tools should be employed to provide sufficient levels of interaction.

- A more demanding issue with online education is how to design and offer content. The current study failed to provide content using synchronous tools which promote communication simultaneously; lectures were merely created in PowerPoint and posted online for students to view at their convenience, lessening the online courses to simply threaded discussions and forums. To correct this problem, the use of streaming audio and video coupled with PowerPoint presentations as well as web conferencing is recommended not only to promote interaction simultaneously but also to promote an online environment in likeness of the traditional classroom.
- The instructor-centered approach was used in year 2 and 3 of this study as a means of controlling course activities and student participation and disseminating information. Flexibility has been cited as one of the prevailing advantages to taking online courses. In as much, students have the flexibility of completing assignments at their convenience with the option of working ahead. However, to enable students to work leisurely and ahead, all course material should be finalized and posted on the web site at the beginning of the course requiring upfront design and development, not development as the course progresses.
- The instructor repeatedly noted that students were using the book to look up answers to the quizzes. To avoid the problem of cheating, online exams must embrace structured questions or other assessment methods that represent intellectual activity that require students to apply, analyze, synthesize, and/or evaluate the concepts they have learned rather than the regurgitation of simple recall or recognition of facts. (Krathwohl, Bloom & Masia (1973).

CONCLUSION

The current study set out to assess the academic performance of students in both the traditional and e-learning formats. The results, while consistent with the predominance of the current literature reviewed, indicate that the e-learning format offers flexibility with no loss of performance.

The 2003 Sloan Survey of Online Learning polled academic leaders . . . and asked them to compare the online learning outcomes with those of face-to-face instruction; a majority said they are equal. (Roach, 2003, p. 1).

From the prevailing research, we can conclude that the use of the Internet and the World Wide Web to abet in the development of Web-based courses is a growing trend that cannot go unnoticed (Rungtusamatam et al, 2004; Simonson, 2006; Fornaciari and Forte, 1999). The data gathered in this study can inform future planning and implementation of online instruction. Although significant differences in performance were not generally reported in the reviewed studies, there are many challenges to overcome if we are to make e-learning a rewarding experience.

REFERENCES

Ali, A., & Elfessi, A. (2004). Examining students performance and attitudes towards the use of information technology in a virtual and conventional setting. *The Journal of Interactive Online Learning, 2*(3), 1–9.

Alldredge, J., & Som, N. (2002). Comparison of multimedia educational materials used in an introductory statistics method course. *Proceedings of the Sixth International Conference on Teaching Statistics*. The Netherlands: International Statistics Institute.

ANTA. (2003). *What is flexible learning? Australian flexible learning framework*. Retrieved from http://flexiblelearning.net.au/aboutuswhatisfl.htm

Backroad Connections Pty Ltd. (2003). *Definitions of key terms used in e-learning (version 1.00)*. Australian flexible learning framework quick guides series, Australian National Training Authority. Retrieved from http://flexiblelearning.net.au/guides/keyterms.pdf

Best, J., & Kahn, J. (1998). *Research in education* (8th ed.). Needham Heights, MA: Allyn and Bacon.

Buchanan, E., Brown, M., Casanova, J., Wolfram, D., & Xie, H. (2000). Web-based and traditional instruction: A systematic study of student and instructor perceptions from a graduate MLIS program. *Teaching with Technology Today*, *7*(1), 1–3.

Carbonaro, M., Dawber, T., & Arav, I. (2006). A comparison of students' performance under full-time and part-time, and online conditions in an undergraduate nursing microbiology course. *Journal of Distance Education*, *21*(1), 51–61.

Carey, J. (2001). Effective student outcomes: A comparison of online and face-to-face delivery modes. *DEOSNEWS*, *11*(9), 1–19.

Connolly, T., MacArthur, E., Stansfield, M., & McLellan, E. (2007). A quasi-experimental study of three online learning courses in computing. *Computers & Education*, *49*(2), 345–359. doi:10.1016/j.compedu.2005.09.001

Corey, S. (1953). *Action research to improve school practices*. New York: Teachers College Press.

Ellis, R., Goodyear, P., Prosser, M., & O'Hara, A. (2006). How and what university students learn through online and face-to-face discussion: Conceptions, intentions, and approaches. *Journal of Computer Assisted Learning*, *22*(4), 244–256. doi:10.1111/j.1365-2729.2006.00173.x

Fields, P., & Collins, P. (2005). An assessment of student performance in an introductory statistics hybrid course. *Proceedings of the 55th Session, International Statistical Institute*.

Fornaciari, C., & Forte, M. (1999). Distance education as a strategy: How can your school compete? *Journal of Management Education*, *23*(6), 703–719. doi:10.1177/105256299902300608

Gagne, M., & Shepherd, M. (2001). A comparison between a distance and a traditional graduate accounting class. *T.H.E. Journal*, *28*(9), 58–65.

Hilton, S., & Christensen, H. (2002). Evaluating the impact of multimedia lectures on student learning and attitudes. *Proceedings of the Sixth International Conference on Teaching Statistics*. The Netherlands: International Statistics Institute.

Hoban, G., Neu, B., & Castle, S. (2002). *Assessment of student learning in an educational administration online program*. Paper presented at the American Education Research Association (AERA) Annual Meeting, New Orleans, Louisiana.

Johnson, S., & Aragon, S. (2003). An instructional strategy framework for online learning environments. *New Directions for Adult and Continuing Education*, *100*, 31–43. doi:10.1002/ace.117

Keegan, D. (1988). On defining distance education. In D. Sewart, D. Keegan & B. Holmberg (Eds.), *Distance education: International perspectives* (pp. 6-33). London/New York: Routledge.

Krathwohl, D., Bloom, B., & Masia, B. (1973). *Taxonomy of educational objectives. The classification of educational goals. Handbook II: Affective domain*. New York: David McKay Co., Inc.

McFarland, D., & Hamilton, D. (2005). Factors affecting student performance and satisfaction: Online vs. traditional course delivery. *Journal of Computer Information Systems*, *46*(2), 25–32.

McFarland, K., & Stansell, J. (1993). Historical perspectives. In L. Patterson, C. Santa, C. Short & K. Smith (Eds.), *Teachers are researchers: Reflection and action*. Newark, DE: International Reading Association.

McLaren, C. (2004). A comparison of student persistence and performance in online and classroom business statistic experiences. *The Decision Journal of Innovative Education, 2*(1), 1–10. doi:10.1111/j.0011-7315.2004.00015.x

Nofke, S., & Stevenson, R. (Eds.). (1995). *Educational action research: Becoming practically critical*. New York: Teachers College Press.

Paulsen, M. (2002). *Online education systems: Discussion and definition of terms*. NKI Distance Education. Retrieved from http://home.nettskolen.com/~morten

Roach, R. (2003). Survey says online learning equal to classroom instruction. *Black Issues in Higher Education, 20*(16), 44.

Rungtusanatham, N., Ellram, L., Siferd, S., & Salik, S. (2004). Toward a typology of business education in the Internet age. *Decision Sciences Journal of Innovative Education, 2*(2), 101–120. doi:10.1111/j.1540-4609.2004.00040.x

Sapp, D., & Simon, J. (2005). Comparing grades in online and face-to-face writing courses: Interpersonal accountability and institutional commitment. *Computers and Composition, 22*(4), 471–489. doi:10.1016/j.compcom.2005.08.005

Stansfield, M., McLellan, E., & Connolly, T. (2004). Enhancing student performance in online learning and traditional face-to-face class delivery. *Journal of Information Technology Education, 3*, 173–188.

Ury, G. (2004). A longitudinal study comparing undergraduate student performance in traditional courses to the performance in online course delivery. *Proc ISECON*, 21, 1-7.

Vrasidas, C., & McIsaac, M. (2000). Principles of pedagogy and evaluation for Web-based learning. *Educational Media International, 37*(2), 105–112. doi:10.1080/095239800410405

Watts, H. (1985). When teachers are researchers, teaching improves. *Journal of Staff Development, 6*(2), 118–127.

Zhang, J. (2002). Teaching statistics online: Our experience and thoughts. *Proceedings of the Sixth International Conference on Teaching Statistics*. The Netherlands: International Statistics Institute.

Chapter 7
Examining Individual Students' Perceptions of Curiosity Utilizing a Blend of Online and Face-to-Face Discussions:
A Case Study

Ronnie H. Shroff
The Hong Kong Institute of Education, Hong Kong

ABSTRACT

Research has established that the exploratory behavior of an individual student has a positive effect on learning and academic achievement. However, very little is known about the impact of a blended learning approach on individual student curiosity and whether combinations of online and face-to-face learning activities significantly enhance student exploratory behavior. This chapter assesses the effects of blended learning on perceived individual student curiosity, utilizing a blend of online and face-to-face discussions. This research collates elements from the theories of curiosity. A qualitative research methodology was utilized for the purpose of the research. Data were obtained through in-depth and semi-structured one-on-one interviews with undergraduate students. Results from the qualitative study showed that individuals' perceptions of curiosity were strongly supported. The results of our study may suggest that future research should explore more deeply, the importance of technology on learning and academic achievement (Alavi & Leidner, 2001). For example, specific studies could address various aspects of online learning and instruction, such as an individual's patterned ways of thinking, feeling and reacting. These interconnected thoughts, feelings and behaviors, may reflect the differences in motivational behavior between an individual and groups.

INTRODUCTION

Colleges and universities share a common mission to educate their students in the best possible way, by creating environments where students are intellectually challenged, where current and relevant subject matter is disseminated in a professional manner and where lifelong learning and high standards of professional education are fostered.

DOI: 10.4018/978-1-60566-852-9.ch007

Given the technologies of the 21st century, we ask the question, how can educators successfully accomplish this mission? Universities world-wide are currently facing a restructuring of traditional educational paradigms. What is emerging within this restructuring is a blended learning model that combines the best practices of online and face-to-face formats (2005; Boyle, Bradley, Chalk, Jones, & Pickard, 2003). Blended learning offers the convenience of the online format without the loss of face-to-face contact (Dziuban, Hartman, & Moskal, 2004). By combining face-to-face and computer-mediated elements into a blended learning activity, the learning activities become more authentic for the students. Moreover, when technology is used as a tool to support students in performing authentic tasks, the students are in a better position to define their goals, make decisions and evaluate their progress (Leidner & Jarvenpaa, 1995).

Both online and face-to-face delivery has the potential to facilitate environments where: (1) meaningful and authentic learning takes place; (2) construction of knowledge is promoted; (3) collaboration and conversation (between and among students and instructors) is supported; and finally, (4) individual student curiosity and exploratory behavior may be significantly increased. However, a major problem we encounter is that we presently lack accurate information on to how to effectively make use of blended learning environments in order to effectively promote the active learning, collaboration and problem solving skills of individual students. It is not only difficult to assess how students learn but also how well they are able to adapt to these learning environments.

The following research question seeks to assess the effects of perceived curiosity of individual students utilizing a blended learning approach: Are perceptions of individual student curiosity higher in online discussions compared to traditional face-to-face discussions, utilizing this type of blended learning approach? The intention of this research is to create a blended learning platform that allows students to interact and collaborate in both online and face-to-face settings. Interaction and collaboration is one of the most important components of learning experiences in both on-line and face-to-face environments (Jonassen, Peck, & Wilson, 1999; Vygotsky, 1978). Collaborative inquiry offers a different model of learning from that provided by traditional lecture and classroom-based methods (Ocker & Yaverbaum, 2002). However, recently developed instructional and communication technologies can facilitate the collaborative learning process for students by adding structure to their group experiences and giving them additional tools to support their work (Hiltz, 1990; Warschauer, 1997).

This research has long-term significance for students, instructors, institutions and society at large. The information that can be gained from assessment can be invaluable in facilitating students' higher-order cognitions, active learning and self-regulated learning. The use of a blended learning approach also has the potential to change the nature of learning environments and the ways in which we design both online and face-to-face activities to support intellectual development, including the explorative strategies involved in learning. Examining individual students' perceptions of curiosity, utilizing a blended learning approach, should play a pivotal role in enhancing learning and furthering this research. Considerable discussions emanating from academic debate and research surround the emergence of blended learning environments. This paper firstly seeks to integrate and synthesize content regarding (a) blended learning environments and (b) curiosity. The paper concludes with a discussion of the results and the implications of these results.

BLENDED LEARNING ENVIRONMENTS

Currently many universities are exploring what is referred to as a unique combination of blended learning, in which a portion of the learning activities have been moved online. Blended learning is course delivery that utilizes more than one method of providing information to the learner (Garrison & Kanuka, 2004). This concept has become increasingly more prevalent, with the introduction of new technologies, which have offered innovative instructional delivery mechanisms that ultimately create new blends. The term blended learning is used to describe the utilization of computer-based online curriculum delivery with a mix of instructor-led face-to-face classroom delivery (Osguthorpe & Graham, 2003). Blended learning has been utilized by the teaching profession as an addition to a classroom capability and is usually synonymous with instruction that involves a mix of face-to-face and online instruction (Novak, Gavrin, Christian, & Patterson, 1999). As faculties consider realigning their courses to this new delivery format, many issues arise, including the perception that teaching online is the same as teaching face-to-face (Bleed, 2001).

In the past decade, there has been an increase in utilization of educational technology by educators. Dede (1996) warns that merely using technology as a tool for learning, instead of as a means to deliver appropriately designed content, will surely lead to failure. This technology is not valuable unless it is properly and effectively incorporated into the content and methodology of the course. Instructors need to employ the appropriate technology by creating an educational platform that interests, excites and motivates students to learn. These platforms can subsequently also serve as portals to more in-depth advanced information, if a learner wishes to proceed further than the required curriculum (Vaughan, 2007).

The main component that differentiates blended from face-to-face instruction is the use of more than one delivery method, which includes the use of computer-based instruction that can be implemented in a traditional classroom-based format (Thorne, 2003). The involvement of students in the blended learning environment is the key to their success in the learning process. In both online and face-to-face instruction, the learners and instructors interact, share ideas and generally try to support one another throughout the learning cycle (Boyle, 2005). This type of collaborative learning has been found indispensable for learners to integrate new information with existing knowledge, in order to create new ideas (Bosworth & Hamilton, 1994). The learners are better able to assimilate new information and solve problems when working in collaboration with others (Ocker & Yaverbaum, 2002). The unique feature of collaborative learning is its emphasis not only on individual learner effort but also on group coordination, shared understanding and even confrontation to achieve a common goal (Bosworth & Hamilton, 1994; Edelson, Pea, & Gomez, 1995) .

Blended learning is an approach that optimizes learning by incorporating the use of technologies with regular class-based teaching strategies, depending on the requirements of the course and its learner (Osguthorpe & Graham, 2003). These practices can be in the form of regular classroom instruction coupled with online activities, self-paced tutorials, online assessment and online surveys, all of which help to facilitate learning. Once classroom and online delivery have been implemented successfully, the focus can be shifted to a combination of the two. The combination or "blend" would allow for increased flexibility, responsibility and control to students for their learning activities (Garrison & Kanuka, 2004). For example, both face-to-face and online delivery can facilitate access to worldwide sharing of ideas and knowledge (Boyle, Bradley, Chalk, Jones, & Pickard, 2003). These types of situations encourage an individual to seek information, explore ideas and make him or her feel the need to resolve any ambiguity or obtain more information about the topic (Kashdan & Fincham, 2004). Thus, an individual needs a representative learning environment in which his or her explorations may be conducted and a blend of both online and face-to-face discussions, best serves this purpose (Keller, Schneider, & Henderson, 1994).

CURIOSITY

Research into curiosity and exploration concerns itself primarily with describing and explaining exploratory behavior. Explanations based on everyday experience often incorporate the notion of an active individual pursuing particular content-related goals (Kashdan & Fincham, 2004). That individual is not simply motivated; instead he or she is "curious" about some matter or content. Existing scientific discussions neglect the concept of curiosity research in areas of motivation (Kashdan & Fincham, 2004).This is especially surprising in light of the fact that, as early as 1949, Berlyne (1950), the original founder of research on curiosity, dealt extensively with the relation between curiosity and exploratory behavior. It may therefore, be useful to consider in greater detail, those aspects of exploratory behavior that traditionally have been essential components in theories of curiosity.

In interpreting curiosity, research approaches based on drive theories, theories of activation (Berlyne, 1960) or cognitive theories, have typically exhibited a general psychological perspective. Investigations were inclined to center on phenomena that can be described and explained in terms of general laws of human behavior. Researchers, for example, have focused on differences in behavior and on explanations or predictions of individual differences in light of personality characteristics. These researchers have assumed motivational factors to be the source of these differences in the field of exploratory behavior. Numerous methods for descriptions of various degrees of curiosity, in the sense of an exploratory motive, have been developed. Typical examples would be the theories, conceptions and methods pertaining to "seeking curiosity" (Livson, 1967), "sensation seeking" (Zuckerman, 1971), "variation motivation" (Pearson & Maddi, 1966), "cognitive orientation" (Kreitler & Kreitler, 1976) and "experience-producing tendencies" (Henderson, 1989).

Berlyne's (1954) Optimal Stimulation Theory asserts that an individual's behavior is mediated by his or her need for a moderate (optimal) level of stimulation (Berlyne, 1954). Berlyne's (1960) work focused on determining which properties of stimuli evoke curiosity in an individual. According to his theory, the arousal leading to curious behavior is most often induced by the "collative" properties of a stimulus – ambiguity, novelty, incongruity and complexity (Berlyne, 1960). He later extended his theory to include "epistemic curiosity" which leads to "epistemic behavior," the function of which is to "build up knowledge" (Berlyne, 1965).

Over the past few years, progress has been made toward the development of approaches that abandon a global conceptualization of curiosity in favor of process variables. In recent years, several studies (E. L. Deci & R. Ryan, 1985; Harter & Connell, 1984) have shown that when conditions of curiosity are created, conceptual learning, creative thinking and the quality of learning increase dramatically. Deci and Ryan (1985) argued that even seemingly trivial or purely illusory choices have significant benefits on learning motivation and that curiosity is also promoted by placing learning in meaningful and exciting contexts.

Thus, autonomous activity and conscious goal-orientation represent fundamental aspects of exploration and may indicate how an individual's content-specific preferences influence his or her exploratory behavior. A theory of curiosity useful in describing everyday activity should, for instance, yield insights into whether and in what ways specific exploration is influenced by the presence or absence of content preferences. The conceptualization of curiosity to be presented in this research paper is based on the theoretical consideration of the effect of person-environment relationships. It is assumed that individual development is determined largely by the quality and course of an individual's relationships to the social environment. Continual interaction with other individuals, objects, events and areas of subject matter (i.e. content) leaves behind traces in both that individual and the environment. Each experience adds to and differentiates an individual's store of knowledge. Person-environment engagements thereby play a crucial role in shaping an individual's motivational structure.

Various research approaches deal with curiosity (Berlyne, 1960; Keller, Schneider, & Henderson, 1994) in predicting feelings of relatedness. Curiosity is related to social engagement because exploratory behavior is a powerful contributor to individual well-being that can interfere with social relatedness. Curiosity appears to increase opportunities for fulfilling social relatedness needs and is associated with enhanced goal pursuit, performance and individual well-being. Individuals have a need to feel related to the environment and this need provides a desire to act upon the environment (Berlyne, 1950). These desires to explore, discover, understand and know are inherent to an individual's nature and are central motivators for his or her behavior (Spielberger & Starr, 1994).

Curiosity, defined by Berlyne (1954) as a drive that is reduced by the acquisition of knowledge, has been hypothetically linked to learning and cognitive ability (Berlyne, 1978; Dember & Earl, 1957; Loewenstein, 1994). According to Berlyne (1978), curiosity is the impetus to explore and understand our environment. Berlyne (1954) promoted an Optimal Stimulation Theory of exploratory behavior, conceptualizing curiosity as a drive to reduce perceived uncertainties. According to his theory, individuals endeavor to sustain a preferred level of interaction with the environment. Uncertainty raises the level of arousal and curiosity motivates individuals to seek out stimuli, which reduce that uncertainty, thus decreasing the arousal to a more optimal level. As such, Berlyne (1978) considered curiosity and exploratory behavior central to learning by discovery and explicated that such learning leads to greater intellectual potency.

Malone and Lepper (1987) suggested that curiosity is directly related to the outcomes of motivation. According to their theory, curiosity is divided into two categories - sensory curiosity and cognitive curiosity. Sensory curiosity involves gaining an individual's attention through his or her senses, such as light, sound, smell, touch and taste. Examples of stimulating sensory curiosity include the use of colorful textbooks, educational materials that appeal to an individual's senses and educational computer programs. For instance, educational computer games use graphics, color, sound, movement and video to attract and sustain the individual's attention. Many a time, without even the conscious knowledge of an individual, the stimulation of his or her sensory curiosity leads to an engagement in the learning process (Malone, 1981).

Alternately, cognitive curiosity is stimulated by the prospect of modifying an individual's current cognitive level (Walker, Greene, & Mansell, 2006). It involves creating cognitive dissonance and challenging the learner's current cognitive structure. Cognitive structure is challenged by a conflict between incompatible existing attitudes or ideas. Sensory and cognitive curiosity can be created and designed in various types of environments to make individuals think and learn. Through the use of interactive curricula or environments, an individual becomes a part of the learning process and in turn, his or her levels of motivation increase (Parker & Lepper, 1992). Additionally, by challenging an individual's cognitive structure, he or she learns and builds upon his or her knowledge base (Malone & Lepper, 1987). Berlyne and Frommer (1966) stated that individuals are more likely to be curious, explorative or investigative if they encounter something that is new, complex, incongruous or surprising (Berlyne & Frommer, 1966).

Figure 1. Overview of research

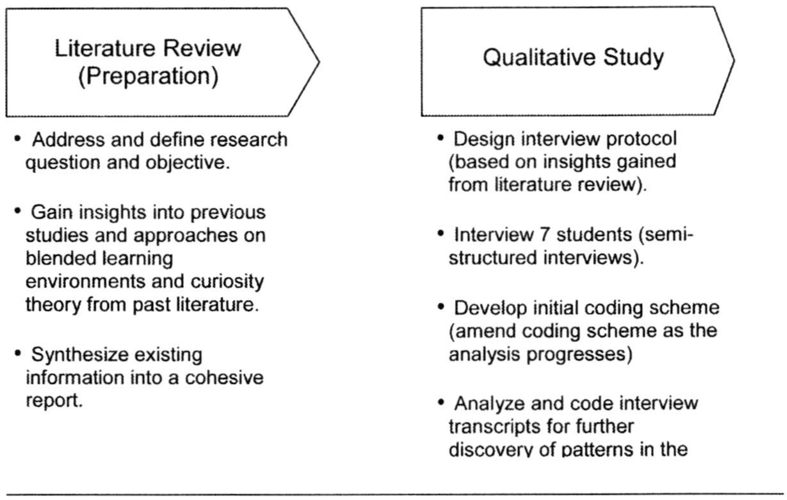

RESEARCH METHODOLOGY

A qualitative research approach was used to help clarify the following research question: Are perceptions of individual student curiosity higher in online discussions compared to traditional face-to-face discussions, utilizing a blended approach? A summary of the two stages of this research is outlined below (see Figure 1). As mentioned below, the preparatory stage consisted in conducting a thorough literature review, followed by the qualitative study that provided a conceptualization and interpretation of the results.

The objective of this study was to examine individual students' perceptions of curiosity utilizing a blended learning approach. Each of the techniques employed in the qualitative study are described below to explain their purpose and application to the study. The techniques are listed as steps in the order in which they were conducted (see Table 1).

Based upon previous literature on curiosity, a case study protocol was designed. The case study protocol was developed from a combined literature review of this paper and research question and then supplemented by the framework developed. By applying a theoretical interpretive model to the findings, the findings were mapped on to the curiosity construct. In a previous exploratory study, we had examined the implications of various other learning activities on aspects of intrinsic motivation in e-learning (Shroff, Vogel, Coombes, & Lee, 2007; Vogel, Shroff, Kwok, & Coombes, 2002). Based on a review of the above literature, we proposed that perceptions of individual curiosity will be higher in online discussions compared to face-to-face discussions. When activities heighten curiosity, then an individual is naturally involved and driven to learn because his or her motivation is increased. If curiosity is to be stimulated, the role of the environment is to provide an individual with activities/opportunities to explore.

Specifically, this study is intended to better understand individuals' perceptions of curiosity in the context of online discussions and face-to-face discussions. This study is limited to a blend of online discussions and face-to-face discussions, because, as our prior research suggests, this blended approach has the potential to influence a wide spectrum of factors directly related to individual curiosity and these factors, thus appear as a favorable context to study the subject.

Table 1. Path of inquiry

	Method	Tools
PREPARATION	- Developed case study protocol - Designed interview protocol - Selected and contacted student subjects - Scheduled interviews - Developed initial coding scheme	- Use of framework and constructs gained from literature review
DATA COLLECTION	- Interviewed 7 FB students via semi-structured interviews - Transcribed interviews	- Interviews scheduled and conducted
DATA ANAYLSIS	Detailed analysis – Within case: - Preliminary analysis – within case- (summarizing) - Detailed analysis (coding)	- Summarized transcripts (to capture main impression) - Coded interviews - Developed summary/overview tables for each case.

For example, student-student interaction is seen by Cifuentes et al (1997) as a powerful force for supporting learning and by Klemm (1999) as a means for ensuring participation, which is critical based on his view that, "Learning is best accomplished when the learner is actively engaged in the process." In particular, online discussions allow for the development and expansion of an individual's capacities, by presenting increased "think time," and furthermore, by providing a transcript of dialogue that can be read and re-read, giving that individual the opportunity to clarify his or her thoughts in writing and decreasing the pressures of face-to-face discussions.

Background of Study

The research plan comprised the use of online technology-supported and face-to-face discussions to assess the effects of perceived curiosity of individual students utilizing a blended learning approach. Students enrolled for the BBA program constituted a large pool of available subjects, who qualified satisfactorily within the context and purpose of this study.

Course Structure

FB2501 "Management of Information Systems (MIS2)" was an undergraduate course offered to BBA students in the School of Information Systems at the City University of Hong Kong. This course provided students with an understanding of the role of computer-based information systems in business organizations. Emphasis was placed on management and technical concepts essential to business applications and management control of information systems. Procedures and controls used in maintaining communication channels were an integral part of the course. On completion of this course, participants were able to:

1. Understand the concept of an Information System and the crucial role it plays in all organizations.
2. Explain how to leverage the use of human and capital assets through Information Technology.
3. Recognize the technologies needed to implement Information Systems.
4. Outline how Information Systems are developed.
5. Assess the risks involved in the development of Information Technology.
6. Evaluate the costs and benefits of Information Technology use.

Technology

The specific type of learning activity employed in this research, was online discussions using the "Virtual Classroom" tool of the "Blackboard" online learning platform. The "Virtual Classroom" has increasingly becoming a much wider used platform, from which it is easier to teach a broad range of different topics and it also provides an opportunity for participants to engage in collaborative discussions. The "Blackboard Virtual Classroom" consists of two parts - a whiteboard and a chat room. The whiteboard area allows an instructor to display web pages and to draw on them. The chat room allows students and an instructor to communicate with each other and consists of three pages, the "Chat Panel," "Questions" and "User Info."

The "Chat Panel" is the default panel, the chat room where participants enter messages in the "Text Entry Box" (Figure 2 below). Once they press "Enter," all the participants in the chat room are able to see the comments posted in the chat display area. The "Questions" section allows participants to type questions to the instructor. When the instructor responds, participants are able to see both the question as well as the response(s) from the instructor. The "User Info" section lists the participants who are currently logged into the "Blackboard Virtual Classroom."

When using the "Blackboard Virtual Classroom," each participant sits in front of a computer terminal. The computer screen is divided into two halves. The participant composes messages on the bottom half and when ready, hits the send button. The message appears immediately on the upper half of every participant's screen, which also contains all the entries posted by all the participants. This screen is scrollable, making it is effortless for participants to read or re-read carefully what others have been discussing. The entries are listed in chronological order, with identifiable names of senders. The participants can read each others' entries at their own pace on the upper screen and thereafter, type in messages at leisure on the lower screen, without interference from incoming messages. These types of programs have introduced the possibility of real-time, synchronous, many-to-many discussions, used either by the whole class or by small groups within the class.

Figure 2. Example of Virtual Classroom. ©2009 Ronnie H. Shroff. Used with permission.

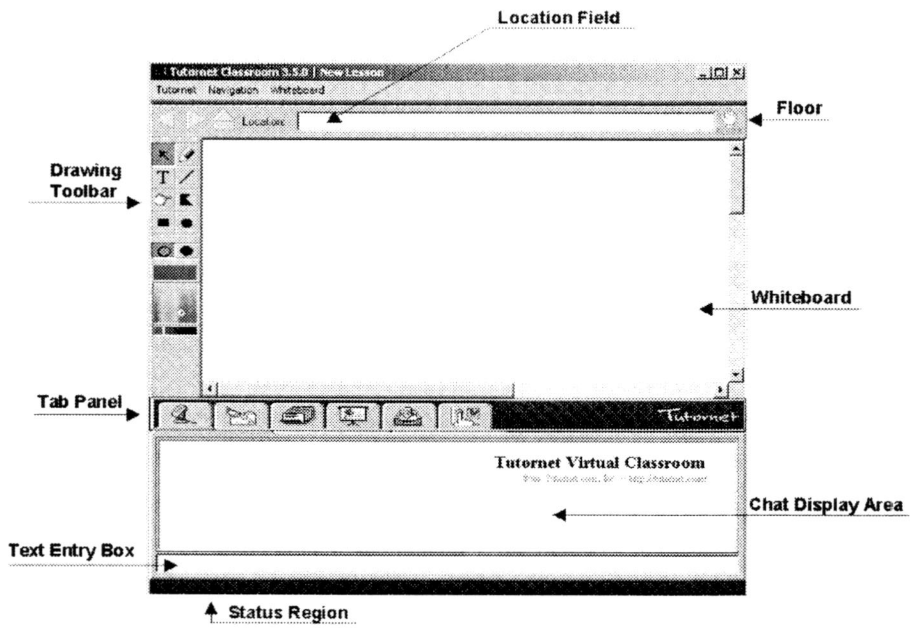

Teaching Methods as the Course Framework

When designing the learning activity, the Teaching Assistant (i.e. the researcher) was mindful about applying the content material to the course, and thereby meeting the course objectives. The Teaching Assistant was also versatile in the the use of "Blackboard." Designing and implementing the course activities was a challenging part of this course. Given that learning outcomes and course content had been defined clearly, the Teaching Assistant had to decide between varieties of activities to achieve these goals. A combination of activites and tasks, within the mix of technology-supported online discussions and face-to-face discussions were tailor made for this purpose. Activities for both technology-supported online discussions and face-to-face discussions were designed to reflect real-world complexities, in order to promote student-student dialogue, idea sharing and articulation of views.

Procedure

Classroom activities were organized around whole-class discussions and revolved around forums and debates for both technology-supported online discussions and face-to-face discussions. Both online discussions within "Blackboard" and face-to-face discussions were used to support student-student and student-instructor collaboration, to promote the free flow of ideas. Combining the unique characteristics of synchronous communications utilizing "Blackboard," with various common course goals, offered students the following useful educational tools:

1. A break from the classroom environment, which permits students to relax and creates a certain level of excitement about and engagement in class discussions.
2. A chance to participate in "real-life" scenarios directly related to their writing assignments.
3. Direct exposure to the importance of voice/tone in written communication, due to the immediate feedback students get from what they submit to the group.
4. An opportunity for students to test their preconceptions about how society "works," by eliminating certain factors such as appearances or membership of social groups and then examining whether and how their online groups work differently from "regular" societal exchange.
5. Experience portraying a favorable self-image, face and persona through language in real time.
6. Activities in both the online versus face-to-face discussions were designed to allow students to engage in discussions, thereby demonstrating ideas, posing questions, offering insights, advancing suggestions and revealing a broader and deeper understanding of the issues at hand.

The Research Setting

Students currently enrolled in the Bachelor of Business Administration (BBA) program and taking the FB2501 "Management of Information Systems (MIS2)" course, constituted a large pool of available interviewees that fit well within the context and purpose of this study. Interviewing a student sample from the BBA program helped to ascertain the generalizability of this study across populations. In addition, casting a wider net in the data collection stage, helped to cross-check data and served, "As a strategy that added rigor, breadth and depth to [the] investigation", (Denzin & Lincoln, 1994). For this study, we interviewed a total of seven students enrolled in the BBA program. A total of seven interviews appeared to be reasonable, both with respect to the goals of this study and the feasibility involved for the purpose of the study.

Respondents were selected using a two-stage sampling procedure. In the first stage, the FB2501 "Management of Information Systems (MIS2)" course was selected and in the second stage individuals were chosen from the FB2501 course. Seven students who were exposed to the online and face-to-face discussions were interviewed from the course. The selection of this course was based on the following criteria: Firstly, this course provided a rich opportunity for applying both technology and non-technology support to both online and face-to-face classroom environments. Secondly, learning activities in the form of online and face-to-face discussions were structured into the design and organization of the course. We expected students to engage in "expert-like" ways of thinking, acting and problem solving (i.e. making interpretations, engaging in negotiations, providing rationales and reaching conclusions) in both the online and face-to-face discussions.

Interviews for the FB2501 course students took place during the first half of semester B. Resources used in interviewing included paper, a recorder, recording tapes, writing instruments and a quiet place for conducting the interviews. The unit of analysis for this data collection was the individual (i.e. the student). In-depth interviews were planned and conducted using a printed, standardized instrument as an interview guide for semi-structured interviews. The interview protocol minimized bias by providing a basis for a consistent sequence and approach to interviews (see Appendix). This was done by adopting consistent wording for the applicable questions and by asking each question in the same way to each participant, in order to minimize bias.

The procedures used for conducting the interviews were performed as follows: Participants were first scheduled for a 60(sixty)-minute session in a private room. They were asked to read and sign the informed consent form, following which they were asked if they had any pertinent questions for the researcher. The description of the research was read, which allowed for the participant to ask any questions to clarify the nature of the study and his or her expectations for participation. Following the project description, participants were asked a series of open-ended questions in a semi-structured format from the interview guide. If a question did not apply in the context of a particular participant, we skipped to the applicable question. Participants were encouraged to describe situations in significant detail and were asked follow-up questions to draw emerging meanings (Rubin & Rubin, 1995).

Case Study Measures

A semi-structured interview outline was developed to study the impact of the online and face-to-face discussions on the construct of perceived curiosity chosen from the literature and research model previously described. Measures were developed for the following construct of perceived curiosity covered in the interviews - that perceptions of individual curiosity will be higher in online discussions, as compared to face-to-face discussions (Shroff, Vogel, Coombes, & Lee, 2007). Questions relating to individual perceived curiosity were asked, such as the extent to which the online and face-to-face discussions promoted the ability of an individual to investigate, study or analyze - look into or explore, etc. The following three measures are factors supporting the degree of perceived curiosity in the online and face-to-face discussions. Perceived curiosity was measured (see Table 2) by the extent to which these factors were present or not present in the assigned activity.

The interview questions were generated using the construct of curiosity in the literature review and research model. The construct of curiosity is highlighted in the work on "The Self-Determination Theory" by Deci and Ryan (1985) and related work on curiosity by Berlyne (1954) and others (Dember & Earl, 1957; Keller, Schneider, & Henderson, 1994). Individual students with

Table 2. Measures of curiosity

Discover	Get to know or become aware of or make a new finding (Spielberger & Starr, 1994) .
Explore	The potential ability of an individual to investigate and explore the relationship between the tasks and his or learning abilities (Keller, Schneider, & Henderson, 1994).
Query	A request for information or posing a question in an attempt to search for information (Henderson, 1989).

acceptable English skills were selected to be interviewed from the FB2501 course. The objective was to interview them with the motive of exploring the influence of online and face-to-face discussions, relative to the construct of curiosity. Semi-structured interviews were used with leading open-ended questions, so that participants were able to reflect on the meaning of their experiences during the interviews and thus engage themselves in a deeper exploration of the meaning ascribed to their motivational behavior.

Data Analysis Procedures

In our data analysis, information was represented in the form of matrices that displayed information (tabular information showing relationships among categories of information) in a spatial format, thereby presenting that information systematically to the reader (Miles & Huberman, 1984) as well as enabling the identification of the coding procedures to be used, in order to reduce information to themes/categories (Tesch, 1990). We expected the categorization and themes to emerge from: (1) Ongoing comparison; (2) Themes generated from the literature review; (3) Themes embedded in instrument questions; (4) Themes embedded in research questions; (5) A combination of any of the above. The stages of the coding process (Figure 3) are shown below:

Coding was guided by a coding scheme that was derived from constructs and ideas found in the relevant literature (a so-called start-list of

Figure 3. Coding process

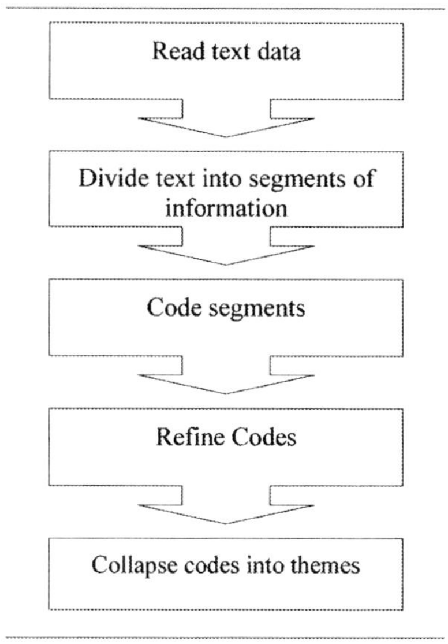

codes). Data refinement included selecting and thus simplifying the data that appeared in the transcriptions. The objective was to code the categories and group and organize these categories, so that conclusions could be reasonably drawn and verified. Data were displayed in matrices (see Table 3 for example), thereby illustrating the patterns and findings from the data.

Analysis and coding of the data transcripts, presented in matrices and displays, were used to visualize and represent the data, thus enabling further discovery of patterns in the issues raised by the participants.

Table 3. Classification for coding of interview responses

Construct/ Concept	Code	Measure	Sub-Code
Curiosity	CU	Discovery	CU-DIS
		Exploring	CU-EXP
		Query	CU-QUE

ANALYSIS OF QUALITATIVE RESULTS

The qualitative data relating to students' perceptions in the online discussions provided a valuable overview of the overall student experience and the results are discussed herewith in detail. Our results are summarized in Table 4 below, aligned with the embedded units design, with "+" and "-," indicating positive and negative comments, respectively based on the coding scheme illustrated above in Table 3. For example, "+CU" under Interviewee 1, indicates a positively related comment with respect to the construct of "perceived curiosity (CU)" and measure of "exploring," indicated by sub-code CU-EXP.

If we examine the issues from the construct of curiosity previously discussed as illustrated in Table 3, we find that perceived curiosity (CU) was positively (indicated by "+") supported by all seven interviewees and recognized in the online discussions with regard to discovery (CU-DIS), exploration (CU-EXP) and query (CU-QUE). We interpreted from the following statements that perceptions of individual perceived curiosity are higher in online discussions, as compared to face-to-face discussions.

For example, Interviewee 1 noted that, "If I typed in my own comments and didn't look at theirs, they will tell me that next time I need to look more at their comments, their opinions and not just formalize my own, so I need to explore (CU-EXP) different options. The online discussions made me disclose more information than face-to-face and I got more responses from my colleagues which helped me to build stronger interactions."

Interviewee 2 explained, "...sometimes you want to say something but you find that others have already pointed it out, so it will encourage you to search for more points so you can add more opinions. The online discussion provided guidance and gave me opportunities to explore (CU-EXP) from different angles. For example, when my instructor or colleagues posted some thought-provoking questions (CU-QUE) or some surprising statements, I felt the need to explore the conflict, until it was resolved and then posted my solutions and comments."

To summarize, there was agreement among students that the online discussions were motivating and invoked their curiosity. As Interviewee 3 stated:

"Quite motivated I think. I haven't fully adapted to it, but I think it has many advantages like new ideas...hmmm...may be more complete opinions and things...it's quite good. For example, I felt motivated to raise questions (CU-QUE) and test my own knowledge like brainstorming and answering questions posted by my colleagues. The online discussion also helped me to foster my own curious (CU-EXP) ways by adding more questions and looking from different perspectives....and this helped me to build my own confidence."

Table 4. Summarized results

Interviewee 1	Interviewee 2	Interviewee 3	Interviewee 4	Interviewee 5	Interviewee 6	Interviewee 7
+CU (CU-EXP)	+CU (CU-EXP) (CU-QUE)	+CU (CU-QUE) (CU-EXP)	+CU (CU-DIS)	+CU (CU-QUE) (CU-EXP)	+CU (CU-DIS) (CU-EXP)	+CU (CU-DIS)

As Interviewee 4 declared:

"Hmmm…I will motivate myself to think about more points and offer more information to others and then we can form our solution in our group. I felt motivated because a lot of different opinions rush to you and a lot of fresh ideas come to your mind .I was able to find the solutions for myself and come up (CU-DIS) with new ideas."

The online discussions encouraged "independent learning," while "managing" teaching and learning with reduced tutor contact and use of online technology, which was largely perceived by students as desirable and effective. Commenting on this, Interviewee 5 said, "I think I am highly motivated by using the online discussion. For example, I had a strong desire to know the facts (CU-QUE) and to monitor my progress, investigate (CU-EXP) different perspectives…and my performances made me feel good as I was able to share my feelings with others and feel a sense of closeness."

Thus, the online discussions enabled and encouraged a "learning to learn" approach and we had proof of this, as is evident from the following opinions of Interviewee 6:

"As I mentioned before, with the online discussions, we can learn from others but we have to concentrate more, while it is easier to move onto other topics with the face-to-face discussions. As we could chat about other things very easily, the online discussions increased our efficiency. Posting comments enhanced my expression and I felt more fluency and able to elaborate and be more creative in my thinking."

"I think it's also highly effective because of the information ways…the ways the information is provided and also I said it's more efficient to use this, because we cannot discuss about some stupid things. So I feel it is [online discussions] very effective in assisting my learning. It also gave me a desire to learn the facts, the desire to know (CU-DIS) and also investigating (CU-EXP) different possibilities"

Moreover, our findings from the qualitative study illustrated that some students would have preferred to attend the online discussions at their own convenience or participate from wherever they were. As a student pointed out, "I think only this course has provided the online discussions and we have only been able to discuss in the class, in this tutorial and we don't have time to discuss online outside of the class on other occasions."

Finally, a more widely held perception among students was that the skills of presentation and communication in the online discussions were also useful and convenient from a more practical standpoint. For example, Interviewee 7 was of the opinion that, "Of course we pay more attention to both the skills of presentation and skills from the book during the presentation. The presentation is mixed with those most useful things and that's the part I like very much. The online discussions helped us to list important points to reach agreement on which is the most important success factors and then this helps us to present more effectively, make new findings (CU-DIS)."

From an overall perspective, the results demonstrated that students were comfortable using technology supported online discussions, through application of the "Blackboard Virtual Classroom." Students excelled in the use of the "Blackboard Virtual Classroom" and these online discussions demonstrated strong support for the construct of perceived curiosity.

DISCUSSION

Most of the comments generated by students in the interviews were consistent in supporting the construct of curiosity and its measures. The following emergent trends were noticeable:

- Compared to face-to-face discussions, all students perceived that online discussions aroused their curiosity, given the rich nature of the discussions and the more personal interactions with each other and the tutor. These types of synchronous activities seemed more familiar to them and gave them ample opportunities to influence and further explore the directions of the topics under discussion.
- A significant benefit arising from the online discussions was that these discussions compelled students to give more serious thought to the issues being discussed online and the effects the use of technology has on their learning behaviors.
- Yet another noteworthy advantage of communicating via computers was an individual development of thoughts and ideas, feeling part of or a sense of inclusion in an online community, gaining insights about different people and learning from each other. This also included the advantages of overcoming isolation, enhancing personal self-esteem and confidence and finally, making it appear to be less threatening to be able to contact others. Students felt that by utilizing computers for online discussions, they could learn faster, become more creative and write better. They accepted that they had more control over their learning behaviors and more opportunities to practice their written English dialogue skills. Resulting from these advantages, the online discussions appeared to enhance their curiosity for learning.
- Compared to face-to-face discussions, participants in the online discussions seemed less apprehensive about being evaluated by others and more willing to participate in the discussions. They felt less affected by wait-time, turn-taking and other elements of traditional face-to-face interactions, thereby enabling them to participate as much as they wanted to in the discussions, along with opportunities for gainful contributions being more uniformly distributed among them.
- Students who were shy or felt inhibited in face-to-face discussions, found a "voice" in online discussions and tended to participate more actively in these discussions.

The subjects, whom we interviewed for this study, appeared to derive pleasure from the online discussions, because these discussions provided them with a level of surprise, conflicting discrepancy and novelty. Curiosity is stimulated, when something in the physical environment attracts an individual's attention or when there is an optimal level of discrepancy between his or her present knowledge and skills and what these could be, if the individual engaged in an activity. Most of the subjects in this study were participating in online discussions for the very first time, and were able to assimilate this new experience into their schemata. Individual curiosity seemed to have been further aroused as the online discussions placed participants in active roles of exploration, investigation and discovery, thereby, enabling them to use the electronic interface in meaningful ways, so as to awaken their innate sense of curiosity. Our results showed that the online discussions positively enhanced individual student perceptions of curiosity. In addition, online discussions supported feedback in the form of verbal rewards, such as praise or positive comments generated by the students. Overall, our students found that the online discussions aroused their curiosity and permitted them to make their own decisions, exercise control and set their own pace in the online activities.

Designing technologies to stimulate curiosity is more about designing effective strategies that are more appropriate for existing and available technologies. Lowenstein explained curiosity, in terms of an information-gap and the need to seek information in order to close that gap (Loewenstein, 1994). Curiosity is both a state and a trait. As a state, curiosity is commonly experienced by all individuals, wherein all events arouse a state of curiosity in almost all individuals. However, curiosity is also a trait which is much more typical of some individuals than others. In this context, the trait varies between individuals, in that some individuals will see some events as intriguing or strange or peculiar, while other individuals will consider those events as holding little interest for them (Spielberger & Starr, 1994). This differentiation should be an important consideration in designing for various technologies.

Not only is it necessary to be concerned about which design strategies will stimulate curiosity in a situation-specific context, but it is also imperative to address an individual's differences, in his or her pre-disposition to be curious when presented with novel, incongruous, complex and unfamiliar stimuli (factors that stimulate curiosity). This would be especially relevant in designing interactive learning environments, such as online discussions that could extend an individual's state of curiosity into what Csikszentmihalyi (1988) refers to as flow - where just the right amount of stimulation leads to intrinsic motivation. Online discussions, for example, could be used in such a way as to encourage extended exploration on a regular basis, such that they contribute to increasing trait curiosity.

In summary, research on the construct of curiosity has typically been seen as a positive factor supporting individual intrinsic motivation. This type of exploratory and curious behavior is performed for its own sake, independent of external reinforcements, consequently promoting conditions for intrinsic motivation to occur. Thus, activities that appeal to curiosity or invoke exploratory behavior are thought of as intrinsic and performed for intrinsic reasons.

LIMITATIONS

There are several limitations of the present study that need to be considered. The key limitations center around: (1) Generalizability between groups and individuals (2) Mediating factors (3) Potential for bias (4) Over-interpretation of the findings with a lack of triangulation.

To elaborate, firstly, the results of this study cannot be generalized between groups and individuals. Since the unit of analysis of this study is the individual student, the findings of this study cannot directly be generalized at the group level of analysis. Secondly, this study does not take into account mediating factors such as individual beliefs and values. The fact that the learners are individuals, with their own predetermined beliefs and values, may have a significant impact on their motivational dispositions. The motivation for taking the course is an important mediating factor, because different students may take the course for a variety of different reasons and therefore, their expectations for course success may differ. Similarly, a certain amount of inquisitiveness about the subject matter is important, from the viewpoint that not all students may be enrolled in the course because they find the course content interesting or intriguing. In addition, the level and type of skills (i.e. teamwork and communication) of individual students may differ and thus affect their motivational behavior. For example, a student experienced in working in teams may show a higher degree of motivation to engage in team discussions, as compared to a student with no experience of working in teams.

The third limitation observed in this study was a potential for bias. For example, because the construct of perceived curiosity was composed of an individual's perceptions of personal phenomena, self-report methods were necessary. Nonetheless, future work can reduce these potential confounds via longitudinal designs, objective procedures and behavioral measures. The fourth limitation addresses an over-interpretation of the findings with a lack of triangulation. Future research may benefit from using other sources of data such as computer file exchange, electronic meeting logs and online discussion transcripts. Data could be analyzed in relation to specific key participants, settings, behavior and activities, relevant to the theoretical framework and the emergent interests and outcomes. Additionally, other dependent variables, such as fantasy (Malone & Lepper, 1987; Parker & Lepper, 1992) and control (Harter & Connell, 1984), referred to earlier and creativity (Amabile, 1996), could also extend the scope of future studies.

FUTURE RESEARCH DIRECTIONS

For future research, we would strongly suggest investigating various aspects of Malone and Lepper's research on individual variables such as fantasy, playfulness and control (Malone & Lepper, 1987). Valuable information can be garnered from such research. For instance, Malone and Lepper (1987) mentioned that, the extent to which individuals are treating technology systems, "Not as tools to achieve external goals, but as toys to use for their own sake," increases the fantasy and control aspects of the system. This may actually explain why the male gender tends to dominate the field of computers and technology systems - this is because research has found that they tend to view the computer as a toy and not as a tool (Giacquinta, Bauer, & Levin, 1993).

The above suggestion for future research could potentially build upon our results, because such research may be essential in order to improve our understanding of the effects of perceived curiosity of individual students utilizing a blended learning approach. For example, the results of this study can be used as base-line data for future quantitative studies. In addition, the qualitative results garnered from this study may also enable the development of improved methods of integrating technology into the classroom environment and can consequently be used as a knowledge construction tool, in which individual students work together in a collaborative setting. Such a learning environment allows students to actively discover their own thought processes and apply new knowledge appropriately.

CONCLUSION

With reference to the main effects of online discussions and face-to-face discussions on individual perceived curiosity, the findings of the qualitative study indicated that online discussions were found to lead to a more positive perception of an individual's curiosity compared to face-to-face discussions. The subjects, whom we interviewed for this study, seemed to derive pleasure from the online discussions, because these discussions provided them with a level of surprise, conflicting discrepancy and novelty. Individual curiosity could have been further aroused, if the online discussions had placed participants in active roles of exploration, investigation and discovery, to enable them to use the electronic interface in meaningful ways, so as to awaken their innate sense of curiosity. When activities heighten curiosity, then an individual is naturally involved and driven to learn.

An individual's ability to explore the environment proficiently is an increasingly meaningful trait that defines his personality. By its very nature, an individual's motive (i.e. curiosity) to explore the environment is presumably an innate behavior that enables him or her to gain information about an object or his or her environment. Research on curiosity and its subsequent exploratory behavior, could help us make decisions about designing strategies into learning environments such as multimedia, web, online discussions etc., that trigger and sustain individual curiosity and the motivation to learn. Keeping this in mind, it would be interesting to investigate different online discussion platforms that lead to a higher probability of invoking individual curiosity, where such activities lead to prolonged individual engagement, new learning and ultimately, to intrinsically motivated behavior. This study is a cautious yet assured step towards understanding the effects of blended learning on perceived curiosity of individual students.

REFERENCES

Alavi, M., & Leidner, D. E. (2001). Research commentary: Technology-mediated learning-a call for greater depth and breadth of research. Information Systems Research, 12(1), 1–10. doi:10.1287/isre.12.1.1.9720doi:10.1287/isre.12.1.1.9720

Amabile, T. M. (1996). Creativity in context. Boulder, CO: Westview Press.

Berlyne, D. (1950). Novelty and curiosity as determinants of exploratory behavior. The British Journal of Psychology, 41, 68–80.

Berlyne, D. (1954). A theory of human curiosity. The British Journal of Psychology, 45, 180–191.

Berlyne, D. (1960). Conflict, arousal, and curiosity. New York: McGraw Hill.

Berlyne, D. (1965). Curiosity and education. In J. D. Krumboltz (Ed.), Learning and the educational process (pp. 67-89). Chicago: Rand McNally.

Berlyne, D. (1978). Curiosity and learning. Motivation and Emotion, 2, 97–175. doi:10.1007/BF00993037doi:10.1007/BF00993037

Berlyne, D., & Frommer, F. (1966). Some determinants of the incidence and content of children's questions. Child Development, 37, 177–189. doi:10.2307/1126438doi:10.2307/1126438

Bleed, R. (2001). A hybrid campus for a new millennium. EDUCAUSE Review, 36(1), 16–24.

Bonk, C., & Graham, C. (2005). Handbook of blended learning: Global perspectives, local designs. San Francisco, CA: Pfeiffer Publishing.

Bosworth, K., & Hamilton, S. J. (1994). Collaborative learning: Underlying processes and effective techniques. San Francisco: Jossy-Bass.

Boyle, T. (2005). A dynamic, systematic method for developing blended learning. Education, Communication, and Information. Special Issue on Blended Learning, 5(3), 221–232.

Boyle, T., Bradley, C., Chalk, P., Jones, R., & Pickard, P. (2003). Using blended learning to improve student success rates in learning to program. Journal of Educational Media, 28(2-3), 165–178. doi:10.1080/1358165032000153160doi:10.1080/1358165032000153160

Cifuentes, L., Murphy, K., Segur, R., & Kodali, S. (1997). Design considerations for computer conferences. Journal of Research on Computing in Education, 30(2), 177–210.

Csikszentmihalyi, M. (1988). The flow experience and its significance for human psychology. In M. Csikszentmihalyi & I. S. Csikszentmihalyi (Eds.), Optimal experience: Psychological studies of flow in consciousness (pp. 57-97). New York: Cambridge University Press.

Deci, E. L., & Ryan, R. (1985). Intrinsic motivation and self determination in human behavior. New York: Plenum Press.

Deci, E. L., & Ryan, R. M. (1985). The general causality orientations scale: Self-determination in personality. Journal of Research in Personality, 19, 109–134. doi:10.1016/0092-6566(85)90023-6doi:10.1016/0092-6566(85)90023-6

Dede, C. (1996). Emerging technologies in distance education for business. Journal of Education for Business, 71(4), 197–204.

Dember, W. N., & Earl, R. W. (1957). Analysis of exploratory, manipulatory, and curiosity behaviors. Psychological Review, 64, 91–96. PubMed doi:10.1037/h0046861doi:10.1037/h0046861

Denzin, N. K., & Lincoln, Y. S. (1994). Handbook of qualitative research. Thousand Oaks, CA: Sage.

Dziuban, C. D., Hartman, J., & Moskal, P. (2004). Blended learning. Educause Center for Applied Research Bulletin, 7, 1–12.

Edelson, D. C., Pea, R. D., & Gomez, L. (1995). Constructivism in the collaboratory. In Constructivist learning environments: Case studies in instructional design. Englewood Cliffs, NJ: Educational Technology Publications.

Garrison, D. R., & Kanuka, H. (2004). Blended learning: Uncovering its transformative potential in higher education. The Internet and Higher Education, 7(2), 95–105. doi:10.1016/j.iheduc.2004.02.001doi:10.1016/j.iheduc.2004.02.001

Giacquinta, J. B., Bauer, J. A., & Levin, J. E. (1993). Beyond technology's promise. Cambridge: Cambridge University Press.

Harter, S., & Connell, J. P. (1984). A model of children's achievement and related self-perceptions of competence, control, and motivation orientation. Advances in Motivation and Achievement, 3, 219–250.

Henderson, B. B. (1989). Individual differences in exploration: A replication and extension. The Journal of Genetic Psychology, 149, 555–557.

Hiltz, S. R. (1990). Collaborative learning: The virtual classroom approach. Technological Horizons in Education Journal, 17(10), 59–65.

Jonassen, D., Peck, K., & Wilson, B. (1999). Learning with technology: A constructivist perspective. Upper Saddle River, NJ: Merrill Publishing.

Kashdan, T. B., & Fincham, F. D. (2004). Facilitating curiosity: A social and self-regulatory perspective for scientifically based interventions. In P. A. Linley & S. Joseph (Eds.), Positive psychology in practice (pp. 482-503). New Jersey: Wiley.

Keller, H., Schneider, K., & Henderson, B. (1994). Curiosity and exploration. Berlin: Springer-Verlag.

Klemm, W. (1999). Eight ways to get students more engaged in online conferences. The Journal of Higher Education, 26(1), 62–64.

Kreitler, H., & Kreitler, S. (1976). Cognitive orientation and behavior. New York: Springer.

Leidner, D. E., & Jarvenpaa, S. L. (1995). The use of information technology to enhance management school education: A theoretical view. MIS Quarterly, 19(3), 265–291. doi:10.2307/249596 doi:10.2307/249596

Livson, N. (1967). Toward a different construct of curiosity. The Journal of Genetic Psychology, 111, 73–84. PubMed

Loewenstein, G. (1994). The psychology of curiosity: A review and reinterpretation. Psychological Bulletin, 116(1), 75–98. doi:10.1037/0033-2909.116.1.75doi:10.1037/0033-2909.116.1.75

Malone, T. (1981). Toward a theory of intrinsically motivating instruction. Cognitive Science, 3, 333–369.

Malone, T., & Lepper, M. (1987). Making learning fun: A taxonomy of intrinsic motivations for learning. In Aptitude, learning, and instruction, vol. 3, cognitive and affective process analyses. New Jersey: Lawrence Erlbaum.

Miles, M. B., & Huberman, A. M. (1984). Qualitative data analysis. A sourcebook of new methods. Beverly Hills, CA: Sage.

Novak, G., Gavrin, A., Christian, W., & Patterson, E. (1999). Just-in-time teaching: Blending active learning with Web technology. New York: Prentice Hall Series in Educational Innovation.

Ocker, R., & Yaverbaum, G. J. (2002). Collaborative learning environments: Exploring student attitudes and satisfaction in face-to-face and asynchronous computer conferencing settings. Journal of Interactive Learning Research, 12(4), 427–448.

Osguthorpe, R., & Graham, C. (2003). Blended learning environments definitions and directions. The Quarterly Review of Distance Education, 43(3), 227–233.

Parker, L., & Lepper, M. (1992). The effects of fantasy contexts on children's learning and motivations: Making learning more fun. Journal of Personality and Social Psychology, 62, 625–633. PubMed doi:10.1037/0022-3514.62.4.625doi:10.1037/0022-3514.62.4.625

Pearson, P. H., & Maddi, S. R. (1966). The similes preference inventory: Development of a structured measure of the tendency toward variety. Journal of Consulting Psychology, 30, 301–308. doi:10.1037/h0023540doi:10.1037/h0023540

Rubin, I. B., & Rubin, H. J. (1995). Qualitative interviewing: The art of hearing data. Thousand Oaks: Sage.

Shroff, R. H., Vogel, D. R., Coombes, J., & Lee, F. (2007). Student e-learning intrinsic motivation: A qualitative analysis. Communications of the Association for Information Systems, 19(12), 241–260.

Spielberger, C. D., & Starr, L. M. (1994). Curiosity and exploratory behavior. In H. F. O'Neil, Jr. & M. Drillings (Eds.), Motivation: Theory and research. Hillsdale, NJ: Erlbaum.

Tesch, R. (1990). Qualitative research: Analysis types and software tools. New York: Falmer.

Thorne, K. (2003). Blended learning: How to integrate online and traditional. London: Kogan Page.

Vaughan, N. (2007). Perspectives on blended learning in higher education. International Journal on E-Learning, 6(1), 81–94.

Vogel, D., Shroff, R. H., Kwok, S., & Coombes, J. (2002, September 2-4). Student e-learning intrinsic motivation: A qualitative analysis. Paper presented at the Pacific Asia Conference on Information Systems, Tokyo, Japan.

Vygotsky, L. S. (1978). Mind in society. Cambridge, MA: Harvard University Press.

Walker, C. O., Greene, B. A., & Mansell, R. A. (2006). Identification with academics, intrinsic/extrinsic motivation, and self-efficacy as predictors of cognitive engagement. Learning and Individual Differences, 16(1), 1–12. doi:10.1016/j.lindif.2005.06.004doi:10.1016/j.lindif.2005.06.004

Warschauer, M. (1997). Computer-mediated collaborative learning: Theory and practice. Modern Language Journal, 81(5), 470–481. doi:10.2307/328890doi:10.2307/328890

Zuckerman, M. (1971). Dimensions of sensation seeking. Journal of Consulting and Clinical Psychology, 36, 45–52. doi:10.1037/h0030478doi:10.1037/h0030478

APPENDIX

Student Interview Protocol

For Case Study on Individuals' Perceptions of Curiosity

(Note: Interviews will be conducted with FB2501 students. This document focuses on the student interview protocol)

[Interviewer Note: As the opening of the interview, the interviewer will introduce himself and provide a brief idea of the interview objective]

[Interviewer Note: The following demographic and general questions will be used to provide additional background and engage the interviewee in talking about the topic area]

Demographics

Personal information (introduction icebreaker)

a. Can you give me a brief overview of yourself?
b. What general aspects of education do you find most interesting?

The Course in General

1. In general, why did you choose to study this course?
2. What are your course expectations?

[Interviewer Note: The type of learning activity to be examined within the FB2501 course is the online discussions using "Virtual Classroom" of "Blackboard". The following sections strive to examine the use of the "Virtual Classroom" relative to the theoretical construct of curiosity underlying this interview.]

Perceived Curiosity

If curiosity is to be stimulated, the role of the environment is to provide an individual with activities/ opportunities to probe and explore (Keller, Schneider, & Henderson, 1994; Spielberger & Starr, 1994). Questions relating to individual perceived curiosity were asked, such as the extent to which the online and face-to-face discussions promoted the ability of an individual to investigate, study or analyze - look into or explore, etc.

3. Compared to the face-to-face discussions, did the online discussions arouse your curiosity about the topics being discussed?
4. Compared to the face-to-face discussions, did the online discussions encourage you to probe and explore a variety of issues you might not have otherwise considered? What are some specific examples?

[Interviewer Note: the focus of the following section would be to get some specific feedback related to technology support that may inhibit or encourage the degree of exploratory behavior]

Technology Support

5. Overall, how self-motivated were you in the online discussions compared to the face-to-face discussions? Can you provide some specific examples
6. How effective were the online discussions in assisting you in your learning compared to the face-to-face discussions?

Final Comments

7. Are there any other things you would like to add or comment upon?

Chapter 8
Online Discussion and E-Mentoring Strategies in Blended Continuing Education Courses

Lung-Hsiang Wong
National Institute of Education, Singapore

Chee-Kit Looi
National Institute of Education, Singapore

ABSTRACT

This study analyzes online discussions in a course portal that supplemented class discussion in three continuing education courses. Our student groups were full-time professionals who studied on a part-time basis. We use and adapt some elements of Henri's model for content analysis to quantitatively and qualitatively analyse the online discourse (Henri, 1992). Transcript content analyses show that students' messages were on-task, thoughtful, and indicative of student-initiated learning and a good amount of peer help. While other studies have studied effective discussion through similar forums or computer-mediated instruction, we emphasize the role of the e-mentors in promoting and mediating the discussions. We discuss factors that contributed to the effective use of the discussion forums for fostering learning, including e-mentors' enthusiasm in responding to the messages, and e-mentoring strategies. We also induce several strategies adopted by the e-mentors in facilitating online forum discussions.

INTRODUCTION

In this chapter, we analyze online content arising from student discussions in a Knowledge Portal (KP) which supported three postgraduate courses in an institute that typically consist of both classroom and online components, i.e., they are blended learning courses. Our student groups were full-time professionals who studied for a Masters in Software Engineering (SE) or Knowledge Engineering (KE) on a part-time basis. To support student-student and student-instructor online interaction outside of the classroom, a number of collaboration features are provided, such as an online discussion forum, chat room, protected folders, group space and content

DOI: 10.4018/978-1-60566-852-9.ch008

access tracking in the portal. We collected a variety of evidence regarding the usage of the portal, in particular that of the discussion forums.

As Guzdial & Turns (2000) noted, simply making a discussion forum available does not mean that it will be used effectively to enable learning. Guzdial, Ludovice, Realff, Morley & Carroll (2002) did an extensive use of their CoWeb collaboration tool in a variety of Math, Engineering and Computer Science courses. CoWeb supports anchored collaboration which is an online discussion. The researchers pointed to a variety of causes for lack of collaboration, including too much competition, a sense of learned helplessness, and faculty issues.

Our study aims to contribute to this discourse. In particular, we study the role of e-mentor facilitation of the online forums for an audience of students who typically are very busy because they also hold full-time jobs. We are especially interested in studying e-mentoring and assistance to analyze online e-mentors' interaction styles, such as social and cognitive acknowledgement, questioning, direct instruction, modeling, and encouragement and facilitation of discussion. Not many of the studies of online content analysis focus on the roles and strategies played by the online instructors or e-mentors. Doing a content analysis, we induce several e-mentoring strategies adopted by the course e-mentors in facilitating and promoting online discussions. Our research questions are:

1. For the adult students of the blended learning courses supported by KP, what are their participatory attitudes and their posting patterns on the online forums on the KP?
2. What are the online forum facilitation strategies exercised by the e-mentors of the KP that are not only theory-grounded but are efficacious in being able to boost the quantity and the quality of the students' postings?

LITERATURE REVIEW

Frameworks for online analysis of online activity abound in the literature (Blake & Rapanotti, 2001; Rourke, Anderson, Garrison & Archer, 2001). As online collaborative learning proliferates, there is a need for evaluation and instructional frameworks that will help researchers, educators, and policy-makers evaluate students' online collaboration. In a review of research methodologies in online collaborative environments, Henri (1992) has developed one of the most sophisticated cognitive analysis models for online interaction. She delineated five dimensions related to the quality of the messages:

1. The quantitative posting rate of the participants.
2. Content that reflects the social dimension of conference interchanges.
3. Content relating to the interactive dimension of the conference.
4. Content indicating the application of cognitive skills.
5. Content showing metacognitive skills.

In our context, the Henri (1992) framework was chosen to evaluate the effectiveness of the online discussion group because it allowed for analysis of a range of aspects of an online discussion, the level of participation in the form of usage statistics, the nature of the interaction between contributors, and an indication of the learning process through an analysis of the cognitive activity evident in the message content.

Hara, Bonk & Angeli (2000) analysed online discussion in an applied educational psychology course in which they adopted the technique of getting students to be a "starter" and "wrapper" of discussions. A starter is supposed to read the material so that she can explain it to the others and foster the discussion, while the wrapper is supposed to summarize and bring closure to the discussion. They used Henri's (1992) model for content analysis of computer-mediated communication to qualitatively analyze the electronic discourse. Their study showed that students were using high level cognitive skills such as inferencing and judgment as well as metacognitive strategies related to reflecting on experience and self-awareness. Weekly conference activity graphs revealed that student electronic comments became more interactive over time, but were highly dependent on the directions of discussion starter.

Asynchronous, online discussions are a relatively new, student-centered form of learning with respect to traditional way of highly structured, didactic instruction that most of the present adult learners are used to. As such, the learners have to be convinced of the effectiveness of online discussion as a learning tool. If the learners perceive and experience online discussion as a valued process, they will then be more likely to participate actively in it (Rogers, 1995). As was also found in other studies (Greer, McCalla, Vassileva, Deters, Bull & Kettel, 2001), "knowledge investment by the authorities" in a course seems to have an important influence on usage. The participation of the e-mentors is critical at the outset of a course to stimulate usage of the system. There is much that e-mentors can do to promote and build increasingly productive use of the medium to scaffold the learners in achieving independent and socio-constructivist learning (Salmon, 2004). Indeed, e-mentoring is a craft that has general principles and strategies – that can be learned (Collison et al, 2000). Good e-mentors know when and how to take part, to provide expert input, to act as a peer, and to stay silent (Salmon, 2004).

From a survey of the returns of a questionnaire completed by 135 online instructors, Beaudin (1999) found that the online instructors rated the following as the top four techniques for keeping asynchronous online discussion on topic: (1) Carefully design questions that specifically elicit on-topic discussion; (2) Provide guidelines to help online learners prepare on-topic responses; (3) Reword the original question when responses are going in the wrong direction; (4) Provide discussion summary on a regular basis. Lim & Cheah (2003) studied the perceptions and experiences of pre-service teachers on the roles of their tutors in the online discussion forum and proposed six techniques (although they positioned them as (tutor's) "roles") to address the learners' needs: (1) Setting meaningful task; (2) Guiding participants in the 'technicality' of online discussion; (3) Participating actively by answering queries, providing feedback and posing conflicting views to elicit thinking/reflection; (4) Keeping the discussion focused; (5) Drawing conclusions and providing content expertise; (6) Recommending resources for extension of learning.

Berge (1991), Paulsen (1995), and Mason (1995) divided the typical responsibilities of online instructors in three similar categories: organizational (or managerial), social, and intellectual (or pedagogical). In turns, Anderson, Rourke, Garrison & Archer (2001) proposed the notion of "teaching presence" in the context of computer conferencing, defined as "the design, facilitation and direction of cognitive and social processes for the purpose of realizing personally meaningful and educationally worthwhile learning outcomes." The framework consists of three categories – design and organization (overlapping of "organizational" and "pedagogical"), facilitating discourse (predominantly "social"), and direct instruction (predominantly "pedagogical"). The conceptual framework could be used for understanding, measuring and improving the important function of teaching presence within asynchronous online discussions. However, as Wozniak & Silveira (2004) has noted, there has been little research that specifically looks at the type of instruction or strategies required for learners to interact effectively with each other beyond describing the general roles of the e-mentors during asynchronous discussion.

STUDY DESCRIPTION

In this study, we analysed three runs of two courses offered by the above-mentioned KP portal which included two runs of the Masters of Technology Genetic Algorithms (GA-1 and GA-2) course, and the Intelligent Agents (IA-1) course. A total of 139 student places were taken up for GA-1, GA-2and IA-1. The courses combined live and online approaches to instruction, i.e., five week of live instruction in class concurrent with the use of the Knowledge Portal that continues until the course examination date. All of the students were full-time professionals with at least one basic degree. Most of their jobs or professions were related to Information and Communication Technologies with a small number of other students coming from various technical backgrounds like mechanical, civil or bio engineering. As far as we know, most of the students did not have prior experience in e-learning or in education-oriented online forums before they were enrolled in these courses.

The system, which is an integral part of the Institute of Systems Science (ISS) Community Portal, was developed using the open-source and the Python programming language. The course portal for organizes learning materials such as PowerpointTM slides used in the classroom sessions, and resources (such as useful web links). Figure 1 shows a screenshot of the discussion forum used for GA-2. The portal has a e-Mentor center which provides facilities to support forum-related activities such as tracking the number of contributions sent by each student, viewing all contributions by a student, sending template-emails to students based on their participation patterns, and providing a student audit trail such as log-in, log-out, the objects she accessed and at what times. Figure 2 shows a screenshot that summarizes some postings for the user.

We coded the forum discussions post-mortem by categorizing individual student postings into "problem", "explanation", "proposal", "disagreement", "comment" and "summary". Subsequently, we analyzed the posting patterns of the discussion forums by working out the week-by-week descriptive statistics of the categories of postings. Concomitantly, we studied the e-mentors' postings to mine or induce e-mentoring strategies that have proven effective in boosting the quantity and the quality of subsequent student postings. We then mapped or associated individual strategies to relevant prior literature and frameworks to see if these strategies are theoretically grounded or even theory challenging. It is hoped that our compilation of the strategies could become a guide or tool for e-mentoring practitioners in motivating students to effectively participating in such peer learning activities.

FINDINGS

Electronic Participation Findings

We analyzed the number of threads posted, the average number of messages per thread, and the average number of messages sent per student in a course (see Table 1). A total of 590 messages were posted in all the online discussions. On the average, 2.8, 5.4 and 2.4 messages were posted by each student in GA-11, GA-2 and IA-11 respectively. 10%, 18% and 15% of the messages in GA-11, GA-2 and IA-11 were contributed by the e-mentors, respectively.

Putting the online discussions in the context of the overall course which comprises mainly classroom sessions and workshops, there were lively, animated, and dynamic discussions during the classroom sessions. The e-mentors also made efforts to read the issues and discussion points in the forums, and subsequently raised and summarized these issues in the classroom sessions. These inter-weaving of conversations, online and in-class, allow more thoughtful and deep thinking of the concepts, skills and practical issues covered in the traditional classroom. They are indications that the social space for students to build common

Figure 1. Screenshot of discussion forum for GA-2. ©2009 Wong Lung Hsiang. Used with permission.

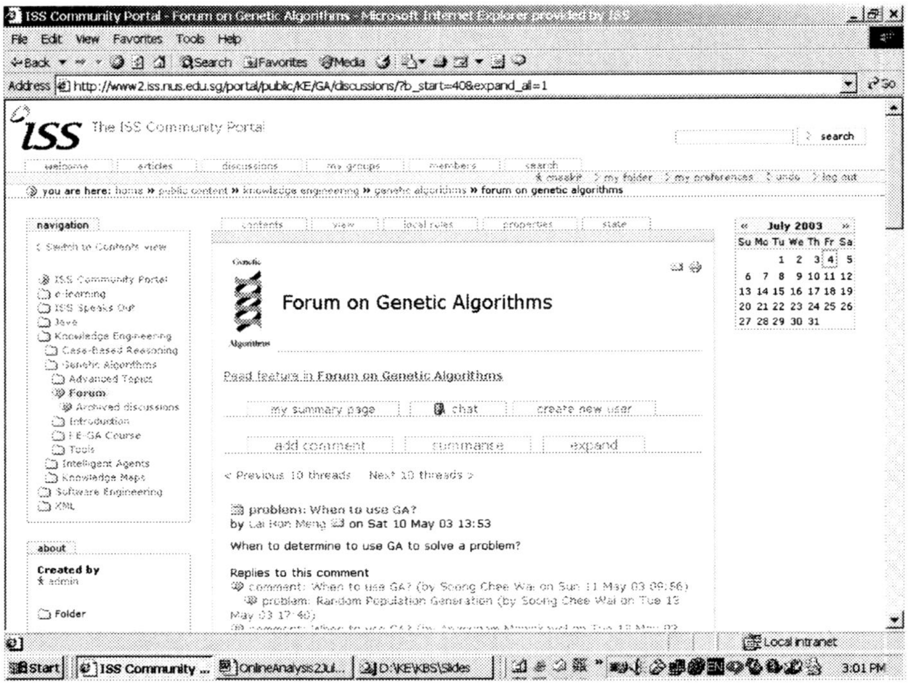

Figure 2. Screenshot of summary page in discussion forum for GA-2. ©2009 Wong Lung Hsiang. Used with permission.

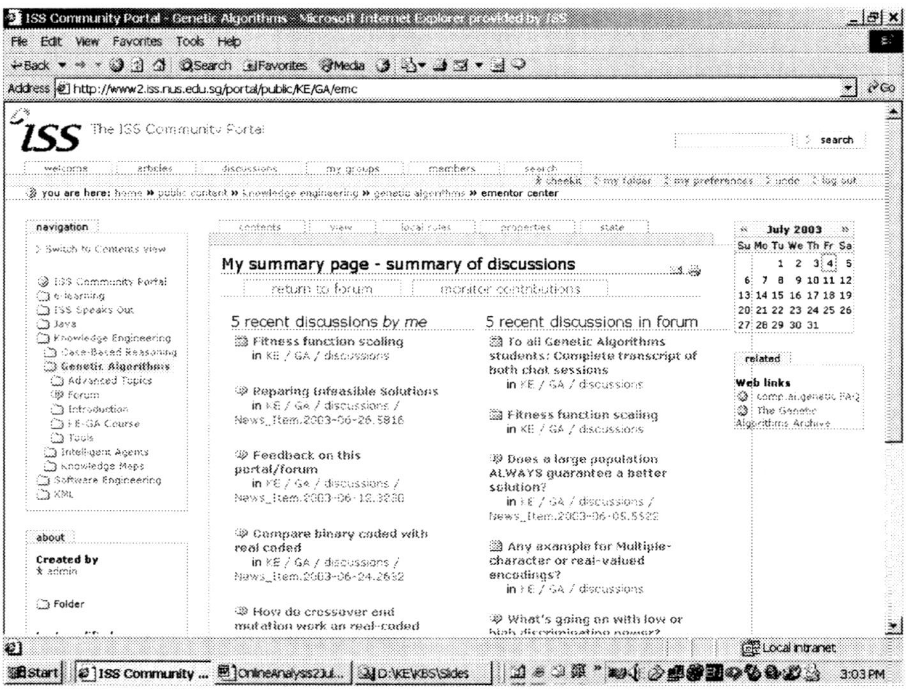

Table 1. Participation rates of the 3 courses

	GA-1	GA-2	IA-1	All courses
# of students	65	43	29	137
total # of threads created	66	75	35	176
total # of messages posted	200	274	116	590
# of messages posted by instructor 1	10	15	9	34
# of messages posted by instructor 2	9	34	10	48
# of messages posted by students	181	225	102	508
avg # of messages per thread	3.0	3.7	3.3	3.4
avg # of messages per student	2.8	5.2	3.3	3.7

knowledge and intersubjectivity extends beyond the electronic conference (Hara, Bonk & Angeli, 2000). They are also indications that learning arises from the set of activities in a classroom, and the KP environment is one support for those activities (Guzdial & Caroll, 2002).

Many of the message threads are started by students who posted the message to resolve their lack or misunderstanding arising from the classroom discussions. Here is an example of a message started by a student in GA-1 who could not follow the classroom discussions even after reading the course materials:

Schemata in GA - 101

I've been trying to understand what this "Schemata in GA" is for some time now, but I still could not figure out what it's all about (even after going through the course materials). Can we start some discussion on this topic? I'd like to know (probably from lay man's view first) what's its importance to GA and how it can be used in real situations by citing examples that you may have. Everyone is welcomed to contribute anything as long as it will help people like me understand "Schematas" more.

Here are students' comments when asked if they found classroom discussion more useful or forum discussion more useful:

Both are useful. In-class discussion, we could be able to get answer or correction immediately; while forum discussion enable us to post question or discussion with sufficient time of reflection.

The classroom discussion was more useful as it helps me to clarify doubts straightaway. However, it lacks the records of other students' discussions which might prove useful as well. The forum on the other hand store records of other discussion but lacks the spontaneity of classroom discussion. So I believe a combination of these 2 is good.

To elicit participation, the e-mentors of the three courses had made conscious efforts to log on regularly to model good discussions. The two runs of GA in two successive years bear out some positive evidence of sustainability. The experiences of the e-mentors in running the first run seem to be useful in making more effective use of the forum in the second run.

E-Mentoring Strategies

Perhaps the most important contribution of this study is our identification, analysis and compilation of the effective e-mentoring strategies arouse which has the potential of becoming prescriptive strategies for future forum facilitators. As we have been trying our best to make the list of strategies as comprehensive as possible, we have also tried to glean such strategies from other courses running on the same KP like C++ Programming and IT Project Management.

On the other hand, in developing their "teaching presence" framework, Anderson et al. (2001) iidentified and coded typical indicators of each of the following categories in the postings of several online forums of some postgraduate courses offered by their university, namely, design and organization, facilitating discourse, and direct instruction:

- Design and organization: e.g., setting curriculum; designing methods; establishing time parameters; utilizing medium effectively; establishing netiquette;
- Facilitating discourse: e.g., identifying areas of agreement/disagreement; seeking to reach consensus/understanding; encouraging, acknowledging or reinforcing student contributions; setting climate for learning; drawing in participants; assessing the efficacy of the process;
- Direct instruction: e.g., presenting content/ questions; focussing the discussion on specific issues; summarizing the discussion; confirming understanding; diagnosing misconceptions; injecting knowledge from diverse sources; responding to technical concerns.

The examples of dissections of the e-mentors' postings cited in the paper (e.g., "This week we will be discussing ..." or "I think we are getting a little off track here" as indicators of "design & organization" and "facilitating discourse" respectively) demonstrate the e-mentors' conscious application of e-mentoring strategies even though the authors do not explicitly position them as such – instead, the sub-categories are part of the coding scheme. This framework is well-grounded in a model of Community of Inquiry (Garrison, Anderson & Archer, 2000) that prescribes crucial elements for teachers and students to co-construct better understanding in the subject matters, which was one of the major goals of the KP portal's forum facilitation practice. Therefore, we adopt this framework for analyzing and explaining the strategies that we have identified.

Books on e-mentoring or e-coaching (e.g., Collison et al., 2000; Salmon, 2000; Bender, 2003; Watkins, 2005; Shank, 2007) have suggested different types of strategies for promoting online discussions. Analyzing the messages in the three forums, we unraveled a number of specific strategies used by the e-mentors to stimulate participation and contribution. We distinguish two types of strategies: proactive strategies, where e-mentors start a discussion thread, and reactive strategies, where e-mentors respond to students' postings. The classification is analogous to Henri's (1992) classification of all postings (by e-mentors or students in education-oriented discussion forums) as "independent statement" (a posting that initiates a thread) and "explicit response" (a posting that is directly linked to a previous message). We feel that it is a useful distinction from the practitioner's point of view.

We identified the following e-mentor's proactive strategies:

1. Starting all the major topic threads
2. Asking an open-ended, opinionated relevant question at the early stage of the course
3. Asking the students to relate the subject matter to real-life situations
4. Designing a proposing or critiquing task
5. Linking thread topics to appropriate resources or activities
6. Breaking a complex question down into more than one posting
7. Challenging the students to reflect their overall impression of the subject matter or review their own learning objective(s) towards the end of the course
8. Stimulating examples and counter-examples
9. Entrapping the students (perhaps by asking a misleading question and then provide a counterexample)

We identified the following e-mentor's reactive strategies:

1. Summarizing/Regulating a thread that lacks focus (convergence)
2. Summarizing in the middle of a discussion thread
3. Re-formulating a student's problem
4. Inviting student who has posted existing resource to summarize or comment on it
5. Putting the question back to the students based on the empirical or hands-on work they have done, or their past experiences
6. Modelling how to answer a question or part-of, and prompting the other students to respond to the rest of the questions
7. Holding back your views to let other students participate in the discussion
8. Stimulating student to compare and contrast the concept in question with related concepts that she already knows
9. Entrapping the students (perhaps by asking a misleading question and then provide a counterexample)

Proactive Strategy I: Starting all the Major Topic Threads

Many researchers have documented the challenge to the e-mentor of synchronizing activities so that the students feel 'in sync' with the rest of the class (Salmon, 2004). On the other hand, Laurillard, Stratfold, Luckin, Plowman & Taylor (2000) argue that the teacher's task is to create a narrative path through the mediated instruction and activity such that students are aware of the learning goals and activities in which they participate – especially if the instruction and the activities are to take place in a non-linear learning medium like online discussion forum.

This strategy may provide a solution to these issues. The motivation of this strategy is to ensure the forum's comprehensive coverage of all major topics or modules or chapters in the course. For each topic, the e-mentor decides whether to post a "plain" initial message to kick off the discussion to ask some open-ended questions that could stimulate discussion, or to design a relevant online task or case study. Before the course, he designs one or a few questions or tasks for each module of the course. After the course has kicked off, he posted each of them at strategic timing – usually 'in sync' with the recommended starting time of learning each corresponding module. Hence, this strategy could be viewed as a meta-strategy as it reinforces a structure throughout the whole course of an online forum while the e-mentors may apply different strategies in designing individual messages that kick start topic discussions.

Proactive Strategy II: Asking an Open-Ended, Opinionated Question at the Beginning

The e-mentors should understand that students may be self-conscious regarding the quality and quantity of their contributions to the discussion, particularly during the initial weeks of the classes (McCracken, 2006). In the following example, the IA e-mentor adopted the proactive strategy of asking an open-ended, opinionated relevant question at the early stage of the course. The objective of this strategy is to encourage the students who are new to the subject to post personal, perhaps superficial views yet without the pressure to "get it correct." The challenge is getting the students to be courageous enough to be heard and make their first postings. The strategy may follow through to invite the students, in the same posting, to revisit the thread and post their revised views towards the end of the course. This will assure the students that their first postings are not "the end of the story" but they are welcome to revise their views later – to eliminate their mental pressure to "get it correct" and the fear of being embarrassed by posting "wrong" thoughts. Hence, this strategy is a perfect "setting climate for learning" indicator under "facilitating discourse" of the teaching presence framework.

Here is an example of such a message posted by the e-mentor in IA-1:

Topic: Is Agent Technology old wine in new bottle?

Many IT professionals have been skeptical in Agent Technology, calling it "old wine in new bottle." This is probably because plenty of software developers have been loosely using the cool, trendy term of "agents" to describe their relatively "conventional" software, even though some of those do incorporate some intelligence.

Please share with us how do you find this argument (i.e., how do you perceive "agents") prior to completing our course. By the end the course, you may revisit your arguments to see if you wish to change your thoughts.

This message resulted in the longest thread of messages, 19 in all, which was seen in the three forums.

Proactive Strategy III: Asking the Students to Relate the Subject Matter to Real-Life Situations

The e-mentor encourages the students to think of how the knowledge they have just learned could be applied to real-life situations. This strategy is especially good for the early stage of the course, where the students' motivation and enjoyment in forum participation come from personal and experiential communication (Preece, 1999). The challenge is not to pressurize the students to offer opinion as we would expect from a practicing professional or expert but to encourage them to be creative and imaginative. Therefore, similar to Proactive Strategy II, such a strategy is helpful in setting a good climate for learning and sharing. Here is an example at the beginning of the GA-1 online discussions:

Topic: Discussion item 1: Examples of GA applications in your everyday life

To get you started in this discussion forum, we've got a simple ice breaker - describe an application of GA in your everyday life. Feel free to take liberties with reality, to propose possibly outrageous problems or solutions.

No matter what your take is, you will need to describe in detail the problem at hand, why you think GA is applicable, how you think GA can be applied to solve the problem, a detailed model of the problem, and the advantages and disadvantages of the solution.

It's your turn now!

Proactive Strategy IV: Designing a Proposing or Critiquing Task

The motivation of this strategy is to stimulate the students to propose and critique the given materials or the proposals made by their counterparts. E-mentors need to be creative in designing such tasks, for example, dramatic or controversial cases which could foster extensive student interaction (Bonk, et al., 2001). Yet the tasks should be relatively simple so that they could be carried out on the forum and they are engaging and attractive to the students, as suggested by (Klemm, 1998). The tasks should be open-ended such that the information can be interpreted and discussed from multiple perspectives and alternative solutions can be generated (Veerman & Veldhuis-Diermanse, 2001). Students may also be broken into pairs or groups to facilitate a lower level but perhaps more intimate peer learning. A higher level challenge is to ensure that the task is not just an 'add on', but an integral part of the learning environment (McKenzie & Murphy, 2000).

Here is an example that we have gleaned from the IT Project Management forum – the e-mentor presented a case study and then created six sub-threads to let the students discuss on the case in depth and in an organized manner:

Case Study: Project Tracking and Control

... (case description omitted) ...

Sub-thread 1: What are the considerations to compute anticipated or predicted end-date based on progress to date?

Sub-thread 2: Should we predict future performance based on increased man-effort?

Sub-thread 3: What are your comments on the difference between planned and actual spend in task 1 to 8?

Sub-thread 4: What are the constraints on the project, e.g., when must the software be completed?

Sub-thread 5: In terms of the current progress on the project, what observations can be made on the completed tasks and what could be the explanation?

Sub-thread 6: How would you proceed to draw the Gantt Chart that show actual progress, starting from the first task?

Proactive Strategies V: Linking Thread Topics to Appropriate Resources or Activities

Since the forum participants are already online, checking out various Internet resources on the issues discussed would be convenient and invaluable. Thus, the e-mentor should organize and make easily available the widest possible range of resources for learning (Addesso, 2000). The motivation of this strategy is to foster supplementary discussion on and perhaps collaborative learning in "official" assignments, readings, projects, exercises, or in the context of blended learning, the latest or upcoming topic to be taught at the 'live' classroom sessions. E-mentors need to know how to initiate the discussion on each activity in a compelling manner and stimulate individual students to share knowledge and opinions instead of providing information overload to the students.

Proactive Strategy VI: Breaking a Complex Question down into more than One Posting

The motivation is to guide students through a step-by-step thinking process and reduce their confusion in dealing with complex problems. E-mentors need to make sure that each question is relatively easy so that at least one student will post an answer; and the e-mentor could post subsequent questions. Here is an example that we have gleaned from the C++ Programming forum:

Topic: Problerm: Object Slicing

Author: Mary (e-mentor)

Heard of Object Slicing Problem?

Topic: Explanation: Object Slicing

Author: Shanti (student)

When we are "passing a derived object by value" to a function that takes a "base object by value" may cause a problem known as "object slicing". Every additional data member declared in the derived object should be omitted. The resultant object contains only the data members declared in the base class.

Topic: Problem: Object Slicing & Exception Handling

Author: Mary

Yes, that's a good explanation. Can you relate this to exception handling? Could this happen when you catch exceptions by value?

Proactive Strategy VII: Challenging the Students to Reflect their Overall Impression of the Subject Matter or Review their own Learning Objective(s) towards the End of the Course

The motivation is to stimulate the students to synthesize what they have learnt from a high-level holistic perspective and to internalize the knowledge learned. E-mentors ask the right questions so that they are not too heavy to, and yet thought-provoking. The strategy can proceed with the e-mentor briefly presenting both positive and negative existing views (perhaps with provocative words) to stimulate thinking. Here's an example from GA-2:

Topic: Your View on GA

Can you share your views of GA as we are close to finishing the classroom sessions of this course? Maybe you are inspired ... we can learn much from biology or we can have a good shot at deriving good solutions to not-well-understood optimization problems, or you are thinking - so what? what's the big deal as it is just another optimization technique?

This could be a companion strategy for Proactive Strategy II, "Asking an opinionated, open-ended question at the beginning." An e-mentor may utilize both strategies at the beginning and the end of a course respectively. In the thread generated with Proactive Strategy VII, the e-mentor may consider advising the students to compare their present views on the course with their earlier views as posted in the earlier thread generated with Proactive Strategy II.

Proactive Strategy VIII: Stimulating Examples and Counter-Examples

The motivation is to stimulate the students to examine the knowledge or skills from different directions, under different situations or exceptions. It involves the students in analytical thinking as they are required to understand not only the content as a whole but also the constituent parts involved in its structure (Bender, 2003). The challenge is to identify arguable, open-ended or exception-prone pieces of knowledge in order to apply this strategy.

Topic: Building blocks - some additional notes

I would like to re-inforce some of the concepts in the session on Theoretical Foundations & Practical Issues. We introduce the idea that GAs process not only individual chromosomes but also, implicitly, schemata or schemas. A schema is a set of individuals in the search space. Think of a GA as directing the search towards schemas *containing highly-fit regions of the search space. Consider individuals coded as bit (binary) strings. < text omitted > E.g. suppose we have a problem for which an individual solution is represented as "02278294" using a number representation. Suppose further that this problem contains 2 subproblems, the solutions to which are represented by non-overlapping sets of genes. Suppose the first subproblem is represented by the 2nd & 3rd genes, so that its solution can be described by the schema X22XXXXX and that the second uses genes 5 & 7, and is solved by members of the schema XXXX8X9X. So, these 2 schemata are building blocks which can be combined to form a better solution X22X8X9X. Now, can you think of more examples (problems and their solution encoding)? Can you also think of other counter-examples to this idea of building blocks (I presented one such example in the class)?*

Proactive Strategy IX: Entrapping the Students (perhaps by Asking a Misleading Question and then providing a Counterexample)

Prior knowledge might cause some stickiness to old, incorrect ideas and unconscious resistance to change. Even if instructors have taught well, the students may not understand correctly if the teacher remains unaware of the way students think (Bender, 2003). The motivation of this strategy is to bring students through a critical thinking process which is appropriate for correcting students' misconceptions. The challenge is to carefully phrase your questions and responses without offending, satirizing or discouraging the students.

We have presented the proactive strategies induced from the empirical data. We next discuss the reactive strategies we induced from our analysis of the online discussions.

Reactive Strategy I: Summarizing/ Regulating a Thread that Lacks Focus

The objective is to steer the discussion onto the "right" track, i.e., increase the relevancy of subsequent postings, by stimulating new or alternative interpretations. The mentor needs to strike a balance between being too open-ended and the provision of a specific sense of direction to steer the discussion towards. It might involve making a judgment on whether the lack of focus would be actually beneficial to the discussion as it might encourage alternative ideas.

Reactive Strategy II: Summarizing in the Middle of a Discussion Thread

Similar to the notions of "weaving" (Salmon's, 2004) or "landscape" (Collison, Elbaum, Haavind & Tinker, 2000), the e-mentor gleans some insights from various posts to generate further dialogue or to juxtapose and stimulate deeper meaning or application. The goal is to prompt students to reflect on the progress of the discussion and to contribute new thoughts. This is consistent with Anderson et al.'s (2001) assertion that the teacher's summary could serve to develop and delineate the context in which knowledge growth has taken place. The challenge is to understand the difference between the "wrapping-up summary" and the "discussion extending summary," and invoke one of them at the appropriate time. The e-mentor needs to judge whether the discussion should continue to evolve if there is still room for further exploration, or to wrap it up if the discussion has become "saturated".

Reactive Strategy III: Re-Formulating a Student's Problem

The crux of this strategy is that instead of posting a direct reply to a student's message, either clarify, rephrase or re-negotiate the definition or discussion in the problem to guide the student towards a clearer or more obvious thinking direction, which could still reach the same or a similar conclusion. This is a strategy which has been addressed by Winiecki (1999) as well. The challenge in applying this is to determine the student's cognition, work out alternative ways of expressing the problem, and possibly predict her thinking process after the problem is rephrased. Here is an instance of the strategy applied in GA-2:

Topic: GA's memory

Author: Manick

Can GA get into an infinite loop?

As we learnt in the last lecture, GA does not have any memory about its previous generations. If it is true, is there a possibility to get the same old population after many cycles of "Selection, Cross-over and mutation". Can GA get into a kind of infinite loop?

Topic: GA's memory: Consider it from a problem space perspective

Author: Peter (e-Mentor)

Hi Manick,

I'd like to paraphrase your question in a slightly different way - consider the problem from the perspective of a complex problem space.

Remember those difficult problem spaces we looked at in class? There were hilly ones, plateaus and even egg cartons.

So, what would be the consequence of the GA optimisation process under such circumstances?

By the way, this question is not addressed to Manick alone but to the whole class. What do the rest of you think about this?

Reactive Strategy IV: Inviting the Student who has Posted an Existing Resource to Summarize or Comment on it

This strategy emerges as some students posted the URLs of content-related web resources without giving any comment or summary. The e-mentors then made such a request to ask the student to analyze and appraise the online resources, thereby boosting other students' interests to go through and co-assess them (Watkins, 2005). Students would not only evaluate the resources for quality and reliability, but should also be encouraged to discuss how their contents are (or could not be) linked to the course materials and earlier discussion threads. They are encouraged to seek meaningful integration or synthesis of the online resources with what they have already learned. The challenges in implementing this strategy successfully include phrasing your request so that the student will comply, and possibly briefly offering her own view or set some relevant problems out of the posted resource to stimulate further discussion.

Reactive Strategy V: Putting the Question back to the Students Based on the Empirical or Hands-On Work they have Done

In this example, the e-mentor responded briefly to a student's question on whether there is any methodology of formulating the penalty function in GA, and then turned it back to all the students.

Topic: GA - Penalty Function

<text omitted>The penalty function should compute to some value that penalizes the fitness value, but should not dominate it (i.e. the quantum of the penalty function should be a fraction of the fitness function). In this way, we can allow for the "slight" violation of some soft constraints - provided the solution is still an acceptable solution.

What experience did you have with the different penalty functions in the case studies?

Reactive Strategy VI: Modelling how to Answer a Question or Part-of, and Prompting the Other Students to Respond to the Rest of the Questions

This strategy seeks to promote peer learning and interaction. The challenge is to decide which part and to what extent the e-mentor should give away the answers and stimulate further discussion. In this example, the e-mentor responded to a student message that was laden with many questions:

Topic: GA vs Constraint Programming (CP)

Author: Sandy (student)

Lesson 1 examples using Evolver appears to run in cycles, at times instable with no end in sight, even with the best prior knowledge on crossover & mutation rates. CP (e.g. using OPL) seems to be able to solve these classes of problems more elegantly, with better UI.

Is this perspective accurate? If so, why bother using Evolver, or GA in general for these classes of problems? Or OPL has GA within? Or is GA related to CP? Or GA can do other problems that CP can't?

Topic: GA vs Constraint Programming (CP)

Author: Peter (e-mentor)

In constraint programming (CP), we have a set of hard constraints to satisfy. CP will reduce the search space (using constraint satisfaction techniques) into the set of feasible values which satisfy all the hard constraints. <text omitted>

A GA handles constraints somewhat differently. One way is to include a penalty term in the fitness function. This is called a soft constraint and it is equivalent to allowing the solution to violate a constraint by trading solution quality against penalty (I will cover this in the session on Theoretical Foundations & Practical Issues). <text omitted>

You have a lot of questions in your one message:) Can the others comment or answer some of the other questions? (e.g. what type of problems are suitable for a GA solution? for a CP solution?)

Six messages by students followed after this thread trying to address the different questions.

Reactive Strategy VII: Holding back your Views to let Other Students Participate in the Discussion

E-mentors as "guide on the side" (versus "sage on the stage") have been advocated by the literature (e.g., Collison et al., 2000; Salmon, 2004). As McCracken (2006) stated, virtual interactions in online learning communities is ideally a collaborative inquiry process as a result of design by e-mentors through a willingness to relinquish traditional classroom direction to prioritize collaboration and discourse, and the ability to allow students responsibility in their own learning processes and outcomes. In this strategy, the e-mentor seeks to avoid situations where the students hold back after reading what they perceived to the "authoritative" view or answer from the e-mentor. In the context of our student culture, the power distance is large, and hence there is the danger of e-mentor inadvertently bringing a closure to a discussion thread. The challenge in implementing this strategy is to decide when to hold back or whether part of instead of whole of the e-mentor's views could be given to stimulate a more meaningful discussion.

Reactive Strategy VIII: Stimulating the Student to Compare and Contrast the Concept in Question with related Concepts that she already knows

This strategy may train the students in how to cope with the lack of information by processing (e.g., generalizing, specializing, etc.) their existing knowledge, that is, it becomes a process of unlearning and relearning. The challenge in applying this strategy is about how to "pick and match" students' existing knowledge that is related to the present concept in question. At the same time, the e-mentor must prevent possible interpretations of advocacy and control seeking in order to create and maintain a spirit of open dialogue (Collison et al., 2000). We gleaned the following example from the Fundamentals of Knowledge Engineering course where the students discussed about various AI search algorithms:

Topic: Hill-Climbing Algorithm

Author: Leonard

For Hill-climbing method, we choose the next node to expand, by comparing how "promising" each node is, and selecting the most promising one. In the Road Traversal Problem, many peers I have spoken to, judge how promising the next node is, by taking that node's Euclidean distance to the destination. In my approach, however, I decided that the level of promise shown by any node X, should be the sum of (link cost between current node and node X) + (Euclidean distance from node X to destination).

<text omitted>Comments please?

Topic: Hill Climbing Algorithm

Author: L.H. (e-Mentor)

Does anybody think this modified Hill-Climbing Algorithm looks like A Algorithm? Would you like to make a comparison between A* and the proposed algorithm?*

(Two students then discussed in depth the differences between the two algorithms and agreed that the modified Hill Climbing Algorithm was indeed a more efficient algorithm. To wrap up the discussion, the e-Mentor posted another reply to point out a major limitation of the original Hill Climbing Algorithms which the proposed modification did not solve despite bearing some resemblance with the more powerful A* Algorithm.)

Reactive Strategy IX: Entrapping the Students (perhaps by asking a Misleading Question and then providing a Counterexample)

This strategy is similar to Proactive Strategy IX ("Entrapping the students") except that it occurs in the e-mentor's reply to a student's posting which may reflect a misconception.

Content Coding and Analysis

Transcript content analyses showed that students were able to help peer students in answering questions, and providing explanations, comments and summaries of various messages in a discussion thread. Several students posted questions and comments on issues that extend the teaching covered in class. As one student put it,

The forum does help increase my understanding because there were questions or opinions in there that I would have never had thought of.

One lurker who did not participate still found the forum useful:

I found it is very useful. I followed the forum postings closely and learned a lot. Personally I felt bad in not participating in the forum. In my case it took some time for me to catch-up the concept of GA. I spent some time on learning the basics. By the time I get familiar with basics, the course gets completed by 70%. I was away from forum, as I got answers for my doubts from my fellow students or from the forum itself. But later I realized I should post those questions in the forum. It may be useful for others.

As e-mentors, we created a learning environment where students were in charge of their own learning. We did not structure any activity that would require them to use the forum. However, we did post leading questions especially in the initial stages to stimulate participation. In the GA-2 course, we have added a feature that requires the message poster to tag the contribution as one of problem/question, explanation, proposal/idea, disagreement, comment or summary. A problem/question is someone wanting an issue resolved, and an explanation is one such response. A proposal/idea may be an alternative response that takes a look at the problem from a fresh perspective; additionally, a proposal/idea may also be used by students with a bright idea that he or she may not have encountered in the literature or lecture sessions.

Almost all of the discussion threads were initiated by students who posted the message as a "problem" type or to a lesser extent, "comment" type. A message posing a "problem" is typically followed by responses which are:

1. "comments" by different posters
2. "explanations" by different posters
3. more "problem" messages, in which students posed their version of a related problem

This suggests that many students used the forum as a mechanism to seek solutions to any problem or question they have.

We can loosely map the scheme we are using with Hara's cognitive skills coding:

- Problem -> Elementary Clarification
- Explanation -> In-depth Clarification OR Judgment
- Proposal -> Elementary Clarification OR Inferencing OR Application of Strategies
- Disagreement -> Judgment
- Comment -> In-Depth Clarification
- Summary -> In-depth Clarification OR Inferencing

Like (Hewitt & Teplovs, 1999), we observed that messages acquired most of their responses in the first few days after they are initially posted to the forum, and the odds of a response drops dramatically with time.

Table 2 shows the quantitative data of the forum discussion weekly for GA-1. Classroom sessions lasted only for the first 5 weeks. The online discussions continued to be active in the 6th and 7th weeks, and lasted until the 13th week just before the course examinations were held. At the time when the course was running, the KP does not require the poster to tag the message into the contribution type. Thus the types were coded post-mortem by one of the GA e-mentors. The majority of postings were "comments" with a good number of "problems", "explanations" and "proposals." We observed that students themselves provide a good number of explanations and comments, indicating a good amount of peer help. Students also posted personal experiences, comparisons and contrasts, and references from readings.

Table 3 shows the quantitative data of the forum discussion weekly for GA2003. Classroom sessions lasted only for the first 5 weeks. The number of messages increases from Week 1 to Week 4 and peaked there. Student continued to participate from Week 5 onwards even though the course has completed all the classroom sessions.

Unlike GA-1, the tagging of the messages for GA-2 into the contribution types was done by the message contributor. A walkthrough of the contents of the messages shows that in general the contribution type is an accurate label for the message, except that many students seem to use "Comments" as a modest way to describe their message even though it has elements of an explanation. Table 3 also shows that the majority of contributions are "Comments" which is the typical way the students tagged their messages when they responded to a "Problem" or "Proposal". Only two "Summary" comments were posted by the e-mentor which shows that students were not yet at the level of synthesizing concepts and issues. There is also a low number of "Disagreements" which reflected the non-confrontational stance of the messages.

Table 4 shows the quantitative data of the forum discussion weekly for IA2002. At the time when the course was running, the KP did not require the poster to tag the message into the contribution

Table 2. Message contribution types exhibited in GA-1[1]

Week	Problem	Explanation	Proposal	Disagreement	Comment	Summary	TOTAL
week 1	0	0	1	0	4	0	5
week 2	4	5 (1)	3 (2)	0	4 (1)	0	16
week 3	17 (1)	9 (1)	3	1	23 (3)	1	54
week 4	3	4 (3)	2	0	7	0	16
week 5	3	6 (1)	10 (1)	0	10 (3)	1	30
week 6	2	5 (1)	6	1	6	0	20
week 7	4	10	18	4	6	0	42
week 8	0	2	0	0	4	0	6
week 9	0	0	0	0	0	0	0
week 10	0	0	0	0	0	0	0
week 11	0	0	0	0	0	0	0
week 12	0	1	2	0	6	0	9
week 13	0	1 (1)	1	0	0	0	2
Total	33	43	46	6	70	2	200

Table 3. Message contribution types exhibited in GA-2

Week	Problem	Explanation	Proposal	Disagreement	Comment	Summary	TOTAL
week 1	5 (2)	1	9 (1)	0	6 (2)	0	**21**
week 2	7 (1)	1	5 (1)	0	15 (4)	2 (2)	**30**
week 3	7	13 (4)	7	1	13 (2)	0 (1)	**41**
week 4	18	17 (12)	9 (2)	3	29 (2)	0	**76**
week 5	12	4	7 (1)	5	17	0	**45**
week 6	1	4 (2)	7	1	7 (1)	0	**20**
week 7	3	2 (2)	2	0	0	0	**7**
week 8	5 (1)	3	0	0	6 (1)	0	**14**
week 9	0	1	0	0	2	0	**3**
week 10	1	0	0	0	1	0	**2**
week 11	7	4 (4)	0	0	3 (1)	0	**14**
week 12	0	0	0	0	1	0	**1**
Total	**66**	**50**	**46**	**10**	**100**	**2**	**274**

type. Thus the types were coded by one of the IA e-mentors. A large number of postings were "problem" or "explanation." We observed that students themselves provided a good number of explanations and comments, indicating a good amount of peer help.

Our analysis revealed that some of the messages were fairly deep in terms of information processing. We had messages that challenged the prevailing wisdom taught in class. Here's a "disagreement" sent by a student in GA-1:

It was mentioned during the lecture that replacement repair method is applicable when the optimal solution lies in the centre of feasible region whereas non-replacement is applicable when there are many disjoint feasible and optimal solution lies in the border of feasible regions. I don't quite agree with this recommendation. I feel that it should be based on whether the repair method violates the theoretical foundation of GA. If we are using schemas to analyse the theory behind GA, we know that schemata of short defining length, low order and above average fitness will receive exponentially increasing trails in future generations. Lets take the case study 1 in our lecture notes for example.

Table 4. Message contribution types exhibited in IA-1

Week	Problem	Explanation	Proposal	Disagreement	Comment	Summary	TOTAL
week 1	3 (1)	5	1 (1)	4	5(1)	0	18 (2)
week 2	3	13 (2)	6	3 (1)	10	3 (3)	38 (6)
week 3	0	3	0	2	2	0	7
week 4	5	5	0	0	3	0	13
week 5	2	9 (8)	2	3 (2)	1	0	17 (10)
week 6	9	5	3	2	4	0	23
Total	22 (1)	40 (10)	12 (1)	14 (3)	25(1)	3 (3)	116 (17)

DISCUSSION

By providing a course portal that allows the access of all the course materials and an online forum, students would have more time to reflect on course content and make in-depth cognitive and social contributions than would be possible in a traditional classroom. Our students are full-time professionals. The amount of time they spent online depends on the time they have allocated to the course. If they can only put in a certain number of hours, they would naturally spend most of those hours in the classroom where they feel their learning experience is optimized.

Online discussions allowed the less vocal students to contribute equally and made in-class discussions more interesting. Brush, Bargeron, Grudin, Borning & Gupta (2002) reported that integrating the online and in-class discussions was challenging. Rather than serving as a starting point for in-class discussions, the online discussions often competed with the classroom discussions. Students who participated frequently online seemed uninterested in addressing the same issues in-class with the rest of the students.

Guzdial et al. (2002) quotes the condition called learned helplessness from Bruer (1993), in which if the student is confused, he may not want to seek help, perhaps to avoid admitting the confusion. Seeking and receiving help can lead to achievement, but students have to seek the help (Webb & Palincsar, 1996). We have some students who felt that if they asked questions or replied to questions, they might appear foolish to others:

As a SE student and relatively new to the concept of GA i found myself and others in great difficulty to comprehend the subject itself, let alone participating in the forum.

I agree, personally I myself feel reluctant to reply to other people's opinions because I'm afraid that I might put in dumb replies which might not be helpful to the others in the forum.

This is further compounded by the fact that many of the students are from Singapore, China and India, where a culture of not speaking up is more of the norm, as one student has put it,

For those who come from foreign lands where their native language is not English, then I can understand their difficulty in speaking English in public and their shyness because of this. When we were younger, during our primary & secondary school days we were thought (NOTE: should be "taught") more to listen than to question. But during these modern times I think we should have outgrown this mould.

On the other hand, we would like to further analyze our identified e-mentoring strategies as below. Our categorization of e-mentor's proactive and reactive strategies is based on a simple rule – either a strategy is applied to launch a new thread or to reply to an existing (e-mentor- or student-initiated) thread. Still, at least three pairs of proactive-reactive strategy pairs are essentially the same strategies applied in different situations, namely, Proactive Strategy III and Reactive Strategy V, Proactive Strategy VI and Reactive Strategy VI, and Proactive Strategy IX and Reactive Strategy VIII. The entire set of the identified strategies have also "covered" almost all the techniques identified by Beaudin (1999) or proposed by Lim & Cheah (2003) as stated in the "Literature Review" section of this paper.

A key principle of constructivism is that the meanings or interpretations that people give to incoming information depend on their previous mental models and maps of the topic area or issue, drawn from experience (Seel, 2001). Appropriate challenges and arguments will foster deeper thinking and reflection (Salmon, 2004). Many of the above identified strategies may well fit into this notion. Some examples are: Proactive

Strategy IV, VI, VII, VIII and IX, and Reactive Strategy I, II, VIII and IX that stir the students to unlearn and relearn which may result in revising of their previous mental models; and Proactive Strategy III, and Reactive Strategy V that guide the students to tap on their experience (or creating new experience, in the case of Proactive Strategy IV) in making meanings of the theories and skills they have learned.

Indeed, many of the same instructional skills routinely used to facilitate interaction and participation in traditional classrooms can be transferred to Web-based environments (McCracken, 2006). Many of the strategies that we have gleaned bear a resemblance with teacher's inquiry strategies as inductively identified by Collins & Stevens (1982) by analyzing the transcripts of face-to-face Socratic dialogues, for example, raising examples and counterexamples, entrapping the students, etc. Nevertheless, adaptation is required when such strategies are transferred to this new medium of computer network (e.g., Co-applying "assessing the efficacy of the process" with other strategies as specified in the "teaching presence" framework). New affordances that were previously unavailable to traditional classroom discussion can be exploited (e.g., tapping on Internet resources), while the new learning management issues arose from the asynchronous, anytime-and-anywhere mode of discussions need to be addressed too (e.g., "Establishing time parameters" in the "teaching presence" framework).

Table 5 summarizes how the e-mentor's strategies that we have identified are mapped to the "teaching presence" framework.

The mapping shows that many of the strategies span more than one of the three categories identified in the "teaching presence" framework. In fact, the framework does not advocate a clear distinction among the categories. For example, the authors argue that the facilitation of discourse is not just the social dimension of computer conferencing; rather, it is usually integrated within direct instruction and in situ design of instructional activity. Many of the forum facilitation strategies that we have identified echo the argument, namely, Proactive Strategy I, II, VII and Reactive Strategy I, III, IV, VI. Indeed, with the right content and phrasing in the e-mentor's postings as we have discussed, any strategy could result in greater participations and at the same time stimulating the students' cognitive thinking. In other words, these strategies could play an important role in facilitating social-constructivism and community of inquiry.

One notable point is that one of the online discussion forums that Anderson et al. (2001) analyzed in developing their "teaching presence" framework involved several e-mentor-appointed student moderators during the later weeks of the course who performed a substantial part of the teaching presence role. This led the authors to name the element of the community of inquiry as "teaching presence" rather than "teacher presence". McDonald & Reushle (2002) echoed such an arrangement by advocating teacher-triggered, student-facilitated interactions, and that facilitation roles should be rotated among the students. Similarly, we believe the strategies that we have identified could also be applied by "high-ability" students for spontaneously carrying out peer coaching – if an e-mentor is able to not only set the climate for learning, but also peer coaching in her online forum. In fact, in our case study, the GA-1 e-mentor had been inviting individual "high-ability" students to summarize selected threads (i.e., performing Reactive Strategy I & II), which would become a good starting point to stimulate, if not explicitly appoint, peer mentoring among the students.

CONCLUSION

Our exploratory investigation reveals that e-mentors use a variety of different strategies for facilitating online forum discussions. Our list of strategies is by no means an exhaustive one

Table 5. Mapping forum facilitation strategies to the "Teaching Presence" framework

Strategies	**Mapping to Anderson *et al.*'s "Teaching Presence" Framework (2001)**
(Proactive strategies)	
Starting all the major topic threads	DO – Setting curriculum; Designing methods; Establishing time parameters FD – Drawing participants DI – Presenting Content/Questions
Asking an open-ended, opinionated question at the early stage	FD – Setting climate for learning; Drawing participants DI – Confirming understanding
Asking the students to relate the subject matter to real-life situations	FD – Setting climate for learning; Drawing participants
Designing a proposing or critiquing task that could be conducted on the forum	DO – Setting curriculum; Designing methods DI – Confirming understandings
Linking thread topics to appropriate resources or activities	DI – Injecting knowledge from diverse sources; Confirming understandings
Breaking a complex question down into more than one posting	FD – Drawing in participants
Challenging the students to self-reflect towards the end of the course	FD – Drawing in participants DI – Confirming understanding
Stimulating examples and counter-examples	DI – Confirming understanding; Diagnosing misconceptions
Entrapping the students	DI – Confirming understanding; Diagnosing misconceptions
(Reactive strategies)	
Summarizing/Regulating a thread that lacks focus	FD – Assessing the efficacy of the process DI – Summarizing the discussion
Summarizing in the middle of a discussion thread	DI – Summarizing the discussion
Re-formulating a student's problem	FD – Drawing in participants DI – Confirming understanding
Inviting student who has posted existing resource to summarize or comment on it	FD – Drawing in participants DI – Summarizing the discussion; Confirming understanding
Putting the question back to the students based on their past experiences	FD – Drawing in participants
Modelling how to answer a question or part-of, and prompting the other students to respond to the rest of the questions	FD – Drawing in participants DI – Presenting Content/Questions
Holding back your views to let other students participate in the discussion	FD – Drawing in participants
Stimulating the students to compare and contrast the concept in question with related concepts that she already knows	DI: Confirming understanding; Diagnosing misconceptions
Entrapping the students	DI – Confirming understanding; Diagnosing misconceptions

(DO = Design & Organization; FD = Facilitating Discourse; DI = Direct Instruction)

and needs to be extended and refine further from analyses of more online forum discussions with different instructional and learning contexts. The discussion forums for the three courses were meant to support, complement and supplement online discussions in a blended course deliver mode. Other contexts for using discussion forums might be that the e-mentor creates a case study or scenario and guides the students through it using the discussion forum, in which case he might adopt different or more strategies to guide the discussion.

We point out a few issues that help to highlight the differences between positive and negative adoptions of the discussion forums. The context of the students should be considered. The students are mostly busy professionals who have to cope with the demands of coursework. Naturally, they cannot be blamed for taking the path of least effort to fulfill their course requirements. If students do not expect to collaborate in a course or they do not see the benefits, they probably would not. While student reticence to collaborate may be a factor here, we believe that other factors are more significant. The time, effort put in and e-mentoring strategies adopted by the e-mentors to moderate the discussions are also factors in the success of the forums. The e-mentors have to invest a good amount of time and effort to ensure the successful participation of the discussion forum. While finding that faculty is busy is certainly not new, we realize from talking to our colleagues who are more hesitant in using discussion forums for their courses that they might also have problems in coming up with ideas for learning activities that necessitate the use of the forum.

One limitation of this study is that the relationship between the two major components of its outcomes - "the identification of the e-mentoring strategies" and "the coding and (statistical) pattern analysis of the students' postings" can be explored further. More work needs to be carried out in designing a new coding scheme that covers and at the same time discern both e-mentors and students' postings. A fresh round of coding effort with the new scheme and the subsequent statistical and/or discourse analysis may lead to a better understanding of how individual e-mentoring strategies might influence the dynamics of the student-student and student-teacher discourses on the forums.

More careful questioning of a wide variety of student and faculty collaboration users and non-users would provide better insight into the questions of how and when collaborative activities are adopted. Our findings suggest more hypotheses that could be explored further to determine their generality. The study has also provided us with a framework for the analysis of online interactions in subsequent blended learning courses.

ACKNOWLEDGMENT

The work described here was conducted when the authors were researchers at the Institute of Systems Science, National University of Singapore. We would like to credit the institute for providing us the opportunity for doing this work.

REFERENCES

Addesso, P. (2000). *The online teaching guide: A handbook of attitudes, strategies, and techniques for the virtual classroom.* Boston, MA: Allyn & Bacon.

Anderson, T., Rourke, L., Garrison, D. R., & Archer, W. (2001). Assessing the teaching presence in a computer conferencing context. *JALN, 5*(2).

Beaudin, B. P. (1999). Keeping online asynchronous discussions on topic. *JALN,* 3(2).

Bender, T. (2003). *Discussion-based online teaching to enhance student learning: Theory, practice, and assessment.* Sterling, VI: Stylus Publishing.

Berge, Z. K. (1991). Facilitating computer conferencing: Recommendation from the field. *Educational Technology, 15*(1), 22–30.

Blake, C. T., & Rapanotti, L. (2001). *Mapping interactions in a computer conferencing environment.* The Netherlands: Euro-CSCL2001.

Bonk, C. J., Malikowski, S., Angeli, C., & Supplee, L. (2001). Holy COW: Scaffolding case-based "conferencing on the Web" with preservice teachers. *CRLT Technical Report No. 15-1.* Bloomington, IN: Indiana University.

Bruer, J. T. (1993). *Schools for thought: A science of learning in the classroom.* Cambridge, MA: MIT Press.

Brush, A. J., Bargeron, D., Grudin, J., Borning, A., & Gupta, A. (2002). Supporting interaction outside of class: Anchored discussions vs. discussion boards. *Proceedings of Computer Support for Collaborative Learning 2002.*

Collins, A., & Stevens, A. L. (1982). A cognitive theory for inquiry teaching. In P. Goodyear (Ed.), *Teaching knowledge and intelligent tutoring* (pp. 203-230). Norwood, NJ: Ablex.

Collison, G., Elbaum, B., Haavind, S., & Tinker, R. (2000). *Facilitating online learning: Effective strategies for moderators.* Madison, WI: Atwood Publishing.

Garrison, D. R., Anderson, T., & Archer, W. (2000). Critical inquiry in a text-based environment: Computer conferencing in higher education. *The Internet and Higher Education*, *2*(2-3), 87–105. doi:10.1016/S1096-7516(00)00016-6

Greer, J., McCalla, G., Vassileva, J., Deters, R., Bull, S., & Kettel, L. (2001). Lessons learned in deploying a multi-agent learning support system: The i-help experience. [Amsterdam, The Netherlands: IOS Press.]. *Proceedings of AIED, 2001*, 410–421.

Guzdial, M., & Carroll, K. (2002). Explaining the lack of dialogue in computer-supported collaborative learning. *Proceedings of CSCL 2002.* Retrieved from http://newmedia.colorado.edu/cscl/18.html

Guzdial, M., Ludovice, P., Realff, M., Morley, T., & Carroll, K. (2002). When collaboration doesn't work. *Proceedings of the International Conference of the Learning Sciences* (pp.125-130). Mahwah, NJ: Lawrence Erlbaum Associates.

Guzdial, M., & Turn, J. (2000). Effective discussion through a computer-mediated anchored forum. *Journal of the Learning Sciences*, *9*(4), 437–469. doi:10.1207/S15327809JLS0904_3

Hara, N., Bonk, C. J., & Angeli, C. (2000). Content analysis of online discussion in an applied educational psychology. *Instructional Science*, *28*(2), 115–152. doi:10.1023/A:1003764722829

Henri, F. (1992). Computer conferencing and content analysis. In A. R. Kaye (Eds.), *Collaborative learning through computer conferencing: The Najaden papers* (pp.115-136). New York: Springer.

Hewitt, J., & Teplovs, C. (1999). An analysis of growth patterns in computer conferencing threads. [CSCL]. *Proceedings of Computer Support for Collaborative Learning, 1999*, 232–241.

Kim, K.-J., & Bonk, C. J. (2002). Cross-cultural comparisons of online collaboration. *JCMC, 8*(1).

Klemm, W. R. (1998). Eight ways to get students more engaged in online conferences. *T.H.E. Journal.* Retrieved on April 23, 2008, from http://www.thejournal.com/magazine/vault/A1997.cfm

Laurillard, D., Stratfold, M., Luckin, R., Plowman, L., & Taylor, J. (2000). Affordances for learning in a non-linear narrative medium. *Interactive Media in Education.* Retrieved on April 23, 2008, from http://www.jime.open.ac.uk/00/2

Lim, C. P., & Cheah, P. T. (2003). The role of the tutor in asynchronous discussion boards: A case study of a pre-service teacher course. *Educational Media International*, *40*(1), 33–48. doi:10.1080/0952398032000092107

Mason, R. (1991). Moderating educational computer conferencing. *DEOSNEWS, 1*(19).

McCracken, H. (2006). *Furthering connected teaching and learning through the use of virtual learning communities*. Retrieved on April 30, 2008, from http://www.e-mentor.edu.pl/_xml/wydania/17/359.pdf

McDonald, J., & Reushle, S. (2002). Charting the role of the online teacher in higher education: Winds of change. *Proceedings of ASCILITE'02*, Auckland, New Zealand.

McKenzie, W., & Murphy, D. (2000). 'I hope this goes somewhere': Evaluation of an online discussion group. *Australian Journal of Educational Technology*, *16*(3), 239–257.

Paulsen, M. P. (1995). Moderating educational computer conferences. In Z. L. Berge & M. P. Collins (Eds.), *Computer-mediated communication and the online classroom in distance education*. Cresskill, NJ: Hampton Press.

Preece, J. (1999). Empathic communities: Balancing emotional and factual communication. *Interacting with Computers*, *12*, 63–77. doi:10.1016/S0953-5438(98)00056-3

Rogers, E. M. (1995). *Diffusion of innovations*. New York: The Free Press.

Rourke, L., Anderson, T., Garrison, D. R., & Archer, W. (2001). Methodological issues in the content analysis of computer conference transcripts. *International Journal of Artificial Intelligence in Education*, 12.

Salmon, G. (2004). *E-moderating: The key to teaching and learning online (2nd ed.)*. Abingdon, UK: Taylor & Francis.

Seel, N. M. (2001). Epistomology, situated cognition, and mental models: 'Like a bridge over troubled water.' . *Instructional Science*, *29*(29), 403–427. doi:10.1023/A:1011952010705

Shank, P. (Ed.). (2007). *The online learning: 95 proven ways to enhance technology-based and blended learning*. San Francisco, CA: John Wiley & Sons.

Veerman, A., & Veldhuis-Diermanse, E. (2001). Collaborative learning through computer mediated communication in academic education. In P. Dillenbourg, A. Eurelings, & K. Hakkarainen (Eds.), *European perspectives on computer-supported collaborative learning* (pp. 625-632). Maastricht, The Netherlands: University of Maastricht.

Watkins, A. (2005). *E-learning activities: Making online learning interactive*. San Francisco, CA: John Wiley & Sons.

Webb, N. M., & Palincsar, A. S. (1996). Group processes in the classroom. In D. C. Berliner & R. C. Calfee (Eds.), *Handbook of educational psychology* (pp. 841-873). New York: Macmillan.

Winiecki, D. J. (1999). Keeping the thread: Adapting conversational practice to help distance students and instructors manage discussions in an asynchronous learning network. *DEOSNEWS*, *9*(2).

Wozniak, H., & Silveira, S. (2004). Online discussions: Promoting effective student to student interaction. *Proceedings of ASCILITE Conference 2004*.

ENDNOTE

1 The notation 5(1) means that out of the 5 messages, 1 is posted by one of the e-mentors.

Chapter 9
A Case Study of Infusing Web 2.0 Tools for Blended Learning:
Virtual Presentations as an Alternative Means of Assessment

Yiu Chi Lai
The Hong Kong Institute of Education, Hong Kong

Eugenia M. W. Ng
The Hong Kong Institute of Education, Hong Kong

ABSTRACT

In the era of Web 2.0, students are not restricted to search and collect information from existing Internet resources. They are expected to be able to collaborate, create, and share new information on the Web through different tools. On the other hand, students of this era are also familiar with sharing multimedia contents on the Internet. We can also observe that presentations are not limited to face-to-face and university students should be able to present virtually using multimedia technology. It seems that Web 2.0 tools open another space for the assessment modes for teachers. This study aims to describe an innovative practice of having two groups of student teachers conducting a virtual presentation about their final assignments, which could either be videos or other digital formats. One group of students was final year undergraduate while another group consisted of post-graduate Diploma of Education student teachers. For the purpose of the study, the virtual presentation materials were uploaded to a learning management system (LMS) platform to enable the two different classes to comment each other's work within one week. Thereafter, the data collected from tracked statistics provided by the learning platform and students' reflections of this interclass activity were analyzed and compared with each other. It was found that most of the participants were positive about this new presentation approach and ready to accept it as a part of the assessment. However, the undergraduate students were more active in participating in virtual presentations of both classes. Furthermore, their attitudes were influenced by the tutors' participation. Thus, it is suggested that tutors involved in virtual presentations should play an active role and give encouragement to their students regularly.

DOI: 10.4018/978-1-60566-852-9.ch009

INTRODUCTION

With the rapid development of the Internet since mid 1990, Information Technology (IT) has presented a new arena for learning and teaching worldwide. In particular, Web 2.0 tools provide a huge, untapped resource for educators because of their potential to enhance learning in virtually any environment. They also offer a real opportunity to create a classroom without walls (Barlow, 2008). We expect that our students can be able to collaborate, create and share new information on the Web through various Web 2.0 tools such as social bookmarking systems, blogs, wikis, social networks, video sharing platforms, etc. Students can learn from blogs and wikis as well as from traditional textbooks and they prefer using their "clicker" to indicate understanding instead of raising their hands (Conrad, 2008).

Furthermore, students of this era are familiar with production of multimedia contents and have no difficulties to share them with others through various communication technologies. However, most existing learning and teaching resources are still confined to the traditional text format. Similarly, most learners are assessed in plain text formats, rather than multiple presentation formats, though Web 2.0 tools have opened another space for the assessment modes for teachers. "It is widely accepted that assessment must be designed to reflect course pedagogy, aims and objectives. Networked courses require the course designers to rethink the assessment strategy if it is to reflect the aims of the course and appropriately assess the skills developed during the course," (Macdonald, Weller, & Mason, 2002, p. 9). In the study, the researchers attempted to make use of a Web 2.0 tool: a Learning Management System (LMS) platform to conduct virtual presentations. These presentations were considered as an alternative means of assessment. In addition, the virtual presentation component may be able to supplement face-to-face contact time and also very useful to enrich the online interaction.

The following section proceeds to describe the pertinent literature review to justify using IT as a tool and medium for peer assessment. The review will be followed by a discussion of the research methodology and findings. Finally, the conclusion of the research and future directions will be discussed.

LITERATURE REVIEW

The traditional mode of learning requires rote learning facts and procedures and, thereafter, learners are assessed for their command over the content and the knowledge they have acquired. Vygotsky (1978) was amongst the pioneers who suggested a constructivist approach to learning which emphasized learning through social interaction, which included social relations and interactions with social artifacts such as linguistic symbols, to enable individuals to construct new knowledge from their experiences. Bruner (1986) believes that learning is an active social process in which learners construct new ideas of concepts based on current knowledge. Lave and Wenger (1991) regard both the physical as well as the social environment as being crucial to the learning process. Jonassen, Peck and Wilson (1999) argue that learning is more engaging and interesting when learners are stimulated by sounds and images. Furthermore, Jonassen, Howland, Moore and Marra (2003) suggest that technologies such as video, hypermedia and the Internet are excellent tools to learn with. Their emphasis is on problem solving and they address how the Internet can be used to foster community building. Oliver (2007) points out the needs to redesign technology integration course to leverage new Web 2.0 tools that have been created with web collaboration, sharing and/or new information creation in mind.

Assessment has a long history in both the Eastern and Western worlds and the role of assessment was mainly used for selection purposes in the past. Morris (1995) points out that assessment is one of the basic components of a curriculum and there are six major reasons for carrying out an assessment: grading, selection, mastery, guidance, prediction and diagnosis. He also explains that teacher requires information about pupils which is immediate and which helps them to plan their lessons and to obtain rapid feedback on the pupils' learning. However, the views on assessment are ever changing. Biggs (1996) argues that assessment should be designed to support learning rather than select learners. Chan and Van Aalst (2004) believe that the current trend is to assess for learning rather than assessment of learning. Berry (2008) also points out that the fundamental principle of assessment for learning is making strong connection between assessment and learning. Besides, in the assessment for learning model, assessment should be used to promote, induce, and reinforce learning.

Brown and Knight (1994) present a theory of formative assessment. They argue that feedback must be rapid and provided at an appropriate point in the learning process, in order to be effective. They point out that it will be even more appropriate if the feedback is diagnostic and prescriptive so that recipients of such feedback can actually utilize it to guide their future learning. The capability and potential of IT undoubtedly fits the requirements of providing timely feedback. Macdonald, Weller and Mason (2002) suggest that, "Networking opens up possibilities for enhancing formative feedback to students through peer review, when scripts are posted electronically for comment and review" (p.10). Indeed, the effectiveness of conducting peer assessments online has been examined in detail, and thereafter, analyzed and confirmed by various studies. These studies showed positive results for online collaborative assessment (Buchanan, 2000; Kwok & Ma, 1999; Thelwall, 2000). Chang (2001) further confirms that most students have a positive attitude towards a web-based portfolio system's assistance in the personal learning process and its outcomes. Furthermore, Lin, Liu and Yuan (2001) also argue that students are more willing to critique online as they can post their comments anonymously. Similarly, it was found that student teachers who utilize peer assessment, outperform their counterparts who do not use peer assessment and the former also unequivocally alter and amend their perceived views of assessment, instruction and the role of the educator (Sluijsmans, Brand-Gruwel, & Van Merrienboer, 2002).

In recent years, online interaction was also thought to be an essential supplement of face-to-face interaction. Blended learning is widely used today in many higher education institutions and it is commonly used to describe a solution that combines several different educational delivery methods, such as collaboration software, web-based courses, and computer communication media with traditional face-to-face instruction (Mortera-Gutiérrez, 2006). Besides, blended learning has created new opportunities for students to interact with their peers, faculty, and content, inside and outside of the classroom (Vaughan, 2007). Ridgway, McCusker and Pead (2004) point out that "High assessments explify curriculum ambitions, define what is worth knowing, and active classroom practices" (p.2). They also believe that e-assessment can not only support current educational goals but also facilitate the assessment of problem solving, and process skills such as understanding and representing problem, controlling variables, generating and testing hypotheses, and finding rules and relationships. The Joint Information Systems Committee (JISC) (2007) also argues that e-assessment can increase the range of what is tested. It can provide evidence of both cognitive and skills-based achievements and ways that are durable and transferable.

The reviewed literature has reminded the authors of this study that assessment should be used to support learning and online peer assessment may be a wise alternative. Moreover, the emerging Web 2.0 tools definitely provide new opportunities for sharing and knowledge creation. Therefore the authors implemented the study as follows: students were required to conduct virtual presentations on a Web 2.0 enabled LMS platform and they were encouraged to give constructive feedback and comments for improvement, instead of allotting grades to their peers, due to conflict of interest.

RESEARCH METHODOLOGY

As using virtual presentation as an assessment component in a blended learning environment is a completely new concept, we start the research as a case study. Robson (1993) points out that case study is "a strategy for doing research which involves an empirical investigation of a particular contemporary phenomenon within its real life context using multiple sources of evidence" (p.146). As the case study approach can cope with complexity (Johnson, 1994), it is useful for exploring purposes (Robson, 1993). This helps the researchers to investigate the complex interactions among the student participants. In the following sections, we will focus on the participants, course design, assessment task and methods of analysis.

Participants

The study was conducted at the Hong Kong Institute of Education (HKIEd), which is the major teacher education provider in Hong Kong. There are two groups of participants from three classes in the study: One-year full-time PGDE (Secondary) programme (thereafter FT PGDE), Two-year part-time PGDE (Secondary) programme (thereafter PT PGDE) and Four-year full-time BSc(MAIE) programme (thereafter MAIE). Most MAIE students are straight from secondary school, whilst some FT PGDE students have just graduated from universities but some have 1-2 working experiences. Some PT PGDE students are teachers, some work as supporting staff at schools and some work in companies. Table 1 summarizes their backgrounds.

As Information Technology is not a core subject in secondary school curriculum, the number of student teachers in IT Major is small. In order to increase the sample size, the researchers tried to bring students studying similar modules but of different courses together. However, the sample size is still not big enough, so it only favors the case study approach.

Course Design and Timetabling Arrangement

From Table 1, we can observe that students from three different groups were involved in the study. There are several reasons to combine these three groups together:

Table 1. Summary of the backgrounds of the PGDE and MAIE students

	PGDE Group	MAIE Group
Level	Post-graduate	Undergraduate
Subject Discipline	Information Technology	Mathematics and Information Technology
Programme	PGDE(Secondary) IT Major *One-year full-time or two-year part-time professional teacher education course at HKIEd for graduates with IT or related disciplines from other universities.*	BSc(Mathematics and IT Education) *Four-year joint programme, conducted by the Hong Kong University of Science and Technology (HKUST) and a one-year professional teacher education course at HKIEd.*
Mode of delivery	30 face-to-face contact hours supplemented with online tasks	39 face-to-face contact hours supplemented with online tasks
No. of participants	9 Yr 1 student teachers - 4 Full-Time PGDE students (Male-3, Female - 1) 5 Part-Time PGDE students (Male-5, Female - 0)	13 Yr 4 student teachers (Male – 8; Female -5)

- They need to study the same set of curriculum and teaching methods modules in IT at HKIEd.
- The size of virtual community can be increased.
- Students can receive feedback from others with different backgrounds.

The timetabling arrangement was a little bit complicated in order to cater for the needs of both PT and FT students. There was also a combined class arrangement for PT and FT PGDE students. Figure 1 shows the sequence of the three curriculum and teaching methods modules offered in their programmes. As seen from their study paths, it was expected that they would have sufficient knowledge to give constructive comments to their fellow participants, whilst providing opportunities for the practice of relevant assessment skills. During the period of this study, MAIE students took the module titled "Supporting Information Technology in Schools." The objective of the module is "To develop participants' ability to coordinate and manage issues related to ICT Management in school." The PGDE students took the module titled, "Learning and Teaching of Selected Topics in Information Technology." The objective of the module is "To enhance participants' ability to select appropriate strategies to create learning environments for their students that foster learning and teaching of ICT subjects." Obviously, the experience in conducting virtual presentations can contribute to the knowledge in ICT Management and Strategies to create learning environments. We decide to bring these students together in a virtual learning environment in the study.

Assessment Tasks

As these three groups of students were attending two different modules, they need to complete different assignments in order to fulfill the module requirements. Table 2 shows their assignment tasks and weighting of each component. The following discussion will focus on virtual presentation activity rather than on their overall learning and teaching activities.

It is a very common practice for student teachers to give a presentation prior to submission of their assignments. However, this type of presentation should not be restricted to class presentation when most new LMS platforms allow us to conduct presentation in a virtual manner. As the participants are potential IT teachers in schools, they are expected to be adept and proficient in creating a virtual presentation by using video or self-running slide show.

In the study, they were instructed to express the core essence of their assignment using video or other digital formats such as a PowerPoint slides embedded with voice narration before uploading the presentation materials to the LMS platform. This would enable them to acquire feedback from peers in their class, along with feedback from peers with diverse backgrounds and also instructors of two modules. The MAIE students were required to present their final individual essay, whereas the PGDE students' virtual presentations were on their group project, where one group consisted of Full-Time students and the other group consisted of Part-Time students. It was suggested that student teachers should give constructive comments on at least two of their peers' projects.

Analysis of the New Practice

After the virtual presentation was over, the practice of incorporating virtual presentation as an assessment component was analyzed in the following ways:

1. We obtained the descriptive statistics from the tracking function of the LMS platform.
2. For probing the usefulness and limitations of the practice, two instruments were used. A focus group meeting for the MAIE student group was conducted to brainstorm the issues of the new practice that were interesting to

Figure 1. Study paths of the FT PGDE, PT PGDE and MAIE students

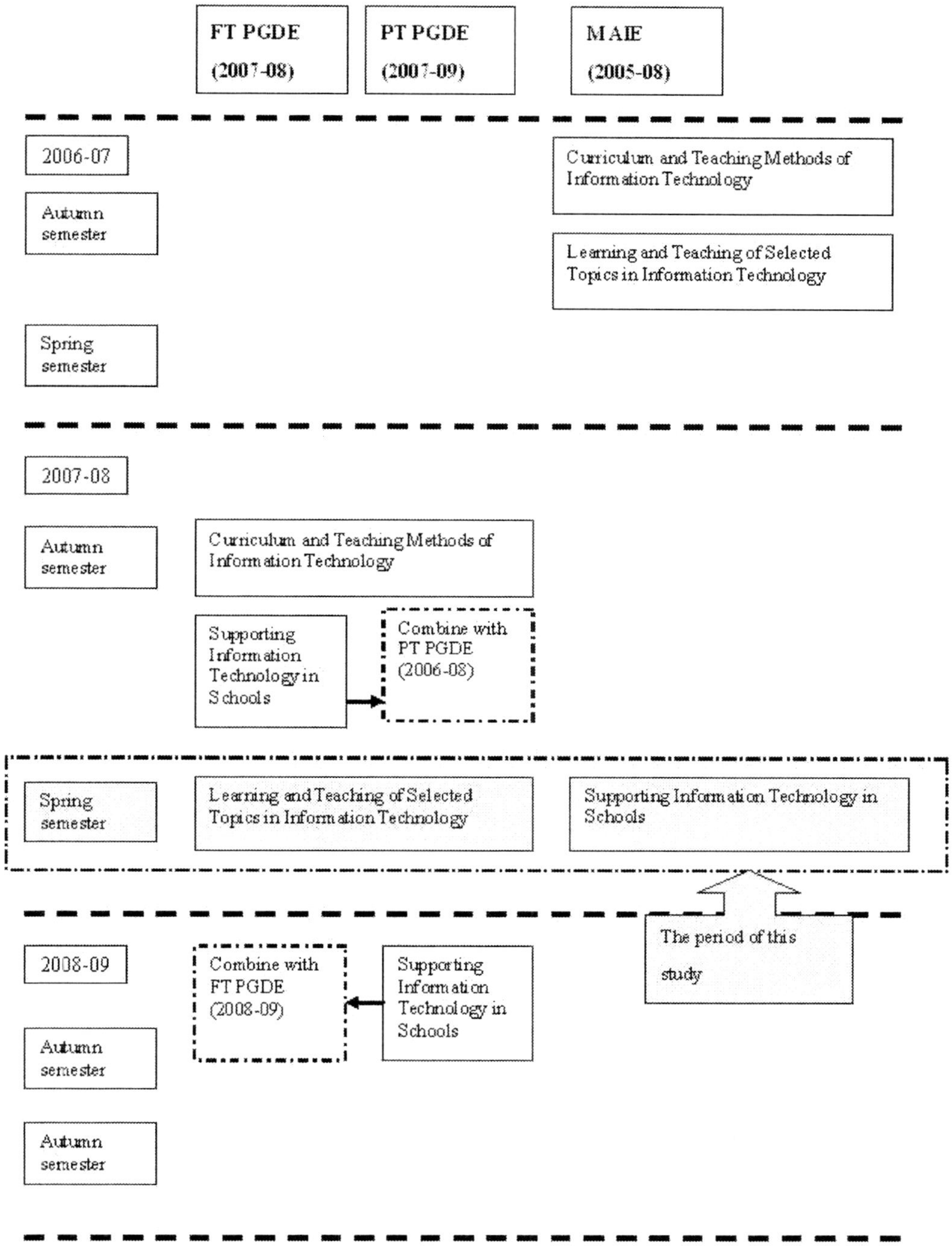

follow. Then the information gathered in the meeting was used to inform the researchers what kinds of data should be collected from their individual reflective reports.

3. Furthermore, tutors' reflections are also useful for giving a deeper understanding about the issue under investigation.

Table 2. Assignment tasks and weighting of each component for PGDE and MAIE students in the modules involved in the study

Group	PGDE Students (FT and PT)		MAIE Students	
Module attended	Learning and Teaching of Selected Topics in Information Technology		Supporting Information Technology in Schools	
Assessment	(a) A group project *To design and create a web site to serve as virtual learning community for secondary school IT students; elucidate and explain very logically how this community could be employed to enhance teaching and learning of IT and the methods by which it could be appropriately applied in a computer class.* **[enhanced with a virtual presentation component]**	70%	(a) A group project *To complete a small practical task that can illustrate an innovative use of IT in schools.*	20%
	(b) An individual report *Write an individual report, to analyze the problems and strengths for building a virtual learning community in his/her teaching practice or own school.*	30%	(b) An individual report *Write a report on any critical issues related to the module content.* **[enhanced with a virtual presentation component]**	70%
			(c) Class participation *Online and face-to-face activities*	10%

The linkage between the research tools in the study is depicted in Figure 2.

DATA ANALYSIS AND RESULTS

After the deadline for uploading digital presentations to the LMS platform, the virtual presentation began and lasted for one week. During that week, the participants were allowed to give comments and to have dialogue exchanges at any time. The study ended after the PGDE students had performed their presentations as the PGDE programme had a later assignment submission deadline. There were two main data sources from the LMS platform:

- The presentation and dialogue exchanges on the discussion forum and
- The descriptive statistics provided by the tracking function

However, these data, mainly quantitative in nature, cannot provide us in-depth understanding of the usefulness and limitations of virtual presentations. We also need qualitative data from students' and tutor's reflection in order to have a holistic view on this innovative practice.

Findings from Discussion Forum of LMS Platform

Although the PGDE students' presentation was in a group, it was found that each group had constructed at least one presentation in video format. The FT PGDE students had made two video presentations in Windows Media Video format and also paste additional links of other Internet resources like online videos as supplementary information about their presentation. On the other hand, the PT group used both videos and PowerPoint slides embedded with voice narration for their virtual presentation. They tried to demonstrate how to use their e-learning centre with a video (see Figure 3). For the thirteen MAIE presentations, most of them preferred to use PowerPoint slides with embedded voice narration rather than videos. Only one student presented his individual report with video. We can also observe that most virtual presentations were uploaded to the LMS platform almost on the day of submission, as the deadline loomed close (see Figure 4).

Figure 2. Linkage between the research tools in the study

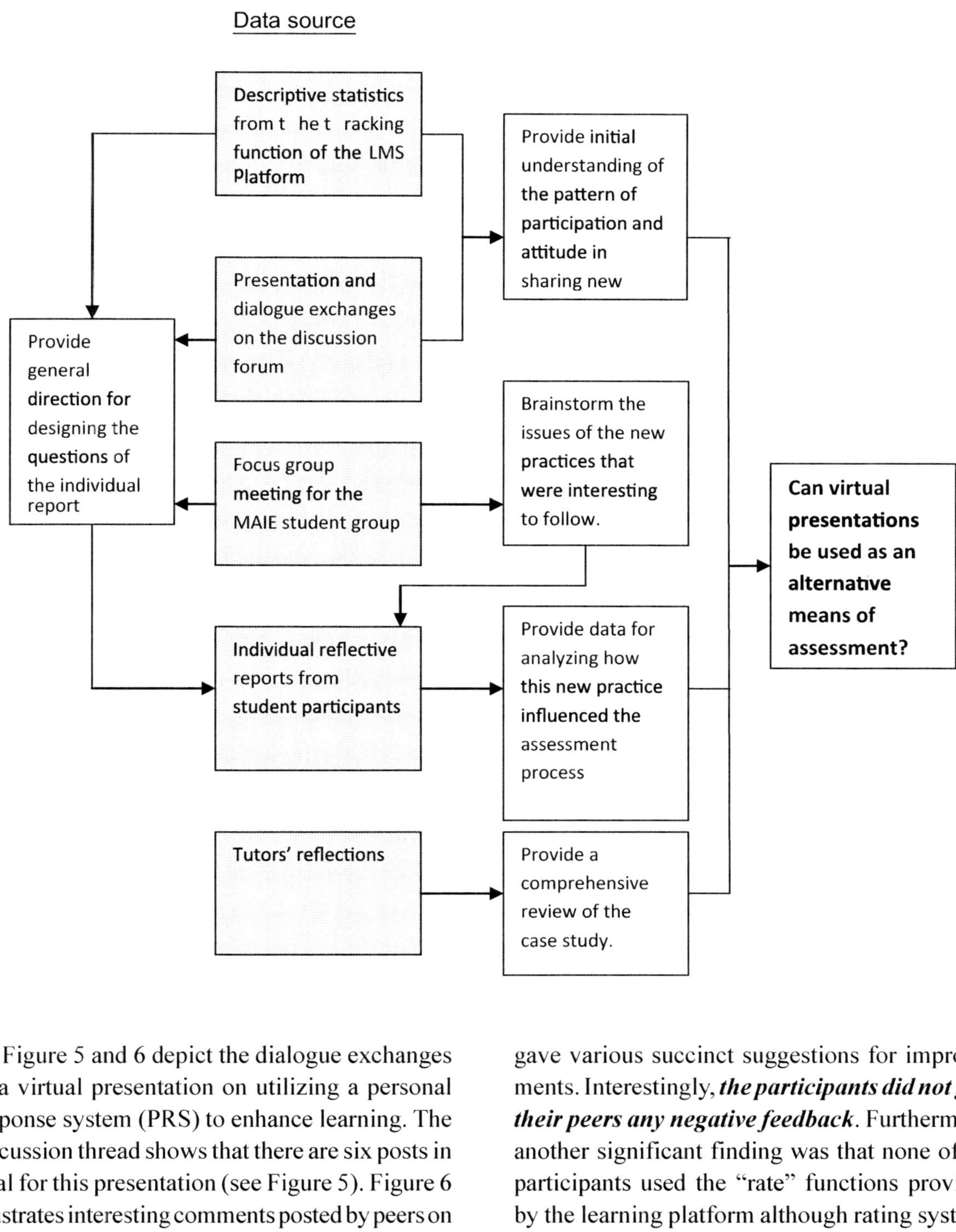

Figure 5 and 6 depict the dialogue exchanges of a virtual presentation on utilizing a personal response system (PRS) to enhance learning. The discussion thread shows that there are six posts in total for this presentation (see Figure 5). Figure 6 illustrates interesting comments posted by peers on the virtual presentations. A noteworthy observation was that ***peers characteristically gave positive feedback on the contents of the presentations*** and gave various succinct suggestions for improvements. Interestingly, ***the participants did not give their peers any negative feedback***. Furthermore, another significant finding was that none of the participants used the "rate" functions provided by the learning platform although rating systems are common in most Web 2.0 applications like *youtube* (http://www.youtube.com/).

Findings from Tracking Functions of the LMS platform

As the Institute is using Blackboard online learning platform as our LMS platform, we can get a lot of useful descriptive statistics from its tracking functions. The statistics about the number of postings, number of views of threads, accessing times and number of hits can help us interpret the degree and pattern of their participation in the virtual presentation period quantitatively.

Number of Postings for a Post from Each Class

Table 3 shows the statistics of postings for each class. The data show that students were more active in providing feedback to peers in their own class rather than student participants of another class. In particular, PGDE students were specifically reluctant to comment the work of MAIE students. The number of postings by MAIE students was relatively higher as they had to submit individual presentations, rather than a group presentation, as required of the PGDE students.

Figure 3. A group of PGDE students uploaded a video presentation

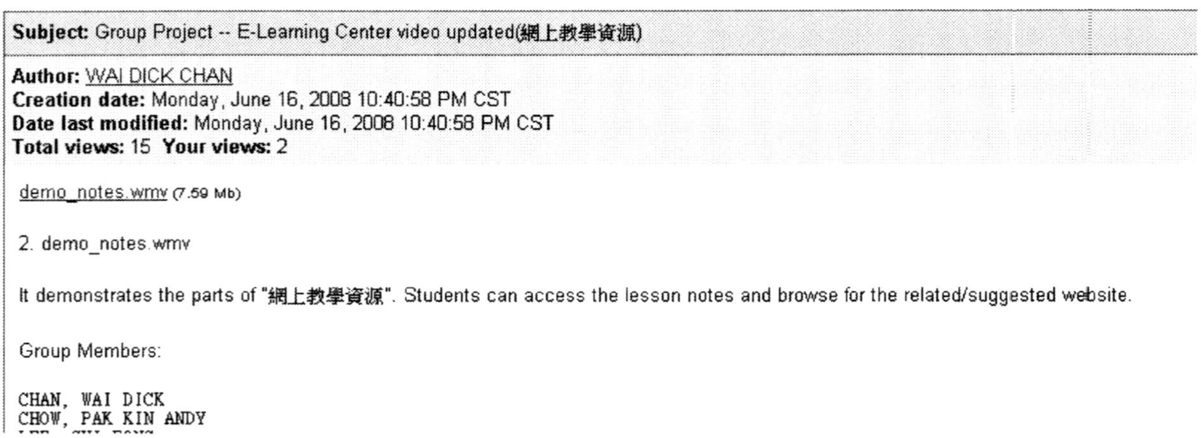
Subject: Group Project -- E-Learning Center video updated(網上教學資源)

Author: WAI DICK CHAN
Creation date: Monday, June 16, 2008 10:40:58 PM CST
Date last modified: Monday, June 16, 2008 10:40:58 PM CST
Total views: 15 **Your views:** 2

demo_notes.wmv (7.59 Mb)

2. demo_notes.wmv

It demonstrates the parts of "網上教學資源". Students can access the lesson notes and browse for the related/suggested website.

Group Members:

CHAN, WAI DICK
CHOW, PAK KIN ANDY

Figure 4. Sample illustration of students' virtual presentation topics

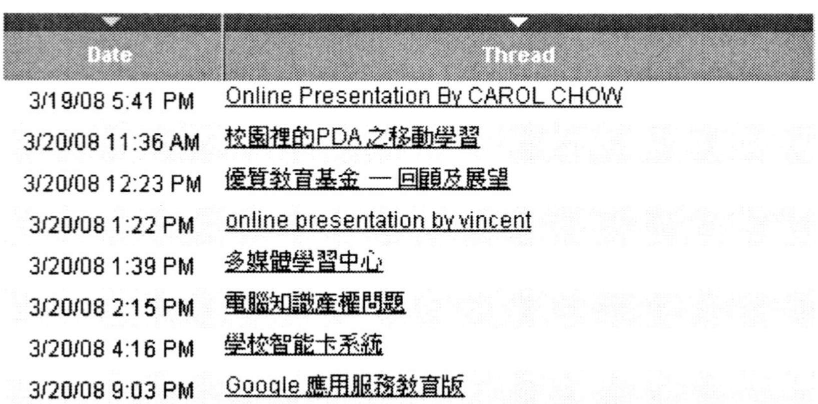

Date	Thread
3/19/08 5:41 PM	Online Presentation By CAROL CHOW
3/20/08 11:36 AM	校園裡的PDA之移動學習
3/20/08 12:23 PM	優質教育基金 — 回顧及展望
3/20/08 1:22 PM	online presentation by vincent
3/20/08 1:39 PM	多媒體學習中心
3/20/08 2:15 PM	電腦知識產權問題
3/20/08 4:16 PM	學校智能卡系統
3/20/08 9:03 PM	Google 應用服務教育版

Number of Views of Threads

The LMS also tracked data about the number of views of the threads by the participants. The number of views was much higher than the number of postings, around ten times that of the total postings. Figure 7 shows that the MAIE students also had more views than the PGDE students and it was interesting to note that the PT students were more active than the FT students. It seems that MAIE students were more active in joining the virtual presentations. However, we need to be aware that the number of views merely measures the number of hits, so we are unable to predict the duration or the amount of time spent on each view. It is also possible that participants viewed some postings more than once. As mentioned above, this type of data can only provide quantitative instead of qualitative information.

Access Pattern in a Day and the Number of Hits in Each Hour

As the virtual presentations were conducted in an asynchronous mode, the participants could review

Figure 5. Sample illustration of students' presentations and dialogue exchanges

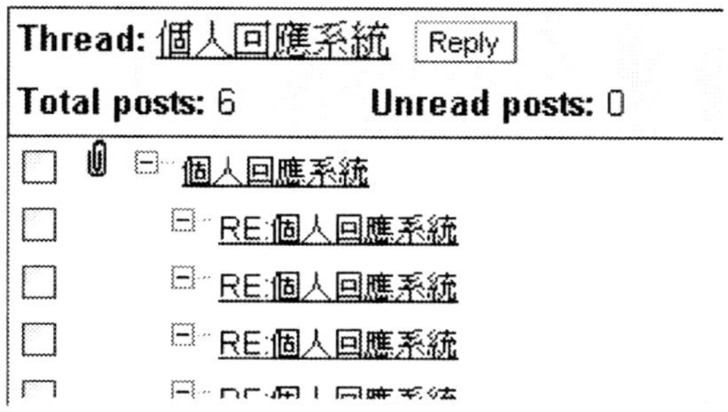

the presentation and make comments at any time. Figure 8 clearly reveals a specific pattern that the participants followed in the study. They usually took advantage of the flexibility provided to access the learning platform at different hours of the day. As Hong Kong is a "sleepless" town, the participants were quite active around the hours near midnight. This phenomenon is indicated from a peak around mid-night in Figure 8.

Figure 6. Sample illustration of students' comments on PRS virtual presentations

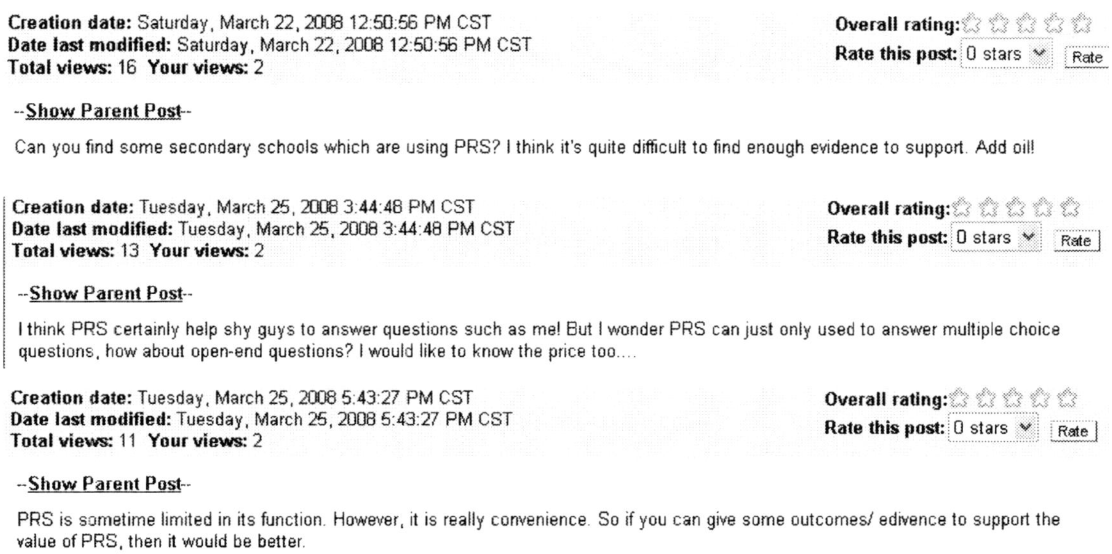

Table 3. Tracked statistics of postings on students' presentations

Group	No. of total postings on their presentations	No. of postings from MAIE students	No. of postings from PGDE Students	No. of postings from the instructor
MAIE	80	66 (82.5%)	1 (1.25%)	13 (16.25%)
PGDE(FT)	27	8 (29.63%)	19 (70.31%)	0 (0%)
PGDE(PT)	24	6 (25.00%)	17 (70.83%)	1 (4.17%)

Findings from Participants' Reflections

The quantitative data enumerated in the above pages, undoubtedly show that MAIE students were more active than PGDE students. However, quantitative data cannot provide us in-depth understanding of the idea of virtual presentation. We also need qualitative data from students' and tutor's reflection in order to understand the full picture of infusing virtual presentation in blended learning. Robson (1993) states that "using more than one method in an investigation can have substantial advantages, even though it almost inevitably adds to the time investment required" (p.290). He also points out that one important benefit of multiple methods is in the reduction of inappropriate certainty. The quantitative data from the LMS platform and the qualitative data from students' and tutors' reflections can be used to complement each other. In this study, the descriptive statistics from the LMS platform were used to provide general understanding of the pattern of participation and attitude in sharing new information, but the reflections can be used to analyze how this new practice influenced the assessment process. Furthermore, the integration of reflective practice into the curriculum for initial and continuing education, especially for professionals such as teachers, nurses and social workers (Boud & Walker, 1998), has been prevalent over the past 10 years. This practice addresses issues such as the alignment of learning objectives with assessment outcomes and the assessment of reflective practice, including dealing with disclosure and

Figure 7. Tracked statistics of students' and instructor's views

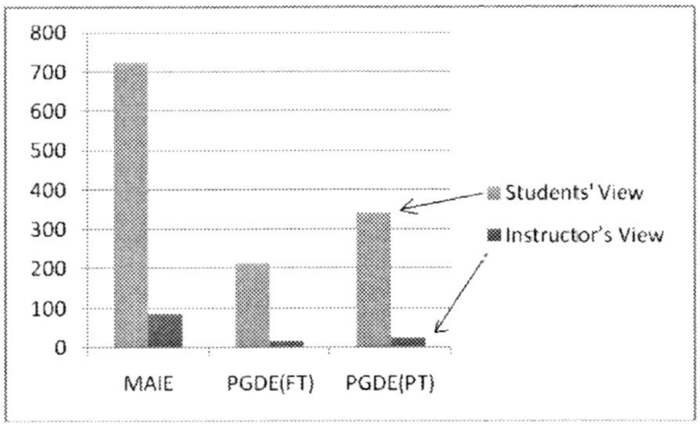

Figure 8. Access pattern in a day and the number of hits in each hour

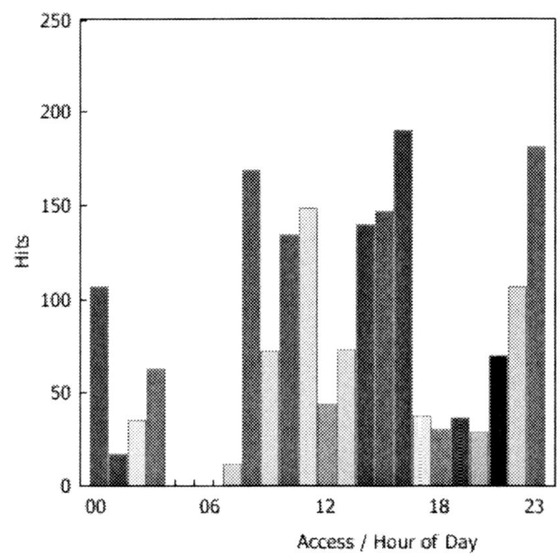

providing feedback, and collaboration, group work and plagiarism. Boud and Walker further suggest, "It is important to frame reflective activities within the learning context in which they are taking place" (p.193). Therefore, the authors of this study adopted a combined method and attempted to obtain qualitative information from their reflections.

The results from the students' reflective reports are summarized in Table 4. Key concepts of the reflections are tallied. This table depicts the top ten student comments: positive on the right and negative on the left for easy comparison. Here are some important points that can be observed:

- Most of them (9 students in total) agreed that giving comments on other's work was easier when using virtual presentation.
- Six MAIE students opined that it was more flexible in terms of space and time to produce and to listen to virtual presentations but only one PGDE student cited this important point.
- Four MAIE students embraced this new experience as none of them had practised participating in virtual presentations, prior to this study. It was also apparent that none of the PGDE students was enthusiastic about this novel and innovative practice.

There are several possible reasons for having different attitudes towards this new practice. As the PGDE students have a stronger IT knowledge and experience than the MAIE students, it is relatively difficult to arouse their interest with technologies that are already known to them. Actually, provision of flexibility is often perceived as a de facto standard for online applications. Moreover, the assessment for PGDE students was based on the performance of their own group, some students may prefer to spend more time on their individual assignment. It seems that the PGDE students just tried to give a minimum effort to fulfill the assignment requirement. It implies that individual presentation is preferable for virtual presentation. In addition, the PGDE tutor, who was worried about his comments on students' work, might inhibit further comments from other students and he preferred to be an observer in the study. The data show that the tutor should take a more active role in the process. This might explain why the PGDE students were less enthusiastic about this innovative practice.

Further examination of their reflections revealed that both groups offered more positive feedback as expected (Chang, 2001) rather than

Table 4. Ten notable phrases from students' reflections on virtual presentations

Positive feedback on Virtual Presentation	MAIE	PGDE	Total	Negative feedback on Virtual Presentation
It was easier to give comments on other's work.	4	5	**9**	
	3	3	**6**	Preparation took me more time.
It was more flexible in terms of space and time to produce and to listen to virtual presentations	5	1	**6**	
	3	2	**5**	I was unable to get instant feedback from peers
I was able to learn more from other's presentations	3	1	**4**	
I felt less pressure (could re-work again, did not have to face the audience)	3	1	**4**	
This was a new experience	4	0	**4**	
I was able to transfer the skills to secondary school settings	2	1	**3**	
It was easier to present the ideas	0	2	**2**	
I was able to foster generic skills	2	0	**2**	

negative feedback on the virtual production and sharing. Moreover, the following issues have been pointed out by the students:

Flexibility and Drawbacks for Teaching and Learning

Its flexibility is highlighted by the positive comments like "easier to give comments on other's work", "more flexible in terms of space and time to produce and to listen to virtual presentations", "easier to present ideas" etc. Some positive comments from their reflective reports were:

It is interesting to have virtual presentations as I haven't done it before. .... We can express ourselves freely, we can be confident when doing the virtual presentation. We may feel nervous and not confident if we present in front of people. – A MAIE student

The adoption of virtual presentation is a good and efficient idea of presenting an individual report online. Not only does it save time, but also allows us the flexibility to watch the presentation anytime we wish and then to give our comments. – A PGDE (PT) student

However, two of the students debated that:

The drawback of virtual presentations is that they are less efficient as compared with presentations in class, as we are not sure when others will give us feedback and then, there is a delay for us to reply to the feedback too. – A MAIE student

I prefer traditional presentation as it can help me to develop confidence and presentation skills. – A PGDE(FT) student

How Can Virtual Presentation Be Used to Support Assessment for Learning?

Its usefulness in supporting assessment for learning is highlighted by the positive comments like "able to learn more from other's presentation", "less pressure", "able to foster generic skills" etc. Some positive comments from their reflective reports are:

When we compare with the group presentation during the class time, we feel that using virtual presentation can reduce our stress and help us create a better product. - A MAIE student

The virtual presentation helped me to gear up my production skills. Whilst watching others' presentations, I learnt more of how to choose a topic and how to produce visual effects. This has also reminded me to add video production as one of the exercises for my own students'. – A PGDE(PT) student

It is an innovative method of learning to encourage a discussion and an exchange of ideas between two classes. It brought two classes together to exchange opinion which benefits learning as the topics we are discussing are similar or even the same. - A MAIE student

When I view my own virtual presentation, I can reflect and this helps to foster self-learning. – A PGDE (FT) student

Being a commentator of virtual presentations, we can know more about the topic through dialogue exchanges and their presentation documents. If we have missed some points, we can listen to the virtual presentation again. – A MAIE student

Apart from understanding how virtual presentation can give benefit to knowledge creation as Web 2.0 tools usually do, it is equally important to know if the participants like sharing their products and ideas through this means. The authors tallied key concepts and it was encouraging to conclude that students felt they could receive distinct and diverse opinions, rather than merely opinions from students in their own class (Jonassen, Howland, Moore, & Marra, 2003), due to their different and varied backgrounds (see Figure 9). Some students also reflected that the virtual presentations enabled students to improve their communication skills and it was a less tedious exercise than class presentations. There were fewer comments on inter-class activity but one of the students did suggest having inter-class competitions as such competitions would be more stimulating and challenging. Another student expressed that the inter-class activity had added meaningful value to their overall learning experience.

Nevertheless, we can conclude that:

1. The new practice provides flexibility for teaching and learning. However, some IT students do not appreciate this feature as they assume that it is a basic requirement for online applications.
2. Virtual presentation provides a convenient means for students getting opinions from other participants. In fact, this innovative practice can facilitate active participation and sharing. Thus, virtual presentation can be used to support assessment for leaning.

LMS enables and facilitates inter-class exchanges easily and conveniently as it could be very difficult for two classes, especially the part-time students, to participate in face-to-face activities due to time-tabling problems.

Figure 9. Students' reflections on inter-class activity

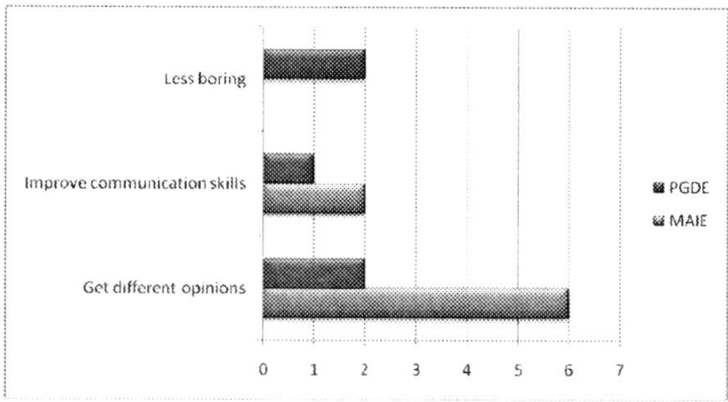

Course Tutors' Reflections

It was the first time that the authors collaborated to embark on an exploratory study of a new practice. The study involved months of planning and effort and was an endeavor to execute and achieve a set goal, through diligent application and synergistic study. However, the authors did face a dilemma in implementation, for they had a module outline to follow, and they had to adapt those guidelines to comply with this new study. The authors felt that it was more convenient to give feedback to virtual presentations as they could bestow their full concentration and attention when watching the students' virtual presentations in their own offices, rather than in the classrooms. Furthermore, the discussion time for classroom presentations is usually too limited. On the contrary, the authors had more time to offer constructive comments and positive feedback in virtual presentations. The tutors also observed the following important points in this case study.

The Tutor Should Actively Take Part in the Virtual Presentation Process

One of the course tutors hesitated to give comments on students' work as he thought that it might inhibit the comments from other participants. He preferred to be an observer in the study. Unfortunately, the students in his group were less motivated and more passive. It seems that regular encouragement for participation is needed for virtual presentation.

The Effectiveness of Virtual Presentation Is Affected by the Nature of Assignment, the Participants' Attitude and Their Academic Background

The tutors also observed that it was difficult to ask every member of a group to pay equal effort in the process. It seems that an individual presentation can force students to take up more responsibility. Besides, the law of diminishing returns may apply to the PGDE students and they may find some so-called innovative technology solutions boring.

Nevertheless, the study provided the tutors a solid experience on using virtual presentation in student assessment. Table 5 summaries their views on virtual presentation and classroom presentation after the study.

Technically, the course tutors thought that virtual presentation as an assessment component is still new and requires further fine-tuning. It would be more appropriate to use it for improving the quality of their assignments and facilitating assessment for learning. Thus there is no intention to consider their performance in virtual presentation seriously to be part of their final assessment grade.

CONCLUSIONS AND FUTURE DIRECTIONS

This article discusses a new attempt to infusing a Web 2.0 tool for blended learning and using virtual presentation as an alternative means of assessment. In the study, the virtual presentations were conducted in an asynchronous mode and the presentation materials were in forms of videos or electronic slides embedded with audio narration. In spite of a dearth of adequate financial and human resources, this study demonstrates that integrating technology with learning, teaching and assessment can be effectively accomplished with the application of creative ideas and innovative practices.

Peer assessment can be easily supported with Web 2.0 enabled LMS platform that provides tools for enhancing participation, sharing resources and ideas, giving ratings and comments, etc. The majority of student teacher participants expressed their enthusiasm with the new experience and did not encounter any unforeseen obstacles in creating a virtual presentation. Through the use of virtual presentation as a means of assessment, the participants can refine their knowledge of their assignment topic and also learn more from others' presentations. Furthermore, the assessment activities not only helped participants to understand different methods to integrate IT to provide a seamless learning and assessment experience, but also equipped them with the training necessary to be better prepared and organized while using different digital formats when teaching at schools. It seems that this innovative assessment practice is closely related to the curriculum for IT teachers. This practice can enrich their knowledge in using virtual learning environment which is considered to be core knowledge for today's IT teachers. The verification of the study echoed Macdonald, Weller and Mason's (2002) suggestion that the learning platform had provided flexibility for peer assessment.

The student teachers received more positive feedback with this practice and at the same time it was found that they were not too keen on contributing suggestions. The findings, therefore suggested that our student teachers are ready to take on the role of producers of digital productions but lack the conviction to be assertive in expressing their critical comments on work presented by their peers. However, they tended to give more comments to their own class rather than to another class. It was encouraging to discern that student teachers thought that the new assessment method could be applied successfully in secondary

Table 5. Virtual presentation vs classroom presentation (or face-to-face presentation)

Aspect	Element	Virtual Presentation	Classroom Presentation
Mode of delivery	Time	Asynchronous/ Synchronous; Span a relatively longer duration, for example, a day to several weeks.	Synchronous; Fixed schedule
	Place	At any place with Internet access.	Usually at school
	Participants	Not limited, but a critical mass is preferred; Not bounded by course enrollment.	Number of participants depends on the venue size, course structure, schedule etc.
Teaching and learning	Teaching strategies	More guidelines and supervision required; Most teachers are not familiar with virtual presentations; Active participation preferred.	Easily handled by most teachers.
	Subject contents	Suitable for topics that require more time to explore or for controversial issues	Suitable for most cases.
	Teacher's comments	More time to gather information; Relatively more accurate; Instant feedback not guaranteed	Quality of comments and advices heavily depends on the teacher's preparation.
	Assessment	Useful for improving assignment quality through peer assessment; Individual presentation encourages more participation.	Normally for grading purpose
	Students' Communication Skills	Knowledge of presentation and ICT skills are equally important; A means for improving communication skills	Knowledge of ICT skills is relatively less important although it is still an advantage.
	Interaction among participants	More collaboration expected; Inter-groups interaction not guaranteed.	Not guaranteed; It depends on the topic and peers' experience.
Technology	Hardware & Software	Usually web-based;	Can be presented orally or with presentation software.
	Social implication	Students should be able to access Internet at home for optimizing the benefits of virtual presentation.	The problem of digital divide can be neglected.

schools. Although most of their comments were merely encouraging and supportive, they seldom asked questions for the purpose of clarifications nor did they offer constructive comments to their peers to improve their work. Some of them even preferred to have traditional classroom presentations. Nevertheless, the following points have been confirmed in the study:

- The new practice provides flexibility for teaching and learning but IT student teachers may perceive that it is a de facto standard for online applications.
- Virtual presentation can facilitate active participation and sharing and thus it can be used to support assessment for learning. However, its effectiveness will be affected by the nature of assignments, participants' attitude and the tutor's involvement.
- Information technology can be used for more than text communications with some creative ideas.

DIRECTIONS FOR FUTURE STUDIES

The study indicates that there is an urgent need for a cultural change for assessments. Traditional assessment is always used for grading, not learning purpose. With the emerging Web 2.0 tools, different formats of assessments through virtual presentation, blogging, social networks may become feasible. It is worth to explore these new formats of assessment and see how these forms of assessment can be used for learning especially inter-class activities. Besides, as blended learning becomes mature and popular in higher education, it is meaningful to develop more strategies for online peer assessment. In addition, teacher educators should help student teachers broaden their mind and encourage them to become more flexible, objective and tolerant to giving and receiving comments from their peers. In the meantime, student teachers should be better prepared to assess and support the work of their peers in peer assessment. As Ridgway, McCuster and Pead (2004) remind us that the issue for e-assessment is not if it will happen, but rather, what, when and how it will happen. Several aspects are also worth to be explored in the future such as the considerations of the gender and learning styles of the participants. However, it is dangerous to generalize the findings from a single case study. The authors hope that more cases can be done in different settings and in different countries. Moreover, longitudinal research is inevitably considered necessary to examine whether virtual presentation can add value to the overall learning and assessment experiences of student teachers.

ACKNOWLEDGMENT

The authors are very thankful to all learners for participating and allowing the authors to cite their work. Generous financial support from the Hong Kong Institute of Education for their Teaching Development Project entitled, "Creating a virtual learning community via video production and sharing", Activity 3298, is also acknowledged.

REFERENCES

Barlow, T. (2008). Web 2.0: Creating a classroom without walls. *Teaching Science*, *54*(1), 46–48.

Berry, R. (2008). *Assessment for learning*. Hong Kong: Hong Kong University Press.

Biggs, J. (1996). Assessing learning quality: Reconciling institutional, staff, and educational demands. *Assessment & Evaluation in Higher Education*, *21*, 5–15. doi:10.1080/0260293960210101

Boud, D., & Walker, D. (1998). Promoting reflection in professional courses: The challenge of context. *Studies in Higher Education*, *23*(2), 191–206. doi:10.1080/03075079812331380384

Brown, S., & Knight, P. (1994). *Assessing learning in higher education*. London: Kogan Page.

Bruner, J. S. (1986). *Acts of meaning*. Cambridge, MA: Harvard University Press.

Buchanan, T. (2000). The efficacy of a World Wide Web mediated formative assessment. *Journal of Computer Assisted Learning*, *16*, 193–200. doi:10.1046/j.1365-2729.2000.00132.x

Chan, C. K. K., & Van Aalst, J. (2004). Learning, assessment, and collaboration in computer-supported environments. In J. W. Strijbos, P. A. Kirschner, R. L. & Martens (Eds.), *What we know about CSCL and implementing it in higher education* (pp. 87-112). Boston, MA: Kluwer Academic Publishers.

Chang, C. C. (2001). Construction and evaluation of a Web-based learning portfolio system: An electronic assessment tool. *Innovations in Education and Teaching International*, *38*(2), 144–155. doi:10.1080/13558000010030194

Conrad, D. (2008). Reflecting on strategies for a new learning culture: Can we do it! *Journal of Distance Education, 22*(3), 157–161.

Johnson, D. (1994). *Research methods in educational management*. Harlow: Longman.

Joint Information Systems Committee (JISC). (2007). *Effective practice with e-Assessment: An overview of technologies, policies, and practice in further and higher education.* Retrieved on March 10, 2009, from http://www.jisc.ac.uk/media/documents/themes/elearning/effpraceassess.pdf

Jonassen, D. H., Howland, J., Moore, J. C., & Marra, R. M. (2003). *Learning to solve problems with technology: A constructivist perspective*. Upper Saddle River, NJ: Merrill/Prentice Hall.

Jonassen, D. H., Peck, K. L., & Wilson, B. G. (1999). *Learning with technology: A constructivist perspective*. Upper Saddle River, NJ: Merrill.

Kwok, R., & Ma, J. (1999). Use of a group support system for collaborative assessment. *Computers & Education, 32*, 109–125. doi:10.1016/S0360-1315(98)00059-1

Lave, J., & Wenger, E. (1991). *Situated learning: Legitimate peripheral participation*. Cambridge, UK: Cambridge University Press.

Lin, S. S. J., Liu, E. Z. F., & Yuan, S. M. (2001). Web-based peer assessment: Feedback for students with various thinking styles. *Journal of Computer Assisted Learning, 17*, 420–432. doi:10.1046/j.0266-4909.2001.00198.x

Macdonald, J., Weller, M., & Mason, R. (2002). Meeting the assessment demands of networked courses. *International Journal on E-Learning, 1*(1), 9–18.

Morris, P. (1996). *The Hong Kong school curriculum: Development, issues, and policies (2nd ed.)*. Hong Kong: Hong Kong University Press.

Mortera-Gutiérrez, F. (2006). Faculty best practices using blended learning in e-learning and face-to-face instruction. *International Journal on E-Learning, 5*(3), 313–337.

Oliver, K. (2007). Leveraging Web 2.0 in the redesign of a graduate-level technology integration course. *TechTrends, 51*(5), 55–61. doi:10.1007/s11528-007-0071-3

Ridgway, J., McCusker, S., & Pead, D. (2004). *Literature review of e-assessment*. Bristol, UK: Futurelab. Retrieved on March 10, 2009, from http://www.futurelab.org.uk/resources/documents/lit_reviews/Assessment_Review.pdf

Robson, C. (1993). *Real world research.* Oxford: Blackwell.

Sluijsmans, D. M. A., Brand-Gruwel, & Van Merrienboer, J. (2002). Peer assessment training in teacher education: Effects on performance and perceptions. *Assessment & Evaluation in Higher Education, 27*(5), 443–454. doi:10.1080/0260293022000009311

Thelwall, M. (2000). Computer-based assessment: A versatile educational tool. *Computers & Education, 34*, 37–49. doi:10.1016/S0360-1315(99)00037-8

Vaughan, N. (2007). Perspectives on blended learning in higher education. *International Journal on E-Learning, 6*(1), 81–94.

Vygotsky, L. S. (1978). *Mind in society: The development of higher psychological processes.* Cambridge, UK: Harvard University Press.

Chapter 10
Reflective Practice, Professional Learning, and Educational Partnerships:
Effecting Change in Classroom Settings

Chris Brook
Curtin University of Technology, Australia

Graeme Lock
Edith Cowan University, Australia

ABSTRACT

In light of current interest in teacher education, this chapter presents an outcome of a study that sought to explore ways that the classroom practices and status of teachers might be improved. The enquiry used a model of professional learning that incorporated blended learning, reflective practice, performance management processes, authentic experiences, and tertiary learning to encourage change in classroom settings. Teacher insights were explored and their classroom practices analysed to identify any change in teacher behaviours that might be attributed to participation in the learning program. Findings suggest that teachers are largely dissatisfied with conventional approaches to professional development believing them to be separate from the classroom experience and ineffective in bring about change. However, teachers in this study found that a blended learning setting that fostered an intentional connection between theory and practice and collaborative learning provided a strong learning experience that translated to change in classroom practice.

INTRODUCTION

Many contemporary scholars assert that the role of the teacher is pivotal in the quality of student learning experience (Darling-Hammond, 2000; Hill & Rowe, 1998; Hattie, Clinton, Thompson & Schmidt-Davies, 1995; Hattie, 2003). Given the extensive body of literature exploring effective teaching and learning practices (Dewey, 1929; Piaget, 1955; Vygotsky, 1978), it could reasonably be assumed that contemporary classroom practice would be informed by research findings. However, there is strong evidence that this is not the case

DOI: 10.4018/978-1-60566-852-9.ch010

(Cognition and Technology Group at Vanderbilt, 1993; Newman & Cole, 2004) with some scholars arguing that school based learning has continued in a teacher centred manner despite evidence highlighting the limitations of this approach (Laurillard, 1997). Some scholars argue that school based learning is essentially separate from learning in the lived in world in several ways: school learning largely promotes individual endeavour and cognition, school learning concentrates on promoting 'pure thought' and abstract representations and symbol manipulation is favoured in school learning. Finally, school learning promotes generalised, theoretical principles and skills. In contrast, learning in the lived in world values situation-specific capabilities, shared learning experiences, the effective use of tools and actions that are closely connected to the actual context of objects and events (Resnick, 1987). Newman (2004) suggests that this separateness might be described as a problem of *ecological validity* whereby schooling is systematically different from everyday practices.

Some researchers posit the outcome of professional training activities is often a mere ten to fifteen percent of knowledge transfer from the leaning setting to the work place as a consequence of this separateness (Broad & Newstron, 1992; Burke & Baldwin, 1999; Facteau, Dobbins, Russell, Ladd, & Kudisch, 1995). It has been further suggested by Herrington (1997) that 'school based and university learning are at risk of being isolated, irrelevant and marginalised from mainstream real world activity and performance. It has been argued that the apparent separation of theory and practice is a consequence of a focus on a discrete body of knowledge separated into subject areas that characterises traditional classroom settings (Herrington 1997). In addition, traditional classroom settings are often characterised by a prescribed timeframe and are removed from the realities of the lived in world. It has also been suggested that educational research has often been conducted without thought to connections between theory and practice (Reeves, 2000; Tanner, 1998). These assertions suggest that the constraints of the classroom setting and ill conceived goals of researchers compound separateness between theory and practice.

These views suggest that, in many instances, current educational practices do not reflect contemporary learning theory, are frequently divorced from the lived in world and are regularly not meeting the educational needs of stakeholders.

This situation suggests a need for enquiry into the ways that contemporary teaching and learning theory might be embedded in the practices of teachers to facilitate pedagogic change in classrooms in ways that overcome the limitations of these settings. In addition, there appears to be a strong need to explore ways to connect the goals of the researcher with those of the practitioner and to explore the influence these factors might have on knowledge transfer from the learning setting to the workplace.

Technologies

Many questions are currently being asked regarding the capacity of learning technologies to meet these educational needs in some way. Some scholars see this technology as potentially an economic vehicle to offer more access to education at a reduced cost (see Hiltz, 1998 p. 55; Holt & Thompson, 1998). Others see it as yet another fad in education that will go the way of radio and television, both of which promised to revolutionise education, but did not (Cuban, 1986 p. 74). Yet another faction sees technology as providing an opportunity to revolutionize the way we teach, providing the rich learning experiences that educators have advocated for many years (e.g. Hiltz, 1998; Palloff & Pratt, 1999; Saettler, 1990).

Those researchers, who advocate a change in the way we teach in order to take advantage of the potential of technologies, often cite theories of learning that report the role of social engagement in the construction of knowledge as a vehicle for change. It has been further suggested that encouraging reflective practice provides a strong framework for bringing about change in teacher behaviours. Schön (1987) suggests the artistry of being a reflective practitioner lies at the heart of being a highly effective teacher. It is the ability to constantly and critically self-evaluate one's program, methods, lessons, pedagogy, strategies and students' individual performances that distinguish these teachers. Effective teachers have the capacity to adapt and change their teaching in response to the needs of the students both *in the moment* and over a longer period of time. Reflective practice or *reflection-in-action* is acquired over time through experience in real classrooms in different contexts. Perry (2001) suggest that video provides an excellent medium for case studies that might include the key elements of reflective practice (Stigler & Hiebert, 1999). Stigler and Hielbert pioneered the use of video for the analysis of teaching practice in the Third International Mathematics and Science Study and continued by others (Powell, 2005).

However, current understanding of the ways in which technologies might be used as a vehicle for educational change remains in its infancy. It is not clear in what ways the intentional combination of technologies including video and online communication and educational theory might influence the transfer of knowledge from the learning setting to the classroom practice of teachers.

Research Questions

In response to this research need, this enquiry sought to explore the following questions:

1. What learning supports do teachers require to engage in quality reflective practices?
2. In what ways do teacher attitudes toward their own teaching alter as a consequence of engaging in reflective practices?
3. In what ways might video be used to facilitate reflective practice and how might this influence teachers' practice?
4. In what ways does a context sensitive learning experience influence the transfer of knowledge from the learning setting to practice?
5. In what ways does a performance management process inform and support teacher professional learning?

BACKGROUND

This study was a collaborative endeavour between Edith Cowan University (ECU) of Western Australia and Ballarat and Clarendon College (BCC) of Victoria (Australia). ECU is a lead provider of both undergraduate and postgraduate teacher education programs in Australia. The university has a strong history of innovative instruction that connects theory to practice. In recent years BCC has invested heavily in teacher professional development and the use of video to support learning. The College has four observation classrooms equipped with multiple audio and video cameras supported by a control room with two way mirrors. Conscious of the investment in both technology and teacher professional learning the College approached ECU with a request to develop a framework that would take full advantage of the available resources to improve the quality of teaching in their school. This study is an outcome of that project.

METHODOLOGY

The quest for both fundamental understanding and application of findings were the guiding factors in the selection of both the research paradigm and methodology. Accordingly, this study seeks to engage in *use inspired basic research* (Stokes, 1997) with a dual focus on practical application of findings and a contribution to a growing theoretical knowledge base. Two further factors influenced the methodology adopted for this inquiry. The first was the context specific nature of the learning experience and the second was the desire to ensure congruence between the goals of the researcher and those of the industry partner (Reeves, 1999, 2000). Acknowledging that qualitative and quantitative paradigms are not mutually exclusive (Patton, 1990) both paradigms were used according to need.

In accordance with these influencing factors a Grounded Theory (Strauss, 1987) approach was chosen due to the inductive nature of generating theory from close contact with the empirical world (Patton, 1990). In the tradition of Grounded Theory data collection strategies were embedded in the experiences, actions and behaviours of the actors involved requiring a case study approach to the inquiry (Willig, 2001). An instrumental case considered an exemplar model (Willig, 2001) was selected for this study. This approach accounted for the context specific nature of the teaching and learning experience providing for the generation of theory from the actions of expert practitioners. This method also fostered a connection between the goals of the researcher and those of the practitioner.

The selection of data collection methods was guided by the nature of case study research that required a certain level of *triangulation* (Willig, 2001), and the context specific nature of the teaching and learning experience. Data collection methods included: interviews, observations, questionnaires, video analysis and the institution performance management processes. These methods allowed participants to describe their experience, allowed an objective interpretation of the experience and provided a way to quantify outcomes.

Questionnaire

A demographic questionnaire was employed to collect data on individual characteristics that might influence teaching practices including teacher experience, qualifications and years at the school. The questionnaire was also used to collect data on individual teacher's perceptions of their classroom practice prior to engaging in the learning experience. Participating teachers were asked to complete the questionnaire at the beginning of the course.

An Attitudinal Survey

A survey was employed to collect data on teacher attitudes toward their own professional practice, their learning experience, the performance management process and their perceptions of knowledge transfer from the learning setting to the classroom. The survey was completed at the beginning and the end of the program to identify any shift in attitudes that might be attributed to participation in the program.

Interviews

Interviews were used to account for the teachers' understanding of the teaching and learning experience and the transfer of knowledge. Interview methods were sensitive to the teachers' understanding and interpretation of the experience (Willig, 2001) and were conducted in the early stages of course delivery to establish baseline data and latter stages of course delivery to ascertain any variation.

OBSERVATIONS

Potential incongruence between what the interviewee says and what actually happens was explored through the inclusion of an observational data collection strategy (Becker & Blanch, 1970). Observations of the workplace behaviours of participating teachers were made to gauge the extent of knowledge transfer from the teaching and learning setting to classroom practices. These observations of workplace practices were made before teachers engaged in the learning experience, during the learning experience and then three months after the learning experience was complete. Observations followed a structured approach proposed by Kiddler (1981).

1. What should be observed?
2. How should observations be recorded?
3. What procedures should be used to try to assure the accuracy of the observations?
4. What relationship should exist between the observer and the observed, and how should such a relationship be established.

The observation schedule provided the opportunity to measure teacher practices and experiences before, during and after the learning experience. Observations were supported through the use of video technologies from the performance management process. This approach ensured that teacher practice was recorded as a semi-permanent record that could be analysed and referred to over time. This feature provided the observer the opportunity to refer back to the practice as if they were referring to the actual event (Merriam, 1998).

DATA ANALYSIS

Resulting qualitative data sets were analysed using a constant comparative approach (Patton, 1990). Qualitative data were coded according to emergent themes. Themes were constantly compared with emergent categories to establish a best fit with the data set. Quantitative data collected through the survey were analysed using descriptive statistics in accordance with the limitations of a relatively small sample size.

THE CASE STUDY DESIGN

Adopting a case study approach to the research methodology is holistic in nature (Willig, 2001) allowing the study of professional learning in the context within which it exists. The case study methodology affords a focus on the particular rather than the general and facilitates theory generation (Willig, 2001). While case study methodology was well suited to the goals of the research it was necessary to specify the type and design of case study that was used. A single case study approach is considered useful to test a well formulated theory or may be used when the case may represent an extreme or unique case of intrinsic interest or the case may be revelatory (Yin, 1994).

Prior to engaging in the selection of cases to be included in the study it was necessary to identify the difference between *the case* and *the object to be studied* (Hamel, 1993). Following the distinction drawn by Hamel (1993), a learning community was identified as the object of study while the case was the actual display of this phenomenon. Considering that the same case may be used to study different phenomenon (Bromley, 1986) it was necessary to state that the interrelationship between pre-existing conditions and forms of engagement and activity that facilitate community development were of interest in this study (Willig, 2001).

THE SETTING

Learning Program Design

In response to the needs of participants the course was designed to be delivered in a blended setting incorporating three face to face lectures and workshops and the equivalent of ten weeks online delivery. To model the intentional connection between theory and practice, participants were made aware that the learning program was designed according to guidelines espoused in contemporary literature. Reflective dialogues (Powell, 2005), situated cognition (Herrington & Oliver, 1995), and community development in online settings (Brook & Oliver, 2003) guided the design of the learning program. Guidance was also taken from university requirements of a Master of Education unit that included a minimum workload of 36 hours of instruction or the equivalent online workload and a maximum of three appropriately sophisticated assessment points. In line with the school performance management process, teachers were required to video their classroom practice biannually. This video became the vehicle for analysing and reflecting on the act of teaching.

The course began with a review of contemporary literature investigating the apparent separation between education theory and classroom practice. Following a brief review of this literature participants were asked to post a short comment on discussion boards. This activity was intended to be non-threatening and provide a meaningful way for participants to explore the learning management system and initiate online dialogue with the instructors.

Participants were provided with a brief summary of the perceived benefits of reflective practice and were encouraged to explore a selection of current literature exploring aspects of reflective practice. Participants were encouraged to extend their reading beyond the provided literature and were given an in-depth review of the reflective dialogue model used by Powell (2005).

When reflecting on their classroom practices participants were asked to consider:

- *Intentions and purpose*
- *Self awareness*
- *Practical reflection*
- *Technical reflection*
- *Perceptual awareness*
- *Critical reflection*

This framework was presented as a useful mechanism to guide reflections, but was not presented as a mandated approach. Participants were encouraged to select the approach to reflective practice that they believe provided a *good fit* with the needs.

The nine discrete characteristics of situated learning environments identified by Herrington and Oliver (1995) were central to course design:

- *Provide authentic context that reflect the way the knowledge will be used in real life*
- *Provide authentic activities*
- *Provide access to expert performances and the modelling of process*
- *Provide multiple roles and perspectives*
- *Support collaborative construction of knowledge*
- *Provide coaching and scaffolding at critical times*
- *Promote reflection to enable abstraction to be formed*
- *Promote articulation to enable tacit knowledge to be made explicit*
- *Provide for integrated assessment of learning within the tasks* (p 181)

All learning activities were based in the professional practices of participants. A common symbol system was established through reference to contemporary literature (Louden, Rohl, Barratt-Pugh, Brown, Cairney, Elderfield, House, Meiers, Rivalland, & Rowe, 2005). Participants were exposed to expert performances through viewing the practices of others and required to engage in a collaborative analysis of that practice. Lecturers acted as facilitators of the learning experience providing appropriate coaching and scaffolding. Reflective practice was facilitated through an analysis of actual classroom practice articulated through the common symbol system. All learning activities were linked directly to classroom teaching and the assessment schedule and participants were encouraged to articulate their learning through a conference presentation.

Central to course design was the notion of a common symbol system. It was acknowledged that in order to share knowledge and experiences there is a real need to ensure common understanding. This was facilitated through the six dimensions of quality literacy teaching and the corresponding teaching practices identified in the 2005 *In Teacher's Hands* study (Louden et al., 2005).

- Participation: (Attention, Engagement, Stimulation, Pleasure and Consistency)
- Knowledge: (Environment, Purpose, Substance, Modelling, Metalanguage and Explanations)
- Orchestration: (Awareness, Structure, Flexibility, Pace and Transition)
- Support: (Responsiveness, Explicitness, Persistence, Assessment, Feedback and Scaffolding)
- Differentiation: (Connection, Variation, Inclusion, Individualisation and Challenge)
- Respect: (Warmth, Rapport, Credibility, Citizenship and Independence)

This framework provided a common symbol system for communication and was used in combination with a model of reflective practice to explore the individual teacher's classroom practice.

A record of classroom practice was facilitated through the use of video and observational classrooms. Purpose built observational classrooms were available in the school setting. These classrooms utilised two way mirrors, multiple video cameras and strategically located microphones to record the practices of teachers and the activities of students. Observational classrooms had been in use in the setting for some time and were considered a key aspect of the teaching and learning program; as such their use was likely to result in accurate record of classroom activities. The resulting video was analysed by the classroom teacher or in collaboration with other teachers using computer software.

Some scholars (Bonk & Wisher, 2000; Hiltz, 1998; Palloff & Pratt, 1999) propose that the social phenomenon of community might be put to good use in the support of online learning. Given the blended nature of this learning setting intentional action was taken to promote a sense of community (McMillan & Chavis, 1986) among participants. Figure 1 shows the Learning Community Development Model (LCDM) developed by Brook & Oliver (2004) as a useful framework for both exploring and promoting community development in online settings.

Care was taken to ensure that many of the presage factors that have been shown to present barriers to community development (Brook & Oliver, 2005) were overcome. To ensure reliable communication a well supported, easily accessed and reliable learning management system was used. To avoid unhealthy system promoted conflict among participants, assessment was based on a pass or fail system with no limit set on the number

Figure 1. The learning community development model © 2004 Brook & Oliver. Used with permission.

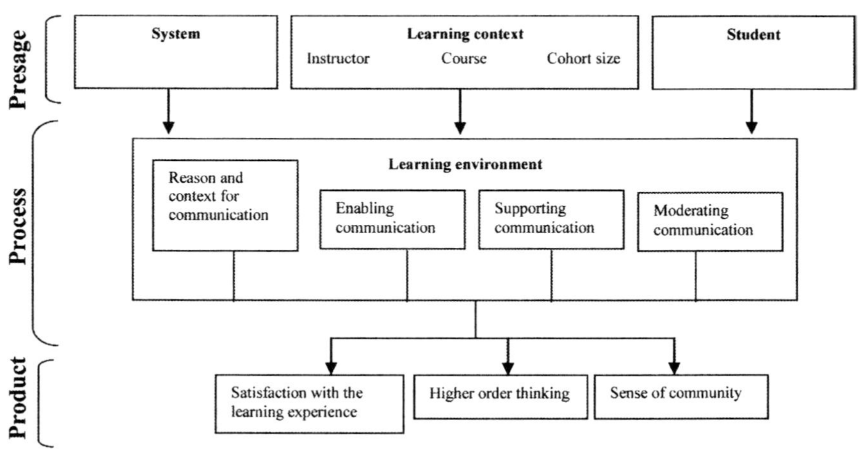

of participants who could achieve a pass grade. The instructors had extensive technical, pedagogic and social skill sets, the course itself was suited to collaborative endeavours and the cohort size was within recommended numbers. Participants were selected on a voluntary basis to ensure a willingness to participate and were informed of the collaborative nature of this learning setting prior to engagement.

Following the process component of the LCDM the reason and context for participation was driven by the opportunity to increase learning, reduce workload and *work smart* by linking professional learning with performance management and classroom practice. The instructors established regular and meaningful meetings both online and face to face and maintained and appropriate pace for communication. A code of conduct was established to support communication and participants were encouraged to express themselves while accepting their responsibility to listen to others. The instructors took an active role in communication weaving the contributions of others and prompting deep thinking through critical reflection and further enquiry.

Over 100 teachers were invited to take part in the course with six volunteering. Although school administrators were welcome to engage, they chose not to in light of their reduced classroom workload. However, intentional action was taken to ensure school administrators were informed of course progress and included in scheduled course related face to face meetings.

Results

All six participating students volunteered to take part in the research project associated with the course of study. Table 1 introduces the volunteers and provides relevant descriptive details.

The demographics of the group suggest that participants in this learning program were familiar with the school setting. All participants had at least three years experience teaching in the school and many have management responsibilities in addition to classroom teaching. In addition, Charles is characterised as an experienced practitioner (20 years teaching) with senior management responsibilities. These characteristics suggest a cohort of experienced practitioners who are active in school management and decision making processes.

All participants identified experience in attending professional learning programs. Table 2 shows the nature of professional learning programs attended, the participant response to that program and the perceived impact on classroom teaching.

Table 1. Roles and responsibilities of participating students

Name	Years at the school	Main responsibilities
Allan	3 years	Years 11-12 Information Technology and pastoral care
Charles	20 years	Years 5,6,7,8, and 9 Head of Middle School
Jan	7 years	Years 7-12 English
Ross	6 years	Years 7-12 Science and Chemistry, Maths, Personal Futures Physical Education
Susan	4 years	Years 7-12 English
Stuart	3 years	Year 4 – 12 music Head of Music and Performing Arts

Table 2. Perceptions of professional learning programs attended

Nature of professional learning	Comments	Perceived impact on Classroom Teaching
School developed professional learning	Found to be seriously deficient	Limited
External professional learning	Haven't related to classes taught Usually one-offs, with no follow-up. Lag time. Information limited and constrained Very sceptical of the ones that give you activities and games to do in the classroom, without the reasons behind them. You need the theory.	Limited
Conferences	Not much to bring home and to work with	Limited

Participants identified three forms of professional learning commonly attended. That which is developed at the school level, that which is provided by external agencies and conferences.

When asked to describe the value of previous professional learning experiences participants commented that the professional learning developed at the school level was seen to be seriously deficient and resulted in only a limited impact on classroom teaching. Professional learning provided by external agencies was also perceived to have limited impact on classroom teaching. Participants commented that this form of professional learning was seen to be separate from the classroom practices of teachers, lacked a connection with educational theory and presented a limited or constrained view of teaching. Conferences were also perceived to have little impact on classroom teaching, as attendees tended to make limited connections between the conference presentation and the classroom practices of attendees.

Responses suggested that participants were largely unsatisfied with their recent professional learning experiences, as these experiences had not provided the desired learning outcome or connection with classroom teaching.

Despite being largely unsatisfied with previous learning experiences, participants provided a strong indication of what they valued in the current professional learning activity. Table 3 presents what participants identified as positive aspects of the professional learning experience under investigation.

Participants identified several common aspects of the course they believed to be useful in promoting their learning. These included opportunities to connect contemporary teaching and leaning theory with their own classroom practices. In addition, participants articulated a belief that the learning experience would have a positive impact on their classroom teaching and an appreciation of the opportunity to engage in structured reflective practice. Common threads also included the enjoyable nature of the course, an appropriate pace and structure for learning.

Course Design

Close analysis of the data set revealed a number of factors that were seen to influence the teachers' opportunity to engage in quality reflective practices. A review of contemporary literature suggests that in general terms teachers consider themselves to be reflective practitioners, but that reflection tends to be shallow in nature and perhaps more aligned to *thinking about what one is doing* rather than critical reflection. As might be expected, teachers in this enquiry articulated a belief that they engaged in quality reflective practice prior to the commencement of the learning program. However, analysis of the data set suggests this might not be the case. The following section presents the data analysis using the research questions as a framework.

Table 3. Positive aspects of this professional learning program

Name	Perceived benefit	Comments
Allan	Connecting with classroom practice	Enjoyed it. Been an eye-opener. Enjoyed most of the readings.
Charles	Sees himself as stepping out of classroom teaching role, but also knee-deep in it. Looking at what kind of coaching he would like: getting significant staff input. Being able to teach the teachers, and enhance own learning (because of the need to look at it from two perspectives: teacher and student)	Allowed me to look at my personal and professional needs Flexibility of the course allowed development of my own professional learning, and to develop skills and craft as teacher and leader within the school.
Jan	Being able to combine teaching theory and practice.	Good option and resources. Range of ideas with enough crossover to see common threads. Good having other people at school doing it. Enrolling was easy
Ross	Actually links into teaching. Reflective practice is valuable. Looking at different ways of reflecting	Pretty good Enrolment process tricky. Working at a distance tricky
Susan	Being able to draw on more experienced teachers' knowledge, and look at my own practice in the classroom.	Being able to draw on more experienced teachers' knowledge, and look at own practice in the classroom.
Stuart	It's going to benefit my teaching in every way.	Enjoying it. This is some of the best professional learning activities you can do. Gives an opportunity to reflect on own practice and that of individuals. Set timeframe is good, or else would just keep pushing it back.

What Learning Supports Do Teachers Require to Engage in Quality Reflective Practices?

The participants in the study emphasised four key support aspects, the first of which was the use of a peer group learning model. They commented that the already established peer learning model within the school provided valuable background to the work they undertook within this project. In particular, they emphasised the confidence they gained from such support and the "binding experience" gained by working with others who shared the same context and objectives. Second, the group members were positive about the university staff providing immediate responses to questions. They identified the immediacy of this feedback as being both critical and highly valued. This is exemplified in a comment by Charles, "Instant support from the ECU staff has been great – strategic alliance with a tertiary institution has been very beneficial to take the helicopter view as critical friends." Overall, a statement by Jan neatly summaries these first two aspects, "Email contact and online discussions with ECU staff was fantastic and together with staff contact here was enough to get me through."

The school teaching staff also identified the importance of personal visits throughout the year by the university academics. These visits were made possible by the funding attached to this project and prove to be crucial to the school staff, who suggested that they were critical to sustaining the group's interest and giving the sense that academics cared about their research and them as individuals. Stuart summarised the importance placed on this aspect when he stated that, "(The) one-to-one interviews really helped develop focus" and "(I) really liked the personal interest shown by the ECU staff."

The final learning support, which received comment, was the incentive of academic credit to complete the professional learning. It was seen by the group as being critical to sustain motivation and contributed to all members of the group completing the first year of the course.

Members of the group also suggested that a change to the structure might have provided another learning support. They commented that the order of unit delivery might be changed so that the final unit was focused on active reflection. This change, they argued, would allow them to build on the scaffolding of learning from the previous three units. Within this unit, they thought that more opportunity could be provided to reflect as a group, with a symposium or reflection point, facilitated by ECU, to be built into the unit structure.

In What Ways Do Teacher Attitudes Toward Their Own Teaching Alter as a Consequence of Engaging in Reflective Practices?

All members of the group commented that although engaging in postgraduate study while continuing to teach necessitated a considerable amount of extra work, it was both manageable and worthwhile. Their comments in response to the questions associated with this research question can be categorised into three themes.

First, they discussed how they have been inspired to learn more and engage in the rigour of postgraduate study. The inspiration and rigour they experienced took them out of a sense of complacency and gave them more of a sense of purpose in their teaching. Second, the group members commented that, in addition to their reflective practice becoming routinised, their postgraduate study gave them more structure and deliberation within this process. Ross commented:

We used to think that we were talking about our teaching, but really we were talking superficially about our students. Now our conversations are really about teaching – this is a very big change.

Third, these teachers described how they had made the link between theory and their own teaching practice. This link, they argued, resulted in significant and validated (through video observation) improvement in their teaching. Ross neatly summarised this improvement when stating,

Yes. It has underlined the value of the review section of a lesson at the beginning and end. Shows that what you expect students to know isn't always so, so there needs to be a structure to the review process and that's what you researched." Those who were in administrative positions also outlined improvements in this aspect of their roles due to the professional learning involved in this project.

In What Ways Does a Context Sensitive Learning Experience Influence the Transfer of Knowledge from the Learning Setting to Practice?

Unanimously, the teachers who participated in this project were vociferous when stating that there had been a definite transfer of knowledge from the learning setting to practice, with consequent improvements to their teaching and administrative tasks. Participating in this professional learning program, and the associated reading and research had provided a helicopter view for reviewing their own teaching and administrative practices. In relation to this transfer of knowledge, Jan a participant in the study stated,

Definitely had an impact on my classroom practice, and especially early on because the knowledge was coming from outside the school, so definitely supplemented changes that I was making to my teaching.

Group members also indicated that the impact of this knowledge transfer, which they discussed with both the school administration and other members of the teaching staff, resulted in wider changes to the school culture and policy. Two examples were cited to describe the former. First, teachers in the school developed a common language with which to discuss teaching and participate in professional dialogue. Second, the results of the project have assisted teachers to make links at a variety of levels: school, department, learning areas and the classroom.

Participants indicated that developing a common language for talking about their teaching was instrumental in promoting reflective practice. Through the common language teachers were able to engage in dialogue that promoted much deeper reflections than simply *thinking about what they were doing.* Ross commented:

Has allowed me to reflect on my practice – that was superficial before – now I have tools to dig deeper."

In what ways does a performance management process inform and support teacher professional learning?

Two themes emerged from the group members' responses to interview questions related to this aspect of the research. First, while they believed the project had shown the close links between the school's performance management process and teacher professional learning, they acknowledged that confusion about the purpose and implementation of performance management still existed. As observed by Jan

Gave a sense of direction and a framework to use for management for performance and that was a big improvement for credibility of the performance management process. In the past there has been some resentment because of the previously subjective way things have been commented on in performance management, but using the Classroom Observation Schedule gave a common language to use for performance management.

The second theme identified that support from the school administration had been critical to the success of this project. The teachers considered that the effort they had put into the professional learning was valued at senior managerial level.

In what ways might video be used to facilitate reflective practice and how might this influence teachers' practice?

Members of the group were in total agreement that the use of video was a very powerful tool for reflecting on teaching. In making this comment they identified the necessity of using a common observation framework and suggested watching oneself teaching is the only way to see what is happening in the classroom. The observation framework provided them with a lens for self-analysis, allowing them to compare reality with self perception. Comments from Ross and Jan summarise the group's thoughts:

I was able to see more of what was happening in the classroom rather than having an idealised view – positive or negative – of my practice." Jan commented, "Although we've had a look at our own teaching before watching through the Classroom Observation Schedule framework gave specific insight on teaching practices rather than superficial things.

While acknowledging the usefulness of video to facilitate reflective practice, the group members commented on the confronting nature of such a practice. However, all suggested that this confrontation can be overcome. As observed by Stuart, "I would feel it was more confronting if viewed by others, but even that would be okay if sufficiently prepared."

Discussion

An exploration of participating teachers past professional learning experiences identified three forms of professional learning typically attended: externally provided professional learning session, school based professional learning and conference based professional learning. Teacher perceptions of the value of these forms of professional learning varied, but were generally negative.

School based professional learning was described as *seriously deficient*, professional learning delivered by providers external to the school were depicted as *one off sessions with no follow up*, conferences were criticised for the lack of connection with the realties of teachers. Importantly, all participants identified that learning presented through the three models of delivery had limited influence on their classroom practice.

This finding is in keeping with contemporary literature that describes a separation between educational theory, professional learning and classroom practice. However, the findings of this study suggest that the design of a professional learning program can improve the transfer of knowledge from the learning setting to the classroom. By comparison with the types of professional learning in which these teachers had previously participated, this program incorporated performance management, authentic experiences, reflective practices and tertiary learning. The professional learning program was delivered using a blended mode that included face-to-face lectures and workshops, together with the equivalent of 20 weeks of online learning; 10 weeks per semester.

Course features included reflective practice, basing learning activities on the professional practices of the participants; the use of a common symbol system; the use of video and observational classrooms; and the promotion of a sense of community among the six teachers. The findings of the study present interesting reading when compared with the existing literature on professional learning. Comments from the participants revealed that the authenticity of the learning experiences, that is, the explicit link between the program and their teaching roles in this program contributed to the definite transfer of knowledge from learning setting to practice. One of the key design elements of this professional learning course, the use of video, was seen by the participants to be a powerful tool in reflecting on their teaching. In addition, the use of a blended approach to courses delivery incorporating both face to face instruction and online communication proved an essential design element. This combination of *learning spaces* facilitated the ongoing sense of togetherness between students and academic staff essential to a quality learning experience.

Limitations

Due to the small sample size in this study, the generalisability of the findings requires some discussion. The teachers in this group were highly motivated to participate in this project, linked partly to the incentive of a postgraduate qualification. If the lure of a postgraduate qualification was removed, and the study enlarged to include all teachers in the school, would the findings have been the same? Did the small size of the group, which enabled them to develop a sense of camaraderie, influence the findings? Working with a hundred teachers, not all of whom might be highly motivated, would present another set of challenges in designing and delivering a professional learning program.

CONCLUSION AND FURTHER RESEARCH

This study demonstrated that it is possible to develop a learning setting that promotes change in practice by incorporating what we already know about teaching and learning. Insight suggests that course design should be derived from established learning theory. In this case, the program was designed around reflective dialogues (Powell, 2005), situated cognition (Herrington & Oliver, 1995), and community development in online settings (Brook & Oliver, 2003). The program was delivered in a blended mode, which included authentic tasks, the use of video and a common symbol system. According to the study's participants, the program design and delivery resulted in a definite transfer of knowledge from the learning setting to practice; an indicator of an effective program.

Findings suggest that an effective learning program will demonstrate a direct link between learning activities contemporary research and classroom practice. Results from this study indicate that these factors motivated initial and continuing participation in the learning program and were seen to be instrumental in effecting change in classroom practice. A further finding is that accreditation appears to be a factor that motivates participation. In addition, evidence suggests that the professional standing of teachers within both the school and community setting was positively influenced through their participation in this learning experience.

In the case of this study participants acknowledged the usefulness of blended learning incorporating online communication with the instructors, the face-to-face meetings were critical to the success of the program. This finding provides a basis for further research into the-nature of a *blended learning* setting that incorporates aspects of flexible learning supported by face to face instruction and support. In addition, a pivotal factor in effective learning programs appears to be support, awareness and engagement from senior administrators. In the case of this study all participants recognised the importance the senior administration team played in the success of the learning program. Issues to be considered in future research include investigating whether this study might be replicated on a larger scale, in a different school setting or with different content.

REFERENCES

Becker, H., & Blanch, G. (1970). Participant observation and interviewing: A comparison. In W. J. Filstead (Ed.), *Qualitative methodology*. Chicago: Markham.

Bonk, C. J., & Wisher, R. A. (2000). Applying collaborative and e-learning tools to military distance learning: A research framework. Retrieved on July 2, 2002, from http://www.publicationshare.com/docs/Dist.Learn(Wisher).pdf

Broad, M. L., & Newstron, J. L. (1992). *Transfer of training: Action packed strategies to ensure high payoff from training investments*. Reading, MA: Addison-Wesley.

Bromley, D. B. (1986). *The case study method in psychological and realted disciplnes*. Chichester: John Wiley.

Brook, C., & Oliver, R. (2003). Online learning communities: Investigating a design framework. *Australian Journal of Educational Technology, 19*(2), 139–160.

Brook, C., & Oliver, R. (2005). *Exploring system factors that influence community development in online settings.* Paper presented at the World Conference on Educational Multimedia, Hypermedia, & Telecommunications, Montreal, Canada.

Burke, L., & Baldwin, T. (1999). *First break the rules: What the worlds greatest managers do differently*. New York: Simon & Schuster.

Cognition and Technology Group at Vanderbilt. (1993). Toward integrated curricula: Possibilities from anchored instruction. In M. Rabinowitz (Ed.), *Cognitive science foundations of instruction* (pp. 33-55). Hillsdale, NJ: Lawrence Erlbaum Associates.

Cuban, L. (1986). *Teachers and machines: The classroom use of technology since 1920 by Larry Cuban*. Teacher's College Press.

Darling-Hammond, L. (2000). Teacher quality and student achievement: A review of state policy evidence. *Educational Policy Archives, 8*(1).

Dewey, J. (1929). *The sources of a science of education*. New York: Liveright.

Facteau, J. D., Dobbins, G. H., Russell, J. E. A., Ladd, R. T., & Kudisch, J. D. (1995). The influence of general perceptions of the training environment on pretraining motivation and perceived training transfer. *Journal of Management*, *21*, 1–25. doi:10.1016/0149-2063(95)90031-4

Hamel, J. (1993). *Case study methods*. London: Sage.

Herrington, J. (1997). *Authentic learning in interactive multimedia environments*. Unpublished doctoral dissertation, Edith Cowan University, Perth.

Herrington, J., & Oliver, R. (1995). *Critical characteristics of situated learning: Implications for the instructional design of multimedia.* Paper presented at the Ascelite, University of Melbourne.

Hill, P., & Rowe, K. J. (1998). Modelling student progress in studies of educational effectiveness. *School Effectiveness and School Improvement*, *9*(6), 310–333. doi:10.1080/0924345980090303

Hiltz, S. R. (1998). *Collaborative learning in asynchronous learning environments: Building learning communities.* Paper presented at the Web-Net 98 World Conference of the WWW, Internet and Intranet Proceedings, Orlando, Florida.

Holt, D., & Thompson, D. (1998). Managing information technology in open and distance education. *Distance Education*, *19*(2), 197–227. doi:10.1080/0158791980190203

Kiddler, L. H. (1981). *Sellitz, Wrightsman, & Cook's research methods in social relations* (4th ed.). Austin, TX: Holt, Rinehart, and Winston.

Laurillard, D. (1997). *Rethinking university teaching a framework for effective use of educational technology*. New York: Routledge.

Louden, W., Rohl, M., Barratt Pugh, C., Brown, C., Cairney, T., Elderfield, J., et al. (2005). *In teachers' hands*. Perth, WA: Edith Cowan University.

McMillan, D., W., & Chavis, D. M. (1986). Sense of community: A definition and theory. *Journal of Community Psychology*, *14*, 6–23. doi:10.1002/1520-6629(198601)14:1<6::AID-JCOP2290140103>3.0.CO;2-I

Merriam, B. S. (1998). *Qualitative research and case study applications in education*. San Francisco: Jossey-Bass.

Newman, D., & Cole, M. (2004). Can scientific research from the laboratory be of any use to teachers? *Theory into Practice*, *43*(4), 260–268.

Palloff, R., & Pratt, K. (1999). *Building learning communities in cyberspace*. San Francisco: Josey-Bass Publishers.

Patton, M. Q. (1990). *Qualitative evaluation and research methods*. Newbery Park, CA: SAGE Publications, Inc.

Perry, G., & Talley, S. (2001). Online video case studies and teacher education: A new tool for preservice teacher education. *International society for technology in education, 17*(4), 26-31.

Piaget, J. (1955). *The construction of reality in the child*. London: Routledge.

Powell, E. (2005). Conceptualising and facilitating active learning: Teachers' video-stimulated reflective dialogues. *Reflective Practice*, *6*(3), 407–418. doi:10.1080/14623940500220202

Reeves, T. (1999). A research agenda for interactive learning in the new millennium. Retrieved on July, 29, 2001, from http://it.coe.uga.edu/~treeves/EM99Key.html

Reeves, T. (2000). *Enhancing the worth of instructional technology research through design experiments and other development research strategies.* Paper presented at the International Perspectives on Instructional Technology Research for the 21st Century, New Orleans, LA.

Resnick, L. (1987). Learning in school and out. *Educational Research*, *16*(1), 1–10.

Saettler, P. (1990). *The evolution of American educational technology.* Englewood, CO: Libraries Unlimited, Inc.

Schön, D. (1987). *Keynote: Educating the reflective practitioner.* Paper presented at the AETA Annual Conference, Washington, D.C.

Stigler, J. W., & Hiebert, J. (1999). *The teaching gap*. New York: Free Press.

Stokes, D. E. (1997). *Pastuer's quadrant: Basic science and technological innovation*. Washington, D.C.: Brookings institution Press.

Strauss, A. L. (1987). *Qualitative analysis for social scientists*. New York: Cambridge University Press.

Tanner, D. (1998). The social consequences of bad research. *Phi Delta Kappan*, *79*, 344–349.

Vygotsky, L. S. (1978). *Mind in society: The development of higher psychological processes* (M. Cole, V. John-Steiner, S. Scribner & E. Souberman, Trans.). Cambridge: MA: Harvard University Press.

Willig, C. (2001). *Introducing qualitative research in psychology adventures in theory and method.* Buckingham: Open University Press.

Yin, R. K. (1994). *Case study research: Design and methods*. London: Sage.

Chapter 11
Allegheny Women's Biotechnology Workforce Collaborative:
Investing in Disadvantaged Populations with Technology

Michelle Zuckerman-Parker
Allegheny-Singer Research Institute, USA

Christine Compliment
Allegheny-Singer Research Institute, USA

Megan Rodella
Allegheny-Singer Research Institute, USA

Garth Ehrlich
Allegheny-Singer Research Institute, USA

J. Christopher Post
Allegheny-Singer Research Institute, USA

Allysen Todd
Community College of Allegheny County, USA

James Schreiber
Duquesne University, USA

ABSTRACT

The Allegheny Women's Biotechnology Workforce Collaborative (AWBWC) is a research based educational intervention designed to support participants with "lifelines" using blended learning as they further their education and enter the biotechnology workforce. This holistic educational approach provides didactic instruction with a focus on individualized learning using technology to foster personal skill development and mentoring from industry professionals. The AWBWC participants live at 60% below the poverty level

DOI: 10.4018/978-1-60566-852-9.ch011

and 90% have been victimized. This comparative study is based on a new model and its impact upon achievement. The quantitative data includes participant grade point average (GPA), technology usage, and rate of attrition. The qualitative data includes emails, text messages, focus group and face-to-face interviews. Additionally, anecdotal evidence indicates the children of participants have increased self-esteem, perform better in school as measured by GPA, and desire to pursue higher education.

INTRODUCTION

Once an industrial giant, Pittsburgh, Pennsylvania has undergone a transformation from steel city to a biomedical research hub, a region in need of a qualified science, technology, engineering, math (STEM) and healthcare workforce. In an area where blue-collar jobs were once plentiful, there are now economically depressed communities with many families, most headed by women, who seek an opportunity to regain their economic independence. Many of these women were displaced early from academics or the workplace for a variety of circumstances, such as teen-age pregnancy, economic or domestic difficulties or the learned hopelessness that comes from living in a depressed community located on the north shore of the city. The Northside is composed of a diverse group of 14 identifiable neighborhoods. Their demographics represent the greater Pittsburgh community at large, half are African American and half are Caucasian, (see Table 1). Participants of the **Allegheny Women's Biotechnology Workforce Collaborative** (AWBWC) represent a cross section of the Northside community at large: 47% are African American, 53% are Caucasian., ages range from 19-50 with 41 children in total. Nearly all of the participants, 75%, receive public assistance and most, 40%, are second generation on public assistance and 53% have a family member incarcerated. The federal government identifies "socially and economically disadvantaged individuals" as those who have been subjected to racial or ethnic prejudice or cultural bias and who have limited capital and credit opportunities, 113 CFR §124.103. According to 2008 HHS Poverty Guidelines, the poverty line for a 3 person household is $17,600, but the average AWBWC 3 person household is $7,324 annually or 60% below poverty level. In spite of this economic hardship, these women are resilient and determined to get an education, begin a career and get off public assistance. Many yearn for the opportunity to make a difference for themselves but more specifically for their children.

The conditions these families live in are not conducive to learning advanced complex domains

Table 1. Neighborhood demographics

	Northside	Pittsburgh	Pennsylvania
Population of area	48,000[1]	297,061[4]	9,987,926[4]
Poverty rate	22.3%[2]	22.2%[4]	12.1%[4]
Unemployment rate	5.1%[1]	7.4%[4]	6.2%[4]
Drop-out rate	37%[3]	29%[3]	1.9%[5]
Percent of ages 25+ w/o high school diploma	24%[1]	18.1%[4]	13.8%[4]

1- (Northside United, 2008)

2- (Pittsburgh United, 2007)

3- (RAND Education, 2006) Northside data from Oliver High School

4 – (American Community Survey, 2006)

5- (Pennsylvania Department of Education, 2007)

such as biotechnology. Even as they attempt to enter education in the traditional manner, their efforts are often interrupted when preparing a sandwich at lunchtime or putting children to bed. Gun violence and fatalities are common in their communities which to a certain extent has desensitized them to the situation. The current program discussed below began with the observations by Dr. J. Christopher Post of patients in his Ear, Nose and Throat clinic located on the Northside of Pittsburgh . "These mothers are resilient, intelligent, inquisitive, and eager to learn with technology," Dr. Post explained at the first advisory council meeting (2007).

He believed intrinsically these women had the essential characteristics required to be a scientist. From these observations, the mission became a call to provide these disadvantaged women with a second chance at an education and provide them with an opportunity to work in a growing field that would lead to long-term stable employment. The AWBWC model tailor fits individual education needs for participants to successfully complete the academically rigorous courses through the use of blended technologies for academic and personal support.

By providing these women with an educational intervention steeped in blended learning, with therapists available to resolve traumatic experiences, the overall goal of the program is to provide these women with the support needed that can help each individual be successful. The technology allows the program to be much more student centric because we can tailor needs and assistance.

LEARNING THEORY AND THE AWBWC

Informal Learning Principles

Currently, the traditional didactic learning model provides some student with an academic opportunity which meets their individual needs. Bonk, Kim, and Zeng (2006) provide Standard Blended Learning Model, but does this work for disadvantaged populations? Based on the attrition rates of 60-80% depending on race, from American Community Colleges, the Blended Learning Model provides a starting point and allows others to proceed in the right direction. Still, the problem remains; the traditional didactic learning model will not work with this demographic. A new model is needed which is a modification of the traditional with blended learning. A starting point has been provided but it is missing the mark. We proposed a collective holistic learning community which used blended learning. And, we considered how well it works.

According to Shank and Brown (2007, p. 2-3), "Education is a basic human process." Teaching and learning occur every day in every sort of setting and social situation (Shank & Brown, 2007). However, education has been skewed heavily toward formal learning especially within schools. As a result, the types of learning that go on in informal learning situations with nontraditional media have been under- utilized in contemporary education. A consequence of this singular learning focus is the fact that assessment is viewed toward such formal learning structures as objectives (Gerber, Marek & Cavallo, 2001). While there are some notable successes (McNeil & Dixon, 2005; Chapman, Ramondt & Smiley, 2005) by and large informal learning ends up being under-used and under-assessed. In order to correct this situation we need to take a closer look at how learning works on its own terms, in its own context (Pekarik, 2002). A large amount of social and academic learning occurs through the use of the technologies in formal settings for these women.

Participatory Learning

Barab, Hay, Barnett, and Keating (2001) define participatory learning environments (PLEs) as systems that " engage students in the construction of products requiring practices that embody complex concepts, necessitate collaboration, and contextualize learning within contexts in which problem solving and inquiry are fundamental aspects of the learning process" (Barab et al., 2000; Barab et al., 2001). In other words, participatory learning facilitates meaningful meaning making. According to Bonk and Cunningham (1998, p. 379), "during the dialogue process, people learn how to think together - not just in the sense of analyzing a shared problem or creating new pieces of shared knowledge, but in the sense of occupying a collective sensibility, in which the thoughts, emotions, and resulting actions belong not to one individual, but all of them together." Such a classroom is effervescent because the educator allows the students to truly experience the creative aspects inherent in scientific discovery. Students design their own experiments rather than follow recipes in the textbook and build upon their own knowledge with new information in collaboration with other students."

Blended Learning and Non-Traditional Students

Although blended learning is appropriate for digital natives, it is applicable to adults returning to school. Swan and Garrison (2006) developed theoretical frames for defining blended learning. Most importantly, they define it as an integration of face-to-face and online modalities, not a simple substitution. The design of such courses and programs ought to maximize the value of the experience by selecting modalities based on their suitability for achieving instructors' goals. Swan and Garrison (2006) are particularly concerned with developing communities of inquiry that support "social presence" (i.e., that employ technologies in such a way that students are able to "project themselves socially and emotionally as 'real' people"), "cognitive presence" (i.e., that afford ample opportunities for students to engage in discovery, application, and debate regarding the subjects at hand), and "teaching presence" (i.e., the capacity of instructors to structure and guide the learning process so that the outcomes of student inquiry can be assessed and verified as "educationally worthwhile learning outcomes."

Vignare et al. (2006) provide a synopsis of theoretical and practical concerns relevant to defining blended learning and identifying best practices in the design, development, management, and evaluation of hybrid and blended courses. Of particular interest is the authors' emphasis on the value of building knowledge communities with technology. Graham (2006) describes the importance of a mindful approach to course re-design and of identifying appropriate situations for employing technology and effective technology-enhanced learning practices based on research, evaluation, and the sharing of experiences. Twigg (2003) identified a range of categories of blends, from uses of technology that simply substitute online activities for face-to-face equivalents to fully online courses that either eliminate face-to-face contact altogether or replace it with on-demand tutoring. Graham notes that these categories can constructively be reduced to three. "Enabling Blends" do not involve pedagogical change, but instead seek to provide an equivalent experience to that experienced by face-to-face students. They are intended to address "issues of access and convenience" for distance students or those who prefer flexible schedules. "Enhancing Blends" add technology-enhanced materials to the course to extend it (i.e., by providing additional course experiences than might otherwise be possible in the normal classroom setting) or to improve students' experience (i.e., by providing technology-enhanced alternatives that afford students more choice about what activities they pursue and when and how they pursue them).

Graham (2006) provides useful examples of enhancing blends in his description of programs like those at the University of Waikato in New Zealand that are stratified into four categories of blends, from those in which online components are supplementary and not required through those that require students to complete some, most, or all of their work online, each entailing appropriate pedagogical changes and support resources. "Transforming Blends" radically alter pedagogy by giving students the freedom to direct their own learning. Technology is used to immerse students in authentic environments that enhance their understanding of real-life performances (e.g., in virtual reality and simulation environments in which decision-support prompts and diagnostic data can be layered on top of sensory input).

"For many participants, school presents a choice between their social and personal lives and their intellectual engagement in school. What appears to be a lack of interest in learning may therefore not reflect a resistance to learning or an inability to learn. On the contrary, it may reflect a genuine thirst for learning of a kind that engages one's identity on a meaningful trajectory and affords some ownership of meaning." (Wenger, 1998, p. 270). "The processes of learning and the transfer of learning are central to understanding how people develop important competencies. Learning is important because no one is born with the ability to function competently as an adult in society" (Bransford, 2000, p 51). Self reflection, "who I am as a person" in conjunction with metacognition, "what I think about my thinking" allow insight into parts of one's self not revealed in other settings. According to Palloff and Pratt (1999) "when an opening is created through which participants can reflect on change, participants are likely to note the changes" (p. 139). It is this introspection which encourages conscious and critical reflection regarding the content under consideration. When this process takes place by a group of participants within a community, it maximizes the benefits and potential of the educational process.

According to Hughes (2005), "improved education and greater educational opportunity will drive long-term economic growth and reduce income inequality at the same time. Today's income gap narrows as an individual's education grows; education contributes to equity and a rising middle class as well as long-term economic growth. Using educational technology will allow a new talent in science and engineering for global leadership. This approach to education requires pedagogy linked to learning styles" (p. 433). Hughes suggests, "We must understand the cognition patterns of participants who grew up on VCRs, MTV, video games, and instant messaging, and devise ways of organizing pedagogy to enable them to use their skills and perspectives in yet more creative ways." (Woodrow Wilson International Center for Scholars, 2006, p. 15) It is imperative that "We must educate our students to work between disciplines, reflecting the new and growing multi-disciplinarily of research and innovation" (p. 16).

For example, community colleges would be wise to reach out to their new participants earlier and more aggressively in such areas as orientation, academic advising, and financial aid. Community colleges typically lose about half of their participants prior to the participants' second year, Sanders noted (2008). Community college participants are "more vulnerable" (p. A25). However, they are also highly motivated. Sixty-eight percent of the respondents in the survey said they strongly agreed with the statement, "I have the motivation to do what it takes to succeed in college" (p. A25). Dropping out, they said, would come only because of too many demands on time and money.

Research specific to collaboration by Hootstein (as cited in Guthrie, 2001) and Zahorik (as cited in Guthrie, 2001) found "professors believe that social collaboration in the classroom will increase interest in the content of learning" (¶27). Interestingly, with regards to gender issues in the technology-rich collaborative learning environments of middle school, "the data suggest that not only are girls and boys similar with regard to attitudes about computers and group work, but that during collaborative learning activities, girls may actually participate more actively and persistently regardless of the nature of the task" (Goldstein & Puntambekar,2005, p. 505).

Specific to higher education learning environments, when collaborative learning was purposely infused within college level course, "Central to the design of the course was our pedagogical commitment, which involved moving away from lectures and toward immersing participants within a learning environment that they actively participate and engage in processes associated with scientific investigations" (Barnet, Barab, & Hay., 2001, p 304). Podcasting provides an alternative form of learning. It creates a classroom where participants are actively engaged in sharing, discussing, and learning from one another. Podcasting shifts learning responsibilities from teacher-centered lectures to a more participant-oriented environment.

Although the benefits of collaborative learning provide participants with the potential for great results, the proper use of this technique by educators is critical. Additionally, some contend this process of learning provides "playtime." However, with clear guidelines of expectations and the use of rubrics for assessment, there is no issue about "playing around" and not staying on task. Participants realize this is "real work." Fortunately, there are free resources available online to develop rubrics for group learning environments such as Rubistar (Advanced Learning Technologies in Education Consortia [ALTEC], 2006) and Technology (2007).

Constructivism emphasizes the importance of the context in which participants work and the importance of collaborative learning. According to Miao, Fleschutz, & Zentel (1999, p.2), "no strict curriculum guides participants through the learning issues, rather the environment as a whole stimulates them to construct knowledge for themselves." From separate voices of ideas and opinions, communities of practice form. "Communities of practice help weave broader value webs created by relationships and exchanges which in turn create extended knowledge systems" (Wenger, McDermott, & Snyder, 2002, p. 220). Collaboration "refers to the social discourse among participants in a learning community that enables them to see perspectives and to construct knowledge socially from text" (Guthrie, 2001).

FRAMEWORK

To address the lifetime of affliction and trauma from living in poverty, dealing with the transition into an academic culture and constant tug between these worlds, we use Bronbenbrenner's Social Ecology of Human Development Model as a macro model to understand the complex lives these women live in each day. We use blended learning technologies to help these participants negotiate and succeed within their life-worlds.

Cell phones, email and Instant Messenger play an important role in this process as the myriad of human development and social science issues have been unearthed. The nexus of issues are adult learning, age advance juvenile delinquency, early trauma, and restorative practices. Counseling provides participants' the ability to mediate environmental stressors whereby the AWBWC is identified pictorially in Figure 1: Bronfenbrenner's Social Ecology of Human Development (Santrock, 1996, p. 51). In addition to the technology, the program brings together several large neighborhood organizations in service to address the economic and financial needs of a region, and more particularly, a community.

This critical linkage incorporates principles of andragogy and blended learning to develop strategies for changing behaviors, and thereby contribute to success in both the participants' personal lives and their future workplace opportunities. Organized around the generosity of local philanthropic gifts to ASRI, AWBWC is comprised

Figure 1. Bronfenbrenner's social ecology of human development (Santrock, 1996, p. 51)

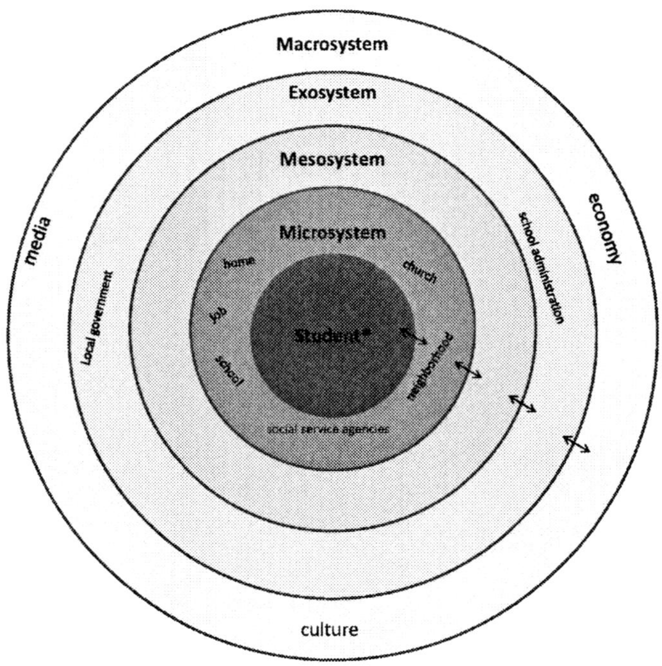

* Student encompasses theories of Maslow, Piaget, Erikson, Vygotsky, & Freud
↔ AWBWC acts as mediating influence across and within systems, specifically operating within the meso-, micro-, and exosystems

of local stakeholders in education, healthcare, research, civic organization, philanthropy and potential Science, Technology, Engineering and Math (STEM) and healthcare employers.

In this study, we aim to address the following research questions:

1. Does the use of blended learning lead to academic success for these participants?
2. Does the use of blended learning lead to successful navigation of personal issues?
3. How much informal learning is occurring related to academic content?
4. Does the social connection component of the program benefit the participants academically and/or socially?
5. Which participants seem to benefit from the program? What is unique about them in comparison to those who are not as successful or successful at all?

GENERAL PROGRAM DESCRIPTION

The AWBWC is a three-year program that provides both didactic instruction to increase scientific literacy, and personal development group sessions to improve life skills in both formal and informal learning environments. While enrolled, participants of the AWBWC program receive paid college tuition, laptop computers, textbooks, school supplies, and free daycare.

The AWBWC participants are enrolled at the Community College of Allegheny College (CCAC) to earn an Associate's Degree in Biotechnology. Additionally, a staff of two people dedicated to the success of the AWBWC cohorts provides extensive case management around the clock. The AWBWC program director and a licensed clinical social worker provide the vital conduit between the participants and the learning community that is fostering this successful model.

Learning Community

In addition to the use of technology, the AWBWC employs a learning community model. The learning community is composed of the professors who facilitate the educational process for the participants of the AWBWC program. Each week this group of professors meets to review the accomplishments of each participant in the program with the personnel of the AWBWC, including a director, licensed clinical social worker and research assistant. From these meetings, the AWBWC personnel work with the participants of the AWBWC to help connect them with the resources needed to increase their success.

Additionally, these meetings provide opportunities for the professors to collaborate and develop lessons with the AWBWC personnel to maximize exposure to timely topics of biotechnology for the participants of the AWBWC. This translates into innovative teaching with technology like podcasting. As such, the learning community is pivotal to the success of the program because working with adult learners warrants different contextualization of content and life experiences.

The learning community is a partnership among the professors, administration and program directors working on behalf of the participants. This group is enhanced by efficiency, expediency, and mutual interests, 'community' places greater emphasis on relationships, shared ideals, and a strong culture. Collectively, the learning community is relentless in questioning the status quo, seeking new methods, testing those methods, and then reflecting on the results. This commitment to continuous improvement is evident in an environment in which innovation and experimentation are viewed not as tasks to accomplish or projects to complete, but as ways of accomplishing tasks. Most importantly, assessment was based on results rather than intentions because it is our goal to set these students up for success.

Technology

The infusion of technology throughout the AWBWC program is a strategy to increase achievement. Technology increases access of the following tools in a timely manner: communication, educational resources, and specialized laboratory equipment. These tools provide mechanisms allowing participants to get the information they need and apply the knowledge gained in a real laboratory environment thus increasing academic achievement and the proficiency of these specialized skills set.

Ubiquitous and specialized technologies are incorporated throughout the AWBWC program. For example, cell phones, laptop computers, podcasts, etc are utilized. To follow are three examples of how technology is used.

1). Cell Phone Text Message: When a participant needs information about how to solve an algebra homework problem after class has concluded and the professor is no longer available during office hours, she is able to text message other participants. As soon as the message is received, another participant shares the URL of an online tutorial, i.e.: www.purplemath.org, which she is familiar with. If the receiver is unable to speak immediately because she is preparing dinner for her family, a simple text message, "later" is sent. However, empowered with knowledge specific to their individual learning style, if the sender receives resources contrary to her identified learning style from the sender, another message is sent requesting another type of assistance, i.e.: auditory rather than textual or podcasts. This ability to ask for specific types of assistance using technology immediately when the need arises has been instrumental in the success of the participants.

2). Personal Laptops: Each participant receives a laptop computer integrated with internet connectivity allowing each member of the cohort a mechanism to facilitate the exchange of English paper drafts between cohort members in a timely fashion on any day and from any location providing hyperlinks to various educational resources to reference during the editing process. The ability to work at any time from any location is a tremendous asset for these participants. First, access to a personal laptop computer reduces the anxiety associated with waiting on campus at a computer lab when they have limited time to be away from home. Secondly, the ability to do homework away from a home environment that is not conducive to the learning process is an enormous benefit. Many of the participants live in areas laden with gang violence, gunshots and drug dealers.

Furthermore, for many of these participants their home is not a safe place for them to keep the laptop computers so they often leave them at another residence. When the laptops are used, typically this occurs either on campus or somewhere other than the participant's primary residence. The fact that the participants have made these arrangements for the storage of a laptop computer speaks to their dedication and commitment. As a result of the threat of theft posed by keeping the laptops at home, their size and weight, cell phones have been a preferred instrument of choice.

3). Podcasts: For many learners, hearing material in class while the instructor is presenting doesn't provide instruction. To aid in their learning process, digital recording devices are used to capture the information and then listen again while class notes are reviewed. However, for some students, a particular instructor may not provide the level of detail needed to understand the concepts which they are accountable for knowing on examinations. Furthermore, for some learners, the textbook is not always helpful. To aid these learners, the use of podcasts have been implemented. Using personal computers, the participants are able to download podcasts specific to content covered in class from iTunes and numerous other websites. Additionally, many cell phones provide the functionality to store and play .mp3 files. These cell phones provide the same functionality of popular iPods or other digital storage devices. By accessing these podcasts, the participants who are auditory learners have an opportunity to review material in a meaningful way. These learners prefer to have information explained to them because the written words are not as valuable as those they hear.

Through the various types of technological exchanges, participants get to know each other as people. Being able to resource materials that meet a specific need is empowering. Typically, once a source has been discovered, this information is shared rather than hoarded. This "team spirit" or "sisterhood" emanates throughout each group of participants. During face-to-face weekly group sessions in addition to regular classes, the participants learn more about the other participants in the group. Although the participants in the AWBWC represent diverse backgrounds exemplified across all demographics, these participants share one dream, collectively they strive to reach a common goal, to graduate with an Associate's Degree in Biotechnology and provide a better life for their families.

Additionally, unlike traditional college students, these participants have a personal stake in the program. They know participation in this program is a gift, a second chance, and they value the opportunity immensely. When one participant is in need, whether her child is sick or her washer machine flooded the basement, immediately they help each other while simultaneously contacting the AWBWC staff to keep all apprized of the situation. As a result of the cohort model, the participants are also able to share their strengths with each other. It is not uncommon for the participants to text message or call each other or the staff when questions arise.

This exchange of knowledge fosters and exemplifies organic communities of practice. A validation of what each woman knows is inherent in the process as they share with each other. The attrition of < 5- 30% compared to 60-80% nationally is accredited to extensive case management and use of instructional technology. Using a learning community in conjunction with a cohort model and instructional technology, the AWBWC maintains constant communication and fosters academic achievement. Additionally, the children of participants are proud of the academic achievements. This pride transcends into their own academic achievement.

RESEARCH METHOD

Design

This is Design Experiment (DE) because the program involves multiple cohorts that will experience different programs over time as adjustment decisions based on the evaluation component (Brown, Campione, Webber, & McGilley, 1992). This is also a DE based research study because the researchers are interested in an iterative approach to the program, developing theories, putting theories in "harm's way" (Cobb, Confrey, di Sessa, Lehrer, & Schauble, 2003, p 9), and developing knowledge that can be shared with practitioners (Cobb, et al). In addition, to answer our questions and interrogate our beliefs about how learning, engagement, and success should work in this program, we will use a multi-method design and data collection process (Tashakkori & Teddlie, 1998). Finally, the rationale for multiple types of data is also supported by the fact we need to triangulate data to make warranted claims for the program overall (Miller, 2003).

Participants

Participant Recruitment was facilitated by a simple easy to read flyer provided to all stake holders, local workforce investment boards and faith-based organizations as part of a program awareness campaign. Once a person contacts us, we begin a multi-phase screening process, that included phone interviews, face to face interviews, and a rubric to ascertain issues related to criminal history, drug and alcohol use, educational completion and experience levels, and motivation.

Data

The long-term indicators of the AWBWC's success are completion, obtaining employment in the STEM fields and providing a research based model which is exportable to other communities and other demographics. For this particular component of this study, the data are academic achievement, interviews, electronic data from email and text messages, computer usage, podcast usage, group sessions, and PDS (post-traumatic stress disorder) instrument. (Foa, EB, Cashman, L, Jaycox, LH, Perry, K (1997). The validation of a self-report measure for PTSD: The Posttraumatic Diagnostic Scale. Psychological Assessment, 9, 445-451.) PDS (Foa,et al, 1997) is a 49-item self-report instrument that assesses adult PTSD symptoms. It is unique among adult PTSD scales in that it assesses all DSM-IV criteria for PTSD. Each item is rated on a Likert scale from 0 (not at all) to 3 (5 or more times a week). Internal consistency of the entire scale is .92 with the 3 PTSD cluster sub-scales ranging from .78 to .84. Test-retest reliability was .83; construct validity revealed a sensitivity rate of .89 and specificity rate of .75 when compared to structured interview.

Counseling Issues

Developmentally appropriate advising for each individual is conducted using various instruments for assessment. This is based on the concept that academic success is an intrinsic aspect to student growth. Additionally, undiagnosed mental health issues are examined and psychotherapy is implemented. Participants learn how to learn and understand gaps in their own knowledge. For those who have tried to study and are still unsuccessful according to grades, learning disabilities and undiagnosed mental health needs often presents additional emotional challenges that affect the individual and consequently the social support relationship. The emphasis is on the importance of balancing the social and emotional needs of students with LD and mental health needs with their academic goals. It is critical that social support programs consider the possibility that some students with LDs and mental health issues that are participating in their programs may need at least as much social as academic support. Based on the data collected, 100% of the participants have post traumatic stress disorder, PTSD, using the PDS. Once a participant has been identified with depression, an anxiety disorder or bipolar we work with them in concert with their therapists. Nearly all of the participants who have been identified with a mental health issue and require medications have been identified When the women confide in us that they are afraid to fill the prescription we help them consider options. This communication typically occurs between the participants and the staff via technology since these issues doesn't occur during school hours. For example, one student shared how helpful it was to meet with a therapist after being apprehensive for weeks as her anxiety grew.

The long-term success will be seen with the increase in minority women in the STEM fields in the region. A second long-term success is the transition for many of the targeted population from dependent to independent members of society. The evaluation will also provide essential information in order to acquire more in-depth and nuanced understanding of the dynamics of learning, both formal and informal situations, with this particular population.

RESULTS

Below we provide the results of this study by the question asked.

RQ1. Does the use of blended learning lead to academic success for these participants?

We observed an increase in academic achievement by engaging participants of the AWBWC with ubiquitous technology, (cell phone text messages, email, and podcasts), which with they are already comfortable. Not all of the participants are enrolled in the same courses during the same semester; therefore, each participant has different set of grades as indicated on the two tables Available in appendix x. Both Tables, Table 2; Participant Grades and Extenuating Circumstance and Table 3; Participant Background, Current Status, Current Physical and Psychological Area of Concern, Technology Usage in the Program, and Cumulative GPA provide insight into the academic standing and it's relationship to technology in terms of frequency of use.

From Table 2, an overview of the participants' changes in test scores is provided. Note, we do not have control over the quality of the assessment instruments used. However, from the data, participants who consistently used the ubiquitous technology or made changes to include the use of technology outperformed those who did not access these blended learning tools at all. As such, GPA and attrition rates directly relate to use of technology: 1) 100% of the participants who have been using the technology to learn and to reflect are doing well are achieving or surpassing aca requirements or have been able to improve their standing in the program, 2) 100% of the participants who did not use the technology at a moderate (requested level) to learn or reflect were not able to do well and are no longer in the program.

Table 3 Participant Background, Current Status, Current Physical and Psychological Area of Concern, Technology Usage in the Program, and Cumulative GPA. the column labeled "Technology Usages" provides insight re: frequency as identified: 1) "High" refers to a participant who meets and surpasses required use, increased frequency with text messages, emails and phone plus traditional face to face, 2) "Moderate" refers to a participant who meets requirements via text messages, emails and phone plus traditional face to face, 3) "Nominal" refers to marginal frequency with technology or face to face (later explained by participants as their culturalizaltion. They are ashamed to share personal situations which are to be kept in the family because family business

Table 2. Participant grades and extenuating circumstances

	Developmental	Math	Science	Extenuating Circumstances
Student 1	n/a	95+	95+	Yes, each semester
Student 2	From 60 to 80/70	From 40 to 68	From 40 to 65	Currently on Medical W
Student 3	90	90	83	n/a
Student 4	90	From 60 to 90	From 60 to 80	Past Medical W in the past because of abortion; school didn't think she would return, but she did
Student 5	90	90	From 70 to 89	Took one semester off before but came back, school never thought that would happen
Student 6	90	30 to 40 to 60	60 to 68	Withdrew this semester because frustrated with fear of failure
Student 7	n/a	This is a kicker, academic placement exam had high scores and she was placed out of pre algebra stuff but she had to repeat math classes because she failed	From 68 to 85	Immaturity and fear of manic depression diagnosis
Student 8	90	Has taken math class over but gets it now - from 63 to 87	Does really well in science, loves science From 67 to 87	You name it, she has had it
Student 9	90	From 78 to 92	From 82 to 89	You name it, she has it
Student 10	80/70	Very strong in math, 97	From 50 to 70	Son killed last semester, high blood pressure, sleep apnea
Student 11	n/a	Always a strong 72	Always a strong 72	Chemistry professor, suicide threat, previous rape, daughter of minister, etc
Student 12	90	From 80 to 86	From 80 to 86	Leery of people and Quick to judge people and usually on target
Student 13	90	Strong in math, 90s	From 50 to 75	She is very shy and timid; terrified she is dying of cancer because doctor told her there was a growth on her thyroid. It took her months to go back to dr and find out she will live, lives in constant fear of something
Student 14	70	Struggles with math 60 to 78	Struggles with science 58 to 67	Each semester there is a major crisis, this time it is the pregnancy
Student 15	90	83 to 92	73 to 79	
Student 16	90/80	74 to 82	62 to 78	Mom passed away and dad is homeless
Student 17	70	30-60	70	
Student 18	70	65-80	50-65	
tudent 19	70/60	30-59	59-71	
Student 20	n/a	n/a	47-70	
Student 21	70/60	20-50	50-60	
Student 22	70/60	30-59	50-60	

Note: A = 90-100, B = 80 - 89, C = 70 - 79, D = 60 - 69, F = > 60

Table 3. Participant background, current status, current physical and psychological area of concern, frequency of technology usage in the program, and cumulative GPA

	Current status	Current issues	Tech Usages	Cum GPA
Caucasian, early 30, north side resident	Medical W MRSA	Rape, Abusive boyfriend, abortion, PFA, court appearance, etc	High	From 4.0 to A/B this semester because of crap situation, B will not count because of W
African-American, early 40, north side resident	Medical W Depression	Unexpected pregnancy – abortion and then son with heart transplant sick and daughter paralyzed	Nominal because she was brought up to keep family business to herself. When she changed this, improvement	C/D average 1.5 4A 3B 2C 1D
Caucasian, early 40, non northside	Doing well	Unemployed husband, 3 kids, she works full time, anxiety disorder being treated	High	Consistently A/B 3.5
Caucasian, early 30, non northside	Doing better	Unmarried, 3 kids, had an abortion to stay in school, high anxiety. Took a medical withdrawal and returned	From low to high	From D tc B/C 1.0 to 2.5
Caucasian, early 30, non northside	Doing well	Married, 2 kids, had to take a semester off because she is the care giver of two elderly parents	HIGH	B/C 2.5
Caucasian, early 30, non northside	Medical W because undiagnosed LD and working towards unresolved Mental Health issues	Unmarried, 2 kids, taking semester off because she is freaking out with sense of failure even though she is working hard	moderate	C/D 1.5
Caucasian, early 20, northside	Doing better	Just diagnosed with bipolar	From low to HIGH	From D to B/C 1.5 to 2.5
Caucasian, early 20, northside	Doing better	Raped, house broken into, car vandalized,	From low to HIGH	From D to B/C 1.0 to 2.5
African American, early 20, northside	Doing better	Raped at 2, lives in public housing, brother deals drugs, autistic kid, horrible situation, just now getting therapy	From moderate to HIGH	From D to C 1.0 to 2.0
African American, early 40, northside	Medical W	Her son was killed and her blood pressure is over the top, she has horrible sleep apnea, and clinically depressed	NOMINAL	D 1.0
Caucasian, early 20, northside	Doing better	Rape, professor in position of authority knew she was suicidal and she lost focus for a while but doing well, executive functioning	From moderate to HIGH	From D to B/C 1.0 to 2 5
Caucasian, early 40, non northside	Doing well	Police officer with pension, 4 kids, no husband, high anxiety	HIGH	Consistently B/C 2.5
African American, early 20, northside	Doing better	Absolutely no self-esteem, very abusive family situation, now working with scientists and mentors and therapist and other sources but professors keep telling her she is too far in the hole to come out	Moderate	C/D 1.5
African American, early 20, northside	Medical W	Just got pregnant after finally getting onto birth control, 1 child, boyfriend in and out of picture	Nominal	D/F 1.0
African American, early 40, non northside	Doing better	Pension as a police officer, anger management 180 better, 3 children, no husband	From nominal to Moderate	From D to B/C 1.0 to 2.5

Table 3. continued

	Current status	Current issues	Tech Usages	Cum GPA
African American, early 40, non northside	Doing better	Pension as a police officer, anger management 180 better, 3 children, no husband	From nominal to Moderate	From D to B/C 1.0 to 2.5
African American, early 20 northside	Doing better	Only child, father is homeless, mother passed away, still dealing with grief, immaturity issues	From nominal to Moderate	From D to B/C 1.0 to 2.5
Caucasian, 40, northside	Working AGH	Couldn't stand the failure with math even though she tried and tried	Nominal	D 1.0
African American, early 40 northside	SSI illness	Unable to focus on school because of medical condition, 3 kids, mother lives with her, Too many issues in her life and she didn't want to talk about it, left after third week of program	low	D/F 1.0
African American, early 40 northside	MIA	Too many issues in her life and she didn't want to talk about it, left after third week of program	low	D/F 1.0
African American, early 40 northside	Working AGH	Too frustrated to be struggling with math failure and needed a job so she is working and taking advantaged of in-house training and tuition reimbursement for career advancement	Low	D/F 1.0
African American, early 40 northside	Changed Major/ MIA	She has 3 kids, she was selling drugs to pay for rent, and boyfriend was abusive. She didn't have transportation	Low	D/F1.0
African American, early 20 northside	Working/GED	She has 2 kids, no husband, needed a job and uncomfortable with her academic abilities because she did not have a GED. She wants to return	Low	D/F\ 1.0
African American, early 40 northside	Changed Major	Drug abuse history, therapist told her to change majors, still grieving with the loss of her son who was shot and killed	Low	D/F 1.0

is private) and 4) "Low" refers to frequency of contact with technology or face to face.

RQ2. Does the use of blended learning lead to successful navigation of personal issues?

We observed an increase in the successful navigation of personal issues by engaging participants of the AWBWC with comprehensive social support. At the onset of the program, we suggested participants call or email if they needed help. Immediately, we were barraged with phone calls for help. These requests ranged from fear to come to campus the first day, not wanting to wait in line for registration and help with trauma after gunshots ricochet around their kitchen. Our phones were literally ringing off the hook. The blended learning for facilitated navigation of personal issues which includes form of contact: Participants and program staff meet for one hour each week for group sessions on campus plus provide individual personal meetings upon request. Within a few months, after weekly group sessions were used to identify various resources available, and individual meetings were used to identify strategies, participant phone call frequency declined dramatically. During face-to-face sessions, participants would share how they dealt with the situations using the resources provided. (See Table 4 in Appendix).

Example of Data Collected

As part of the hyperarousal of PTSD, people cannot concentrate and tend to sleep poorly. According to Dr. Tony Mannarino, "these two symptoms have a significant impact on cognitive functioning and performance," (Personal Communication March 10, 2009). Additionally, the internalization of failure has manifested itself with self-sabotaging or avoidance, characteristics indicative of the PTSD. Participants of the AWBWC often share their experiences with "re-experiencing, avoidance/numbing, and hyperarousal," p. 405 (Cohen & Mannarino, 2004) which are symptoms related to PTSD. It is these personal issues which historically have prevented AWBWC participants from success. Using technology, the staff works regularly with the women individually and as a group on how to mediate stressful situations both related and unrelated to the academic experience. For example, in an attempt to help the participants deal with these manifestations during the two most stressful times of the academic year namely, midterms and final exams, the following email was sent to the participants after talking about obstacles to success during a weekly group session on March 2, 2009.

dear ladies,
i know you are all stressed.
i am trying to identify just how stressed you are. midterms and finals are stressful times for students. yes, being a student is stressful. being a mom is stressful. being a mom and student is incredibly stressful
there are many ways we can help you deal with the stress. however, being part of a program should not add to your stress. we are here to help you succeed.
from the bottom of my heart, i hope you know, XXX and i have been listening to you and trying to advocate on your behalf
if you think there is something else we should know, please write an email
be as detailed as you are comfortable with and let us know from your perspective what are the root causes of your stress today....
i would love to know your thoughts about the following...
what if you were able to withdraw from a class this semester and deal with the underlying issues causing the stress, would you mind if there was a delay in your graduation?
would you be willing to work on the underlying issues?
as always, we appreciate your input and look forward to hearing from you.
kind regards,
XXX

The common message throughout the responses is that although the participants are enrolled in a psycho education program, they are still disadvantaged. Contrary to popular belief, enrollment in this program does not negate issues associated with being disadvantaged. However, the fact remains the issues which impact each participant's life are historically what prohibited them from other educational. If left unchecked, this situation will only be further exacerbated because the participants are more stressed and unable to learn. These situations prompt the participants to recognize the need to learn with many challenges facing them yet with less time. Access to technology provides them a conduit to assistance when they need it. The following response regarding a participants desire to address the issue of stress is best exemplified in the following:

AWBWC response on March 2, 2009

"Morning Doll, YESSS! If given the oppertunity, I would love to work on my underlying issues and "fix" me! But seriously, for me the issues are dealing with loss, mainly because it will be one year soon of my moms' passing and emoitionally I am getting worse (I think). I know that things that I need to talk about and get advice on but I don't know exactly how to communicate it to others. Now with you and [her] I am comfortable,

although there are things that happened to me that I still don't like to remember or deal with, but it is this one thing that has a hold of me and I am afraid to bring it to the light because it has the potential to destroy other people's lives and I really don't think I can handle that. So there it is, well I am in the library researching for english. Smooches, XXX

In addition to email responses to writing prompts, participants use technology with the staff as mechanism for psychological support with personal issues. For example, after receiving a text message from a participant who was feeling anxious about seeing a therapist for the first time, this medium of communication allowed for quick and private exchanges. The quality of exchange between the participants and staff is amazing. When a participant was beaten by her boyfriend and needed to get emergency medical attention in the ER, a simple text message, "I need help" was sent. After the participant and staff sat in the ER studying together they used technology to discretely share information when they could not meet face to face. Resources were identified to obtain legal assistance and psychological services without family members knowledge. However, this use of technology is not restricted to requesting help in times of need. Rather, participants often share with each other and store to save an email or text message from the staff because it was meaningful. For example, when a woman in the program was feeling overwhelmed and spent time with the staff identifying strategies to deal with the situations, she was happy to report good news when she left the therapist's office feeling better about herself (see Response A in appendix)

Ironically, when a phone is not available due to financial limitations, participants share their phones with each other to contact each other or the staff. On occasion, participants have gone to the computer lab on campus and waited in line for internet access when it is not available at home. They maintain contact with each other and the staff by "checking in." This is done not to make them feel like prison paroles rather because they have requested the structure and guidance to keep them focused. For example, a participant was beaten up by her boyfriend when he bashed her bedroom door in at 3am. She needed a restraining order, and she work nights in a bar because the father of her children was not consistent with child support. Although she doesn't qualify for public assistance, this participant stays in contact, any way she can. See Appendix Response B for a text message exchange which shows how a participant who needs to be in contact, shares good news and updates with the other women.

RQ3 How much informal learning is occurring related to academic content? We are also interested in what students are doing in non-classroom settings (informal) together that fosters academic success.

To answer this, we have been interviewing the participants about the out of class activities. This robust qualitative data indicates informal learning takes place while participants are walking to classes, eating in the cafeteria, and using free time available. Participants share a common dream and motivate each other. To others, it is a place of emotional support, with deep sharing and bonding with close friends. Some see community as an intense crucible for personal growth. For others, it is simply a place to pioneer their dreams" (McLaughlin & Davidson, 1994, 471, as cited in DuFour & Eaker,, 1998, xii). Exemplars of the organic community of practice, which have evolved follow:

When we started classes we became even closer. We created study groups that morphed into support groups. I would never have made it through the exams, the bad days, the overall experience if I didn't have these women cheering me on every day and allowing me to do the same for them. (AWBWC Response C: Personal Communication November 2007)

We have a support network, we help each other both academically and personally. (AWBWC Response D: Personal Communication February 9, 2008)

I couldn't succeed if given a scholarship, we cooperate with each other, we work together, we learn together, we want the same goal and push each other. (AWBWC Response E: Personal Communication October 11, 2008)

This group of women gives me the help with daily tasks so I can keep my eye on the goal, to graduate. (AWBWC Response F: Personal Communication January 26, 2009)

Time on campus is a luxury. Participants must race home to pick up their children from the bus stop. Technology enhances the opportunity to continue face to face informal learning opportunities via email exchanges, text messages and phone calls. This conduit between the participants allows them extended "campus time" to explore thoughts and ideas once home.

Additionally, the staff uses this technology to assist participants academically. For example, PPT and online academic tutorials are shared via email. Topics range from academic guidance regarding study habits to metacognitive activities. Blended learning also provides participants a safe environment for exploration. For those who are excessively inattentive, impulsive and hyperactive, a much-needed written format and structure exists for scaffolding.

According to self-assessments conducted during the initial intake (August 2007) by participants, historically, this population has failed academically because of "extreme procrastination, disorganization, trouble making deadlines, and impulsive behavior." In an effort to allow participants to reflect about their learning throughout the program, weekly email prompts are sent. This is a time and place allowing participants to be truthful, especially if they are shy or uncomfortable talking about such issues face to face. (See Appendix for Email A)

Additionally, as a group the women have a collaborative spirit and they share resources rather than hoard information. Prior to exams, the women meet to review their notes and study together. When one woman completes a course which another woman will enroll in the next semester, it is not uncommon for them to share notes with each other and tutor each other from this position of previous experience, even if both participants have different professors with different assignments. The content is the same and the bond within this group is strong.

RQ 4 Does the social connection component of the program benefit the participants academically and/or socially?

From the academic perspective, we see the social connection as a major influence on the success and perseverance of these women. A specific example from "Laura" who is 24 and a single mother with two children, one diagnosed with Autism, on public assistance. She stated,

"Going back to the classroom was frightening." There were times this spring she doubted she would make it, but the group would have none of it. One woman even told her that if she wasn't in class she would show up outside her house with a megaphone. "They won't let me quit,"

Participants have changed their socialization habits also. When there is free time on campus, participants sit together in the cafeteria and in other common areas. The bond which has formed during these twenty months has solidified this group of women, as exemplified when a woman loses her son to a random act of violence When participants are off campus, they phone each other. When they are not studying or caring for children, it is not uncommon for participants to use Facebook and online social networking to touch base with each other.

RQ 5 Which participants seem to benefit from the program?

Caucasian women, n= 2, >30 years of age who did not grow up in poverty are perceived by their professors as doing the best academically but this does not mean they benefit from the program. The women who are benefiting, n=13, the most are those who are able to continue in the program and deal with the psychosocial issues which have prevented them from success in the past. Those who use the technology to contact the staff and each other because they need help, whether someone to talk to them or someone to identify resources, are able to benefit, whether they are in need of a late night pep talk or the opportunity to share with someone that they did well on an assignment. The use of technology has fostered these relationships and those who use it outperform those who do not. The following examples typify the exchanges.

January 31, 2009 8:46 pm

AWBWC Response G: Ok. Thanks 4 the support. I am not going to quit

Staff: Giving up is not an option! Tell yourself you can do it and you will

AWBWC Response G1: I know!

March 12, 2009 12:31 pm

AWBWC Response H: I GOT a B ON MY PAPER!!

Staff: Whoooo hoo good for you

AWBWC Response H2: Thank u

Staff: You earned it! Be proud

AWBWC Response H3: With help

Feb 20, 2009 10:07 am

AWBWC Response I: I got an A- on my English paper!

Staff: You rock

Additionally, the older women, n=2, with children seem to benefit from the program more than the younger women with children. We attribute part of this to maturity from increased life experiences. Those who have not been successful in the program were in a place in their lives where the circumstances were such that they were not able to deal with the psychological impacts. Of all the participants who have left the program, only two are no longer in contact with us. All of the others have pursued another educational program better suited to their academic needs. This lateral attrition will be considered over time because "approximately 45 percent of students who begin postsecondary studies at community colleges in the United States have not completed a degree or enrolled elsewhere six years later" (Fast Fact, 2005).Fifteen women from the twenty-two who are enrolled. Although some have taken a semester off they have each returned and this is unprecedented. Those who leave our biotechnology program enroll in other STEM or Healthcare programs available at CCAC. Most critical is the understand that these participants need time to deal with extenuating circumstances rather than removed from an educational program because of attendance policies. Without this perspective of the participants and the reality they live in, successful systemic change is unlikely. A specific example of a successful failure is demonstrated in one participant who left the program, but was able to obtain a better job because of her new skill and knowledge sets.

DISCUSSION

This program has embraced the participatory learning model and infused the blended learning theory to provide these women an opportunity to succeed in post-secondary education. The program creates the participatory environment where these women can create knowledge and develop skills together. The blended learning allows them to work more flexibly at the moments they have the opportunity to work. Though most of them are a member of the "Digital Native" cohort, this is the first opportunity for them to engage with their peers in this flexible world through technology. The traditional didactic classroom works to deliver basic academic information for them, but the learning truly occurs among these through their group meetings and the use of the technology to academically advance.

This same pairing of technology and participation is helping them negotiate the life stressors that most post-secondary students do not have. They use the technology to keep the group together. Given the mobility rates traditionally associated with this population, we are pleased with the current rate of participation. Twenty months later, participants are better able to mediate the stressors in their environments as identified in the Bronbenbrenner's Social Ecology of Human Development Model.

More specifically, for a demographic with 100% PTSD, technology provides a safe haven for participants to express themselves, a medium to reduce stress and access people to help them mediate the stress. Traditional resources such as online tutorials in concert with social support with technology provide participants an opportunity to share themselves when they need someone to listen. This group historically has failed academically because of their inability of attention, planning, concentration, managing time and completing tasks, and making thoughtful decisions have been problematic.

Larger Theoretical Areas

Furthermore, due to the victimization rate of 90% the key to making participants feel comfortable and welcome means placing them in small groups with their peers. A recent study investigating Kingsborough's (2003) student learning communities indicates greater academic success for participants. Community means different things to different people. To some it is a safe haven where survival is assured through mutual cooperation. The participants who were struggling academically and/or social emotionally, once they realized we were there to help them, used resources and improved within a maximum of two weeks. This change of behavior persisted over semesters. Typically, when such situations occur, according to Dr. Allysen Todd, the Dean of Academic Affairs, students are so traumatized, they stop coming to school and receive failing grades, making them ineligible for future opportunities. This successful navigation of personal issues is possible because of the relationships fostered by phone calls, emails and text messages.

Program Related

We have learned that even with the level of support provided, the program has not been for everyone. That is a key piece of information as a push for student-centric programs receives more attention. We do need to know the who, where, what, why, and how of this program so that we can more accurately target participants and ensure their success. Because of the students who have left, we understand where a different program needs to be created with a different entry trajectory in order to give them the more opportunities to build their academic strength and self-efficacy for specific courses and content. We have noticed that older women who left program were more likely to show up for weekly 1 hour meetings rather than engage in technology or communicate about issues preventing them from academic success. Finally, it is the combination of blended learning environments, blended social support, and a program that works in a design experiment mode with a focus of success for each participant that has made this program as successful as it is today.

CONCLUSION

From our preliminary data, technology leads to higher GPA because "lifelines" are more accessible when needed. This in turns reduces attrition as exhibited when a comparison is done with peers not participating. AWBWC participants who used technology as part of a blended learning framework experienced increased achievement compared to those who did not. However in the process of gathering the data, we quickly recognized that access to technology or the digital divide still persists and mediated that situation. When GPA is the metric, those participants who use cell phones, email, and practice with the high tech lab equipment earned higher GPA than those who do not. Interestingly, the participants who did not achieve academically are those who did not engage with either traditional modes of communication or technology. To this end, Dr. Christopher Post, creator of the AWBWC program has stated, "We believe this program will empower underserved women in our community, fostering a heightened sense of dignity and pride that accompanies a rewarding career and the ability to better care for their families both socially and financially."

FUTURE RESEARCH DIRECTIONS

From our experience, the myriad human development and social science issues have been unearthed with the AWBWC and funding and research is needed for quality academic programming, which includes psychosocial support for high risk populations. However, before participants begin the didactic portion of the program, this model should include participants with safe and affordable housing, access to quality health care, and access to public transportation in order to level the playing field. We believe with a clean bill of health for the children and participants as well as access to the requisite additional resources, cognition and increased academic achievement will provide statistically significant results. Without proper attention to these basic human needs, the manifestations of symptoms related to acute stress disorder and post traumatic stress disorder will continue to prevent participants from achieving academic and personal success.

Translational research provides a mechanism that underscores the need to get more information to increase knowledge in specific sectors of social science allowing for the construction, replication, and re-replication enlightened because of research. Using both quantitative and qualitative data collection future research, grounded in the literature will provide insight from literature to generate a hypothesis then test.

Furthermore, we need to redefine remediation, motivation and performance on their own terms as we continue to identify what it is about the AWBWC model which makes it successful. This research has direct bearing on the training for community colleges and community members who aim to help keep this demographic academically engaged in the learning process. Such research has direct bearing on the training of K-12 educators to provide quality-learning opportunities.

Despite the fact that the US spends more money than any other nation per child on education, our students are not actively engaging in the learning process. A professional community of educators and social scientists linked with technology has many advantages today. We have the ability to create a community based system of interventions that provides all students with additional time and support when they experience difficulty in their learning. The AWBWC is an example of a model where the thorny issues of lessons learned are applied.

Dialogue A

March 4, 2009 3:30 pm

AWBWC Response A1: Hey I got a appointment on Friday at 820

Staff: Great

AWBWC Response A2: That's the earliest day and time available

March 6, 2009 10:07 am

AWBWC Response A3: I went 2 see the psychiatrist. And he put me on sum medication

Staff: Did talking help

AWBWC Response A4: Yes. A lot. He also gave me sum good advice

Staff: Wonderful, please let us know what we can do to help

March 6, 2009 4:42 om

AWBWC Response A5: Yes. A lot. He also gave me sum go

Staff: Just 2 take it easy. Quit worrying and stressing so much. Things like that

Staff: Great!!! And remember, we are here for you too

AWBWC Response A6: I know. Thanx 4 your support. I luv u guys

Staff: We love you too

AWBWC Response A7: I know thanx

March 11, 2009 12:32om

AWBWC Response A8: Ok. Thankx

Staff: Hope you are feeling better. You have been on my mind...

AWBWC Response A9: I have been feeling better a little bit. Thanx 4 ur concern

Dialogue B

AWBWC Response B1 to Staff 3/3/2009 11:31 AM>>>

Just checking in my phone charger is lost... so I can't call. But I'm ok and I'm doing well so I'll call you tommorrow. And just so you know I'm taking off Thurday night so that I am well rested for my Mid-Term. I'm thinking an "A"

from Staff to AWBWC participant

Tuesday, March 3, 2009 1:21:02 PM

good...

did you get my email about your chem lab grade???

please talk to the professor

don't give up

and please tell me something...

when will you stop working during the week at the bar?

you really should work at ASRI during the week

they want you here

and it would be awesome for you...

please

please

please

please

think about it

From AWBWC Response B2 to Staff

Tuesday - March 3, 2009 3:26 PM

I got the Chem Lab and will talk to the preofessor.. I'm working on it.. And I'm workingn on the bar situation .. I'll keep you posted.

Thanks XXXX,

Email A (Personal Communication March 2, 2009)

"I am aware that for this entire half semester I have been distracted and I know that scares you but please trust me when I say this.. I am not ready to be counted out just yet. I hope that you know that I am capable because I know that about myself. I just lost my way for awhile. But I'm finding it and I have to tell you I'm ready.

I've been thinking about why things have gone the way they have and why I sarted out strong and well just gave up trying. And at first I said it was because of what happened with XXX.. Then I decided it was the baby.. and I'm sure to some extent these things distratced me (hurt me). Especially the baby. But when I really thought about it I decided that mostly I was just buying time and I'll tell you why.

There was something so scary about seeing the end of this program... I felt like I was losing more than I was gaining, I know let me explain. When I started this group I had no self-esteem I had really no friends and I was isolated from pretty much everything else going on in the world. Then I began this journey with these women that were just like me and we picked each other up and dusted each other off and I never felt more apart of something. It didn't occur to me until recently that these things meant more to me than the degree. This might not make too much sense to you but this is what I felt like. I felt like once this thing ended and we all went our seperate ways that our lives would just continue on and this part of me (this thing that transformed every ounce of my being) would be just a memory. A great memory but just a memory. I was afraid that I would go back to being the person I was and that this person (the one I think I became) would be sort of like a shadow of me.

I realize now that I can never go back to being that woman who was ok with being counted out by the world. The woman who agreed when people said I was nothing and that I could never be anything. I never want to feel that way again. But I assume that once you realize your worth and realize your potential you can never go back to that.

And so XXXX, now that your eyes are crossed and tired from reading this extremely long e-mail just please don't count me out. I'm going to show you just how worth it I am (and then you can brag)."

REFERENCES

2006*American Community Survey.* [census data file]. Washington, D.C.: United States Census Bureau. Retrieved on November 11, 2008, from http://factfinder.census.gov/home/saff/main.html?_lang=en

Anderson-Levitt, K. M. (2006). Ethnography. In J. L. Green, G. Camilli, P. B. Elmore, A. Skukauskaitė & E. Grace (Eds.), *Handbook of complementary methods in education research* (pp 279-296). Mahwah, NJ: Erlbaum.

2008 Associates degree & certificate producers rankings 2008. *Community College Week, 20*(21), 24-40.

Barab, S. A., Hay, K. E., Barnett, M. G., & Keating, T. (2000). Virtual solar system project: Building understanding through model building. *Journal of Research in Science Teaching, 37*(7), 719–756. doi:10.1002/1098-2736(200009)37:7<719::AID-TEA6>3.0.CO;2-V

Barab, S. A., Kay, K. E., Barnett, M., & Squire, K. (2001). Constructing virtual worlds: Tracing the historical development of learner practices. *Cognition and Instruction, 19*(1), 47–94. doi:10.1207/S1532690XCI1901_2

Barnet, M., Barab, S. A., & Hay, K. E. (2001). The virtual solar system project: A stellar exercise in modeling celestial bodies. *Journal of College Science Teaching, 30*(5), 300–304.

Berg, B. L. (2007). *Qualitative research methods for the social sciences* (6th ed.). Boston: Allyn and Bacon.

Bonk, C. J., & Cunningham, D. J. (1998). Searching for learner-centered, constructivist, and sociocultural components of collaborative educational learning tools. In C. J. Bonk & K. S. King (Eds.), *Electronic collaborators: Learner-centered technologies for literacy, apprenticeship, and discourse*. Mahwah, NJ: Erlbaum.

Bonk, C. J., Kim, K., & Zeng, T. (2006). Future directions of blended learning in higher education and workplace learning settings. In C. J. Bonk & C. R. Graham (Eds.), *Handbook of blended learning: Global perspectives, local designs* (pp. 550-568). San Francisco, CA: Pfeiffer Publishing.

Bransford, J. D. (with Cognition and Technology Group; Vanderbilt University). (2000). Adventures in anchored instruction: Lessons from beyond the ivory tower. In R. Glasser (Ed.), *Advances in instructional psychology: Vol. 5*. Mahwah, NJ: Erlbaum.

Brown, A. L., Campione, J., Webber, L., & McGilley, K. (1992). Interactive learning environments: A new look at learning and assessment. In B. R. Gifford & M. C. O'Connor (Eds.), *Future assessment: Changing views of aptitude, achievement, and instruction* (pp. 121-211). Boston: Academic.

Career Voyages. (2005). *Biotechnology high growth industry profile* [brochure]. Washington, D.C.

Chapman, C., Ramondt, L., & Smiley, G. (2005). Strong community, deep learning: Exploring the link. *Innovations in Education and Teaching International, 42*(3), 217–230. doi:10.1080/01587910500167910

Cobb, P., Confrey, J., diSessa, A., Lehrer, R., & Schauble, L. (2003). Design experiments in educational research. *Educational Researcher, 32*(1), 9–13. doi:10.3102/0013189X032001009

Cohen, J. A., & Mannarino, A. P. (2004). Posttraumatic stress disorder. In T. H. Ollendick & J. E. March (Eds.), *Phobic and anxiety disorders in children and adolescents: A clinician's guide to effective psychosocial and pharmacological interventions*. New York: Oxford University Press.

Davies, A., Ramsey, J., Linderfield, H., & Couperthwaite, J. (2005). A blended approach to learning: Added value and lessons learnt from students' use of computer based materials for neurological analysis. *British Journal of Educational Technology, 36*(5), 839–849. doi:10.1111/j.1467-8535.2005.00506.x

DeVol, R., Koepp, R., Wallace, L., Bedroussian, A., Murphy, D., Wong, P., et al. (2005). *The greater Philadelphia life sciences cluster: An economic and comparative assessment*. Philadephia: The Milken Institute.

Eaker, R. E., & Dufour, R. (1998). *Professional learning communities at work: Best practices for enhancing student achievement.* Bloomington, IN: Solution Tree.

Fast fact: Learning communities program at Kingsborough Community College improves test scores. (2005, November 23). Retrieved on March 20, 2009, from http://www.mdrc.org/area_fact_25.html

Goldstein, J., & Puntambekar, S. (2005). The brink of change: Gender in technology-rich collaborative learning environments. *Journal of Science Education and Technology, 13*(4), 505–522. doi:10.1007/s10956-004-1471-1

Graham, C. (2006). Blended learning systems. Definitions, current trends, and future directions. In C. Bonk & C. Graham (Eds.), *The handbook of blended learning: Global perspectives, local designs*. San Francisco: John Wiley and Sons.

Guthrie, J. T. (2001). *Contexts for engagement and motivation in reading* [electronic version]. Retrieved on October 23, 2006, from http://www.readingonline.org/articles/art_index.asp?HREF=/articles/handbook/guthrie/index.html

Ho, D. (2007, August). Harlem program finds ways to help kids, revive a community. *Cox News Service.*

Hughes, K. H. (2005). *Building the next American century: The past and future of American economic competitiveness*. Washington, D.C.: Woodrow Wilson Center Press.

Kruger, D. (1981). *An introduction to phenomenological psychology*. Pittsburgh, PA: Duquesne University Press.

Levers, L. L., & Hawes, A. R. (1989). Drugs and gender: A women's recovery program. *Journal of Mental Health Counseling, 12*, 527–531.

McNeil, B., & Dixon, L. (2005). *Success factors in informal learning: Young adults' experiences of literacy, language, and numeracy*. London: NRDC. (ISBN 1905188102)

Miao, Y., Fleschutz, J. M., & Zentel, P. (1999, December). Enriching learning contexts to support communities of practice. In C. M. Hoadley & J. Roschelle (Eds.), *Proceedings of the 1999 Conference on Computer Support for Collaborative Learning*, Palo Alto, CA. Retrieved on June 14, 2007, from http://portal.acm.org/citation.cfm?id=1150289

Miller, S. (2003). Impact of mixed methodology and design on inference quality. In A. Tashakkori & C Teddlie (Eds.), *Handbook of mixed methods in social and behavioral research* (pp 423-456). Thousand Oaks, CA: Sage.

Northside United. (2008). *Northside demographics factsheet*. Pittsburgh, PA. Retrieved from http://www.pittsburghunited.org/sites/default/files/attached_files/NSDemographics.pdf

Palloff, R., & Pratt, K. (1999). *Building learning communities in cyberspace: Effective strategies for the online classroom*. San Francisco, CA: Jossey-Bass.

Pekarik, A. J. (2002). Feeling or learning? *Curator, 45*(4), 262–264.

Pennsylvania Department of Education. (2007, August). *Public secondary school dropouts in Pennsylvania in 2005-06*. Harrisburg, PA: J. Bobek.

Pittsburgh, U. N. I. T. E. D. (2007, August). *Racial & economic disparities on Pittsburgh's northside*. Pittsburgh, PA. Retrieved from http://www.pittsburghunited.org/research/08/aug/19/racial-economic-disparities-on-pittsburgh%E2%80%99s-northside

RAND Education. (2006, July). *Estimating graduation and dropout rates with longitudinal data: A case study in the Pittsburgh public schools* (WR-372-PPS). Pittsburgh, PA: J. Engberg & B. Gill. Retrieved from http://www.rand.org/pubs/working_papers/WR372/

Rendell, E. (2008, January). *Keynote address at the National Science Foundation: Science education and workforce development: Key challenges for the states workshop*. Washington, D.C.

Sander, L. (2008, March 28). At community colleges, a call to meet new students at the front door. *The Chronicle of Higher Education*, A25.

Santrock, J. W. (1996). *Child development* (7th ed.). Madison, WI: Brown & Benchmark Publishers.

Schackner, B. (2008, July 6). AGH, CCAC team up to offer pioneering program to train biotech technicians. *Pittsburgh Post Gazette*, B-1. Retrieved from http://www.post-gazette.com/pg/08188/895111-298.stm

Shank, G., & Brown, L. (2007). *Exploring educational research literacy.* London: Routledge.

Stufflebeam, D. L. (2001). Evaluation models. *New Directions for Evaluation, 89*, 7–98. doi:10.1002/ev.3

Swan, K., & Garrison, R. (2006, May). *Pedagogical principles*. Panel discussion presentation at the Sloan-C Workshop on Blended Learning in Higher Education, Chicago, IL. Retrieved from http://www.uic.edu/depts/oee/blended/workshop/presentations/Pedagogical%20Principles.pdf

Tashakkori, A., & Teddlie, C. (1998). *Mixed methodology: Combining the qualitative and quantitative approaches.* Thousand Oaks, CA: Sage.

Twigg, C. (2003). Improving learning and reducing costs: New models for online learning. *EDUCAUSE Review, 38*(5), 28–38.

van Manen, M. (1990). *Researching lived experience: Human science for an action sensitive pedagogy*. Albany, NY: State University of New York Press.

Vygotsky, L. (1978). *In mind in society*. (Trans. M. Cole). Cambridge, MA: Harvard University Press.

Wenger, E. (1998). *Communities of practice: Learning, meaning, and identity.* Cambridge, UK: Cambridge University Press.

Wenger, E., McDermott, R., & Snyder, W. M. (2002). *Cultivating communities of practice*. Boston: Harvard University Press.

Wilson, B. G. (1995). Situated instructional design: Blurring the distinctions between theory and practice, design and implementation, curriculum and instruction. In M. Simonson (Ed.), *Proceedings of Selected Research and Development Presentations*. Washington D.C.: Association for Educational Communications and Technology.

Woodrow Wilson International Center for Scholars. (2006). *Funding the foundation: Basic science at the crossroads* [brochure]. Washington, D.C.: K. Hughes & L. Sha.

Zuckerman-Parker, M. (2008). Andragogy and technology. In L. A. Tomei (Ed.), *Encyclopedia of information technology curriculum integration* (pp. 30-36). Hershey, PA: Idea Group Publishing.

APPENDIX

Table 4. Contact through use of technology (frequency)

	Formal	Informal	Other Tech Usages	Range	Cum GPA
Caucasian, early 30, north side resident	4meetings/month Plus 2 f2f/month	4email/month	150/month	For 20 months, she has been consistently in touch	From 4.0 to 3.5 this semester because of medical withdrawl
African-American, early 40, north side resident	3meetings/month Plus 2 f2f/month	2email/month	50/month	When she needs helps she calls otherwise no contact	2.0
Caucasian, early 40, non northside	4meetings/month Plus 2 f2f/month	4email/month	150/month	For 20 months, she has been consistently in touch	3.5
Caucasian, early 30, non northside	From 2meetings/month To 4meetings/month Plus 2 f2f/month	From 2mail/month to 4email/month	50/month . to 150/month	For the first 16 months, some contact, now consistently in touch	From D to B/C
Caucasian, early 30, non northside	4meetings/month Plus 2 f2f/month	4email/month	150/month	For 20 months, she has been consistently in touch	B/C
Caucasian, early 30, non northside	4meetings/month Plus 2 f2f/month	4email/month	150/month	For 20 months, she has been consistently in touch	C/D
Caucasian, early 20, northside	From 2meetings/month to 4meetings/month Plus 2 f2f/month	From 2mail/month to 4email/month	50/month to 150/month	For the first 16 months, some contact, now consistently in touch	From D to B/C
Caucasian, early 20, northside	From 2meetings/month to 4meetings/month Plus 2 f2f/month	From 2mail/month to 4email/month	50/month to 150/month	For the first 16 months, some contact, now consistently in touch	From D to B/C
African American, early 20, northside	From 2meetings/month to 4meetings/month Plus 2 f2f/month	From 2mail/month to 4email/month	50/month to 150/month	For the first 16 months, some contact, now consistently in touch	From D to C
African American, early 40, northside	2meetings/month	2email/month	50/month	For 20 months, she has been in touch	D
Caucasian, early 20, northside	From 2meetings/month to 4meetings/month Plus 2 f2f/month	4email/month	From 50/month to 150/month	For the first 16 months, some contact, now consistently in touch	From D to B/C
Caucasian, early 40, non northside	4meetings/month Plus 2 f2f/month	4email/month	150/month	For 20 months, she has been consistently in touch	Consistently B/C
African American, early 20, northside	4meetings/month Plus 2 f2f/month	3email/month	100/month to 150/month	For the first 16 months, some contact, now consistently in touch	C/D
African American, early 20, northside	2meetings/month	2email/month	50/month	For 20 months, she has been in touch	D/F
African American, early 40, non northside	From 2meetings/month to 4meetings/month Plus 2 f2f/month	From 2mail/month to 4email/month	From 50/month to 150/month	For the first 16 months, some contact, now consistently in touch	From D to B/C
African American, early 20 northside	From 2meetings/month to 4meetings/month Plus 2 f2f/month	From 2mail/month to 4email/month	From 50/month to 150/month	For the first 16 months, some contact, now consistently in touch	From D to B/C
Caucasian, 40, northside	4meetings/month Plus 2 f2f/month	1email/month	10/month	While in program for 9 months, rarely in touch	D
African American, early 40 northside	2meetings/month	1email/month	10/month	While in program for 12 months, rarely in touch	D/F
African American, early 40 northside	3meetings/month	1email/month	10/month	While in program for 9 months, rarely in touch	D/F

Table 4. continued

	Formal	Informal	Other Tech Usages	Range	Cum GPA
African American, early 40 northside	2meetings/month	1email/month	10/month	While in program for 3 months, rarely in touch	D/F
African American, early 40 northside	2meetings/month	1email/month	10/month	While in program for 3 months, rarely in touch	D/F
African American, early 20 northside	2meetings/month	1email/month	10/month	While in program for 3 months, rarely in touch	D/F
African Amerian, early 40 northside	3meetings/month	email/month	Never	While in program for 3 months, rarely in touch	D/F
totals					

Chapter 12
Blending Classroom Activities with Multi-User Virtual Environment for At-Risk Primary School Students in an After-School Program:
A Case Study

Lee Yong Tay
Beacon Primary School, Singapore

Cher Ping Lim
Edith Cowan University, Western Australia

ABSTRACT

This chapter documents how a group of 14 academically at-risk Primary 5 students have been engaged in academic related tasks in an after-school program mediated by a game-like 3D multi-user virtual environment (MUVE), Quest Atlantis (QA). The case study explores the possibilities and potentials of using the game-like 3D MUVE for the re-engagement of this group of academically at-risk students. From the observation notes, interviews with the students and students' activities in the MUVE, the two main elements in the MUVE that have been found to engage the students are: 'play and fun' and 'recognition and affirmation of performance.' However, these engaging elements alone could not purposefully engage these students. Non-ICT activities such as orientation tasks, support by teachers, and the careful selection of authentic assignments are necessary to further enhance their engagement with their learning.

INTRODUCTION

Various studies of Singapore schools have shown that the main factors that influence students' academic performance include socio-economic status and attitudes toward school life. However, there are studies that have shown that teachers and teacher knowledge do make a difference regardless of social background. Hill and Rowe (1998), and Cuttance (1998, p. 1158-9) indicate that 'up to 55% of the

DOI: 10.4018/978-1-60566-852-9.ch012

variation in individual learning outcomes lies between classrooms within schools'. It would appear that if teaching effectiveness can be improved by developing teacher knowledge about how to engage students in richer and more relevant learning tasks, the outcomes for students will be improved. The focus on standards, grades, and outcome measures is in direct opposition to the idea of designing learning environments that are more likely to engage students. Learner engagement is paramount to learning success; where engagement entails mindfulness, intrinsic motivation, cognitive effort and attention. By undervaluing rich complex, and engaging, processes and strategies for learning, classroom activities that require active inquiry and deep conceptual understandings are often rare in schools.

By contrast, the gaming industry has informally engaged students and motivated them to invest significant amounts of time in tasks which relate to effective game play but not to tasks on which they are typically assessed. This revolution began with the simple two-dimensional arcade games and has progressed to the virtual reality three-dimensional (3-D) multi-user role-playing game of today. Harnessing the excitement and engagement among students playing computer games bears considerable potential for schools to capture the intensive engagement of students (Lim, Nonis, & Hedberg, 2006). 3D multi-user games with their multimedia elements situated within a community of players provide opportunities for players as learners to engage in literacy through modalities of interpretation and expression (Gee, 2003). This paper documents how a group of 14 academically at-risk Primary 5 students (aged 11) are engaged in academic related tasks in an after-school program mediated by a 3D game-like multi user virtual environment (*MUVE*) – *Quest Atlantis* (*QA*). At-risk students are those who constantly not performing up to the expected academic standards over the years. The findings suggest that for the after-school program to engage these students, the *MUVE* has to be supported by non-ICT face-to-face activities designed and carried out by the teacher – taking up the learning opportunities and addressing the limitations of both virtual and face-to-face learning environments.

LITERATURE REVIEW

Quest Atlantis – Multi-User Virtual Environment

Quest Atlantis (*QA*) is a 3-D virtual learning environment developed by the Center for Research on Learning and Technology (CRLT) at Indiana University. The Center is committed to explore and develop appropriate applications of ICT to improve teaching and learning in diverse settings. This environment is built for students, ages of 8 to 12, who have given up on themselves as learners. It is the belief of CRLT that *QA* with its deep content and challenging game-like activities will motivate these academically at-risk students. Students explore and move around freely in the 3D virtual world as questers with their own avatars. There is also an online synchronous chat for students to discuss topics of interest and collaborative works. On the right hand side of this environment, students can access their emails, forums, view their accumulated points and *lumins*, *quests*, as well as update their personal information.

QA allows students to travel to various virtual spaces and carry out educational activities known as *quests*. Each *quest* is a curricular task designed to be entertaining and yet educational in nature. In order to complete these *quests*, students have to complete real world activities that are socially and academically meaningful. All *quests* involve both content-area findings and personal reflection by the student. This is done with the aim of fostering critical thinking and meta-cognition. Developers of *QA* believe that students learn best when they are actively engaged in the learning process, with an emphasis on inquiring into domain-related problems. The basic philosophy of inquiry-based learning is to make learning more meaningful, more transferable to various situations out of a specific context, and more conducive to self-directed life-long learning (Lim, Nonis, & Hedberg, 2006).

The Engaging Elements in Computer Games and Game-Like Environments

Several authors suggest that there are engaging elements found within such a game-like *MUVE* (Cordova & Lepper, 1996; Dickey, 2005; Gee, 2003; Lim, Nonis, & Hedberg, 2006; Malone & Lepper, 1987). The following engaging design elements are found within the *QA MUVE* according to the frameworks and methods as proposed by the various authors mentioned above. These design elements are: (1) affiliation and cooperation with others; (2) challenge; (3) clear goals and standards; (4) competition; (5) opportunity to try and try again; (6) control and choice; (7) play and fun; (8) fantasy; (9) moving up the levels; (10) multimodal output and input; and (11) recognition and affirmation of performance.

Cordova and Lepper (1996), in their experimental study examine the effects of 3 complementary strategies on the learning process – contextualization, personalization, and provision of choices – for enhancing students' intrinsic motivation. The experiment involves five conditions: (a) generic fantasy – no choice; (b) generic fantasy – choice; (c) personalised – no choice; (d) personalised – choice; and (e) no-fantasy control group. In the basic control condition, students are engaged in two computer-based learning games in an unembellished form. In the other four experimental conditions, the same learning activities are embedded in simple fantasy contexts. It is observed that there are no significant differences between the experimental condition and the students' gender or grade. However, significant differences are observed in the students' intrinsic motivation, learning, perceived competence, and level of aspiration for students in all the experimental groups. The authors add that there is no reason to believe that these findings are dependent on the use of the computer. However, the authors also caution that the use of motivational embellishment strategies of the sort used in their experiments may not always have such beneficial effects. For example, these techniques may not be effective with older children or adults, given that the interest in such fantasies may decrease with age. It may also not be as effective for children who are already highly motivated and task-oriented as it could be seen as more of a distraction and time-wasting nuisance to them. There are also issues of novelty and habituation as it is likely that the positive effects of such techniques may diminish over time if they are used too frequently.

From one perspective, the addition of extra game-like elements is seen as likely to be distracting and to impair learning. At the very least, it will make learning less efficient. From the other viewpoint, the addition of such motivational devices is seen as likely to enhance children's attention to the material presented and their active processing of it. ..... In addition, the provision of a concrete and familiar visual representation or a conceptual "point of view" may further promote retention of the material learned or enhance the child's ability to transfer that learning to other settings. (Lepper & Chabay, 1985, p. 220)

Dickey (2005) observes that the following aspects of game design fit into the existing model of engaged learning: (1) Focused goals, (2) Challenging tasks, (3) Clear & compelling standards, (4) Protection from adverse consequences for initial failures, (5) Affirmation of performance, (6) Affiliation with others, (7) Novelty & variety, and (8) Choice.

Gee (2003) suggests 36 learning principles from good video games (video and computer games) that can be applied in the learning of content areas in the classrooms. Good video games have a great deal to teach us about how to facilitate learning, even in domains outside games, even in school (Gee, 2003). Real learning is often associated with pleasure which ultimately is a form of play. However, schools often dismiss this principle.

Good games are complex, challenging, and long; they can take 50 or more hours to finish. If a game cannot be learned well, then it will fail to sell well, and the company that makes it is in danger of going broke..... good games have to incorporate good learning principles in virtue of which they get themselves well learned. (Gee, 2003, p. 57)

Proponents of engaged learning also argue that learners can become meaningfully engaged in the learning environment by being provided with activities that allow them to play an active role and make judgments about progress toward defined goals (Schlechty, 1990 as cited in Dickey, 2005).

Lim, Nonis, and Hedberg (2006) list the following elements that help in the engagement of students in the *QA* 3D *MUVE*. They are: (1) Immersion and Interaction; (2) Inquiry-Oriented Learning and Scaffolding (3) Game-like Experience and Rewards; and (4) Opportunities for Collaboration. According to the authors, the *QA* allows students to be immersed and interact within the 3D *MUVE*. They add that:

QA is different from traditional role-playing games as it allows the students to leave the virtual environment and accomplish quests in the physical world. For example, a student will look for a quest online and read the resources available. Thereafter, he/she may proceed out to the real world, carry out an experiment or conduct an interview. The data collected is then interpreted and analysed before he/she submit the completed quest to the council online. (p. 6)

Lim, Nonis, and Hedberg (2006) caution that the extent to which these opportunities are taken up depends on how *QA* is situated in the learning environment. Participation in *QA* may trigger changes in the activities, curriculum and interpersonal relationships in the learning environment, and may be reciprocally affected by the very changes it causes (Lim, 2002).

Malone (1981) generates three main elements that "Make video games fun": Challenge, fantasy, and curiosity. Malone and Lepper (1987) synthesise the various factors to design environments that are intrinsically motivating from many research studies. Factors such as challenge, curiosity, control, fantasy, competition, cooperation, and recognition are found to promote intrinsic motivation amongst learners. They define intrinsic motivation simply in terms of what people will do without external inducement. Intrinsically motivating activities are those that people engage in for no reward, but the interest and enjoyment that accompany them.

It appears that computer and video games could be used as tools to engage students in educationally related activities. Hopefully by being engaged and spending more time and effort in such activities, students can achieve better performance in school related activities. The wide prevalence of research initiatives, conferences, books, and software that focus on educational games suggest that computer and video games will have a part to play in education, just as all media before they have been used for learning (Dempsey, Haynes, Lucassen, & Casey; 2002; Rieber, 1996; Rosas et al., 2003; Squire, 2005; Stewart, 1997).

Table 1 is an attempt to summarise the engaging design factors and elements found within *QA* according to the frameworks and methods as proposed by the various authors mentioned above. The engaging design factors and elements are: (1) affiliation and cooperation with others; (2) challenge; (3) clear goals and standards; (4) competition; (5) opportunity to try and try again; (6) control and choice; (7) exploration, discovery, curiosity, play, fun, and variety; (8) fantasy; (9) moving up the levels; (10) multimodal output and input; and (11) recognition and affirmation of performance. A brief description of design factors and elements found in *QA* are listed in Table 1.

These design factors and elements are also discussed and evaluated for its effectiveness in engaging and motivating the students in performing academic related activities within the after-school program and within *QA*. The impact of these proposed design elements found within *QA* would be looked into and further discussed in the later sections to evaluate their potential in engaging and motivating students in completing academic related activities and tasks in an after-school setting.

THE ESSENTIAL FACTOR TOWARDS A SUCCESSFUL AFTER-SCHOOL PROGRAM

Research studies seem to suggest that after-school program is a good way to re-engage and motivate at-risk students (Beck, 1999; Cole, 1998; Cooper, Valentine, Nye, & Lindsay, 1999; Cosden, Morrison, Gutierrez, & Brown, 2004; Girod, Martineau, & Zhao, 2004). This is regardless of whether the focus of the program is on academic performance, bonding towards school, or usage of technologies, in a community setting, or within a school setting. More importantly, it is the commitment of the teachers or other adults who are running such programs with the basic aim of enriching the young minds, boosting their confidence, and valuing school related activities.

Beck (1999) reports that formal after-school programs can make a difference in the academic performance of students and some schools are even implementing their own on-site after school curricula. She conducts a study at the Manchester Youth Development Centre and identifies six salient elements for the successful implementation of such initiatives. The factors are: (1) provision for both structure and autonomous space, (2) focus on academic achievement, (3) program is culturally consistent, (4) large core of committed authoritative adults, (5) child centred activities, and (6) safe place. There are clear rules and routines within the program and at the same time, have autonomous space that may be described as "wiggle room". The academic component offers the extra time on task and instructional support provides additional educational opportunity. Time is also given for students to complete their homework. It is important to be aware and understand the culture, family background and belief systems of the students. The presence of adults who genuinely care for the students and are capable of disciplining them, if the need arises, is also important. The students and the children are the focus of this program. Lastly, safety includes protection from outside hazards and safety within the environment.

Cole (1998) reports the successful implementation of the Fifth Dimension and *KLICK!* after-school programs respectively. The Fifth Dimension combines both practical and pedagogical concerns in the design of computer-mediated activities. The need to merge students' interests in play and arcade-style games with interest in educationally effective games is considered. The second goal is to create activities with opportunities for written and oral communication about the goals and strategies used in problem solving. Third, is the awareness of repeated findings that girls engage in computer-based activity less than boys. Hence, the promotion of communicative writing is one area of computer involvement to attract the girls. Fourth, it is also the aim of the program to design the activity to be intrinsically motivating for the children who are involved in the program.

Cooper, Valentine, Nye, and Lindsay (1999) report the relationships between five after-school activities (homework, television viewing, extra-curricular activities, other types of structured after-school groups, and jobs) and academic achievement. After-school activities that are directly related to achievement (homework),

Table 1. Engaging and motivating design elements that are found in QA

No.	Design Factors and Elements	Brief Description of Design Factors and Elements found in Quest Atlantis
1.	**Affiliation and Cooperation with Others** (Dickey, 2005; Gee, 2003; Lim, Nonis, & Hedberg, 2006; Malone & Lepper, 1987)	There are two forms of communication available in – synchronous and asynchronous. Both forms of communication have the potential of engaging students in collaborative tasks where learning is viewed as a social process that involves building connections: (a) connections among what is being learned and what is important to the learner; (b) connections among what is being learned and those situations in which it is applied; and (c) connections among the learner and other learners with similar goals.
2.	**Challenge** (Dickey, 2005; Gee, 2003; Malone & Lepper, 1987)	In order to rebuild and restore the lost wisdom, the *Atlantian* council came up with a series of *quests* to challenge students to participate in their *quests* and share their knowledge with the *Atlantian* on how to save *Atlantis*. The inquiry nature of the *quests* provides opportunities and challenges for students to research into other cultures, analyse newspaper articles, interview members of the community and use software to come up with a meaningful document. The inquiry-oriented learning processes of information collection, interpretation, and analysis, and personal reflection to foster critical thinking and meta-cognition empower and enhance learning engagement. The *quests* in *QA* also provide template-based response documents with guiding questions, web links and keywords as scaffolds to direct students' attention to the successful completion of the *quests*. The *Atlantian* council opened a virtual environment known as the *OTAK* Hub as a form of communication between Earth and *Atlantis*. Students are able to interact with the digital artefacts in the *OTAK*.
3.	**Clear Goals and Standards** (Dickey, 2005)	Goals and standards are clearly spelled out for each and every *quest* assigned to the students.
4.	**Competition** (Malone & Lepper, 1987)	This point system (*lumins* and *cols*) is transparent to all users within the environment. It provides some form of competition among the users as well. The points that they obtain from playing a game often appeal to them and motivate them. It is very common to observe that they compare and compete with their peers to demonstrate progress and superiority in the game.
5.	**Opportunity to try and try again** (Gee, 2003)	Students are required to continuously refine and resubmit *quests* that are not accepted by the *Atlantian* council (a role played by the teachers).
6.	**Control and Choice** (Dickey, 2005; Gee, 2003; Malone & Lepper, 1987)	They can also create their own avatars (virtual characters) and control them. The avatars can perform basic actions like wave, dance, jump with joy, and etc. Found in the eleven worlds (with three villages in each world) are games and simple interactivities to enhance the curiosity of the students.
7.	**Play and Fun** (Dickey, 2005; Gee, 2003; Lim, Nonis, & Hedberg, 2006; Malone & Lepper, 1987)	The 3D virtual world allows students to explore, discover, and enhance their curiosity. The 3D world provides a platform for play and fun. There is a variety of *quests* in the 11 worlds available within *QA*.
8.	**Fantasy** (Lim, Nonis, Hedberg, 2006; Malone & Lepper, 1987)	*QA* attempts to situate the students in the fantasy of rebuilding and reconstructing the "arch of wisdom". Students are introduced the back-story at the onset of the program. Students are known as *questers* to restore order in the virtual world of *QA*.
9.	**Moving up the levels** (Gee, 2003; Lim, Nonis, & Hedberg, 2006)	The *quests* assigned to students follow a step-by-step sequence from easier ones to more difficult and complex *quests*.
10.	**Multimodal Output and Input** (Gee, 2003)	The *quests* within *QA* do not consist of only text. Teacher prepared worksheets, URL links to relevant website, hands-on sessions, and interaction within the 3D world are found in the *quests* assigned to students. Students are required to produce multimodal output such as screen capture, scanned images, hand drawn posters, and etc. Students' outputs are not restricted to text only.
11.	**Recognition and Affirmation of Performance** (Gee, 2003; Lim, Nonis, & Hedberg, 2006; Malone & Lepper, 1987)	Through the point system called *lumins* students are given recognition for their contributions when they successfully submit the *quests* to the *Atlantian* council. For the other activities, they can collect *cols*, gems and minerals, jewellery, trading cards, maps, and etc. in their *Q-Pack* These increase the probability of student engagement.

fostering of a positive identification with school (extra-curricular activities and other types of structured after-school programs), or both are positively related to students' achievement in school. On the other hand, activities that displace school (television viewing), replace school identity with other identities (employment or jobs), or both are negatively related to achievement. According to the authors, it seems safe to say that parents and educators can profitably focus on the students' after-school activities as a potentially important influence on achievement.

Cosden, Morrison, Gutierrez, and Brown (2004) report their reviews on the effects of after-school activities on school success. They observe that most of the after-school programs that address academic needs are designed to serve at-risk students and youths. These programs are typically broad-based and designed to promote self-esteem, enhance school bonding, and motivation which serve as a protective role to help students maintain their academic standing. After-school homework programs seem to benefit children who are at risk for school failure. Although after-school homework programs provide structure, supervision, and academic assistance, there are other types of extracurricular activities that may be beneficial to these children and would be unavailable if they were to attend the homework programs. The authors stress the importance of non-academic extracurricular activities – including sports, service clubs, and art activities – that are often associated with school engagement and achievement. These activities increase connectedness to the school and help to build students' strengths, self-esteem, and positive social networks.

Girod, Martineau, and Zhao (2004) also report their positive findings on the *KLICK!* (Kids Learning In Computer Clubhouses!) program. *KLICK!* is a computer clubhouse supporting positive, engaging, and innovative after-school activities for teenaged students. The students spend time, voluntarily, at the computer clubhouse creating web pages, surfing the internet, chatting on-line, filming and editing digital movies, and playing games. The *KLICK!* clubhouse is filled with networked computers, scanners, digital cameras, laser printers, and a server. Latest software to manage and edit digital video, author web pages, and chat interactively with other clubhouses are also available. There are numerous projects going on in a clubhouse. Many *KLICK!* Teens who contribute to the consortium newsletter, participate in video games and robotics competitions, are employed by teachers and community members to provide computer training and assistance. In addition, they also maintain the extensive local clubhouse and community websites.

THE STUDY

The purpose of this study rather than a specific methodology defines this research study. The main aim of this study was to look into the effectiveness and subsequent formative improvements of the intervention of using the 3D game-like *MUVE* In order to understand and describe the processes which involved teachers, students and the 3D *MUVE*, a more qualitative research approach was used to engage and motivate 14 academically at-risk students in an after-school program.

Background of the Study

This study is a collaborative project with a primary school in Singapore, the Centre for Research on Learning and Technology (CRLT) at Indiana University, and National Institution of Education / Nanyang Technological University, Singapore. It builds on earlier research studies on the implementation of Quest Atlantis in the United States (Barab, Thomas, Dodge, Carteaux, & Tuzun, 2005) and Singapore (Lim, Nonis, & Hedberg, 2006).

This was a one year case study conducted in 2006. A total of 14 students were identified based on their previous year's academic performance.

They were the ones with the lowest examination scores among their cohort of about 240 students. Students in this after-school program were required to stay back for one and a half hour twice weekly.

Students' Engagement with Quests

The *QA* after-school program started off with orienting the students to the 3D virtual environment as well as the expected behaviour of the students when they were online or within the *QA* virtual learning environment. It was made clear to the students that the *quests* were related to the work done in their normal classes. However, they would be using more of the computer and other forms of technologies to complete their q*uests* (or assignments).

At the very beginning of the orientation, all the students were shown a video of the back story of *Quest Atlantis*. The back story was about the deterioration of the *Atlantis* after it was handed over to the previous ruler's son and daughter with the passing of the former leadership. Students, who were also known as questers, in this 3D online virtual environment, were to help the *Atlantian* Council to restore the 'arch of wisdom' by completing the *quests* that were assigned. The restoration of the 'arch of wisdom' would stop the deterioration of the *Atlantis* world.

A structured inquiry approach was adopted during the initial phase and many of the subsequent sessions. Students were usually gathered in front of the computer laboratory and the teachers who were conducting the lesson would outline the basic agenda of the session and what was expected from the students. The teachers would then demonstrate how certain tasks could be completed. After which, the students would be assigned a computer each to login into the 3D virtual environment to complete the tasks they were assigned.

Following the orientation *quests*, students were also taught technical skills such as how to take a photograph (screen capture) of the characters within the virtual world, make a bracelet as well as collect maps, trading cards, user manuals, gems, minerals, and discovery tools. The students were also given a round-neck *QA* T-shirt each after the orientation phase of the program. This was done to promote students' sense of belonging to the *QA* after-school program. The same number of *lumins* and *cols* were awarded automatically by the system when the *quests* submitted were accepted by the *Atlantian* Council, which was role-played by the teachers who were running the after-school program. Additional *cols* were also given to the students by the teachers when they had successfully completed additional tasks assigned by the teachers or when they exhibited desirable behaviour such as helping a friend in completing their *quests*. Teachers could award *cols* but not *lumins*.

Students did not complete all the orientation *quests* as suggested by the teachers as they were often distracted by the 3D space and animated digital artefacts within *QA*. As a result, some of the students only started doing the orientation quests after many reminders from the teachers.

After the orientation phase, the students were often re-gathered in front of the computer laboratory for a short briefing before each session. It was as a form of advance organiser on how certain *quests* could be done, followed by the students working with the computer on the *quests* at their own time. Lim (2004) suggests the use of advance organiser as a strategy to teach student "learn how to learn online". He also suggests the use of scaffolding to address students' lack of knowledge. As a form of scaffolding given to the students, teachers assist the students when they needed any assistance. The students were also given the freedom to explore and do their own *quests* with permission from the teacher. But, only a handful of the students took the initiative to work on the *quests* of their choice. The students were also encouraged to attempt any *quest* when they were at home. However, it was observed that the students preferred to follow the instructions of the teachers. Only students who were more independent attempted a few additional *quests* on their own accord after seeking permission from the teachers.

Many, if not all, the students were often observed to be engaged with the 3D space in the virtual environment and playing with their favourite online games, such as *Maple SEA*, *HABBO Hotel*, *Adventure Quest*, to name a few. Students usually engaged themselves in these online game sites before and after the program. They would come in earlier and stayed back later to make use of whatever possible opportunities they had to visit these game sites. At times, they visited these sites when they thought that the teachers were not watching. Other than earning their *lumins* through the submission of *quests*, they also spent considerable amount of time collecting digital artefacts and *cols* in their respective *Q-Packs*. However, they were also aware of the expectations of the teachers, that is, to attend the program and submit the *quests* as expected of them.

For the students, the computer and *QA* were used as tools to access and play their favourite online games. In addition, students also used the *QA* 3D space to work on and submit their *quests*, get their *lumins*, *cols* and digital artefacts, and communicate with their *QA* classmates and other questers who were online. The students were attracted by the game-like design elements and this could be further exploited to draw out the intended outcomes.

Students' engagements with the *quests* were basically teacher guided. Some of the students were more enthusiastic in doing the *quests* so as to earn more *lumins* and *cols* which allowed them to *luminate* the petals of their respective *Shard Flowers*, change their avatars, and exchange for digital artefacts in the virtual environment. However, some were less engaged with the *quests* but were more interested in the collection of digital artefacts from exploring the 3D space of the virtual learning environment. It was evident that the game-like design elements alone could not engage the students in academic related activities.

RESEARCH DESIGN AND METHODS

A case study approach is used in this study to look into the effectiveness of the intervention of the use of a 3D *MUVE* to re-engage a group of academically at-risk students in an after-school program. The students were selected based on their academic performance. This project aims to re-engage this group of students in academic related tasks and activities. A case study approach is used as this program is a "case" of the implementation of a 3D *MUVE* in an after-school setting within a school context. The interest is on both the commonalities and uniqueness of this case. Most importantly, it is on what we can learn from and share about this case. Although case study seems to be a poor basis for the purpose of generalization to inform about future practices, the case will be studied at greater length and the recurrent activities, problems, and responses will be considered. Hence, generalization could then be drawn up. "For the most part, the cases of interest in education and social service are people and programs. Each one is similar to other persons in many ways and unique in many ways" (Stake, 1995, p. 1).

Case study research is not a sampling research. Hence, it is not the primary intent of this case study to understand other cases. According to Stake (1995, p. 4), it may be useful to try to select cases that are typical or representative of other cases, but a sample of one or a sample of just a few is unlikely to be a strong representation of others. The most important criterion of using a case study as a research method is to maximise what we can learn. Certainly, the intervention experience with this group of students could be used to inform the educational practitioners about the future practices and remedies for this group of students regardless of which school they belong to.

A constant theme that appears in the literature of case study research is triangulation, the use of multiple sources of evidence in data collection (Yin, 1994; Stake, 1995; Gillham, 2000b; Merriam, 1998). The most important advantage presented by using multiple sources of evidence is the development of converging lines of inquiry. Findings or conclusion is likely to be much more convincing and accurate if it is based on several different sources of information. With multiple approaches within a single study, we are likely to illuminate or nullify some extraneous influences (Yin, 1994; Stake, 1995). In this case study, triangulation addresses the problems of validity and reliability.

The different research methods used in this study acted as a means of triangulation. The findings were derived and triangulated from the various research methods listed below. For instance, observation notes of the after-school program was triangulated with interviews with the students, and the students' activities in the virtual environment to enhance validity and trustworthiness of this study.

The following research methods were used in the data collection and analysis:

1. Observation Notes – Observation allows the gathering of rich data in natural settings. Rich data means a better description and understanding of what goes on in a particular process. The focus of the observation notes were on the teacher-student, student-teacher interactions, and behaviour of the students during the after-school program. Observation notes were recorded after each after-school session for analysis.
2. Interviews and Interactions with Students – Interviewing could be one of the most common and most powerful ways to try to understand the individual or a group (Fontana & Frey, 1994). One of the main purpose of the interview sessions with the teachers is to reconcile a common discrepancy between what they say about themselves and what they actually do (Gillham, 2000a). Hence, the interviews with the teachers and also students would act as a form of triangulation against what is observed from the researchers' perspective.

All the 14 students who were involved in the *QA* after-school program from the beginning were interviewed informally and individually throughout the study. These interviews were conducted either during the after-school program or immediately after the after-school sessions. Each student was interviewed at least twice. They were interviewed individually so that the responses from the student could be independent and not influenced by the others. In addition, it was also to avoid the very dominant or opinionated students from biasing the results obtained from the interviews as the more reserved students might be hesitant to talk. These sessions took the form of informal interviews; basically in the form of an informal chitchat session during the after-school program to check on the students' responses and reactions towards their progress and how they felt about the program. The students were one of the most important elements in this research, especially in the area of their motivation and engagement with the use of the 3D *MUVE*.

The interview questions were generated after observation of the students in the after-school program and interactions with the students during the after-school program. The questions asked were mainly on how they felt about the after-school program, what were the factors that motivated them to attend the sessions and what were the elements found within *QA* that motivated and engaged them in the completion of quests

3. Students' Activities in the *MUVE* – The *QA* virtual learning environment provides a very comprehensive teacher module that captures each and every student's activities within the online learning environment. For instance, detailed students' activities, such as the number of quests assigned, number of quests each individual student had attempted, and the number of *lumins* awarded could be retrieved from the teacher's module. Students' chat log could also be retrieved through this module. This module was used

to retrieve information on the number of quests students had completed, the number of *lumins* they earned, number of *cols* they had collected in their respective *Q-Packs*, and the number of logins to this virtual learning environment.

The whole research setting happened naturally with many variables within the school context in an after-school remediation program that was conducted twice weekly. Constant discussions and reflections were done to fine-tune the implementation of this program and the introduction of the type of *quests* that best captivate the attention of the students. One central focus was to look into how the different elements within the *QA* environment motivate and engage the students with school related activities and how these elements could inform theories in educational *MUVE* design, engagement, and motivation. In addition, the students were not treated like subjects. Instead, they were treated as partners of this program and were constantly consulted on how they would like the program to be.

In this case study, data analysis with each method, between methods and with the case took place together with the data collection and data processing. The ongoing analyses helped to remove biases and errors that had crept into the fieldwork and fine-tune the research methods to reflect a better understanding of the setting. The data collected was continually subjected to cross checking with the various sources of data.

In short, the points of discussion were derived from the various sources of data, which were cross-examined within each method and between methods. The design elements within *QA* that could engage the students were established through interview sessions with all the students and this was further triangulated with their activities with *QA*, and the observation notes.

FINDINGS AND DISCUSSION

This chapter reports the findings – students' interaction with the engaging elements in *QA* from the observation notes, interviews with students, and students' activities in the *MUVE*.

Students' Interaction with the Engaging Elements in QA

Several game-like elements were found in *QA*. These elements were outlined in the earlier section. They would be discussed in relation to the *QA* after-school program. It was observed that students seemed to be engaged with seven of these eleven game-like elements found in *QA*.

The **play and fun** elements found within the *QA*'s 3D space attracted and engaged the students. In addition, the **recognition and affirmation of performance** also motivated the students to attempt and submit their *quests*. Other design elements such as the **affiliation and cooperation with others, challenge, clear goals and standards, competition, and control and choice** also showed potential for engaging the students. The reactions of the students to these design elements would be discussed in greater detail in the following sections that follow.

Affiliation and Cooperation with Others

The after-school program had created some sort of exclusiveness and affiliation amongst this group of students. The 3D online game-like virtual learning environment, that is, *QA*, also provided the group with an identity in the school, especially amongst the Primary 5 students. The after-school program was commonly known as "*QA*" to the selected students, other students in the school, and fellow teachers.

It was observed that students worked in pairs doing their *quests* and other activities on many occasions during the after-school program. The virtual environment also provided a possibility for co-questing, that is, forming groups for the submission of *quests* within the environment. Some of the students, used the communicative tools found within the environment on their own accord, especially the synchronous chat that provided just-in-time and on-demand type of interactions with other participants of *QA* which included students in the after-school program, as well as local and overseas students who were also present in the virtual environment. Collaboration amongst the students was mainly via the online chat. However, the content of the emails, chats, and telegrams was mainly socially motivated rather than content related discussions.

Challenge

The element of challenge was not very evident in engaging this group of students, especially for those *quests* that were closely tied to the school curriculum and syllabus. Although the *quests* were designed to challenge the students, quite a number of them were rather similar to the type of assignments given in their daily classes. As many of the *quests* were mainly text-based inquiry type of questions, some of the students found it difficult even to achieve the minimum requirements. It was the reminders and assistance by the teachers who conducted the program that drove the submission of these curriculum related *quests* amongst the students.

However, students seemed to be more engaged with the more authentic type of *quests*, such as those that required students to help clean up a nearby river banks and solve mysteries within the virtual environment. Students were observed to be more challenged by these *quests*.

Clear Goals & Standards

The goals and standards required were clearly spelt out for each *quest,* with narration to help students who could not read well. The objectives of each *quest* were further reinforced and elaborated by the teacher who conducted the lesson to help the students focussed on the tasks that they had to do. Students also helped one another to clarify doubts they had through face-to-face interactions during the after-school program. Although this element was not very apparent and did not come out distinctively, it had indirectly helped the students to be more focused towards the tasks they were supposed to complete.

Competition

The point system, that was the *lumins* and *cols*, was transparent to all the users within the virtual environment. Students did compare their performance amongst themselves, although it was not very apparent and did not really come out strongly in the interviews with the students. Two girls did share that they liked the competition with others.

Yvonne shared that she could show off the number of *lumins* and *cols* to her friends. "… if I *lumin*ate…, I will show off and go tell others," she exclaimed. One of the students also reflected that it was a form of contest to her to get more *lumins* as compared to her friends. "When you get more *lumins* mean you win," she shared.

Opportunity to Try and Try Again

In *QA*, students were given the opportunities to continuously refine and resubmit their *quests* that were rejected by the *Atlantian* council members who were role-played by the teachers. They were allowed to resubmit their *quest* as many times until they were accepted by the council. There were no penalties for any *quests* not accepted by the council.

However, several students commented that it was very frustrating when they were asked to resubmit their *quests* repeatedly. For instance, although several students shared that they would continue to submit even after many rejections, they was not forthcoming in terms of behaviour in the resubmission of *quests*. One of them lamented that, "... I tried doing the *quests* and submitting them but sometimes the council does not accept them." When I asked him whether he would resubmit his *quests*, his answer was positive that he would resubmit even for the third or fourth time. He also expressed his frustration regarding the rejection of the *quests* he had submitted.

Control & Choice

Students liked the control and choice over their avatars and where they wanted to go in the online game-like virtual environment. However, the same could not be said for the *quests* that they needed to do.

Basically, there were two different groups of students. One group of students was rather independent with their submission of *quests* while the other group was less focused and spent quite a considerable amount of time just loitering and wandering about within the 3D environment. There was this constant struggle that when the students were given a choice, many of them would spend too much time on the 3D space rather than on the completion and submission of the *quests*.

Play & Fun

The hot favourite amongst the students was to explore, discover, and satisfy their sense of curiosity, especially in the 3D environment, where they played around with the gym, cars, and boats. The student quickly shared what they could do with the cars and boats in the 3D environment with the others and shortly, all of them would be taking turns to have a ride on either the cars or the boats. They were also able to explore and discover new things within the *MUVE*. It was actually the students who taught the teachers, including myself, many features/elements that they had found in the virtual environment.

Throughout the after-school program, it was observed that students were very interested in the 3D environment, especially playing with the cars, airplanes, yacht, and gym. Those who were a little more creative even played hide-and-seek within the 3D environment. At times, the students visited other game sites when teachers were not looking at them. The 3D *MUVE* could really engage the students. Unfortunately, it was not in doing their *quests*. The virtual environment could entice them to be involved in computer game-like play such as controlling the cars, airplanes, and yachts. The 3D environment was a constant distraction. However, we could not imagine the *MUVE* without it. The 3D environment played quite a significant role in attracting the students to come to the after-school program as they were allowed to explore, discover, and satisfy their sense of curiosity. There were instances where the students were so distracted by it that teachers had to disable the 3D space so as to get them to focus on the *quests*. The 3D environment was the main attraction and without it, the students seemed to be very restless during the period where the 3D space was disabled. Students found it very captivating even if they were to just move around and explore the 3D environment with their friends. Students exchanged notes on how and what to do in the various worlds that were available to them. Some had even gone into the hidden worlds through online chat with their overseas counterparts. We learned a lot from the students in this aspect. The 3D environment was play, fun, and possibly variety to the students. From the above findings, the 3D environment was indeed a source of attraction, especially to the students.

Fantasy

Generally, the students understood the back story of *Quest Atlantis*. However, it was observed during the interviews that some were not very convinced with the existence of the *Atlantian* council. Below were the interview dialogues between the interviewer and two of the students. The dialogues were their thoughts about the fantasy and back story of *Quest Atlantis* and the *Atlantian* council. "I don't believe there is a Council," one of them shared during her interview. "All those teachers involved in *QA*. They mark the *quests*. I don't believe that there is Council... I don't believe that. That are not real, it is false." When interviewed, the other students reflected that she was still doubtful and she confirmed that a couple of her friends did not believe in it. Some of the students even approached teachers to ask whether they were the ones who gave feedback on their assignments online. Through the interactions with the students, it seemed that this element of fantasy was not prominent in engaging the students to submit their *quests*.

Moving up the Levels

The whole design and plan for the after-school program was to engage the students in a step-by-step manner with the easier *quests* to be done first, followed by the more complex and difficult ones. Simple orientation *quests* were first introduced, followed by the more complex *quests*. This approach had, in its limited ways, encouraged the students to attempt some of the *quests*.

Multimodal Output & Input

A variety of *quests* was assigned to the students, ranging from online worksheets type to *quests* that required the students to interact with the digital characters in the 3D environment. Students were also required to produce multimodal types of output as part of their submissions such as screen captures, scanned images, and hand drawn maps. It had, to some extent, engaged students who were not inclined to text and writing.

Recognition & Affirmation of Performance

Most, if not all, students reflected that the *lumins*, *cols*, avatars, and digital artefacts did motivate them to submit *quests* that were assigned to them. This was especially evident from the interview sessions with the students. Although the main focus during the after-school program was for the students to complete their *quests,* the students actually spent quite a considerable amount of time learning from one another and exchanged ideas on how they could go about collecting more items in their *Q-Packs* and how to use their *cols* to exchange for things that they wanted. One of the students was delighted when he gained enough *lumins* to change his avatar to one with an eagle on its shoulder. The student actually figured out on his own how he could change his avatar. This created some talks and discussion amongst the students, too.

As much as the teachers would like to draw out the intrinsic motivation of the students in academic related activities, it seemed to suggest that extrinsic forms of motivation such as the points system within the 3D *MUVE*, that is, the *lumins* and *cols* were more able to encourage the students to submit *quests*, even those who were not so engaged and motivated. The *lumins* earned allowed the students to *luminate* their respective petals of the *Shard Flower*. In addition, the *lumins* also permitted the students to change their avatars (changing to one with an eagle on the shoulder). Some students shared during their interviews that they would like to do more *quests* so that they could get more *lumins* to change their respective avatars. *Cols* were the currency in the *QA* environment that allowed the students to rent land, buy digital artefacts, to name a few. Students were also interested in getting more *cols* to buy more digital artefacts and land. The digital artefacts they collected and bought were kept in their *Q-Packs*. One of the more savvy students even conducted a sharing session on how to use *cols* to buy land within the environment as many of the students would like to know how to do it. They spent considerable effort and time to collect all these in their respective *Q-Packs*. Students were more engaged with the non-academic activities that seemed to be more meaningful to them than the academic ones.

The findings suggested that the play elements found within the *QA*'s 3D space attracted and engaged the students. In addition, the recognition and reward system also motivated the students to attempt and submit their *quests*. Other design elements such as the affiliation and cooperation with others, challenge, clear goals and standards, competition, and control and choice also showed potential for engaging the students. However, it was observed that these engaging elements alone, which were found within the *QA MUVE*, were not sufficient in engaging these students in completion of *quests* (i.e., inquiry-based tasks and activities). The students' engagement with the *quests* found within the virtual learning environment is discussed in greater details in the next section.

NON-ICT ACTIVITIES THAT FURTHER FACILITATED THE STUDENTS' ENGAGEMENT

The above discussion highlighted how a technological tool such as *QA* could be used to facilitate the learning of a group of academically at-risk students depended very much on how it was being used. Although the *QA* virtual learning environment provided the students with opportunities to engage themselves in the learning process, it could not be assumed that these opportunities would be taken up (Crane, 2000). Lim (2004) also put forward that learners may lack the learning strategies, knowledge, and attitude to work through the online learning environment. It was observed that non-ICT activities planned and carried out by the teachers were crucial in further facilitating the engagement of the students. Without these non-ICT activities, the effectiveness of the ICT tool would be compromised.

In order to better engage these students, orientation program was planned and conducted to address the issue of lack of learning strategies in the students by providing the necessary opportunities for students to learn and explore the *QA* virtual learning environment. The *QA* after-school program started off with orienting the students to the 3D virtual environment as well as the expected behaviour of the students when they were online or within the *QA* virtual learning environment. Lim (2004) suggests that in order to address the lack of learning strategies, students need to be provided with "learn how to learn online" sessions so that students do not get lost due to the navigation aspects of the interface. A structured inquiry approach was adopted during the *QA* sessions. Students were usually gathered in front of the computer laboratory and the teachers who were conducting the lesson would outline the basic agenda of the session and what was expected from the students. The teachers would then demonstrate how certain tasks could be completed. Advance organisers in the form of relevant and inclusive introductory materials to provide students with a structure that could guide them on a given learning activity as they work through the learning environment. After which, the students would be assigned a computer each to login into the 3D virtual environment to complete the tasks they were assigned.

In order to address the lack of knowledge, teachers and the researchers monitored the progress of each student and provided necessary technical and content knowledge when students were in doubt with navigating within the virtual environment or uncertain with the *quests* they were working on.

As for the lack of appropriate attitude, Lim (2004)suggests the use of authentic activities such as problem-solving (solving of authentic problems) and simulating activities. In order to enhance the students attitude towards their *quests* the teachers and researchers designed authentic and problem-solving type of *quests* to even better engage the students. Students were shown a video of the back story of *QA* to situate them as questers seeking knowledge to restore the 'arch of wisdom' so to stop the deterioration of the *Atlantis* world.

LIMITATION OF STUDY

There were three main limitations in this research. Firstly, this case study provided little basis for generalization. Nevertheless, the context of the study is elaborated in detail to address this limitation – a rich content is provided. According to Stake (1995, p. 4), it may be useful to try to select cases that are typical or representative of other cases, but a sample of one or a sample of just a few is unlikely to be a strong representation of others. However, the primary intent of this case study was not to understand the other cases. The main purpose was to maximise what we could learn from this case study on how the use of a 3D *MUVE* could be used to re-engage academically at-risk students in school related work.

The second limitation was our assumptions and biases as we are directly involved implementation of the research. Recognizing that our assumptions and biases could affect the data collection and its outcome, the data collection process, data analysis within each method, between methods, and within the case took place alongside data collection and data processing. Having ongoing analysis had two advantages. First, they helped to undo errors in the field. Observation notes were recorded after each session and completed very promptly. This allowed time for us to look through these notes and reflect upon how the data collection processes could be fine-tuned along the way. Second, the ongoing analysis provided opportunities to refine the research methods to reflect a better understanding of the context. There were continuous efforts to triangulate the observations and the interviews conducted. However, at times, it was obvious that the interpretation of the researchers as well as that of the participants mediated all the data. To address this, we constantly questioned our own assumptions. I also regularly checked our observations with the teachers who were involved in this research project.

The third limitation was the students who were involved in the after-school program. They were a group of students who were the weakest among their cohort and were not very fluent in their English language as many did not speak English at home and with their friends. This was an issue during the informal interviews with them as they needed much probing and remained rather quiet with open-ended type of questions. This limitation was recognised during the on-going data collection process and other sources of data, such as the students' online activities via the *QA* teachers' module, were used to complement the interviews.

CONCLUSION AND FUTURE TRENDS

This paper has highlighted the potentials and possibilities of the use of a game-like virtual environment in the engagement of a group of academically at-risk students. The engaging elements within the virtual environment attracted the students but additional non-ICT activities are needed to support them in the completion of academically related tasks and activities, which are known as *quests* in this virtual environment.

QA was more than a tool to the students. Some of the design elements within this game-like *MUVE*, such as the 3D space, *lumins*, *cols*, avatars, and digital artefacts became something that the students sought after. The students who were involved in the after-school program were not intrinsically motivated towards the *quests* but they were extrinsically motivated by the 3D space, *lumins*, *cols*, avatars, and digital artefacts. Hence, these elements could be further capitalised to bring about the desired behaviours amongst the students. In essence, *QA* played the role of a tool to facilitate learning, it also played the role of enticing and attracting the attention of the students. Lepper, Corpus, Iyengar (2005) suggest that "working to enhance both intrinsic motivation and the internalisation of extrinsic motivation may help to maximise – or, at least, to minimise the loss of – children's motivation to learn" (p. 193). The authors further propose that intrinsic and extrinsic motivation can and do coexist. They argued that although not all activities could be designed or made intrinsically motivating, the internalisation of extrinsic motivation could be potentially useful and informative as a supplement to intrinsic motivation.

In other words, the engaging elements mentioned above could be used as a supplement to enhance the intrinsic motivation of the students. Non-ICT based activities such as orientation activities, advance organisers, learning how to learn in an online virtual environment, teachers' guidance, and use of more authentic tasks are also necessary and crucial to further bring out the potentials of this game-like *MUVE*. This observation again illustrated the importance of the need to develop appropriate pedagogical strategies to better engage our students.

Hence, further studies could be conducted to look what teaching pedagogies would be more suited to bring out the potentials of such game-like *MUVE* to enhance the extrinsic and the intrinsic motivation of the students for learning in a school setting. An in-depth study could also be carried out to look into what are the necessary socio-cultural conditions for such an educational innovation to flourish within a school setting. In addition, a more comprehensive experimental study could also be conducted to look into the effectiveness of such a program in enhancing the academic results of these pupils.

REFERENCES

Amory, A., Naicker, K., Vincent, J., & Adams, C. (1999). The use of computer games as an instructional tool: Identification of appropriate game types and game elements. *British Journal of Educational Technology*, *30*(4), 311–321. doi:10.1111/1467-8535.00121

Barab, S. A., Thomas, M., Dodge, T., Carteaux, R., & Tuzun, H. (2005). Making learning fun: Quest Atlantis, a game with guns. *Educational Technology Research and Development*, *53*(1), 86–107. doi:10.1007/BF02504859

Beck, E. L. (1999). Prevention and intervention programming: Lessons from an after-school program. *The Urban Review*, *31*(1), 107–124. doi:10.1023/A:1023200500215

Cole, M. (1998). *Cultural psychology: A once and future discipline*. London: First Harvard University Press.

Cooper, H., Valentine, J. C., Nye, B., & Lindsay, J. J. (1999). Relationships between five after-school activities and academic achievement. *Journal of Educational Psychology*, *91*(2), 369–378. doi:10.1037/0022-0663.91.2.369

Cordova, D. I., & Lepper, M. R. (1996). Intrinsic motivation and the process of learning: Beneficial effects of contextualization, personalization, and choice. *Journal of Educational Psychology*, *88*(4), 715–730. doi:10.1037/0022-0663.88.4.715

Cosden, M., Morrison, G., Gutierrez, L., & Brown, M. (2004). The effects of homework programs and after-school activities on school success. *Theory into Practice*, *43*(3), 221–226.

Crane, B. E. (2000). *Teaching with the Internet: Strategies and models for K-12 curricula*. New York: Neal-Schuman Publisher.

Cuttance, P. (1998). Quality assurance reviews as a catalyst for school improvement in Australia. In A. Hargreaves, A. Lieberman, M. Fullan & D. Hopkins (Eds.), *International handbook of educational change: Part 11* (pp. 1135-1162). Dordrecht: Klwer Publishers.

Dempsey, J. V., Haynes, L. L., Lucassen, B. A., & Casey, M. S. (2002). Forty simple computer games and what they could mean to educators. *Simulation & Gaming, 33*(2), 157–168. doi:10.1177/1046878102332003

Dickey, M. (2005). Engaging by design: How engagement strategies in popular computer and video games can inform instructional design. *Educational Technology Research and Development, 53*(2), 67–83. doi:10.1007/BF02504866

Fontana, A., & Frey, J. H. (1994). Interviewing: The art of science. In N. K. Denzin & Y. S. Lincoln (Eds.), *Handbook of qualitative research* (pp. 361-376). Thousand Oaks, CA: SAGE Publications Inc.

Gee, J. P. (2003). *What video games have to teach us about learning and literacy*. NY: First Palgrave Macmillan.

Gillham, B. (2000a). *The research interview*. New York: Continuum.

Gillham, B. (2000b). *Case study research methods*. New York: Continuum.

Girod, M., & Martineau, J., & Zhao. (2004). After-school computer clubhouses and at-risk teens. *American Secondary Education, 32*(3), 63–76.

Hill, P. W., & Rowe, K. (1998). Modelling student progress in studies of educational effectiveness. *School Effectiveness and School Improvement, 9*(3), 310–333. doi:10.1080/0924345980090303

Lepper, M. R., & Chabay, R. W. (1985). Intrinsic motivation and instruction: Conflicting views on the role of motivational processes in computer-based education. *Educational Psychologist, 20*(4), 217–230. doi:10.1207/s15326985ep2004_6

Lepper, M. R., Corpus, J. H., & Iyengar, S. S. (2005). Intrinsic and extrinsic motivational orientations in the classroom: Age differences and academic correlates. *Journal of Educational Psychology, 97*(2), 184–196. doi:10.1037/0022-0663.97.2.184

Lim, C. P. (2002). A theoretical framework for the study of ICT in schools: A proposal. *British Journal of Educational Technology, 33*(4), 411–421. doi:10.1111/1467-8535.00278

Lim, C. P. (2004). Engaging learners in online learning environments. *TechTrends, 48*(4), 16–23. doi:10.1007/BF02763440

Lim, C. P., Nonis, D., & Hedberg, J. (2006). Gaming in a 3D multi-user virtual environment (*MUVE*): Engaging students in science lessons. *British Journal of Educational Technology, 37*(2), 211–231. doi:10.1111/j.1467-8535.2006.00531.x

Malone, T. W. (1981). Toward a theory of intrinsically motivating instruction. *Cognitive Science, 5*(4), 333–369.

Malone, T. W., & Lepper, M. (1987). Making learning fun: A taxonomy of intrinsic motivations of learning. In R. E. Snow & M. J. Farr (Eds.), *Aptitude, learning, and instruction: Vol 3. Cognitive and affective process analysis* (pp. 223-253). Hillsdale, NJ: Lawrence Erlbaum.

Merriam, S. B. (1998). *Qualitative research and case study applications in education*. San Francisco: Jossey-Bass Publishers.

Rieber, L. P. (1996). Seriously considering play: Designing interactive learning environments based on the blending of micro-worlds, simulations, and games. *Educational Technology Research and Development, 44*(2), 43–58. doi:10.1007/BF02300540

Rosas, R., Nussbaum, M., Cumsille, P., Marianov, V., Correa, M., & Flores, P. (2003). Beyond Nintendo: Design and assessment of educational video games for first and second grade students. *Computers & Education, 40*(1), 71–94. doi:10.1016/S0360-1315(02)00099-4

Squire, K. (2005, August). Changing the game: What happens when video games enter the classroom? *Innovate, 1*. Retrieved on August 30, 2006, from http://www.innovateonline.info/index.php?view=article&id=82

Stake, R. E. (1995). *The art of case study research.* Thousand Oaks, CA: SAGE Publications, Inc.

Stewart, K. M. (1997). Beyond entertainment: Using interactive games in Web-based instruction. *Journal of Instruction Delivery System, 11*(2), 18–20.

Yin, R. K. (1994). *Case study research: Design and methods* (2nd ed.). Thousand Oaks: SAGE Publications.

Chapter 13
Comparing Face-to-Face with Blended Learning in the Context of Foreign Language Education

Kosmas Vlachos
Hellenic Open University, Greece

ABSTRACT

The discussion presented in this chapter is based on the findings of a post doctoral research, which compared face-to-face with blended learning in the field of foreign language education and the learning of English in Europe. The studying conditions that are present in each of these two modes are explored and juxtaposed in order to draw the reader's attention to a number of benefits that spring from blended learning, namely the development of skills and strategies, the cultivation of positive attitudes towards learning, the promotion of literacies, and the unfolding of communicative competence. Specifically, as we assert in this chapter, it follows from our research that the combination of blended learning with cross cultural online collaboration supports the construction of foundational and new literacies, enhances the development of linguistic, pragmatic, strategic, sociolinguistic, and intercultural competences, and boosts students' cognitive, metacognitive, and social strategies, as well as their critical thinking skills. Overall, the chapter emphasizes the need for blended learning in foreign language education.

INTRODUCTION

Integrating computer assisted language learning (CALL) in the teacher led lessons in the classroom has been an issue of study in foreign language education over the last few years. The proponents of CALL claim that ubiquitous computing is an integral part of modern life and, consequently, computers cannot be seen simply as tools that facilitate learning; they are to be viewed as sources of linguistic knowledge and as the means that allow students to communicate, internalize previous knowledge and set the foundations for acquiring new. On the other hand, teacher led tuition is considered to be critical, especially in the school context, due to the fact that foreign language learning needs to be organized and well-structured if it is to be effective. Blended learning, which combines online and

DOI: 10.4018/978-1-60566-852-9.ch013

off-line learning modes, provides students with chances for computer mediated language learning at school and/or at home, while at the same time teacher led classes guide and encourage them to take the next step to knowledge.

In this chapter we argue for blended learning and discuss the language learning and pedagogical benefits that spring from its application in foreign language education. We draw evidence from a post doctoral research, in which we compared and contrasted face-to-face with blended learning. Collating and exploring the two specific learning modes shed light on a number of critical to language learning issues, such as the construction of a social learning environment in class that simulates real-life communication and the development of a methodology that offers students ample opportunities, on the one hand, for exposure to authentic input and production of output and, on the other, for consolidating and expanding new knowledge. The comparison between the two modes allows us to examine in depth the new goals that have emerged in foreign language education and information communication technologies (ICT), i.e. the construction of new literacies, communicative competence and learning strategies, and to investigate the extent to which these goals can be accomplished.

Apart from the introduction and the conclusion, the chapter includes four main sections. The first, the background section, introduces the reader to some basic concepts regarding blended learning and foreign language education and discusses the goals of English language learning in the present ICT era. The second section acquaints the reader with our research, whereas the third one presents and discusses our findings, by means of making close reference to the theoretical principles and concepts presented in the first section. The fourth section analyses our proposals for future implementation, while the conclusion includes some recommendations for future research.

BLENDED LEARNING AND FOREIGN LANGUAGE EDUCATION IN SCHOOLS, THEORETICAL PERSPECTIVES

Definition, Practices and Pedagogy

Blended learning has been explored the last few years. Scholars, researchers and practitioners have been studying the inherent characteristics which compose effective learning and teaching practices and analyzing the benefits that emanate from its application. A broad definition could be that blended learning is viewed as the procedure where more than one learning/teaching modes are being used and different learning styles are supported, with a view to improving learning (Singh & Reed 2001). This chapter refers specifically to the combination of face-to-face tuition in the classroom and online teaching methods to facilitate language learning. In this educational process of combining classroom work with technology mediated learning, the realization of the teaching goals and the learning benefits are of primary importance. Although a major advantage of educational technology lies in its ability to motivate students, the teacher's prime consideration is first, to set specific learning goals and then decide on the delivery modes and the technologies that will realize these aims.

Specifically, as it is supported in the relevant literature, tutors and course designers who adopt blended learning practices need to take a number of factors into consideration, before deciding which learning modes and technological applications they will use (Ausburn 2004; Bonk & Graham 2005; Chapelle 2001). First, it is suggested that they make a needs analysis research and take into account their students' preferred learning styles, interests and intelligences. Second, it is recommended that they consider the conditions and parameters that constitute their learning context and teaching situation: Factors, such as the teaching time they have at their disposal, the resources that are available in their institution and the students' potential for self-access and self-study at home, need to be seriously considered. Last but not least, it is suggested that educators take into consideration the learning outcomes that are expected to be realized. In other words, only after they have considered and examined carefully the learning goals, are tutors able to make selections across the applications and the learning activities that will optimize learning, which in the case of this chapter is the learning of English.

In foreign language education the effective combination of face-to-face learning with tuition that is accomplished with the aid of educational technology has been systematically investigated for more than three decades. Scholars, such as Beatty (2003), Cummins (1996), Levy & Stockwell (2006), Warschauer (1996 & 1998), Warschauer & Kern (2000), Warschauer & Whitaker (1997), Willis (2001) to name but a few, have been arguing for the systematic integration of educational technology and internet activities in the foreign language programs. The advances in ICT and the new trends in pedagogy and in applied linguistics have enriched and expanded the blended learning modes and the possibilities they offer to consolidating and expanding a foreign language.

Nowadays, there is a considerable number of blended learning possibilities the tutor can take advantage of in a foreign language program. Online multimedia language learning programs, thesauri, digital dictionaries and concordancers are used in combination with face-to-face tutorials to assist students in developing an understanding of how the linguistic system of the target language works. Furthermore, the world wide web (hereafter web) is used for web quests, i.e., the learning process in which students navigate the web to retrieve information, which they elaborate to create projects with the aim of consolidating and enriching the linguistic and non linguistic knowledge they have acquired in their non electronic lessons. Moreover, asynchronous and synchronous online communication with the aid of the email, blogs, wikis, multiplatforms of communication and videoconferencing are combined with face-to-face lessons in the classroom to enable students to develop both their productive (speaking and writing) and social skills in the foreign language.

There is no doubt that online learning brings immediate and up-to-date information to the classroom. A primary goal for many teachers using the web and online communication is to harness their motivational quality. Motivation has always been a key issue in education. Ideally, teachers attempt to make their students develop intrinsic interests in the subjects being taught so that they will pursue learning on their own (Dornyei 2001 & 2003; Fox 1998). Research has proved that the use of online learning activities in foreign language education seems to fill the criterion of promoting intrinsic motivation, as students see the internet as a modern and useful tool that enables them to be connected with the world (Cooper & Selfe 1990; Moras 2000; Pennington 2004; Peterson 1997). Except for retrieving information, students create their own materials which they share with partner classes or with the whole world. This possibility adds a great deal of interest as it provides communication with a real audience and enables students to exceed the borders of the physical classroom (Vlachos & Athanasiadis 2005).

Additionally, integrating online activities in foreign language lessons on a regular basis gives the students the opportunity to control their own learning (Beatty & Nunan 2004; Vlachos 2005; Williams 2002). Working under the umbrella of social-constructivist pedagogy, students can work at their own pace, take initiatives, make research and collect information to synthesize digital texts. They can cooperate and communicate electronically with other students and use sound, music and graphics so that they create multimodal texts in the student-friendly environment of educational technology, which gives them freedom to develop their own personal styles and intelligences and, therefore, take control of the learning process (Warschauer 2001 & 2005). Online activities encourage students to become autonomous and develop learning strategies and skills that will help them broaden their educational horizons. However, interaction with authentic sources and communication with native and non native speakers of the target language cannot replace teacher led lessons in the areas of the language system, such as grammar and syntax. Educational technology practices cannot be treated as stand alone elements in the multidimensional learning process of the foreign language, which aims at the fostering of skills, competencies, strategies and literacies (Kamberi & Vlachos 2003).

Blended learning, which combines both online learning and classroom teacher led tuition, caters for the development of students' linguistic knowledge, communicative experiences and new literacies. The ultimate goal in foreign language education is for students to develop the construct of communicative competence along with a number of strategies, that will help them "learn how to learn" and cope with the difficulties communication in the foreign language entails, as well as a number of new literacies that will enable them to use the foreign language to function in modern multilingual societies. Therefore, as we support in Vlachos (2006a), mastering a foreign language in schools is a complex and demanding learning procedure in which teacher led instruction is central, due to the fact that students and especially young learners need support, encouragement and guidance in the learning process, which is progressive and life-long, since it is going to continue and be enriched throughout the students' lives.

The Aims of Foreign Language Education in a Blended Learning Environment: Communicative Competence, New Literacies and Learning Strategies

Communicative Competence

As it has already been explained in the previous subsection, the fundamental goal in foreign language education and by extension in the learning of English as a foreign language (hereafter EFL) is for students to develop the construct of communicative competence. Since the 70s the communicative approach has prevailed in foreign language learning. This approach, which has evolved throughout the years, views language as a system of meanings, notions and linguistic functions, which is used for communication and needs to be studied within the social and cultural contexts where it is used. More specifically, the communicative approach sees language as a complex system through which we express ideas, facts, thoughts and values, in other words cultural reality. As we explain in detail in Vlachos (2006b) communicative competence is a construct which consists of a number of sub competences (competences hereafter), skills, and knowledge that is being gradually built thanks to the linguistic, social and intercultural experiences the student gains in her/his life. Specifically, the construct of communicative competence comprises the following competences:

- The linguistic competence, which includes knowledge in the linguistic system of the target language (syntax, grammar, vocabulary and phonology). This knowledge helps students express themselves with accuracy so that the meanings they create can be comprehensible (Papaefthymiou-Lytra 1987; Van Ek 1977; Widdowson 1972 & 1979).
- The pragmatic competence, which refers to the student's ability to produce coherent and cohesive speech that enables her/him to communicate complex meanings, to argue and to produce sophisticated speech (Canale & Swain 1980; Widdowson 1983). In written discourse, where the student does not always have signs as to whether the reader comprehends the meanings conveyed through the text, the development of pragmatic competence is of great

significance and it is, therefore, one of the most important aims in the teaching of writing skills (Vlachos 2000 & Athanasiadis in press).

- The strategic competence, which concerns the skills and the linguistic and non linguistic techniques the student needs to develop so that she/he can make herself/himself understood in speech acts. In particular, the ability to anticipate difficulties and gaps in communication and to rephrase meanings, to use body language and paralanguage and to adjust the speed of his/her speech delivery constitute components of the strategic competence (Ellis 2003; Lee 2000).
- The sociolinguistic competence, which regards the student's skills and knowledge that enable her/him to communicate effectively taking into consideration social factors, such as her/his interlocutors' social class, educational level, ethnic origin, sex, age etc. (Canale & Swain 1980; Dubin & Olshtain 1986; Hymes 1967 & 1972). When communicating, speakers of the foreign language need to adjust what they say and how they say it according to the social context the interaction is placed in. They need to consider factors, such as a. the formality of the situation, b. the status of the people they address themselves, c. their interlocutors' possible educational background, d. what their interlocutors' expectations from this interaction might be and adjust their verbal behavior accordingly etc.
- The intercultural competence, which is centred on the students' capacity to use the foreign language to discover and relate to new people from various and diverse social and cultural contexts (Vlachos 2007). According to the intercultural perspective in foreign language education, students need to go beyond the acquisition of the linguistic system of the target language and to be engaged in an active exploration of the cultural identities of the social groups that use the target language. As Byram (1994 & 2000) puts forward, students should learn not to be influenced by stereotypes, to exhibit understanding and tolerance towards the 'otherness' of their interlocutors in a communicative event, to be positive and to promote communication and interaction. Furthermore, it is essential that they should be given opportunities to appreciate their own cultural identities and to learn how to approach and interact with representatives of other cultures, using the target language (Byram & Fleming 1998; Dendrinos 2001; Papaefthimiou-Lytra 1996 & 2004; Vlachos 2008).

New Literacies

As technology creates new possibilities for EFL learning, students need to develop new literacies to exploit these potentials. Several years ago the term 'literacy' in language learning was mainly associated with the students' abilities in reading and writing. These abilities, which in this chapter will be called 'foundational literacies', include phonemic awareness, knowledge in the grammar and syntax of the language, word recognition and vocabulary knowledge, understanding the meaning of new words from the context they are embedded, comprehension, inferential reasoning, producing well spelled texts, moving forward and backwards in the stages of the writing process while composing texts, responding to literature etc. Nowadays the term ' new literacies' refers to skills, strategies and knowledge the students progressively build in order that they will ultimately become able to adapt to the changing ICT and the new learning contexts that are created and to use digital and non digital sources to enhance their understanding of topics and issues. These literacies permit students to use sources in print, the web, computer mediated communication (hereafter CMC) and other ICT to find answers to questions by locating information, critically evaluating it and reconstructing it (Gardner 1999; Leu et all 2004).

Today EFL students become literate by learning to read, to understand and to interpret the words, the symbols, the graphics, the art work and the photos, in other words the data, which synthesize electronic and non electronic multimodal texts. They need to learn to decode, evaluate, compare and interpret multiple representations from different disciplines. They need to learn to select and to use different representational media to express themselves when composing written discourse. As various new genres appear in communication, such as the art of graffiti or the language of the email and blogs, the teaching of productive skills is being enriched and widened to encompass the new forms of interaction. What is more, EFL students need to learn to modify the style, the register and the formality of the discourse they use, judging by the rhetorical situation, the media they select and the intended audience.

Therefore, it is necessary for EFL students to be trained to develop new literacies (Shetzer & Wasrchauer 2000) such as:

- using search engines to locate information;
- selecting information according to their needs and purposes;
- critically evaluating the information accessed and gathered;
- interpreting multimodal texts;
- using the word processor effectively to produce grammatically and syntactically well- formed texts;
- selecting art work, graphics and photos that illustrate the meanings they intend to convey through their multimodal texts;
- knowing how to use the email to communicate effectively;
- participating in online discussions and bulletin boards;
- using multiplatforms or multi-device e-learning systems to communicate synchronously and asynchronously with other students with a view to creating online projects;
- accessing online learning resources, such as dictionaries and thesauri, to refine the way they express themselves.

It is made clear in the relevant literature that the new literacies are built on foundational literacies (Leu 2000; Spires & Estes 2002; Sutherland-Smith 2002). As reading and writing become even more critical in our ICT world, being the language skills mostly used in digital environments, foundational literacies form the basis on which new literacies are constructed. Due to the fast evolution of ICT and the competences that are demanded on the part of the student, it is essential for EFL education to focus on both the development of foundational and new literacies. As we explain in the sections that follow, it can be concluded from our research that blended learning seems to be the answer to the challenge of catering for both types of literacies. The combination of face-to-face tuition with computer-based learning offers tutors opportunities, on the one hand, for teaching basic language components in the areas of syntax, grammar, phonology and vocabulary and, on the other, to design digital, communicative activities that foster the development of new literacies.

Learning Strategies (Cognitive, Metacognitive & Social)

In an EFL blended learning environment, building the construct of communicative competence and promoting foundational and new literacies presuppose students' engagement in critical inquiry learning (Kinzer 2003; Kinzer & Leander 2003; Tyner 1998), whose prerequisites are student autonomy and the development of learning strategies and skills. According to Ellis & Sinclair (1989), in foreign language education students can be trained to self-study. They can also learn to activate the appropriate strategies that not only facilitate their learning but also make it more pleasant and, hence, more effective. Research has evidenced that the more we understand how we can learn better, the more pleasant learning becomes. It has also demonstrated that self-learning, cooperative learning and investigative learning become sources of inspiration leading to student autonomy (Dickinson 1987; Papaefthymiou-Lytra 2004). In this learning context the cognitive actions students take in order to make learning more self-controlled, more self-directed, easier and more pleasant, are defined as learning strategies (Oxford 1990).

In this chapter we deal with three types of learning strategies:

- Cognitive strategies, which help students approach, understand and produce new content information. Using the grammar and syntax control of the word processor, resorting to reference materials, such as online dictionaries and thesauri, classifying lexical items and concepts, taking notes in abbreviated forms, summarizing the main points of a text with a view to reproducing its content, relating new information to previous knowledge, using prior knowledge to assist understanding of new information, inferencing the meaning of unknown words from the context they are placed and using symbols and mental or either actual images to remember new information are some instances of cognitive strategies (O' Malley & Chamot 1990).
- Metacognitive strategies, which permit students to control learning through planning, organizing and evaluating their own progress. Previewing the main ideas of the material to be studied and learned, rehearsing the language that will be needed for completing a communicative activity, planning and sequencing the main ideas that are to be transmitted through communication, checking and judging one's own comprehension and production of messages, locating types of mistakes one usually makes with a view to avoiding them in the future and, finally, setting new educational goals and seeking opportunities for more learning are some examples of metacognitive strategies (Chamot & O'Malley 1996; Wenden 1991).
- Social strategies, which allow students to interact with other people. Some instances of social strategies are: eliciting additional explanation from their interlocutors, providing clarifications that promote communication, rephrasing, working together with peers to solve problems, receiving and exploiting feedback from interlocutors and teachers, providing feedback, etc (O' Malley & Chamot 1990). In social learning environments, such as online platforms of communication, the development of social strategies is vital since it caters for the creation of dialogue among students who come from different social and national backgrounds. This cross cultural dialogue adds a sense of purpose to foreign language learning as students see the target language as the means that allows them to interact with representatives of other cultures.

All three types of strategies support the development of communicative competence in a social learning environment. In the sections that follow we present the research we conducted and we compare blended learning with face-to-face learning with a view to examining the extent to which each one of these methodologies enhances competences, literacies and strategies.

THE RESEARCH STUDY

The conducted research lasted for two consecutive school years and involved two projects: A blended learning project, in which participated three classes of students from three different European primary schools, and a face-to-face project in which took part the students of a class from a Greek primary school. The research compared face-to-face with blended learning in the context of EFL. The ultimate learning goals of both projects were to help the participating students develop the competences that constitute the construct of communicative competence, to start building foundational and new literacies and to get used to taking advantage of cognitive, metacognitive and social strategies. In both projects we created social learning environments, which allowed students to get involved in an effective learning process by means of communication, interaction and cooperation. Both projects ran at the same time and were evaluated on the basis of the same criteria.

The Blended Learning Project

In the blended learning project computer assisted language learning and in particular asynchronous online collaboration was regularly and systematically integrated into the foreign language program of three classes of primary school students from Finland, Spain and Greece, aged 10-11, in the form of an asynchronous online networking scheme. The scheme was called "The Euro e-pals". The three primary schools that participated were the Savonlinna Normaalikoulu school from Finland, which belongs to the Savonlinna Normaalikoulu University; the C.P. San Agustin school from La Orotava, Tenerife, Spain; and the 9th primary school of Zografou, Athens, Greece. The Savonlinna school participated with a class of 20 students, the C.P. San Agustin with a class of 22 students and the 9th primary school of Zografou with a class of 18 students. All learners were at an approximate age of 10 years when the "Euro e-pals" started in March 2004. The participating students, in groups of 3-4 children, collaborated online, exchanged cultural information, expressed ideas, feelings and attitudes and negotiated meanings with the aim of creating multimodal electronic texts that were, eventually, published in an interactive-publishing online platform, which had been specifically constructed by the researcher to facilitate the students' online interaction.

Regarding computer equipment, all three participating schools offered the necessary facilities, i.e. computer laboratories with broadband internet connection. As concerns the students' knowledge in computers, before the project the participating students had not received any formal instruction in computer operation. Therefore, they were not familiar with word processing, accessing the web and using the email for online communication. In the process of the project, they were taught to use the interactive-publishing online platform, the word processor, the e-mail and the web to retrieve information. Developing the students' computational skills was integrated in the project lessons and was seen as an integral part of the EFL learning and cross cultural collaboration. As it was reported by the teachers who worked for the blended learning project, when "The Euro e-pals" was completed all the participating students had cultivated basic skills in the specific computational areas.

Throughout the duration of the blended learning project, seven teaching/learning units were completed. Table 1 presents the titles of the units. Each teaching/learning unit included an asynchronous online exchange of multimodal electronic letters among the sixty students of the participating European classes, as well as the production of multimodal electronic reports, in which the students described the information they had collected online through the electronic letters and commented on the similarities and differences between their culture and the cultures of their overseas partners. The students worked in groups. There were six groups of students in each country. Each group had taken the name of a species of animals which is met in the country the children lived. Table 2 presents the names and the matching of the groups. For the completion of every teaching/learning unit presented in Table 1, the groups of students presented in Table 2, exchanged information among each other and negotiated meanings. For instance, the Ladybirds exchanged electronic multimodal letters with the Eagles and the Whales and gathered information, which they used to compose multimodal electronic reports that provided comparisons across the cultures involved in the project.

For the teaching of each one of the teaching/learning units and the effective organization of the asynchronous communication, a learning-teaching framework was created. The framework, which was named as "The framework of intercultural asynchronous online communication" (IAOC framework), was founded on Willis' (1996) Task-Based Learning Framework. Each teaching/learning unit was designed by the researcher and taught by the participating teachers following the three stages of the IAOC framework. The stages of the framework included:

Table 1. The titles of the seven teaching/learning units that were completed

1. "Making friends, introducing ourselves and our school"
2. "How do you celebrate Easter?
3. "The Olympic Games"
4. "The Environment"
5. "Christmas traditions in different parts of Europe"
6. "Providing an ending to a story"
7. "Health habits at school and at home"

Table 2. The names and the matching of the groups

Greek Groups	Finnish Groups	Spanish Groups
Ladybirds	Eagles	The Whales
Sparrows	Black Hawks	Canaries
Crickets	Angry Weasels	Lizards
Cats	Crawling Snakes	The Pigeons
Nightingales	Spiders	Dolphins
Butterflies	Arctic Foxes	Verdino Dogs

1. The preparation of the students, which was realized through face-to-face learning in the classroom. In this stage the students carried out communicative activities that prepared them for the online communication which was to follow. The researcher created learning materials that were available online and taught by the three participating teachers. The materials focused on the topic of the teaching/learning unit that was being taught and presented vocabulary and structures that were meant to be used by the students throughout their online interaction, which was to follow in the next stage. Figure 1 presents a teaching/learning activity that was available online and prepared the students for the composition of the multimodal electronic letters and reports of unit 7 "Health habits at school and at home".
2. The asynchronous online communication, which included a. the composition of electronic, multimodal letters and the synthesis of the electronic, multimodal reports. Both types of texts were uploaded and published in the interactive-publishing online platform. To produce both types of electronic texts, students used the word processor and online dictionaries, worked in groups and exchanged feedback within the borders of the physical classroom. Specifically, the groups of students were encouraged to discuss their texts with other groups from their class, to share ideas, to cooperate on expression and to improve each others' texts. Figure 2 presents some of the electronic multimodal letters the Greek students prepared to present information regarding the Olympic Games in Greece.
3. The language focus stage, in which the learners studied and analyzed the form of the English language. The learners looked critically at some linguistic elements used at the second stage and made observations

Figure 1. An example of an online learning activity taught at the preparatory stage of the IAOC framework

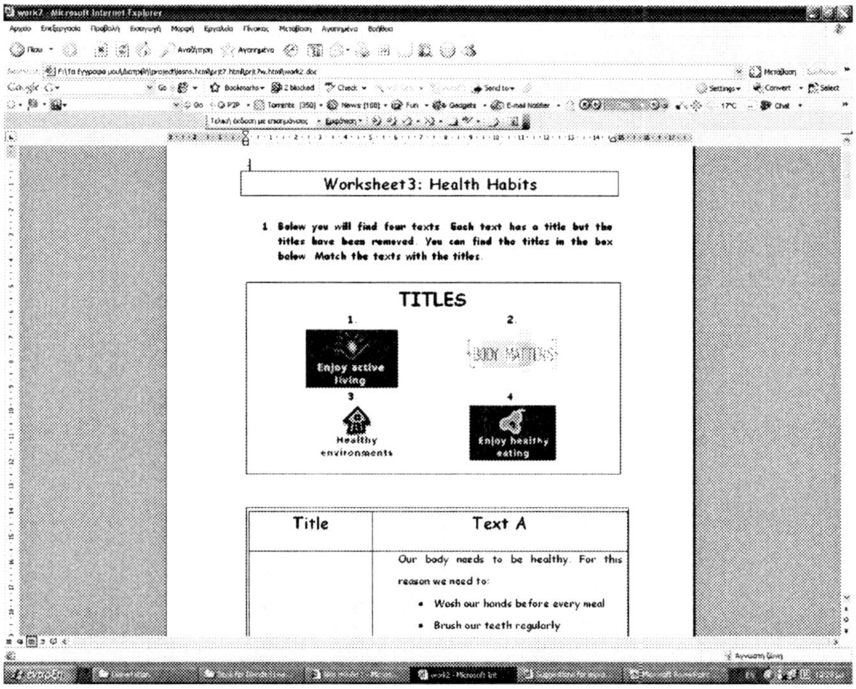

Figure 2. Some electronic multimodal texts the Greek students prepared to present information about the Olympic Games in Greece)

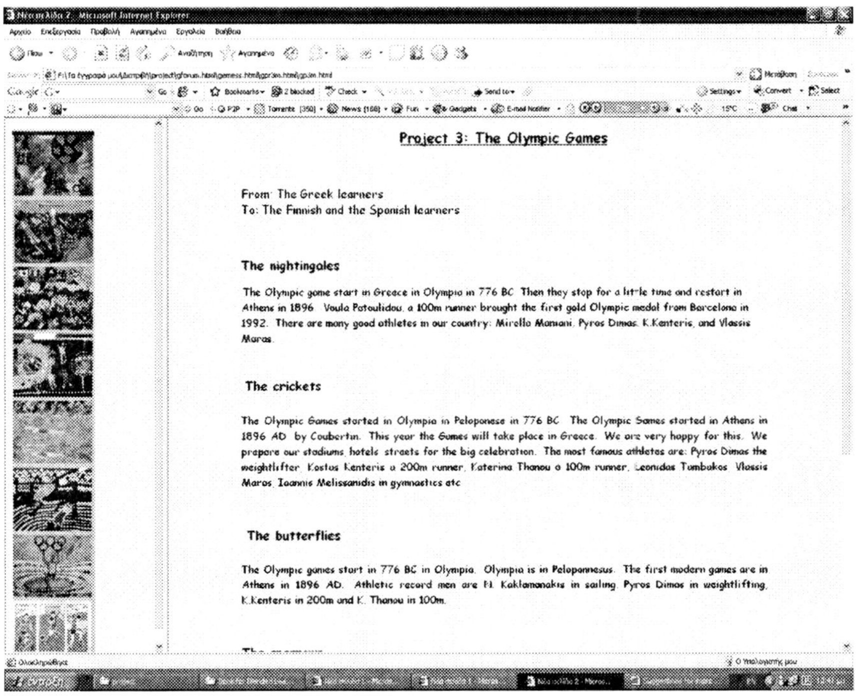

as concerns their function in the linguistic system and/or their function in communication. They practised words, phrases and patterns to build accuracy and confidence. The language focus analysis was taught in the classroom mostly through face-to-face learning but occasionally students used concordancers to access corpora that provided them with linguistic examples and online thesauri for alternative expressions, synonyms and antonyms.

The Face-to-Face Project

The eighteen students of the face-to-face project were taught the same teaching/learning units, linguistic items, language functions and text types as the Greek "Euro e-pals" networked students. Still, the students of the face-to-face project exchanged information and negotiated meanings among each other only in a face-to-face mode in the classroom and, therefore ICTs were not used at all. In the face-to-face project the teacher used the Task-Based Learning Framework, as this is presented in Willis (1996). Specifically, regarding the stages of each teaching/learning unit:

- First, the teacher prepared the students so that they would compose texts that would contain cultural information (Easter & Christmas traditions, environmental problems in the local area, health habits etc). The students in groups elaborated the topic, gathered information from texts in print, brainstormed and discussed what types of information and ideas could be included in their texts. The teacher also presented relevant vocabulary and linguistic items and activated background knowledge.
- Next, the groups of students composed their texts, which they exchanged with other groups in their classroom, made comparisons across the texts and commented on them. Since there were not recipients of the students' texts from another country or from another region of the same country, who would be interested in learning new information which they would not be familiar with, there was no information gap. Therefore, the students of this group used English and face-to-face interaction to present cultural information from their country, most of which was known to everybody in the class.
- Last, the language focus section followed, where the students observed and analysed the linguistic phenomena, the text types and the genres they had used in the second stage. Similarly to the students of the blended learning project, the students of the face-to-face project examined linguistic elements, syntactical patterns and collocations critically and observed their function in the linguistic system. The only resources they used were limited to printed materials.

DATA COLLECTION AND ANALYSIS

Both the eighteen "Euro e-pals" networked students from the blended learning project and the eighteen students of the face-to-face project attended lessons in schools in Athens, Greece and were taught by the same teacher of the English language. Before starting teaching each one of the above mentioned Greek classes (phase 1), the teacher gave the students of both classes a placement test and a questionnaire (questionnaire 1, appendix 1) gathering information on the productive language skills they had already developed, namely writing and speaking. At the end of the first year of the research, when three out of the seven teaching/learning units had been completed, the students of both classes were given a progress test (phase 2). When the seven teaching/learning units had been completed at the end of the second year of the research (phase 3), the teacher gave a final test to the students of both Greek classes, as well as the same questionnaire (questionnaire 1) the students had filled in phase 1 to fill in again. In addition, the teacher gave a second questionnaire (questionnaire 2, appendix 2), which gathered information on the students' attitudes, the learning skills and strategies they had built, the competencies and the new literacies they had constructed and their plans regarding future EFL learning. As regards the three tests, the activities investigated the development of the students' linguistic, pragmatic and sociolinguistic competences; they tested their knowledge in grammar, syntax, vocabulary as well as their reading and writing skills. The three tests provided the researcher with the opportunity to examine quantitavely to what extent the Greek students had been benefited from blended learning in comparison to the students who had been taught only through the face-to-face mode. All students answered the same tests and questionnaires, i.e. the topics and the questions were common for the students of both classes. Table 3 presents schematically the data collection methods and the learning areas that were explored in each one of the three phases.

The students' replies to questionnaires 1 and 2 were rated statistically with cluster analysis, a method that categorizes data in clusters (groups) on the basis of common characteristics (Athanasiadis 1995). Furthermore, tables with frequencies and rates were formed. The software that was used for the analysis was SPAD 4.5. The statistic analysis of the students' replies to the questionnaires helped the researcher to make comparisons across the two Greek classes, concerning issues such as attitudes, motivation and the development of literacies, of skills and strategies, of communicative competence and of knowledge that had been fostered and cultivated.

Finally, the electronic multimodal reports the five groups of students of the blended learning project had produced throughout the completion of the seven teaching/learning units were compared and contrasted with the texts the five groups of students of the face-to-face project had created (phase 4). Discourse analysis was used. The texts were evaluated and rated on the basis of a series of criteria, which referred to expression, content, structure, formatting & artistic design and effectiveness in terms of communication. The rates were processed statistically with cluster analysis. Tables with frequencies and rates were formed as well. This analysis assisted us in making comparisons in terms of linguistic and communicative knowledge across the groups of the Greek students who participated in the two projects.

THE FINDINGS OF THE RESEARCH: PRESENTATION & DISCUSSION

Linguistic Competence, Attitudes to Learning and Motivation

As it has already been explained in the previous section, both the eighteen students of the blended learning project in Greece (blended learning students or blended learning group hereafter) and the eighteen students of the face-to-face project (face-to-face students or face-to-face group hereafter) were taught by the same Greek teacher (teacher hereafter), who regularly provided the researcher with comparative reports upon the progress of the two groups. In her first report, the teacher explained that the face-to-face students were more enthusiastic about participating in a research project and were more positive about the social learning environment that had been created in their EFL lessons. Compared with the blended learning students, the students of the face-to-face group enjoyed cooperating and working in groups more.

According to the teacher's first report, an additional element which was in favor of the face-to-face group was that it comprised students whose learning records and test results in the past had been better than those of the students of the blended learning group. This

Table 3. Data collection methods and learning areas being researched

Phase	Group	Data Collection	Learning areas being researched
1	Blended learning group & Face-to-face group	Questionnaire 1	Writing & speaking skills developed before the beginning of the projects.
		Placement test	Pragmatic & sociolinguistic competences; grammar, syntax, vocabulary; reading & writing skills.
2	Blended learning group & Face-to-face group	Progress test	Pragmatic & sociolinguistic competences; grammar, syntax, vocabulary; reading & writing skills.
3	Blended learning group & Face-to-face group	Questionnaire 1	Writing & speaking skills developed by the time the two projects had been completed.
		Questionnaire 2	Students' attitudes; learning skills; cognitive, metacognitive and social strategies; new literacies and future plans.
		Final test	Pragmatic & sociolinguistic competences; grammar, syntax, vocabulary; reading & writing skills.
4	Blended learning group & Face-to-face group	The multimodal electronic texts the blended learning students had produced were compared with the texts the face-to-face students had created; discourse analysis	Expression, content, structure, formatting & artistic design and effectiveness in terms of communication.

comment was confirmed by the results of the placement test, in which the average score of the face-to- face group was 67%, whereas that of the blended learning group was 58%. Following the teachers' argument, the 9% difference between the two groups was due to the fact that the blended learning group included four less motivated students, who sometimes tended to be indifferent and unwilling to participate in the lessons. This lack of motivation created a challenge for the teacher and the researcher, who expected that the blended learning mode would enhance both the levels of motivation and test scores.

At the end of the first year of the research, when the progress test was given to the students of both groups, the results were in favour of the blended learning group who scored an average 65,5% as opposed to the 63,4% of the face-to-face group. When the two projects were completed, after two years of learning, the results of the final test were again in favour of the blended learning group who scored an average 71,8% as opposed to the 66,2% of the face-to-face group. Figure 3 illustrates the two groups' performances in the placement, the progress and the final test.

It is worth mentioning, though, that the face-to-face students had constant 5% precedence over the blended learning ones in the scores which referred to pure linguistic exercises, where their knowledge in grammar, syntax and vocabulary was tested. It seems that the extended face-to-face tuition they received in the classroom drew their attention to structures and form. On the contrary, when it came to communicative reading and writing tasks, where students had to skim and scan texts and to produce effective texts in terms of meaning and linguistic accuracy, the blended learning group had constant 10% precedence over the face-to-face group, a difference that was not detected when the students had completed the placement test. Figure 4 illustrates the performances of the two groups: a) in task 4 of the progress test and b) in task 4 of the final test. In both tasks the students were expected to read information, which they

Figure 3. The two groups' performances in the three tests

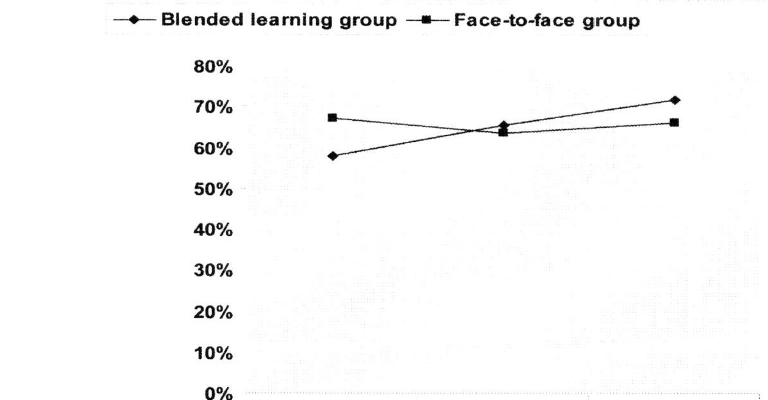

	Placement test	Progress test	Final test
Blended learning group	58%	65,50%	71,80%
Face-to-face group	67%	63,40%	66,20%

elaborated and reconstructed in order to produce letters. The highest mark a student could be given in each of these tasks was 25.

It can, therefore, be supported that the systematic online communication the blended learning students experienced, the methodical use of the word processor with its syntax and grammar control, the interactive-publishing online platform of communication, where they could instantly upload and download multimodal electronic materials, and, last but not least, the face-to-face guidance they received from their teacher and peers strengthened their communicative reading and writing skills. This assertion is enhanced by

Figure 4. The two groups' performances in communicative reading and writing tasks in the progress and the final test

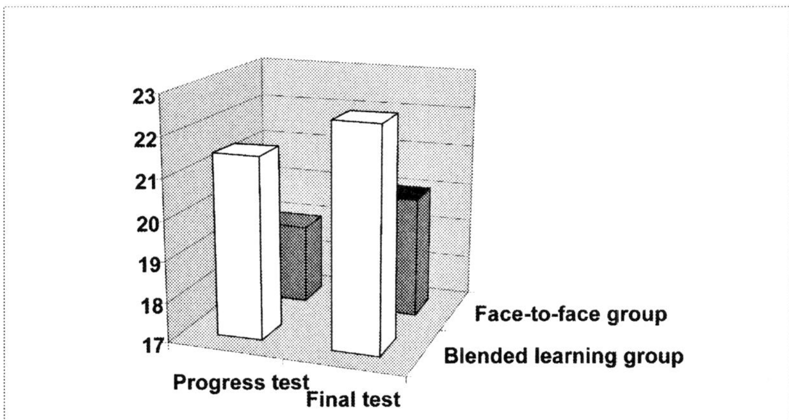

	Progress test	Final test
□ Blended learning group	21,5	22,5
▩ Face-to-face group	19	20

the teacher's comment, who in her final report, while comparing the two groups, explained that the blended learning students managed to do better than the face-to-face students because in the process of cross cultural communication the former students had cultivated the legitimate aspiration to create interesting, well written and comprehensible multimodal texts that would attract their overseas interlocutors' attention. She also added that blended learning students wished to disseminate elements of their culture and expressed interest in learning more about their interlocutors' ways of life. Although they had not been very positive about the idea of blended learning and cross cultural online communication in the beginning, later they became highly motivated and set off a learning journey of exploring new knowledge and acquiring new experiences. The questions they uploaded in the platform of communication and addressed to their foreign interlocutors indicated their intention to cover new areas of knowledge and their willingness to make comparisons across habits and civilizations. Hence, it appears that blended learning and cross cultural communication create positive attitudes to learning, boost motivation and guide students in the paths of learning how to learn.

Intercultural, Strategic, Pragmatic and Sociolinguistic Competences

Analysing the data we collected from the "Euro e-pals" networking scheme, we concluded that the networked students in all three countries, Greece, Spain and Finland, progressively developed intercultural awareness. Specifically, the three teachers who participated in "The Euro e-pals" networking scheme confirmed through the reports they systematically sent to the researcher that their students strengthened their national identity and became proud of their cultural and social background. Having processed the students' replies to the questionnaires, we found out that the 97% of the blended learning students accepted that systematic cross cultural online communication and blended learning enriched their intercultural knowledge and experiences. A 57% of them realized that the particular project helped them to learn more about their own civilization, habits and ways of life.

Furthermore, according to the Spanish, the Greek and the Finnish teachers' reports, the networked students learnt to take into serious consideration the cultural and linguistic otherness of their interlocutors, while collaborating on a local level and producing multimodal texts that would be uploaded in the interactive-publishing online platform of communication. They became more conscious of the fact that their online partners originated from diverse cultural and national backgrounds, had been brought up in dissimilar natural environments, spoke different L1s and, therefore, had disparate perceptions of the world. Hence, the networked students developed sociolinguistic and intercultural competences.

In addition, the three teachers observed that while composing and revising their texts, their students progressively became aware of the fact that they could make language mistakes, while expressing themselves in the target language, misled by the syntactical patterns, the word order, the notions and the functions of their mother tongue. The Greek teacher commented that, while selecting a folk story to narrate to their European partners, the Greek networked students (the students who in this chapter are called blended learning students) communicated with their interlocutors abroad and investigated whether in the Finnish language nouns have gender suffixes, as they do in the Greek language. In other words, the blended learning students built the ability to anticipate difficulties that could burden communication and tried to find solutions that would facilitate it. They, therefore, developed strategic competence.

Moreover, according to the cluster analysis and the evaluation of the multimodal electronic texts we conducted, the blended learning students' texts were better than those of the face-to-face ones in the criteria which referred to coherence, cohesion and effectiveness in terms of communication. Figure 5 illustrates the four clusters that include the groups of students and the characterizations they received for their texts on the basis of the seven criteria. Clusters 3 and 4 include groups of students whose texts were characterized as very good and excellent respectively in a number of criteria, whereas clusters 1 and 2 contain groups whose texts were characterized as weak or good. It can be observed that four of the five blended learning groups of students are placed in clusters 3 and 4, whereas only 2 of the face-to-face groups of students are sorted in the specific clusters. In addition, the blended learning students' texts were not only more coherent and richer in meanings but they were more appropriate in terms of text type and genre selection as well. It seems that due to the fact that there was always an information gap present in cross cultural communication, the blended learning students, who were curious to learn more about the topic being explored, were encouraged to choose the genre, the text type and register that would facilitate interaction. Consequently, it can be deduced that the blended learning students became more skilful as regards pragmatic competence.

It should be highlighted, though, that the fact that students of both projects were being prepared on the use of different genres and text types by their teacher through face-to-face tuition before the production of texts, played a critical role because it helped them produce better texts. Still, it is highly likely that the texts the face-to-face students generated were not as effective on the basis of the particular criteria (coherence, cohesion and effectiveness in terms of communication) as the texts of the blended learning students because, although the former students had composed them in a social learning environment, there was still absence of interest for writing and communication, since the face-to-face students had known each other for long and there was no real information gap in the communication that took place in the classroom.

It can, thereafter, be asserted that when blended learning is integrated with systematic cross cultural online communication, EFL students are offered more opportunities for developing sociolinguistic, intercultural, strategic and pragmatic competences. In Vlachos (2007) and Vlachos and Papaefthymiou-Lytra (2008) we explore in detail the issues of communicative competence and intercultural and language awareness and we discuss how these are promoted in a blended

Figure 5. The four clusters that include the groups of students and the characterizations they received for the electronic multimodal texts they produced

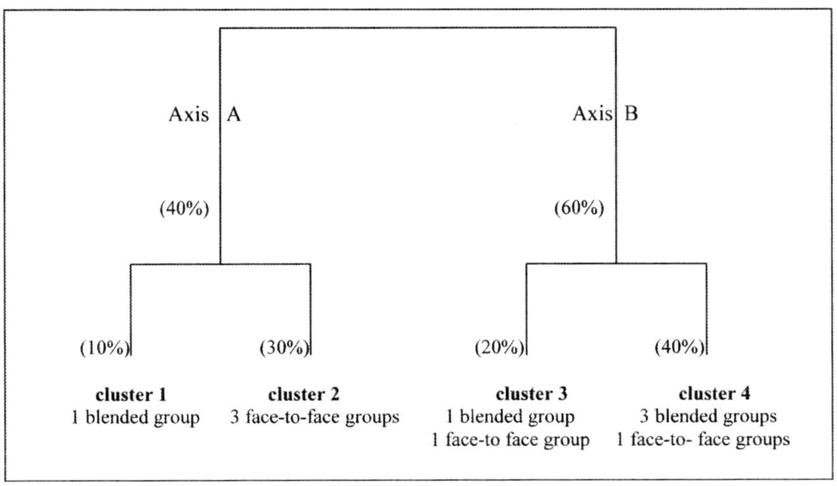

learning environment with the aid of cross cultural communication activities.

Literacies and Metacognitive Awareness

Having observed the learning procedure in both the face-to-face and the blended learning groups in Greece, we concluded that the students of both groups built foundational literacies. At the end of the two projects the teacher reported that the Greek students of both groups exhibited considerable progress in areas such as grammar, syntax, vocabulary and comprehension. The students' replies in questionnaire 1 indicated this progress, as the majority of them (80%) realized that they had improved in the specific areas. The results of the progress and the final test confirmed the teacher's comments and the students' replies. However, it should be noticed that, as we have already explained, at the end of the two projects the face-to-face students seemed to be slightly better at pure linguistic knowledge (syntax and grammar), whereas the blended learning students were better at reading and writing.

Furthermore, it has to be mentioned that the Finnish, the Spanish and the Greek teachers pointed out in the feedback they sent to the researcher that, apart from the literacies analysed in the previous paragraph, their students soon got used to studying carefully the information they selected from the electronic texts they had received, critically evaluating it and comparing it to their life experiences. The students also used to cross reference the information they had collected to check up on the similarities and differences and sometimes they surfed the web for more information or asked their overseas partners for clarifications. It is, hence, felt that blended learning and the systematic integration of cross cultural online communication encouraged students to be engaged in critical enquiry, in which they reflected and evaluated the content and the originality of the online texts they were processing.

Learning Strategies (Cognitive, Metacognitive & Social)

Concerning learning strategies, it was found out that both the face-to-face and the blended learning students were given opportunities for building strategies due to the fact that in both contexts social learning environments had been created. Yet, blended learning was more effective because of the methodical incorporation of online collaboration, the access to hypermedia and the use of the word processor. It was observed that the blended learning students became more autonomous and were more successful in developing metacognitive awareness, i.e. knowing how and what to do to enhance learning.

Specifically, it was noticed by the Greek teacher that both the face-to-face and the blended learning students built cognitive and social strategies. According to the teacher, the students from both modes of learning got used to collaborative writing and got accustomed to peer editing, i.e. the process in which the groups exchanged the texts they had produced and made suggestions as to how each others' texts could be improved. This procedure generated discussion in the classroom and helped the students to learn to spot mistakes, exchange views and consult reference materials (grammar books, course books etc) with the aim of ameliorating content and expression. The students of both groups discussed their texts, exchanged ideas, improved others' texts and finally learned what cognitive and social strategies to follow to correct their own mistakes. They got used to cooperating effectively and providing feedback without criticizing each others' errors, because they realized that collaboration and the friendly atmosphere in the classroom facilitated learning.

Yet, the blended learning students, who had been engaged in more critical thinking since they had been exposed to a larger variety of media and had experienced cross cultural interaction, were found to have built metacognitive strategies, which enabled them to plan, organize and evaluate learning. The Greek teacher of the blended learning group noticed that her students became aware of such factors as their purpose and intended readers, while making decisions on the content, the genre, the language functions, the layout and the style of the text they were about to produce. They made charts that outlined the organization of the texts they were planning to compose. They resorted to online thesauri and created webs with the lexical items they would include. They consciously moved in a recycling mode from planning to drafting, reviewing, replanning and revising. Finally, they systematically re-examined their texts from a reader's perspective to estimate whether the texts were comprehensible. The Spanish and the Finnish teachers explained in their reports that their networked students followed similar strategies when composing their texts.

Moreover, it was reported by the Greek teacher that, on a local level, the Greek blended learning students cooperated among each other better than the face-to-face students, as they were more willing to share skills and knowledge with other students with a view to improving their literacies and to disseminating cultural information. The social strategies they built allowed them to share their individual expertise and to teach their literacies to others. This finding suggests that blended learning supports the exchange of learning skills and strategies among students and tutors within a world of multiple new literacies framed by the ICTs.

It can, thereafter, be asserted that in a blended learning environment cognitive, metacognitive and social strategies assist students in their quest for new literacies since they direct them towards selecting the appropriate mental activities that will facilitate the development of new expertise. By orchestrating the exchange of new literacies and by consciously building learning strategies and communicative competence, EFL students broaden their skills in communication and their potentials for effective language learning.

TEACHING IMPLICATIONS AND PEDAGOGICAL PROPOSALS

Digital Applications and Learning Activities that Enhance Communicative Competence, New Literacies and Learning Strategies

As it can be inferred from our research, in an EFL blended learning environment, all competences that constitute the construct of communicative competence, literacies and learning strategies can be accommodated. The linguistic competence and foundational literacies are being built through face-to-face tutorials in the classroom, where the students study and observe the linguistic elements of the language, as well as through computer applications that provide corpora with linguistic examples, drill, practice, tutorial explanation, testing instruments and corrective feedback.

The pragmatic competence can be catered for, on the one hand, through writing practice with the aid of the word processor and its spelling, grammar and syntax control and, on the other hand, through the synchronous and asynchronous applications of online communication that enable students to interact with other students of the target language or native speakers. Face-to-face tutorials with the teacher and peer correction in the classroom guide students in the development of coherence and cohesion in discourse and of cognitive strategies. Online communication, on the other hand, permits students to practise what they have been taught in face-to-face tutorials and it encourages them to test whether the meanings they produce can be easily understood by their online interlocutors. Thereafter, online communication helps students to build metacognitive strategies.

In addition, online communication and especially videoconferencing provide students with opportunities for building their strategic competence. While working online and completing cooperative tasks, students learn to anticipate difficulties in communication, to adjust their rate of speech delivery, to rephrase and to elaborate meanings. They get used to expressing themselves in such a way that communication in the foreign language can be effective.

Sociolinguistic and intercultural competences are catered for through the cognitive and socio cognitive applications of educational technology. The generation of cognitive programs provides applications and digital resources in which students interact with the computer, working on meanings with cultural associations. These programs enable students to cultivate cognitive strategies, as they encourage them to use critical thinking to reproduce cultural content, to relate new information to previous knowledge and to use prior knowledge to assist understanding of new information. As we explain in detail in Lambropoulos et al (2005), these applications illustrate the social context(s) the target language is placed. An example of such a resource is the BBC schools site (www.bbc.co.uk/schools), which can be used as a source for project work or for simulation activities.

Furthermore, as we argue in Vlachos (2006b), CMC enables students of different origins to develop social strategies as it lets them exchange cultural and social information, expand their knowledge on cultural elements and social codes, suspend disbelief about each others' practices and interpret and relate these practices. In CMC, introductory face-to-face lessons that precede online interactions prepare students for the difficulties they might encounter and provide them with linguistic expressions, structures and vocabulary they will need while attempting to offer more information. These introductory lessons stimulate students to develop their metacognitive strategies, i.e. to control learning through planning and organizing, to preview the activities that are to be completed and to rehearse the language that will be used throughout communication.

Moreover, in CMC online collaborative activities students are given opportunities to enrich and expand their cognitive strategies since they resort to the grammar and syntax control of the word processor and to dictionaries and thesauri to elaborate expression and to organize the concepts and meanings of the electronic texts they create. Moreover, CMC follow up, face-to-face classroom activities, in which students reflect on the social and intercultural experiences they gained, help them accommodate new knowledge. These activities enhance the development of metacognitive strategies as they direct students towards locating the types of mistakes they made throughout the online interaction and set expectations for future online encounters and new learning goals. Eventually, CMC stimulates students to learn how to operate all their literacies, learning strategies and competences as well as to respect their interlocutors' gender, age and social status in real time communication.

Teacher's Roles

As it results from our research and as it is supported in the relevant literature, the teacher's role in blended learning should not be underestimated (Teeler & Gray 2000; Tsitouridou & Tsolakidis 2001; Tsolakidis & Tsitouridou 2001; Vlachos 2008; Warschauer & Whittaker 1997). The teacher needs to act as a facilitator, who guides the students in online learning, designs appropriate communicative activities and encourages them to look critically at the linguistic system of the target language, to make observations, to internalize new linguistic structures and vocabulary and eventually to build their linguistic and non linguistic knowledge.

Blended learning intensifies the need for skillful management on the part of the teacher. It poses new challenges: challenges to investigating her/his students' learning styles and to locating the technological applications that suit these styles; challenges to planning, to time management, to organizing interaction, to taking advantage of her/his students' technological expertise and initiatives, to encouraging them to experiment with new ideas and technologies and to drawing their attention to the linguistic aspects of the digital and non digital texts being processed. Finally, blended learning poses challenges to helping students gain metalinguistic awareness of genres and discourses, to assisting them in developing learning strategies, skills and literacies and to evaluating the activities and the learning outcomes.

LIMITATIONS OF THE CONDUCTED RESEARCH

Our research could have been further enhanced if there had been face-to-face groups in the Finnish and Spanish schools which participated in "The Euro e-pals" networking scheme. This prospect could have given us the opportunity to draw more sound conclusions since a larger number of students would have participated in the research, fact which in turn, would have enabled us to make more in-depth comparisons across nations, cultures and educational systems. Moreover, the research could have been strengthened if it had embraced participants from other continents beyond Europe. In this case we would have been able to examine how the two learning modes work in studying environments where students, teachers, curriculum designers and people in general have different philosophies, ideologies, frames of reference, priorities and educational goals.

CONCLUDING REMARKS AND RECOMMENDATIONS FOR FURTHER RESEARCH

In this chapter we compared face-to-face with blended learning and argued for blended learning in foreign language education and in EFL in particular. We drew evidence from our post doctoral research and we asserted that blended learning combined with cross cultural online networking enhances the development of linguistic, pragmatic, strategic, sociolinguistic and intercultural competences. We also put forward that blended learning supports the construction of foundational literacies and promotes the development of new literacies. Moreover, we maintained that blended learning and online collaboration boost students' cognitive, metacognitive and social strategies, help them develop critical thinking skills and metacognitive awareness and encourage them to share ICT literacies. In addition, we explored the role of the teacher in a blended learning environment and argued that she/he has the role of the guide, who organizes learning and encourages the exchange of ICT expertise.

Blended learning opens up new prospects in foreign language education. Still, a lot of research remains to be done. It would be interesting to investigate how effective blended learning can be in the acquisition of less commonly taught/learnt foreign languages. The research conditions in this case could be different if compared with our research. This is so because very few online sources use languages other than the major international and, therefore, online communication would be the main digital means of learning. We also believe that it is worthwhile exploring blended learning in the area of content and language integrated learning (CLIL). It would be important to know if blended learning can be effective in content learning in subjects like geography, maths, history, science, etc, when this knowledge is delivered and acquired through a foreign language. Extensive research of this type may prove that blended learning can be equally rewarding when the learning goals relate both to content and to language. Last but not least, as we have already discussed in the limitations section of this chapter, it would be interesting to compare blended with face-to-face learning across educational systems with different philosophies.

Overall, we believe that thanks to blended learning and the ICT development, students will have a more active role in the future. They will seek knowledge using all possible electronic and non electronic media. Learning will never be totally complete since both students and teachers will continue to process diverse online sources of information, to cooperate with students and teachers from other parts of the world, to develop their capacities in employing new technologies and to learn languages with a view to gaining new experiences.

ACKNOWLEDGMENT

The post doctoral research presented in this chapter was supervised by Professor Sofia Papaefthymiou-Lytra, who the writer would like to thank for her invaluable help and support. The research was conducted in the Department of English Language and Civilization of the School of Philosophy of the Kapodistrian University of Athens, Greece.

REFERENCES

Athanasiadis, E. (1995). *Correspondents and cluster analysis, applications, and examples*. Athens: New Technologies.

Ausburn, L. J. (2004). Course design elements most valued by adult learners in online education environments: An American perspective. *Educational Media International*, *41*(4), 327–337. doi:10.1080/09523980420003 14820

Beatty, K. (2003). *Teaching and researching CALL*. Harlow: Longman.

Beatty, K., & Nunan, D. (2004). Computer-mediated collaborative learning. *System*, *32*, 165–183. doi:10.1016/j.system.2003.11.006

Bonk, C., & Graham, C. (2005). *Handbook of blended learning: Global perspectives, local designs.* San Fransisco, CA: Pfeiffer Publishing.

Byram, M. (1994). *Teaching and learning language and culture*. Bridgend: WBC Ltd.

Byram, M. (2000). Intercultural communicative competence: The challenge for language teacher training. In A. Mountford & N. Wadham-Smith (Eds.), *British studies: Intercultural perspectives* (pp. 95-102). Essex: Longman.

Byram, M., & Fleming, M. (1998). *Language learning in intercultural perspective. Approaches through drama and ethnography*. Cambridge: Cambridge University Press.

Canale, M., & Swain, M. (1980). Theoretical bases of communicative approaches to second language teaching and testing. *Applied Linguistics*, *1*(1), 1–47. doi:10.1093/applin/1.1.1

Chamot, A. U., & O'Malley, J. M. (1996). The cognitive academic language learning approach (CALLA): A model for linguistically diverse classrooms. *The Elementary School Journal*, *96*(3), 259–273. doi:10.1086/461827

Chapelle, C. (2001). *Computer applications in second language acquisition: Foundations for teaching, testing, and research.* Cambridge: Cambridge University Press.

Cooper, M. M., & Selfe, C. L. (1990). Computer conferencing and learning: Authority, resistance, and internally persuasive discourse. *College English*, *52*(8), 847–869. doi:10.2307/377388

Cummins, J. (1996). *Negotiating identities: Education for empowerment in a diverse society*. Los Angeles: Association for Bilingual Education.

Dendrinos, B. (2001). *The politics of ELT*. Athens: The University of Athens Publications.

Dickinson, L. (1987). *Self-instruction in language learning*. Cambridge: Cambridge University Press.

Dornyei, Z. (2001). *Teaching and researching motivation*. Harlow: Longman.

Dornyei, Z. (2003). *Attitudes, orientation, and motivation in language learning: Advances in theory, research, and applications*. Oxford: Blackwell Publishing.

Dubin, F., & Olshtain, E. (1986). *Course design*. Cambridge: Cambridge University Press.

Ellis, G., & Sinclair, B. (1989). *Learning to learn English: A course in learner training*. Cambridge: Cambridge University Press.

Ellis, R. (2003). *Task-based language learning and teaching*. Oxford: Oxford University Press.

Fox, G. (1998). The Internet: Making it work in the ESL classroom. *The Internet TESL Journal,* 4/9. Retrieved on August 28, 2001, from http://www.aitech.ac.jp/~iteslj/Articles/Fox-Internet.html

Gardner, H. (1999). *Intelligence reframed: Multiple intelligences for the 21st century*. New York: Basic Books.

Hymes, D. (1967). Models of the interaction of language and social setting. In J. McNamara (Ed.), Problems of bilingualism. *Journal of Social Issues*, 23, 8-28.

Hymes, D. (1972). On communicative competence. In J. B. Pride & J. Holmes (Eds.), *Sociolinguistics*. Harmondsworth: Penguin Books.

Kamberi, K., & Vlachos, K. (2003). Teaching second/foreign languages using the task based approach and online networking. In the *Proceedings of the 1st International Conference ICT in Diaspora*, Greek Embassy in London, UK (pp. 17-31).

Kern, R. (2000). *Literacy and language teaching*. Oxford: Oxford University Press.

Kinzer, C. K. (2003). The importance of recognizing the expanding boundaries of literacy. *Reading online, 6*(10). Retrieved on November 17, 2008, from http://www.readingonline.org/electronic/elec_index.asp?HREF=/electronic/kinzer/index.html

Kinzer, C. K., & Leander, K. (2003). Technology and the language arts: Implications of an expanded definition of literacy. In J. Flood, D. Lapp, J. R. Squire & J. M. Jensen (Eds.), *Handbook of research on teaching the English language arts* (pp. 546-566). Mahwah, NJ: Erlbaum.

Lambropoulos, N., Christopoulou, M., & Vlachos, K. (2005). Cultural-based language learning objects in CALL. In P. Zaphiris & G. Zacharia (Eds.), *User–centred computer aided language learning* (pp. 22-43). Hershey, PA: Idea Publishing.

Lee, J. (2000). *Tasks and communicating in language classrooms*. Boston: McGraw-Hill.

Leu, D. J., Jr. (2000). Literacy and technology: Deictic consequences for literacy education in an information age. In M. L. Kamil, P. B. Mosenthal, P. D. Pearson & R. Barr (Eds.), *Handbook of reading research* (Vol. 3, pp. 743-770). Mahwah, NJ: Erlbaum.

Leu, D. J., Kinzer, C. K., Jr., Coiro, J., & Cammack, D. W. (2004). Toward a theory of new literacies emerging from the Internet and other information and communication technologies. In R. B. Ruddell & N. Unrau (Eds.), *Theoretical models and processes of reading* (pp. 1570-1613). Newark, DE: International Reading Association. Retrieved on November 17, 2008, from http://www.readingonline.org/newliteracies/lit_index.asp?HREF=leu/

Levy, M., & Stockwell, G. (2006). *CALL dimensions: Options and issues in computer-assisted language learning.* Mahwah, NJ: Lawrence Erlbaum Associates.

Moras, S. (2000). Computer assisted language learning (CALL) and the Internet. Retrieved from http://www3.telus.net/linguisticsissues/CALL.html. Last access: 28/8/2001

O'Malley, J. M., & Chamot, A. U. (1990). *Learning strategies in second language acquisition.* Cambridge: Cambridge University Press.

Oxford, R. (1990). *Language learning strategies: What every teacher should know*. New York: Newbury House.

Papaefthimiou-Lytra, S. (1987). *Language awareness and foreign language learning*. Athens: The University of Athens Press.

Papaefthimiou-Lytra, S. (1996). Integrating culture in the curriculum. In A. Tsopanoglou (Eds.), The sociolinguistic dimension in the teaching and learning of modern languages. *G.A.L.A.*, 7, 234-252. Thessaloniki: Greece.

Papaefthimiou-Lytra, S. (2004). Multipolar intercultural competence. In E. Joyce & A. Sougari (Eds.), *Challenges in teacher education* (pp. 15-25). Thessaloniki: Aristotle University, Department of English Language & Civilization.

Pennington, M. C. (2004). Electronic media in second language writing: An overview of tools and research findings. In S. Fotos & C. Browne (Eds.), *New perspectives on CALL for second language classrooms* (pp. 69-92). Mahwah, NJ: Lawrence Erlbaum Associates.

Peterson, M. (1997). Language teaching and networking. *System*, *25*(1), 29–37. doi:10.1016/S0346-251X(96)00058-9

Shetzer, H., & Warschauer, M. (2000). An electronic literacy approach to network-based language teaching. In M. Warschauer & R. Kern (Eds.) *Network-based language teaching: Concepts and practice* (pp. 171-185). Cambridge Applied Linguistics, Cambridge University Press.

Singh, H., & Reed, C. (2001). *A white paper: Achieving success with blended learning*. ASTD State of the Industry Report, American Society for Training & Development, Centra Software. Retrieved on November 17, 2008, from http://chriscollieassociates.com/BlendedLearning.pdf

Spires, H. A., & Estes, T. H. (2002). Reading in Web-based learning environments. In C.C. Block & M. Pressley (Eds.), *Comprehension instruction: Research-based best practices* (pp. 115-125). New York: Guilford.

Sutherland-Smith, W. (2002). Weaving the literacy Web: Changes in reading from page to screen. *The Reading Teacher*, *55*, 662–669.

Teeler, D., & Gray, P. (2000). *How to use the Internet in ELT.* Harlow: Longman.

Tsitouridou, M., & Tsolakidis, C. (2001). Teachers and ICTs. In the *Proceedings of the European Symposium on E-Learning and Continuing Education, Thematic Network in University Continuing Education, THENUCE Conference* (pp. 55-65), University of Ioannina.

Tsolakidis, C., & Tsitouridou, M. (2001). The need for primary teachers' training in information and communication technologies. In the *Proceedings of the European Symposium on E-Learning and Continuing Education, European Thematic Network in University Continuing Education, THENUCE Conference* (pp. 67–73), University of Ioannina.

Tyner, K. (1998). *Literacy in a digital world: Teaching and learning in the age of information*. Mahwah, NJ: Erlbaum.

Van Ek, J. A. (1977). *The threshold level for modern language teaching in schools*. London: Longman.

Vlachos, K. (2005). Online discourse communities and task based learning in foreign language education. *Annals of the University of Craiova*, *4*(9-10), 129–138.

Vlachos, K. (2006a). Online networking and the teaching of English as a foreign language to young learners: A methodological framework. In J. Bardos (Ed.), *HUSSE papers, Proceedings of the Seventh Biennial Conference* (Vol. B, pp. 618-625) Hungary: Veszprem.

Vlachos, K. (2006b). *The use of the Internet and asyncronous online networking for the learning and consolidation of English as a foreign language in European primary schools.* Unpublished doctoral dissertation, University of the Aegean, Rhodes, Greece.

Vlachos, K. (2007). The contribution of online collaboration in the development of learners' intercultural communicative competence and European understanding. In G. Kapsalis & A. Katsikis (Eds.), *Proceedings of the Conference 'Primary Education and the Challenges of Our Times'* (pp. 212-220). Ioannina: University of Ioannina.

Vlachos, K. (2008). Developing intercultural awareness through computer assisted language learning (CALL). In the *Proceedings of the International Conference of the University of Athens: Language in a Changing World.* University of Athens Publications.

Vlachos, K., & Athanasiadis, E. (2005). Online networking and the teaching of second/foreign languages to young learners through project work. *Themes in Education, 6*(1), 29–44.

Vlachos, K., & Athanasiadis, E. (in press). Foreign language development and consolidation through multipolar online networking. In the *Proceedings of the International Conference 42nd Linguistics Colloquium in Rhodes*, September 27-30, 2007. Rhodes: University of the Aegean.

Vlachos, K., & Papaefthymiou-Lytra, S. (2008). Collaboration through asynchronous online networking and the learning of foreign languages. In L. A. Tomei (Eds.), *Encyclopedia of information technology curriculum integration* (Vol. A, pp. 63-70). Hershey, PA: IGI Global.

Warschauer, M. (1996). Comparing face-to-face and electronic communication in the second language classroom. *CALICO Journal, 13*(2), 7–26.

Warschauer, M. (1998). Interaction, negotiation, and computer-mediated learning. *Papyrus News: Language Learning & Technology Journal.* Retrieved on July 18, 2006, from http://www.insa-lyon.fr/Departements/CDRL/interaction.html

Warschauer, M. (2001). Online communication. In R. Carter & D. Nunan (Eds.), *The Cambridge guide to teaching English to speakers of other languages* (pp. 207-212). Cambridge: Cambridge University Press.

Warschauer, M. (2005). Sociocultural perspectives on CALL. In J. L. Egbert & G. M. Petrie (Eds.), *CALL research perspectives* (pp. 41-51). New York: Lawrence Erlbaum Associates.

Warschauer, M., & Kern, R. (2000). *Network-based language teaching: Concepts and practice.* Cambridge Applied Linguistics, Cambridge University Press.

Warschauer, M., & Whittaker, P. F. (1997). The Internet for English teaching: Guidelines for teachers. *The Internet TESL Journal,* 3/10. Retrieved on July 18, 2006, from http://www.aitech.ac.jp/~iteslj/Articles/Warschauer-Internet.html

Wenden, A. (1991). *Learner strategies for learner autonomy.* Cambridge: Prentice Hall International.

Widdowson, H. (1972). The teaching of English as communication. *English Language Teaching, 27*(1), 15–19.

Widdowson, H. (1979). *Explorations in applied linguistics*. Oxford: Oxford University Press.

Widdowson, H. (1983). New starts and different kinds of failures. In A. Freeman, I. Pringle & J. Yalden (Eds.), *Learning to write: First language/second language*. London: Longman.

Williams, P. (2002). The learning Web: The development, implementation, and evaluation of Internet-based undergraduate materials for the teaching of key skills. *Active Learning in Higher Education*, *3*, 40–53. doi:10.1177/1469787402003001004

Willis, J. (1996). *A framework for task-based learning*. Harlow: Longman.

Willis, J. (2001). Making the best of technology: Lessons from the past. In P. Brett (Ed.), *CALL in the 21st century* [CD ROM]. Whitstable: IATEFL.

APPENDIX 1

Speaking & Writing Skills

Please use the following symbols:

Symbol Characterization

- \- I cannot do this yet
- ! I can sometimes do this
- !! I can do this easily

NOTE: Columns 1 and 3 were filled in by the student. Column 1 was filled before the beginning of the projects and column 3 when the projects were completed. Columns 2 and 4 were completed by the teacher. Column 2 was filled before the beginning of the projects and column 4 when the projects were completed.

Table 4. Questionnaire 1

	Spoken Interaction	**1**	**2**	**3**	**4**
1	I can introduce myself or a friend of mine				
2	I can use greeting and leave-taking expressions				
3	I can say simple things about myself, my free time, my likes and dislikes, my family, my home, my school but I need some help from my teacher				
4	I can say simple things about myself, my free time, my likes and dislikes, my family, my home, my school without my teacher's help				
5	I can ask other children simple questions about where they live, people they know, things they have, what they like				
6	I can understand other children when they answer to my questions if they speak clearly and slowly				
7	I can describe past events and use phrases like "last weekend", "last Christmas" with my teacher's help				
8	I can talk about things that will happen in the future and use phrases like " next week", "tonight", "this weekend" with my teacher's help				
9	I can describe past events and use phrases like "last weekend", "last Christmas" without my teacher's help				
10	I can talk about things that will happen in the future and use phrases like " next week", "tonight", "this weekend" without my teacher's help				
	Writing				
11	I can fill in a grid with information about myself (my name, address, telephone number, hobbies)				
12	I can write a greeting card, for example a birthday card				
13	I can write a simple postcard (for example with holiday greetings)				
14	I can write a simple message to ask a friend some questions				
15	I can write a simple message to answer to some questions				
16	I can write sentences and simple phrases about myself and my family				
17	I can write a simple text that describes my friend, my school, my town				

APPENDIX 2

Questionnaire 2: Project Evaluation

Please use the following symbols:

Symbol Characterization

- \- No
- ! I think yes, but I am not very sure
- !! Yes

Table 5. Questionnaire 2

	MOTIVATION	
1	Did you like using the computer and the Internet to communicate with children from another country?	
2	Did you like learning new things about Spain, Finland and the Spanish and Finnish people?	
3	Did this project help you to learn to cooperate well with the members of your group?	
4	Would you like to participate in similar projects in the future?	
	TECHNOLOGY	
5	Did this project make you improve your typing skills?	
6	Did this project make you learn to change fonts in your texts?	
7	Did this project make you learn to insert pictures and graphics in your texts?	
8	Did this project make you learn to save a file?	
9	Did you try to experiment with the computer to produce good looking texts?	
10	Did the project help you to learn to search the web to find and select information and artwork?	
11	Did you learn to employ platforms of communication to upload texts in the internet and to download texts and media from the Internet?	
12	Did you learn to make use of hyperlinks to access hypermedia?	
13	Do you intend in the future to consult online dictionaries and thesauri to refine the texts you produce?	
14	Do you intend in the future to use the email and the English language to communicate with other people?	
	CULTURE	
15	Did you learn new things about the life and the people in Finland and Spain? For example did you learn how the Finnish and the Spanish celebrate Christmas or what they do to protect the environment?	
16	Did you ever try to find more information about Spain and Finland from the Internet or a book?	
17	Will you use the Internet or a book to learn more things about Finland and Spain or another European country in the future?	
18	Did this project make you learn more things about the life and the people in your country?	
	LANGUAGE	
19	Can you write a short letter describing your Christmas customs?	
20	Can you write a short article describing the environmental problems you have in your school and in your town?	
21	Can you write a short report describing how people in another country celebrate Easter?	
22	Can you narrate a story in the past?	
23	Did you try to speak in English with your fellow students and your teacher when you worked on the project?	
24	Do you think that the project stimulated you to speak in English?	
25	Did you learn new vocabulary from the texts you received from the Finnish and the Spanish learners?	
26	Did this project help you remember and use words you already knew in English?	
27	Did this project help you learn to find and correct the mistakes in your texts without your teacher's interference?	

Section 3
Cultural Differences Studies

Chapter 14
When Cultures Meet in Blended Learning:
What Literature Tells Us

Chun Hu
University of Sydney, Australia

ABSTRACT

This chapter presents a literature review of the blended learning projects that involved learners from different cultures. The studies reviewed essentially addressed two issues: the feasibility of cross-cultural blended learning and leaner differences in such a learning environment. While the studies overwhelmingly reported the benefits of using the Internet to create opportunities for students to learn with peers from other cultures, they also highlighted issues of cultural impact on learner behaviors. Learner differences reported included approaches to asking questions, collaborating with others and preferences in the way they made use of technologies. Patterns emerged from the review, implying some design considerations for planning cross-cultural blended learning. It seems that successful cross-cultural blended learning programs need committed teaching teams who make decisions on curriculum choices, learning tasks and assessments, and which technology tools to use; and who skillfully handle issues of language barriers, project management, and preparation of learners.

INTRODUCTION

Blended learning, also referred to as flexible learning and hybrid learning, is becoming a norm on our campuses. Growing numbers of teachers use information and communication technologies (ICT) to complement conventional face-to-face lectures/ seminars. Although some ICT tools such as multimedia resources have long been used in teaching/ learning, only in the last decade has the Internet been increasingly integrated into teaching and learning process. Teachers use learning management system (e.g. Blackboard, WebCT) to manage course documents, to distribute course materials, and to conduct synchronous chats and asynchronous discussions. Students use discussion forums to share ideas and to collaborate in projects; and they use chat and email to communicate with peers and instructors.

DOI: 10.4018/978-1-60566-852-9.ch014

More and more teachers and academics initiate collaborations with their counterparts in other schools/universities at home and abroad in order to provide additional learning opportunities for their students.

Blended learning is more than a combination of two media: instructor-led and technology-led activities. The notion "the medium is the message" (McLuhan, 1964) appears inappropriate to describe technology use in education, as we all know from our own experiences that medium of instruction itself does not necessarily affect student learning. Take face-to-face instruction - our most familiar instructional mode - for example. Not all teachers are created equal in terms of their abilities of brining effective learning experiences to students. Successful teachers are more likely to be those who skillfully select and structure their teaching methods that motivate learners and relate learning experiences to learners' knowledge-levels, interests and needs (Yoon & Lim, 2007). Effective blended learning depends more on teachers' instructional design and methods than their technical skills. "Methods are necessary and unique, but media are not" (Cobb, 1997, p. 24).

Through a literature review, this chapter intends to provide academics, teachers, researchers and professionals who are interested in involving teachers and students from different cultures in their blended learning activities with an introduction to the research development in the area. Specifically, the chapter will present a summary of relevant research studies; their underpinning theoretical frameworks, methodologies used, and examples of the projects involving learners and teachers from culturally diverse backgrounds across geographic and time zones. Attempts are made to draw inferences from the literature reviewed on design considerations for planning cross-cultural blended learning activities. The chapter is divided into four sections: (1) background - rationale, sources of the studies to be reviewed; (2) summary of the studies reviewed - theoretical frameworks, examples of cross-cultural blended learning projects, methodologies used and design considerations inferred; (3) future trends; and (4) conclusion.

BACKGROUND

For the purpose of the discussion, a definition by Osguthorpe and Graham (2003) on blended learning is adopted. The purpose of "blended learning approach is to find a harmonious balance between online access to knowledge and face-to-face human interaction" (p. 228). Blends of blended learning may involve the mixing of online and face-to-face learning activities, student or instructors with a number of goals including pedagogical richness, access to knowledge, and social interaction (p. 231). Blended learning share a similar component with distance learning, i.e. information and communication technology. Distance learning, according to the U.S. Department of Educational Research and Improvement, is "the application of telecommunications and electronic devices which enable students and learners to receive instruction from some distant location" (Bruder, 1989, p. 30). However, blended learning is not the same as distance learning and does not have a vital element of Keegan's (1988) definition of distance learning, i.e. "the quasi-permanent separation between teacher and student throughout the length of the learning process" (p. 10).

When Cultures Meet in the Internet

The rapid penetration of the Internet ushered in an era where educational activities can be conducted on a global stage involving teachers and learners from different cultures and nations. Education has become global in terms of its diverse student population due to the flexible delivery system of online learning (Jarvis, 1999; Mason, 1998). With increasing interactions among teachers and teachers, teachers and students, students and students from different cultural backgrounds, understanding and tolerance of cultural differences are needed to reach successful learning outcomes (Pinhey, 1998).

Using the Internet to connect geographically distributed and culturally diverse learners is not new. As early as the 1980s, Levin and his colleagues (Levin, Riel, Miyake & Cohen, 1987) created an Inter-Cultural Network connecting participants from universities, secondary schools and even upper primary school levels in the US, Mexico, Japan and Israel. Through this network, participants engaged in solving a common problem, for instance the shortage of water, from the perspectives of their own community. They sent and received email, reading and analyzing messages from other participants, and learned to transfer solutions used elsewhere to their own community.

Compared with the 1980s' technologies, we now have much faster Internet speed and more sophisticated ICT tools. More importantly, the Internet has become an inseparable part of our modern life, and technical skills, which once upon the time a major hurdle, are not problems for many teachers and students. As growing numbers of teachers and students use blended learning to teach or learn with others from cultures different from theirs, there is a concern of how learning activities may be designed and carried out to benefit learners from different cultural backgrounds. While there is an emerging body of literature on using blended learning involving culturally diverse learners, the area of research is still in its infancy and research evidence is scarce.

In comparison, there is a longer history and more research evidence on designing web sites (not necessarily educational web sites) for users from other cultures. Culture is "the collective programming of the mind which distinguishes the member of one group or category of people from another" (Hofstede, 1997, p. 260). Historically, studies on cross-cultural web design use communication transmission model, focusing on the links between culture and web usability (the ease with which users use the Internet to search information and communicate with others). Culture is examined by using cultural factors and cultural markers. Cultural factors include power distance, uncertainty avoidance, masculinity vs. femininity, individualism vs. collectivism, time orientation (Hofstede, 1997); and low and high context cultures (Hall & Hall, 1989). For instance, it is believed that in low context cultures (i.e. Western cultures), people express their intentions and positions directly, while in high context cultures such as Asian cultures, people tend to deemphasize direct expression in their messages, hide implicit meanings behind words, and use ambiguous language or even silence to maintain harmony with other people (Hall & Hall, 1989). Cultural markers refer to the preferences of different cultures to signs or symbols.

Cross-cultural web design research with an emphasis on the links between culture and web usability is rationalized by the notion that culturally constructed and shared domains of knowledge serve to structure and constrain people's experiences thus forming cultural models (Li, 2002). As receivers and processors of information mediated by the Internet, web users' ways of using the Internet are presumably influenced by a complex blend of cultural contexts within which users live. In other words, people from different cultures are inclined to behave differently on and off-line. A study of over 250 Hong Kong and US web users showed that users in Hong Kong tended to use the Internet for social communication more than those in the US (Chau, Cole, Massey, Montoya-Weiss & O'Keefe, 2002). It is imperative that web designers be aware of the differences between themselves and the cultural groups for whom they are designing and understand the impact of cultural issues (del Galdo, 1996); and web sites designed for people of other cultures must match users' cultural characteristics and accommodate the way people communicate in those cultures (Nielsen, 1993). For example, use of visual or written metaphor, language cues, and navigation controls can create a look and feel matching the cultural expectations of the users for that particular culture (Smith, Dunckley, French, Minocha & Chang, 2004). "A misuse of other symbols, colors, and metaphors can unintentionally offend or alienate learners" (Rogers, Graham & Mayes, 2007, p. 205).

It is worth mentioning that cultural model plays an important role in the research of learning styles. The rationale is that individuals within a culture, when compared with members of another culture, tend to have a common pattern of learning (Oxford & Anderson, 1995). For instance, using Hofstead's theory, Salili (2001) found that in a large power distance culture, such as China, teachers usually keep reasonable distance from students to get the class in full control; informal in-class communication and using first names are regarded as inappropriate (Myers, Zhong & Guan, 1998). However, generalizations such as these are refuted by other researchers. In a study investigating teacher-student email communication, Zhang (2006) contended, "little in-class interaction does not indicate little out-of-class interaction, since the pastoral role of Chinese teachers requires an on-going, extra-curricular involvement with students" (p. 37).

The questions here are: what is blended learning like when it involves teachers and learners from culturally diverse backgrounds; do learners from different cultures behave differently in a blended learning environment; what are the challenges for teachers to carry out cross-cultural blended learning activities; what are the challenges for students to participate in cross-cultural blended learning activities; what are the theories currently used to study cross-cultural blended learning; and what are the design issues related to cross-cultural blended learning?

Objectives of the Chapter and Sources of the Review

The objectives of this chapter are to find answers to the questions raised above by means of a literature review of published peer-reviewed journal articles. Knowledge of where the filed stands would help those who are interested in adding a cross-cultural component to their blended learning experience. The sources of the review were identified from three electronic databases: ProQuest 5000, ScienceDirect and PsychInfo. Online searches were performed during the period of 15 to 31 August 2008. A combination of search words of blended learning and each of the following was used: national culture, cultural factor, cultural variable, cross-cultural, cultural difference, intercultural, and multicultural. The searches did not restrict the years of publications. Disappointingly, the searches yielded only seven journal articles.

Consequently, further online searches were conducted by using the combinations of each of these keywords - flexible learning, elearning, online learning, web design, interface design, web usability, graphic symbols, email, online discussion, discussion forum and CSCL – and each of the keywords - national culture, cultural factor, cultural variable, cross-cultural, cultural difference, intercultural, and multicultural. The searches did not set limit on the years of publications. The searches yielded 151 journal articles. Criteria were set to focus the literature review on using blended learning in formal educational contexts where learners are from at least two different cultures or ethnic groups. Using the set criteria, articles were excluded from the review if they reported (1) a course/program that was entirely online (i.e. there were no face-to-face interactions); (2) a study whose learners were from the same culture; (3) a program that was not part of formal curriculum (e.g. controlled lab experiment, extra-curriculum activity); (4) a program that was part of international collaboration yet learners from different countries did not have any direct interactions;

Table 1. The articles reviewed in the chapter

Author(s)	Year	Cultures Involved	Curriculum Area/Topic	Technologies Used
(1)				
Van Ryssen & Godar	2000	Belgium, US	International marketing	Project website, email
Winner & Shields	2002	Bahamas, US	English – Introductory writing	Web postings, electronic bulletin board, email
Buchanan, Wilson & Gopal	2008	South Africa, UK, & US	Racism (Criminal Justice)	Project website, online readings, asynchronous discussion forums
Evans, Suzuki, Begg & Lam	2008	Japan & UK	Clinical genetics	Project website, discussion forum
(2)				
Freedman & Liu	1996	Asian Americans – Hmong, Cambodia, Vietnam, Lao	Art, Social Studies, Creative Writing	Word-processing software, HyperStudio, email
Liang & McQueen	1999	China, Fiji, Hong Kong, Korea, New Zealand, the Philippines, South Africa, Taiwan, US	Adult continuing education	Email
Cifuentes & Murphy	2000	Americans - Caucasians & Hispanics	English	Email, videoconferencing
Shih & Cifuentes	2003	Taiwan & US	English as a Foreign Language	Discussion forums, email
Kim & Bonk	2006	Finland, Korea, & US	Educational Psychology	Discussion forums
Vinagre	2008	Spain & UK	English, Spanish	Email
Yudko, Hirokawa & Chi	2008	Caucasian, Asian, Pacific Islander, African American, Latino, & Native American	Communication	Online readings; video-recorded lectures

and (5) a position paper where personal views were expressed without any supporting data or evidence. After the elimination, 11 journal articles were selected for the review.

Broadly defined, the selected studies served two purposes: (1) to provide evidence that the Internet could create an opportunity for students to learn with learners from other cultures; and (2) to provide evidence or rebut the notion that learners from different cultures have different learning styles and preferences when engaging in cross-cultural learning activities. Table 1 lists the studies to be reviewed in these two categories.

The review here is by no means a comprehensive coverage of the development in the filed of cross-cultural blended learning. The author is fully aware that this literature review did not cover all the published peer-referred journal articles on the topic due to a number of reasons. First, all the articles identified were from the electronic versions of printed journals. Automatically excluded from the search results were the articles that appeared in a journal that does not have electronic version. Secondly, the three electronic databases used may not be comprehensive enough to include all the peer-referred journals. Furthermore, there are many books, book chapters, conference papers and unpublished doctoral dissertations that are devoted to the area of cross-cultural blended learning. Therefore, what is being discussed here may represent only a small portion of the knowledge that is intended to be discovered. Nonetheless, readers could use this chapter as a prelude to a fascinating yet under-explored area of cross-cultural blended learning.

WHEN CULTURES MEET IN BLENDED LEARNING

This section is divided into four parts: (1) rationales and underpinning theoretical frameworks of the studies reviewed, (2) summaries of the studies, (3) methodologies used in the studies, and (4) design considerations inferred from the studies reviewed.

Underpinning Theoretical Frameworks

The studies reviewed took different approaches to investigating the phenomenon of blended learning activities involving learners from different cultures. Generally, two underpinning theoretical perspectives were employed in the studies: (1) cultural factors, and (2) socio- cultural theory. When none of these theoretical frameworks was specified, the studies seemed to intend to fill a gap in the research literature, e.g. "there is very little evidence in the literature about online learning shared between students … in different countries" (Evans, Suzuki, Begg & Lam, 2008, p. 27).

From the Perspective of Cultural Factors

Researchers holding such a perspective view learners, whose culture may sit at the extreme ends of the continuum of Hofstede's (1986) national culture model, behave differently in a blended learning environment because cultural distinctions are manifested in educational contexts, and learners from different cultural backgrounds learn differently. Researchers attempted and, in some cases, succeeded in providing evidence to support this notion.

While acknowledging computer networked environment could lead to a form of education in which "students could develop a better understanding of similarities and differences between themselves and people with them they could otherwise have little contact" (Freedman & Liu, 1996, p. 44), the researchers argued that students with different ethnic backgrounds had different attitudes about the experience with technology, and attention to this aspect of learners would help contextualize technology use in learning. In the same fashion, Liang and McQueen (1999) contended, "technology may or may not suit the learners' characteristics and their prior learning style" (p. 26). In studying adult learners' behaviors in an email-mediated learning experience, they concluded, "e-mail interactive learning was more effective for peer-oriented learners, such as most of the Western students in this case" (P. 26).

Other researchers question the legitimacy of indiscriminately applying theories originated from the West to designing learning in non-Western cultural contexts. Shih and Cifuentes (2003) explored cultural issues related to online intercultural learning and communication by Taiwanese and US students. They argued, using "recommended methods based on Western experience does not necessarily meet the needs of Asian learners. Close examination of learning facilitated by the new telecommunication technologies should be carried out prior to fully adopting these new technologies as learning tools" (p. 83).

Kim & Bonk (2006) investigated online collaborative behaviors among pre-service teachers from Finland, Korea and the US, "to ferret out how their collaborative behaviors are different across cultures and its implications for designing and facilitating online collaboration among culturally diverse learners" (p. 2). The researchers pointed out that learning through multicultural collaboration was not an easy task. Their research found that learners from three cultural groups being investigated were different in the levels of cross-cultural participation and exhibited distinctive online collaborative behaviors. "Therefore, a growing body of knowledge of cultural issues in computer-supported collaborative learning is needed to inform us of how to foster online collaboration among multicultural learners" (p. 2).

From the Perspective of Socio-Cultural Theory

All the studies reviewed used computer-medicated communication (CMC) and computer supported collaborative learning (CSCL) to connect learners from different locations. Some authors explicitly owed their studies to socio-cultural theory, asserting that learning occurs in cultural contexts and all knowledge is socially mediated (Vygotsky, 1978 cited in Kim & Bonk, 2006), and social interaction and discourse help student's cognitive development. For instance, Winner and Shields (2002) integrated cross-cultural peer review into an English writing class based on Vygotsyian theory: "writing is more than a product, ... a process; writing is a relation, a social relation that is first shared between two ore more people in community and it subsequently internalized, individualized, and made concrete by the individual" (p. 275).

Teachers holding the perspective of socio-cultural theory took advantage of ICT's affordances in supporting interactive, distributed and collaborative learning; and used it to create "opportunities for students to share their experiences with people of other cultures and to learn from perspectives and experiences of others" (Cifuentes & Murphy, 2000, p. 71). Through sharing information and negotiating meanings of such information with others, participants in these studies actively constructed knowledge to develop new understanding. In addition to enhancing cognitive development, social interaction and discourse via CMC and CSCL are viewed as avenues to provide practical experiences for university students, many of whom after graduation will work at jobs requiring them to interact with people from other countries. Researchers advocated that faculty "... make available to students, within the normal curriculum, the experience of working in global alliance" (Van Ryssen & Godar, 2000, p. 50). Cross-cultural blended learning exposes "students to multi-identity discussions across differences in ways they otherwise would not be exposed to in their respective university settings" (Buchanan, Wilson & Gopal, 2008, p. 681); and helps them "to transform into more tolerant and respectful citizens when they include opportunities to develop relationships with people from diverse cultures and backgrounds" (Cifuentes & Murphy, 2000, p. 71). For teachers, cross-cultural blended learning activities raise "interesting challenges and exciting opportunities in respect of academic collaboration and the development of learning and teaching strategies" (Buchanan et al., 2008, p. 671).

It should be pointed out that although socio-cultural theory was reckoned as a theoretical framework in some studies, not all the important concepts of the theory were sufficiently addressed in these studies. For instance, the concept of Vygotsky's Zone of Proximal Development was not elaborated in the studies reviewed. Evidently, there are a number of areas that future studies should look into, for example - how teachers help students and how students from different cultures help one another to create new knowledge; and how the process of using technological tools and information help to develop new understanding.

Examples of Cross-Cultural Blended Learning Projects

In this section, the main points of each of the 11 journal articles will be summarized. In general, all the studies reported positive impact on learners. Learner differences were found in their approaches to asking questions, collaborating with others, and preferences to ways of using technologies. However, the studies also reported similarities among learners from different cultural backgrounds.

Enhanced Cultural Understandings

Cross-cultural blended learning "lend itself to exposing students to multi-identity discussions across differences in ways they otherwise would not be exposed to in their respective university settings" (Buchanan et al., 2008, p. 681). The studies reviewed overwhelmingly reported the benefits of cross-cultural blended learning. It is not clear whether it could be the result of so-called publication bias which suggests that negative results be less likely to be published (Reginald, 1964; Rothstein, Sutton & Borenstein, 2005). Most cross-cultural blended learning projects took place in higher education settings. Only two studies reported projects at secondary school level. Regardless the levels of institutional settings, cross-cultural blended learning appeared to have enhanced participants' cultural understandings.

In a study by Cifuentes & Murphy (2000), 15 8th graders in a school on the Texas side of the border with Mexico used email and videoconferences to work on a Cultural Connection project with students in a partner school near Huston. The Cultural Connection project was jointly created by two teachers over four months of online communication, and was intended to promote collaboration and multicultural understanding among students across geographic locations. Of the 15 8th graders, 14 were identified as at-risk, 13 were Hispanic and two Caucasians. Ten participants from the partner school were gifted-and-talented 5th graders (seven were Caucasians). Throughout a school year, the students from both schools engaged in nine extended activities in their English classes. They wrote about their home lives, their goals, thoughts and stories and created multimedia presentations using HyperStudio. They shared their multimedia presentations, discussed readings and debated issues via videoconferences.

Cifuentes & Murphy's (2000) article focused on the students at the border school. The researchers reported encouraging results based on the data collected from multimedia portfolios, written reflections of teachers and students, and interviews with the students. The yearlong project reportedly helped improve the students' understandings of their counterparts whose cultures and social circumstances were different from theirs. For instance, at the beginning of the year, the students at the border school thought their counterparts were "wealthy and trouble free" (p. 75). By the end of the year, the students reported their common interests with their partners and respect for differences. Among other positive outcomes reported was the students' aspiration for academic achievement. When the program first started, no students "introduced themselves with images of college or careers. By the end of the year, however, 11 of 15 students indicated that they intended to go to college and all expressed interest in successful careers" (p. 76). The "students matured and acquired cultural sensitivity" and also showed "increased poise, communication and leadership skills, and comfort and proficiency with technology indicated their growth in self-concept. ... the finding is consistent with research indicating that stereotypes can be broken down through telecommunication partnership" (Cifuentes & Murphy, 2000, p. 80).

Similar positive outcomes were reported by Winner and Shields (2002). In their study, Winner and Shields (2002) described a writing project participated in by the students from the Bahamas and the US. The project was centered around a literacy autobiography, one of the four pieces of the writings that the Bahamas students were doing in a 15-week semester. The US students also had an assignment on literacy autobiography. The literacy autobiographies by the students from both universities were uploaded onto a web site for the students to read and respond via email in and outside the class. In addition, an electronic bulletin board was set up for the students to use informally to get to know one another and exchange ideas. Again, this article focused on one group of participants, in this case the students from the Bahamas. The project was reportedly well received by the Bahamas students. As observed by the researchers, once starting to share their stories via email, "the Bahamian students and the U.S. students were able to collaborate, ... to create a community of writers free from many of the power struggles prevalent in face-to-face communities" (Winner

& Shields, 2002, p. 279). "This online writing collaborative helped the students embrace this principle of community knowing and of fostering some sense of connectedness among the students" (Winner & Shields, 2002, p. 280).

Another study (Buchanan et al., 2008) involved students from three universities of South Africa, the UK and the US. In a period of four weeks, a total of 51 students (31 from the UK, 7 from South Africa and 3 from the US) engaged in an online forum "International Online Race Conference". The forum was part of Social Difference and Inequality module of a BA (Hons) Criminal Justice course in the UK university. The South African students participated in the online forum as part of their Victim Studies module of Honors Degree in Criminology, and the US students took part in the forum as part of their Social Work for Social Justice Program. The students read three assigned papers and participated in an asynchronous discussion forum accompanying each reading. They submitted an online 1,000-word reflective account with a portfolio demonstrating their learning in relevance to the three forums. The participants not only had different nationalities, but also were culturally diverse - all but one of the UK students were white, six of the seven South African students were either black or Indian, and the three US students were Caucasian, multi-racial (Native American and Caucasian) and Hispanic respectively. The researchers concluded from a survey that most students felt positive about studying the issue of racism with students from other countries. The positive impacts summarized by the researchers included: international dimension and richness of the discussion with students from different socio-political-cultural contexts, and the flexibility that allowed the students to study at their own time.

Still another study (Van Ryssen & Godar, 2000) described a collaborative international marketing project between one Belgium and two US universities. To commence the project, the students communicated via email and formed partnerships with students from another country (Belgium or the US) to prepare a marketing report. In groups of four, 33 groups of students chose a product for their marketing reports. The students from each country made an analysis of their respective "home markets" and then combined those analyses into the final report which included a comparison of the Belgium and US markets, stressing the similarities and strategies on how the needs of each target market were to be met by the parts of the marketing mix such as product, price, promotion and place. The report counted for 20% and 35% of the students' course grades in the respective universities. Van Ryssen and Godar (2000) reported that through the collaboration the students learned a wide range of skills: the Internet related tools, collaborative intercultural work, marketing techniques and marketing theory. The students showed improvement in communication skills, idiomatic language, understandings of differences in cultural values, and knowledge of each other's cultural backgrounds.

Learner Differences

A number of studies reviewed focused on behavioral differences among learners from different cultures in blended learning activities. Five studies reported how learners from Asian heritages differed from non-Asian learners (Freedman & Liu, 1996; Liang & McQueen, 1999; Shih & Cifuentes, 2003; Evans, Suzuki, Begg & Lam, 2008; Kim & Bonk, 2006). The study by Freedman and Liu (1996) investigated the learning behaviors of a group of Asian American high school students in a technology integrated interdisciplinary curriculum. In a 10-week curriculum, the students from three classes (Art, Social Studies and Creative Writing) investigated their cultural backgrounds and taught other students about that background in class and over the Internet. The students formed email pen pals with students from two schools in other states, one predominately white school and another on a Native American reservation. The topics of email included family, school, community and social issues, and the students also discussed specific aspects of their culture. The three curriculum subjects were well integrated. For instance, the students would write on a topic in Creative Writing class using word processing, then, they would draw pictures using computer software in Art class. They sent their work to the students in other states via email, discussing and replying to email responses form their counterparts.

Freedman and Liu's (1996) data collection focused on 21 Asian American 8th graders involved in this curriculum. Eighteen of these students were Hmong, and the rest were Cambodian, Vietnamese and Laotian. Freedman and Liu (1996) used "Asian American students" to refer to the 21 participants, distinguishing those of Hmong heritage from the rest in some instances. The study reported various differences between the Asian and non-Asian students. While the Asian American students indicated in the questionnaire and interviews that they had no difficulties in using computers, the observations showed that they "tended to work on a technical, rather than creative level. They only mechanically manipulated the software they used in the class" (p. 51). Compared with their non-Asian peers, the Asian American students preferred using email to other computer uses, and they used the computer differently. For instance, they would sit silently in front of the computer and would not start to work until they were asked to. Whereas other students would start working right away or even before they were asked to. The researchers interpreted this behavior as Asian American students being not used to experiential learning. Although the Asian American students tended to stay together as a group both in and outside of school, they were interested in their email correspondents' lives, and were positive towards communicating with them online. The girls seemed particularly more positive about cross-cultural relations than their non-Asian peers. Interestingly, the students discussed in email the issues that they would not talk about with their non-Asian classmates in person.

Somewhat similar behavior patterns of Asian learners were reported by Liang and McQueen (1999). In this study, the researchers investigated perceptions held by adult Asian and Western learners in respect to the role of teacher, and their consequent behavior patterns in email-mediated interactive learning activities. The participants in this study were 18 Asian and Western adult learners (aged 24-55) enrolled in a 12-week credit course. The course had regular face-to-face interactions, group work and email interactions. The learners were originally from China, Fiji, Hong Kong, Korea, New Zealand, the Philippines, South Africa, Taiwan and the US. Through a questionnaire and interviews, the researchers found that the learners from Asian and Western cultures differed in their expectations about the role of the teacher and their learning styles. Most Asian learners were tutor-oriented while most Western learners were peer-oriented. The researchers suspected that the Asian learners' orientation was a result of the educational system in their home countries. The Asian learners expected the tutor to offer information. In contrast, most Western learners believed that more interaction among students should be encouraged. The Western learners were active when provided with opportunities to communicate with fellow students via email, and they felt that "they received more information from the co-learners than from their instructors via email interactive learning style" (Liang & McQueen, 1999, p. 27) which led the researchers to conclude, "e-mail interactive learning was more effective for peer-oriented learners, such as most of the Western students in this case, than for the tutor-oriented learners" (P. 26).

In a more recent study, Shih and Cifuentes (2003) reported 40 Taiwanese college English students' experience in online learning interactions with US pre-service teachers who were trained to teach English as a foreign language and Social Studies. In a period of 10 weeks, the US students acted as tutors and corresponded with the Taiwanese students via email as part of their course requirements. All the Taiwanese and US participants contributed to an online forum set up exclusively for them. In addition, there were two forums where both Taiwanese and US participants were encouraged to submit cultural and technical questions according to their interests and needs, yet only one Taiwanese and two US participants initiated discussions over the 10 weeks. Shih and Cifuentes' (2003) analysis was based on the data collected on the Taiwanese students via interviews and questionnaires as well as web logs. The researchers found that the Taiwanese students "were reluctant to express their ideas on the board because they felt uncomfortable having their ideas appear in this public space" and "they did not want to lose face or express what they considered valueless opinions in front of their fellow students" (p. 86). Rather, they preferred one-on-one interaction via email, although email communication experienced some hiccups largely due to language and cultural differences. For instance, the Taiwanese students were uncomfortable about the seemingly expressive styles used by their US tutors and felt offended by their direct critiques. They "claimed that they felt that they should apologize or express their gratitude because they senses impatience in the tutors' messages that so bluntly stated a point of view", and "several misinterpretations of meaning of behavior took place because the students were not used to those behaviors, and analyzed them from the Taiwanese perspective" (p. 87). Had the Taiwanese students tried to clarify these situations, misunderstanding could have been resolved. Unfortunately, "the Taiwanese reserved and nonconfrontational manner impeded such clarification" (p.87).

The fourth study that compared Asian and non-Asian learners reported how medical students from two universities in Japan and the UK used a purposely-built website to learn clinical genetics (Evans et al., 2008). In this two-week project, the UK students were paired with Japanese students to form a group of 16 students. Because there were more UK students, the UK students who did not have Japanese partners served as control groups. After being presented with a scenario of a family with a history of phenylketonuria, the students read the case online, engaged in online discussions, and wrote a letter supposedly from a consultant to the family practitioner. The working language of the project was English and the Japanese students were provided with language support. In addition to online interactions, the students on both campuses organized their own face-to-face discussions with peers and instructors. The researchers evaluated the project by using the results of the students' writings, a questionnaire and analysis of online postings. A paired t-test showed no significant differences in the results of the writings by the students from the two universities. The questionnaire showed that the website was more favored by the Japanese students; but the UK students found the case and task more interesting than the Japanese students. The UK students also favored the information and comments given by the tutors more than their Japanese counterparts.

Finally, a study by Kim and Bonk (2006) investigated online collaborative behaviors of students from Finland, Korea and the US. The participating students in this study were enrolled in an undergraduate educational psychology course in their respective universities. Prior to the study, all the students had a school experience. In a period of 10 weeks, the students had their regular face-to-face classes and web-based activities. In the web-based activities, they posted their own cases, either individually or in a group, in relevance to their school experience and initiated case discussion. The students were required to summarize the discussions on the cases that they had initiated. Through the analyses of the web postings, the researchers found a number of differences among the students from three cultures. The Korean students postings demonstrated higher percentage (24%) of "seeking input" than both Finnish students (12.7%) and US students (21%), indicating high social activities. A higher level of reflection was observed among the Finnish students. For instance, all the students were required to write summaries of their discussions at the end of each case discussion. While the Finnish students posted thoughtful summaries of their case discussions and reflected on the various perspectives and comments posted to their case situation, the Korean and US students seldom summarized the discussions or put postings related to their cases. Further, different behaviors were observed in feedback seeking and giving. The US students' feedback seeking and giving tended to be action-oriented, and the Finnish students tended to seek feedback or opinions that are more theory-driven. In terms of social action behaviors, the discourses of the Finnish and US students showed that they were very much task-focused; while the Korean students tended to be more social online and shared personal feelings or concerns related to participating in the discussion forums.

Vinagre's (2008) study was one of the two articles reviewed that compared learners from two Western countries. The study compared the politeness strategies used by students in collaborative email exchanges by analyzing 22-email messages exchanged between Spanish students who studied advanced English and UK students who studied beginners or intermediate Spanish. The Spanish students initiated the email exchange by introducing themselves with information such as where they lived, what they were studying. The messages were written half in English and half in Spanish. Responses by the UK students used the same language strategy. The analysis of email messages revealed that the Spanish students used a total of 218 politeness strategies verses 165 politeness strategies used by the UK students. Interestingly, instead of attributing the differences to cultures as in the studies summarized above, the researcher suspected that the higher use by the Spanish students was due to their competence in the target language (advanced vs. beginner, and intermediate) as the UK students' use of politeness strategies increased by 11.51% when they wrote in English as opposed to Spanish. Similarly to Vinagre (2008), Van Ryssen and Godar (2000), whose Belgium-US collaborative project was summarized in the earlier section of this chapter, did not relate the observed differences between the Belgium and US students to national culture. Instead, hiccups in the communication were attributed to the students' lack of cultural knowledge of language because "Belgium society is multilingual ... The use of English came natural to the Belgium participants" (p. 55).

Variations Outside the "Norm"

We must rectify the impression that learners from certain cultures are deemed to behave in set patterns, such as "Asian students are rote learners and surface learners who use memorizing as a learning strategy" (Samuelowicz, 1987; Ballard, 1991, cited in Samarawickrema, 2005, p. 51); and members of the same culture are to behave similarly in blended learning activities. Even from the limited studies reviewed, it is evident that there are variations within cultural groups. Liang and McQueen (1999) found in their study that older native English speaking learners appeared to be more interested in the cultures of different ethnic groups, and especially those with low ICT skills preferred interactions with the whole class. In contrast, younger native English speaking learners preferred to work with those who were similar to themselves, and were less willing than the older native English speaking students to spend time trying to communicate with non-native English speaking students. Furthermore, Liang and McQueen (1999) found similarities in older learners (the researchers did not define the age range). Regardless of the cultural backgrounds, this group of learners felt intimidated speaking in class. Email-mediated interactive learning enabled this group of students "to express their thoughts more fully and honestly" (p. 28).

In the study by Kim and Bonk (2006), Korean students whose culture is classified as a collective one, which encourages the development of group identities and cooperation, did not exhibit more collaborative behaviors than those from individualistic cultures. In this study, the students were given the choice of writing their cases individually or in groups. While the Finnish students wrote their cases in pairs or groups, the Korean students wrote theirs individually, so did the US students whose culture is considered an individualist one that gives priority to one's own goals and to defining one's identity in terms of personal attributes.

Finally, a study by Yudko, Hirokawa and Chi (2008) investigated rural students' attitudes toward the online aspect of blended learning. The participants of the study were university students taking a Communication course in a rural area in Hawaii. The participants were between 18 and 25, and were from culturally diverse backgrounds (slight over 1/3 were Caucasians and the rest were Asians, Pacific Islanders, African Americans and other ethnic groups). The class had two lectures per week, and class notes and video recorded classes were available to the students 24/7. At the end of the course, the students filled out a seven-item questionnaire. The survey result showed an overall positive attitude towards the blended learning approach. There was a positive relationship between computer/Internet literacy and perceived usefulness of online materials and new online learning modalities. However, the researchers did not find any differences between students' positive attitude toward online component of blended learning and their demographics.

Methods Used to Study Cross-Cultural Blended Learning

Table 2 lists the methods used in the studies reviewed (in the order of method and year of the publication). Almost all the studies were qualitative in nature; one used quantitative method (Yudko et. al., 2008); and two used a mixed-method approach (Freedman & Liu, 1996; Evans et al., 2008). Content analyses of email messages and discussion forum postings appeared to be the most popular data collection method, followed by questionnaire and interview.

A distinct similarity was observed in the studies reviewed in this chapter. All the studies focused on the online component of blended learning, and did not provide much information on how face-to-face teacher-led classroom activities complemented the online components. Such a phenomenon can be interpenetrated in a number of ways. As can be seen from the research questions, these articles meant to investigate either the feasibility of using the Internet to connect learners from difficult cultures, or behavioral differences among learners in a cross-cultural online learning environment. As a result, the complementary part of face-to-face interaction was not an intended part of the investigation. Few articles briefly mentioned teachers' role in cross-cultural learning activities. For instance, some tutors emailed students to encourage their participation (Shih & Cifuentes, 2003). Others "contributed equally to the facilitation of the groups online" (Evans et al., 2008, p. 28). Still, others "provided case feedback and served as mentors. … not only in their own conference but also in other conferences … e.g. Finish students received feedback from both American and Finnish mentors on their case discussions" (Kim & Bonk, 2006, p. 5). Face-to-face classroom interactions were hardly mentioned in the articles reviewed. When mentioned in rare cases, functions of teacher-led sessions appeared to be around students' online cross-cultural communication. For instance, when the question brought up by students as to whether it should be $2.935 million or $2,935 million, the teachers discussed in their "respective classes the differences in communication" (Van Ryssen & Godar, 2000, p. 57).

As survey method (questionnaire) was a common technique used for data collection, much of what we have learned about online aspects of cross-cultural blended learning activities is

Table 2. Research methods used in the studies reviewed

Author(s)	Year	Purpose/Research Questions of the Study	Method/ Data Source
Van Ryssen & Godar	2000	- Does the use of Internet-related tools create an opportunity for students to learn from experiences rather than the processing of information in textbooks? - What are the advantages and drawbacks of Internet-enhanced environment? - Under what condition can the educational results of the use of such tools be optimized? (p. 50)	Narrative accounts
Winner & Shields	2002	"how the web can reinforce the power of language and communication by building a bridge between socially, culturally, geographically, economically, and ethnically distinct students" (p. 274)	Narrative accounts
Liang & McQueen	1999	"We examined the learner's expectation of the teacher, the preferences by which these learners communicated with their learning peers, the conformity issue and the impact of language barrier". (p. 26)	Questionnaire; observation; interviews
Cifuentes & Murphy	2000	"In what ways, if any, did the Cultural Connections experiences affect (a) multicultural understanding, and (b) self-concept for the broader-school teacher and her students" (p. 70)?	Multimedia portfolio; written reflections of teachers & students; interviews with students
Shih & Cifuentes	2003	"... this study explores the cultural issues and phenomena of online intercultural learning and communication" (p. 85).	Analysis of web postings, email & computer conference response; mid-term & post-connection survey; reflective journal entries; interviews
Kim & Bonk	2006	- Are there differences in learner's online collaborative behavior cross cultures? If so, how are they different? - How do learners feel about the international collaboration experience? - What are the implications of such cross-cultural differences for designing and facilitating collaborative learning among culturally diverse learners? (p. 3).	Content analysis of conference transcripts; post-connection questionnaire
Buchanan, Wilson & Gopal	2008	"... the method of integrating students from different parts of the world online to cross-culturally explore issues such as racism appears effective, cheap and relatively easy to obtain" (p. 681)	Online questionnaire, descriptive statistical analysis
Vinagre	2008	"how participants in asynchronous collaborative exchange comply with certain social and interactional rules, namely politeness strategies in language use" (p. 1023)	Content analysis of email messages
Freedman & Liu	1996	What are the characteristics of Asian American students learning while using computers for multicultural understanding? (p. 45)	Content analysis of email; participant observation; interviews; questionnaire; journal entries
Evans, Suzuki, Begg & Lam	2008	"Whether medical students from 2 different cultures can learn effectively from a shared web-based learning environment" (p. 27)	Content analysis of web postings; questionnaire, descriptive statistical analysis
Yudko, Hirokawa & Chi	2008	- Are student attitudes towards combining distance learning techniques with traditional lecture positive? - Does this new approach impact the students' regular class attendance? - Do students believe that they are benefiting from the use of this new technology? (p. 1218)	Questionnaire; descriptive statistical analysis

limited to learners' self-reported perceptions/behaviors. There was inadequate information on how students used different elements of blended learning to complement each other; how interactive and collaborative features of asynchronous technology enabled learners to impart opinions, viewpoints and experiences; or how such learning adventures impacted their intercultural ways of thinking and behaving.

Implications for Designing Cross-Cultural Blended Learning

This section will summarize some inferences drawn from the studies reviewed, by relating the discussion to relevant literature. Undoubtedly, there are problems in drawing precise conclusions on how cross-cultural blended learning activities should be designed from the 11 studies reviewed. Nevertheless, even if the studies reviewed here are treated only as a rough guide, certain patterns emerged and some implications could be inferred. The review seemed to suggest that design of cross-cultural blended learning activities should take into considerations of (1) curriculum choice, (2) activity management, (3) language issues, and (4) preparation of learners.

Curriculum Choice for Cross-Cultural Blended Learning Activities

Curriculum choice for blended learning activities seems to be one the most important factors influencing learning outcomes. The studies summarized in this chapter covered a wide range of curriculum areas: communication, English for speakers of other languages, international marketing, medicine, teacher education, and high school interdisciplinary curricula. The studies appear to suggest that it be imperative that desired learning outcomes of each participating institution be integrated; and the Internet be used to complement the achievement of these outcomes. Furthermore, activities are more likely to attract participation if they focus on a specific academic topic and learning tasks are relevant to learners. Take the study by Feedman and Liu (1996) for example. The Asian American students tended to sit quietly in front of the computer and would not start to work until they were asked to. However, "when the assignment related to the Asian students life, they worked more quickly and easily" (p. 52). When learners do not see the relevance in the tasks given, what is described by Shih and Cifuentes (2003) will likely happen. During a period of 10 weeks, only one Taiwanese and two US participants put postings in the forums even though all the participants were encouraged to submit cultural and technical questions according to their interests and needs.

Closely related to curriculum choice are decisions on what is to be learned online, what is to be learned in face-to-face classroom situations, and which ICT tool is to be used. Liang and McQueen (1999) suggested, "to balance the learning style of learners with various cultural backgrounds, the percentage between online interactive learning and conventional face-to-face lecture/group discussion should be carefully determined" (p. 28). This is in line with what has been advocated in blended learning literature. It is argued that teachers need to decide what objectives can best be achieved through online learning activities, what can best be accomplished in the classroom, and how to integrate these two learning environments (Dziuban, Hartman & Moskal, 2004). Hofmann (2006) recommended that the first step be matching learning objectives with a medium that does it the best. Learning objectives requiring memorization might lend itself best to online self-directed/paced activities where students can practice as many times as they want to and get immediate feedback from the most "patient" teacher – the computer. Similarly, learning objectives aiming knowledge absorption may benefit from online activities where students are put "in situations which compel them to read, speak, listen, think deeply" (Dodge, 2001, p.6).

In general, online communication takes longer and is not easy to use in solving complex problems (Yoon & Lim, 2007). "Thick" technologies, such as audio/video conferencing, are faster and more efficient than "lean" technologies such as email (Chou, 2004). However, they are not always suitable for cross-cultural blended learning activities "apparently because time differences would have made it very impractical" (Van Ryssen & Godar, 2000, p. 53). On the other hand, "lean" technologies such as synchronous discussion and email may help reduce communication barriers for learners who have to use another language, although it may increase obstacles of writing. Nonetheless, researchers found that "compared to the barriers of speaking caused by accent difference or incorrect pronunciation, the barrier of writing style was perceived as less troublesome by the learning peers" (Liang & McQueen, 1999, p. 28). Furthermore, decision-making needs to take into account which part of the learning outcomes will benefit the most from collaborating with learners from another culture. For instance, Shih and Cifuentes (2003) observed that, "Asian learners believe that neither the instructor nor the student should be led to lose face. Therefore, situations that may cause anyone to lose face, such as large group web-boards, should be avoided" (p. 88).

Besides choice of curriculum subject area and topics, many other factors could also impact learners' participation in cross-cultural blended learning activities, such as individuals' work ethics and their interests in the cultures of their collaborators. "Cultural barriers can be alleviated when the need for collaboration and the nature of the joint activity is made clearly evident to the students" (Bannon, 1995 cited in Kim & Bonk, p. 17). Involving potential cross-cultural learning participants in the planning of learning tasks may help create relevant activities that learners are interested in participating in.

Managing Cross-Cultural Blended Learning Activities

Like any other successful educational program, effective cross-cultural blended learning relies on efficient planning and management. The studies reviewed seemed to have suggested a few areas that must receive serious attention at the planning stage, namely a committed teaching team who makes important decisions on choices of learning task and assessment, and managing learning activities.

A common pattern was observed on how cross-cultural blended learning projects emerged – individual teachers' interests and initiatives. In the high school project (Freedman & Liu, 1996), "students were selected because the teachers of these classes wanted their students to have contact through the computer network with students who had other cultural backgrounds" (p. 46). In the Belgium-US project, one teacher emailed another one with a message: "I've seen the web pages of your course and was wondering if you would like to collaborate on a project" (Van Ryssen & Godar, 2000, p. 51). Still, in the UK-US-South Africa project (Buchanan et al., 2008), two teachers started collaboration after meeting during a social work conference, and the third teacher joined them after attending the project presentation at another conference a year later. Once teachers got connected, they spent a lot of time planning and making decisions on all aspects involved in the collaboration, including choices of curriculum subject area and ICT tool. In many situations, "the relationship between the two teachers did not begin with face-to-face meetings" (Cifuentes & Murphy 2000, p. 77). A trusting relationship seems to be a key to a productive project. As pointed out by two teachers; "we doubt that the project would have been a success had we not taken that time to get acquitted" because their "length discussions not only led to clarity about aims, processes, and responsibilities, but also were necessary to build mutual understanding and trust" (Van Ryssen & Godar, 2000, p. 53).

As part of planning, teachers needed to create detailed guidelines for students to accomplish learning tasks assigned. The more detailed description given to students, the easier it appeared for students to follow. A good example of a detailed guideline is found in Vinagre (2008). In this study, Spanish students studying English exchanged email with UK students who were studying Spanish. Detailed instructions given to the students included:

Vocabulary: make note of the new words you learn, either from your partner of from the use of dictionary;

Culture: what aspects related to your partner's culture and way of life have you learned about? Compare them with your own and give your opinion briefly (p. 1032).

Not all the studies provided information on whether their cross-cultural blended learning activities were part of formal assessments. Assessment or not, it did not seem to impact the quality of student work. Take Van Ryssen and Godar's project (2000) for example. The marketing plan that the Belgium and US students generated from online collaboration counted for 20% and 35% of the course assessment in respective universities. Nevertheless, "what students collected and finally wrote up about their products was sometimes very scant. For most groups, it was certainly below what we would have accepted as a quick and dirty market analysis" (p. 57).

Again, not all the studies mentioned how students teamed up with students from another culture. In those that did provide such information, grouping was done in two ways – teacher assigned groups and groups of free choice. While teacher assigned groups were able to embark on learning activities right away, the process of free choice grouping was time-consuming. Normally, students would put a posting introducing themselves and their topics of interests. Those who were interested in the same topics would reply, and a team might be formed after a few rounds of email exchanges. There are certainly advantages and disadvantages in each grouping method. For those who prefer free-choice grouping, Van Ryssen and Godar's (2000) remark may help. In their observation, "the teams who had been very explicit about what they wanted to do, and those teams that had been very vague or not outspoken at all, had more difficulties in finding partners" (p. 54). The groups that had the least trouble finding partners were those that "presented themselves with a clearly stated interest, without stressing their own choices too much" (p.54). As for the timing of grouping, Liang and McQueen (1999) recommended: "to find idea group work partners, it may be better to defer the formation of learning groups until after a reasonable time of communication among learning peers" (p. 28).

Language Issues

English was used as the working language in all the studies reviewed in this chapter. On the surface, language did not seem to be a barrier for non-native English speaking learners. For instance, Japanese students "were able to communicate in English better than had been anticipated by their teachers" (Evan et al., 2008, p. 30), and "many US students and instructors acknowledged the high level of English skills displayed in the postings from Finnish participants" (Kim & Bonk, 2006, p.8). Nonetheless, levels of non-native English speaking students' participation seemed to imply otherwise. In Kim and Bonk's (2006) study, the students from each of the three countries also had access to the forums of two other countries. While the Finnish students posted an average of one posting in the US forum, the US students posted an average of 2.6 postings in the Finnish forum. The Korean forum generated 163 postings, of which 101 (62%) were entered by the Korean students, 15 (9%) by the Finnish students, and 47 (29%) by the US students. This made the researchers suspect "whether language expertise, self-confidence, or online experience as a factor" (Kim & Bonk, 2006, p. 8).

When working with a language that is not their mother tongue, learners may feel like being in a foreign environment dominated by another culture, and may not be motivated or be able to perform their best. In the study by Liang and McQueen (1999), non-native English speaking learners with low English language ability preferred to work with those who had a similar level of English language ability. When not online, non-native English speaking students preferred to discuss the project in their native language. Even when language support was offered, non-native English speaking students may still be disadvantaged largely because they "find that learning academic concepts in English is more challenging and are therefore distanced from the concepts and find the topic less engaging than native speakers" (Evans et al., 2008, p. 32). What was pointed out by Liang and McQueen (1999) may be true, that in email-mediated learning, learners "can catch the meaning by reading some key words from the email context, and they also have enough time to comprehend the meaning of some words by using tools such as a dictionary" (p. 28). Possibilities of proofreading their messages and editing their messages before sending them out may help reduce the stress level experienced by learners with low proficiency of the working language. Still, language support should be on the agenda when planning cross-cultural blended learning activities.

Preparing Learners for Cross-Cultural Blended Learning

Students new to cross-cultural blended learning activities may experience various problems. In addition to the language barrier mentioned above, challenges in encountering people whose cultures, values and habits are different from theirs could be overwhelming. As culture is embedded in language, barriers to cross-cultural communication exist even for non-native English speakers with high language proficiency. In the study by Shih and Cifuentes' (2003), the Taiwanese participants were students of English as a Foreign Language, and presumably had certain levels of competency in English. However, this did not prevent them from feeling offended by their US tutors because of their limited knowledge of how English language was used in social contexts. As for whether students should be prepared for cross-cultural interactions prior to such experiences, there seemed to be two opposite opinions. Some researchers believe that teachers should prepare their students by informing them of the complexity of cross-cultural interaction with inductions to the theories of cross-cultural communication. In the study by Shih and Cifuentes' (2003), the US pre-service teachers received instruction on Hofstede's four dimensional model prior to their online experience "to avoid misunderstandings and discrepancies in expectations ... become acquainted with thinking patterns, expression styles, and characteristics of the culture involved" (p. 89). When learners are encouraged to make a little effort learning about the other culture, unnecessary frustration caused by ignorance may be reduced. In the study reported by Winner and Shields (2002), one US student asked a Bahamas student in the electronic bulletin board "if everyone in the Bahamas drank out of coconuts and lived in grass huts" (p. 279). The Bahamas student "seemed especially challenged to defend her cultural identity via this writing collaborative" (p. 279). Kim and Bonk (2006) suggested that teachers prepare students for cross-cultural online learning by showing them "examples or case transcripts highlighting cultural differences in communication styles. If learners are aware of different communication styles across cultures, they will become more competent in understanding their differences and figuring out how to cope with such differences" (p. 17).

Not everyone agreed with this approach. Van Ryssen and Godar (2000) argued, "allowing the students to uncover these problems themselves helps them also work on solutions themselves" (p. 59), and "instead of learning about them, they learned from them" (p. 57). As an alternative to pre-experience preparation, Van Ryssen and Godar (2000) suggested: "during and after the project, professors must help students give meaning to what they experience by referring to a framework for interpreting cultural differences" (p. 59), and they "spent significant time debriefing students with Hofstede's (1997) paradigm" (p. 57) at the completion of their project.

FUTURE TRENDS

This literature review intended to find answers to the questions: what is blended learning like when it involves teachers and learners from culturally diverse backgrounds; do learners from different cultures behave differently in blended learning activities; what are the challenges for teachers carrying out cross-cultural blended learning activities; what are the challenges for students participating in cross-cultural blended learning activities; what are the theories currently used to study cross-cultural blended learning; and what are the design issues related to cross-cultural blended learning?

The review appears to have answered some of these questions, if not all. But, more questions arose that need to be investigated in future studies. The studies reviewed essentially addressed two issues in cross-cultural blended learning: feasibility of and leaner differences in cross-cultural blended learning. We learned that it is possible for teachers to integrate a cross-cultural component into their curriculum by using the Internet. We were presented with evidence that the Internet could create an opportunity for students to learn with learners from other cultures, but were also cautioned of various issues that teachers should be aware of. We were informed that learners from different cultures have different learning styles and preferences when engaging in online cross-cultural learning activities.

The studies reviewed were published in a period of 12 years (1996-2008), with two published in the 1990s and the rest in the 2000s. The lack of the published studies on cross-cultural blended learning indicates the inadequacy of the research in the area. Eleven peer-reviewed journal articles were chosen for the analysis because they fit the criterion: they were components of a formal curriculum consisting of teacher-led face-to-face interactions and online activities. However, a closer look at these articles revealed that what is being reported was primarily the online part of a blended learning course. Face-to-face classroom situations/interactions and instructor-led activities from a cultural perspective were hardly mentioned or discussed. Evidently, this is an area that future studies could look into. For instance, future studies could compare and contrast non-technology supported learning activities from a cultural perspective, such as how teachers help students and how students from different cultures assist one another to create new knowledge. Future studies may also explore the issues from socio-cultural perspectives, such as how the concept of Vygotsky's Zone of Proximal Development is experienced in cross-cultural blended learning.

The chapter shows that issues relating to cultural differences continue to be a focus of investigation throughout the 12 years when the studies reviewed were published, implying that the issue continues to be an interest. Cultural differences were found among learners in their approaches to asking questions, collaborating with others, and preferences to ways of using technologies. In some cases, differences were significant enough to be a concern. Awareness of cultural differences is undoubtedly helpful to those who are interested in embarking on cross-cultural blended learning. However, perhaps, it is more important that future studies go beyond the stage of creating awareness. Rather, they could explore strategies of how to deal with the differences that may impede cross-cultural learning activities.

Future studies could also investigate how sharing and dissemination of information via online interaction and collaboration with learners from different cultures impact learners' intercultural ways of thinking and behaving. For instance, verbal feedback in CSCL environment may be different for learners from collectivistic and individualistic cultural backgrounds. In collectivistic cultures, learners are "very concerned about loss or gain of their collective face in their pursuit of achievement" (Salili, 1994, p. 646) as "the individual's identity is derived from the social group rather than from his or her own attributes" (Hui,

1988 cited in Salili, 1994, p.637). Would interaction with learners from an individualistic culture help change behaviours of the learners who are from a collectivistic culture?

Future research on cross-cultural blended learning could also benefit from a new direction taken by the research in cross-cultural web design. In recent years, researchers in cross-cultural web design have begun to investigate cultural differences in the way humans process information. Researchers holding such a position believe that focus on computer-mediated communication is not enough; there is a need for exploring the cultural cognitive style of web users (Faiola & Matei, 2005). Cognitive style is a collection of strategies premised on how individuals differ when processing information (Ford, Wood & Walsh, 1996), influenced by the environment/culture in which one resides. Anthropological and psychological studies of general cognitive processes continue to suggest that cognitive styles are connected to culture (Faiola & Matei, 2005). Empirical evidence shows that analytical processes operate on different inputs for different people and in different situations and cultures (Nisbett & Norenzayan, 2002). For instance, Faiola & Matei (2005) found that American and Chinese Internet users performed information-seeking tasks faster when using web contents created by designers from their own cultures. Perhaps, future blended learning studies may explore the impact of learning designers' cultural backgrounds on student learning.

Finally, research on cross-cultural blended learning should take into account recent social, economical and technological developments in the world. This chapter seems to suggest that cross-cultural blended learning activities be more likely to take place in developed (e.g. the UK) and emerging (e.g. Korea) economies. Of all the studies reviewed, only one described a collaborative project between the students from a developing country (the Bahamas) and the developed world (the US). As globalization progresses and technologies become accessible in more parts of the world, it is likely that more Bahamas-US collaborative type projects will emerge, and more learners from diverse cultures will mix in the same learning environment. It is true that cultural differences will exit for many years to come; it is also possible that in an increasingly globalized world learners are becoming more adaptable when working with "foreigners". Cultures are changing, and changes are accelerated by Internet penetration. Take China for example. By the end of June 2009, China's population of Internet users reached 338 million (CNNIC, 2009), the world's largest Internet user group. China now has 102.7 million online forum participants and 181.8 million bloggers (an increase of 12.9% and 12.2% respectively from December 2008). With this kind of development, the question needs to be asked whether the conventional wisdom, such as Asian learners do not want to express their opinions in public, is still valid. It would be interesting to explore how learners in different cultures have managed to adapt to an international norm; and whether frequent Internet use has the potential of turning those from traditionally public-speech-shy cultures to active participants in an online learning environment.

CONCLUSION

The field of research on cross-cultural internet-mediated learning has come a long way since the Inter-Cultural Network (Levin et al., 1987). Progress has been made since Freedman and Liu (1996) wrote, "cultural issues concerning… ways of knowing, attitudes about technology, and communication ethics have yet to receive adequate attention in relation to computer networking" (p. 44). Nevertheless, our understanding of how people learn in cross-cultural environments is still limited.

The studies reviewed overwhelmingly reported the benefits of cross-cultural blended learning activities, suggesting their potentials to ensure the widest possible impact of students' learning experience. However, like any other kind of learning design, connecting to learners from other cultures will not automatically warrant effective learning. Teachers and academics need to carefully design all components of cross-cultural blended learning activities, and diligently facilitate their students' online learning experiences. Moreover, they should constantly reflect on their cross-cultural blended learning design. In addition to examining students learning outcomes, teachers should evaluate and assess the fit of each delivery medium (Yoon & Lim, 2007), and make improvement. Only by adopting such an approach will the likelihood of achieving intended learning goals be enhanced.

ACKNOWLEDGMENT

The author wishes to thank two anonymous reviewers for their valuable comments and suggestions, and also wishes to thank Mr. Neville Ellis for proofreading the manuscript.

REFERENCES

Bruder, I. (1989). Distance learning: What's holding back this boundless delivery system? *Electronic Learning*, *8*(6), 30–35.

Buchanan, J., Wilson, S., & Gopal, N. (2008). A cross cultural virtual learning environment for students to explore the issue of racism: A case study involving the UK, USA, and SA. *Social Work Education*, *27*(6), 671–682. doi:10.1080/02615470802201804

Chau, P. Y. K., Cole, M., Massey, A. P. M., Montoya-Weiss, M., & O'Keefe, R. M. (2002). Cultural differences in the online behavior of consumers. *Communications of the ACM*, *45*(10), 138–143. doi:10.1145/570907.570911

Chou, C. (2004). A model of learner-centered computer-mediate interaction for collaborative distance learning. *International Journal on E-Learning*, *3*(1), 11–19.

Cifuentes, L., & Murphy, K. (2000). Promoting multicultural understanding and positive self-concept through a distance learning community: Cultural connections. *Educational Technology Research and Development*, *48*(1), 69–83. doi:10.1007/BF02313486

CNNIC. (2009). The 24th statistical report on the Internet development in China (第**24**次中國互聯网絡发展狀况統计報告**)**. Retrieved on September 16, 2009, from http://www.cnnic.cn/html/Dir/2009/07/15/5637.htm

Cobb, T. (1997). Cognitive efficiency: Toward a revised theory of media. *Educational Technology Research and Development*, *45*(4), 21–45. doi:10.1007/BF02299681

Del Galdo, E. M. (1996). Culture and design. In E. M. Del Galdo & J. Neilsen (Eds.), *International user interfaces* (pp. 74–87). New York: John Wiley & Sons.

Dodge, B. (2001). FOCUC: Five rules for writing a great webquest. *Learning & Learning with Technology*, *28*(8), 6–9.

Dziuban, D., Hartman, J., & Moskal, P. (2004). Blended learning. *Educause Centre for Applied Research Bulletin*, *7*, 1–12.

Evans, P., Suzuki, Y., Begg, M., & Lam, W. (2008). Can medical students from two cultures learn effectively from a shared Web-based learning environment? *Medical Education*, *42*(1), 27–33.

Faiola, A., & Matei, S. (2005). Cultural cognitive style and Web design: Beyond a behavioral inquiry into computer-mediated communication. *Journal of Computer-Mediated Communication*, *11*(1), 375–394. doi:10.1111/j.1083-6101.2006.tb00318.x

Ford, N., Wood, F., & Walsh, C. (1994). Cognitive styles and searching. *Online and CDROM Review*, *18*(2), 79–86. doi:10.1108/eb024480

Freedman, K., & Liu, M. (1996). The importance of computer experience, learning processes, and communication patterns of multicultural networking. *Educational Technology Research and Development*, *44*(1), 43–59. doi:10.1007/BF02300325

Hall, E. T., & Hall, M. R. (1989). *Understanding cultural differences*. Yarmouth, ME: Intercultural Press.

Hofmann, J. (2006). Answers to those questions that keep you up at night. In C. Bonk & C. Graham (Eds.), *The handbook of blended learning: Global perspectives, local designs* (pp. 27-40). San Francisco: Pfeiffer.

Hofstede, G. (1986). Cultural differences in teaching and learning. *International Journal of Intercultural Relations*, *10*, 301–320. doi:10.1016/0147-1767(86)90015-5

Hofstede, G. (1997). *Cultures and organizations: Software of the mind*. New York: McGraw-Hill.

Jarvis, P. (1999). Global trends in lifelong learning and the response of the universities. *Comparative Education*, *35*(2), 249–257. doi:10.1080/03050069928017

Keegan, D. (1988). Problems in defining the field of distance education. *American Journal of Distance Education*, *2*(2), 4–11.

Kim, K. J., & Bonk, C. J. (2006). Cross-cultural comparisons of online collaboration. *Journal of Computer-Mediated Communication*, *8*(1), 1–21.

Levin, J. A., Riel, M., Miyake, N., & Cohen, M. (1987). Education on the electronic frontier: Teleapprentices in globally distributed educational contexts. *Contemporary Educational Psychology*, *12*, 254–260. doi:10.1016/S0361-476X(87)80030-9

Li, J. (2002). A cultural model of learning: Chinese "heart and mind for wanting to learn." . *Journal of Cross-Cultural Psychology*, *33*, 248–269. doi:10.1177/0022022102033003003

Liang, A., & McQueen, R. (1999). Computer assisted adult interactive learning in a multi-cultural environment. *Adult Learning*, *11*(1), 26–28.

Mason, R. (1998). *Globalizing education: Trends and applications. Routledge studies in distance education*. New York: Routledge.

McLuhan, M. (1964). The media is the message. New York: Mentor.

Myers, S. A., Zhong, M., & Guan, S. (1998). Instructor immediacy in the Chinese college classroom. *Communication Studies*, *49*, 240–254.

Nielson, J. (1993). *Usability engineering*. New York: Academic Press.

Nisbett, R. E., & Norenzayan, A. (2002). Culture and cognition. In H. Pashler & D. L. Medin (Eds.), *Stevens' handbook of experimental psychology: Vol. 2: Cognition* (3rd ed., pp. 561-597). New York: John Wiley & Sons.

Osguthorpe, T., & Graham, R. (2003). Blended learning environment. *Quarterly Review of Distance Education*, *4*(3), 227–233.

Oxford, R. L., & Anderson, N. J. (1995). A cross-cultural view of learning styles. *Language Teaching*, *28*, 201–215. doi:10.1017/S0261444800000446

Pinhey, L. A. (1998). *Global education: Internet resources*. ERIC Digest. ED417124.

Reginald, S. (1964). The importance of negative results in psychological research. *Canadian Psychology*, *5*(4), 225–232.

Rogers, P., Graham, C., & Mayes, C. (2007). Cultural competence and instructional design: Exploration research into the delivery of online instruction cross-culturally. *Educational Technology Research and Development*, *55*(2), 197–210. doi:10.1007/s11423-007-9033-x

Rothstein, H., Sutton, A., & Borenstein, M. (2005). *Publication bias in meta-analysis: Prevention, assessment, and adjustments.* Chichester: Wiley.

Salili, F. (1994). Age, sex, and cultural differences in the meaning and dimensions of achievement. *Personality and Social Psychology Bulletin*, *20*(6), 635–648. doi:10.1177/0146167294206002

Salili, F. (2001). Teacher-student interaction: Attributional implications and effectiveness of teachers' evaluative feedback. In D. A. Watkins, & J. B. Biggs (Eds.), *Teaching the Chinese learner: Psychological and pedagogical perspectives* (pp. 77-98). Hong Kong: Comparative Educational Research Center.

Samarawickrema, R. G. (2005). Determinants of student readiness for flexible learning: Some preliminary findings. *Distance Education*, *26*(1), 49–66. doi:10.1080/01587910500081277

Shih, Y., & Cifuentes, L. (2003). Taiwanese intercultural phenomena and issues in a United States-Taiwan telecommunication partnership. *Educational Technology Research and Development*, *51*(3), 82–90. doi:10.1007/BF02504555

Smith, A., Dunckley, L., French, T., Minocha, S., & Chang, Y. (2004). A process model for developing usable cross-cultural Web sites. *Interacting with Computers*, *16*(1), 63–91. doi:10.1016/j.intcom.2003.11.005

Van Ryssen, S., & Godar, S. (2000). Going international without going international: Multinational virtual teams. *Journal of International Management*, *6*, 49–60. doi:10.1016/S1075-4253(00)00019-3

Vinagre, M. (2008). Politeness strategies in collaborative e-mail exchanges. *Computers & Education*, *50*, 1022–1036. doi:10.1016/j.compedu.2006.10.002

Winner, T., & Shields, T. (2002). Breaking the island chains: A case study exploring the intricate powers of language shared on the World Wide Web. *Computers and Composition*, *19*, 273–284. doi:10.1016/S8755-4615(02)00129-9

Yoon, S. W., & Lim, D. (2007). Strategic blending: A conceptual framework to improve learning and performance. *International Journal on E-Learning*, *6*(3), 475–489.

Yudko, E., Hirokawa, R., & Chi, R. (2008). Attitudes, beliefs, and attendance in a hybrid course. *Computers & Education*, *50*, 1217–1227. doi:10.1016/j.compedu.2006.11.005

Zhang, Q. (2006). Immediacy and out-of-class communication: A cross-cultural comparison. *International Journal of Intercultural Relations*, *30*, 33–50. doi:10.1016/j.ijintrel.2005.06.006

Chapter 15
Online Literacy among Students and Faculty:
A Comparative Study between the United States and Eastern European Countries

Plamen Miltenoff
St. Cloud State University, Minnesota, USA

John H. Hoover
St. Cloud State University, Minnesota, USA

Galin Tzokov
Paisii Khilendarski University, Bulgaria

ABSTRACT

Based on the recent proliferation of online education and the ongoing technological revolution, this research focused on interaction of students and faculty as a main contributor to the success of online education. During 2003, a survey was distributed to convenience samples of faculty members and students from the Midwest of the U.S. and three Eastern European countries. The data reflects students' and faculty members' opinions about the state of technology, online communication, and instruction. The results confirm findings from the literature about the existence of a digital divide between developed and emerging nations. Although Eastern European respondents don't benefit from the technology base of their American correspondents, their satisfaction and comfort with technology remains relatively strong. The digital divide may result from administrative rigidity; Eastern European students enjoy less access to computer labs, due to fewer and less flexible hours. Faculty members and administrators remain entrenched in "old" technologies such as e-mail, whereas Millennials expect newer communication tools and prefer synchronous ones. Considering the available technology, online assessment is employed relatively inconsistently. Libraries as technology providers are perhaps underutilized particularly in Bulgaria, Moldova, and Macedonia.

DOI: 10.4018/978-1-60566-852-9.ch015

INTRODUCTION

The rapidly increasing number of online classes and programs prompt researchers and educators to focus on learner engagement (Andrews & Haythornthwaite, 2007; Condrad & Donaldson, 2004; Finkelstein, 2006). Students rate instructiveness as a critical course satisfaction factor (e.g., Burnett, et al., 2007; Gould & Padavano, 2006; Green, et al., 2006;Young & Norgard, 2006); engagement is positively associated with levels of academic achievement (e.g., Bell, 2007; Lee et al., 2006) and motivation measures (e.g., Bennett & Lockyer, 2004; Kawachi, 2003; Schrum et al., 2007).

The existence of online environments is made possible by the technological revolution and the advent of the Internet's connectivity. The online environment both thrives on and generates technological advancements; offering space and time alternatives over traditional classrooms. As a result of the changes in delivery modalities, it is essential to explore the effects of online and hybrid offerings on teaching and learning processes. In the course of the last decade, online learning technologies underwent significant change. Mullinix and McCurry (2003) propose a detailed taxonomy for instructional modalities (Fully in-class, Web-supplemented, Web-enhanced, Web hybrid, Fully-online). Face-to-face, hybrid, and fully online are currently the most commonly employed types. The ever-increasing application of information technology appears to have produced a nexus between face-to-face and online modalities referred to as distributed learning (Vrasidas & Glass, 2002). The shift toward distance education utilizing online tools for instruction and communication turned many face-to-face classrooms into hybrid operations (Young, 2002). Definitions of hybrid classrooms vary significantly, mostly due to disagreements over technological applications (Schrum & Hong, 2002). Three elements, however, appear in nearly all descriptions: hybrid instructional systems require (a) the existence of electronic infrastructure and (b) a professoriate skilled in the use of new technologies and (c) college students sophisticated enough to make use of hybrid offerings. The subject purpose of this chapter is to study the degree to which adult educators in the Midwestern U.S.A. and Eastern Europe effectively employ the instructional technologies typically part of hybrid environments.

The leaders in distance education include Pacific countries such as, but not only, Australia, New Zealand, Canada, and the United States (Stephenson, 2002). This is not a coincidence as countries of vast territories, sparse population and ability to invest in distance education most likely forge ahead in the use of online systems. Given the preeminence of Pacific Rim countries in instructional technology application, we employed the U.S. as a benchmark for comparison with Eastern European nations.

BACKGROUND

The primary American University (hereafter Midwestern University) selected for investigation is described as a master's college or university (subdivision = larger program) in the Carnegie classification system (http://www.carnegiefoundation.org/classifications/). The university, located in the Northern Midwest, provided over 130 undergraduate majors and 52 master's programs at the time of the investigation. The student population was just under 16,000. In many ways, Midwestern University is typical of U.S. comprehensive universities in terms of technology use—if slightly above the infrastructure curve. In terms of technology application, prestigious private colleges and universities, along with larger land grant and flagship institutions, tend to be slightly further along the adaptation curve than does Midwestern University; two-year colleges and technical schools tend to lag behind.

At the time that the study was conducted, Midwestern University was experiencing, as did many other institutions, a rapid increase in the availability of educational technology resources. Over 150 courses per annum were fully online at the time of the study, with one nationally-recognized M.S. program being fully online serving students in over 20 U.S. states and 15 countries. Because of the breadth of network and support services, Midwestern University achieved a top 50 (out of more than 500 comparable institutions) Intel ranking of "most wired" campuses.

The existence of infrastructure does not assure that instructors or students will adopt new technologies—or that they will take maximum advantage of them. While Midwestern University boasts of online programs and subscribes to course management software, many faculty members have not tapped the richer potential of instructional technology. However, most professors (about 85%, it is estimated) who employ course maintenance software (about 75% of the total), do so to support face-to-face courses. Thus, it might be argued that by default, Midwestern University educators employ a hybrid model; what is not clear is the extent to which this blend of online and face-to-face approaches is used effectively. It has been argued that the training of prospective teachers has not kept up with the technology needs and preferences of students in American public schools. Teachers often encounter students, so-called Millennials, whose expertise with electronic devices and the Internet exceeds what educators experience in college (Prensky, 2001). Perhaps this situation is somewhat expected given the rapid growth in available hard- and software.

On the other side of the global spectrum are countries from the developing world, which fall behind, despite efforts such as the $100 laptop initiative (http://laptop.media.mit.edu/) and similar projects aimed at bridging the digital divide (Read, 2007). For example, Bulgaria, Macedonia and Moldova enjoy proximity to Western Europe and thus connectivity with a well-developed Internet grid; yet they lag far behind European Union standards and requirements for hardware, software, and Internet connectivity. Experts estimate that Bulgaria remains a decade behind Western nations in the process of building an information society (Report e-Bulgaria, 2006).

In some respects, Eastern European academics manage to keep close, if not move ahead of their Western European colleagues in instructional technology. In order to bridge the digital gap, the Bulgarian government disseminated significant strategic plans, including one on e-education. Between 2002 and 2005, Bulgarian academic institutions added over 250 computer labs; a large number of educational institutions in Bulgaria provide wireless Internet connection, thus initiating the transition toward mobile learning. Bulgarian educators have developed several in-house Course Management Systems (CMS) and about 15 distance education centers have been formed.

Twenty years ago, like Moldova and Macedonia, Bulgaria was part of the Soviet economic and political system. Since then, Bulgarians have elected to democratize their government and national institutions; in January 2007 Bulgaria formally joined the European Union (Popov & Pironkova, 2007). While Macedonia and Moldova are not yet part of the European Union, their governmental development, education in particular, evolved very similarly to their Bulgarian counterparts.

The higher education system in Bulgaria was codified in 1995 to reflect the nation's democratic changes. According to the Law for Higher Education, educational instructions in the country are now provided by both public and private institutions. The main educational entities are universities, colleges, specialized higher education schools and academies. Universities manifest a three-level structure. Four-year education, which concludes with a bachelor degree, is followed by a fifth- year resulting in an M.S.; eligible students may elect to pursue a doctoral degree, typically a three year commitment (Bekhradnia, 2005).

Such progress cannot overshadow the fact that in 2002 the computer/student ratio in the American University in Bulgaria (AUBG, http://

www.aubg.bg/) was about eight times higher than the ratio at state institutions (National Evaluation and Accreditation Agency's Newsletter, 2002, p. 399). In the following two years efforts increased (educational institutions equipped with schools and/or upgraded computers, Internet access, students' and faculty training, etc.). According to the National Evaluation and Accreditation Agency (http://www.neaa.government.bg), in 2005, the ratio improved to 8 per 100, from 4 computers per 100 students in 2001. Educational institutions also boosted their presence on the Internet and upgraded their Internet connection to broadband and wireless. For the same period about 68% of the higher education institutions used CMS and about 150-200 courses contained multimedia content. Nonetheless, the overall technological state of the country remains considerably behind that of Western Europe.

Macedonia and Moldova are representative of former Soviet-type states in that their educational systems were shaped by highly centralized governments. After the disintegration of the Soviet Union and Yugoslavia, Moldova and Macedonia struggled to reshape the content of their educational and technological systems, though remaining behind Western Europe and the United States. Similarly to Bulgaria, however, young people find a way to connect—often employing Internet cafes and cellular phones. Faculty members evidence awareness of current technological trends, even if they cannot always apply them.

The investigation described below was designed to allow the characterization of instructional technology use in the U.S.A., Bulgaria, Macedonia, and Moldova.

METHOD

The U.S. educational institutions were situated in the Midwest, as described above, whereas Bulgarian respondents worked at or attended major Bulgarian universities in the capital and in rural districts. The Moldovan respondents represented a large university situated in a rural region. Macedonian respondents hailed from a university in the capital city (Skopje).

The sample included 145 faculty members and 873 students.

Responses from the United States and Bulgaria were collected in the fall of 2002. Moldovan responses were collected in the spring of 2003 and Macedonian ones in the fall of 2003. Students and faculty members, the majority representing education programs, in Bulgaria and the U.S. completed questionnaires in 2002.

The first author developed a questionnaire based on a review of extant literature (The E-Learning Committee, 2002; Hiltz, 1995; Albion, 2001; Hoover & Steffens, 2003). The questions were grouped into the following categories of topical issues: (1) satisfaction with technology services at the institution (including items related to access) (2) comfort with instructional technology; (3) [levels of] use of various online communication techniques; (4) application of online assessment and evaluation; and (5) the role of the library in supporting instructional technology (Appendix A and B). Student and faculty surveys were distributed to some respondents from Bulgaria and Moldova as paper copies and online to the rest of the respondents. English, Bulgarian, and Russian (for Moldova) versions of student and faculty instruments can be obtained by e-mailing the first author. Responses from paper surveys were entered in MS Excel spreadsheet and imported into the SPSS statistical package. All data were processed via SPSS. Data employed to produce figures are available upon request.

ANALYSIS

In a preliminary analysis, differences between online and paper surveys were examined for 5 items. As no significant differences accrued, survey format was not treated as in independent vari-

Table 1. Numbers and percents of the sample by status and nation

	U.S.A		Bulgaria		Macedonia		Moldova		Row TOTAL	
Status	N	%	N	%	N	%	N	%	N	%
Professors	36	25	40	28	2	1	67	46	145	100
Students	326	37	270	31	56	6	214	25	873	100
Column Percent		62		59		7		71		

able. The present investigation is best described as descriptive, with few a priori hypotheses posited. Statistical treatments must thus be interpreted cautiously as the sample was gathered as a matter of convenience. We found it difficult to identify a target population in this initial investigation from which to select. Thus, all statistical treatments fail the test of random sampling. Statistical tests were employed to provide a sense of whether levels of variables differed enough that they did not occur as a function of pure chance.

Unless otherwise specified, the conventions of causal comparative or ex post facto research were maintained. The general approach was non-parametric, as the behavior (e.g., reliability and validity) of any possible scales derived from the questionnaire would not be known ahead of time (exceptions are noted, see Table 1). For nearly all of the analyses performed below (see Table 1 for specifics), the 5-choice Likert-type instrument was reconfigured to three levels. Agree and Strongly Agree (or other response choices, see Table 1) were combined, the neutral response choice was retained, while Disagree and Strongly Disagree were combined. Pertinent values were cross-tabulated with this three-level response (categorical) variable, with family-wide error rate managed via the Bonferroni method. As can

Table 2. A mapping of the variables and brief explanations

Question Category	Figure	Description of Question(s)/ Analyses
Background of research question	1	Number of participants disaggregated by age categories, country, and status (professor vs. Student)
Satisfaction with technology	2	Percent of **students** expressing satisfaction with various aspects of instructional (and other) technologies by country
Satisfaction with technology	3	Percent of **faculty members** expressing satisfaction with various aspects of instructional (and other) technologies by country
Satisfaction with technology by modality	4	Percent of respondents reporting positive attitude (satisfaction) toward technology applications (across modalities)
Use of computer laboratories	5	Percent of **faculty members** confirming personal use of the computer lab at their institution
Use of computer laboratories	6	Percent of **students** confirming personal use of the computer lab at their institution
Instructional use of selected technologies	7	Percent of **students** utilizing online communication technology for learning
Instructional use of selected technologies	8	Percent of **faculty members** utilizing online communication technology for learning
Instructional use of selected technologies	9	Percent of respondents reporting use of various technology modalities for providing feedback
Administrative: labs and libraries	10	Percent of respondents reporting that library is important technology provider
Administrative: labs and libraries	11	Percent of **students** agreeing that they experience various levels of access to computer labs
Administrative:labs and libraries	12	Percent of **faculty members** reporting levels access to computer labs by country.

be seen in Table 2, the results of each descriptive analysis is presented by means of a figure.

In a first section (represented by Figures 2 to 4), differences between advanced (represented by U.S.A. data) and emerging societies (represented by Bulgaria and the other Eastern European countries) in satisfaction with technology are examined. Via the same set of analyses, differences between students and professors are also investigated. In a second section, the use of technology among students and faculty of different university majors is laid out (See Figures 5 and 6). In the third, instructional use of online communication modalities is investigated (Figures 7 to 9). In addition, the role of libraries and access to computer labs is analyzed (Figures 10 to 12).

RESULTS

Descriptive data for age is shown in Figure 1, where age was divided into bivariate distributions, roughly at the median for each group. Faculty ages were divided at age 40 (40 and less vs. 41 or greater), while student age was subdivided at age 25 (and above vs. 24 and below). As can be seen in Figure 1, American faculty members tend to be younger than their colleagues in the three Eastern European countries. It might be expected that members of a younger faculty may be more technologically savvy. However, Berger (2007) pointed out that this is not always the case in the U.S. American students are also unique in the impressive number of "returning" or "life-long" students. It may turn out that [especially returning] American students will adopt technology more slowly compared with their "Millennial" Eastern European counterparts.

Technological State of the Institutions

Each of the five items tapping "state of technology" proved statistically significantly different between American and the East European respondents (Figure 2 and Figure 3), with Americans rating the current state of infrastructure higher (e.g., agreeing with items worded in terms of use) than did their Eastern European peers. A set of four cross tabulations, one for each of technology modality, and chi square tests were run, Response Choice (3 levels, Agree = positive attitude, Neutral, Disagree) by Country (U.S., Moldova, Bulgaria, and Macedonia) ; the Bonferroni adjustment for family-wide error-rate was employed to adjust alpha levels. Only percent agree is shown in Figures 2 and 3 "Agree," in this case means that the state of technology met expectations or was of "high quality." The difference applies for both faculty members and students, though it is worth noting that, within country, students tended to rate the state of instructional technology higher than did their faculty counterparts.

Figure 1. Age of faculty members and students

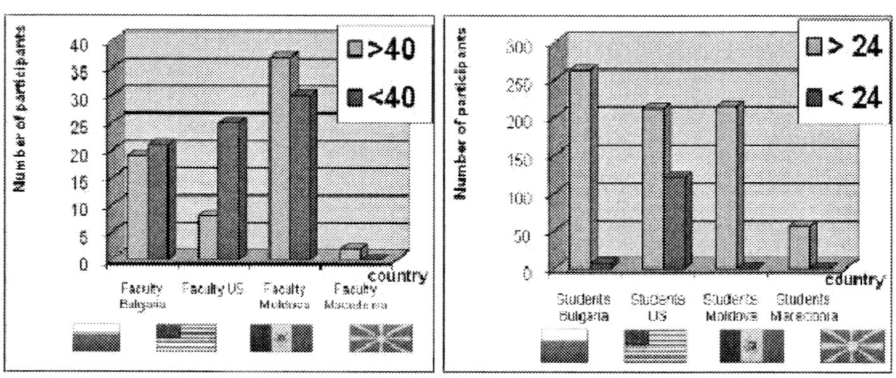

Figure 2. Percent of students expressing positive attitude toward aspects of technology use

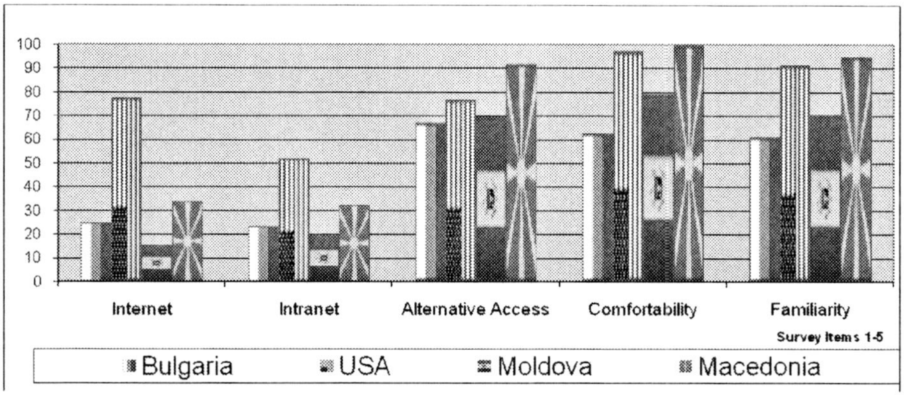

It appears that a discrepancy exists between the technological status (quality of Internet and Intranet connectivity) between U.S. institutions of higher learning (IHE) versus Eastern European universities (Бюлетин на НАОА, 2002, p. 399). However, Figure 2 shows, Eastern European respondents report technological comfort and familiarity at levels that equal or exceed their American counterparts.

A comparison of "satisfaction" levels (e.g., agreement across items that technology is employed effectively) of faculty members and students is displayed in Figure 4. Mean response across technology modalities were divided as follows: 1.00 to 2.499 = Disagree, 2.50 to 3.49 = Neutral, and 3.50 to 5.00 = Agree). Two Response Choice (3-level, as described) X Country (4 levels) cross tabulations were run for the case of students (Figure 5) and faculty members (Figure 6) . "Agree that modality is of high quality" was interpreted in terms of satisfaction. Satisfaction levels between faculty members and students did not vary significantly by country. It was expected that more U.S. respondents would express satisfaction (agree used effectively). The fact that the level of satisfaction among the respondents from the Eastern European countries vary significantly across status designations (Faculty Members vs. Students) is worth further exploration. In 2003, the University in Moldova included in this investigation was still not connected via fiber-optic to the Internet.

Figure 3. Percent of faculty members expressing positive attitude toward aspects of technology use

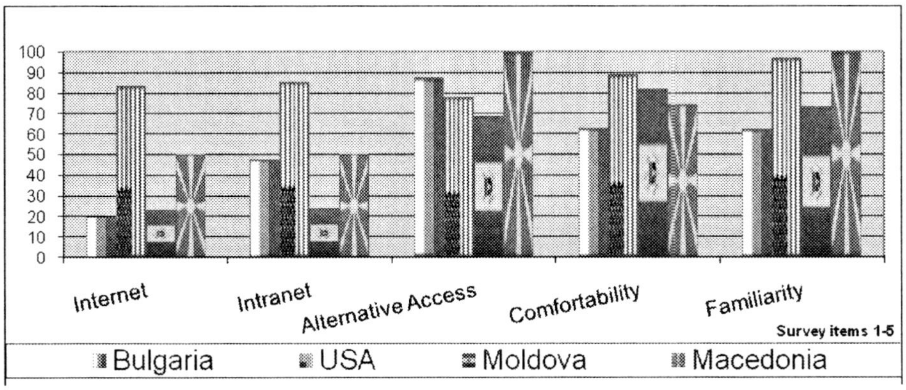

Figure 4. Faculty versus student satisfaction with technology by country

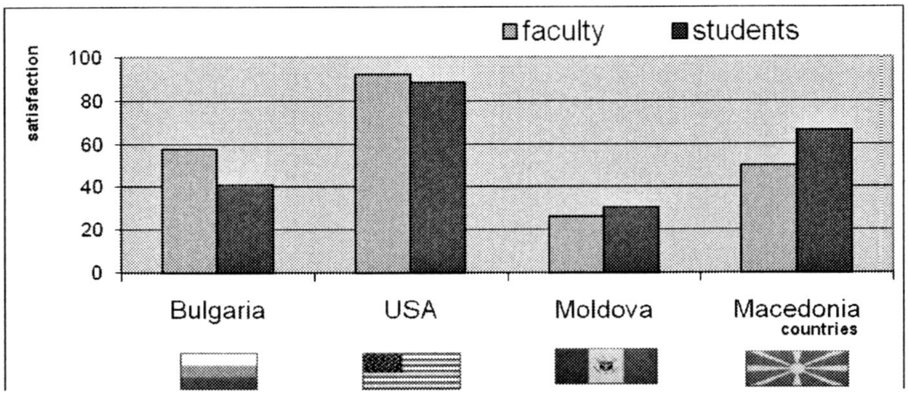

Figure 5. Percent of faculty members reporting use of computer lab by country and discipline area (value = 0 for Macedonian faculty respondents)

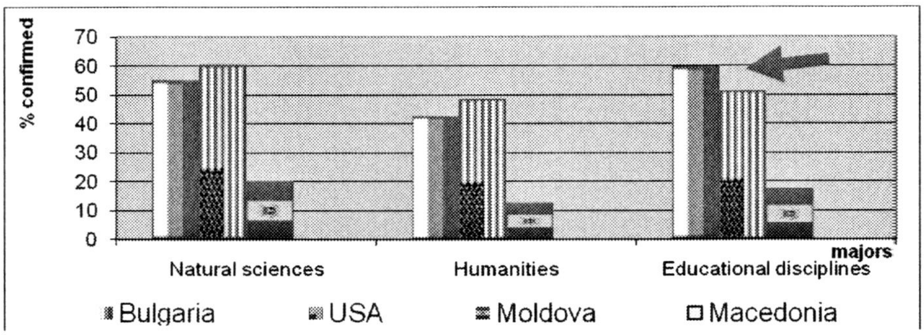

Figure 6. Percent of students reporting use of computer lab by country and discipline area

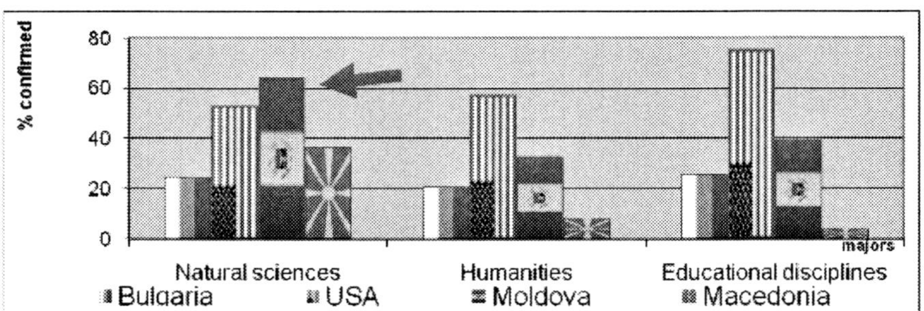

Use of the Computer Lab at the Educational Institutions by Major

Mean response of faculty members across five "lab use" items were divided as follows: 1.00 to 2.499 = Disagree, 2.50 to 3.49 = Neutral, 3.50 to 5.00 = Agree). Two cross tabulations (and accompanying chi square tests) were run, Response Choice (3-level) X Country (4 levels), one for students and one for faculty members. The difference between the U.S. and the other three countries on connectivity proved statistically significant. It is not

Figure 7. Percent of students utilizing online communication technology for learning

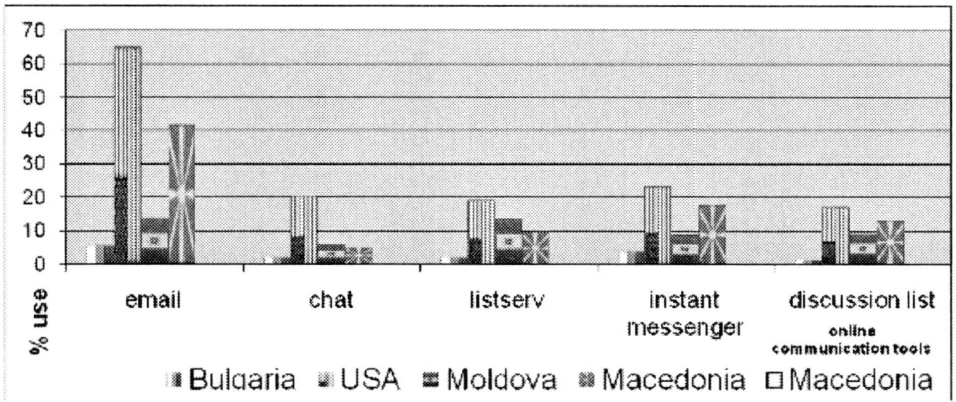

surprising that both American faculty members and students tended to use computer labs in the educational process at rates higher than did their Eastern European counterparts (Report e-Bulgaria, 2006). On the other hand, Bulgarian faculty members in education and Moldovan natural science students surpassed their American counterparts in lab use; a fact worth further investigation, at least according to informant ratings (mostly education majors).

Computer lab use differed by discipline across countries. American students majoring in education, according to ratings made by all respondents, demonstrate the highest rate of computer lab usage in comparison with other majors. These results probably accrued to the fact that in 2002, students in the natural sciences tended to own computers whereas higher numbers of education majors did not at that time. Further investigation on such digital inequality among majors can bring clarity and improve the plan of action for general application of technology in education.

Use of Online Communication in the Educational Process

Mean response of students across six "instructional-use/communication" items, were divided as follows: 1.00 to 2.499 = Not Used, 2.50 to 3.49 = Neutral, 3.50 to 5.00 = Used). A Response Choice (3-levels) X Country (4 levels) cross tabulation was calculated, with an accompanying chi square test to test for significance.. The difference between the U.S. and the other three countries, taken together, was statistically significant. For the year 2002, the five most popular types of electronic communication in academia were the following: email, chat, listservs, instant messaging and discussion lists. With the exception of email, however, the rest were scarcely used, even in the United States, with its putatively more advanced state of technology. A red flag for the Eastern European countries is that faculty use of electronic communications is greater than that of students. It would be expected that students enjoy access to technology at higher rates and they are able to communicate online to a significant degree (Stephenson, 2002). In 2002, Eastern European educators reported significantly higher use of instructional email then did their American counterparts, whereas American students, as expected, use e-mail more frequently. Significantly, e-mail is presently the official means of communication at most U.S. campuses. However, by 2006, American students asserted that email is no longer their favorite communication tool (Carnevale, 2006). Results (see Figure 7 and 8) suggest that university administrators and faculty members might be slow in responding to students' needs, particularly young student-consumers' preferences for online communication modalities.

Figure 8. Percent of faculty members utilizing online communication technology for learning

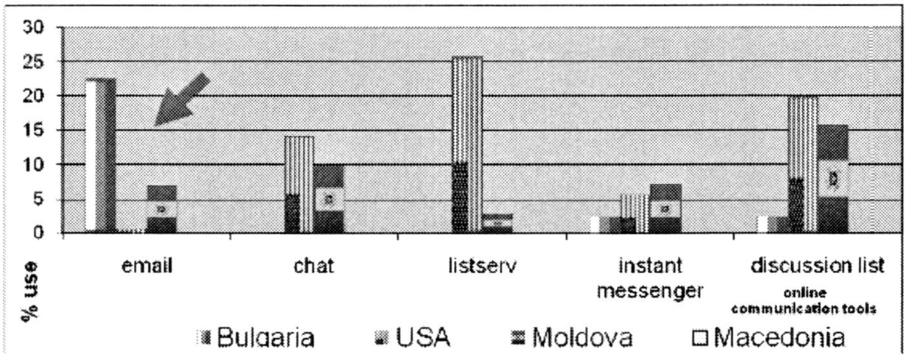

Online Assessment and Feedback

The results of the statistical analysis for items related to provision of feedback and assessment are displayed in Figure 9. A set of two chi square tests, one for student data, one for faculty data were run on the cross tabulations (e.g., Country by Response Selection [Agree, Neutral, Disagree], with agree meaning that one either uses the method for feedback [faculty members] or experiences feedback on assignments via e-technology [students]). As was typical, the Bonferroni method was employed to adjust family-wide error rate problems engendered by running a family of two tests. While the Eastern European users are adjusting to the use of online communication tools for instructional interactions, their use-levels [for assessment] lag behind their American counterparts. In 2002-2003, Course Management Systems (CMS)[1] such as Blackboard/WebCT (http://www.blackboard.com/us/index.Bb?SERV1) rapidly gained popularity. One of the very popular modes of CMS is "Grades," which can explain the drastic difference in responses regarding assessment. The results reveal low levels of online instructional assessment and feedback in both North American and Eastern Europe, though use was significantly higher in the U.S., with the exception of e-mail. Standard benchmarks for assessment and evaluation in online learning environments is needed for

Figure 9. Use of online technology to provide feedback/assessment by country and status

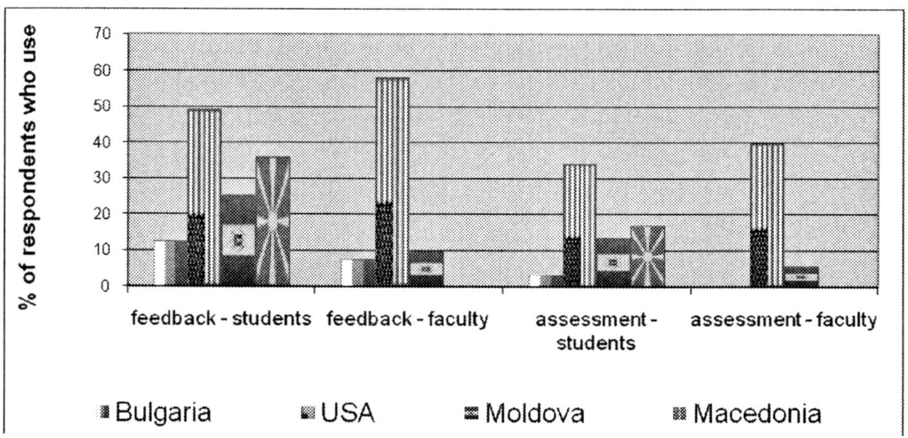

future comparisons of this type. CMS software is becoming popular outside of the United States, as evidenced by the advent of such open source tools as Moodle (http://moodle.org/) (Nagel, 2008). As of this writing, CMS is not the only suitable online assessment tool, with the advent of new e-conferencing tools[2] such as Elluminate [http://www.elluminate.com/], and Adobe Connect [http://www.adobe.com/products/connect/], etc.). These packages allow for synchronous teaching and learning interactions.

Role of Libraries as Technology Providers

A set of two 2 tests (one for student data, one for faculty responses) was calculated for Country by Response Selection (Seldon, Neutral, Often) cross tabulations (Bonferroni adjustment). Two important outcomes emerge from the results displayed in Figure 10. One concerns the role of libraries at academic institutions. Faculty members and students within nations expressed very similar views of library-based technology services. Both students and faculty members in Bulgaria evidenced negative views about their libraries' role in providing technology. In contrast, American students and instructors viewed libraries positively in this provider role. The second issue is the role of the academic library per se. Even at American institutions only 60% of respondents viewed libraries as campus technology centers. The changing role of the library as provider of technology instruction is clearly noted by the American Library Association (Fidishun, 2001). On the other hand, a palpable and growing gap exists between library services and culture and expectations by Millennials[3]. Perhaps the Eastern European institutions will view these American results as a benchmark for change in the role of the library—depending upon whether or not, or to what degree, this fits with universities' intellectual culture.

Representatives of the American Library Association call for libraries to become campus technology hubs (Fidishun, 2001); the locus for cutting-edge technology—especially its dissemination; this is an entirely new, but potentially positive role for librarians. Such stance is recognized by the European Union's "Information Society" (http://ec.europa.eu/information_society/index_en.htm). However, while Eastern Europeans proved familiar with this trend, Internet cafes, not the library, remain the place where many young people access technology (Dimchev & Miltenoff, 2006).

The issue of the library's role is further complicated by the "disconnection between library culture and the millennial generation values"

Figure 10. Percent of respondents reporting that library is important technology provider

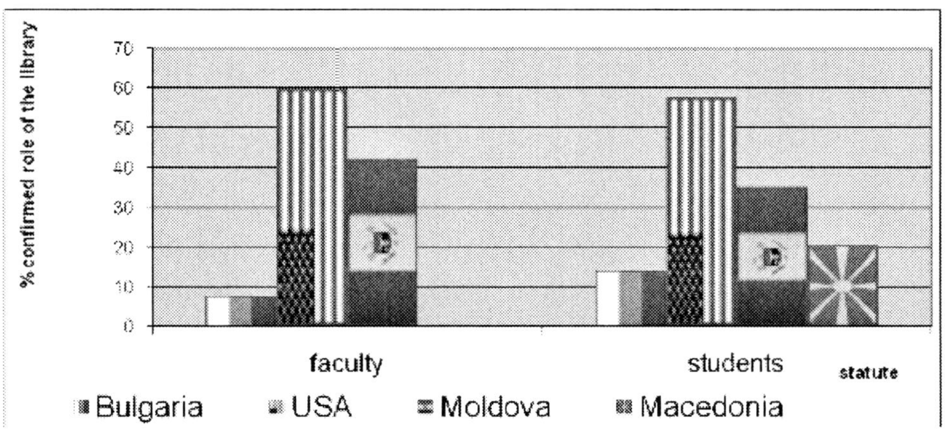

Figure 11. Percent of students reporting levels access to computer labs by country

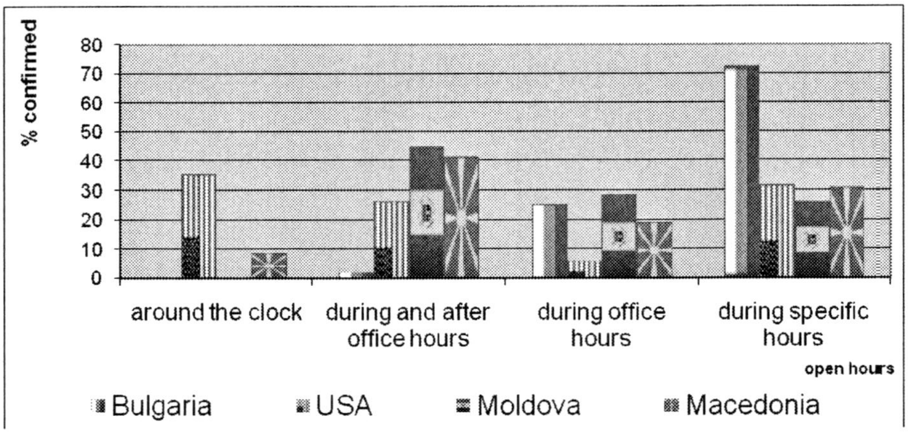

(Thomas & McDonald, 2006, p.4). Some experts claim that further delay in turning libraries into campus technology hubs pushes students away and slows the adoption of instructional technology (Albright & Nworie, 2008; Oden et al., 2001; Senn Breivik & Gee, 2006).

Access to Computer Labs

An item was developed via which information was requested about the temporal availability of the computer labs. A set of four chi square tests (over choices of when tech labs are open), for the Country by Response Selection (Selected Vs, not selected) cross tabulations were calculated (error rates adjusted via the Bonferroni method). As shown in Figure 11 and 12, faculty members and students reported differential levels of technology access. Around-the-clock use of computer labs potentially produces an advantage for American students. However, these data must be interpreted cautiously given the following two factors: First, overall time-of-use should be controlled in future studies. Perhaps Eastern Europeans adjust their

Figure 12. Percent of faculty members reporting levels access to computer labs by country

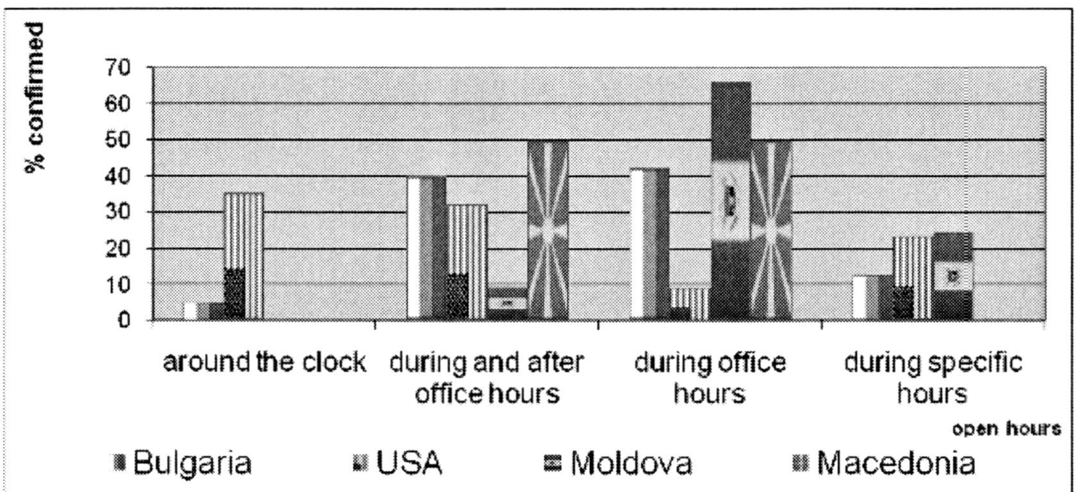

daily schedules thus attaining as many lab hours as do their American counterparts. Second, quality-of-use factors were not addressed by the questionnaire, producing the possibility that Eastern European students may use labs more strategically and intensively during the hours available to them. Little educational advantage would accrue, for example, to American students playing computer games at 2:00 A.M. Also, assistance with technology and course content would probably overlap with lab hours (in assessment of learning effects). However, the most parsimonious interpretation remains that American students enjoy greater access to instructional technology via university labs then do Eastern European postsecondary learners. Access issues most likely remain the single most important factor in assessing the digital divide between students in the U.S. and those in Moldova, Bulgaria, and Macedonia.

LIMITATIONS

This project sought to compare online communication in education of two rather different educational systems from four different countries, three of them on the have-nots side of the digital divide. Cultural differences were taken into account, especially when translating the instrument in four different languages. The researchers were seeking to establish a cultural parallel when asking the questions in the survey and interpret, rather than translate the English version into Russian, Bulgarian and Macedonian. The researchers are fully aware of the complex cultural issues. On the other hand, the researchers were interested in an initial assessment of differences between the four countries. A comprehensive, culturally and anthropologically un-biased study would required significantly more time and finances than did this exploratory work. Based on these findings, researchers should consider expanding the scope of the research and turning it into a multi-disciplinary and multi-cultural comparison of how online communications vary across borders and educational systems. Other than the fact that four countries were involved, the present methods did not allow findings to be organized around cultural differences. It is essential to move to this deeper level of interpretative sophistication. Despite the language difficulties, the exploration of the cultural context suggests the need to apply ethnographic approaches to international investigations of online and hybrid methods.

CONCLUSION

Online education is a global trend and is not solely a domain of developed countries. Online education may open a venue for developing countries to educate their populace more economically than is possible in traditional bricks-and-mortar settings (Bollag & Overland, 2001; Dhanarajan, 2001). Online interaction is a key factor for the success of online education. It increases students' motivation thus boosting retention and presumably achievement.

With some already-noted exceptions, the present data match the extant literature. A digital divide exists between developed and developing countries. Eastern European universities lag behind in hardware and bandwidth availability and the faculty members and students are well aware of it. It is important to note that the structure of the faculty and student body in the United States and Eastern Europe varies significantly; this influence acceptance in technology in education can be an important topic for future research. The following findings are defensible from the present data:

- Eastern European faculty members and students use alternate modalities (e.g. Internet cafes, home computers) to access hardware and bandwidth more so than do their North American counterparts.
- Eastern European faculty members' and

students' satisfaction and comfort with technology is relatively strong, even in comparison these values with respondents in the U.S.A.

- In Eastern Europe, Education students use computer labs, but not as often as do students from other disciplines. Eastern European respondents use campus labs less often, perhaps because the labs are open for fewer hours per day. Administration of computer lab use in Eastern European universities can probably be improved by expanding hours and securing access during unconventional times.
- Faculty members and administrators may not be effectively responding to students' preferred modalities for online communication. Specifically, more emphasis should probably be placed on interactive communication tools other than e-mail. We suspect that Millennials want faculty members to move from asynchronous to synchronous tools, even in hybrid courses.
- Online assessment is employed relatively infrequently, considering the technology and options available, even in 2003.
- Libraries as technology providers are perhaps underutilized particularly in Bulgaria, Moldova, and Macedonia.

RECOMMENDATIONS

Two major recommendations based on the survey include revising and supporting the role of academic libraries by scholastic officials and planners, who could also profitably work toward provision of 24/7 lab access. It remains to be determined whether libraries are the most effective institutions for managing technology access in Eastern Europe; this question remains a fertile target for researchers and policy analysts. Other issues that deserve the attention of policy makers and investigators include the following:

- Universities in Eastern European countries need to improve technology performance (Internet and Intranet) to support both pure online and hybrid courses.
- Libraries must replace Internet cafes as convenient and safe places for young people to access courses.
- Future studies of lab use should include metrics related to learning outcomes and such control variables as effective use (study versus gaming, for example), strategic use (students scheduling use effectively during open sessions), and staffing patterns (whether or not, or to what degree, technology and content assistance is available during open hours).

We posed essentially two questions about faculty and student satisfaction in working with technology. Future investigators can consider other parameters to better evaluate levels of satisfaction (e.g., involve cross-cultural studies and psychometric benchmarks to more precisely define and measure satisfaction relative to availability and use). The improvement of faculty and student satisfaction can lead to a better and faster application of technology in higher education. Survey results revealed some unexpected outcomes: (1) instructors/professors and students at U.S. institutions clearly did not employ technology to its full potential in 2003. Computer labs in Moldovan, Bulgarian, and Macedonian universities remain dormant for the greater part of the week (evenings, nights and weekends).

In conclusion, maximization of hybrid instruction will require practiced e-technology skills on the part of both instructors and students. Internalizing such skills will allow instructors to think more about the nail and less about the hammer as they creatively weld effective face-to-face instruction, existing technologies, and emerging technologies. As of 2003, some gaps were noted both in technology use and support; it is interesting to note that that a preliminary analysis of data from 2007 revealed very similar patterns to the information noted here (Miltenoff, Hoover & Tzokov, 2008). It is imperative that policy makers create systems to fill in these gaps.

REFERENCES

Albion, P. R. (2001). Some factors in the development of self-efficacy beliefs for computer use among teacher education students [electronic version]. *Journal of Technology and Teacher Education, 9*(3), 321-347. Retrieved on November 1, 2002, from http://www.aace.org/dl/index.cfm/fuseaction/View/paperID/6502

Albright, M., & Nworie, J. (2001). Rethinking academic technology leadership in an era of change. *Educause Quarterly, 31*(1), 14-23. Retrieved on August 22, 2008, from http://connect.educause.edu/Library/EDUCAUSE+Quarterly/RethinkingAcademicTechnol/4607

Andrews, R., & Haythornthwaite, C. (2007). *The sage handbook of e-learning research*. Thousand Oaks: SAGE.

Bekhradnia, B. (2005). *Обзорен преглед на висшето образование в България*. (An overview of higher education in Bulgaria). Sofia.

Bell, P. (2007, Summer). Predictors of college's student achievement in undergraduate asynchronous Web-based courses. *Education, 127*(4), 523–533.

Bennett, S., & Lockyer, L. (2004, September). Becoming an online teacher: Adapting to a changed environment for teaching and learning in higher education. *Educational Media International, 41*(3), 231–244. doi:10.1080/09523980410001680842

Berger, C. (2007). The millennium student: And now, evidence for the millennial instructor! *Educause Resource Center*. Retrieved on February 17, 2007 from http://www.educause.edu/ELI071/Program/10825?PRODUCT_CODE=ELI071/SESS39

Bollag, B., & Overland, M. A. (2001). Developing countries turn to distance education. *Chronicle of Higher Education, 47* (40), 29-31. Retrieved November 1, 2007, at: http://chronicle.com/weekly/v47/i40/40a02901.htm

Burnett, K., Bonnici, L., Miksa, S., & Joonmin, K. (2007, Winter). Frequency, intensity, and topicality in online learning: An exploration of the interaction dimensions that contribute to student satisfaction in online learning. *Journal of Education for Library and Information Science*, *48*(1), 21–35.

Carnevale, D. (2006, October). E-mail is for old people. *Chronicle of the Higher Education, 53*(7). P. A27. Retrieved on February 14, 2007, from http://chronicle.com/weekly/v53/i07/07a02701.htm

Conrad, R., & Donaldson, A. (2004). *Engaging the online learner: Activities and resources for creative instruction*. San Francisco, CA: Jossey-Bass.

Dhanarajan, G. (2001). Distance education: Promise, performance, and potential. *Open Learning, 16*(1), 61-68. Retrieved on November 1, 2007, from http://search.ebscohost.com/login.aspx?direct=true&db=aph&AN=4041530&site=ehost-live

Dimchev, A., & Miltenoff, P. (2006). Books, libraries, media, and new information technologies: Seeking the balance. The new information technologies (NIT) and the risks for the coming generation. *Proceedings of the International Scientific Conference "Children and Libraries,"* October 5-8, 2005, Belgrade, Yugoslavia. Retrieved on February 6, 2009, from http://web.stcloudstate.edu/pmiltenoff/ioc_2006/balance_nit.doc

Fidishun, D. (2001, March). People servers vs. information providers: The impact of service orientation on technology training. *Information Technology and Libraries, 20*(1). Retrieved on December 12, 2008, from http://www.ala.org/ala/mgrps/divs/lita/ital/vol20/number1/fidishun.cfm

Finkelstein, J. (2006). *Learning in real time: Synchronous teaching and learning online*. San Francisco, CA: Jossey-Bass.

Gould, M., & Padavano, D. (2006, May). 7 ways to improve student satisfaction in online courses. *Online Classroom*, 1-2.

Green, M., Hilken, J., Friedman, H., Grossman, K., Gasiewski, J., Adler, R., & Sabini, J. (2005, March). Communication via instant messenger: Short- and long-Term Effects. *Journal of Applied Social Psychology*, *35*(3), 445–462. doi:10.1111/j.1559-1816.2005.tb02130.x

Hiltz, S. R. (1995). *The virtual classroom: Learning without limits via computer networks*. Norwood, NJ: Ablex Pub.

Huck, S. (2004). *Reading statistics and research* (4th ed.). Boston, MA: Pearson/Allyn and Bacon.

Kawachi, P. (2003, April). Initiating intrinsic motivation in online education: Review of the current state of the art. *Interactive Learning Environments*, *11*(1), 59–82. doi:10.1076/ilee.11.1.59.13685

Kumpulainen, K., & Renshaw, P. (2007, April). Cultures of learning. *International Journal of Educational Research*, *46*(3/4), 109–115. doi:10.1016/j.ijer.2007.09.009

Lee, J., Carter-Wells, J., Glaeser, B., Ivers, K., & Street, C. (2006, Spring). Facilitating the development of learning community in an online graduate program. *Quarterly Review of Distance Education*, *7*(1), 13–33.

Miltenoff, P., Hoover, J., & Tzokov, G. (2008). Interaction among students and faculty: A comparative study. *Proceedings of Informing Science and IT Education conference*, 2008, Varna, Bulgaria.

Mullinix, B. B., & McCurry, D. (2003, September/October). Balancing the learning equation: Exploring effective mixtures of technology, teaching, and learning [electronic version]. *The Technology Source*. Retrieved on November 20, 2008, from http://technologysource.org/article/balancing_the_learning_equation/

Nagel, D. (2008, January). Open source poised for surge in education. *THE Journal*. Retrieved on January 30, 2008, from http://www.thejournal.com/articles/21900

National Evaluation and Accreditation Agency's Newsletter. Бюлетин на НАОА (2002). *4*. Sofia.

Oden, R., Temple, D., Cottrell, J., Griggs, R., Turney, G., & Wojcik, F. (2001). Merging library and computing services at Kenyon College: A progress report. *Educause Quarterly, 24*(4), 18-25. Retrieved on August 22, 2008, from http://www.educause.edu/ir/library/pdf/EQM0141.pdf

Popov, N., & Pironkova, M. (2007). *Образователната система в България* (Educational system in Bulgaria). Sofia.

Prensky, M. (2001). *Digital natives, digital immigrants.* Retrieved on December 15, 2008, from http://www.marcprensky.com/writing/Prensky%20-%20Digital%20Natives,%20Digital%20Immigrants%20-%20Part1.pdf

Read, B. (2007). 'A digitally isolated Africa.' *The Wired Campus of Chronicle of Higher Education*. Retrieved on October 26, 2007, from http://chronicle.com/wiredcampus/article/?id=2447

Report e-Bulgaria. Доклад е-България. (2006). Фондация «Приложни изследвания и комуникации». София. Retrieved on February 15, 2007, from http://www.daits.government.bg/projects.php

Schrum, L., Burbank, M. D., & Capps, R. (2007, July). Preparing future teachers for diverse schools in an online learning community: Perceptions and practice. *The Internet and Higher Education, 10*(3), 204–211. doi:10.1016/j.iheduc.2007.06.002

Schrum, L., & Hong, S. (2002, July). Dimensions and strategies for online success: Voices from experienced educators. *JALN*, 6(1), 57-68. Retrieved on October 26, 2007, from http://www.aln.org/publications/jaln/v6n1/v6n1_schrum.asp

Senn Breivik, P., & Gee, G. (2006). *Higher education in the Internet age: Libraries creating a strategic edge*. Westport, CN: Praeger Publishers.

Stephenson, J. (Ed.). (2002). *Teaching & learning online: New pedagogies for new technologies*. London: Kogan Page.

The E-Learning Committee. (2002). *E-learning committee survey on Web enhanced and Web based teaching*. St. Cloud State University. E-mail correspondence with R. Kolb, E. Kang & J. Burgeson.

Thomas, C., & McDonald, R. (2006). Disconnects between library culture and millennial generation values. *Educause Quarterly, 26*(4). Retrieved on February 5, 2007, from http://www.educause.edu/apps/eq/eqm06/eqm0640.asp?print=yes

Vrasidas, C., & Glass, G. V. (Eds.). (2002). *Current perspectives on applied information technologies: Distance education and distributed learning* [electronic version]. Greenwich, CT: Information Age Publishing. Retrieved on December 1, 2002, from http://www.infoagepub.com

Young, A., & Norgard, C. (2006, April). Assessing the quality of online courses from the students' perspective. *The Internet and Higher Education, 9*(2), 107–115. doi:10.1016/j.iheduc.2006.03.001

Young, J. (2002). 'Hybrid' teaching seeks to end the divide between traditional and online instruction. The *Chronicle of Higher Education*, A33. Retrieved from http://chronicle.com/free/v48/i28/28a03301.htm

ENDNOTES

1 Briefly on CMS: http://en.wikipedia.org/wiki/Course_management_system

2 Briefly on e-conference tools: http://en.wikipedia.org/wiki/Webinar

3 Briefly about the Millennials: http://en.wikipedia.org/wiki/Millennials, otherwise, Howe, N. & Strauss, W. (2000). *Millennials Rising: The Next Great Generation*. New York: Vintage Books) (Thomas & McDonald, 2006).

APPENDIX A

In conjunction with Shoumen University "St. Konstatin Preslavski" and St. Cloud State University.

INFORMATION TECHNOLOGY LAB

Faculty Survey

Please answer this questionnaire regarding information technologies in your University. When asked about the *computer lab*, please consider a lab with various types of software and Internet connection.

Please respond the best you can. You will be using the scale shown in Table 3.

Table 3. Scale symbols

SD	D	N	A	SA
STRONGLY DISAGREE	DISAGREE	NEUTRAL	AGREE	STRONGLY AGREE
NA	**R**	**S**	**O**	**VO**
NOT AT ALL	RARELY	SOMEWHAT	OFTEN	VERY OFTEN

Please circle the responding value.

You may complete this questionnaire (see Table 4) using email (pmiltenoff@stcloudstate.edu) and/or using the following Web site: http://web.stcloudstate.edu/pmiltenoff/survey/survey_f.html

Table 4. Faculty survey

	Statements	***Responses*** **strongly disagree disagree neutral agree strongly agree**						
1.	The speed and quality of the university Internet connection meets my expectations	SD	D	N	A	SA		
2.	The university Intranet connection (your campus Local Area Network) meets my expectations	SD	D	N	A	SA		
3.	I use alternative means to access Internet and use a computer (at home, public library, Internet cafes, at friends, etc.)	SD	D	N	A	SA		
4.	I am comfortable with the use of technology (computer, Internet, VCR, projector, cellular, ATM machines, etc.)	SD	D	N	A	SA		

5.	I am familiar with the use of technology (computer, Internet, VCR, projector, cellular, ATM machines, etc.)	SD	D	N	A	SA	
		strongly disagree	**disagree**	**neutral**	**agree**	**strongly agree**	
6.	Faculty in math, information science, and other computer-related majors use computer lab at the university	SD	D	N	A	**SA**	No such majors
7.	Faculty in technical related fields use computer lab at the university	SD	D	N	A	**SA**	No such majors
8.	Faculty teaching sciences use computer lab at the university	SD	D	N	A	**SA**	No such majors
9.	Faculty teaching art and other majors like history, psychology, sociology, etc. use computer lab at the university	SD	D	N	A	**SA**	No such majors
10.	Faculty teaching education use computer lab at the university	SD	D	N	A	**SA**	No such majors
		Not at all	**Rarely**	**Somewhat**	**Often**	**Very often**	
11.	Faculty at your university use *email* as a part of the learning process	NA	R	S	O	**VO**	
12.	Faculty at your university use *chat* use as a part of the learning process	NA	R	S	O	**VO**	
13.	Faculty at your university use *listserv* use as a part of the learning process	NA	R	S	O	**VO**	
14.	Faculty at your university use *instant messaging* (instant messenger: ICQ, MSN Messenger, Yahoo Messenger and/or AOL Instant Messenger) as a part of the learning process	NA	R	S	O	**VO**	
15.	Faculty from your university participate in virtual discussion groups as a part of the learning process?	NA	R	S	O	**VO**	
16.	Faculty from your university provide feedback using various electronic means (e.g. email, chat, listserv, instant messaging, etc.)	NA	R	S	O	**VO**	

17.	Faculty from your university provide assessment and evaluation using online communication means (e.g. email, chat, listserv, instant messaging, etc.)	NA		R	S	O	**VO**
18.	Library plays important role in providing access to technology (e.g. VCR, projectors, laptop, Internet access, etc.)	NA		R	S	O	**VO**
19.	Please specify when do faculty have access to the computer lab at your university.	'Round the clock	During office and after office hours		During office hours	During specific hours	
20.	Demographic info:	Age:	Gender:	Years of Teaching:			
21.	Please reflect any other forms for virtual communications, which have been omitted in this questionnaire and faculty at your University use.						
22.	Please share your opinion, who do you think benefits more of the use of technology: faculty or students						
23.	Please share your opinion about any other topics that relate to the use of technology in education						

We appreciate your participation!

APPENDIX B

In conjunction with Shoumen University "St. Konstatin Preslavski" and St. Cloud State University.

INFORMATION TECHNOLOGY LAB

Students' Survey

Please answer this questionnaire regarding information technologies in your University. When asked about the *computer lab*, please consider a lab with various types of software and Internet connection.

Please respond the best you can. You will be using the scale shown in Table 5.

Table 5. Scale symbols

SD	**D**	**N**	**A**	**SA**
STRONGLY DISAGREE	DISAGREE	NEUTRAL	AGREE	STRONGLY AGREE
NA	**R**	**S**	**O**	**VO**
NOT AT ALL	RARELY	SOMEWHAT	OFTEN	VERY OFTEN

Please circle the responding value

You may complete this questionnaire (see Table 6) using email (pmiltenoff@stcloudstate.edu) and/or using the following Web site: http://web.stcloudstate.edu/pmiltenoff/survey/survey_s.html

Table 6. Student survey

№	Statements	Responses: strongly disagree	disagree	neutral	agree	strongly agree	
24.	The speed and quality of the university Internet connection meets my expectations	SD	D	N	A	SA	
25.	The university Intranet connection (your campus Local Area Network) meets my expectations	SD	D	N	A	SA	
26.	I use alternative means to access Internet and use a computer (at home, public library, Internet cafes, at friends, etc.)	SD	D	N	A	SA	
27.	I am comfortable with the use of technology (computer, Internet, VCR, projector, cellular, ATM machines, etc.)	SD	D	N	A	SA	
28.	I am familiar with the use of technology (computer, Internet, VCR, projector, cellular, ATM machines, etc.)	SD	D	N	A	SA	
		strongly disagree	**disagree**	**neutral**	**agree**	**strongly agree**	
29.	Students in math, information science, and other computer-related fields use computer lab at the university	SD	D	N	A	SA	No such majors
30.	Students in technical related fields use computer lab at the university	SD	D	N	A	SA	No such majors
31.	Students majoring in sciences use the computer lab at the university	SD	D	N	A	SA	No such majors
32.	Students majoring in art and other majors like history, psychology, sociology, etc. use the computer lab at the university	SD	D	N	A	SA	No such majors
33.	Students majoring in education use the computer lab at the university	SD	D	N	A	SA	No such majors
		Not at all	**Rarely**	**Somewhat**	**Often**	**Very often**	
34.	Students at your university use *email* as a part of the learning process	NA	R	S	O	VO	
35.	Students at your university use *chat* use as a part of the learning process	NA	R	S	O	VO	
36.	Students at your university use *listserv* use as a part of the learning process	NA	R	S	O	VO	

37.	Students at your university use *instant messaging* (instant messenger: ICQ, MSN Messenger, Yahoo Messenger and/or AOL Instant Messenger) as a part of the learning process	NA	R	S	O	VO
38.	Students from your university participate in virtual discussion groups as a part of the learning process?	NA	R	S	O	VO
39.	Students receive feedback using various electronic means (e.g. email, chat, listserv, instant messaging, etc.)	NA	R	S	O	VO
40.	Students receive assessment and evaluation using online communication means (e.g. email, chat, listserv, instant messaging, etc.)	NA	R	S	O	VO
41.	Library plays important role in providing access to technology (e.g. VCR, projectors, laptop, Internet access, etc.)	NA	R	S	O	VO
42.	Please specify when do students have access to the computer lab at your university.	'Round the clock	During office and after office hours	During office hours	During specific hours	
43.	Demographic info:	Age:	Gender:	Major:		
44.	Please reflect any other forms for virtual communications, which have been omitted in this questionnaire and students at your University use.					
45.	Please share your opinion, who do you think benefits more of the use of technology: faculty or students					
46.	Please share your opinion about any other topics that relate to the use of technology in education					

We appreciate your participation!

Chapter 16
The Efficacy of Security Awareness Programs from a Cross-Cultural Perspective

B. Dawn Medlin
Appalachian State University, USA

Charlie C. Chen
Appalachian State University, USA

ABSTRACT

Different cultures have different technological capabilities and, therefore, face a diverse set of security challenges. Increasing security awareness training can alert users to the existence of security vulnerabilities and threats. A user's ability to understand these threats and vulnerabilities can empower them to take preventive and corrective actions in the event of such problems. This study proposes that users adopt situational awareness learning that is more receptive to high individualists than low individualists in their ability to increase their security awareness levels, which include comprehension, projection, and actions. We conducted an intercultural study to investigate if users from the U.S. and Taiwan exposed to the same situational awareness learning would have different performance in security awareness outcomes. Our findings confirmed that security awareness is cultural-ware learning, and our proposed situational awareness is a more useful learning approach to high individualists than low individualists.

INTRODUCTION

Lack of security awareness on the part of human beings can present security technology challenges that can often result in negative consequences. As an example, anti-virus software can alert one to suspicious emails, however, some users may go ahead and open those emails without even thinking of their potential adverse consequences. Other security breaches, such as identity theft, and dumpster diving, can also be caused by users' carelessness and lack of knowledge. Technological solutions are effective only if users know how to utilize them. Security-savvy users may be able to act by detecting or predicting problems and next taking the appropriate actions to prevent and correct security breaches. Improving security awareness is a preventive measure which is, much less costly and certainly more effective than being reactive to costly situations.

DOI: 10.4018/978-1-60566-852-9.ch016

Security awareness training is an effective approach in making users aware of the importance of securing their surrounding environment (O'Boyle, 2008). International firms, such as Daimler-Chrysler (Grant, 2007), consider employee security awareness as one of the key performance indicators of a successful security operation. Members of the European Network and Information Security Agency (ENISA), representing 67 government departments and private companies in nine European countries, are actively conducting internal and external auditing to assess their actual state of security awareness (Filipek, 2007). Although different countries may have different states of security awareness, increasing that awareness is unequivocally important for that may be affected.

This study will investigate the efficacy of web-based information security awareness programs from a cross-cultural perspective. Subjects from Taiwan and the United States participated in web-based programs, which were created to enhance their security awareness knowledge level. Both pre- and post-tests were given to assess both cultures' receptivity to the use of technology-driven security awareness programs.

BACKGROUND

Information security deals with issues related to authorization, authentication, availability, integrity, non-repudiation, and privacy. These security issues are invariably very dissimilar within different countries. A cross-cultural study on the awareness of users in the area of availability shows that Chinese users are less aware of spyware and viruses than their U.S. counterparts (Schmidt, 2008). In the privacy area, a report on Internet Enemies shows that 13 countries have been exercising a more rigorous censorship than most countries (Reporters without Borders, 2008). For instance, China filters online information based on key words and has the world's largest prison for online dissidents. Belarus bans anti-government websites via the use of denial of services. Libya owns the main Internet service provider, the General Post and Telecommunications Company (GPTC), and if their citizens spread online information that can endanger the country's authority they could face the death penalty. All of these examples demonstrated that national security concerns can easily compromise personal privacy. Thus, it is important that residents in any county be aware of privacy-related security risks.

Security issues manifest themselves in various forms in different cultures. Countries establish different codes of conducts related to the use of information and communication technologies (ICT) in order to improve information security awareness and ethics (Bia and Kalika, 2007). Culture is the habitual method of doing things over time (Hofstede, 1993). Culture influences are acceptable ways to process information, such as labeling, languages, and symbols (Triandis, 1995). Moreover, culture defines an individual's societal role and prescribes guiding principles in relation to security threat reactions. As a result, culture has influenced the formation of many security measures, such as national security policies, information ethics, security training, privacy, etc. It is therefore imperative to incorporate the culture into the design of IT applications (e.g. security awareness training systems) to improve their perceived values (Agrawal and Haleem, 2003) and adoption (Montealegre, 1998).

The increase of security awareness and cautious behavior at the individual's level can improve the information security performance of an organization (Albrechtsen, 2007). Thus, the focus of security awareness training must be developed according to the needs of individual users in different countries and in their different cultures.

Improving Security Awareness via Situational Awareness Approach

Awareness is "realization, perception or knowledge" according to Merriam-Webster dictionary. Security awareness is the knowledge and attitude a general user possesses in order to protect personal physical and information assets. For instance, a user needs to remember logging off computer whenever leaving his/her office. Virus protection software needs to be updated regularly. As we are ubiquitously connected via the Internet, information confidentiality, integrity and availability is easily compromised when users lack awareness of security risks. Security awareness is role-based learning, thus highlighting the need for a clear definition in relation to the roles and responsibilities of a user within the IT system of an organization. Awareness of security risks and the availability of counter measures pose the first line of defense to secure information assets from internal and external threats. The goal of security awareness is to instill general users with a natural reflex for all security threats, according to Computer and Network Security Task Force (2008). Security awareness can result in the reduction of human-related errors, including theft, fraud and misuse of information assets (Drevin, kruger and Steyn, 2007). Through the use of training and education users can learn the necessary skills and knowledge to perform IT security control activities.

Situational awareness is a user's perception, understanding, and the ability to predict changes to environmental dynamics. Business activities that primarily deal with challenges in situational awareness include aviation, air traffic control, and military command and control, and power plant operations. Situational awareness makes users aware of their surroundings as well as the environmental elements and their contextual meanings (Endsley, 1995). Facilitating this awareness in their working environment allows employees to form a mental model to both understand the current risks of a situation and to predict and possibly prevent the potential adverse effects of these risks. Most users are not sensitive to information security threats in their surrounding environment. As reported by Wilson and Hash (2003), an organization can potentially protect itself from security threats by simply improving a user's level of security awareness in their working environment (Wilson and Hash, 2003).

Mental models are "mechanisms whereby humans are able to generate descriptions of system purpose and form, explanations of system functioning and observed system states, and prediction of future states" (Rouse and Morris 1985). A complete mental model of security awareness is to be aware of different forms of security threats, understand how these threats work and predict potential outcomes of allowing them to continue. The awareness is about the perceptions of security threats, since not all of them are obvious.

A comprehensive security framework consists of three basic components: people, technology and process (Kark et al., 2007). None of these components alone can secure the environment. Security awareness is to address security issues related to people. An improvement in security awareness of people can identify potential security risks, and resort to technological solutions or business process transformation. General users with a higher security awareness level can quickly address those risks and respond to them than users may be able to with a lower level of awareness. Lack of security awareness of general users can confer the other two key components useless. Thus, it is important to first and foremost improve the security awareness level of general users. For example, a user with a higher security awareness level can better sense impending security threats. Laptop theft and run-of-the-mill virus infections are two typical security incidents that can easily be prevented and minimized if users learn to lock their computer and use anti-virus software to check suspicious emails. These two security incidents alone account for $20 million U.S. dollars of loss, according to a 2008 Computer Security

Institute/U.S. Federal Bureau of Investigation survey with 131 respondents (http://www.gocsi.com/forms/csi_survey.jhtml).

A complete mental model of security awareness is to be aware of different forms of security threats, understand how these threats work and predict potential outcomes of allowing them to continue. The awareness is about the perceptions of security threats, since not all of them are so obvious. A user with a higher security awareness level can better sense impending security threats then those users who are unaware of the security threats that surround them. This is the rudimentary form of a mental model that can be derived from the situational awareness-learning program. Perceptions can arouse interest, thereby leading to a greater understanding about how the identified threats function. Comprehension is the second level of learning outcomes resulting from situational awareness programs. Taking actions in response to security risks is the third level of learning outcomes.

Comprehension resulting from situational security awareness programs can assist in more efficiently forming a coherent mental model of the studied subjects, and the appropriate plan of action can be taken to cope with the situation (Sarter and Woods, 1991; Fracker, 1991). Situational awareness, according to Endsley and Garland (2000), is an effective user-centered learning approach that improves the perception, comprehension and projection ability of users to secure their surroundings (Endsley and Garland, 2000).

Situational security awareness training immerses an individual into his/her familiar environment to improve the efficiency of processing information. To successfully implement the training, it is important to align the cultural factors (values, beliefs and assumptions) of users with the managerial practices (Hofstede, 1993; Kirkman and Shapiro, 1997). It is plausible that situational security awareness training is a more efficient alternative than the traditional face-to-face training in improving security awareness levels.

Security Awareness Levels of General Users Vary with Cultures

People in different cultures have different levels of security sensitivity depending upon their social and technical environments. In addition, these socio-technical backgrounds have resulted in the formation of varying security awareness levels of general users in relation to security risks. Due to differences in information communications and telecommunication (ICT) infrastructure, varying forms of security risks (e.g. external, internal, virtual, physical and natural risks) have been formed. This process has gradually shaped the way public users perceive and respond to security threats. Take for instance the individualism (IDI) dimension. Individuals in high IDI cultures are self-oriented and believe in individual decision-making initiatives (McCoy, Galleta and King, 2005). Collectivists react more negatively to job insecurity than individualists (Probst and Lawler, 2006).

Security awareness is a user-involvement exercise as previous evidences indicated. As such, high IDI individuals care about their personal privacy and know that the government has a very small role to play in protecting their personal privacy. Additionally, these individuals understand that in order to increase their knowledge of security awareness the responsibility is theirs and not the governments. In contrast, and as seen in different countries and cultures, personal privacy right are often yielded to the government if the collective interests of the society as a whole are greater than that of an individual's personal privacy desires. As an example, the government of the People's Republic of China asked the cooperation of multinational enterprises, such as Google, to release personal communication records about an individual citizen suspected of violating national interests (Turban, Leidner, McLean and Wetherbe, 2008). This example shows a clear contrast that individual security awareness level is higher in the high IDI culture than in the low IDI culture.

As previously stated, within the realm of security management, individualism is a salient cultural dimension that can have potential influence on an individual's security awareness. Power distance pertains to topics related to social inequality. Masculinity addresses topics related to gender-based decision making process. Uncertainty avoidance discusses topics related to social issues. A cursory search of key words of "security" and "culture" in the databases ABI/Inform Complete and Business Source Complete showed that ample opportunities exist to bridge these two areas of study. Standardization is more receptive to people from high power distance, high uncertainty avoidance and high-context cultures (Newburry and Yakova, 2006). In this logic, standardization of security policy and infrastructure could be more receptive to people from those cultures. Lack of studies on the cultural influence in relation to security management should therefore focus on the investigation of whether the issue of the IDI cultural dimension has any particular influence on the effectiveness of security awareness training programs.

High Individualists Have a Higher Individual Security Awareness Level

To validate our propositions that information security awareness levels of individuals vary with their culture, we first examined the relationship between the individualistic culture and security awareness level. The goal of this study is to propose hypotheses to test if situational security awareness programs have varying effects on the improvement of security awareness levels of general users. If so, are people from high individualistic cultures more receptive to situational awareness training programs than people from low individualistic cultures?

Individualists (Americans) react more positively to job insecurity, whereas collectivists (Chinese) react negatively (Probst and Lawler, 2006). President Bush's plan to privatize the Social Security system was deeply rooted in the individualism culture, according to the Democratic senator Max Baucus (Harrington, 2005). Online behaviors are another form of individualism-collectivism culture. Collectivists (e.g. Japan and Turkey) have a predisposition to associate security issues with financial risks, whereas individualists (US, UK and Denmark) are inclined to accept security as a part of products or services (including quality, convenience and satisfaction) or privacy issues (Kucuk, 2002). For this reason, collectivists are less receptive to online individual banking, because its perceived risks are higher than traditional physical banking (Charbaji and Jannoun, 2005).

National cultures have a systematic influence on the adoption decision of emerging technologies (Steers, Meyer and Sanchez-Runde, 2008). High individualism cultures have a positive effect on the perceived usefulness, perceived enjoyment and perceived ease of use of mobile Internet services (Lee, Choi, Kim and Hong, 2007). The influence of individualism culture has altered the perceptions of security and technology to secure individual assets. Individualists have a higher tolerance of risks and are more willing to adopt web-based security technology. Therefore, in comparison with the traditional F2F training approach, situational awareness training is a more innovative approach. Individualists are more likely to perceive the usefulness of this training approach and appreciate its potentials.

The purpose of security awareness is to instill the skills that users need in order to perform IT security control activities. According to Endsley (1995), users need to first become aware of security vulnerabilities in their surroundings, then predict future happenings of security incidences due to these vulnerabilities, and next to take the appropriate actions to resolve security breaches if they should occur (Endsley, 1995). Moreover, users who are able to predict potential adverse effects of these risks can assist in minimizing their effects should they surface.

The effectiveness of the situational training approach adopted in this study is to improve the three levels of security awareness - comprehension, projection and actions - that can potentially vary the degree of the individualism culture because of the unique nature of the "felt-involvement" which is embedded in this training approach. Situational and intrapersonal are two important elements of the "felt-involvement" feature (Richins and Bloch, 1986). Situational awareness training is to deliberately create a "felt-involvement" learning atmosphere so that users can easily immerse themselves into security situations.

We suspect that high individualists are more likely to be receptive to situational awareness learning than low individualists because the "felt involvement" feature creates less cognitive pressure on learners and ease the comprehension process. As the comprehension process is improved, projection and actions-taking process can be enhanced correspondingly. We therefore propose the following hypothesis.

- H1: Security Awareness Levels
- Hypothesis H1a: High individualists have a higher 1st level of security awareness than low individualists after receiving the situational training approach.
- Hypothesis H1b: High individualists have a higher 2nd level of security awareness than low individualists after receiving the situational training approach.
- Hypothesis H1c: High individualists have a higher 3rd level of security awareness than low individualists after receiving the situational training approach.

RESEARCH METHODOLOGY

This study used Macromedia Flash as the application to develop an animation-based security awareness program based on Endsley's (1995) Situational Awareness Dynamic Decision Making Model and Situation Awareness Global Assessment Techniques. Experimental sessions were conducted with 160 Taiwanese and 100 American subjects to assess if culture is a relevant element to be considered when adopting situational security awareness programs. To understand the moderating effect of culture, we compared results collected from two separate studies in the U.S. and Taiwan with respect to the impact of situational vs. traditional security awareness programs on the improvement of the three aforementioned levels of security awareness. This manipulation control makes it possible to detect the effects of the single independent variable (training method) on training outcomes. With the training method as a control factor, any significant differences between these two studies indicate that the exogenous factors of computer self-efficacy, pre-test security awareness levels, and culture exist.

Course Materials

Two security awareness topics were popular with general users: password usage and desktop security. Users need to know and understand how to create a strong password which would consist of a combination of a certain length, numbers, alpha characters, upper and lower case letters as well as well as the the need to make frequent changes to protect his/her password.

The scope of desktop security includes the use of screen savers, preventing the viewing of information on a computer screen, battery backup devices, and access control, according to NIST-SP-800-50. The authors developed course materials concerning the two aforementioned topic areas while narrowing our research only to one subtopic from each area: (1) creating a secure password (Figure 1) and (2) protecting the physical assets of information that may appear on a desktop. A situational awareness environment was created that would allow the deliverance of these two subtopics (Figure 2). Although it is easy to create a password, practice is often needed in order to create a secure one. Many users are

Figure 1. Creating a secure password

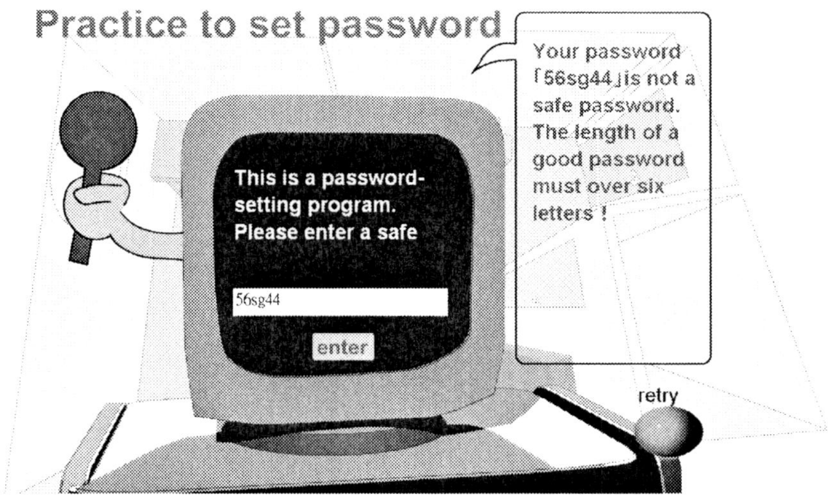

not aware of the importance of creating a strong password or do not know how to create one. A weak password can invite intrusion to personal information property.

This training goes beyond the simple training of just creating a password. In this training, subjects learned testing the strength of password created each time against the following criteria:

1. A secure password needs to have 8 or more characters in length;
2. A secure password combines letters, numbers and symbols;
3. A secure password randomizes the order of the password combination;
4. A secure password avoids sequences or repeated characters;
5. A secure password mixes uppercase and lowercase numbers and letters.

Figure 2. Protecting physical assets of information on a desktop

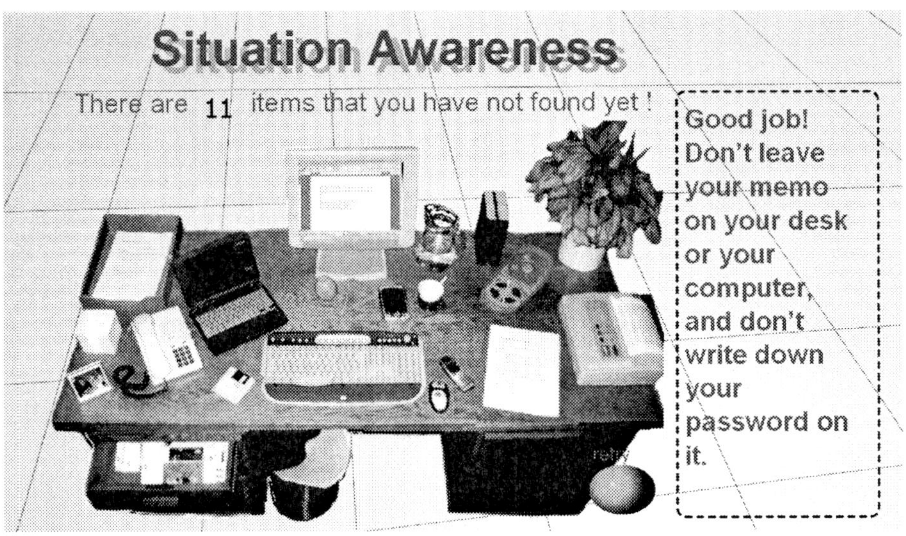

Desktop clearance is another security topic often underestimated by general users. Many users left login ID, password, customer's contact information, and mobile phone number on a notepad or a notebook. Very few users log off computers or bring computers with them when walking out for a business meeting or taking a break. The ignorance of desktop clearance can result in identity theft, and stolen of information properties. In this training, there are 10 information properties deliberately hidden on a desktop. Subjects need to discover those 10 items before completing the training. When discovering a new item each time, subjects would read a pop-up message regarding the importance of that item. For instance, when the notebook on computer is discovered and removed, the following message pops up: "Good job! Don't leave your memo on your desk or your computer, and don't write down your password on it." If the wrong item was discovered, another message pops up to redirect the subjects to other items on the desktop. For instance, when clicking on the phone subjects will receive the following message "No! You can leave the telephone on the desk." These two topics are closely related to the security awareness of general users, and often underestimated in the real life.

Measurement Design

The measurements of this study are comprised of an evaluation of computer efficacy and three levels of information security awareness (Appendix I). A pretest was conducted to assess participants' computer efficacy with the survey questionnaire instrument including questions related to computer-related knowledge and existing security awareness levels. These questions were used to assist us in assessing the repository of security knowledge and security awareness levels possessed by the subjects. In addition, we used this survey as a control to monitor the potential compounding effects of these prior competencies on learning outcomes. Further, a statistical test was conducted to assess the effect between experimental and control groups. After participants received training sessions, they participated in a post-test to assess their performance in each of the three levels of security awareness. Two security experts who are certified with the BS7799 security management certificate and two scholars who teach information security courses were invited to modify the survey questionnaire. Native U.S. speakers assisted with the translation of course materials from Chinese to English in order to accommodate the needs of the American students.

Two groups of college students were exposed to situational and traditional face-to-face learning approaches to assimilate security awareness topics. As previously discussed, high individualists would be more likely to perform better in the situational training and low individualists would be more likely to do so in the traditional training. Three levels of learning outcomes were measured at the end of a one-hour learning session.

In order to clearly understand if the training approach contributes to the difference in learning outcomes, subjects were also required to fill out survey questionnaires to self-report their computer self-efficacy and prior experiences related to security training. In addition, subjects were given a scenario to assess their response actions to security threats.

Experimental Subjects and Procedures

One hundred and sixty sophomores from a private university in Taiwan participated in the first round of this study. Another one hundred juniors from a public state university in the U.S. attended the second round. We deliberately compared the U.S. with Taiwanese subjects because American subjects are high individualists (IDV=91) and Taiwanese subjects are low individualists (IDV=17). The intent of this design is to increase the effect size so as to help us control the magnitude of moderating influence of the individualism culture on the relationship between situational awareness and learning outcomes. Effect size is a family of indices to measure the magnitude of influence of a treatment effect (Lipsey and Wilson, 1993). Each group of subjects was equally divided into one of two groups: experimental or control group. The control/experimental group designation was randomly determined before the pre-test in both countries. Subjects from the experimental group received the web-based situational awareness while other subjects from the control group received the traditional face-to-face learning method. Situational awareness treatment was delivered on the Internet, where subjects were instructed while in a lab setting to link to a website where two flash-based execution files were placed. Subjects were instructed to click on the files and begin interacting with the presented course materials. In another words, it was a blended learning approach. Instructors used Microsoft PowerPoint to present the same course materials used in the flash-based situational awareness in slides. It has been commonly known that the learning outcomes of face-to-face instructions are largely depends on the instructor. We took this potential effect into consideration and had the same instructor lecture students in the face-to-face instruction mode for American and Taiwanese subjects, respectively. Although the teacher was Chinese in both experimental settings, he has six years of university level teaching experience in an AACSB College of Business within an American university. It is still probable that the language/accent of the non-native English speaker could still influence the understanding of the content by the subjects. In order to further minimize the potential influence of cross-cultural communication, we developed the same course materials in Chinese and English for Chinese and American subjects, respectively. In addition, a teacher manual was strictly followed.

The "felt-involvement" feature is missing from this step-by-step instruction. For instance, the instructor first explained what constitute a weak password in a presentation slide. Then the instructors enlisted all passwords that are considered as a weak control, such as using birthday as a password, not mixing letter with numbers, and writing down passports and sticking them on a computer screen. Instructors further provided instructions on how to secure passwords and suggested some actions to reset passwords if they were lost. Tables 2 and 3 show the distribution of subjects receiving situational or face-to-face training at Taiwan and the U.S. sites, respectively. American subjects were not equally divided because we randomized these two treatments by class. Four classes participated in this study, with a total of 40 students of two classes receiving situational awareness and a total of 60 students of other two classes receiving the traditional face-to-face instruction. All subjects received 30 minute sessions. This counter-group design can help identify if a situational awareness approach is better than a traditional F2F learning approach at improving the level of security awareness for general users.

Table 2. Experimental design at the Taiwan site

Group	# of Subjects	Pretest	Learning Approach	Post-Test
Experimental Group (Situational Training)				
MIS Major	40	Computer Efficacy	Situational awareness	Information Security Awareness Measurements Scenario
International Business Major	40			
Control Group				
MIS Major	40	Computer Efficacy	Traditional F2F	Information Security Awareness Measurements Scenario
IB Major	40			

Table 3. Experimental design at the U.S. site

Group	# of Subjects	Pretest	Learning Approach	Post-Test
Experimental Group				
Business Major	40	Computer Efficacy	Situational awareness	Information Security Awareness Measurements
Control Group				
Business Majors	66	Computer Efficacy	Traditional F2F	Information Security Awareness Measurements

Statistical Data Analysis

Pre-Test Analysis

Table 4 shows that both the experimental and control groups at the Taiwan site are not significantly different related to general computer efficacy. However, subjects in the experimental group appear to have a significantly higher level of security awareness than subjects majoring in International Business with the p value 0.000 (<0.01).

In contrast, at the U.S. site as shown in Table 5 we also detected a significant difference between the situational awareness group and traditional learning group in the security awareness level. The computer efficacy in general does not vary very much between the experimental and control groups. Samples from both the U.S. and Taiwan sites have many similarities. This commonality of the experimental setting in both countries is a good control to assess if different training approaches can enlarge the differences in training outcomes. It should be noted that the experimental group in both countries tend to have a higher security awareness level before receiving situational training.

Table 4. T-test analysis for low individualists (Taiwanese)

	Sample Size	Computer Efficacy		Security awareness	
		Mean	S.D.	Mean	S.D.
Experimental Group	80	25.50	4.27	30.20	2.83
Control Group	80	24.55	3.86	25.46	4.64
Levene test	F	0.325		11.783	
	P value	0.569		0.001***	

P < 0.05 (*) significant; p < 0.01(**) very significant

Table 5. T-test analysis for high individualists (Americans)

	Sample size	Computer Efficacy		Pre-test Awareness	
		Mean	S.D.	Mean	S.D.
Experimental Group	34	6.38	0.70	5.69	0.59
Control Group	66	5.95	0.90	5.26	0.70
Levene test	F	0.001		9.56	
	P value	0.978		0.003 **	

P < 0.05 (*) significant; p < 0.01(**) very significant

The constraint may aggravate the researching findings in either direction, such as situational training is very effective or not ineffective. However, if the findings at both sites go in the opposing direction, our argument to either support or reject the usefulness of situational security awareness training to high individualists is more convincing. With this logic in mind, the following section will examine the learning outcomes after having experimental and control groups receive situational and traditional security awareness training.

Post-Test Analysis

Table 6 indicates that after receiving either situational or traditional security awareness training, no significant differences in all three levels of security awareness exist between the two groups at the Taiwan site. This indicates that situational awareness does not deliver its anticipated benefits in improving general users' perception, comprehension and projection ability. Control groups that received the traditional training approach can perform as well as the experimental groups that are equipped with better security awareness before the training session took place.

In contrast, situational security awareness training at the U.S. site does help the experimental group surpass the control group in the measurements of all three security awareness levels (Table 7). The Anova test as seen in Table 7 shows that these three performance metrics are all significant ($p = 0.000$ for perception; $p = 0.007$ for comprehension; and $p = 0.009$ for projection).

Furthermore, this indicates that the group of subjects receiving situational awareness training outperformed the traditional group. In addition, the situational awareness training approach is indeed a more effective training approach than the traditional approach at helping general users improve their security awareness levels.

Table 6. Measures of dependent variables between experimental and control groups at Taiwan site

		Group	Size	Mean	S.D.	Levene test		t	P
Post-Test Awareness	SA1	Experimental	80	25.61	3.79	2.121	0.147	-0.255	0.799
		Control	80	25.48	2.99				
	SA2	Experimental	80	24.35	4.28	0.003	0.957	-1.333	0.184
		Control	80	23.46	4.14				
	SA3	Experimental	80	28.53	3.27	0.96	0.757	-0.539	0.590
		Control	80	28.25	3.18				

P < 0.05 (*) significant; p < 0.01(**) very significant

Table 7. Measures of dependent variables between experimental and control groups at the U.S. site

		Group	Size	Mean	S.D.	F value	P
Post-Test Awareness	SA1	Experimental	34	6.30	0.74	13.40	0.000 **
		Control	66	5.70	0.80		
	SA2	Experimental	34	6.27	0.58	7.568	0.007 **
		Control	66	5.84	0.83		
	SA3	Experimental	34	6.45	0.62	7.15	0.009 **
		Control	66	6.06	0.72		

P < 0.05 (*) significant; p < 0.01(**) very significant

DISCUSSION

American users who received the situational security awareness training outperformed those who received the traditional step-by-step instruction. In contrast, Taiwanese users of both experimental and controllable groups had similar performance after receiving respective training approaches. Since the research findings at both sites go in the opposing direction, we are confident in stating that situational security awareness training is more effectively useful to high individualists than high collectivists.

As seen below in Table 8, hypotheses H1a to H1c are supported in the U.S. site, whereas those hypotheses were rejected in the Taiwanese site.

These findings confirm the potential influence of individualism culture as a socio-technical factor concerning the improvement of knowledge surrounding the topic of security awareness. Our study further suggests that the cultural trait, particularly the individualism cultural dimension, is a strong dispositional predictor of the efficacy of situational training applied in the context of security awareness improvement.

The positive influence of the individualist culture also corroborates with the finding in the field of consumer behavior that high individualists have a higher intention than high collectivists to purchase personalized products in an online retailing situation (Moon, Chadee and Tikoo, 2008). This cultural trait also exhibits its influence on the trust formation. For instance, a trustee's perceived ability and integrity are the source of trust to individualists and predictability as benevolent interactions are to collectivists (Branzei, Vertinsky and Camp, 2007). The positive correlation between individualism culture and the efficiency of situational awareness programs has some commonalities between the topics of cultural traits and the acceptance of consumer goods, which in fact involves the fast formation of trust.

It makes no significant difference for collectivists to receive either situational awareness or step-by-step instruction. However, situational awareness programs make individualists aware of their surroundings as well as the environmental elements and their contextual meanings in a more efficient and effective manner. Situational awareness programs are also an effective vehicle to help individualists form a mental model to both understand the current risks of a situation and to predict and possibly prevent the potential adverse effects of security risks and vulnerabilities.

We administered a pre-test for both American and Taiwanese subjects before they were exposed to both situational awareness and traditional face-to-face treatments. The purpose of this pre-test is to evaluate and minimize the impacts of extraneous factors, such as age differences, computer efficacy, experience, ethnical heterogeneity or family profiles. Students from universities in

Table 8. Summary of hypotheses testing

Security Awareness Levels	Hypotheses	U.S. Site	Taiwan Site
SA1	Hypothesis H1a: High individualists have a higher 1st level of security awareness than low individualists after receiving the situational training approach.	Supported ($p = 0.000 < 0.01$)	Rejected ($p = 0.799 > 0.05$)
SA2	Hypothesis H1b: High individualists have a higher 2nd level of security awareness than low individualists after receiving the situational training approach.	Supported ($p = 0.007 < 0.01$)	Rejected ($p = 0.184 > 0.05$)
SA3	Hypothesis H1c: High individualists have a higher 3rd level of security awareness than low individualists after receiving the situational training approach.	Supported ($p = 0.009 < 0.01$)	Rejected ($p = 0.590 > 0.05$)

both the U.S. and Taiwan were either juniors or seniors. They were all full-time students, despite the studied American school is a public university and Taiwanese school is a private university. About 99% of the American students are Caucasian, and 100% of the students from Taiwan are native Taiwanese. Therefore, the potential impact of ethnical diversity is minimal. It is highly probable that all the variables this study deliberately controlled have negligible effects on learning outcomes. We are confident that the impact of individualism culture on the efficacy of situational awareness learning does exist and that we must pay attention to these factors.

LIMITATIONS

This study has two major limitations. The first limitation is derived from the presupposition that all of the U.S. participants were IDIs and that all Taiwanese were collectivists based on Hofstede's prior study. This assumption and our data lead us to believe that the experimental group in the U.S. "improved" their security awareness compared to the control group while the experimental group in Taiwan did not improve their security awareness compared to the control group. However, Hofstede's study was completed more than 15 years ago. As Taiwanese become more open and international in today's interconnected physical and digital worlds, some Taiwanese may have acquired new behaviors from the Western society. A national culture has at least three layers, consisting of cultural traditions (e.g. shared languages, and beliefs), and subcultures (common identity), and cultural universals (e.g. body languages) (Tylor, 1920). It is probable that subcultures may have changed or caused influences over time. It may be necessary to find a separate survey instrument just to measure the degree of individualism with respect to the studied subjects.

Another potential limitation of this study is the choice of students as participants. Practitioners who have been exposed to security risks could have different degrees of sensitivity in relation to security risks. As such, the security awareness levels of practitioners could be dissimilar to those of students. We purposely administered the pretest to assess and minimize the negative influence of the limitation. Other demographical variables, such as computer self-efficacy, could affect the outcomes of this study. These exogenous variables could potentially add noise to our research results. However, we did not control and manage these variables.

FUTURE TRENDS AND RESEARCH

Security awareness is growing in acceptance by the international community to combat physical and electronic security threats caused by human behaviors. Cisco conducted a global study to investigate the gap between security awareness and actual behavior of 1,000 remote workers and 1,000 IT decision makers in 10 countries (Business Wire, 2006). The gap exists and has variation among these 10 countries. Countries with a large gap are becoming the vulnerability to today's worldwide Internet security. This study offers a cross-cultural perspective on how to narrow the gap via the customization of effective situational security awareness training approaches for users with different cultural backgrounds.

Security awareness training has received much attention to its efficacy at enhancing information security awareness for general users. For instance, a recent study shows that after the training general users could be more competent at using strong passwords with decreased reliance of technical support (Charoen, Raman and Olfman, 2008). Security awareness can also minimize physical and electronic security breaches caused by social engineering techniques (Kamal, 2008).

This study extends the importance of security awareness to the international level. We direct attention to the influence of cultures on the efficacy of the situational awareness training approach. Different testing results at Taiwan and the U.S. sites present cultural implications and opportunities for future research. As we have seen in our research, low individualists appear less receptive to situational awareness training than high individualists. More specifically, high individualists have a higher level of security awareness than low individualists after receiving situational training.

Individualism is the sole cultural dimension investigated in this study. Our findings indicate that the situational awareness training approach is an effective tool to high individualists.

CONCLUSION

Security awareness is an important issue that all individuals must be concerned with as information is transferred around the globe. Global citizens also react differently to security awareness as would be expected due to differing cultures and the emphasis that is placed on individualism. Certainly, awareness of the risks and safeguards is the first line of defense that can be employed by any individual, but how individuals address these risks can be very dissimilar in different cultures. Findings of this study provide insights on how to address the security awareness challenges faced by different cultures via a proposed training approach.

As previously mentioned, our solution is effective in these two cultures and can be expanded to other cultures in order help better secure today's online global environment. Future study can examine how effective this training approach would be in other cultural dimensions, including masculine, power distance, uncertain avoidance, and long-term perspective. The question and future research remains "How can we best or most effectively train individuals in relation to security awareness on a worldwide basis?"

REFERENCES

Agrawal, V. K., & Haleem, A., & Sushil. (2003). Successful implementation of business process reengineering and computer based information systems: Awareness and training program (NIST SP 800-50). *National Social Science Journal*, *20*(2), 1–16.

Albrechtsen, E. (2007). A qualitative study of user's view on information security. *Computers & Security*, *26*(4), 276–289. doi:10.1016/j.cose.2006.11.004

Bia, M., & Kalika, M. (2007). Adopting an ICT code of conduct: An empirical study of organizational factors. *Journal of Enterprise Information Management*, *20*(4), 432–446. doi:10.1108/17410390710772704

Branzei, B. O., Vertinsky, I., & Camp, R. D. (2007). Culture-contingent signs of trust in emergent relationships. *Organizational Behavior and Human Decision Processes*, *104*(1), 61–82. doi:10.1016/j.obhdp.2006.11.002

Business Wire. (2006, November 13). *Global security study: Helpdesk calls on the rise, 2007 spending to increase.*

Charbaji, A., & Jannoun, S. E. L. (2005). Individuality, willingness to take risk, and use of a personal e-card: A Lebanese study. *Journal of Managerial Psychology*, *20*(1), 51–58. doi:10.1108/02683940510571649

Charoen, D., Raman, M., & Olfman, L. (2008, February). Improving end user behaviour in password utilization: An action research initiative. *Systemic Practice and Action Research*, *21*(1), 55–72. doi:10.1007/s11213-007-9082-4

Computer and Network Security Task Force. (2008). *Resource kit for national cyber security awareness*. Retrieved on January 27, 2009, from http://www.educause.edu/security/resourcekit/7479?time=1233090643

CSI/FBI. (2006). *Computer crime and security survey*. Retrieved on August 12, 2007, from http://www.gocsi.com/forms/fbi/csi_fbi_survey.jhtml

Drevin, L., Kruger, H. A., & Steyn, T. (2007). Value-focused assessment of ICT security awareness in an academic environment. *Computers & Security*, *26*(1), 36–43. doi:10.1016/j.cose.2006.10.006

Endsley, M. (1995). Measurement of situation awareness in dynamic systems. *Human Factors*, *31*(1), 65–84.doi:10.1518/001872095779049499

Endsley, M., & Garland, D. (2000). *Experimental analysis and measurement of situation awareness*. Daytona Beach, FL: Embry-Little University Press.

Ess, C. (2006). Ethical pluralism and global information ethics. *Ethics and Information Technology*, *8*(4), 215–226. doi:10.1007/s10676-006-9113-3

Filipek, R. (2007). European nations make security a high priority. *The Internal Auditor*, *64*(5), 15–17.

Floridi, L. (2006). Four challenges for a theory of information privacy. *Ethics and Information Technology*, *8*(3), 109–119. doi:10.1007/s10676-006-9121-3

Fracker, M. (1991). *Measures of situation awareness: Review and future directions.* OH: Armstrong Laboratories, Wright Patterson Air Force Base.

Grant, I. (2007). DaimlerChrysler security drive targets 360,000 staff. *Computer Weekly,* 4-8.

Harrington, J. (2005, August 16). Sen. Baucus relishes resisting Bush's social security privatization plan. *Knight Rider Tribune Business News*.

Hofstede, G. (1993). Cultural constraints in management theories. *The Academy of Management Executive*, *7*(1), 81–94.

Kamal, M. (2008). The psychology of IT security in business. *Journal of American Academy of Business*, *13*(1), 145–150.

Kirkman, B. L., & Shapiro, D. L. (1997). The impact of cultural values on employee resistance to teams: Toward a model of globalized self-managing work team effectiveness. *Academy of Management Review*, *22*, 730–357. doi:10.2307/259411

Kucuk, S. U. (2002). The changing consumerism with the Internet: A global perspective. *Journal of Euromarketing*, *12*(1), 41–61. doi:10.1300/J037v12n01_04

Lipsey, M. W., & Wilson, D. B. (1993). The efficacy of psychological, educational, and behavioral treatment: Confirmation from meta-analysis. *The American Psychologist*, *48*, 1181–1209. doi:10.1037/0003-066X.48.12.1181

McCoy, S., Galletta, D. F., & King, W. R. (2005). Integrating national culture into IS reseach: The need for current individual-level measures. *Communications of AIS*, *5*(15), 211–224.

Montealegre, R. (1998). Managing information technology in modernizing 'against the odds': Lesson from an organization in a less-developed country. *Information & Management*, *34*, 103–116. doi:10.1016/S0378-7206(98)00051-2

Moon, J., Chadee, D., & Tikoo, S. (2008). Culture, product type, and price influences on consumer purchase intention to buy personalized products online. *Journal of Business Research*, *61*(1), 31–39. doi:10.1016/j.jbusres.2006.05.012

O'Boyle, S. (2008). IT security: Socially naive or socially aware? *Accountancy Ireland*, *40*(2), 65.

Probst, T. M., & Lawler, J. (2006). Cultural values as moderators of the outcomes of job insecurity: The role of individualism and collectivism. *Applied Psychology: An International Review*, *55*, 234–254. doi:10.1111/j.1464-0597.2006.00239.x

Rouse, W. B., & Morris, N. M. (1985). *On looking into the blackbox: Prospects and limits in the search for mental models* (DTIC#AD-A159080). Atlanta, GA: Center for Man-Machine Systems Research, Georgia Institute of Technology.

Sarter, N., & Woods, D. (1991). Situation awareness: A critical but ill-defined phenomenon. *The International Journal of Aviation Psychology*, *1*, 45–47. doi:10.1207/s15327108ijap0101_4

Schmidt, M. B., Johnston, A. C., Arnett, K. P., Che, J. Q., & Li, S. (2008). A cross-cultural comparison of U.S. and Chinese computer security awareness. *Journal of Global Information Management*, *16*(2), 91–103.

Triandis, H. C. (Ed.). (1991). *Cross-cultural industrial and organizational psychology*. Palo Alto, CA: Consulting Psychologists Press, Inc.

Turban, E., Leidner, D., McLean, E., & Wetherbe, J. (2008). *Information technology for management*. Hoboken, NJ: John Wiley & Sons, Inc.

Wilson, M., & Hash, J. (2003). *Building an information technology security awareness and training program*. Gaithersburg, MD: Computer Security Division, Information Technology Laboratory, National Institute of Standards and Technology.

APPENDIX 1 SURVEY INSTRUMENT

CONSENT FORM

Please read this form carefully, and sign if you agree to participate in the research study given the guidelines in the statement of consent below.

Purpose of the Study

This study is being conducted to investigate how individuals learn to acquire security awareness topics. There are three parts to this study. One part is to learn about how different backgrounds, attitudes, and experiences influence your learning outcomes. A second part is to compare different methods of training individuals to acquire security awareness topics. The third part is to determine how trainees are applying these studied security awareness topics to a hypothetical situation. Your role in the study

You will be receiving 30 minutes of security awareness training. Prior to the training session, you are being asked to complete a number of questionnaires concerning your computer background, attitudes, and experience. You must also prepare solving problems during the training session. During the session, you will be asked to complete some additional questionnaires. Your specific information and performance during the study will be kept completely confidential.

Statement of Consent

I agree to participate in this research study. I agree to keep my role in this study confidential until after the study has been completed by neither discussing the training nor sharing training materials with other employees involved in the study. I understand that I can withdraw from the study at anytime, but agree to maintain confidentiality until the completion of the study.

Name: ____

Signature ____________________________ *Date* ________________

Pre-Test: Part I. The Basic Computer Skills

Please choose your answers that fit best to each question.

Table 9. Computer skills and knowledge

	Strongly Disagree				Strongly Agree
1. I understand the basic procedures of operating systems (e.g. Windows98, WindowsXP, Windows2000)	1	2	3	4	5
2. I understand the basic functions of computer hardware components (e.g. CPU and memory)	1	2	3	4	5
3. I know how to install applications according to instructions	1	2	3	4	5

Table 10. Operating application packages

	Strongly Disagree				Strongly Agree
1. I know basic ways to manage files (e.g. file copy, delete, searching)	1	2	3	4	5
2. I know how to use multimedia presentation applications (e.g. Power Point)	1	2	3	4	5
3. I know how to download and install files	1	2	3	4	5

Table 11. Information Security Awareness

	Strongly Disagree				Strongly Agree
1. Data confidentiality is lost when data is read or copied by unauthorized people.	1	2	3	4	5
2. I understand that what kinds of information are considered as sensitive and cannot be left on desk	1	2	3	4	5
3. I understand what kinds of sensitive information need to be managed	1	2	3	4	5
4. Authorization based on username and password is the first attempt to prevent authorized access	1	2	3	4	5
5. A secured password needs to avoid using meaningful characters (e.g. good). A secured password uses a combination of mixed characters (upper and lower case), number and special characters	1	2	3	4	5

1. Which of the following is the most secured password?
   a. Joseph
   b. Joseph1219
   c. joseph1219
   d. Jo1219Seph
   e. 1219joseph

2. What should not be left on the office desk in order to protect information security?
   1. Notepad (job logs), cellular phone and iPod
   2. Disk, organizational flow chart of the project, and note pad (job logs)
   3. Laptop, disk and organizational flow chart of the project
   4. Cellular phone, note pad (job logs), disk and organizational flow chart of the project
   5. Cellular phone, laptop, organizational flow chart of the project, note pad (job logs), iPod, and disk

Part II. Personal Demographics

1. Gender: □Male □Female
2. Age: □13~16 □17~19 □20~23 □24~27 □28~31 □32 years old and above
3. Educational background: □(1)High school □(2) two-year college □(3) bachelor □(4) master □(5) doctoral
4. Computer experience: □(1)1~3 years □(2)4~6 years □(3)7~9 years □(4) 10 years and above.
5. What do you do with your computer?: □(1) word processing □(2) Internet surfing □(3)gaming □(4) chatting □(5)work-related activities (Check all that apply)

Post-Test: Evaluations of Information Security Awareness in Different Situations

Part III: Situation Awareness

Table 12. 1st level of situation awareness: perception of environmental elements (status, attributes and dynamics)

	Strongly Disagree				Strongly Agree
1. I understand how to manage password (creating, changing frequency and protection)	1	2	3	4	5
2. I know how to protect confidential data (files management, files backup)	1	2	3	4	5
3. I understand the security policy of office desk (screen protection, control of physical visits, prevention of checking screen information, and access permissions of systems)	1	2	3	4	5

Table 13. 2nd level of situation awareness: understanding of the current environment and the ability to integrate pieces of information

	Strongly Disagree				Strongly Agree
1. A laid-off employee can violate laws if he/she continues to use company's email account	1	2	3	4	5
3. I know the purpose of creating secured password for information security?	1	2	3	4	5
4. I know the policy of desk clearance in office?	1	2	3	4	5
5. I know how to securely store confidential data?	1	2	3	4	5

Table 14. 3rd level of security awareness: projection of future situations: prediction and decision making

	Strongly Disagree				Strongly Agree
1. I understand the rules to create secured passwords	1	2	3	4	5
2. I understand that confidential information cannot be left on desk unattended	1	2	3	4	5
3. I understand the adverse effects of losing company's confidential data	1	2	3	4	5
4. I understand the adverse effect of having passwords stolen	1	2	3	4	5
5. I understand how to respond to security attacks (whom to contact? What right things to do?	1	2	3	4	5

Table 15. Part 2. Attention to Security Topics

	Strongly Disagree				Strongly Agree
1. I will pay attention to the routine update of passwords	1	2	3	4	5
2. I will pay attention to the setting of password length	1	2	3	4	5
3. I will pay attention to the use of password combination (characters, upper and lower case, and numbers)	1	2	3	4	5
4. I will pay attention to the protection of mobile devices (e.g. notebook and memory stick)	1	2	3	4	5
5. I will pay attention to the management of sensitive data	1	2	3	4	5

Table 16. Part 3. Decision to Adopt Information Security Solutions

	Strongly Disagree				Strongly Agree
1. I will routinely change my password	1	2	3	4	5
2. I will create secured password	1	2	3	4	5
3. I will protect mobile equipment (e.g. notebook and memory stick)	1	2	3	4	5
4. I will manage sensitive data	1	2	3	4	5

Part IV. Performance of Actions

This part is to understand your actions to secure password and clear desk

Scenarios: Martin is a newly hired consultant to an accounting firm. All newly hired employees are equipped with a laptop. Martin is primarily responsible for introducing and implementing BS7799 (a security awareness program) program in a telecommunication firm. BS7799 is the standard designed by the British Standards Institution (BSI). The major purpose of this institution is to help organizations create an information security management system to manage risks. This standard is a major reference to other information security standards. The project management office is located inside the telecommunication firm. During the implementation process, Martin will access to the most confidential information about the customers of the client, and other information, such as organizational chart, the operational procedure of departments, job responsibilities and roles of employees, interviewing scripts of each department and infrastructure (e.g. locations of tower stations and their capacity, etc.

(1) After obtaining the laptop from the accounting firm, Martin needs to manage his own password. Martin needs to create a new password for his own use of this laptop before begin using it. If you were Martin, which following password is a secured password?

- 1.martin
- 2.martin1219
- 3.Martin1219
- 4.1219martin
- 5.Mar1219Lue

(2) Martin remembers his training of password management before officially working for the accounting firm. One of important topics he learned is about the length of password to secure personal assets. If you were Martin, what would be the length of a secured password?

- 1. At least 4 characters
- 2. At least 5 characters
- 3. At least 6 characters
- 4. At least 7 characters
- 5. At least 8 characters

(3) This morning, Martin worked hard to complete two reports, one on operational procedure, and another on risks assessment and is ready to turn in to his senior management. These two reports were staying on the office desk of Martin. On the screen of his office computer also shows a working report on SOP. "Let's go out for lunch!" said the colleague of Martin. Martin could not wait to go out with his colleague and left office with his colleague immediately. If you were Martin, how would you respond to this situation?

1. Organize those two reports on the office desk before leaving office with colleague
2. Execute screen protection application before leaving office with colleague
3. Store those two reports, save the working report on the screen in a file and close, and organize office desk before leaving with colleague
4. Store those two reports in the drawer and lock the drawer, save the working report on the screen in a file and close, and execute screen protection application before leaving with colleague
5. Store those two reports in the drawer and lock the drawer, and execute screen protection application before leaving with colleague

(4) Martin has the habit of organizing document and tools on the office desk before begin working in a day. However, he always forgets carrying his document and tools with him when he leaves. One day, a senior manager called Martin and asked him to attend an important meeting on the project he is in charge. Martin left his office immediately after receiving the phone call. He also left his cellular phone, laptop that is not logged off, organizational flow chart of the project, disk, and notepad on the computer screen (job logs). What should not be left on the office desk if you were Martin?

6. Notepad (job logs) and cellular phone
7. Disk, organizational flow chart of the project, and note pad (job logs)
8. Laptop, disk and organizational flow chart of the project
9. Cellular phone, note pad (job logs), disk and organizational flow chart of the project
10. Cellular phone, laptop, organizational flow chart of the project, note pad (job logs) and disk

Section 4
Cross-Disciplinary Studies

Chapter 17
Cross Disciplinary Learning in Distance Higher Education:
Empowerment for Sustainable Research Prowess among Professionals in the African Sub-Region

Jonathan O. Osiki
National University of Lesotho, South Africa

ABSTRACT

Adequately selecting and applying the multi-model structure from the backdrop of cross-disciplinary learning in stimulating professionals' research empowerment in distance higher education, is a regular focus of research. How the benefits of research is developed, nurtured, continuously enhanced, and sustained in value-driven academic activities is the direct consequence of learners' emotionality. The study argues that distance learners learn meaningfully when their emotionality is adequate. Using the emotional spiral model, the study in a pre-test, post-test, control quasi-experimental research design evaluated the impact of behaviour techniques subsumed psychotherapeutically in facilitating learners' emotional stability for inducing research competences. The distance learners were initially screened for their fears in research activities and quantitative abilities, and then subsequently allotted into four independent intervention sub-groups. Under the vantage application of psychotherapy, for a four-week out of a six-week maximum teaching-learning encounter, prior to the post-evaluation (i.e. post-test) period, the learners were exposed to the benefits of the reframing techniques, rational emotive bahaviour techniques, assignment method, and the control technique (i.e the non-treatment) group. Utilizing the analysis of variance statistical method at the 0.05 alpha, the findings showed that the participants' research prowess improved tremendously with a statistically significant treatment effect [$F(4, 1052) = 7.52$; $P<0.05$]. It thus concluded that if the research endeavours within the open distance learning would sustain marginal benefits, interdisciplinarity and/or the multi-approach learning methods should be the vogue.

DOI: 10.4018/978-1-60566-852-9.ch017

INTRODUCTION

Cross-disciplinary learning or cross-disciplinary research and how its benefits can be maximized to enhance academic behaviour and professional credibility is an on-going Higher Education investigation, though recently, that of the Distance Higher Education and or the Open Distance Learning. Academics hither-to, especially within the African sub-regions have often maintained the status-quo by not employing, in absolute terms, the marginal benefits accruable through collaborative studies across disciplines. Research activities, among majority of academics, though involve some form of collaboration, especially within similar disciplines; it does not involve, strictly, that of utilizing the benefits of transdisciplinarity and or cross disciplinary learning or cross-disciplinary research . Prominent and value-driven investigations with sustainable research breakthroughs are a good recipe for regional and global development, growth and continued survival in health, socio-economics, politics and improved standard and quality of life. Such research outcomes and or breakthroughs, unequivocally annexes the marginal advantages of the cross-disciplinary learning or cross-disciplinary research. Specifically therefore, the overall spectrum of this chapter is the examination of (a) the interconnectivity of cross-disciplinary learning or cross-disciplinary research to sustainable research empowerment/ prowess of professionals in Distance Higher Education. Other coverage areas are: (b) identification of challenges in cross disciplinary studies; (c) boosting research outcome through effective collaboration; (d) ethical standards in cross disciplinary learning/research; and (e) emotionality and academic/professional empowerment via empirical investigation.

BACKGROUND

An age-long phenomenon in academic institutions of higher learning, which has constituted an unusual and restricted meaningful research impact in higher education, is the continuous and or perpetuation of academic islands (otherwise, academic boundaries or territories). While academic boundaries have some limitedly defined and beneficial merits, however, the annexation of its maximum benefits is not merely in the future perse, but in collaboration, when effective and eventual benefits of cross disciplinary learning and or research approaches would have permeated all known academic programmes. The challenges arising from economic, social, political and health-related issues that should have benefited from the adaptation and sustenance of cross disciplinary methodology and or the pairing and the use of the Blended Method have therefore, for now, rested on the pendulum. Most academics, for instance, within the pure and applied sciences, just like it is the case with other disciplines, who are presently unenthusiastic, in widening their cooperation (otherwise, horizon) would therefore be goaded when empowered, through collaborative research activities following the cross disciplinary paradigm.

Empowering research skills both in terms of knowledge search and shared, its utilization and application are necessary activities for an all-round professional teacher development. How to search for, and apply relevant knowledge, particularly for a sustainable and value-driven research in distancehigher education and or open distance learning is therefore, part of the total package encapsulated in academic and professional teacher behaviour. Knowledge and value-driven research, especially needed to instigate the twenty-first century marginal difference in professional teacher behaviour, that would impact on our national and or sub-regional survival, growth and development, socio-economically, politically and or, in mental health, should necessarily be directed from the perspective of research orientation that annexes, the macrocosm of cross-disciplinary approaches and the blended method. Cross-disciplinary learning and or cross-disciplinary approaches provides important recipe for sound academic interaction that can be instrumental in motivating and sustaining research interest among professionals and with a concomitant influence on academic credibility and competence in distance higher education.

In several ways, studies (Pennington, 2008; Dewulf, Francois, Pahl-Wostl, & Taillieu, 2007; Schaffer, Lei, Reyes, Oakes & Zoltowski, 2006; Levina & Vaast, 2005; Bailey, 2001) have shown the differential benefits in collaborative studies when the sub-categories of Cross-disciplinary learning are used to boost research outcomes. Cross-disciplinary learning and or research provides the basis for interdisciplinary studies and or cooperation outside traditional boundaries, especially that are germane, to a multi-approach environment for the nurture and pursuit of value-driven meanings to life challenges. Studies of this nature may be typical, though they could benefit immensely against the rigidly structured environment, where researches and or learning subsist within common backgrounds as it were, the cases with either the Faculty of Humanities alone, Sciences alone and or Technology. Though, gleaning information, where the benefits of Cross-disciplinary learning and or Cross-disciplinary research have been annexed may sometimes be misleading (i.e. in terms of the adaptation and application of its sub-classification), the Cross-disciplinary learning and or Cross-disciplinary research, unequivocally, are mutually beneficial overall. It subsists and maximally thrives better where the product of research is the outcome of the combined effect of both the lateral and or horizontal and vertical learning approaches.

Specifically discussing some of the peculiar benefits of the Cross-disciplinary learning, especially in boosting research outcome, the studies of Osiki (2008); Osiki & Braimoh (2008); the Uppsala-Stanford-Karolinska project and the Stanford Alliance for a Global Bioinformatics Curriculum (2008) have examined the components of the lateral and or horizontal learning (collaborative method) approach. In the analogy, the horizontal method draws experiences from individuals with common knowledge such as those coming from the (a) 'same department'; (b) 'same faculties but different departments' and (c) 'same department/ faculties but with varied years of entry'. Using the aforementioned analogy does not however exclude the important fact that acknowledges the existence of the multi-specialty areas in some cases, both within each Department and across the faculties. In the very strictest term however, where learners and or group of researchers are drawn across faculties such as Humanities, Social Sciences, Sciences, Medicine, etc; this epitomizes the vertical collaborative approach; and can be more beneficial and impactful in terms of research dividends and breakthrough technologically, socio-economically and or in medicine. The notion, for instance, that the Uppsala-Stanford-Karolinska project convey the horizontal collaborative sub-type, essentially indicates the intersection of many disciplines within biology, genetics, medicine, computer science, and informatics (i.e. either in the applied and or natural sciences), rather than the inter-mixture of programmes in other areas such as theology and religious studies, economics, history and or philosophy. Adapting either the horizontal and or the vertical collaborative approaches alone merely therefore defines an aspect of the multi-dimensionality of Cross-disciplinary learning and or Cross-disciplinary research in boosting distance higher education research and impacting professional teacher development. When academics are adequately empowered, especially via the vertical approach, their academic and professional behaviour gets boosted which then impacts both the research outcome and overall socio-economic transformation of the African sub-region.

The term 'interdisciplinarity' and or 'trans-disciplinarity' has unequivocally been used by several studies (Bruun & Laine, 2006; Kwa, 2002;

Maasen & Weingart, 2000; Weingart, 2000; Weingart & Stehr, 2000) to convey more meanings and to portray some of the possible advantages in the application of Cross-disciplinary learning and or Cross-disciplinary research in enriching academic competences and professional behaviour in teacher development. In the perspective of the researcher, transdisciplinarity argues that complex human problems are better confronted and solved through the adaptation of the multi-model, which defines fundamentally, the cynosure of the cross-disciplinary learning. Buttressing this further, the argument holds for instance, that such human disturbing conditions as HIV/AIDS, and or its opportunistic cases may not only have had the organic patho-etiology as it is being forcefully speculated, but more importantly, the socio-cultural, economic, and fatalistic dimension; which though may presently be ignored, but needs to be investigated.

Identifying Challenges in Cross Disciplinary Studies

Empowering research prowess among professionals, within the backdrop of the distance higher education, and in annexing the benefits of the multi-dimensionality of the cross-disciplinary learning, the modus vivendi and or modus-operandi for its marginal dividends has continued to attract regular attention. While the studies of Collis & Margaryan (2004) reported the outcome of online and blended learning environments based on social-cultural activities, that of Schaffer & Richardson (2004) investigated the effect of technological integration and in Osiki (2007), that of psychotherapeutic outcome, using the benefits of multi-behaviour techniques. Others (Olt, 2008; Taylor, 2007), vehemently discussed academic dishonesty or integrity or both. Olt (2008) and Taylor's (2007) studies easily brought to the fore one of the major challenges both in institutions of higher learning and the distance higher education and or the open distance learning. Whether through the conventional education format and or otherwise, cheating would continue to erode the academic credibility and professional relevance of especially, the twenty-first century distance higher education and or Institutions of Higher Learning. Although various methods are regularly being validated for improving academic integrity and or the amelioration of the different sub-types of academic fraud, and as suggested in both Olt (2008) and Taylor (2007), fundamental among the concern in today's distance higher education, is the pertinent issue, of how to annex the benefits of cross-disciplinary learning as it were, in directing value-driven researches outside the traditional disciplinary specialization. Collaborative studies within defined and or specific specialty zone, apart from typifying the conditions of limited marginal difference, hardly ever sustain the macrocosm of research dividends, needed for national or global breakthrough, in socio-economics, politics, health and significant overall behavioural change within any community.

In the arguments of Strober (2008), while buttressing the relevance of Cross-disciplinary learning and or cross-disciplinary research, submitted that *'disciplinary specialization inhibits Faculty from broadening their intellectual horizon'* while in juxtaposition, Weingart (2000) said that, *'to push the frontiers of knowledge forward and create knowledge that helps to solve the problems of the World, we need not only discovery within disciplines but also integration across them'.* Although, while such other studies like that of Bruun & Laine (2006) had discussed the opinion divide among scholars on the significance and prevalence of interdisciplinarity, Kwa (2002) merely accepted its existence as a matter of 'discourse' but doubted its practicability, especially in absolute terms.

Boosting Research Outcome Through Effective Collaboration/ Breaking of Barriers

The arguments on cross-disciplinary learning and or interdisciplinarity (otherwise, transdisciplinarity) (Weingart, 2000) are mainly conceived to direct and prompt relevant knowledge that would be germane to global importance and or continued relevance amidst endless socio-economic challenges and issues related to political and physical survival that confront mankind. As epitomized therefore by a Nigerian University vision statement (i.e. University of Ibadan, Nigeria), which states that her vision was 'to expand the frontier of knowledge and transform the society through innovation' (http://www.uiadvancement.org/vision_mission.pdf), it becomes reasonable to simply ask, "how does that happen, when, in the obvious circumstances, whether within the African sub-region and or elsewhere, academic territories or barriers have become jealously restrictive?" Though the university of Ibadan, Nigeria vision is both loaded with a lot of meanings and expectations, the vision-specificity is not nonsensical but, rather, summarises what our research outcome, especially in the distance higher education, should epitomise, for the overall transformation, survival and development of the nations of Africa and or elsewhere, technologically, socio-economically, politically and in health. For instance, Cottingham (2002) and Lele and Norgaard (2005) once argued that interdisciplinary hypotheses are difficult to generate even though, according to Pickett, Burch and Grove (1999), the obvious challenges in hypotheses construction and application are imminent because the knowledge base in emerging research areas is by definition, incomplete and erroneous without distinct scope. But Wear (1999) also added when he said that the quagmire in research is due to the fact that the process of building the expected knowledge-base was laden with semantic issues that at best, slow down the process, and at worst, exclude some from the conversation.

Annexing the relevance of interdisciplinarity and or cross-disciplinary learning, in sharpening the research experiences of professionals in distance higher education, and in particular, in the twenty-first century, should also under-score therefore, the importance of the multi-dimensionality of human challenges in health-related issues, socio-economically and otherwise. The issues of HIV/AIDS and its associated conditions for instance, have, without any equivocation, the behavioural and attitudinal components as well as the social and a concomitant multiple implications for national growth, individual, family and collective commitments; with the consequent stress in socio-economic sustainability, political growth and stability, quality of life as well as general wellbeing. While the phenomena impact so much on the availability of knowledge generally, researchers and professionals, across disciplines (i.e transdisciplinarity and or cross-disciplinary learning), can collaborate for a life-time value-driven research outcomes that would be beneficial to national survival. Such studies (Bammer, 2005; Newell, Crumley, Hassan, Lambin, Pahl-Wostl & Underdal, 2005) have reasoned that, cross-disciplinary conceptual integration can be facilitated by employing methodologies that consider the structure of knowledge in cooperating disciplines, such as disciplinary history, epistemology, framing differences, and scales of application. Pennington (2008), using the term 'cross-disciplinary collaboration and learning, even though had acknowledged that obvious challenges exist in applying the conception of the cross-disciplinary learning in boosting research expectation and or learning, quickly said that it was analogous to the ecosystems. According to Pennington, the primary entities involved in collaboration are humans, bodies of knowledge, and tools; and that, having marginal benefits, without doubt, means the effective links within the dynamics.

Even though there are likely challenges that may fraught the operationalization of interdisciplinarity of research and or learning, the twenty-first century distance higher education professionals should, without any over-emphasis, collaborate, using the benefits of cross-disciplinary learning to facilitating the needed solution for the complex human life stresses and the overt improvement, in professional and academic competences. In arguing to support the application of cross-disciplinarity in learning and or research, Pennington (2008) said that every collaboration is unique but composed of a distinctive combination of people in a specific context. Whether the context is however specific or otherwise, what remains obvious, is the product of the context. One collaborative study has, for instance, the possibility of further collaboration, when the outcome of the collaboration has obvious implications for learning, leadership skills, researchers' dependability as well as collective commitments and success. Like the ecosystem therefore, effective collaboration, especially using the benefits of interdisciplinarity and or cross-disciplinary learning would thrive within well regulated goals, rules, norms and sanctions to elicit group discipline and research productivity.

Ethical Standards in Cross Disciplinary Learning/Research

Noting the benefits of interdisciplinarity and or collaboration (otherwise, cooperation) (Pennington, 2008; Paulsen, 2003; Weingart, 2000), fundamental to the challenges confronting either the Higher Education and or the Distance Higher Education down the ages, however, is how to ensure that workplaces' standards are strictly adhered to. According to Adkins, Kenkel & Lim (2008), cheating on college campuses is a long-standing problem that is intensifying. In Braimoh and Osiki (2008), the issue of 'plagiarism', especially in Distance Higher Eucation, was implicated. Using their words, plagiarism in the twenty-first century higher education, though an age-long phenomenon, which is a constant threat in the operationalization of either employee (with emphasis on the academics) and learners' empowerment (otherwise, mentorship), has continued to erode the fundamentals of education. While the overall benefits accruable via the effective utilisation of the cross-disciplinary learning, is indubitable, empowering the professionals' competences and or academic credibility, especially if the higher education and or distance higher education would continue to receive accolades in the twenty-first century and beyond, certain strategies should therefore be teased to standardise and regularize academic activities. The standardization of workplaces ethics should be unambiguously defined and more functional, to elicit the commitments of every stakeholder (i.e. academic facilitators, different supporting staff members-teaching/non-teaching and learners) as well as learners' significant others who may aid and fraudulently abate academic practices at one time or the other.

Even though the application of the cross-disciplinary learning in inducing value-driven research outcome may have lots of advantages in distance higher education, interdisciplinarity however can become uneventful where its principles are neither functional nor adhered to. For instance, when researchers and or learners collaborate and cooperate, increased self-efficacy, retention, higher motivation and willingness for future collaboration occurs, just as group success remains easily predictable when membership loyalty and commitments are not compromised. But, within higher education and or distance higher education, many academics have had their names appended to publications, under the guise of collaboration, but who could not make the slightest contribution to such efforts. In some cases, there are double standards in the operationalisation of, definition and application of professional practices. Offenders in some other quarters cannot be punished where there are instances of threat to human lives and properties. Perhaps, this might provide a good recipe and or explanation to McCabe's (1993) findings. The results had it that in 1993, nearly a third of the faculty members, out of a total number of 1000 that McCabe interviewed across 21 campuses, admitted to observing cheating in their classes but did nothing about it. The fear of law suits, time required in handling cheating incidents and lack of institutional rewards for catching cheating and or offenders were part of the rationalization for the abuses of academic standards (Koch, 2002). Prominent schools noted for their peculiar strictness in honour codes are not equally exempted from the tendency to avoid taking action against academic dishonesty (Adkins et al, 2008). At the university of Virginia, two surveys indicated "significant number of students and professors who'd be unlikely to take action if they suspected cheating" "(Cheating Thrive, USA Today, May, 2001)". In reporting additional dimension, it further said that at Dartmouth, the disciplinary committee dropped all 63 cases of alleged cheating on homework when it concluded that it was impossible to determine who had and had not cheated. At Amherst College, cases of suspected cheating jumped from an average of five a year through much of the 1990s to 1999. The record at the University of California-Berkeley showed that the cases of academic dishonesty doubled between 1995 and 1999. The situation is not different but, with only slight modification in higher education and or distance higher education globally. In some instances, learners simply laugh it up when caught while, generally, they are equally secretive at reporting any misdemeanour.

In mitigating academic fraud, particularly for enhancing the status of the diastance higher education (otherwise, academic and professional credibility), improvement to academic standards should be the product of regular discussion. Using the inferences from the backdrop of researchers in distance higher education and or open distance learning (otherwise, that of the higher education generally), while the product of their cross-disciplinary research collaboration could be regularly assessed/evaluated to impact on their teaching-learning activities, that implicating the learners, on the other hand, could be administered to similar and related testS as evidence for authenticating their task-commitments to intermittent course work. Adkins et al (2008) suggested among others, the development of rapport with online students/academic online contract, discussing the importance of academic dishonesty as well walking the talk. The use of proctored settings and or one-on-one chats for test was also recommended.

Emotionality and Academic/ Professional Empowerment Via Empirical Studies

Discussing the improvement to workplaces' standards and or professional behaviour has a lot of implication for both learners' and or researchers' emotionality in higher education and distance higher education . Pennington (2008) once said that 'collaborations are, in some ways, analogous to the ecosystems; and then added that learning is an inherent part of collaboration. The supposition herein is that under effective surveillance, learners and or researchers are better empowered, using the cross-disciplinary learning for its obvious outcomes. This in part, also depends on a better understanding of how individual learning processes interact in group setting, which invariably prompts collective learning from which group outcomes may emerge (Hutchins, 1995). Essentially, 'every human being emote; and when we do not appreciate the dimension of its impact, whether in its intra-locality and or inter-complexity, it directs how we learn, what we do or do not, how we process given information as well as our idiosyncrasies'. Though more investigations are needed to underscore the importance of emotionality in professional empowerment and academic behaviour, one argument that may not be too nonsensical is the assumption that the dividends in academic and or professional standards are the function of emotional stability. Perhaps, the age-long problem of academic dishonesty and the different fraudulent practices in higher education globally would have found adequate meanings and expected solutions if they were juxtaposed with learners' emotionality and or emotional fluidity.

In the x-ray of the emotional dimension and its implication on the education of the girl-child, Osiki (2008b), argued that the child learns meaningfully when he/she is mentally stable and happy. According to the perspective, emotionality and or emotional preparedness/status is the totality of feeling that predisposes the learner's mental frame and or alertness as well as the readiness that prompts productive learning (academic/ professional behaviour). It is also the function of the individual personal relaxation which can be affected by the attitude of significant persons. Learners' academic and or professional behaviour and, in particular, research empowerment would receive the expected impetus when their self-perception and how they are perceived by others correlate positively (Osiki, 2008c). Furthermore, the argument said that learners' self-perception, how they perceive their self-worth with a concomitant relationship to how they are perceived, their mental wellness, overall happiness, the happiness of others, positive and or negative regards of others, as well as the differential level of personal attitude of significant people are part of the cumulative indices of emotionality. The emotionality of protégés however affects how they are available for the execution of assigned and or self-/jointly-determined tasks and how they are committed to research, especially in distance higher education . Thus, using a theoretical model to boost the illustration (otherwise tagged emotional spiral), the inference is that, like the spiral, the learner's perception of self-worth (which is a function of other factors as personal idiosyncrasies, environmental stimuli, attitude of significant others, etc) has propensity in the determination of his/her tasks-commitedness. The tasks commitments especially adapting the cross-disciplinary learning and or interdisciplinarity can have several levels as: 'never committed', 'lowly committed', 'moderately committed', and 'highly committed'. Irrespective of the learner's commitedness however, tasks commitments directs how skills are acquired; while finally, adequately acquired skills (research empowerment) prompt academic competences, professional credibility as well as the research breakthrough with the consequent sub-regional and or national (otherwise, global) socio-economic sustainability, political stability, technological advancement and better quality of life. When, as the spiral (Figure 1) epitomised below, the learners and or researchers' emotionality is adequately prompted and facilitated, his/her academic and or research apogee then becomes a reality.

The above framework was the foundation of a research empowerment study that spanned through four academic sessions at the University of Ibadan, Nigeria. The programme involved distance learners drawn from the Faculty of Education from where the researcher is presently away on sabbatical/accumulated leave. The distance learners were enrolled in Guidance and Counselling Programme; although they had different combination of teaching subjects' background. The aim of this study was to investigate the relative and differential effectiveness of three behavioural techniques subsumed in psychotherapies in ameliorating learners' emotional tension in the improvement of research writing and reporting skills. Specifically, the focus of the study was to examine how Reframing Technique, Rational Emotive Behavioural Technique (Erbaugh, 2007; Nitko, 2004; Johnson, Huwe, & Lucas, 2000) and the Assignment Method (Continuous Assessment Plan, 2006) can be used both as combinatorial and independent techniques to boost the distance learners' research potentialities. The study is particularly focused to help the distance learners to acquire expected emotional preparedness which is essentially important for meaningful learning. A very critical assumption of the study is that should learners' emotionality be facilitated adequately, the learners have the potentials to ascend and sustain their academic and or research apogee.

Figure 1. Emotional spiral/model (Osiki, 2008d). Copyright Osiki Jonathan Ohiorenuan. Used with permission.

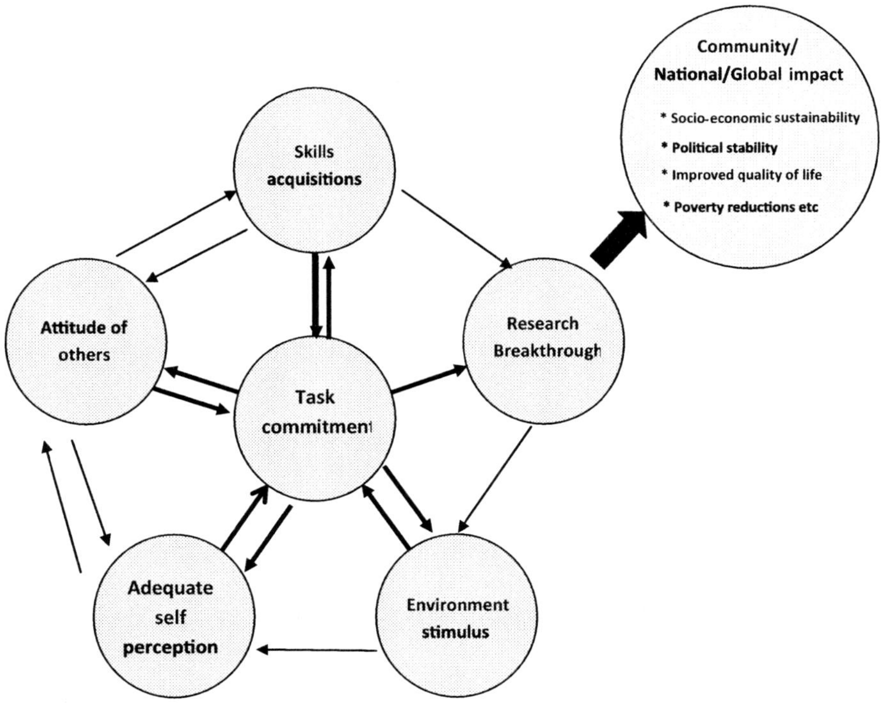

METHOD

The mixed-method approach was utilized to conduct this study spanning through four academic sessions. A total of 1057 distance learners with 398 (37.7%) males and 659 (62.3%) females in the baccalaureate programme in Education and Guidance and Counselling drawn across the 1997, 1998, 1999 and 2000 academic sessions, subsumed into four teams, were treated to a six-week intervention programme in research methodology and project-with course code: Education and Guidance and Counselling (GCE 410). The distance learners (i.e.the participants in the study) had multiple work experiences, marital statuses, and educational variation. While 916 (86.7%) had the National Certificate in Education, others13.3% (141) had the Grade II Teacher Certificates and the diploma as degree admission requirements.

Prior to the evaluation, in each of the academic sessions, the distance learners usually however met for a six-week face-to-face contact lecture period. The face-to-face interactive session was purely meant for review and question time which was done for four weeks while the last two weeks of the six-week period was for the examination. Usually, four out of six weeks of face to face review of lectures and question periods following correspondence are given to the distance learners on campus-format and, or in-school residential interaction form. The four weeks instruction was provided prior to another two weeks of examination (making 6-weeks in all). The distance learners, enrolled in Education and Guidance and Counselling Programme were exposed to the three behavioural techniques subsumed in psychotherapies separately and the non-intervention group, using the four academic sessions (i.e. as a block or stratum) each, for allotment into and combination of psychotherapies (Groups I, II, III and IV) respectively. The intervention periods lasted two hours (double periods) and one-hour (single period), representing three credit hours, thrice weekly during the face-to-face interactive lectures while assignments were provided as take-home for Continuous Assessment. The system was therefore mostly the hybridation type where the distance learning programme was facilitated via the correspondence conducted through regular mails but, had the entire distance learners invited, for a face-to face contact with programme facilitators for six weeks. The six weeks usually include four weeks of question and answer time and or review; and the last two weeks as end-of session evaluative examination. The last two weeks of end-of-session examination ends each and begins another contact academic session.

Data were collected at the intervention levels including the pre-test, post-test and control. The Research Status Inventory was the major research instrument used for data collection. The Research Status Inventory has two sub-sections (i.e. Personal quality and Preference Indicator). The first sub-section was made up of 19 items that require the participants to rate him/herself on how good they are in the sub-component areas of research methodology. The Personal Quality sub-section of the Research Status Inventory was screened following expert judgments in psychometrics for its validity while the reliability value of r (0.85) was obtained using the Cronbach alpha (Allen & Yen, 2002; Cronbach, 1951).

The Preference Indicator so tagged, comprises of two sections 'A' and 'B'. While the first part, which consists of 11 items, tapped information on the participants' emotionality, section 'B' was a proto-type Essay Question, usually moderated by External Examiners, and as part of the regulations in all Degree Examinations monitored by the National University Commission in Nigeria. Such designed examination questions are moderated on the basis of certain criteria some of which are (i) adherence to designed curriculum, (ii) difficulty level, (iii) coverage, (iv) whether verbose, (v) and the response time. The Personal quality (B) is optional and the distance learners were free to decide which four out of the six questions they preferred; but the grading of scripts was patterned after the testing standard rule where all participants' feedback were scored and graded by marking all question one (Q1) across board before all Q2, Q3, Q4, Q5, and Q6 in that order. This was done to reduce both halo effect and discrepancies in script-grading; and it easily allows raters to assess individual position in terms of group performance. The reliability of the PI, which has 6 items in Question Format, and previously administered, and drawn from the Departmental item pool was (r=0.78), following the split half coefficient relationship.

In the assessment of how well the distance learners have achieved and or gained during the application of the intervention package, the research prowess (otherwise, skills) of the distance learners was assessed following the mapping of critical areas in project report writing and after which the distance learners were exposed to 'end-of-course examination'. The critical areas which are embedded in the sub-categories of 'Research Methodology' in Education and Guidance and Counselling (GCE 410) are I.(a).Title of Study (which must be concise and feasible), (b).Abstract, (c).Introduction (background to the Study), (d). Statement of Problem, (e). Research question and, or Hypotheses (f). Objective of the Study (i.e. General and Specific Objectives), (g). Significance of the Study, II. Review of Related Literature (a). Theoretical Framework, (b). Empirical Background; III. Research Methodology- (a). Research Design, (b). Population of Study, (c). Sample and Sampling Techniques, (d). Research Measures, (e). Research Procedure and administration, (f) Data Analysis; IV.Results and Findings (i.e. hypotheses testing and tabular summaries of findings) and discussion of findings. V.Final Chapter (i.e. summary of findings, implication of findings, conclusion of findings, recommendation/ suggestions for further studies); References and appendix (appendices).

The Quasi-experimental and the causal comparative research designs were used in the study. The multiple cases were analyzed for the purposes of empirical evidence and theoretical replication which either (i) predicts similar outcome details; (ii) produces contrasting results but for predictable reasons. The development and validation of theoretical framework are germane for replicability of research procedures (Osiki, 1999; Yin, 1994). The participants in the intervention study were exposed to three psychotherapeutic techniques of (a) Reframing Technique; (b) Rational Emotive Behaviour Technique; (c) Assignment Method and (d) the control group. The rationale for the adaptation of the psychotherapies was to generally find out how their direct application would be useful for modifying the learners' emotional preparedness in boosting the distance learners' research prowess/empowerment. The premise of this study was therefore based on the assumption that distance learners' emotional tension would not be ameliorated to enhance prowess and or skills, especially in research methodology/project when selected behaviour techniques (i.e. Reframing Technique, Rational Emotive Behaviour Technique, and Assignment Method) are subsumed in psychotherapy and applied. Importantly, the assumption was that distance education learners' ability to develop researchable topics, retrieve and apply needed library information, construct acceptable research designs and measures as well as the choice of appropriate statistical methods will not differ significantly when they are exposed to the three selected behaviour techniques. The maturation effects of distance learners were equally assumed to boost the potentialities of the control group (i.e. those without intervention) while equating their outcome research prowess to those of reframing techniques, rational emotive behaviour techniques and the assignment method groups respectively.

Following the aforementioned and stated premise of the study above, three hypothesized statements were therefore generated and tested; and these are:

(i). the distance learners' research prowess will not be significantly different following their exposure to the combined treatment effect of the three behavioural techniques subsumed in psychotherapy and the non-intervention group.

(ii). The distance learners either exposed to the reframing techniques combined with assignment method on one hand and that of the assignment method separately while another group that was exposed to the rational emotive behaviour techniques/assignment method separately will not be significantly different in their research prowess; and (iii).Exposing the distance learners to the individual psychotherapies with a concomitant research prowess will not be significantly different.

Results and Findings

The details reported in this section are sub-divided into the pre-intervention and post-intervention outcomes. The pre-intervention outcome summarizes the details following the administration of the copies of questionnaire tagged the "Research Status Inventory " subsumed in sub-section 'I' (Personal quality) and sub-section II-AI (Preference Indicator); as well as AII (Preference Indicator-Emotionality)

Pre-Intervention Outcome

The initial introductory lecture that was given to the distance learners showed that over 95.64% of the distance learning participants had no previous research orientation and would be happier if research methodology courses and, or dissertation were not made part of University Programme.Other findings as reflected in table 2-'AI'(Appendix 'A') showed that out of 1057 distance learners enrolled differentially for the respective academic sessions, but whose responses were pooled, 986 (93.3%) argued that they would prefer to have a programme that does not include writing research dissertation for submission. Another 879 (83.2%) also said that it were better if dissertation would be made as part of a regular course for instruction and examinable only at the end of academic session while 91.9% reasoned that dissertation should be made optional respectively. Furthermore, while only 16.1% of the participants affirmed to the item-statement, that 'they like research methodology', 83.9% however responded otherwise; and similarly, another 78.4% said that they detest statistical methods.

Post-Intervention Outcome

Hypothesis One

The first hypothesis has it that the distance learners' research prowess will not be significantly different following their exposure to the combined effects of the reframing techniques, rational emotive behaviour techniques, assignment method and the non-intervention group. The findings which utilized Analysis of variance for its computation however showed that it was statistically significant having the main treatment effects as [F (4, 1052) =7.52; P<0.05] (Table 4, appendix 'B'). Furthermore, the group Mean Differential-Scores equally indicated that the participants exposed to the reframing technique (X=71.23) demonstrated major psychotherapeutic gains with more evidence shown in the acquisition of research skills. Other result details showed that the Rational Emotive Behaviour Technique (X=69.56), Assignment Method (X=54.31); and the Control group (X=48.02) respectively, also indicated the treatment gains even though, the observed statistical details reflected the order of their psychotherapeutic importance and or marginal advantages (Tables 5 and 7; Appendix 'B'). Following these computed details and results therefore; it could therefore be argued that psychotherapies would, undoubtedly be beneficial if they are well harnessed to facilitate learning.

A further re-confirmation, apart from that already indicated (see Tables 5 and 7, appendix 'B') and which utilized the least-significant difference test n (Table 7 especially), the Bonferroni correction method (Tables 8 and 9, appendix 'B') was also used to compare the individual Mean-scores within each cell. Both the least-significant difference test n and Bonferroni are two of the examples of post hoc statistics; and as a coincidence, the cell comparison showed that the means were all significant across the cell levels, at alpha 0.05 (see especially Table 9, appendix 'B'). The information which the psychotherapeutic outcome summarizes arguably supports the assertion that, using the cross-disciplinary learning and or the Blended method of instruction to induce expected learning and or distance learners' research prowess has multiplier effects. Directly related to this was the consequence of the behaviour techniques which were encapsulated in the applied psychotherapy in predicting outcome in professionals' behaviour following the intervention. The findings also corroborated other studies (Betts, Zau & Rice, 2003; Lea, Stephenson & Troy, 2003; O'Neill & McMahon, 2007) that found the marginal utility of psychotherapy very relevant as behaviour modification device. Thus, in stimulating adequate academic and or research behaviour, even within the adaptation of either transdisciplinarity (otherwise, the cross-disciplinary learning) and the Blended Method, at the pre-intervention stage, assessing to know, the entry behaviour of the distance learners is germane to the use and application of adequate psychotherapy (or Behaviour Techniques) with the consequent predictability of their research empowerment. When learners are assessed for what they are, their differential-emotionality would be ascertained easily, while the mentor and or the facilitator then knows how to arrange learning strategies/materials to boost expected research behaviour (i.e. information search, access, and application, etc) as it were, and especially for engendering reliable research output as well as academic competences.

Hypothesis Two

In examining the psychotherapy outcome as indicated in the second hypothesis, the participants were exposed to either the combined intervention effect of Reframing Technique/Assignment Method with the Assignment Method alone and, or the Rational Emotive Behaviour Technique/Assigment and Assignment Method alone as well as Reframing Technique/Rational Emotive Behaviour Technique. With the use of the Analysis of variance statistical method, the findings which utilizes the Fisher's value showed that the outcome was statistically significant with [$F(2,1054)=5.07; P<0.05$]; [$F(1,1055)=3.61; P<0.01$ and [$F(2,1054)=9.70; P<0.05$ for all the dimensionalities (Table 6; Appendix 'B'). The outcome of additional computation, as summarized in Table 5, also showed that the combined effects of Refrtaming Technique/Assignment Method ($X= 73.43$), Rational Emotive Behaviour Technique/ Assignment Method ($X=69.91$) and Reframing Technique /Rational Emotive Behaviour Technique ($X=79.34$) were more useful in terms of the skills that the participants gained as compared to other instances where, participants were exposed to single psychotherapy. For the participants who were exposed to the combined treatment effect, only the group which had the Reframing Technique/Rational Emotive Behaviour Technique was more prominent in developing adequate research behaviour in the professionals as ably supported by the choice and construction of feasible research topics, review of relevant literature, selection and application of appropriate research design as well as quantitative techniques among the distance learners. By implication, and as evident in the computed statistical details, the distance learners' academic problem in research prowess was ably facilitated. It was also noticed that the maturation effect of the participants who are in the non-intervention group with Mean-score of 48.02 (table 5) did not boost their research potentialities.

In juxtaposing the above findings with other related studies, and as it corroborated in particular, that of Seligman (1995), the differential-selection and application of psychotherapies is efficacious for prompting and directing academic behaviour. Academic behaviour in distance higher education and or the open distance learning (otherwise, the higher education generally) can be an all-evolving term that includes skill acquisition for academic credibility and performance (including its marginal advantages), research prowess and its sustainability as well as professional competences. Annexing the benefits of transdisciplinarity therefore, learners can be instructed on the effects of collaboration, interconnectivity of disciplines as well as that which implicate the outcome of shared-knowledge.

Hypothesis Three

Finally, the third hypothesized statement which says that, exposing the distance learners to the individual psychotherapies with a concomitant research prowess will not be significantly different was tested by using the student-t statistical method at the 0.05 alpha levels. The computed details as summarized in Table 7 indicated that its findings were statistically significant; and thus, its findings further support the relevance of psychotherapies and, or behaviour techniques for boosting learners' emotionality and its consequent impact in ameliorating learning/research deficiencies and or limitation, and the concomitant boost to research prowess via different application of behaviour modification strategies. As argued by Osiki (2008abc) and which earlier studies (Deacon & Abramowitz, 2004; Barlow, 2002; Seligman, 1995) had equally confirmed, learners' potential to achieve academically, with a sustainable regularity in academic performance and or credibility, professional behaviour as well as impactful subregional research, is a direct function of their emotionality. Thus, the continued dividends of psychotherapy for behaviour modification, with concomitant effects for positive holistic living, which also exemplifies academic concern (including research), has wide empirical evidences (Roth & Fonagy, 2005; Silverman, 2005).

LIMITATION

A very prominent limitation of the study was its inability to directly follow up on the recipients' continuous use of the benefits of the intervention programmes to impact both, on thier academic and professional competences on the one hand, while on the other, research endeavours. being emotionally empowered, particularly as it arguably relates to value-driven research, among the distance learners, can be very instrumental for the long awaited and cumulative breakthrough and dividends for the continuous emancipation from institutional as well as inmdividual research and academic indolence. Following up the distance learners (i.e. the beneficiaries of the intervention), especially longitudinally, should have had an in-built propensity (otherwise, mechanism) to correct future needs of the learners particularly after their qualifications. The study was thus unable to ascertain, if there are, the number of the distance learners that might have continued to utilize the after-effects of the intervention in further research ventures and or graduate academic studies.

CONCLUSION

Facilitating academic/professional competences, for a sustainable value-driven research in distance higher education and or the open distance learning presupposes that programme facilitators or mentors would essentially be prepared to access information on how the learners learn. Learners, and in particular using the backdrop of either transdisciplinarity and or the cross-disciplinary learning can maximize their learning potentials, when their emotionality is understood, its benefits are annexed and consequently applied both in prompting and sustaining academic competences and professional behaviour within workplaces' standards. Selecting and intentionally arranging learning materials as well as adequate behaviour techniques, that are otherwise subsumed psychotherapeutically, are necessary conditions for stimulating meaningful learning in especially the open distance learning. It thus means therefore that, if professionals in the distance higher education and or open distance learning programme, particularly within the African sub-regions, are to benefit from the marginal differences accruable from the selection and application of the multi-model techniques, stimulating research empowerment, with the concomitant dividends, would be nurtured, developed and advanced within inter-disciplinarity and or cross-disciplinary learning. The suggestion therefore, is that which re-echoes the revitalization in the twenty-first century, a new dawn of vigorous academic behaviour that arguably involves research, especially within the African sub-regions, that annexes the benefits of the multi-model structure juxtaposed with cross-disciplinary learning for sustainable and impactful global research dividends.

REFERENCES

(2001, May). Cheating thrives on campus, as officials turn their heads. *USA Today, NewsMax.com Wires*. Retrieved on October 3, 2008, from http://archive.newsmax.com/archives/articles/2001/5/21/ 72734.shtml

Adkins, J., Kenkel, C., & Lim, C. L. (2008). *Deterrents to online academic dishonesty*. Retrieved on February 6, 2008, from http://jwpress.com/JLHE/issues/viii/Deterrents%20to%20online%20academic%20dishonesty.pdf

Allen, M. J., & Yen, W. M. (2002). Introduction to measurement theory. New York: Long Grove IL Waveland Press.

Bailey, K. (2001). Towards unifying science: Applying concepts across disciplinary boundaries. *Systems Research and Behavioral Science, 18*, 41–62. doi:10.1002/sres.364

Bammer, G. (2005). Integration and implementation sciences: Building a new specialization. *Ecology and Society, 10*(2), 6. Retrieved on October 2, 2008, from www.ecologyandsociety.org/vol10/iss2/art6/ES-2005-1360.pdf

Barlow, D. H. (2002). *Anxiety and its disorders: The nature and treatment of anxiety and panic.* New York: Guilford.

Betts, J. R., Zau, A. C., & Rice, L. A. (2003). *Determinants of student achievement: New evidence from San Diego.* San Francisco, CA: Public Policy Institute of California.

Braimoh, D., & Osiki, J. O. (2008). *From empowerment to transformation: A capacity building model for academics in distance higher education institutions in Africa.* Retrieved on October 3, 2008, from http://www.nou.edu.ng/noun/acde2008/acde_en/abstracts/mdg_rpi_odl.html

Bruun, H., & Laine, S. (2006). *Using the self-organizing map for measuring interdisciplinary research.* Retrieved on September 30, 2008, from http://www.stes.fi/scai2006/proceedings/001.pdf

Collis, B., & Margaryan, A. (2004). Applying activity theory to computer-supported collaborative learning and work-based activities in corporate setting. *Educational Technology Research and Development, 52*, 38–52. doi:10.1007/BF02504717

Continuous Assessment Plan. (2006). School principal program, grade P-12 other school personnel program: Professional education unit. University of Kentucky. Retrieved on November 13, 2007, from http://www.coe.uky.edu/acadserv/programs/CA/camadsu3.doc

Cottingham, K. (2002). Tackling biocomplexity: The role of people, tools, and scales. *Bioscience, 52*(9), 793–799. doi:10.1641/0006-3568(2002)052[0793:TBTROP]2.0.CO;2

Cronbach, L. J. (1951). Coefficient alpha and the internal structure of tests. *Psychometrika, 16*(3), 297–334. doi:10.1007/BF02310555

Csikszentimihalyi, M. (1999). Implications of a system's perspective for the study of creativity. In R. J. Sternberg (Ed.), *Handbook of creativity.* Cambridge, UK: Cambridge University Press.

Deacon, B. J., & Abramowitz, J. S. (2004). Cognitive and behavioural treatments for anxiety disorders: A review of meta-analysis findings. *Journal of Clinical Psychology, 60*(4), 429–441. doi:10.1002/jclp.10255

Dewulf, A., François, G., Pahl-Wostl, C., & Taillieu, T. (2007). A framing approach to cross-disciplinary research collaboration: Experiences from a large-scale research project on adaptive water management. *Ecology and Society, 12*(2), 14. Retrieved on January 11, 2008, from http//www.ecologyandsociety.org/vol12/iss2/art14/

Erbaugh, S. E. (2007). *The attributes of psychotherapy for depression.* Retrieved on November 9, 2007, from http://www.healthplace.com/comminities/depression/treatment/therapy/psych_vs_meds.asp

Geen, R. (1994). *Human motivation: A psychological approach.* New York: Wadsworth Publishing.

Hutchins, E. (1995). *Cognition in the wild.* New York: MIT Press.

Johnson, W. B., Huwe, J. M., & Lucas, J. L. (2000). Rational mentoring. *Journal of Rational-Emotive & Cognitive-Behavior Therapy, 18*, 39–54. doi:10.1023/A:1007713804708

Koch, K. (2002). Cheating in schools. *The CQ Researcher, 10*(32), 745–768.

Kwa, C. (2002). Does interdisciplinarity really exist? Retrieved on September 30, 2008, from http://www.easst.net/review/march2002/kwa

Lea, S. J., Stephenson, D., & Troy, J. (2003). Higher education students' attitudes to student-centred learning: Beyond educational bulimia. *Studies in Higher Education, 28*(3), 321–334. doi:10.1080/03075070309293

Lele, S. R., & Norgaard, R. B. (2005). Practicing interdisciplinarity. *Bioscience, 55*(11), 967–975. doi:10.1641/0006-3568(2005)055[0967:PI]2.0.CO;2

Levina, N., & Vaast, E. (2005). The emergence of boundary spanning competence in practice: Implications for implementation and use of information systems. *MIS Quarterly, 29*(2), 335–363.

Maasen, S., & Weingart, P. (2000). Metaphors and the dynamics of knowledge. London & New York: Routledge.

Magnus, P. D. (2007). Distributed cognition and the task of science. *Social Studies of Science, 37*(2), 297–310. doi:10.1177/0306312706072177

Mayer, R. E. (1999). Fifty years of creativity research. In R. J. Sternberg (Ed.), *Handbook of*

McCabe, D. L. (1993). Faculty responses to academic dishonesty: The influence of student honour codes. *Research in Higher Education, 34*, 647–658. doi:10.1007/BF00991924

Newell, B., Crumley, C. L., Hassan, N., Lambin, C., Pahl-Wostl, C., & Underdal, A. (2005). A conceptual template for integrative human-environment research. *Global Environmental Change, 15*, 229–307. doi:10.1016/j.gloenvcha.2005.06.003

Nitko, A. J. (2004). *Continuous assessment and performance assessment.* Retrieved on November 13, 2007, from http://www.moec.gov.jm/project/newhorizons/pdf/assessment/2004/ca/presentation fancy

O'Neill, G., & McMahon, T. (2007). Student-centred learning: What does it mean for students and lecturers? Retrieved on December 14, 2007, from http//www.aishe.org/readings/2005-1/oneill-Mcmahon-Tues_19th_oct_SCL.pdf

Olt, M. R. (2008). *Ethics and distance education: Strategies for minimizing academic dishonesty in online assessment.* Retrieved on February 2, 2008, from http://www.westga.edu/~distance/ojdla/fall53/olt53.html

Osiki, J. O. (1999). The experimental research methodology and randomized controlled trials in psychological investigations: Participants' preference. *Ilorin Journal of Education, 20*(June), 24–37.

Osiki, J. O. (2007). Empowering distance learners' research prowess through the effective utilization of three psychotherapies. *Lesotho Social Science Review, 11*, 97–113.

Osiki, J. O. (2008). Enhancing the academic performance through the identification and psychological management of victims of Asperger syndrome. *Ozean Journal of Social Science, 1*(1), 29–42.

Osiki, J. O. (2008b). Extracurricular activities and teacher attitude to girl-child education and psycho-emotional preparedness. *Indian Journal of Social Science, 17*(1), 73–82.

Osiki, J. O. (2008c). Empowering the culture of quality research within ethical standards in distance education. In T. T. Kidd (Ed.), *Online education and adult learning: New frontiers for teaching practices.* University of Texas Health Science Center.

Osiki, J. O. (in press). Research empowerment in professional teacher development: The effect of blended learning approach in distance education in Africa. In M. M. Mboya (Ed.), *Open and distance learning.* NEPAD

Osiki, J. O., & Braimoh, D. (in press). Management of learning behaviour in higher education: The outcome of cooperative and collaborative approaches, National University of Lesotho Southern Africa. *South African Journal of Higher Education.*

Paulsen, M. F. (2003). *On cooperative learning*. Retrieved on April 28, 2008, from http://www.psychegames.com/cooperative-learning.htm

Pennington, D. D. (2008). Cross-disciplinary collaboration and learning. *Ecology and Society 13*(2), 8. Retrieved on September 26, 2008, from http://www.ecologyandsociety.org/vol13/iss2/art8/

Pickett, S., Burch, W. R. Jr, & Grove, J. M. (1999). Interdisciplinary research: Maintaining the constructive impulse in a culture of criticism. *Ecosystem, 2*, 302–307. doi:10.1007/s100219900081

Roth, A., & Fonagy, P. (2005). What works for whom?: A critical review of psychotherapy research, 2nd ed. New York: Guilford Press.

Schaffer, S. P., Lei, K., Reyes, L., Oakes, W., & Zoltowski, C. (2006). Analyzing cross-disciplinary design teams. Retrieved on September 26, 2008, from http://epics.ecn.purdue.edu/about/papers./FIE2006_crossdisciplinary.pdf

Schaffer, S. P., & Richardson, J. (2004). Supporting technology integration within a teacher education System. *Journal of Educational Computing Research, 31*(4), 421–433. doi:10.2190/V1BX-35NW-7AH6-6MME

Seligman, M. E. P. (1995). The effectiveness of psychotherapy: The consumer reports study. *The American Psychologist, 50*(12), 965–974. doi:10.1037/0003-066X.50.12.965

Silverman, D. K. (2005). What works in psychotherapy and how do we know?: What evidence-based practice has to offer. *Psychoanalytic Psychology, 22*(2), 306–312. doi:10.1037/0736-9735.22.2.306

Strober, M. H. (2008). *Habits of the mind: Challenges for multi-disciplinary engagement.* Retrieved on September 30, 2008, from http://www.stanford.edu/~myras/challenges.pdf

Taylor, B. (2007). *Integrity: Academic and political. A letter to my students.* Retrieved on August 23, 2007 from http://www.mcmaster.ca/cll/resources/nifty.notes/david.godden/Integrity.pdf

University of Ibadan. *Nigeria: The vision for the 21st century*. Retrieved on October 2, 2008, from http://www.uiadvancement.org/vision_mission.pdf

Uppsala-Stanford-Karolinska project and the Stanford Alliance for a Global Bioinformatics Curriculum. (2008). *"Cross-Disciplinary Learning: Bioinformatics."* Retrieved on September 26, 2008, from summit.stanford.edu/pdfs/CDLbioinformatics_tearsheet.pdf

Wear, D. N. (1999). Challenges to interdisciplinary discourse. *Ecosystem, 2*, 299–301. doi:10.1007/s100219900080

Weingart, P. (2000).Interdisciplinarity: The paradoxical discourse. In P. Weingart & N. Stehr (Eds.), *Practicing interdisciplinarity*. Toronto: University of Toronto Press Incorporation.

Weingart, P., & Stehr, N. (2000). *Practicing interdisciplinarity*. Toronto: University of Toronto Press Incorporation.

Yin, R. K. (1994). *Case study research: Design and methods* (2nd ed.). Beverly Hills, CA: Sage.

APPENDIX: A [RESEARCH MEASURE]

Research Status Inventory [ReSI]

Rate yourself on how good you think you are to the following sub-themes in Research Writing and Reporting

Table 1. Personal quality

S/N	Category of sub-themes	Very Good	Moderately Good	Not Good At All
1.	Choosing feasible titles/topics			
2.	Developing issues for background			
3.	Statement of problem			
4.	Rationale for the Study			
5.	Conceptual definition of terms			
6.	objective of the Study			
7.	Review of Related Literature			
8.	Library information Retrieval			
9.	Theoretical Framework			
10.	Empirical Background			
11	Conceptual Model			
12.	Research Questions/Hypotheses			
13.	Research Design			
14.	Sample and Sampling Technique			
15.	Research Measure			
16.	Research Procedure/administration			
17.	Data Analysis/Use of Statistics			
18.	Results and Findings(use of tables)			
19.	Discussion of Findings			

Table 2. Preference indicator [AI]

S/N	Item Category	Yes	No
1.	Research Project is Optional.	971 (98.2%)	17 (1.7%)
2.	I am free to decide between writing a dissertation and, or contributing few articles for journal publication.	314 (77.9%)	89 (22.1%)
3.	There is nothing like writing and submitting dissertation at all.	986 (97.9%)	21(2.1%)
4.	Dissertation is compulsory but I can be free to contract it out for payment	516 (71.8)	203(28.2%)
5.	Dissertation is compulsory and cannot be contracted out.	96 (16.4%)	491 (83.6%)
6.	Dissertation is made part of regular University Programmes that would be taught and examined at the end of session only.	879 (74.7%)	298 (25.3%)

Table 3. Preference indicator [AII]-emotionality

S/N	Item-Type	Yes	No
7.	I like research methodology/project; it prepares me for the future	67 (16.1%))	349 (83.9%)
8.	I hate to do statistics	294 (78.4%)	81 (21.6%)
9.	I would be happier if research project was not compulsory	297 (68.1%)	139 (31.9%)
10.	I just cannot say what my position is with research methodology	211 (73.3%)	77 (26.7%)
11.	Writing and reporting project is what I like the most	79 (21.6%)	286 (78.4%)

APPENDIX B

Tabular Summaries of Computed Statistical Details

Table 4. Analysis of variance (ANOVA) comparing the combined outcome of participants in the intervention conditions (i.e. RT, REBT, AM, CT).

Source of Variation	Sum of Square	df	Mean Square	F-Dist.	P
Main Effect	165.204	4	41.301	7.52	<0.05
RT/REBT/AM/CT	165.204	4	41.301	7.52	<0.05
Explained	165.204	4	41.301	7.52	<0.05
Residual	5783.1813	1053	5.4821		
Total	5948.3853	1057			

$F(4, 1052) = 7.52; P<0.05$

Table 5. Group means-differential scores comparison

Category of Variable	Column (X)
RT	71.23
REBT	69.56
AM	54.31
CT	48.02
RT/AM	73.43
REBT/AM	69.91
RT/REBT	73.47

Table 6. Analysis of variance (ANOVA) comparing the outcome of participants in the intervention conditions (i.e. RT/AM, AM alone, REBT/AM, AM alone and CT).

Source of Variation	Sum of Square	df	Mean Square	F-Dist.	P
Main Effect	372.138	2	186.069	5.07	<0.05
RT/AM	372.138	2	186.069	5.07	<0.05
AM	132.487	1	132.487	3.61	<0.01
CT	95.787	1	95.787	2.61	<0.01
REBT/AM	711.98	2	355.99	9.70	<0.05
Error	38576.41	1054	36.7		
Total	39888.802	1056			

i. $F(2,1054\}=5.07;P<0.05$
ii. $F(1,1055)=3.61;P<0.01$
iii. $F(2,1054)=9.70;P<0.05$

Table 7. Student-t outcome results of intervention group showing mean-scores, standard deviation, t-cal. and the degree of freedom comparison

Category of Variable	N=1057 n	X	SD	t-Cal.	df	P
RT REBT	274 308	71.23 69.56	4.174 6.320	10.02	580	P<0.05
RT AM	274 251	71.23 54.31	4.174 5.341	6.61	523	P<0.05
REBT AM	308 251	69.56 54.31	6.320 5.341	7.64	557	P<0.05
RT CT	274 224	71.23 48.02	4.174 5.801	5.91	496	p<0.05
REBT CT	308 224	69.56 48.02	6.320 5.801	4.85	530	P<0.05
AM CT	251 224	54.31 48.02	5.341 5.801	3.57	473	P<0.05

Table 8. Confidence intervals

Comparison	Mean1 - Mean2	95% CI of difference
1: RT VS. REBT	+ 1.67	+ 0.34 to + 3.00
2: RT VS. AM	+ 16.92	+ 15.52 to + 18.32
3: REBT VS. AM	+ 15.25	+ 13.85 to + 16.65
4: RT VS. CT	+ 23.21	+ 21.74 to + 24.68
5: REBT VS. CT	+ 21.54	+ 20.07 to + 23.01
6: AM VS. CT	+ 6.29	+ 4.82 to + 7.76

Table 9. Statistical significance

Comparison	Significant? (P <0.05?)	t
1: RT VS. REBT	Yes	3.319
2: RT VS. AM	Yes	31.967
3: REBT VS. AM	Yes	28.812
4: RT VS. CT	Yes	41.683
5: REBT VS. CT	Yes	38.684
6: AM VS. CT	Yes	11.296

Chapter 18
Comparing IT and Non-IT Faculty and Students' Perceptions on Blended Learning

Eugenia M. W. Ng
Hong Kong Institute of Education, Hong Kong

ABSTRACT

The successful implementation of blended learning depends on many factors, but the interactions between academics and students far outweigh technology and all other factors put together. However, so far, no satisfactory research has been conducted relating to teacher education or to providing a comprehensive analysis on academic and student teachers' perceptions. For the purpose of this study, thirteen academics were interviewed or attended focus group meetings to share their views on blended learning. Some of them were classified as information technology (IT) academics whilst others were not. The academics had a very positive attitude towards the concept of blended learning and there were no notable differences between IT and non-IT academics. Their findings are also cross referenced with findings from students who participated in a questionnaire survey. There were a total of seventy student teachers, who participated in the survey. Forty-four of them were regarded as IT students whilst the rest was regarded as non-IT students. These two groups of students gave high ratings on most of the questionnaire items. There were some minor differences between the two groups of students but the differences were not very statistically significant. These thought-provoking findings not only serve as practical and beneficial information for The Hong Kong Institute of Education, but they also serve as an invaluable source of knowledge and information for all individuals in the field of teacher education.

INTRODUCTION

Information Technology (IT) has presented a new environment for learning and teaching worldwide since the rapid development of the Internet started in the mid 1990s. IT plays a vital role in the modern world by providing easy access, flexibility and simplicity of communication, supporting multimedia presentations and enabling communication virtually, with anyone, anywhere in the world. IT has

DOI: 10.4018/978-1-60566-852-9.ch018

presented a new arena for learning and teaching, by permeating all aspects of our daily lives. Most universities in developed countries have invested large sums of money in different electronic learning (e-learning) initiatives (Alexander, 2001). Some universities offer online courses, whilst some adopt e-learning tools to complement regular face-to-face lectures.

The author is an academic who educates student teachers. It is inappropriate to replace regular lectures wholly, with online studies for educating student teachers who require good communication skills, interpersonal skills and subject knowledge. Yet it is perceived that there is a need to adopt technology in teaching and learning, in order to enable student teachers to learn contemporary pedagogies and skills through experiential learning. Therefore, a blended learning approach, which means effectively combining face-to-face teaching and learning with e-learning, appears to be the best teaching approach. In fact, there is no agreed definition of blended learning and yet, blended learning usually means to learn through a combination of digital and physical resources and media.

Blended learning provides educators with an additional platform to apply further new teaching strategies and thereby, better equip our future teachers with abilities and skills for independent and life-long learning. The teachers in turn then cultivate these same abilities and skills in their students at schools. However, extra effort needs to be expended by teachers to gain and achieve the positive impact imparted by blended learning. Myers, Bennett, Brown & Henderson (2004) suggested that "these opportunities also increase substantially the time and energy required of faculty to achieve the potential of online learning environments" (p.79). Therefore, the author attempted to uncover the perceptions of both academics and students on blended learning.

The following section will be on pertinent literature research, followed by research findings and discussions. Finally, the conclusion, recommendations and suggestions for future research directions are then made. However, both the literature and research will concentrate more on the e-learning side, as there are far too many face-to-face teaching approaches.

LITERATURE REVIEW

Koschmann (1996) suggests that we are "currently witnessing the emergence of a new paradigm in IT research" (p. 10). He further suggests that this newly emerging paradigm is built on the disciplines of anthropology, sociology, linguistics, and communication science, which focus on language, culture and the nature of the social setting. Indeed, there are different approaches to adopting IT in education and the main advantage lies in the flexibility and convenience of these approaches. IT plays an important role in supporting learning, such as the provision of information in multiple modes, utilizing technologies as mind tools, and scaffolding conversations virtually with anyone in the world (Jonassen, 2000; Jonassen, Peck, & Wilson, 1999). Communication exchanges such as e-mail, wikis and discussion forums provide a flexible and convenient arena for single or multiple users, to discuss a range of topics, synchronously or asynchronously. Messages can be stored, edited and retrieved easily at the discretion of users, without the requirement of sophisticated software. Furthermore, electronic communications enhance learning by enabling students with diverse backgrounds and from differing locations, to obtain and subsequently offer multiple perspectives and solutions to various problems (Lipponen, 2002). In fact, a number of researchers (Applefield, Huber, & Moadlem, 2000; Muukkonen, Hakkarainen, & Lakkala, 2005; Scardamalia, 2002; Woodruff, Brett, MacDonald, & Nason, 1998) have also found that learning environments facilitate student-centered learning.

Factors Affecting E-Learning

There are many critical factors such as technology, pedagogy, attitude, social interactions and content design which affect the success of e-learning. Technological resources such as hardware, software, and communication technologies are important factors affecting user accessibility and reactions to particular aspects of e-learning. The efficiency and potential effectiveness of system design and implementation directly contribute to influencing user behavior (Mowshowitz, 1997). Ginns & Ellis (2007) argued that students' perceptions of teaching quality are closely related to the quality of their learning outcomes. They also found that positive perceptions about e-learning had a higher correlation with deeper learning and astute understanding. A survey conducted on administrators and educators suggested that monetary support, pedagogy and technical competency were the three most critical components for offering quality online courses (Kim & Bonk, 2006).

The attitudes and capabilities of educators and learners when using IT are accepted as important factors influencing the success of e-learning (Hiltz, 1994; Jarvenpaa & Staples, 2000; Larson & Bruning, 1996; McCollum, 1997). Keengwe (2007) found that faculty integration of computer technology positively affected students' perceptions of using computer to improve their learning. Teacher perceptions of technology are also a key factor in adopting learning technologies successfully. When learning technologies are considered to be part of the teaching approach, educators are seen to be more readily integrated. This suggests learning with the technology as opposed to learning from the technology (Jonassen, Howland, Marra, & Marra, 2003). When technology is seen as a tool to assist the learning process, it appears to be more readily adopted and integrated by academic staff. Furthermore, Kanuka (2008) argued that "knowing our own and others' philosophies provides us with the ability to understand the consequences of our technological choices, as well as the effect that our philosophical orientation has on our learners." (p. 93).

Learning design can be subsumed under the term pedagogy. Learning design refers to a variety of ways of designing student learning experiences, which include the sequence of activities and interactions (Oliver, Harper, Wills, Agostinho, & Hedberg, 2007). Boud and Prosser (2002) suggest that a learning design should examine four principles: engage learners; acknowledge the learning context; challenge learners and provide practice. Oliver, Harper, Wills, Agostinho & Hedberg (2007) also suggest that learning design should include the learners' prior knowledge and their desires and thereafter, build on these expectations. However, we cannot assume that all learners are willing to execute the tasks and activities that lead to quality learning, and they need structured learning experiences that are supported by their educators (McLoughlin, 2002).

In a learning environment, interactivity involves the way people think, act and communicate. The relationships and interactions among educators and students are a significant facilitator or inhibitor to teaching and learning in the e-learning mode. It is imperative that members are comfortable with open discussions and decision making, in relation to e-learning (Claver, Llopis, Gonzalez, & Gasco, 2001; Hiltz, 1994). Morrison (2003) suggested that learning activities should be embedded within the learning environment, and that the operation of the mediating tools should be designed to facilitate group coherence and to promote social interaction among learners. "In effective online learning, the instructor acts as facilitator, encouraging students to take charge of their own learning process" (Palloff & Pratt, 2003, p125). In other words, the teaching and learning needs to become a more shared experience. The students' roles also change, and they have to assume responsibility for their own learning. They have to assume the roles of initiators and co-participants in self-regulating learning processes (Collis & Moonen, 2001).

In fact, the success of e-learning depends on the design and interactivity among the diverse elements mentioned above, and these are all influenced by information culture and national culture. Information culture refers to the characteristics of administrators, learners and educators in the use of collaborative information technology for knowledge sharing (Davenport, 1997; Jarvenpaa & Staples, 2000). National culture refers to "the collective programming of the mind that distinguishes the members of one group or category of people from another" (Hofstede, 2001). However, technology is only useful, when it cannot be taught more effectively using another teaching method (Keppell, Au, Ma, & Chan, 2004).

Fjermestad, Hiltz & Zhang (2005) performed a comprehensive review of a hundred empirical studies, on comparing face-to-face versus asynchronous learning networks (combining self-study with substantial, rapid, asynchronous interactivity), up to November 2002. They found that most results are mixed but student learning was established to be significantly better. They also did not find any research related to faculty satisfaction and the most frequently cited disciplines were IT followed by Business and Management (Fjermestad et al., 2005). Subsequently, Alexander & Golja (2007) conducted a study on academics and students' perspective on an e-learning system and yet no comparative analysis was performed, based on their background.

Research Frameworks

In view of the multiplicity of factors which might affect the quality of e-learning, numerous researchers (Alavi & Leidner, 2001; Benbunan-Fich, Hiltz, & Harasim, 2005; Hiltz, 1994) suggested research frameworks to guide research in this area. Benbunan-Fich, Hiltz & Harasim (2005) designed a research framework, an input-process-output model, which is very wide-ranging and comprehensive in its scope. The independent variables (input factors) in this framework include technology, course, instructor and student characteristics; the intervening factor is the learning process; and the dependent variables (outcomes) include access, faculty satisfaction, student learning, student satisfaction and cost effectiveness.

Our institute, The Hong Kong Institute of Educations (HKIEd), has adopted a learning platform since 2000, but no research has been conducted to investigate the perceptions of blended learning within the Institute. In fact, a number of studies have indicated that teacher education does not adequately prepare teachers to teach with technology (Pope, Hare, & Howard, 2002; Selinger, 2001) and in order to successfully implement this, it is suggested that teacher education systems should integrate content, pedagogy and technology (Hughes, 2005; Koehler, Mishra, & Yahya, 2007). During the initial stage of examining the different factors which lead to successful blended learning experiences, the author attempted to explore various input factors such as perceptions of students and faculty members, with regard to their IT competency, e-learning materials and experiences, the value of discussion forums and their preferences of blended learning. In particular, the author endeavored to find out whether IT and non-IT faculty and students have any differences in terms of their perceptions, even though Ginns & Ellis (2007), believed that "evaluating the quality of blended learning experiences is no easy matter, as technologies typically support only part of the learning processes that the students engage in" (p.54). Figure 1 depicts this study in graphic detail.

BACKGROUND

HKIEd is a teacher education tertiary institute in Hong Kong. The Institute has around four hundred and thirty faculty members working in eight departments, based on their specializations. It has realized the potential of utilizing IT to assist learning and in the process has supported many

Figure 1. Research framework

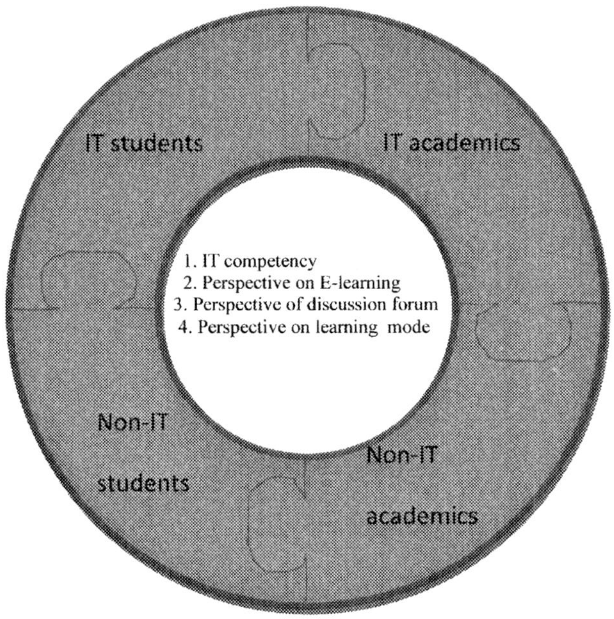

projects related to web-based learning, during the past few years. HKIEd has adopted a popular learning platform, namely Blackboard, to facilitate this new mode of learning. The Office of Information Technology and Services (ITS) (http://www.ied.edu.hk/its/index.htm) supports the hardware and software services of the Institute and is responsible for promoting and supporting the use of IT in the Institute. On the other hand, the Centre for Learning, Teaching and Technology (LTTC) (http://www.ied.edu.hk/lttc/) supports the pedagogical use of Information & Communications Technology (ICT) by helping faculty, through providing educational consulting to faculty members, conducting workshops, organizing seminars and by supporting the overall professional development of academic staff in innovative pedagogies. For the adoption of new technologies and ideas, our Institute has organized various workshops, projects, research seminars and action learning projects. This is indicative of Rogers framework (Rogers, 2003), which says that through the diffusion of innovations framework, evaluators and researchers are able to gain better insight and understanding of the grounds based upon which an educational program results in adoption or rejection of a particular practice.

DATA COLLECTION

A number of teacher educators were invited to share their e-learning experiences by e-mail. Eight of them participated in three separate focus group meetings and five teachers were interviewed individually. The educators' experiences ranged from the beginner user (who had the experience of using the learning platform for team teaching but she planned to use it in the forthcoming semester on her own) to the more experienced users, who had used learning platforms to facilitate learning and teaching and to complement face-to-face teaching, for more than five years. Two of them were from the IT discipline and the rest of the teacher educators were from different disciplines, ranging from Music, English, and Chinese to Physical Education. Two teachers had created a web site for module delivery, while three other educators were regarded as IT experts by their Department. Therefore, a total of seven teacher educators, (in Italics as shown in Appendix 1), could be classified as IT academics, as they were very competent in integrating IT into their teaching and research methods, whilst the rest of the teacher educators could be classified as non-IT academics. For reasons of privacy, in order to protect their identities, the alphabetical letters from 'AA' to 'MM' were used to denote their names. All of them were asked to share their experiences of e-learning through retrospective interviews. Their interviews/focus-group meetings were taped, recorded and transcribed by a research assistant. The transcriptions were sent back to the participants for comments and finally, the revised transcriptions were sent yet again to the academics for confirmation of the transcriptions.

Apart from getting opinions from academics, seventy pre-service student teachers taking the Bachelor of Education (Primary) programme at HKIEd, were requested to answer a questionnaire, in order to have a cross comparison between faculty and students. Forty four of the student teachers had taken an IT module either as an elective or as one of their IT minor studies module. They were primarily Year 1 or Year 2 students and they are classified as IT students for the purposes of this paper. The remaining twenty six participants had taken General Studies as their major of study and did not take IT as their minor or their elective, and they were Year 4 students (hereafter termed non-IT students). The author hopes that the different backgrounds of these student teachers help us to gain more realistic and pragmatic perceptions of blended learning.

The IT students took an IT module with the author. The module material, discussion forum and announcements were put together on Blackboard to facilitate learner-centered learning. The lessons were conducted through a face-to-face method, but one lesson was conducted completely online, to enable the learners to have an authentic e-learning experience. They were required to learn how to use software which had multi-media instructions and related resources on the web site. The IT students were then asked to accomplish a task in groups, which was to be submitted within two weeks, as evidence of their e-learning capabilities and skills. They were also asked to discuss pertinent issues with student teachers in Australia via a discussion forum. The non-IT students had no online lessons but they could have more experience of using the learning platform for supporting learning. The IT student teachers were asked to fill in an online questionnaire during their break time, towards the end of the semester, whilst the non-IT student teachers filled in the same questionnaire, using hard copies, as they had very few computers in their classrooms. The measurement instrument was developed using a five-point Likert-type scale where "1" stands for "Strongly Disagree", "2" stands for "Disagree", "3" stands for "Agree", "4" stands for "Strongly Agree" and "0" stands for "Not Applicable".

FINDINGS AND DISCUSSION

All thirteen participating academics were extremely positive on their e-learning experiences and in particular, they comprehended and accepted the functions of the discussion forum. Non-IT academic AA commented that "e-learning is the current trend for education … students can use it to construct knowledge without time and space constraints". IT academic BB thought that the multiple formats and different channels of communication provided by IT, prompted him to adopt e-learning to foster his own self-learning skills.

IT academic JJ opined that the biggest challenge of blended learning was to instruct and inculcate in learners the discipline to devote equal amounts of time, for participation in both online and face-to-face activities. This was because it was found that some learners could get hooked on participating only in online communications and activities, while not allocating enough time for other activities. Furthermore, non-IT academic II believed that since teaching was only a small and limited part of her life, it was detrimental to her health and well-being, to be encouraged to dedicate twenty-four hours to learning and teaching. However, the true criterion of a good educator is one who would like to improve the quality of teaching and learning. Non-IT academic MM said that "the online learning platform is a good tool to communicate with students and to connect all types of interaction between teachers and students and among students".

Student participants' responses were generally positive on the questionnaire items, as most of the items had more than half the answers which were rated as "agree" or "strongly agree". Any mean score above 2.5 was regarded as "agree". The participants gave the highest rating to "my level of computer competency is good enough to access different materials" (mean of 3.09), followed by, "the course materials are better structured when made online" (mean of 3.03). They however, gave the lowest rating to, "I prefer to take some modules completely delivered online" (mean of 2.26). These low ratings did not suggest that our respondents were negative about blended learning, but only that they are not at ease with wholly online courses. The plausible reason for the low rating this item received could be attributed to that fact that they did not "enjoy reading academic material on-line, as much as listening to instructors in classrooms" (mean of 2.47), even though they believed that "the course materials are better structured when made online" (mean of 3.03).

In general, both academics and student teachers displayed a positive and optimistic attitude about the concept of e-learning (Alexander & Golja, 2007; Ginns & Ellis, 2007). After extracting the general substance of the findings, the following sections aim to discuss the perceptions of educators and learners in greater detail, in particular, to compare IT versus non-IT educators and learners.

Information Technology (IT) Competency

It was found that none of the academics had encountered any major problems, when using the learning platform. All the academics, except one of the IT academics, mastered the functionalities of a learning platform through a trial and error approach, in much the same way as countless academics do, in other parts of the world (Folkers, 2005). Subsequently, two of the participants attended a workshop, which was organized by our supporting unit. Two participants were fortunate to be able take part in projects, which largely relied on assistance from research assistants or project leaders. Two of the participants also sought help from our supporting unit, which had technicians and research assistants. The nature of the assistance they received, varied from assisting the student teachers perform some simple operations such as helping them to create discussion forums and uploading teaching materials; to more complex procedures such as changing the format of files into HMTL format, so that the material appears in a hyperlinked format, rather than sequentially. It was evident that the academics perceived informal learning and mentoring as much more conducive to successful IT implementation, than formal courses and workshops (Granger, Morbey, Lotherington, Owston, & Wideman, 2002). It is indeed encouraging to know that even though our Institute does not have a comprehensive system to prepare educators for e-learning, as some universities such as The State University of New York (SUNY) do, (Shea, Fredericksen, Pickett, Pelz, & Swan, 2001), yet the support system at the HKIEd is more than adequate and satisfactory and is committed to promoting and supporting the use of IT in the Institute.

The students were asked two questions related to IT competency. For the question "easy to use computers", the average was 2.84, which is inclined towards the "agree" side as an average over 2.5 is regarded on the agree side. Similarly,

Table 1. Mean and standard deviation of the perceptions on IT competency

Item	Mean	S. D.
My level of computer competency is good enough to access different materialsf	3.09	0.5
Easy to use computers	2.84	0.65

the mean for the question "my level of computer competency is good enough to access different materials", was 3.09, which suggests that students perceived that they possessed sufficient IT competency to successfully engage in a blend of technology and non-technology supported learning activities.

Interestingly, the mean score for IT students (3.07) was lower than the mean for non-IT students (3.11) for the question "my level of computer competency is good enough to access different materials" and the distribution of ratings can be found at Figure 2. This suggests that the first/second-year undergraduates perceived that they had lower IT competency than final year students which is acceptable. In this study, a t-test was performed to analyze the two sets of data. Results of the t-test showed that there was no statistical significance between the two groups of students for the item "my level of computer competency is good enough to access different materials" (t-test=-0.332, df=68, p=0.741, at the 0.05 level of significance).

My Level of Computer Competency Is Good Enough to Access Different Materials

Figure 3 shows the respondents' rating for the question "easy to use computers", which is mostly positive. The mean scores for both groups of students were almost identical as the mean for IT students was 2.84 and that for non-IT students was 2.85 respectively. A t-test was performed and again it was found that there was no statistical significance between the two groups of students for the item "easy for me to use computers" (t-test = -0.091, df=68, p=0.928, at the 0.05 level of significance).

Easy for Me to Use Computer

The findings suggest that both academics and student teachers were perceived to have good IT competency to adopt e-learning, or rather for adopting an approach, which is a blend of technology and non-technology supported learning activities (Keengwe, 2007). However, it was

Figure 2. Perceptions on "level of computer competency"

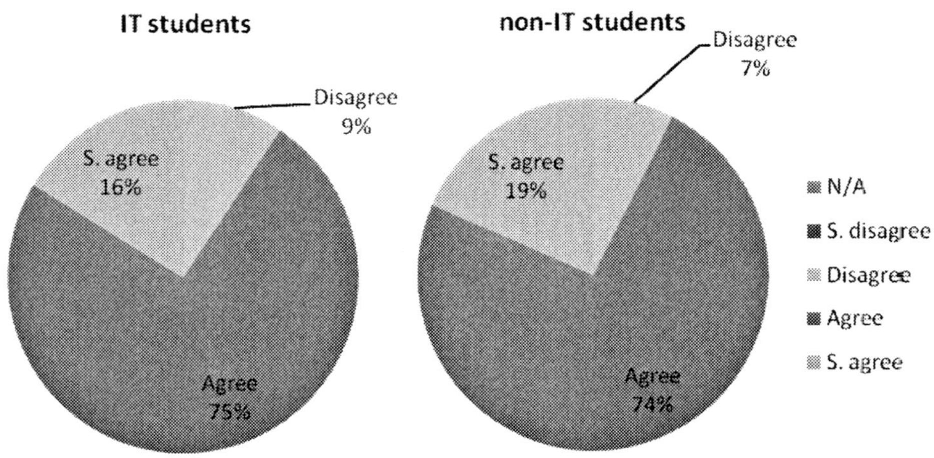

Figure 3. Perceptions on "easy for me to use computer"

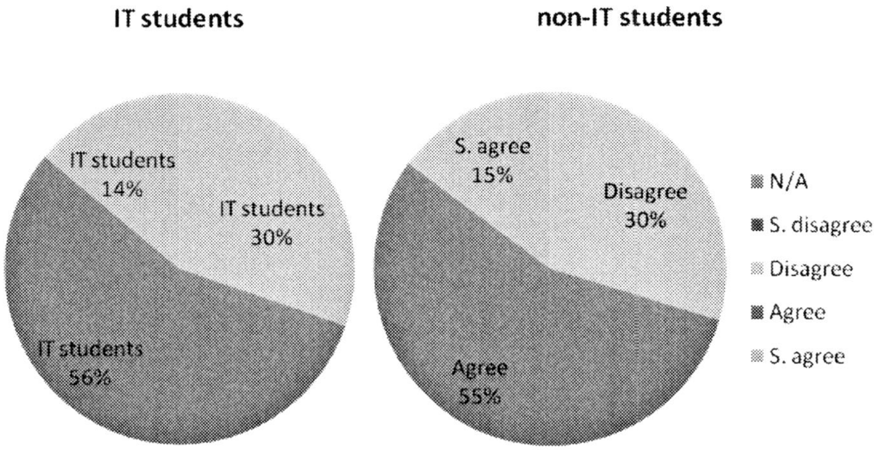

worth noting that there was a difference between IT and non-IT academics, when it came to their willingness to self-learn and imbibe new knowledge. The IT students perceived themselves as possessing a lower level of competency in IT, in spite of studying the subject. Perhaps they were studying at the junior level of university education and would expect to increase their competency during the course of studies.

Perceptions on E-Learning Materials and Experiences

Apart from mastering the techniques of e-learning, the academics in the study, believed that if students understand the need and benefits of e-learning, this alone would motivate them to accept e-learning. IT academic CC commented, "the lecturers have to convince students of the advantages of e-learning. It is useful for them to know this, because very soon, most of the schools in Hong Kong will introduce online learning". IT academic CC further substantiated this fact by stating that, "learner characteristics such as motivation and independent learning capability are two things that make the e-leaning environment successful". Non-IT academic MM said that, "e-learning is more powerful than classroom teaching, because students have more opportunities to learn by themselves". IT academic JJ concurred and thought that e-learning enabled educators to effortlessly provide readily available information from the Internet to learners. He was referring to information available from some government and official web sites. IT academic II adopted blended learning, as he wanted learners to have a range of exciting learning experiences, by including several online games or quizzes as components of his teaching resources.

Some academics adopted blended learning for pedagogical reasons but some adopted blended learning for technical reasons. Non-IT academic FF utilized a learning platform, because it eliminated the need to print out anything for learners, which in turn, freed her from tackling with printing problems. IT academic KK employed a learning platform, as the teaching materials and learners' assignments were composed of numerous computer graphics and visuals. Owing to the very large file size of these graphics, it was virtually impossible to exchange files through the normal mode of emails, and for this reason the learning platform proved to be a valuable advantage. However, the student participants believed that the crucial element is to match the teaching approaches with the content, and their belief aligns with other

Table 2. Mean and standard deviations - perceptions on e-learning

Item	Mean	S.D.
The course content is easier to understand when made online	3.0	0.74
The course content is better illustrated using different digital formats	2.89	0.63
The e-learning experience can enha nce my skills on critical thinking	2.59	0.71
The more e-learning experiences I gain, the better learning effectiveness I have	2.37	0.9

findings (Hiltz, Coppola, Rotter, & Turoff, 2000). All these different reasons, appear to boil down to an academic's intrinsic motivation and desire to provide quality teaching and learning, which in turn match the general descriptions of faculty "entrepreneurs" (Hagner & Schneebeck, 2001), irrespective of their background.

Four questions related to the perceptions of e-learning materials and experiences were asked of our student teachers. The item mean range was from 2.37 (SD = 0.9) to 3.0 (SD = 0.74). Table 2 shows the highest mean score of 3.0 (SD = 0.74) for the item question, "The course content is easier to understand when made online", followed by a mean score of 2.89 (SD = 0.63) for the question, "The course content is better illustrated using different digital formats". The mean score of 2.37 (SD = 0.9) for the item question "the more e-learning experiences I gain, the better learning effectiveness I have", may imply that student teachers found that the e-learning experience enhanced their overall learning skills, without the need to acquire more valuable information or knowledge.

For the item question, "The course content is easier to understand when made online", the mean for both IT and non-IT students was 2.91 and 3.15 respectively, which is somewhat interesting as non-IT students appeared to have given a higher rating to this question (Figure 4). However, the two sets of data confirmed a non-significant difference (t-value = -1.331, p-value = 0.188, df = 68, at the 0.05 level of significance).

The Course Content is Easier to Understand when made Online

Yet again, the mean score for IT students (mean =2.86), was lower than the mean score for non-IT students (mean = 2.96) for the question, "The course content is better illustrated using different digital formats", which is consistent with the findings of the previous question, "The course content is easier to understand when made online". However, the mean scores for both the IT and non-

Figure 4. Perceptions on course content

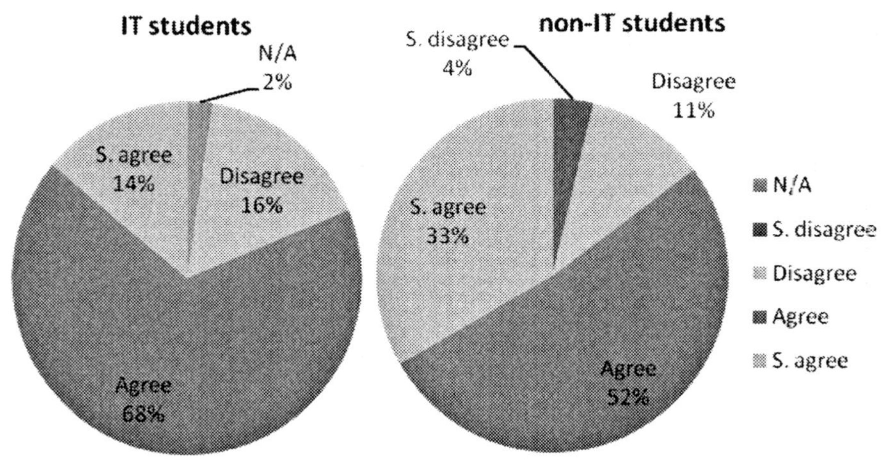

Figure 5. Perceptions on digital formats

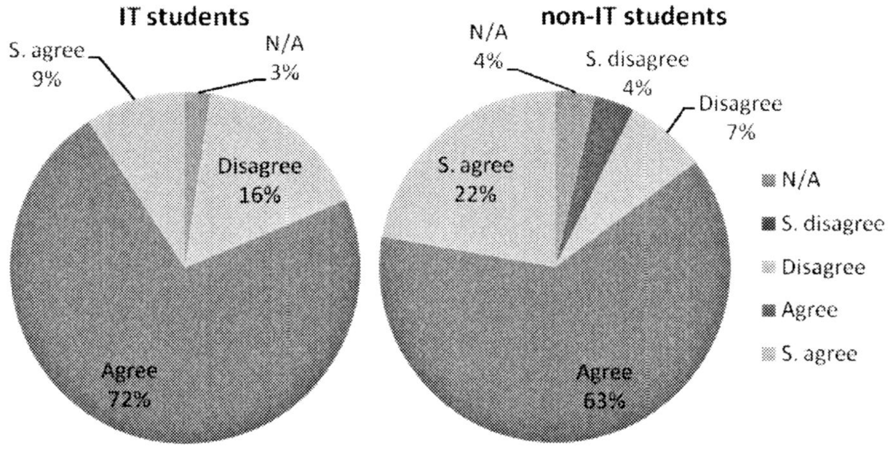

IT groups confirmed a non-significant difference (t-value = -0.543, p-value = 0.589, d.f. = 68, at the 0.05 level of significance) even though Figure 5 shows that there are some differences between two groups of respondents' ratings.

The Course Content is Better Illustrated Using Different Digital Formats

The mean score related to the perceptions of e-learning materials and experiences was again lower for IT students (mean = 2.56), than the mean score for non-IT students (mean =2.63), for the question, "The e-learning experience can enhance my skills on critical thinking". Figure 6 shows that engagement in the e-learning process may have effectively fostered the critical thinking skills of non-IT students as opposed to the IT students. However, the mean scores of both the IT and non-IT students confirmed a non-significant difference (t-value = -0.406, p-value = 0.686, df = 68, at the 0.05 level of significance). Interestingly, the low mean scores for critical thinking

Figure 6. Perceptions on e-learning experiences

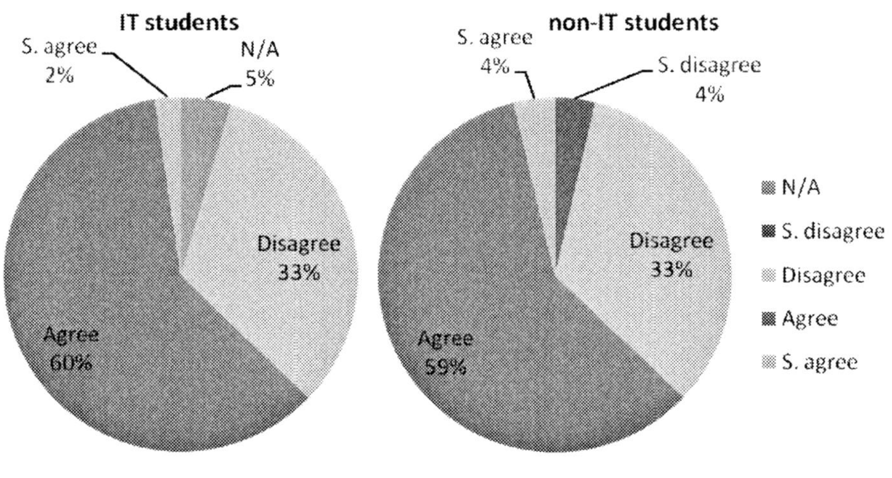

were comparatively different from other research findings (Nagai, Bantz, & Siktberg, 2005; Tan, Turgeon, & Johansson, 2001).

The E-Learning Experience can Enhance my Skills on Critical Thinking

The mean scores of IT and non-IT students were 2.42 and 2.30 respectively for the question, "The more e-learning experiences I gain, the better learning effectiveness I have", which is quite different from their perceptions of e-learning. These findings were indeed encouraging, as they revealed the fact that IT students were aware that they could subsequently improve their learning performance, after gaining more experience. However, the mean score of IT and non-IT students showed a non-significant difference (t-value = 0.548, p-value = 0.585, df = 68, at the 0.05 level of significance) even though Figure 7 shows that there are some differences between the two groups of respondents' ratings.

The More E-Learning Experiences I Gain, the Better Learning Effectiveness I Have

In summary, the above findings suggest that both academics and student teachers had favorable perceptions of e-learning materials and their overall experiences (Alexander & Golja, 2007). There was no perceptible difference between IT and non-IT academics, as all the participants were willing to strive harder, in order to offer quality education. Nevertheless, it was noticed that the IT students consistently had lower preferences on e-learning materials. However, it was encouraging to determine that the IT students believed that the more experience they gained in e-learning, the more effectively this experience would enable them to learn, even though Pang & Penfold (2008) found that students preferred face-to-face tutorials when they had previous e-learning experiences.

Perceptions of Discussion Forum

All the academics in the study used the discussion forums, except for one IT and one non-IT academic. The participants considered the discussion forums a vital and significant function of the learning platform. They firmly believed that the opportunity to participate in the discussion forums was an invaluable tool to them, thus allowing them to participate and engage in textual dialogue outside of class time (Alexander & Golja, 2007). The IT academic who did not use the discussion forum was able to use his own web-based communication tools for engaging in dialogue with the other class participants. The non-IT academic felt it was not necessary to engage in online discussions, because class participants were able to meet and discuss face-to-face in class sessions each week. However, all participants used other means to communicate with each other such as e-mail, discussion groups, blogs and a variety of other communication tools.

The discussion forum was more than just a platform and a means of communication - it also served as a record and log of an individual student's participation in all activities, as well as an archival of discussion transcripts, for later retrieval and student reflection (Lipponen, 2002). For example, non-IT academic AA thought that the record of the discussion enabled her to understand and analyze the learning process of her students, which would not have been possible without the use of the discussion forums. The discussion forums prompted learners to be more reflective, before posting their messages online. The rationale behind this was that posted messages could be read by all individual participants, which demanded careful deliberation on their part, before posting their opinions online. Non-IT academic LL videotaped short presentations of the learners in his class each week, and uploaded these video clips on to the discussion forum. The presenters then had to put their reflections on the presentations on the discussion forum, whilst other learners

Figure 7. Perceptions on e-learning effectiveness

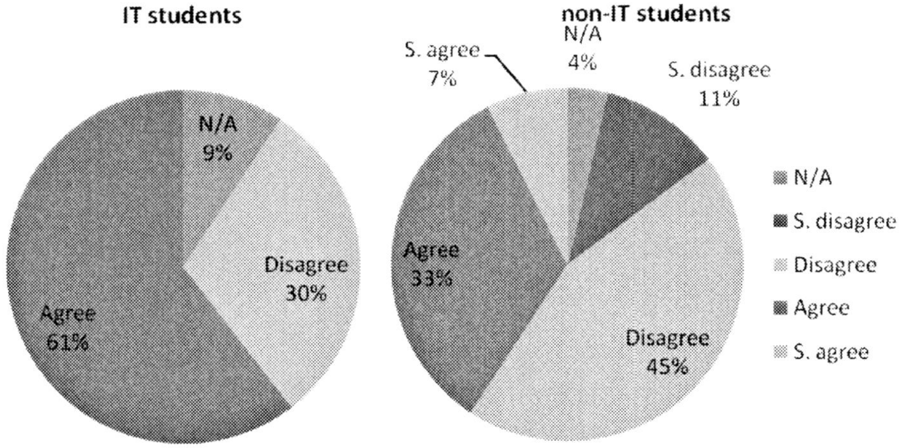

were asked to comment on their presentation skills, prior to the following class. Research has also established that learners consistently rated communication and support from educators and learners, as having a major influence on their learning (Alexander, 2001; Fredericksen, Pickett, & Shea, 2000; Sims, 2003).

Three questions related to the discussion forum were asked of our student teachers in the discussion forum and the responses were moderately favorable. This was relatively different from the academics' perspectives, relating to the use of the discussion forums. The mean score for the question, "It is a constructive supportive way for instructors to comment on and correct my learning by using e-mail or discussion board", was 2.89. As for the question, "I like to take part in discussions about my learning with instructors or other students by using e-mail or discussion board rather than doing the work alone", a mean score of 2.49, suggested that the students received good quality support from their

Figure 8. Perceptions on "support by instructors via e-communication"

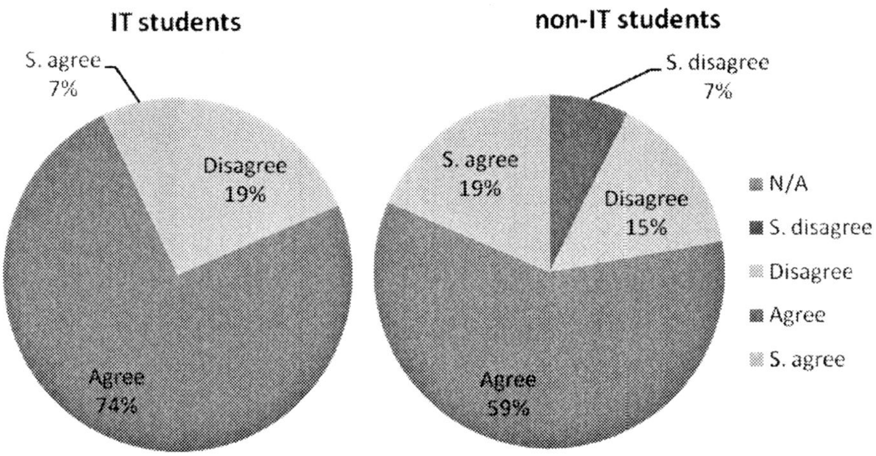

Table 3. Mean and standard deviations - perceptions on e-communication

Item	Mean	S. D.
It is a constructive supportive way for instructors to comment on and correct my learning by using e-mail or discussion board	2.89	0.63
I like to take part in discussion about my learning with instructors or other students by using e-mail or discussion board rather than doing the work alone	2.49	0.7
I prefer to take part in discussion on the discussion board rather than in the classroom	2.44	0.71

instructors, whilst using e-communications. The mean score for the question, "I prefer to take part in discussion on the discussion board rather than in the classroom", was 2.44, which was the lowest score for the three questions related to e-communications.

Figure 8 shows the respondents' rating for the question, "It is a constructive supportive way for instructors to comment on and correct my learning by using e-mail or discussion board", which was mostly positive. The mean score for IT students was 2.88, whereas the score for non-IT students was 2.89, thereby implying that the means were almost identical for both groups. A t-test was performed and it was found that there was no statistical significance between the two groups of students (t-value =-0.33, p-value = 0.973, df = 68, at the 0.05 level of significance).

It is a Constructive Supportive way for Instructors to Comment on and Correct my Learning by Using E-Mail or Discussion Board

Figure 9 shows the respondents' rating for the question, "I like to take part in discussion about my learning with instructors or other students by using e-mail or discussion board rather than doing the work alone", which was mostly positive. The mean score for IT students was 2.58, whereas the score for non-IT students was 2.33. This score suggests that the IT students enjoyed participating in e-communication activities. Although it appeared that there was a difference between the IT and non-IT students, it was found that there was no statistical significance between the two groups of students (t-value = 1.462, p-value = 0.148, df = 68, at the 0.05 level of significance).

Figure 9. Perceptions on "participation in e-communication"

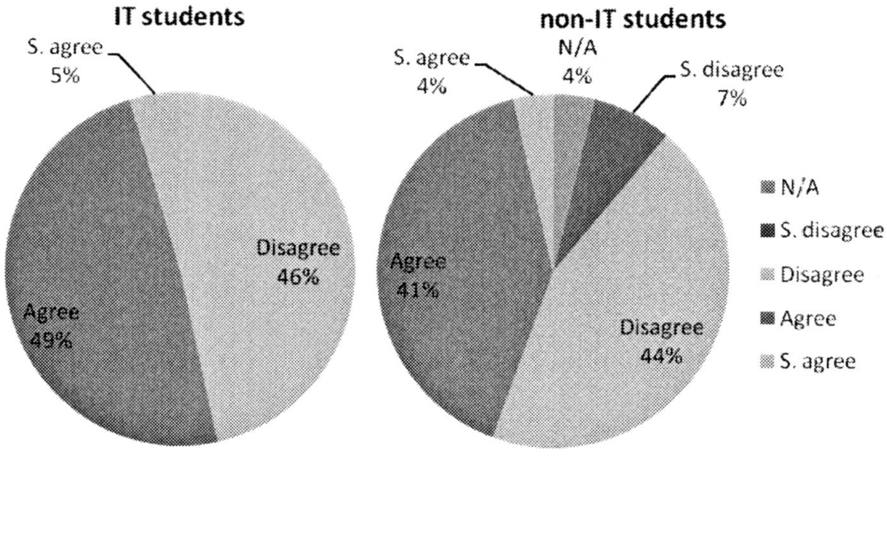

I Like to take Part in Discussion about my Learning with Instructors or Other Students by Using E-Mail or Discussion Board Rather Than Doing the Work Alone

The mean score for IT students was 2.49, which was higher than the score for non-IT students (2.37) for the question, "I prefer to take part in discussion on the discussion board rather than in the classroom". Figure 10 suggests that the IT students were less negative about participating in discussion forums. A t-test was performed but it was found that there was no statistical significance between the two groups of students (t-value = 0.669, p-value = 0.505, df = 68, at the 0.05 level of significance).

I Prefer to Take Part in Discussion on the Discussion Board Rather than in the Classroom

These findings suggest that academics rated the discussion forums much higher than student teachers, even though the latter acknowledged the support that the educators gave them while using electronic communications. There was not much of a perceptible difference between IT and non-IT academics in their interest and enthusiasm, whilst using the discussion forums. However, it appeared that the non-IT academics were more creative in using discussion forums. The IT students preferred participating in the discussion forums, even though their mean score was still rather low. This could be attributed to their positive experiences with their Australian counterparts, which had an affirmative and encouraging impact on their perceptions. The research findings seem contradictory to what we expected in terms of the expected outcomes from both students and academics from other studies. For example, Alexander & Golja (2007) found that students rated their interactions with others on the discussion board as the second most important part of e-learning, whereas the findings also confirmed that academics gave high ratings in terms of providing more information in a timely manner, followed by high ratings in terms of being efficient in making information available.

Preferences on the Mixed Learning Mode

None of the academics believed that any modules should be offered completely online and in fact, considered face-to-face interaction, a vital and significant aspect of teacher education. Most

Figure 10. Perceptions on "discussion online versus face-to-face"

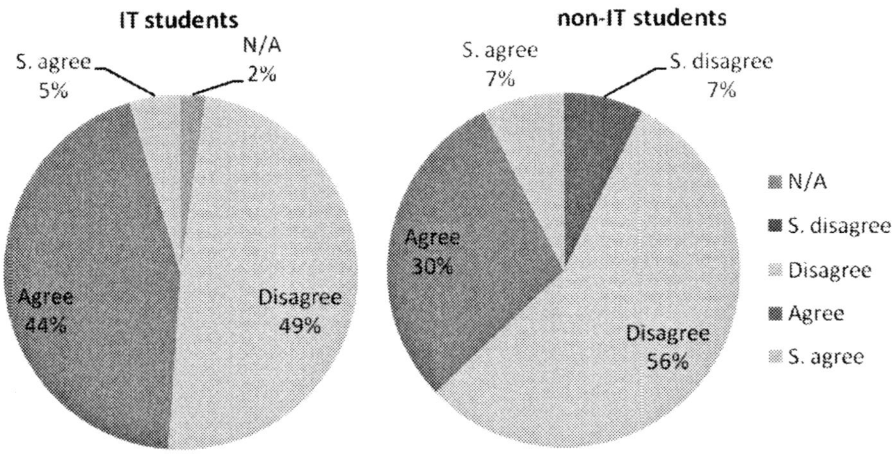

academics opined that about 30% of teaching time could be replaced by online learning, as learners are mature enough to learn at their own time and place. In fact, some of the academics had adopted this mode of learning to help part-time learners cut down on their travelling time. For example, non-IT academic AA had created online discussions to engage learners in peer learning for their project work. The purpose of this activity was to allow learners an opportunity to share their knowledge, to constructively critique each other's work and discuss innovative improvements and new insights. However, all the academics contended that it would be inappropriate to adopt an e-learning mode for a particular module, for example, a model on teaching methods, as learners need to experience different teaching methods and physically participate in a real life teaching practicum.

Four questions related to the mixed learning mode for our student teachers. The item mean range was from 2.29 to 2.47, which is on the lower side and suggests that student teachers tended to disagree with the respective questions.

Interestingly, IT students had higher mean scores (mean of 2.58), than non-IT students (mean of 2.3), for the question, "I enjoy reading academic material on-line rather than listening to instructors in classrooms". When using a t-test

Table 4. Mean and standard deviations - perceptions on mixed learning mode

Item	Mean	S. D.
I enjoy reading academic material on-line rather than listening to instructors in classrooms.	2.47	0.81
I prefer to have more e-learning "lecture" to replace face-to-face learning	2.39	0.77
I learn more using traditional board and chalk method	2.29	0.98
I prefer to take some modules completely delivered online	2.26	0.83

for analysis, the mean of IT and non-IT students showed a non-significant difference (t-value = 1.442, p-value = 0.154, df = 68, at the 0.05 level of significance) even though the ratings from two groups of respondents appear to be different (Figure 11).

I Enjoy Reading Academic Material On-Line rather than Listening to Instructors in Classrooms

Similarly, IT students were more ready to take supplementary e-learning "lectures" as shown by the higher mean (2.44) versus non-IT students (2.37). Figure 12 shows that more non-IT students disagreed with replacing face-to-face lectures by

Figure 11. Perceptions on reading e-materials versus listening to instructors

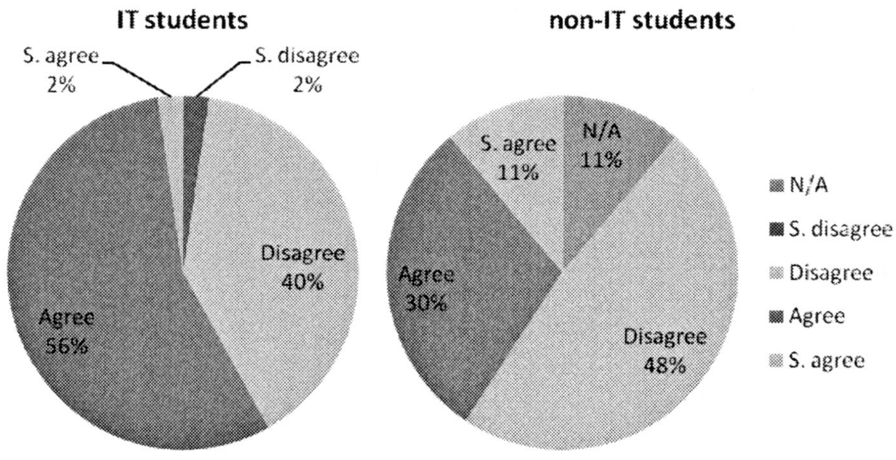

Figure 12. Perceptions on e-lecture versus face-to-face

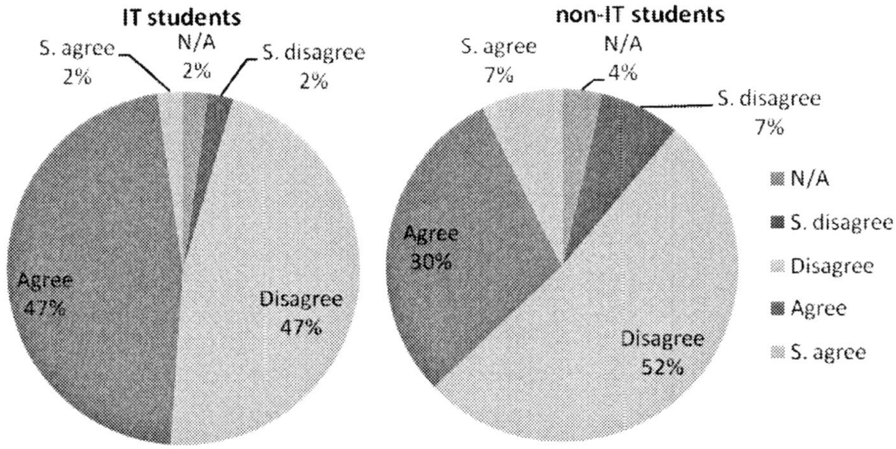

e-lectures. When using a t-test for analysis, the mean of IT and non-IT students showed a non significant difference (t-value = 0.771, p-value = 0.444, df = 68, at the 0.05 level of significance), for the question, "I prefer to have more e-learning "lecture" to replace face-to-face learning".

I Prefer to Have More E-Learning "Lecture" to Replace Face-to-Face Learning

The mean score of IT and non-IT students was 2.16 and 2.48 respectively for the question, "I learn more using traditional board and chalk method", which is lower than the two previous questions on e-learning. Yet the findings are quite contradictory to the question, "I prefer to have more e-learning "lecture" to replace face-to-face learning". In fact, the mean scores for these three questions were all fairly close to each other for both groups of students even though there were some variations among the distribution of ratings (Figure 11, Figure 12 and Figure 13). This may imply that the mean scores and mean standard deviation of the 5-point Likert scale used in our study may be lower compared to what the mean scores and mean standard deviation would be using a 7 or 11-point scale. Once again, the mean of IT and non-IT students showed a non significant difference (t-value = -1.332, p-value = 0.187, df = 68, at the 0.05 level of significance) even though more IT students disagreed with "I learn more using traditional board and chalk method".

I Learn More Using Traditional Board and Chalk Method

Very interestingly, IT students and non-IT students had the same mean score (2.26) for the question, "I prefer to take some modules completely delivered online", which suggested that the mean difference of IT and non-IT students is not significant (t-value = -0.017, p-value = 0.987, df = 68, at the 0.05 level of significance) even though the distributions of the ratings for both groups were not identical (Figure 14). The mean score for this question was the lowest for all questions asked, and this seems logical, since neither primary nor secondary schools have adopted e-learning to replace the traditional face-to-face learning approach.

Figure 13. Perceptions on face-to-face learning method

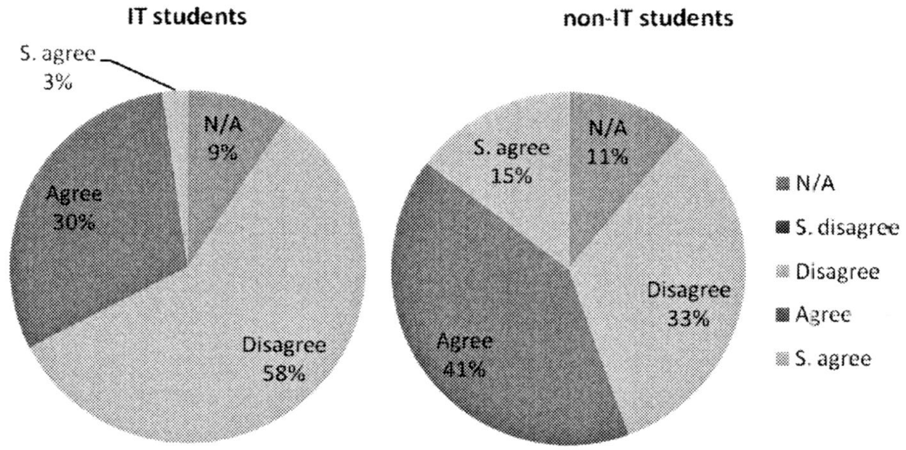

I Prefer to Take Some Modules Completely Online

These findings suggest that neither academics nor student teachers were willing to offer/take lessons completely online, which was completely understandable, as the teaching profession requires good oral communication and face-to-face interaction skills. Results also suggested that there was no noticeable difference between IT and non-IT academics, regarding the total of face-to-face teaching versus online lessons they would like to offer. The IT students in general were less reluctant to have more online lessons, even though both groups of students were not that keen.

LIMITATIONS

It was encouraging to note that thirteen academics volunteered to give their opinions on blended learning and yet, not all of those invited were in actuality, willing to participate in the research. Some of the academics were reticent and diffident

Figure 14. Preferences on complete e-learning mode

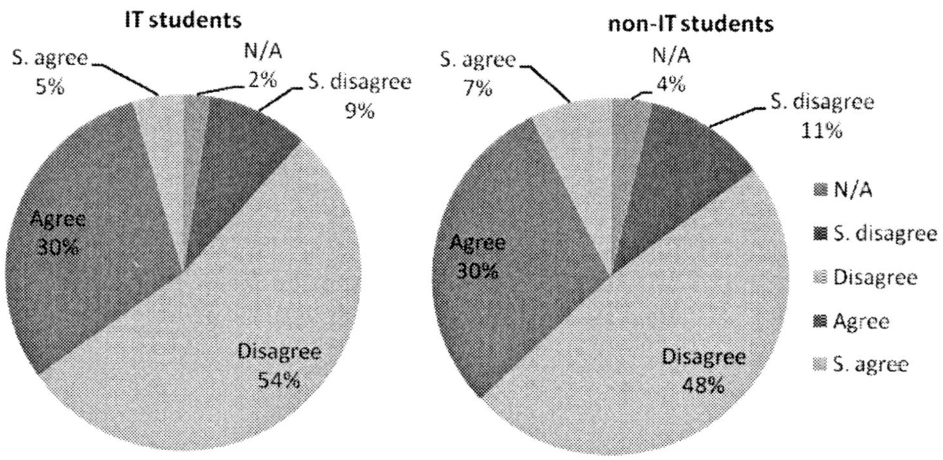

to venture any opinion, yet others did not have any experience with blended learning to share, although they could have presented an interesting and compelling case against utilizing technology to support learning. It was inevitable that the comments received from these participating academics would mostly be positive, constructive as well as innovative. However, these comments were not necessarily representative of the opinions of a vast majority of academics at The Hong Kong Institute of Education (HKIEd).

The author has endeavored to provide various objective views to compare the opinions of IT and non-IT participants, keeping in mind the fact that this was purely an exploratory study, with only a small group of educators and student teachers, who were willing to share their opinions. As the IT student teachers were taught by the author and the non-IT student teachers were taught by another participant, the sample size was deemed too small to represent the views and perceptions of all student teachers. It would have been considerably more significant and convincing if we had sought opinions from all academics who taught the non-IT classes and IT classes and subsequently performed an in-depth analysis of their perceptions on blended learning. Generalizations, thus, have to be dealt with carefully.

CONCLUSION AND IMPLICATIONS

This research provided the first step in exploring the perceptions of faculty and learners on different factors, which affect the successful implementation of blended learning for teacher education and subsequently to find out if there were any differences between IT and non-IT participants. Academics were positive about e-learning or rather the use of a blended learning approach and believed it would make a difference if more assistance were available, in terms of operational support, technological advances and staff development. They used most of the functions provided by Blackboard but almost none of them used the online assessment functions. Discussion forums appeared to be the most controversial function. Most of them embraced discussion forums (Alexander, 2001) but two of them considered them as unnecessary. their project workated arnersnt learning approaches to cater to users. Our supporting units were at all times on hand, to provide ideas and solutions to solve various technical problems. Yet, a fairly large number of academics expressed the need for operational support such as the uploading and designing of teaching materials, due to limited time constraints or the competency to develop preferred electronic resources. This finding is similar to Kim & Bonk's (2006) survey. However, no notable difference was established between IT and non-IT academics.

There are also numerous challenges encountered by teacher educators. Teaching partially online is much more challenging than teaching solely face-to-face, because "You need to design the course and do a lot of preparation work", said non-IT Academic MM. Although participants sincerely believed that online discussions were one of the ways to foster interactivity amongst learners and between learners and educators, it would unquestionably be a challenge to expect learners to participate in discussion forums, when they meet each other in class, on a regular basis. Another inhibiting factor would be the learners' inability to type or rather not being able to type fast enough to get motivated to discuss online. This is particularly true for learners taking Chinese as their major study, because not all learners know how to input Chinese characters. Some of the participants expressed the desire that it would be beneficial if mobile phones or Personal Digital Assistants could be used to download and upload information to and from the learning platform.

It was encouraging that student teachers were positive on most of the items asked, which showed that they were ready to take part in the modules using an e-learning mode, but it also proved that they were unwilling to take modules completely online. When comparing the mean scores of IT and non-IT students, it was noticed that both the groups had almost identical scores for most of the questions. The IT students from year 1 and 2 regarded the e-learning experience as enriching, thus enabling them to learn more effectively than the non-IT students. However, no statistical significance was found between the two groups of students. Student teachers were also positive on most of the items asked, which demonstrated that they were ready to learn equally satisfactorily, if not better, via e-learning under the current environment. They were also prepared to take some modules online, which gave us the confidence to proceed in that direction.

Our findings provided both qualitative and quantitative information on blended learning from academics and student teachers' perspectives. As mentioned in the Limitation Section, the findings are not adequate enough for generalization and there are various modes by which to continue this study. Firstly, we can hold focus group meetings with student teachers and perhaps present questionnaires to different categories of colleagues such as academics, administrators and IT supporting staff, to provide a richer data set. Secondly, perceptions are only the contributory attributes to successful blended learning. We should investigate the process and the learning outcomes (Fjermestad et al., 2005; Ginns & Ellis, 2007; Romanov & Nevgi, 2008) of students, in order to have a more holistic view for any forward planning, and also include more input factors such as gender (Gunn, 2003; Markauskaite, 2005), intrinsic motivation (Shroff, Vogel, Coombes, & Lee, 2007), mode of study (Pang & Penfold, 2008) and level of study (Keengwe, 2007). It is especially important to examine the impact of pedagogies (Kanuka, 2008; Keppell et al., 2004) and the types of assessments on learning (Davies, 2000). Thirdly, a larger sample size will also enable us to gain an in-depth and enhanced understanding of the different independent factors affecting perceptions of blended learning, so that our student teachers are better prepared and therefore inclined more favorably, towards this new mode of learning (and teaching). Lastly, the results would be even more comprehensive and conclusive, if we were able to conduct a small number of cross cultural comparisons with findings from other countries (Henderson, 1996; Hofstede, 2001), to substantiate our own findings and conclusions.

ACKNOWLEDGMENT

I would like to thank my colleagues for their forthright opinions and their willingness to share their experiences with me. I have learnt much from Dr. Shirley Chan, Mr. Tom Chan, Dr. S. H. Chen, Dr. Irene Cheng, Dr. Jane Cheung, Dr. Ming Fai Hui, Dr. Siu Cheung Kong, Dr. Kar-Tin Lee, Dr. Pamela Leung, Dr. Ada Ma, Dr. Ka Ho Tse, Dr. Y. Y. Yeung, and Dr. Christina Yu. I also wish to acknowledge the students who participated in this project and generous funding from HKIEd. Finally, I sincerely thank my research assistants, Diana, Vincent and Wilson for their unstinting support in this research study.

REFERENCES

Alavi, M., & Leidner, D. E. (2001). Research commentary: Technology-mediated learning-a call for greater depth and breadth of research. Information Systems Research, 12(1), 1–10. doi:10.1287/isre.12.1.1.9720doi:10.1287/isre.12.1.1.9720

Alexander, S. (2001). E-learning developments and experiences. Education & Training, 4/5(43), 240–248. doi:10.1108/00400910110399247doi:10.1108/00400910110399247

Alexander, S., & Golja, T. (2007). Using students' experiences to derive quality in an elearning system: An institution's perspective. Educational Technology & Society, 10(2), 17–33.

Applefield, J. N., Huber, R., & Moadlem, M. (2000). Constructivism in theory and practice: Towards a better understanding. High School Journal, 84(2).

Benbunan-Fich, R., Hiltz, S. R., & Harasim, L. (Eds.). (2005). The online interaction learning model: An integrated theoretical framework for learning networks. NJ: Lawrence Erlbaum Associates Publishers.

Boud, D., & Prosser, M. (2002). Appraising new technologies for learning: A framework for development. Educational Media International, 39(3), 237–245. doi:10.1080/09523980210166026doi:10.1080/09523980210166026

Claver, E., Llopis, J., Gonzalez, M. R., & Gasco, J. L. (2001). The performance of information systems through organizational culture. Information Technology & People, 14(3), 247–260. doi:10.1108/09593840110402149doi:10.1108/09593840110402149

Collis, B., & Moonen, J. (2001). Flexible learning in a digital world. London: Kogan Page.

Davenport, T. H. (1997). Information ecology. Oxford: Oxford University Press.

Davies, P. (2000). Computerized peer assessment. Innovations in Education and Training International, 37(4), 346–355.

Fjermestad, R., Hiltz, S. R., & Zhang, Y. (Eds.). (2005). Effectiveness for students: Comparisons of "in-seat" and ALN courses. NJ: Lawrence Erlbaum Associates Publishers.

Folkers, D. A. (2005). Competing in the marketplace: Incorporating online education into higher education-an organizational perspective. Information Resources Management Journal, 18(1), 61–77.

Fredericksen, E., Pickett, A., & Shea, P. (2000). Student satisfaction and perceived learning with online courses: Principles and examples from the SUNY learning network. Journal of Asynchronous Learning Networks, 4(2).

Ginns, P., & Ellis, R. (2007). Quality in blended learning: Exploring the relationships between online and face-to-face teaching and learning. The Internet and Higher Education, 10, 53–64. doi:10.1016/j.iheduc.2006.10.003doi:10.1016/j.iheduc.2006.10.003

Granger, C., Morbey, M. L., Lotherington, H., Owston, R., & Wideman, H. (2002). Factors contributing to teachers' successful implementation of IT. Journal of Computer Assisted Learning, 48(8), 480–488. doi:10.1046/j.0266-4909.2002.00259.doc.xdoi:10.1046/j.0266-4909.2002.00259.doc.x

Gunn, C. (2003). Dominant or different? Gender issues in computer supported learning. Journal of Asynchronous Learning Networks, 7(1), 14–30.

Hagner, P. R., & Schneebeck, C. A. (2001). Engaging the faculty. In C. A. Barone & P. R. Hagner (Eds.), Technology-enhanced teaching and learning, educause leadership strategies (Vol. 5, pp. 1-12). San Francisco: Jossey-Bass.

Henderson, L. (1996). Instructional design of interactive multimedia: A cultural critique. Educational Technology Research and Development, 44(4), 86–104. doi:10.1007/BF02299823doi:10.1007/BF02299823

Hiltz, S. R. (1994). The virtual classroom: Learning without limits via computer networks. Norwood, NJ: Ablex.

Hiltz, S. R., Coppola, N., Rotter, N., & Turoff, M. (2000). Measuring the importance of collaborative learning for the effectiveness of ALN: A multi-measure, multi-method approach. Journal of Asynchronous Learning Networks, 4(2).

Hofstede, G. (2001). Cultures consequences: Comparing values, behaviors, institutions, and organisations across nations. Thousand Oaks, London, New Delhi: Sage Publications.

Hughes, J. E. (2005). The role of teacher knowledge and learning experiences in forming technology-integrated pedagogy. Journal of Technology and Teacher Education, 13(2), 377–402.

Jarvenpaa, S. L., & Staples, D. S. (2000). The use of collaborative electronic media for information sharing: An exploratory study of determinants. The Journal of Strategic Information Systems, 9, 129–154. doi:10.1016/S0963-8687(00)00042-1doi:10.1016/S0963-8687(00)00042-1

Jonassen, D. H. (2000). Computers as mindtools for schools. Upper Saddle River, NJ: Merrill.

Jonassen, D. H., Peck, K. L., & Wilson, B. G. (1999). Learning with technology: A constructivist perspective. Upper Saddle River, NJ: Merrill.

Kanuka, H. (2008). Understanding e-learning technologies-in-practice through philosophies-in-practice. In T. Anderson (Ed.), The theory and practice of online learning (2nd ed., pp. 91-118). Edmonton: AU Press.

Keengwe, J. (2007). Faculty integration of technology into instruction and students' perceptions of computer technology to improve student learning. Journal of Information Technology Education, 6, 169–180.

Keppell, M., Au, E., Ma, A., & Chan, C. (2004). Curriculum development: Making our theories of teaching and learning explicit in technology-enhanced environments. In P. Rogers (Ed.), Encyclopedia of distance learning teaching, technologies, and applications (pp. 492-504). Hershey, PA: Idea Group Publishing.

Kim, K. J., & Bonk, C. J. (2006). The future of online teaching and learning in higher education: The survey says.... EDUCAUSE Quarterly, 29, 9.

Koehler, M., Mishra, P., & Yahya, K. (2007). Tracing the development of teacher knowledge in a design seminar: Integrating content, pedagogy, and technology. Computers & Education, 49(3), 740–764. doi:10.1016/j.compedu.2005.11.012doi:10.1016/j.compedu.2005.11.012

Koschmann, T. (2000). Tools of termlessness: Technology, educational reform, and Deweyan inquiry. Retrieved on March 31, 2007, from http://edaff.siumed.edu/tk/articles/UNESCO.pdf

Larson, M. R., & Bruning, R. (1996). Participant perceptions of a collaborative satellite-based mathematics course. American Journal of Distance Education, 10(1), 6–22.

Lipponen, L. (2002). Exploring foundations for computer-supported collaborative learning. Retrieved on March 20, 2007, from http://www.helsinki.fi/science/networkedlearning/texts/lipponen2002.pdf

Markauskaite, L. (2005, December 4-7). Exploring differences in trainee teachers' ICT literacy: Does gender matter? Paper presented at the Australasian Society for Computers in Learning in Tertiary Education.

McCollum, K. (1997). A professor divides his class in two to test value of online instruction. The Chronicle of Higher Education, 43(24), 23.

McLoughlin, C. (2002). Learner support in distance and networked learning environments: Ten dimensions for successful design. Distance Education, 23(2), 149–162. doi:10.1080/0158791022000009178doi:10.1080/0158791022000009178

Morrison, D. (2003). Using activity theory to design constructivist online learning environments for higher order thinking: A retrospective analysis. Canadian Journal of Learning and Technology, 29.

Mowshowitz, A. (1997). Virtual organisation. Communications of the ACM, 40(9), 30–37. doi:10.1145/260750.260759doi:10.1145/260750.260759

Muukkonen, H., Hakkarainen, K., & Lakkala, M. (2005). Computer-mediated progressive inquiry in higher education. Hershey, PA: Information Science Publishing.

Myers, C. B., Bennett, D., Brown, G., & Henderson, T. (2004). Emerging online learning environments and student learning: An analysis of faculty perceptions. Educational Technology & Society, 7(1), 78–86.

Nagai, S. A., Bantz, D., & Siktberg, L. (2005). Validation of critical thinking skills in online responses. The Journal of Nursing Education, 44(2), 90–94. PubMed

Oliver, R., Harper, B., Wills, S., Agostinho, S., & Hedberg, J. G. (2007). Describing ICT based learning designs that promote quality learning outcomes. London: Routledge.

Palloff, R. M., & Pratt, K. (2003). The virtual student: A profile and guide to working with online learners. San Francisco: Jossey-Bass.

Pang, L., & Penfold, P. (2008). Blending and shaking: Chinese students' perceptions of blended learning in a hospitality and tourism course. Paper presented at the 6th Asia-Pacific (APacCHRIE) Conference and THE-ICE International Panel of Experts Forum, Perth.

Pope, M., Hare, D., & Howard, E. (2002). Technology integration: Closing the gap between what preservice teachers are taught to do and what they can do. Journal of Technology and Teacher Education, 10(2), 191–203.

Rogers, E. M. (2003). Diffusion of innovations (5th Ed.). New York: The Free Press.

Romanov, K., & Nevgi, A. (2008). Student activity and learning outcomes in a virtual learning environment. Learning Environments Research, 11(2), 153–162. doi:10.1007/s10984-008-9038-3doi:10.1007/s10984-008-9038-3

Scardamalia, M. (Ed.). (2002). Collective cognitive responsibility for the advancement of knowledge. Chicago: Open Court.

Selinger, M. (2001). Learning information and communications technology skills and the subject context of the learning. Journal of information technology for teacher education, 10(1&2), 143-154.

Shea, P., Fredericksen, E., Pickett, A., Pelz, W., & Swan, K. (2001). Measures of learning effectiveness in the SUNY learning network. In J. Bourne & J. C. Moore (Eds.), Learning effectiveness, faculty satisfaction, and cost effectiveness (Vol. 2, pp. 303-308).

Shroff, R. H., Vogel, D. R., Coombes, J., & Lee, F. (2007). Student e-learning intrinsic motivation: A qualitative analysis. Communications of the Association for Information Systems, 19(12), 241–260.

Sims, R. (2003). Promises of interactivity: Aligning learner perceptions and expectations with strategies for flexible and online learning. Distance Education, 24(1), 85–103. doi:10.1080/0158791 0303050doi:10.1080/01587910303050

Tan, S. C., Turgeon, A. J., & Johansson, D. H. (2001). Develop critical thinking in group problem solving through computer-supported collaborative argumentation: A case study. Journal of Natural Resources and Life Sciences Education, 30, 97–103.

Woodruff, E., Brett, C., MacDonald, R., & Nason, R. (1998). Participation in knowledge-building communities to promote teaching competency in mathematics. Retrieved on March 14, 2002, from http://www.oise.utoronto.ca/~ewoodruff/cp.htm

APPENDIX 1

Table 5. Profile of participating academics

Academic	Years of Experiences of e-learning with face-to-face learning	Discipline
AA	4	Home economics
BB	7	Science
CC	10	Information technology
DD	3	English
EE	0	Social Science
FF	3	Chinese
GG	1	Design technology
HH	4	Business
II	3	Chinese
JJ	5	Information technology
KK	5	Music
LL	2	Education
MM	3	Physical education

Compilation of References

Abrams, Z. I. (2001). Computer-mediated communication and group journals: Expanding the repertoire of participant roles. *System, 29*(4), 489–503. doi:10.1016/S0346-251X(01)00041-0

Addesso, P. (2000). *The online teaching guide: A handbook of attitudes, strategies, and techniques for the virtual classroom.* Boston, MA: Allyn & Bacon.

Adkins, J., Kenkel, C., & Lim, C. L. (2008). *Deterrents to online academic dishonesty.* Retrieved on February 6, 2008, from http://jwpress.com/JLHE/issues/viii/Deterrents%20to%20online%20academic%20dishonesty.pdf

Agrawal, V. K., & Haleem, A., & Sushil. (2003). Successful implementation of business process reengineering and computer based information systems: Awareness and training program (NIST SP 800-50). *National Social Science Journal, 20*(2), 1–16.

Alavi, M., & Leidner, D. E. (2001). Research commentary: Technology-mediated learning-a call for greater depth and breadth of research. Information Systems Research, 12(1), 1–10. doi:10.1287/isre.12.1.1.9720doi:10.1287/isre.12.1.1.9720

Albion, P. R. (2001). Some factors in the development of self-efficacy beliefs for computer use among teacher education students [electronic version]. *Journal of Technology and Teacher Education, 9*(3), 321-347. Retrieved on November 1, 2002, from http://www.aace.org/dl/index.cfm/fuseaction/View/paperID/6502

Albrechtsen, E. (2007). A qualitative study of user's view on information security. *Computers & Security, 26*(4), 276–289. doi:10.1016/j.cose.2006.11.004

Albright, M., & Nworie, J. (2001). Rethinking academic technology leadership in an era of change. *Educause Quarterly, 31*(1), 14-23. Retrieved on August 22, 2008, from http://connect.educause.edu/Library/EDUCAUSE+Quarterly/RethinkingAcademicTechnol/4607

Alexander, S. (2001). E-learning developments and experiences. Education & Training, 4/5(43), 240–248. doi:10.1108/00400910110399247doi:10.1108/00400910110399247

Alexander, S., & Golja, T. (2007). Using students' experiences to derive quality in an elearning system: An institution's perspective. Educational Technology & Society, 10(2), 17–33.

Al-Hunaiyyan, A., Al-Huwail, N., & Al-Sharhan, S. (2008). Blended e-learning design: Discussion of cultural issues. *International Journal of Cyber Society and Education, 1*(1), 17-32. Retrieved on December 1, 2008, from http://www.academic-journals.org/ojs2/index.php/IJCSE/article/viewFile/401/3

Ali, A., & Elfessi, A. (2004). Examining students performance and attitudes towards the use of information technology in a virtual and conventional setting. *The Journal of Interactive Online Learning, 2*(3), 1–9.

Alldredge, J., & Som, N. (2002). Comparison of multimedia educational materials used in an introductory statistics method course. *Proceedings of the Sixth International Conference on Teaching Statistics.* The Netherlands: International Statistics Institute.

Allen, M. J., & Yen, W. M. (2002). Introduction to measurement theory. New York: Long Grove IL Waveland Press.

Allen, R. (1998). The Web: Interactive and multimedia education. *Computer Networks and ISDN Systems, 30*(16–18), 1717–1727. doi:10.1016/S0169-7552(98)00200-1

Alonso, F., López, G., Manrique, D., & Vines, J. M. (2005). An instructional model for Web-based e-learning education with a blended learning process approach. *British Journal of Educational Technology*, *36*(2), 217–235. doi:10.1111/j.1467-8535.2005.00454.x

Amabile, T. M. (1996). Creativity in context. Boulder, CO: Westview Press.

Amazon.com. (2008). *Amazon Web site*. Retrieved on September 1, 2008, from http://www.amazon.com

Amor, D. (2001). The industrialisation of the Internet gold rush. *Journal of Information Technology Theory and Application*, *3*(4), 20–22.

Amory, A., Naicker, K., Vincent, J., & Adams, C. (1999). The use of computer games as an instructional tool: Identification of appropriate game types and game elements. *British Journal of Educational Technology*, *30*(4), 311–321. doi:10.1111/1467-8535.00121

Anderson, P. (2007). *What is Web 2.0? Ideas, technologies, and implications for education*. JISC Technology and Standards Watch. London: Joint Information Systems Committee. Retrieved on September 1, 2008, from http://www.jisc.ac.uk/media/documents/techwatch/tsw0701b.pdf

Anderson, T., Rourke, L., Garrison, D. R., & Archer, W. (2001). Assessing the teaching presence in a computer conferencing context. *JALN*, *5*(2).

Anderson-Levitt, K. M. (2006). Ethnography. In J. L. Green, G. Camilli, P. B. Elmore, A. Skukauskaitė & E. Grace (Eds.), *Handbook of complementary methods in education research* (pp 279-296). Mahwah, NJ: Erlbaum.

Andrews, R., & Haythornthwaite, C. (2007). *The sage handbook of e-learning research*. Thousand Oaks: SAGE.

Annan, K. (2002). *The role of the state in the age of globalisation, keynote address to conference on globalisation and international relations in the 21st century*. New York: United Nations Publications.

ANTA. (2003). *What is flexible learning? Australian flexible learning framework*. Retrieved from http://flexiblelearning.net.au/aboutuswhatisfl.htm

Applefield, J. N., Huber, R., & Moadlem, M. (2000). Constructivism in theory and practice: Towards a better understanding. High School Journal, 84(2).

Athanasiadis, E. (1995). *Correspondents and cluster analysis, applications, and examples*. Athens: New Technologies.

Ausburn, L. J. (2004). Course design elements most valued by adult learners in online education environments: An American perspective. *Educational Media International*, *41*(4), 327–337. doi:10.1080/0952398042000314820

Backroad Connections Pty Ltd. (2003). *Definitions of key terms used in e-learning (version 1.00)*. Australian flexible learning framework quick guides series, Australian National Training Authority. Retrieved from http://flexiblelearning.net.au/guides/keyterms.pdf

Bailey, K. (2001). Towards unifying science: Applying concepts across disciplinary boundaries. *Systems Research and Behavioral Science*, *18*, 41–62. doi:10.1002/sres.364

Bammer, G. (2005). Integration and implementation sciences: Building a new specialization. *Ecology and Society*, *10*(2), 6. Retrieved on October 2, 2008, from www.ecologyandsociety.org/vol10/iss2/art6/ES-2005-1360.pdf

Barab, S. A., Hay, K. E., Barnett, M. G., & Keating, T. (2000). Virtual solar system project: Building understanding through model building. *Journal of Research in Science Teaching*, *37*(7), 719–756. doi:10.1002/1098-2736(200009)37:7<719::AID-TEA6>3.0.CO;2-V

Barab, S. A., Kay, K. E., Barnett, M., & Squire, K. (2001). Constructing virtual worlds: Tracing the historical development of learner practices. *Cognition and Instruction*, *19*(1), 47–94. doi:10.1207/S1532690XCI1901_2

Barab, S. A., Thomas, M., Dodge, T., Carteaux, R., & Tuzun, H. (2005). Making learning fun: Quest Atlantis, a game with guns. *Educational Technology Research and Development*, *53*(1), 86–107. doi:10.1007/BF02504859

Barlow, D. H. (2002). *Anxiety and its disorders: The nature and treatment of anxiety and panic*. New York: Guilford.

Barlow, T. (2008). Web 2.0: Creating a classroom without walls. *Teaching Science*, *54*(1), 46–48.

Barnet, M., Barab, S. A., & Hay, K. E. (2001). The virtual solar system project: A stellar exercise in modeling celestial bodies. *Journal of College Science Teaching*, *30*(5), 300–304.

Barua, B. (2007). Colonialism, education, and rural Buddhist communities in Bangladesh. *International Education, 37*(1), 60–77.

Bates, T. (1995). *Technology, open learning, and distance education.* London & New York: Routledge.

Bates, T., & Poole, G. (2003). *Effective teaching with technology in higher education: Foundations for success.* San Francisco: Jossey-Bass.

Baudrillard, J. (1983). *Simulations.* New York: Semiotexte.

Beatty, K. (2003). *Teaching and researching CALL.* Harlow: Longman.

Beatty, K., & Nunan, D. (2004). Computer-mediated collaborative learning. *System, 32,* 165–183. doi:10.1016/j.system.2003.11.006

Beaudin, B. P. (1999). Keeping online asynchronous discussions on topic. *JALN,* 3(2).

Beck, E. L. (1999). Prevention and intervention programming: Lessons from an after-school program. *The Urban Review, 31*(1), 107–124. doi:10.1023/A:1023200500215

Becker, H., & Blanch, G. (1970). Participant observation and interviewing: A comparison. In W. J. Filstead (Ed.), *Qualitative methodology.* Chicago: Markham.

Bekhradnia, B. (2005). *Обзорен преглед на висшето образование в България.* (An overview of higher education in Bulgaria). Sofia.

Bell, P. (2007, Summer). Predictors of college's student achievement in undergraduate asynchronous Web-based courses. *Education, 127*(4), 523–533.

Benavot, A. (2006). *The diversification of secondary education: School curricula in comparative perspective.* Working Papers on Curriculum Issues N° 6, International Bureau of Education. Paris: UNESCO.

Benbunan-Fich, R., Hiltz, S. R., & Harasim, L. (Eds.). (2005). The online interaction learning model: An integrated theoretical framework for learning networks. NJ: Lawrence Erlbaum Associates Publishers.

Bender, T. (2003). *Discussion-based online teaching to enhance student learning: Theory, practice, and assessment.* Sterling, VI: Stylus Publishing.

Benhunan-Fich, R., & Hiltz, S. R. (1999). Educational applications of cmcs: Solving case studies through asynchronous learning networks. *Journal of Computer-Mediated Communication, 4*(3).

Benkler, Y. (2006). *The wealth of networks: How social production transforms markets and freedom.* New Haven: Yale University Press.

Bennett, S., & Lockyer, L. (2004, September). Becoming an online teacher: Adapting to a changed environment for teaching and learning in higher education. *Educational Media International, 41*(3), 231–244. doi:10.1080/09523980410001680842

Berg, B. L. (2007). *Qualitative research methods for the social sciences* (6th ed.). Boston: Allyn and Bacon.

Berge, Z. K. (1991). Facilitating computer conferencing: Recommendation from the field. *Educational Technology, 15*(1), 22–30.

Berger, C. (2007). The millennium student: And now, evidence for the millennial instructor! *Educause Resource Center.* Retrieved on February 17, 2007 from http://www.educause.edu/ELI071/Program/10825?PRODUCT_CODE=ELI071/SESS39

Berlyne, D. (1950). Novelty and curiosity as determinants of exploratory behavior. The British Journal of Psychology, 41, 68–80.

Berlyne, D. (1954). A theory of human curiosity. The British Journal of Psychology, 45, 180–191.

Berlyne, D. (1960). Conflict, arousal, and curiosity. New York: McGraw Hill.

Berlyne, D. (1965). Curiosity and education. In J. D. Krumboltz (Ed.), Learning and the educational process (pp. 67-89). Chicago: Rand McNally.

Berlyne, D. (1978). Curiosity and learning. Motivation and Emotion, 2, 97–175. doi:10.1007/BF00993037doi:10.1007/BF00993037

Berlyne, D., & Frommer, F. (1966). Some determinants of the incidence and content of children's questions. Child Development, 37, 177–189. doi:10.2307/1126438doi:10.2307/1126438

Berry, R. (2008). *Assessment for learning.* Hong Kong: Hong Kong University Press.

Best, J., & Kahn, J. (1998). *Research in education* (8th ed.). Needham Heights, MA: Allyn and Bacon.

Betts, J. R., Zau, A. C., & Rice, L. A. (2003). *Determinants of student achievement: New evidence from San Diego.* San Francisco, CA: Public Policy Institute of California.

Bia, M., & Kalika, M. (2007). Adopting an ICT code of conduct: An empirical study of organizational factors. *Journal of Enterprise Information Management, 20*(4), 432–446. doi:10.1108/17410390710772704

Biggs, J. (1996). Assessing learning quality: Reconciling institutional, staff, and educational demands. *Assessment & Evaluation in Higher Education, 21,* 5–15. doi:10.1080/0260293960210101

Biggs, J. B., & Tang, C. (2007). *Teaching for quality learning at university: What the student does,* 3rd ed. Philadelphia: Society for Research into Higher Education and Open University Press.

Bishop, E. B. (2008). *A study of differnces on the effects of parental influence on the self efficacy of first generation and second gerneation college students.* La Verne: AAT 3082008.

Black, P., Harrison, C., Lee, C., Marshall, B., & Wiliam, C. (2003). *Assessment for learning: Putting it into practice.* Maidenhead: Open University Press.

Blackboard Inc. (2008) *Company overview.* Retrieved on October 22, 2008, from http://www.blackboard.com/company/

Blake, C. T., & Rapanotti, L. (2001). *Mapping interactions in a computer conferencing environment.* The Netherlands: Euro-CSCL2001.

Blake, R., Wilson, N. L., Cetto, M., & Pardo-Ballester, C. (2008). Measuring oral proficiency in distance, face-to-face, and blended classrooms. *Language Learning & Technology, 12*(3), 114–127.

Blau, S. R., Hall, J., & Strauss, T. (1998). Exploring the tutor/client conversation: A linguistic analysis. *Writing Center Journal, 19*(1), 19–48.

Bleed, R. (2001). A hybrid campus for a new millennium. EDUCAUSE Review, 36(1), 16–24.

Blight, D., Davis, D., & Olsen, A. (1999). The internationalisation of higher education. In K. Harry (Ed.), *Higher education through open and distance learning, world review of distance education and open learning* (Vol. 1, pp. 15-31). London: RoutledgeFalmer.

Bloxhan, S., & West, A. (2004). Understanding the rules of the game: Marking peer assessment as a medium for developing students' conceptions of assessment. *Assessment & Evaluation in Higher Education, 29*(6), 721–733. doi:10.1080/0260293042000227254

Boghikian-Whitby, S. (2003). *To take or not to take? The future of distance learning: A quasi-experiment comparison of the effectiveness of Internet-based distance learning versus face-to-face classroom.* La Verne: AAT 3081990.

Boghikian-Whitby, S., & Mortagy, Y. (2008). The effect of student background in virtual learning–longitudinal study. In E. B. Cohen (Ed.), *Setting knowledge free: Issues in informing science and infomation technology* (Vol. 5, p. 746). Santa Rosa, CA: Informing Science Press.

Bollag, B., & Overland, M. A. (2001). Developing countries turn to distance education. *Chronicle of Higher Education, 47* (40), 29-31.Retrieved November 1, 2007, at: http://chronicle.com/weekly/v47/i40/40a02901.htm

Bonk, C. J., & Cunningham, D. J. (1998). Searching for learner-centered, constructivist, and sociocultural components of collaborative educational learning tools. In C. J. Bonk & K. S. King (Eds.), *Electronic collaborators: Learner-centered technologies for literacy, apprenticeship, and discourse.* Mahwah, NJ: Erlbaum.

Bonk, C. J., & Wisher, R. A. (2000). Applying collaborative and e-learning tools to military distance learning: A research framework. Retrieved on July 2, 2002, from http://www.publicationshare.com/docs/Dist.Learn(Wisher).pdf

Bonk, C. J., Kim, K., & Zeng, T. (2006). Future directions of blended learning in higher education and workplace learning settings. In C. J. Bonk & C. R. Graham (Eds.), *Handbook of blended learning: Global perspectives, local designs* (pp. 550-568). San Francisco, CA: Pfeiffer Publishing.

Bonk, C. J., Malikowski, S., Angeli, C., & Supplee, L. (2001). Holy COW: Scaffolding case-based "conferencing on the Web" with preservice teachers. *CRLT Technical Report No. 15-1.* Bloomington, IN: Indiana University.

Bonk, C., & Graham, C. (2005). *Handbook of blended learning: Global perspectives, local designs*. San Fransisco, CA: Pfeiffer Publishing.

Bonwell, C. C., & Eison, J. A. (1991). *Active learning: Creating excitement in the classroom*. Washington: George Washington University Press.

Bosworth, K., & Hamilton, S. J. (1994). Collaborative learning: Underlying processes and effective techniques. San Francisco: Jossy-Bass.

Bottery, M. (2000). *Education, policy, and ethics*. London: Continuum.

Boud, D., & Feletti, G. (1991). *The challenge of problem based learning*. London: Kogan Page.

Boud, D., & Prosser, M. (2002). Appraising new technologies for learning: A framework for development. Educational Media International, 39(3), 237–245. doi:10.1080/09523980210166026doi:10.1080/09523980210166026

Boud, D., & Walker, D. (1998). Promoting reflection in professional courses: The challenge of context. *Studies in Higher Education, 23*(2), 191–206. doi:10.1080/03075079812331380384

Boyle, T. (2005). A dynamic, systematic method for developing blended learning. Education, Communication, and Information. Special Issue on Blended Learning, 5(3), 221–232.

Boyle, T., Bradley, C., Chalk, P., Jones, R., & Pickard, P. (2003). Using blended learning to improve student success rates in learning to program. Journal of Educational Media, 28(2-3), 165–178. doi:10.1080/1358165032000153160doi:10.1080/1358165032000153160

Brafman, O., & Beckstrom, R. (2006). *The starfish and the spider: The unstoppable power of leaderless organisations*. New York: Portfolio.

Braimoh, D., & Osiki, J. O. (2008). *From empowerment to transformation: A capacity building model for academics in distance higher education institutions in Africa*. Retrieved on October 3, 2008, from http://www.nou.edu.ng/noun/acde2008/acde_en/abstracts/mdg_rpi_odl.html

Bransford, J. D. (with Cognition and Technology Group; Vanderbilt University). (2000). Adventures in anchored instruction: Lessons from beyond the ivory tower. In R. Glasser (Ed.), *Advances in instructional psychology: Vol. 5*. Mahwah, NJ: Erlbaum.

Branzei, B. O., Vertinsky, I., & Camp, R. D. (2007). Culture-contingent signs of trust in emergent relationships. *Organizational Behavior and Human Decision Processes, 104*(1), 61–82. doi:10.1016/j.obhdp.2006.11.002

Briggs Myers, I., & Cook Briggs, K. (2002). *Myers-Briggs type indicator (MBIT)*. Association for Psychological Type.

Broad, M. L., & Newstron, J. L. (1992). *Transfer of training: Action packed strategies to ensure high payoff from training investments*. Reading, MA: Addison-Wesley.

Broers, N. (2002). Selection and use of propositional knowledge in statistical problem solving. *Learning and Instruction, 12*(3), 323–344. doi:10.1016/S0959-4752(01)00025-1

Bromley, D. B. (1986). *The case study method in psychological and realted disciplnes*. Chichester: John Wiley.

Brook, C., & Oliver. R. (2003). Online learning communities: Investigating a design framework. *Australian Journal of Educational Technology, 19*(2), 139–160.

Brook, C., & Oliver, R. (2005). *Exploring system factors that influence community development in online settings*. Paper presented at the World Conference on Educational Multimedia, Hypermedia, & Telecommunications, Montreal, Canada.

Brown, A. L., Campione, J., Webber, L., & McGilley, K. (1992). Interactive learning environments: A new look at learning and assessment. In B. R. Gifford & M. C. O'Connor (Eds.), *Future assessment: Changing views of aptitude, achievement, and instruction* (pp. 121-211). Boston: Academic.

Brown, S. A. (1999). Assessing practice. In S.A. Brown & A. Glasner (Eds.), *Assessment matters in higher education: Choosing and using diverse approaches*. Buckingham, UK & Philadelphia: Open University Press and Society for Research into Higher Education.

Brown, S., & Knight, P. (1994). *Assessing learning in higher education*. London: Kogan Page.

Bruder, I. (1989). Distance learning: What's holding back this boundless delivery system? *Electronic Learning, 8*(6), 30–35.

Bruer, J. T. (1993). *Schools for thought: A science of learning in the classroom*. Cambridge, MA: MIT Press.

Bruner, J. S. (1986). *Acts of meaning*. Cambridge, MA: Harvard University Press.

Brush, A. J., Bargeron, D., Grudin, J., Borning, A., & Gupta, A. (2002). Supporting interaction outside of class: Anchored discussions vs. discussion boards. *Proceedings of Computer Support for Collaborative Learning 2002*.

Bruun, H., & Laine, S. (2006). *Using the self-organizing map for measuring interdisciplinary research*. Retrieved on September 30, 2008, from http://www.stes.fi/scai2006/proceedings/001.pdf

Buchanan, E., Brown, M., Casanova, J., Wolfram, D., & Xie, H. (2000). Web-based and traditional instruction: A systematic study of student and instructor perceptions from a graduate MLIS program. *Teaching with Technology Today*, *7*(1), 1–3.

Buchanan, J., Wilson, S., & Gopal, N. (2008). A cross cultural virtual learning environment for students to explore the issue of racism: A case study involving the UK, USA, and SA. *Social Work Education*, *27*(6), 671–682. doi:10.1080/02615470802201804

Buchanan, T. (2000). The efficacy of a World Wide Web mediated formative assessment. *Journal of Computer Assisted Learning*, *16*, 193–200. doi:10.1046/j.1365-2729.2000.00132.x

Burke, L., & Baldwin, T. (1999). *First break the rules: What the worlds greatest managers do differently*. New York: Simon & Schuster.

Burnett, K., Bonnici, L., Miksa, S., & Joonmin, K. (2007, Winter). Frequency, intensity, and topicality in online learning: An exploration of the interaction dimensions that contribute to student satisfaction in online learning. *Journal of Education for Library and Information Science*, *48*(1), 21–35.

Business Wire. (2006, November 13). *Global security study: Helpdesk calls on the rise, 2007 spending to increase*.

Byram, M. (1994). *Teaching and learning language and culture*. Bridgend: WBC Ltd.

Byram, M. (2000). Intercultural communicative competence: The challenge for language teacher training. In A. Mountford & N. Wadham-Smith (Eds.), *British studies: Intercultural perspectives* (pp. 95-102). Essex: Longman.

Byram, M., & Fleming, M. (1998). *Language learning in intercultural perspective. Approaches through drama and ethnography*. Cambridge: Cambridge University Press.

Canale, M., & Swain, M. (1980). Theoretical bases of communicative approaches to second language teaching and testing. *Applied Linguistics*, *1*(1), 1–47. doi:10.1093/applin/1.1.1

Carbonaro, M., Dawber, T., & Arav, I. (2006). A comparison of students' performance under full-time and part-time, and online conditions in an undergraduate nursing microbiology course. *Journal of Distance Education*, *21*(1), 51–61.

Career Voyages. (2005). *Biotechnology high growth industry profile* [brochure]. Washington, D.C.

Carey, J. (2001). Effective student outcomes: A comparison of online and face-to-face delivery modes. *DEOSNEWS*, *11*(9), 1–19.

Carless, D. (2005). Prospects for the implementation of assessment for learning. *Assessment in Education*, *12*(1), 39–54. doi:10.1080/0969594042000333904

Carnevale, D. (2006, October). E-mail is for old people. *Chronicle of the Higher Education, 53*(7). P. A27. Retrieved on February 14, 2007, from http://chronicle.com/weekly/v53/i07/07a02701.htm

Carswell, L. (1998). The 'virtual university': Toward an Internet paradigm. *SIGCSE Bulletin*, *30*(3), 46–50. doi:10.1145/290320.283017

Castells, M. (1997). *End of millennium volume three of the information age: Economy, society, and culture*. Oxford: Blackwell.

Castells, M. (2001). *The Internet galaxy: Reflections on the Internet, business, and society*. Oxford: Oxford University Press.

Central Intelligence Agency. (2008). *The world factbook 2008*. Retrieved on January 12, 2009, from https://www.cia.gov/library/publications/the-world-factbook/geos/sf.html

CETIS. (2005). *What is ADL SCORM?* Standards Briefings Series, Centre For Educational Technology Interoperability Standards, UK Joint Information Systems Committee.

Retrieved on December 1, 2008, from http://www.icodeon.com/pdf/WhatIsScorm2_web.pdf

Chamot, A. U., & O'Malley, J. M. (1996). The cognitive academic language learning approach (CALLA): A model for linguistically diverse classrooms. *The Elementary School Journal*, *96*(3), 259–273. doi:10.1086/461827

Chan, C. K. K., & Van Aalst, J. (2004). Learning, assessment, and collaboration in computer-supported environments. In J. W. Strijbos, P. A. Kirschner, R. L. & Martens (Eds.), *What we know about CSCL and implementing it in higher education* (pp. 87-112). Boston, MA: Kluwer Academic Publishers.

Chang, C. C. (2001). Construction and evaluation of a Web-based learning portfolio system: An electronic assessment tool. *Innovations in Education and Teaching International*, *38*(2), 144–155. doi:10.1080/13558000010030194

Chapelle, C. (2001). *Computer applications in second language acquisition: Foundations for teaching, testing, and research.* Cambridge: Cambridge University Press.

Chapman, C., Ramondt, L., & Smiley, G. (2005). Strong community, deep learning: Exploring the link. *Innovations in Education and Teaching International*, *42*(3), 217–230. doi:10.1080/01587910500167910

Charbaji, A., & Jannoun, S. E. L. (2005). Individuality, willingness to take risk, and use of a personal e-card: A Lebanese study. *Journal of Managerial Psychology*, *20*(1), 51–58. doi:10.1108/02683940510571649

Charoen, D., Raman, M., & Olfman, L. (2008, February). Improving end user behaviour in password utilization: An action research initiative. *Systemic Practice and Action Research*, *21*(1), 55–72. doi:10.1007/s11213-007-9082-4

Charron, C., et al. (2006). *Social computing: How networks erode institutional power, and what to do about it.* Forrester Research. Retrieved on September 1, 2008, from http://www.forrester.com/Research/Document/Excerpt/0,7211,38772,00.html

Chau, P. Y. K., Cole, M., Massey, A. P. M., Montoya-Weiss, M., & O'Keefe, R. M. (2002). Cultural differences in the online behavior of consumers. *Communications of the ACM*, *45*(10), 138–143. doi:10.1145/570907.570911

Chou, C. (2004). A model of learner-centered computer-mediate interaction for collaborative distance learning. *International Journal on E-Learning*, *3*(1), 11–19.

Cifuentes, L., & Murphy, K. (2000). Promoting multicultural understanding and positive self-concept through a distance learning community: Cultural connections. *Educational Technology Research and Development*, *48*(1), 69–83. doi:10.1007/BF02313486

Cifuentes, L., Murphy, K., Segur, R., & Kodali, S. (1997). Design considerations for computer conferences. Journal of Research on Computing in Education, 30(2), 177–210.

Clarke, J., & Newman, J. (1997). *The managerial state.* London: Sage.

Claroline. (n.d.) Retrieved on November 21, 2008, from http://www.claroline.net

Claver, E., Llopis, J., Gonzalez, M. R., & Gasco, J. L. (2001). The performance of information systems through organizational culture. Information Technology & People, 14(3), 247–260. doi:10.1108/09593840110402149doi:10.1108/09593840110402149

CNNIC. (2009). The 24th statistical report on the Internet development in China (第**24**次中國互聯网絡发展狀况統计報告**).** Retrieved on September 16, 2009, from http://www.cnnic.cn/html/Dir/2009/07/15/5637.htm

Cobb, P., Confrey, J., diSessa, A., Lehrer, R., & Schauble, L. (2003). Design experiments in educational research. *Educational Researcher*, *32*(1), 9–13. doi:10.3102/0013189X032001009

Cobb, T. (1997). Cognitive efficiency: Toward a revised theory of media. *Educational Technology Research and Development*, *45*(4), 21–45. doi:10.1007/BF02299681

Cognition and Technology Group at Vanderbilt. (1993). Toward integrated curricula: Possibilities from anchored instruction. In M. Rabinowitz (Ed.), *Cognitive science foundations of instruction* (pp. 33-55). Hillsdale, NJ: Lawrence Erlbaum Associates.

Cohen, J. A., & Mannarino, A. P. (2004). Posttraumatic stress disorder. In T. H. Ollendick & J. E. March (Eds.), *Phobic and anxiety disorders in children and adolescents: A clinician's guide to effective psychosocial and pharmacological interventions.* New York: Oxford University Press.

Cole, D. J. (2000). *Portfolios across the curriculum and beyond*, 2nd ed. Thousand Oaks, CA: Corwin Press.

Cole, M. (1998). *Cultural psychology: A once and future discipline.* London: First Harvard University Press.

Collins, A., & Stevens, A. L. (1982). A cognitive theory for inquiry teaching. In P. Goodyear (Ed.), *Teaching knowledge and intelligent tutoring* (pp. 203-230). Norwood, NJ: Ablex.

Collis, B., & Margaryan, A. (2004). Applying activity theory to computer-supported collaborative learning and work-based activities in corporate setting. *Educational Technology Research and Development, 52,* 38–52. doi:10.1007/BF02504717

Collis, B., & Moonen, J. (2001). Flexible learning in a digital world. London: Kogan Page.

Collison, G., Elbaum, B., Haavind, S., & Tinker, R. (2000). *Facilitating online learning: Effective strategies for moderators.* Madison, WI: Atwood Publishing.

Commons, O. E. R. (2008). *OER Commons Web site.* Retrieved on September 1, 2008, from http://www.oercommons.org

Computer and Network Security Task Force. (2008). *Resource kit for national cyber security awareness.* Retrieved on January 27, 2009, from http://www.educause.edu/security/resourcekit/7479?time=1233090643

Condie, R., & Livingston, K. (2007). Blending online learning with traditional approaches: Changing practices. *British Journal of Educational Technology, 38*(2), 337–348. doi:10.1111/j.1467-8535.2006.00630.x

Connolly, T., MacArthur, E., Stansfield, M., & McLellan, E. (2007). A quasi-experimental study of three online learning courses in computing. *Computers & Education, 49*(2), 345–359. doi:10.1016/j.compedu.2005.09.001

Conrad, D. (2008). Reflecting on strategies for a new learning culture: Can we do it! *Journal of Distance Education, 22*(3), 157–161.

Conrad, R., & Donaldson, A. (2004). *Engaging the online learner: Activities and resources for creative instruction.* San Francisco, CA: Jossey-Bass.

Continuous Assessment Plan. (2006). School principal program, grade P-12 other school personnel program: Professional education unit. University of Kentucky. Retrieved on November 13, 2007, from http://www.coe.uky.edu/acadserv/programs/CA/camadsu3.doc

Cooper, H., Valentine, J. C., Nye, B., & Lindsay, J. J. (1999). Relationships between five after-school activities and academic achievement. *Journal of Educational Psychology, 91*(2), 369–378. doi:10.1037/0022-0663.91.2.369

Cooper, M. M., & Selfe, C. L. (1990). Computer conferencing and learning: Authority, resistance, and internally persuasive discourse. *College English, 52*(8), 847–869. doi:10.2307/377388

Cooper, S. T., Tyser, R. W., & Sandheinrich, M. B. (2007). The benefits of linking assignments to online quizzes in introductory biology courses. *Journal of Online Leanring and Teaching, 3*(3). Retrieved on November 21, 2008, from http://jolt.merlot.org/vol3no3/cooper.htm

Cordova, D. I., & Lepper, M. R. (1996). Intrinsic motivation and the process of learning: Beneficial effects of contextualization, personalization, and choice. *Journal of Educational Psychology, 88*(4), 715–730. doi:10.1037/0022-0663.88.4.715

Corey, S. (1953). *Action research to improve school practices.* New York: Teachers College Press.

Cosden, M., Morrison, G., Gutierrez, L., & Brown, M. (2004). The effects of homework programs and after-school activities on school success. *Theory into Practice, 43*(3), 221–226.

Costley, C., & Armsby, P. (2007). Work-based learning assessed as a field or a mode of study. *Assessment & Evaluation in Higher Education, 32*(1), 21–33. doi:10.1080/02602930600848267

Cottingham, K. (2002). Tackling biocomplexity: The role of people, tools, and scales. *Bioscience, 52*(9), 793–799. doi:10.1641/0006-3568(2002)052[0793:TBTROP]2.0.CO;2

Coulby, D., & Zambeta, E. (Eds.). (2005). *Globalization and nationalism in education.* London: RoutledgeFalmer.

Crane, B. E. (2000). *Teaching with the Internet: Strategies and models for K-12 curricula.* New York: Neal-Schuman Publisher.

Creative Commons. (2008). *Creative commons.* Retrieved on September 1, 2008, from http://creativecommons.org

Crebert, G., Bates, M., Bell, B., Patrick, C.-J., & Cragnolini, V. (2004). Ivory tower to concrete jungle revisited. *Journal of Education and Work, 17*(1), 47–70. doi:10.1080/1363908042000174192

Crisp, B. R. (2007). Is it worth the effort? How feedback influences students' subsequent submission of assessable work. *Assessment & Evaluation in Higher Education, 32*(5), 571–581. doi:10.1080/02602930601116912

Cronbach, L. J. (1951). Coefficient alpha and the internal structure of tests. *Psychometrika, 16*(3), 297–334. doi:10.1007/BF02310555

Crystal, D. (2003). *English as a global language* (second edition). Cambridge: Cambridge University Press.

CSI/FBI. (2006). *Computer crime and security survey.* Retrieved on August 12, 2007, from http://www.gocsi.com/forms/fbi/csi_fbi_survey.jhtml

Csikszentimihalyi, M. (1999). Implications of a system's perspective for the study of creativity. In R. J. Sternberg (Ed.), *Handbook of creativity.* Cambridge, UK: Cambridge University Press.

Csikszentmihalyi, M. (1988). The flow experience and its significance for human psychology. In M. Csikszentmihalyi & I. S. Csikszentmihalyi (Eds.), Optimal experience: Psychological studies of flow in consciousness (pp. 57-97). New York: Cambridge University Press.

Cuban, L. (1986). *Teachers and machines: The classroom use of technology since 1920 by Larry Cuban.* Teacher's College Press.

Cummins, J. (1996). *Negotiating identities: Education for empowerment in a diverse society.* Los Angeles: Association for Bilingual Education.

Cushman, K. (2006). *First in the family: Advice about college from first generation students: Your college years.* Providence: Next Generation Press.

Cuttance, P. (1998). Quality assurance reviews as a catalyst for school improvement in Australia. In A. Hargreaves, A. Lieberman, M. Fullan & D. Hopkins (Eds.), *International handbook of educational change: Part II* (pp. 1135-1162*)*. Dordrecht: Klwer Publishers.

Darling-Hammond, L. (2000). Teacher quality and student achievement: A review of state policy evidence. *Educational Policy Archives, 8*(1).

Davenport, T. H. (1997). Information ecology. Oxford: Oxford University Press.

Davies, A., Ramsey, J., Linderfield, H., & Couperthwaite, J. (2005). A blended approach to learning: Added value and lessons learnt from students' use of computer based materials for neurological analysis. *British Journal of Educational Technology, 36*(5), 839–849. doi:10.1111/j.1467-8535.2005.00506.x

Davies, P. (2000). Computerized peer assessment. Innovations in Education and Training International, 37(4), 346–355.

Dawkins, R. (1976). *The selfish gene.* Oxford: Oxford University Press.

Deacon, B. J., & Abramowitz, J. S. (2004). Cognitive and behavioural treatments for anxiety disorders: A review of meta-analysis findings. *Journal of Clinical Psychology, 60*(4), 429–441. doi:10.1002/jclp.10255

Deci, E. L., & Ryan, R. (1985). Intrinsic motivation and self determination in human behavior. New York: Plenum Press.

Deci, E. L., & Ryan, R. M. (1985). The general causality orientations scale: Self-determination in personality. Journal of Research in Personality, 19, 109–134. doi:10.1016/0092-6566(85)90023-6doi:10.1016/0092-6566(85)90023-6

Dede, C. (1996). Emerging technologies in distance education for business. Journal of Education for Business, 71(4), 197–204.

Deibert, R., Palfrey, J., Rohozinski, R., & Zittrain, J. (2008). *Access denied: The practice and policy of global Internet filtering.* Massachusetts: MIT Press. del.icio.us. (2008). *Delicious Web site.* Retrieved on September 1, 2008, from http://del.icio.us

Del Galdo, E. M. (1996). Culture and design. In E. M. Del Galdo & J. Neilsen (Eds.), *International user interfaces* (pp. 74–87). New York: John Wiley & Sons.

Dember, W. N., & Earl, R. W. (1957). Analysis of exploratory, manipulatory, and curiosity behaviors. Psychological Review, 64, 91–96. PubMed doi:10.1037/h0046861doi:10.1037/h0046861

Dempsey, J. V., Haynes, L. L., Lucassen, B. A., & Casey, M. S. (2002). Forty simple computer games and what they could mean to educators. *Simulation & Gaming, 33*(2), 157–168. doi:10.1177/1046878102332003

Dendrinos, B. (2001). *The politics of ELT.* Athens: The University of Athens Publications.

Denzin, N. K., & Lincoln, Y. S. (1994). Handbook of qualitative research. Thousand Oaks, CA: Sage.

Desire2Learn. (n.d.) Retrieved on November 21, 2008, from http://www.desire2learn.com

DeVol, R., Koepp, R., Wallace, L., Bedroussian, A., Murphy, D., Wong, P., et al. (2005). *The greater Philadelphia life sciences cluster: An economic and comparative assessment.* Philadephia: The Milken Institute.

Dewey, J. (1929). *The sources of a science of education.* New York: Liveright.

Dewulf, A., François, G., Pahl-Wostl, C., & Taillieu, T. (2007). A framing approach to cross- disciplinary research collaboration: Experiences from a large-scale research project on adaptive water management. *Ecology and Society, 12*(2), 14. Retrieved on January 11, 2008, from http//www.ecologyandsociety.org/vol12/iss2/art14/

Dhanarajan, G. (2001). Distance education: Promise, performance, and potential. *Open Learning, 16*(1), 61-68. Retrieved on November 1, 2007, from http://search.ebscohost.com/login.aspx?direct=true&db=aph&AN=4041530&site=ehost-live

Dickey, M. (2004). The impact of Web-logs (blogs) on student perceptions of isolation and alienation in a Web-based distance-learning environment. *Open Learning, 19*(3), 279–291. doi:10.1080/0268051042000280138

Dickey, M. (2005). Engaging by design: How engagement strategies in popular computer and video games can inform instructional design. *Educational Technology Research and Development, 53*(2), 67–83. doi:10.1007/BF02504866

Dickinson, L. (1987). *Self-instruction in language learning.* Cambridge: Cambridge University Press.

Digital Ethnography. (2008). *You Tube usage statistics, digital ethnography Web site.* Retrieved on December 1, 2008, from http://ksudigg.wetpaint.com/page/YouTube+Statistics?t=anon

Dimchev, A., & Miltenoff, P. (2006). Books, libraries, media, and new information technologies: Seeking the balance. The new information technologies (NIT) and the risks for the coming generation. *Proceedings of the International Scientific Conference "Children and Libraries,"* October 5-8, 2005, Belgrade, Yugoslavia. Retrieved on February 6, 2009, from http://web.stcloudstate.edu/pmiltenoff/ioc_2006/balance_nit.doc

Dodge, B. (2001). FOCUC: Five rules for writing a great webquest. *Learning & Learning with Technology, 28*(8), 6–9.

Dokeos. (n.d.) Retrieved on November 21, 2008, from http://www.dokeos.com

Doolan, M. A. (2007). 'Group work' scenario: Using Wiki for group work in the context of learning groups and grouping for assessment. *2nd Annual Blended Learning Conference "Supporting the Net Generation Learner,"* University of Hertfordshire, Hatfield. Retrieved on February 29, 2008, from http://perseus.herts.ac.uk/uhinfo/library/w46725_13.doc

Dornyei, Z. (2001). *Teaching and researching motivation.* Harlow: Longman.

Dornyei, Z. (2003). *Attitudes, orientation, and motivation in language learning: Advances in theory, research, and applications.* Oxford: Blackwell Publishing.

Downing, K., & Chim, T. M. (2004). Reflectors as online extroverts? *Educational Studies, 30*(3), 265–276. doi:10.1080/0305569042000224215

Drevin, L., Kruger, H. A., & Steyn, T. (2007). Value-focused assessment of ICT security awareness in an academic environment. *Computers & Security, 26*(1), 36–43. doi:10.1016/j.cose.2006.10.006

Dubin, F., & Olshtain, E. (1986). *Course design.* Cambridge: Cambridge University Press.

Ducatel, K. (1998). *Learning and skills in the knowledge economy.* DRUID Working Paper No 98-2, Danish Research Institute for Industrial Dynamics, Aalborg University. Retrieved on September 1, 2008, from http://www.druid.dk/wp/pdf_files/98-2.pdf

Dunbar, R. (1991). Adapting distance education for Indonesians: Problems with learner heteronomy and a strong oral tradition. *Distance Education, 12*(2), 163–174. doi:10.1080/0158791910120203

Dziuban, C. D., Hartman, J., & Moskal, P. (2004). Blended learning. Educause Center for Applied Research Bulletin, 7, 1–12.

Eaker, R. E., & Dufour, R. (1998). *Professional learning communities at work: Best practices for enhancing student achievement.* Bloomington, IN: Solution Tree.

EC. (2008). *i2010-a European information society for growth and employment.* Brussels: European Commission. Retrieved on September 1, 2008, from http://ec.europa.eu/information_society/eeurope/i2010/strategy/index_en.htm

eCollege. (n.d.) Retrieved on November 21, 2008, from http://www.ecollege.com

Edelson, D. C., Pea, R. D., & Gomez, L. (1995). Constructivism in the collaboratory. In Constructivist learning environments: Case studies in instructional design. Englewood Cliffs, NJ: Educational Technology Publications.

eFront. (n.d.) Retrieved on November 21, 2008 from http://www.efrontlearning.net

EL-Deghaidy, H., & Nouby, A. (2008). Effectiveness of a blended e-learning cooperative approach in an Egyptian teacher education programme. *Computers & Education, 51*(3), 988–1006. doi:10.1016/j.compedu.2007.10.001

Elliott, N., & Higgins, A. (2005). Self and peer assessment–does it make a difference to student group work? *Nurse Education in Practice, 5*(1), 40–48. doi:10.1016/j.nepr.2004.03.004

Ellis, G., & Sinclair, B. (1989). *Learning to learn English: A course in learner training.* Cambridge: Cambridge University Press.

Ellis, R. (2003). *Task-based language learning and teaching.* Oxford: Oxford University Press.

Ellis, R., Goodyear, P., Prosser, M., & O'Hara, A. (2006). How and what university students learn through online and face-to-face discussion: Conceptions, intentions, and approaches. *Journal of Computer Assisted Learning, 22*(4), 244–256. doi:10.1111/j.1365-2729.2006.00173.x

Endsley, M. (1995). Measurement of situation awareness in dynamic systems. *Human Factors, 31*(1), 65–84. doi:10.1518/001872095779049499

Endsley, M., & Garland, D. (2000). *Experimental analysis and measurement of situation awareness.* Daytona Beach, FL: Embry-Little University Press.

Erbaugh, S. E. (2007). *The attributes of psychotherapy for depression.* Retrieved on November 9, 2007, from http://www.healthplace.com/comminities/depression/treatment/therapy/psych_vs_meds.asp

Ess, C. (2006). Ethical pluralism and global information ethics. *Ethics and Information Technology, 8*(4), 215–226. doi:10.1007/s10676-006-9113-3

EU. (2008). Bologna process Web site. Brussels: Benelux Bologna Secretariat. Retrieved on September 1, 2008, from http://www.ond.vlaanderen.be/hogeronderwijs/bologna

Evans, P., Suzuki, Y., Begg, M., & Lam, W. (2008). Can medical students from two cultures learn effectively from a shared Web-based learning environment? *Medical Education, 42*(1), 27–33.

Facebook. (2008). *Facebook Web site.* Retrieved on September 1, 2008, from http://www.facebook.com

Facteau, J. D., Dobbins, G. H., Russell, J. E. A., Ladd, R. T., & Kudisch, J. D. (1995). The influence of general perceptions of the training environment on pretraining motivation and perceived training transfer. *Journal of Management, 21*, 1–25. doi:10.1016/0149-2063(95)90031-4

Faiola, A., & Matei, S. (2005). Cultural cognitive style and Web design: Beyond a behavioral inquiry into computer-mediated communication. *Journal of Computer-Mediated Communication, 11*(1), 375–394. doi:10.1111/j.1083-6101.2006.tb00318.x

Fang, L. (2007). Perceiving the useful, enjoyable, and effective: A case study of the e-learning experience of tertiary students in Singapore. *Educational Media International, 44*(3), 237–253. doi:10.1080/09523980701491682

Fast fact: Learning communities program at Kingsborough Community College improves test scores. (2005, November 23). Retrieved on March 20, 2009, from http://www.mdrc.org/area_fact_25.html

Felder, R. M., & Silverman, L. K. (1988). Learning and teaching styles in engineering education. *English Education, 78*(7), 674–681.

Fidishun, D. (2001, March). People servers vs. information providers: The impact of service orientation on technology training. *Information Technology and Libraries, 20*(1). Retrieved on December 12, 2008, from http://www.ala.org/ala/mgrps/divs/lita/ital/vol20/number1/fidishun.cfm

Fields, P., & Collins, P. (2005). An assessment of student performance in an introductory statistics hybrid course. *Proceedings of the 55th Session, International Statistical Institute*.

Filipek, R. (2007). European nations make security a high priority. *The Internal Auditor*, *64*(5), 15–17.

Fink, D. (2003). *Creating significant learning experiences: An integrated approach to designing college courses*. San Francisco: Jossey-Bass.

Finkelstein, J. (2006). *Learning in real time: Synchronous teaching and learning online*. San Francisco, CA: Jossey-Bass.

Fjermestad, R., Hiltz, S. R., & Zhang, Y. (Eds.). (2005). Effectiveness for students: Comparisons of "in-seat" and ALN courses. NJ: Lawrence Erlbaum Associates Publishers.

Fletcher, R. (1993). *What a writer needs*. Portsmouth, NH: Heinemann.

Floridi, L. (2006). Four challenges for a theory of information privacy. *Ethics and Information Technology*, *8*(3), 109–119. doi:10.1007/s10676-006-9121-3

Folkers, D. A. (2005). Competing in the marketplace: Incorporating online education into higher education-an organizational perspective. Information Resources Management Journal, 18(1), 61–77.

Fontana, A., & Frey, J. H. (1994). Interviewing: The art of science. In N. K. Denzin & Y. S. Lincoln (Eds.), *Handbook of qualitative research* (pp. 361-376). Thousand Oaks, CA: SAGE Publications Inc.

Ford, N., Wood, F., & Walsh, C. (1994). Cognitive styles and searching. *Online and CDROM Review*, *18*(2), 79–86. doi:10.1108/eb024480

Fornaciari, C., & Forte, M. (1999). Distance education as a strategy: How can your school compete? *Journal of Management Education*, *23*(6), 703–719. doi:10.1177/105256299902300608

Foster, J. G., Sheriff, S., & Cheney, S. (2008). Using non-faculty registered nurses to facilitate high-fidelity human patient simulation activities. *Nurse Educator*, *33*(3), 137–141. doi:10.1097/01.NNE.0000312186.20895.50

Fox, G. (1998). The Internet: Making it work in the ESL classroom. *The Internet TESL Journal*, 4/9. Retrieved on August 28, 2001, from http://www.aitech.ac.jp/~iteslj/Articles/Fox-Internet.html

Fracker, M. (1991). *Measures of situation awareness: Review and future directions*. OH: Armstrong Laboratories, Wright Patterson Air Force Base.

Frankola, K. (2001, October). *Workforce*. Retrieved from http://findarticles.com/p/articles/mi_m0FXS/is_10_80/ai_79352432

Fredericksen, E., Pickett, A., & Shea, P. (2000). Student satisfaction and perceived learning with online courses: Principles and examples from the SUNY learning network. Journal of Asynchronous Learning Networks, 4(2).

Freedman, K., & Liu, M. (1996). The importance of computer experience, learning processes, and communication patterns of multicultural networking. *Educational Technology Research and Development*, *44*(1), 43–59. doi:10.1007/BF02300325

Freeman, M., & McKenzie, J. (2002). Spark, a confidential Web-based template for self and peer assessment of student teamwork: Benefits of evaluating across different subjects. *British Journal of Educational Technology*, *33*(5), 551–569. doi:10.1111/1467-8535.00291

Freeman, R., & Lewis, R. (1998). *Planning and implementing assessment*. London: Kogan Page.

Gagne, M., & Shepherd, M. (2001). A comparison between a distance and a traditional graduate accounting class. *T.H.E. Journal*, *28*(9), 58–65.

Gardner, H. (1999). *Intelligence reframed: Multiple intelligences for the 21st century*. New York: Basic Books.

Garrison, D. R., & Kanuka, H. (2004). Blended learning: Uncovering its transformative potential in higher education. The Internet and Higher Education, 7(2), 95–105. doi:10.1016/j.iheduc.2004.02.001doi:10.1016/j.iheduc.2004.02.001

Garrison, D. R., & Kanuka, H. (2004). Blended learning: Uncovering its transformative potential in higher education. *The Internet and Higher Education*, *7*(2), 95–105. doi:10.1016/j.iheduc.2004.02.001

Garrison, D. R., Anderson, T., & Archer, W. (2000). Critical inquiry in a text-based environment: Computer conferencing in higher education. *The Internet and Higher Education*, *2*(2-3), 87–105. doi:10.1016/S1096-7516(00)00016-6

Garrison, D., & Anderson, T. (2003). *E-learning in the 21st century: A framework for research and practice*. London: RoutledgeFalmer.

Garrison, D., & Kanuka, H. (2004). Blended learning: Uncovering its transformative potential in higher education. *The Internet and Higher Education*, *7*(2), 95–105. doi:10.1016/j.iheduc.2004.02.001

Gee, J. P. (2003). *What video games have to teach us about learning and literacy*. NY: First Palgrave Macmillan.

Geen, R. (1994). *Human motivation: A psychological approach*. New York: Wadsworth Publishing.

Giacquinta, J. B., Bauer, J. A., & Levin, J. E. (1993). Beyond technology's promise. Cambridge: Cambridge University Press.

Gibbons, M., Limoges, C., Nowotny, H., Scott, P., Schwartzman, S., & Trow, M. (1994). *The new production of knowledge–the dynamics of science and research in contemporary societies*. London: Sage Publications.

Gibbs, G. (1995). *Assessing student centred courses*. Oxford: Oxford Centre for Staff Development.

Gillham, B. (2000a). *The research interview*. New York: Continuum.

Gillham, B. (2000b). *Case study research methods*. New York: Continuum.

Ginns, P., & Ellis, R. (2007). Quality in blended learning: Exploring the relationships between online and face-to-face teaching and learning. The Internet and Higher Education, 10, 53–64. doi:10.1016/j.iheduc.2006.10.003doi:10.1016/j.iheduc.2006.10.003

Ginns, P., & Ellis, R. (2007). Quality in blended learning: Exploring the relations between online and face-to-face teaching and learning. *The Internet and Higher Education*, *10*, 53–64. doi:10.1016/j.iheduc.2006.10.003

Girod, M., & Martineau, J., & Zhao. (2004). After-school computer clubhouses and at-risk teens. *American Secondary Education*, *32*(3), 63–76.

Glasner, A. (2000). Innovations in student assessment: A system-wide perspective. In S. A. Brown & A. Glasner (Eds.), *Assessment matters in higher education: Choosing and using diverse approaches*. Buckingham, UK & Philadelphia: Open University Press and Society for Research into Higher Education.

Goldstein, J., & Puntambekar, S. (2005). The brink of change: Gender in technology-rich collaborative learning environments. *Journal of Science Education and Technology*, *13*(4), 505–522. doi:10.1007/s10956-004-1471-1

Goldstuck, A. (2002). *The goldstuck report: Internet access in South Africa, 2002*. Johannesburg: World Wide Worx (Pty) Ltd.

Gommlich, K., & Minick, T. (2007). United reinvention of an online teacher education course: From cooperation to collaboration. In E. Hanson-Smith & S. Rilling (Eds.), *Learning languages through technology* (pp. 233-244). Alexandria, VA: TESOL.

Gould, M., & Padavano, D. (2006, May). 7 ways to improve student satisfaction in online courses. *Online Classroom*, 1-2.

Grabe, M., & Sigler, E. (2002). Studying online: Evaluation of an online study environment. *Computers & Education*, *38*(4), 375–383. doi:10.1016/S0360-1315(02)00020-9

Graham, C. (2006). Blended learning systems. Definitions, current trends, and future directions. In C. Bonk & C. Graham (Eds.), *The handbook of blended learning: Global perspectives, local designs*. San Francisco: John Wiley and Sons.

Graham, C. R., Allen, S., & Ure, D. (2003). *Blended learning environments: A review of the research literature*. Unpublished manuscript, Provo, UT.

Graham, G., & Megarry, B. (2005). The social care work portfolio: An aid to integrated learning and reflection in social care training. *Social Work Education*, *24*(7), 769–780. doi:10.1080/02615470500238686

Granger, C., Morbey, M. L., Lotherington, H., Owston, R., & Wideman, H. (2002). Factors contributing to teachers' successful implementation of IT. Journal of Computer Assisted Learning, 48(8), 480–488. doi:10.1046/j.0266-4909.2002.00259.doc.xdoi:10.1046/j.0266-4909.2002.00259.doc.x

Grant, I. (2007). DaimlerChrysler security drive targets 360,000 staff. *Computer Weekly,* 4-8.

Green, H., & Hannon, C. (2007). *Their space: Education for a digital generation*. London: Demos.

Green, M., Hilken, J., Friedman, H., Grossman, K., Gasiewski, J., Adler, R., & Sabini, J. (2005, March). Communication via instant messenger: Short- and long-Term Effects. *Journal of Applied Social Psychology, 35*(3), 445–462. doi:10.1111/j.1559-1816.2005.tb02130.x

Greer, J., McCalla, G., Vassileva, J., Deters, R., Bull, S., & Kettel, L. (2001). Lessons learned in deploying a multi-agent learning support system: The i-help experience. [Amsterdam, The Netherlands: IOS Press.]. *Proceedings of AIED, 2001*, 410–421.

Gunn, C. (2003). Dominant or different? Gender issues in computer supported learning. Journal of Asynchronous Learning Networks, 7(1), 14–30.

Guomundsdottir, G. B. (2005, December). *Approaching the digital divide in South Africa.* Paper presented at the NETREED Conference, Beitostłølen, Norway.

Guthrie, J. T. (2001). *Contexts for engagement and motivation in reading* [electronic version]. Retrieved on October 23, 2006, from http://www.readingonline.org/articles/art_index.asp?HREF=/articles/handbook/guthrie/index.html

Guzdial, M., & Carroll, K. (2002). Explaining the lack of dialogue in computer-supported collaborative learning. *Proceedings of CSCL 2002.* Retrieved from http://newmedia.colorado.edu/cscl/18.html

Guzdial, M., & Turn, J. (2000). Effective discussion through a computer-mediated anchored forum. *Journal of the Learning Sciences, 9*(4), 437–469. doi:10.1207/S15327809JLS0904_3

Guzdial, M., Ludovice, P., Realff, M., Morley, T., & Carroll, K. (2002). When collaboration doesn't work. *Proceedings of the International Conference of the Learning Sciences* (pp.125-130). Mahwah, NJ: Lawrence Erlbaum Associates.

Haag, S., & Cummings, M. (2008). *Management information systems for the inforamtion age* (7th ed.). New York: McGraw-Hill Irwin.

Hagner, P. R., & Schneebeck, C. A. (2001). Engaging the faculty. In C. A. Barone & P. R. Hagner (Eds.), Technology-enhanced teaching and learning, educause leadership strategies (Vol. 5, pp. 1-12). San Francisco: Jossey-Bass.

Hall, E. T., & Hall, M. R. (1989). *Understanding cultural differences.* Yarmouth, ME: Intercultural Press.

Hamel, J. (1993). *Case study methods.* London: Sage.

Hanrahan, S. J., & Isaacs, G. (2001). Assessing self- and peer-assessment: The students' views. *Higher Education Research & Development, 20*(1), 53–70. doi:10.1080/07294360123776

Hara, N., Bonk, C. J., & Angeli, C. (2000). Content analysis of online discussion in an applied educational psychology. *Instructional Science, 28*(2), 115–152. doi:10.1023/A:1003764722829

Harasim, L. M. (1989). Online education: A new domain. In R. Mason & A. Kaye (Eds.), *Mindweave: Communication, computers, and distance education.* Oxford & New York: Pergamon Press.

Harden, R. M., & Hart, I. R. (2002). An international virtual medical school (ivimeds): The future for medical education? *Medical Teacher, 24*(3), 261–267. doi:10.1080/01421590220141008

Hardy, D. W., Ashcroft, J. C., & Abbiatti, M. D. (1996). The motion curricula concept: Technology selection in distance education. Paper presented at the Proceedings of the 12th Distance Teaching and Learning Conference, University of Wisconsin at Madison.

Harland, T. (2005). Developing a portfolio to promote authentic enquiry in teacher education. *Teaching in Higher Education, 10*(3), 327–337. doi:10.1080/13562510500122180

Harrington, J. (2005, August 16). Sen. Baucus relishes resisting Bush's social security privatization plan. *Knight Rider Tribune Business News.*

Harry, K. (Ed.). (n.d.). *Higher education through open and distance learning, world review of distance education and open learning* (Vol. 1, pp. 15-31). London: RoutledgeFalmer.

Harter, S., & Connell, J. P. (1984). A model of children's achievement and related self-perceptions of competence, control, and motivation orientation. Advances in Motivation and Achievement, 3, 219–250.

Hawthorn, D. (2000). *Designing for older users: Display quality versus task complexity.* Paper presented at the OzChi 2000: Interfacing Reality in the New Millennium, The University of Technology, Sydney, Australia.

Hegarty, C. (2006). It's not an exact science: Teaching entrepreneurship in Northern Ireland. *Education + Training, 48*(5), 322-335.

Henderson, B. B. (1989). Individual differences in exploration: A replication and extension. The Journal of Genetic Psychology, 149, 555–557.

Henderson, L. (1996). Instructional design of interactive multimedia: A cultural critique. Educational Technology Research and Development, 44(4), 86–104. doi:10.1007/BF02299823doi:10.1007/BF02299823

Henri, F. (1992). Computer conferencing and content analysis. In A. R. Kaye (Eds.), *Collaborative learning through computer conferencing: The Najaden papers* (pp.115-136). New York: Springer.

Herrington, J. (1997). *Authentic learning in interactive multimedia environments.* Unpublished doctoral dissertation, Edith Cowan University, Perth.

Herrington, J., & Oliver, R. (1995). *Critical characteristics of situated learning: Implications for the instructional design of multimedia.* Paper presented at the Ascelite, University of Melbourne.

Herrington, T., & Herrington, J. (2006). What is an authentic learning environment? In T. Herrington & J. Herrington (Eds.), *Authentic learning environments in higher education.* Hershey, PA: Information Science Publishers.

Herron, F. J., & Wright, V. H. (2006). Assessment in online learning: Are students really learning? In V. H. Wright, C. Szymanski Sunal & E. K. Wilson (Eds.), *Research on enhancing the interactivity of online learning* (pp. 45-64). Greenwich, CT: Information Age.

Hewitt, J., & Teplovs, C. (1999). An analysis of growth patterns in computer conferencing threads. [CSCL]. *Proceedings of Computer Support for Collaborative Learning, 1999*, 232–241.

Hill, P. W., & Rowe, K. (1998). Modelling student progress in studies of educational effectiveness. *School Effectiveness and School Improvement, 9*(3), 310–333. doi:10.1080/0924345980090303

Hilton, S., & Christensen, H. (2002). Evaluating the impact of multimedia lectures on student learning and attitudes. *Proceedings of the Sixth International Conference on Teaching Statistics.* The Netherlands: International Statistics Institute.

Hiltz, S. R. (1990). Collaborative learning: The virtual classroom approach. Technological Horizons in Education Journal, 17(10), 59–65.

Hiltz, S. R. (1994). The virtual classroom: Learning without limits via computer networks. Norwood, NJ: Ablex.

Hiltz, S. R. (1998). *Collaborative learning in asynchronous learning environments: Building learning communities.* Paper presented at the WebNet 98 World Conference of the WWW, Internet and Intranet Proceedings, Orlando, Florida.

Hiltz, S. R., & Turoff, M. (2005). Education goes digital: The evolution of online learning and the revolution in higher education. *Communications of the ACM, 48*(10), 59–64. doi:10.1145/1089107.1089139

Hiltz, S. R., Coppola, N., Rotter, N., & Turoff, M. (2000). Measuring the importance of collaborative learning for the effectiveness of ALN: A multi-measure, multi-method approach. Journal of Asynchronous Learning Networks, 4(2).

Ho, D. (2007, August). Harlem program finds ways to help kids, revive a community. *Cox News Service.*

Hoban, G., Neu, B., & Castle, S. (2002). *Assessment of student learning in an educational administration online program.* Paper presented at the American Education Research Association (AERA) Annual Meeting, New Orleans, Louisiana.

Hodgson, P. (2008). *Building a community of practice through liferay.* Paper presented at the 2008 International Conference on ICT in Teaching and Learning, Hong Kong.

Hodgson, P., & Csete, J. (2007). Creating new learning challenges through ecases [electronic version]. *The Information, Technology, and Educational Change (ITEC) Journal.* Retrieved from http://ejournal.cite.hku.hk/articles/volume2issue2/Hodgson_Csete/Hodgson_Csete.htm

Hodgson, P., & Wong, D. (2008). *Motivation, engagement, and quality of writing through blogs.* Paper presented at the 2008 International Conference on ICT in Teaching and Learning, Hong Kong.

Hodgson, P., Chan, K., & Liu, Y. W. J. (2007). *Learning through e-situated challenges.* Paper presented at the 2007 International Conference on ICT in Teaching and Learning, Hong Kong.

Hofmann, J. (2006). Answers to those questions that keep you up at night. In C. Bonk & C. Graham (Eds.), *The handbook of blended learning: Global perspectives, local designs* (pp. 27-40). San Francisco: Pfeiffer.

Hofstede, G. (1986). Cultural differences in teaching and learning. *International Journal of Intercultural Relations, 10,* 301–320. doi:10.1016/0147-1767(86)90015-5

Hofstede, G. (1993). Cultural constraints in management theories. *The Academy of Management Executive, 7*(1), 81–94.

Hofstede, G. (1997). *Cultures and organizations: Software of the mind.* New York: McGraw-Hill.

Hofstede, G. (2001). Cultures consequences: Comparing values, behaviors, institutions, and organisations across nations. Thousand Oaks, London, New Delhi: Sage Publications.

Hogan, M. P., Pace, D. E., Hapgood, J., & Boone, D. C. (2006). Use of human patient simulation and the situation awareness global assessment technique in practical trauma skills assessment. *The Journal of Trauma, 61*(5), 1047–1052. doi:10.1097/01.ta.0000238687.23622.89

Holt, D., & Thompson, D. (1998). Managing information technology in open and distance education. *Distance Education, 19*(2), 197–227. doi:10.1080/0158791980190203

Hubbard, R. (2009). Learning about e-learning. *Training Journal.*

Huck, S. (2004). *Reading statistics and research* (4th ed.). Boston, MA: Pearson/Allyn and Bacon.

Huffaker, D. (2004). The educated blogger: Using Weblogs to promote literacy in the classroom [electronic version]. *First Monday.* Retrieved on April 8, 2008, from http://www.firstmonday.org/issues/issue9_6/huffaker/#author

Hughes, G. (2007). Using blended learning to increase learner support and improve retention. *Teaching in Higher Education, 12*(3), 349–363. doi:10.1080/13562510701278690

Hughes, J. E. (2005). The role of teacher knowledge and learning experiences in forming technology-integrated pedagogy. Journal of Technology and Teacher Education, 13(2), 377–402.

Hughes, K. H. (2005). *Building the next American century: The past and future of American economic competitiveness.* Washington, D.C.: Woodrow Wilson Center Press.

Hutchins, E. (1995). *Cognition in the wild.* New York: MIT Press.

Hymes, D. (1967). Models of the interaction of language and social setting. In J. McNamara (Ed.), Problems of bilingualism. *Journal of Social Issues,* 23, 8-28.

Hymes, D. (1972). On communicative competence. In J. B. Pride & J. Holmes (Eds.), *Sociolinguistics.* Harmondsworth: Penguin Books.

ILIAS. (n.d.) Retrieved on November 21, 2008, from http://www.ilias.de

INCA. (2008). *International review of curriculum and assessment frameworks Internet archive.* Retrieved on September 1, 2008, from http://www.inca.org.uk

it's learning. (n.d.) Retrieved on November 21, 2008, from http://www.itslearning.com

Jarvenpaa, S. L., & Staples, D. S. (2000). The use of collaborative electronic media for information sharing: An exploratory study of determinants. The Journal of Strategic Information Systems, 9, 129–154. doi:10.1016/S0963-8687(00)00042-1doi:10.1016/S0963-8687(00)00042-1

Jarvis, P. (1999). Global trends in lifelong learning and the response of the universities. *Comparative Education, 35*(2), 249–257. doi:10.1080/03050069928017

Johnson, D. (1994). *Research methods in educational management.* Harlow: Longman.

Johnson, S., & Aragon, S. (2003). An instructional strategy framework for online learning environments. *New Directions for Adult and Continuing Education, 100,* 31–43. doi:10.1002/ace.117

Johnson, W. B., Huwe, J. M., & Lucas, J. L. (2000). Rational mentoring. *Journal of Rational-Emotive & Cognitive-Behavior Therapy, 18,* 39–54. doi:10.1023/A:1007713804708

Joint Information Systems Committee (JISC). (2007). *Effective practice with e-Assessment: An overview of technologies, policies, and practice in further and higher education.*

Retrieved on March 10, 2009, from http://www.jisc.ac.uk/media/documents/themes/elearning/effpraceassess.pdf

Jonassen, D. H. (2000). Computers as mindtools for schools. Upper Saddle River, NJ: Merrill.

Jonassen, D. H., Howland, J., Moore, J. C., & Marra, R. M. (2003). *Learning to solve problems with technology: A constructivist perspective*. Upper Saddle River, NJ: Merrill/Prentice Hall.

Jonassen, D. H., Peck, K. L., & Wilson, B. G. (1999). *Learning with technology: A constructivist perspective*. Upper Saddle River, NJ: Merrill.

Jones, R. H., Garralda, A., Li, D. C. S., & Lock, G. (2006). Interactional dynamics in online and face-to-face peer-tutoring sessions for second language writers. *Journal of Second Language Writing, 15*, 1–23. doi:10.1016/j.jslw.2005.12.001

Jones, S. (2006). Using IT to augment authentic learning environments. In T. Herrington & J. Herrington (Eds.), *Authentic learning environments in higher education*. Hershey, PA: Information Science Publishers.

Juwah, C. (2006). *Interactions in online education: Implications for theory and practice*. London & New York: Routledge.

Kamal, M. (2008). The psychology of IT security in business. *Journal of American Academy of Business, 13*(1), 145–150.

Kamberi, K., & Vlachos, K. (2003). Teaching second/foreign languages using the task based approach and online networking. In the *Proceedings of the 1st International Conference ICT in Diaspora*, Greek Embassy in London, UK (pp. 17-31).

Kanuka, H. (2008). Understanding e-learning technologies-in-practice through philosophies-in-practice. In T. Anderson (Ed.), The theory and practice of online learning (2nd ed., pp. 91-118). Edmonton: AU Press.

Kashdan, T. B., & Fincham, F. D. (2004). Facilitating curiosity: A social and self-regulatory perspective for scientifically based interventions. In P. A. Linley & S. Joseph (Eds.), Positive psychology in practice (pp. 482-503). New Jersey: Wiley.

Katz, J., & Aakhus, M. (Eds.). (2002). *Perpetual contact: Mobile communication, private talk, public performance*. Cambridge: Cambridge University Press.

Kawachi, P. (2003, April). Initiating intrinsic motivation in online education: Review of the current state of the art. *Interactive Learning Environments, 11*(1), 59–82. doi:10.1076/ilee.11.1.59.13685

Keegan, D. (1988). On defining distance education. In D. Sewart, D. Keegan & B. Holmberg (Eds.), *Distance education: International perspectives* (pp. 6-33). London/New York: Routledge.

Keegan, D. (1988). Problems in defining the field of distance education. *American Journal of Distance Education, 2*(2), 4–11.

Keengwe, J. (2007). Faculty integration of technology into instruction and students' perceptions of computer technology to improve student learning. Journal of Information Technology Education, 6, 169–180.

Keller, H., Schneider, K., & Henderson, B. (1994). Curiosity and exploration. Berlin: Springer-Verlag.

Kelly, K. (1994). *Out of control: The new biology of machines, social systems, and the economic world*. Boston: Addison-Wesley.

Keppell, M., Au, E., Ma, A., & Chan, C. (2004). Curriculum development: Making our theories of teaching and learning explicit in technology-enhanced environments. In P. Rogers (Ed.), Encyclopedia of distance learning teaching, technologies, and applications (pp. 492-504). Hershey, PA: Idea Group Publishing.

Kern, R. (2000). *Literacy and language teaching*. Oxford: Oxford University Press.

Khine, M. S., & Lourdusamy, A. (2003). Blended learning approach in teacher education: Combining face-to-face instruction, multimedia viewing, and online discussion. *British Journal of Educational Technology, 34*(5), 671–675. doi:10.1046/j.0007-1013.2003.00360.x

Kiddler, L. H. (1981). *Sellitz, Wrightsman, & Cook's research methods in social relations* (4th ed.). Austin, TX: Holt, Rinehart, and Winston.

Kim, K. J., & Bonk, C. J. (2006). Cross-cultural comparisons of online collaboration. *Journal of Computer-Mediated Communication, 8*(1), 1–21.

Kim, K. J., & Bonk, C. J. (2006). The future of online teaching and learning in higher education: The survey says.... EDUCAUSE Quarterly, 29, 9.

Kinzer, C. K. (2003). The importance of recognizing the expanding boundaries of literacy. *Reading online, 6*(10). Retrieved on November 17, 2008, from http://www.readingonline.org/electronic/elec_index.asp?HREF=/electronic/kinzer/index.html

Kinzer, C. K., & Leander, K. (2003). Technology and the language arts: Implications of an expanded definition of literacy. In J. Flood, D. Lapp, J. R. Squire & J. M. Jensen (Eds.), *Handbook of research on teaching the English language arts* (pp. 546-566). Mahwah, NJ: Erlbaum.

Kirkman, B. L., & Shapiro, D. L. (1997). The impact of cultural values on employee resistance to teams: Toward a model of globalized self-managing work team effectiveness. *Academy of Management Review, 22*, 730–357. doi:10.2307/259411

Klemm, W. (1999). Eight ways to get students more engaged in online conferences. The Journal of Higher Education, 26(1), 62–64.

Klemm, W. R. (1998). Eight ways to get students more engaged in online conferences. *T.H.E. Journal*. Retrieved on April 23, 2008, from http://www.thejournal.com/magazine/vault/A1997.cfm

Knight, P. T. (2002). *Being a teacher in higher education.* Buckingham, UK & Philadelphia: Open University Press and Society for Research into Higher Education.

Koch, K. (2002). Cheating in schools. *The CQ Researcher, 10*(32), 745–768.

Koehler, M., Mishra, P., & Yahya, K. (2007). Tracing the development of teacher knowledge in a design seminar: Integrating content, pedagogy, and technology. Computers & Education, 49(3), 740–764. doi:10.1016/j.compedu.2005.11.012doi:10.1016/j.compedu.2005.11.012

Kolb, A. Y., & Kolb, D. A. (2005, June). Learning styles and learning spaces: Enhancing experiential learning in higher education. *Academy of Management Learning & Education*, 193–212.

Koschmann, T. (2000). Tools of termlessness: Technology, educational reform, and Deweyan inquiry. Retrieved on March 31, 2007, from http://edaff.siumed.edu/tk/articles/UNESCO.pdf

Krathwohl, D., Bloom, B., & Masia, B. (1973). *Taxonomy of educational objectives. The classification of educational goals. Handbook II: Affective domain.* New York: David McKay Co., Inc.

Kreitler, H., & Kreitler, S. (1976). Cognitive orientation and behavior. New York: Springer.

Kruger, D. (1981). *An introduction to phenomenological psychology.* Pittsburgh, PA: Duquesne University Press.

Kucuk, S. U. (2002). The changing consumerism with the Internet: A global perspective. *Journal of Euromarketing, 12*(1), 41–61. doi:10.1300/J037v12n01_04

Kumpulainen, K., & Renshaw, P. (2007, April). Cultures of learning. *International Journal of Educational Research, 46*(3/4), 109–115. doi:10.1016/j.ijer.2007.09.009

Kwa, C. (2002). Does interdisciplinarity really exist? Retrieved on September 30, 2008, from http://www.easst.net/review/march2002/kwa

Kwan, R., & Fong, J. (2005). *Web-based Learning: Technology and pedagogy.* Hong Kong: World Scientific.

Kwok, P. M. H., & Hodgson, P. (2004). *Tea or tears with SARS?* Paper presented at the 38th Academy of Marketing Conference, July 5–7, Cheltenham, England.

Kwok, R., & Ma, J. (1999). Use of a group support system for collaborative assessment. *Computers & Education, 32*, 109–125. doi:10.1016/S0360-1315(98)00059-1

Lam, P., Hodgson, P., & Csete, J. (2007). Enrichment of interaction in online assessments. In S. Frankland (Ed.), *Enhancing teaching and learning through assessment: Deriving an appropriate model.* The Netherlands: Springer.

Lambropoulos, N., Christopoulou, M., & Vlachos, K. (2005). Cultural-based language learning objects in CALL. In P. Zaphiris & G. Zacharia (Eds.), *User-centred computer aided language learning* (pp. 22-43). Hershey, PA: Idea Publishing.

Lanham, E., & Zhou, W. (2003). Cultural issues in online learning: Is blended learning a possible solution? *International Journal of Computer Processing of Oriental Languages, 16*(4), 275–292. doi:10.1142/S0219427903000930

Lanier, J. (2006). *Digital Maoism: The hazards of the new online collectivism. Edge: The third culture.* Edge Foundation, Inc. Retrieved on September 1, 2008, from http://www.edge.org/3rd_culture/lanier06/lanier06_index.html

Larson, B., & Keiper, T. A. (2002). Classroom discussion and threaded electronic discussion: Learning in two arenas. *Contemporary Issues in Technology & Teacher Education, 2*(1), 45–62.

Larson, M. R., & Bruning, R. (1996). Participant perceptions of a collaborative satellite-based mathematics course. American Journal of Distance Education, 10(1), 6–22.

Laurillard, D. (1997). *Rethinking university teaching a framework for effective use of educational technology.* New York: Routledge.

Laurillard, D. (2000). New technologies, students, and the curriculum: The impact of communications and information technology on higher education. In P. Scott (Ed.), *Higher education reformed.* London & New York: Falmer Press.

Laurillard, D. (2002). *Rethinking university teaching: A conversational framework for the effective use of learning technologies*, 2nd ed. London & New York: Routledge-Falmer.

Laurillard, D., Stratfold, M., Luckin, R., Plowman, L., & Taylor, J. (2000). Affordances for learning in a non-linear narrative medium. *Interactive Media in Education.* Retrieved on April 23, 2008, from http://www.jime.open.ac.uk/00/2

Lave, J., & Wenger, E. (1991). *Situated learning: Legitimate peripheral participation.* Cambridge, UK: Cambridge University Press.

Lea, S. J., Stephenson, D., & Troy, J. (2003). Higher education students' attitudes to student-centred learning: Beyond educational bulimia. *Studies in Higher Education, 28*(3), 321–334. doi:10.1080/03075070309293

Leadbeater, C. (2008). *We-think.* London: Profile Books.

Learn.com. (n.d.) Retrieved on November 21, 2008, from http://www.learn.com

Learning, A. N. G. E. L. (n.d.) Retrieved on November 21, 2008, from http://angellearning.com Atutor. (n.d.) Retrieved on November 21, 2008, from http://www.atutor.ca

Lee, C. H., Kim, K., Seo, Y. S., & Chung, C. K. (2007). The relations between personality and lanugage use. *The Journal of General Psychology, 134*(4), 405–413. doi:10.3200/GENP.134.4.405-414

Lee, J. (2000). *Tasks and communicating in language classrooms.* Boston: McGraw-Hill.

Lee, J., Carter-Wells, J., Glaeser, B., Ivers, K., & Street, C. (2006, Spring). Facilitating the development of learning community in an online graduate program. *Quarterly Review of Distance Education, 7*(1), 13–33.

Leidner, D. E., & Jarvenpaa, S. L. (1995). The use of information technology to enhance management school education: A theoretical view. MIS Quarterly, 19(3), 265–291. doi:10.2307/249596doi:10.2307/249596

Lele, S. R., & Norgaard, R. B. (2005). Practicing interdisciplinarity. *Bioscience, 55*(11), 967–975. doi:10.1641/0006-3568(2005)055[0967:PI]2.0.CO;2

Lepper, M. R., & Chabay, R. W. (1985). Intrinsic motivation and instruction: Conflicting views on the role of motivational processes in computer-based education. *Educational Psychologist, 20*(4), 217–230. doi:10.1207/s15326985ep2004_6

Lepper, M. R., Corpus, J. H., & Iyengar, S. S. (2005). Intrinsic and extrinsic motivational orientations in the classroom: Age differences and academic correlates. *Journal of Educational Psychology, 97*(2), 184–196. doi:10.1037/0022-0663.97.2.184

Leu, D. J., Jr. (2000). Literacy and technology: Deictic consequences for literacy education in an information age. In M. L. Kamil, P. B. Mosenthal, P. D. Pearson & R. Barr (Eds.), *Handbook of reading research* (Vol. 3, pp. 743-770). Mahwah, NJ: Erlbaum.

Leu, D. J., Kinzer, C. K., Jr., Coiro, J., & Cammack, D. W. (2004). Toward a theory of new literacies emerging from the Internet and other information and communication technologies. In R. B. Ruddell & N. Unrau (Eds.), *Theoretical models and processes of reading* (pp. 1570-1613). Newark, DE: International Reading Association. Retrieved on November 17, 2008, from http://www.readingonline.org/newliteracies/lit_index.asp?HREF=leu/

Levers, L. L., & Hawes, A. R. (1989). Drugs and gender: A women's recovery program. *Journal of Mental Health Counseling, 12*, 527–531.

Levin, J. A., Riel, M., Miyake, N., & Cohen, M. (1987). Education on the electronic frontier: Teleapprentices in globally distributed educational contexts. *Contemporary Educational Psychology*, *12*, 254–260. doi:10.1016/S0361-476X(87)80030-9

Levina, N., & Vaast, E. (2005). The emergence of boundary spanning competence in practice: Implications for implementation and use of information systems. *MIS Quarterly*, *29*(2), 335–363.

Levy, M., & Stockwell, G. (2006). *CALL dimensions: Options and issues in computer-assisted language learning*. Mahwah, NJ: Lawrence Erlbaum Associates.

Li, J. (2002). A cultural model of learning: Chinese "heart and mind for wanting to learn.". *Journal of Cross-Cultural Psychology*, *33*, 248–269. doi:10.1177/0022022102033003003

Liang, A., & McQueen, R. (1999). Computer assisted adult interactive learning in a multi-cultural environment. *Adult Learning*, *11*(1), 26–28.

Lim, C. P. (2002). A theoretical framework for the study of ICT in schools: A proposal. *British Journal of Educational Technology*, *33*(4), 411–421. doi:10.1111/1467-8535.00278

Lim, C. P. (2004). Engaging learners in online learning environments. *TechTrends*, *48*(4), 16–23. doi:10.1007/BF02763440

Lim, C. P., & Cheah, P. T. (2003). The role of the tutor in asynchronous discussion boards: A case study of a pre-service teacher course. *Educational Media International*, *40*(1), 33–48. doi:10.1080/0952398032000092107

Lim, C. P., Nonis, D., & Hedberg, J. (2006). Gaming in a 3D multi-user virtual environment (*MUVE*): Engaging students in science lessons. *British Journal of Educational Technology*, *37*(2), 211–231. doi:10.1111/j.1467-8535.2006.00531.x

Lin, S. S. J., Liu, E. Z. F., & Yuan, S. M. (2001). Web-based peer assessment: Feedback for students with various thinking styles. *Journal of Computer Assisted Learning*, *17*, 420–432. doi:10.1046/j.0266-4909.2001.00198.x

Lipponen, L. (2002). Exploring foundations for computer-supported collaborative learning. Retrieved on March 20, 2007, from http://www.helsinki.fi/science/networkedlearning/texts/lipponen2002.pdf

Lipsey, M. W., & Wilson, D. B. (1993). The efficacy of psychological, educational, and behavioral treatment: Confirmation from meta-analysis. *The American Psychologist*, *48*, 1181–1209. doi:10.1037/0003-066X.48.12.1181

Littlejohn, A., & Pegler, C. (2007). *Preparing for blended e-learning*. Abingdon: Routledge.

Livson, N. (1967). Toward a different construct of curiosity. The Journal of Genetic Psychology, 111, 73–84. PubMed

Loewenstein, G. (1994). The psychology of curiosity: A review and reinterpretation. Psychological Bulletin, 116(1), 75–98. doi:10.1037/0033-2909.116.1.75doi:10.1037/0033-2909.116.1.75

Loo, R. (2002). A meta-analytic examination of Kolb's learning style preferences among business majors. *Journal of Education for Business*, *5*, 77–85.

Louden, W., Rohl, M., Barratt Pugh, C., Brown, C., Cairney, T., Elderfield, J., et al. (2005). *In teachers' hands*. Perth, WA: Edith Cowan University.

Lund, A., Pierroux, P., Rasmussen, I., Smørdal, O., & Blevis, E. (2007). Pre-conference event for CSCL 2007. *Emerging issues in Wiki research: Knowledge advancement and design*. CSCL 2007. Retrieved on February 29, 2008, from http://design.informatics.indiana.edu/designii/eli/images/8/8c/C wiki_final.pdf

Lynch, M. (2001). *Effective student preparation for online learning*. Retrieved on October 10, 2008, from http://www.elearning.unimass.my/FeaturedSite/archives/000036.ht

Lyotard, J.-F. (1984). *The postmodern condition: A report on knowledge*. Manchester: Manchester University Press.

Maasen, S., & Weingart, P. (2000). Metaphors and the dynamics of knowledge. London & New York: Routledge.

Macdonald, J., Weller, M., & Mason, R. (2002). Meeting the assessment demands of networked courses. *International Journal on E-Learning*, *1*(1), 9–18.

Maddux, C. D., & Johnson, D. L. (1997). The World Wide Web: History, cultural context, and a manual for developers of educational information-based Web sites. *Educational Technology*, *37*(5), 5–12.

Magalhães, A., & Stoer, S. (2003). Performance, citizenship, and the knowledge society: A new mandate for European education policy. *Globalisation, Societies and Education, 1*(1), 41–66. doi:10.1080/1476772032000061815

Magnus, P. D. (2007). Distributed cognition and the task of science. *Social Studies of Science, 37*(2), 297–310. doi:10.1177/0306312706072177

Maier, P., & Warren, A. (2000). *Integrating technology in learning & teaching: A practical guide to educators.* London: Kogan Page.

Malcolm, M. (2005). The exercise of the object: Issues in resource reusability and reuse. *British Journal of Educational Technology, 36*(1), 33–41. doi:10.1111/j.1467-8535.2005.00436.x

Malone, T. (1981). Toward a theory of intrinsically motivating instruction. Cognitive Science, 3, 333–369.

Malone, T. W., & Lepper, M. (1987). Making learning fun: A taxonomy of intrinsic motivations of learning. In R. E. Snow & M. J. Farr (Eds.), *Aptitude, learning, and instruction: Vol 3. Cognitive and affective process analysis* (pp. 223-253). Hillsdale, NJ: Lawrence Erlbaum.

Malone, T., & Lepper, M. (1987). Making learning fun: A taxonomy of intrinsic motivations for learning. In Aptitude, learning, and instruction, vol. 3, cognitive and affective process analyses. New Jersey: Lawrence Erlbaum.

Marcus, A., & Gould, E. W. (2000). Cultural dimensions and global Web user-interface design: What? So what? Now what? *Interactions (New York, N.Y.), 7*(4), 32–46. doi:10.1145/345190.345238

Markauskaite, L. (2005, December 4-7). Exploring differences in trainee teachers' ICT literacy: Does gender matter? Paper presented at the Australasian Society for Computers in Learning in Tertiary Education.

Marshall, H., & Arnot, M. (2008). *Globalising the school curriculum: Gender, EFA, and global citizenship education.* Working Paper No. 17, Research Consortium on Educational Outcomes and Poverty (RECOUP). Cambridge: University of Cambridge.

Martindale, T., & Wiley, D. A. (2005). Using Weblogs in scholarship and teaching. *TechTrends: Linking Research & Practice to Improve Learning, 49*(2), 55–61.

Mason, R. (1991). Moderating educational computer conferencing. *DEOSNEWS, 1*(19).

Mason, R. (1998). *Globalising education: Trends and applications.* London: Routledge.

Matyila, M., & Halland, K. (2004, June). *Using discussion forums in distance education.* Paper presented at the 34th Annual SACLA Conference, Durban, South Africa.

Mayer, R. E. (1999). Fifty years of creativity research. In R. J. Sternberg (Ed.), *Handbook of*

Mayes, T., & de Freitas, S. (2004). *Review of e-learning theories, frameworks, and models. Stage 2 of the e-learning models desk study.* Joint Information Systems Committee (JISC). Retrieved on September 1, 2008, from http://www.jisc.ac.uk/uploaded_documents/Stage%202%20Learning%20Models%20(Version%201).pdf

McAndrew, P. (2005). *What is needed for global e-learning?* Document ID KN6779, OU Knowledge Network. Retrieved on December 1, 2008, from http://kn.open.ac.uk/public/document.cfm?docid=6779

McCabe, D. L. (1993). Faculty responses to academic dishonesty: The influence of student honour codes. *Research in Higher Education, 34,* 647–658. doi:10.1007/BF00991924

McCollum, K. (1997). A professor divides his class in two to test value of online instruction. The Chronicle of Higher Education, 43(24), 23.

McCoy, S., Galletta, D. F., & King, W. R. (2005). Integrating national culture into IS reseach: The need for current individual-level measures. *Communications of AIS, 5*(15), 211–224.

McCracken, H. (2006). *Furthering connected teaching and learning through the use of virtual learning communities.* Retrieved on April 30, 2008, from http://www.e-mentor.edu.pl/_xml/wydania/17/359.pdf

McDonald, J., & Reushle, S. (2002). Charting the role of the online teacher in higher education: Winds of change. *Proceedings of ASCILITE'02,* Auckland, New Zealand.

McFarland, D., & Hamilton, D. (2005). Factors affecting student performance and satisfaction: Online vs. traditional course delivery. *Journal of Computer Information Systems, 46*(2), 25–32.

McFarland, K., & Stansell, J. (1993). Historical perspectives. In L. Patterson, C. Santa, C. Short & K. Smith (Eds.), *Teachers are researchers: Reflection and action.* Newark, DE: International Reading Association.

McKenzie, W., & Murphy, D. (2000). 'I hope this goes somewhere': Evaluation of an online discussion group. *Australian Journal of Educational Technology, 16*(3), 239–257.

McLaren, C. (2004). A comparison of student persistence and performance in online and classroom business statistic experiences. *The Decision Journal of Innovative Education, 2*(1), 1–10. doi:10.1111/j.0011-7315.2004.00015.x

McLaughlin, P., & Simpson, N. (2004). Peer assessment in first year university: How the students feel. *Studies in Educational Evaluation, 30*(2), 135–149. doi:10.1016/j.stueduc.2004.06.003

McLoughlin, C. (2002). Learner support in distance and networked learning environments: Ten dimensions for successful design. Distance Education, 23(2), 149–162. doi:10.1080/01587910220000091 78doi:10.1080/0158791022000009178

McLuhan, M. (1964). The media is the message. New York: Mentor.

McMillan, D., W., & Chavis, D. M. (1986). Sense of community: A definition and theory. *Journal of Community Psychology, 14*, 6–23. doi:10.1002/1520-6629(198601)14:1<6::AID-JCOP2290140103>3.0.CO;2-I

McNamara, M. J., & Deane, D. (1995). Self-assessment activities: Towards autonomy in language learning. *TESOL Journal, 5*(1), 17–21.

McNeil, B., & Dixon, L. (2005). *Success factors in informal learning: Young adults' experiences of literacy, language, and numeracy.* London: NRDC. (ISBN 1905188102)

Meridian, K. S. I. (n.d.) Retrieved on November 21, 2008, from http://www.meridianksi.com

Merriam, B. S. (1998). *Qualitative research and case study applications in education.* San Francisco: Jossey-Bass.

MEST. (2008). *Ministry of Education, Science and Technology.* South Korea. Retrieved on September 1, 2008, from http://english.mest.go.kr

Metrios, S. (2005). Learning objects: A rose by any other name... *Educause Review, 40*(4), 12–13. Retrieved on December 1, 2008, from http://connect.educause.edu/Library/EDUCAUSE+Review/LearningObjectsARosebyAny/40559

Miao, Y., Fleschutz, J. M., & Zentel, P. (1999, December). Enriching learning contexts to support communities of practice. In C. M. Hoadley & J. Roschelle (Eds.), *Proceedings of the 1999 Conference on Computer Support for Collaborative Learning,* Palo Alto, CA. Retrieved on June 14, 2007, from http://portal.acm.org/citation.cfm?id=1150289

Michaelsen, L., Knight, A., & Fink, D. (2004). *Team-based learning: A transformative use of small groups.* VA: Sterling.

Micklethwait, J., & Wooldridge, A. (2000). *A future perfect: The essentials of globalization.* New York: Crown Business.

Miles, M. B., & Huberman, A. M. (1984). Qualitative data analysis. A sourcebook of new methods. Beverly Hills, CA: Sage.

Miller, A. H., Imrie, B. W., & Cox, K. (1998). *Student assessment in higher education: A handbook for assessing performance.* London: Kogan Page.

Miller, S. (2003). Impact of mixed methodology and design on inference quality. In A. Tashakkori & C Teddlie (Eds.), *Handbook of mixed methods in social and behavioral research* (pp 423-456). Thousand Oaks, CA: Sage.

Miltenoff, P., Hoover, J., & Tzokov, G. (2008). Interaction among students and faculty: A comparative study. *Proceedings of Informing Science and IT Education conference,* 2008, Varna, Bulgaria.

Moe, M., Bailey, K., & Lau, R. (1999). *The book of knowledge: Investing in the growing education and training industry.* Global Securities Research and Economic Group and Global Fundamental Equity Research Department. San Francisco: Merrill Lynch and Co.

Montealegre, R. (1998). Managing information technology in modernizing 'against the odds': Lesson from an organization in a less-developed country. *Information & Management, 34*, 103–116. doi:10.1016/S0378-7206(98)00051-2

Montgomery, K., & Wiley, D. A. (2004). *Creating e-portfolios using powerpoint: A guide for educators.* Thousand Oaks, CA: Sage Publications.

Moodle.org. (n.d.) *Moodle.org: About.* Retrieved on November 21, 2008, from http://moodle.org/about/

Moon, J., Chadee, D., & Tikoo, S. (2008). Culture, product type, and price influences on consumer purchase intention to buy personalized products online. *Journal of Business Research, 61*(1), 31–39. doi:10.1016/j.jbusres.2006.05.012

Moras, S. (2000). Computer assisted language learning (CALL) and the Internet. Retrieved from http://www3.telus.net/linguisticsissues/CALL.html. Last access: 28/8/2001

Morgan, A., & Barbour, K. (2008). An initial study into the personality types of undergarduate business students. *Allied Academies International Conference, 13*. Cullowhee: Academy of Educational Leadership.

Morris, J. (2001). Peer assessment: A missing link between teaching and learning? A review of the literature. *Nurse Education Today, 21*(7), 507–515. doi:10.1054/nedt.2001.0661

Morris, P. (1996). *The Hong Kong school curriculum: Development, issues, and policies (2nd ed.)*. Hong Kong: Hong Kong University Press.

Morrison, D. (2003). Using activity theory to design constructivist online learning environments for higher order thinking: A retrospective analysis. Canadian Journal of Learning and Technology, 29.

Mortagy, Y. (2005, June 4). *Online policies and procedures*. (S. Whitby, Interviewer)

Mortera-Gutiérrez, F. (2006). Faculty best practices using blended learning in e-learning and face-to-face instruction. *International Journal on E-Learning, 5*(3), 313–337.

Mowshowitz, A. (1997). Virtual organisation. Communications of the ACM, 40(9), 30–37. doi:10.1145/260750.260759doi:10.1145/260750.260759

Mukhamedyarova, Z., & Cotter, M. (2005). Interactive methods of teaching as a condition for developing students' independent learning skills in Kazakhstan and the U.S. *International Education, 34*(2), 62–72.

Mullinix, B. B., & McCurry, D. (2003, September/October). Balancing the learning equation: Exploring effective mixtures of technology, teaching, and learning [electronic version]. *The Technology Source*. Retrieved on November 20, 2008, from http://technologysource.org/article/balancing_the_learning_equation/

Muukkonen, H., Hakkarainen, K., & Lakkala, M. (2005). Computer-mediated progressive inquiry in higher education. Hershey, PA: Information Science Publishing.

Myers, C. B., Bennett, D., Brown, G., & Henderson, T. (2004). Emerging online learning environments and student learning: An analysis of faculty perceptions. Educational Technology & Society, 7(1), 78–86.

Myers, S. A., Zhong, M., & Guan, S. (1998). Instructor immediacy in the Chinese college classroom. *Communication Studies, 49*, 240–254.

Nagai, S. A., Bantz, D., & Siktberg, L. (2005). Validation of critical thinking skills in online responses. The Journal of Nursing Education, 44(2), 90–94. PubMed

Nagel, D. (2008, January). Open source poised for surge in education. *THE Journal*. Retrieved on January 30, 2008, from http://www.thejournal.com/articles/21900

Nather, K. (2007, July 7). *California community colleges distance education report: Fiscal years 1995-1996 through 2005-2006*. Retrieved on October 10, 2008, from http://website.cccco.edu/Portals/4/AA/Distance%20Education/7-07-DE_Report_Web.doc

National Evaluation and Accreditation Agency's Newsletter. Бюлетин на НАОА (2002). *4*. Sofia.

Nesbit, P. L., & Burton, S. (2006). Student justice perceptions following assignment feedback. *Assessment & Evaluation in Higher Education, 31*(6), 655–670. doi:10.1080/02602930600760868

Newell, B., Crumley, C. L., Hassan, N., Lambin, C., Pahl-Wostl, C., & Underdal, A. (2005). A conceptual template for integrative human-environment research. *Global Environmental Change, 15*, 229–307. doi:10.1016/j.gloenvcha.2005.06.003

Newman, D., & Cole, M. (2004). Can scientific research from the laboratory be of any use to teachers? *Theory into Practice, 43*(4), 260–268.

Ng, C., Yeung, A. S., & Hon, R. Y. H. (2006). Does online language learning diminish interaction between student and teacher? *Educational Media International, 43*(3), 219–232. doi:10.1080/09523980600641429

Ng, M. W. (2008). An alternative learning platform to facilitate usability and synchronization of learning resources. In A. Cartelli & M. Palma (Eds.), *Encyclopedia of information communication technology* (pp. 21-31). Hershey, PA: Information Science Reference.

Nguyen, F. (2004). *Killing two birds with one stone: Creating EPSS through e-learning*. Arizona State University/Intel Corporation, reproduced on the American Society for Training & Development Web site. Retrieved on September 1,

2008, from http://www.astd.org/NR/rdonlyres/8F40492E-4850-4F5AB74B0D3C25C4BF61/5840/W206forWeb.pdf

Nicol, D. (2007). E-assessment by design: Using multiple-choice tests to good effect. *Journal of Further and Higher Education, 31*(1), 53–64. doi:10.1080/03098770601167922

Nielson, J. (1993). *Usability engineering.* New York: Academic Press.

Nisbett, R. E., & Norenzayan, A. (2002). Culture and cognition. In H. Pashler & D. L. Medin (Eds.), *Stevens' handbook of experimental psychology: Vol. 2: Cognition* (3rd ed., pp. 561-597). New York: John Wiley & Sons.

Nitko, A. J. (2004). *Continuous assessment and performance assessment.* Retrieved on November 13, 2007, from http://www.moec.gov.jm/project/newhorizons/pdf/assessment/2004/ca/presentation fancy

NMC/EDUCAUSE. (2007). *2007 horizon report.* Joint publication of the New Media Consortium (NMC) and EDUCAUSE. Retrieved on September 1, 2008, from http://www.nmc.org/horizon

Nofke, S., & Stevenson, R. (Eds.). (1995). *Educational action research: Becoming practically critical.* New York: Teachers College Press.

Norget, K. (2007). Decolonization and the politics of syncretism: The Catholic Church, indigenous theology, and cultural autonomy in Oaxaca, Mexico. *International Education, 37*(1), 78–97.

Norris, M., West, S., & Gaughan, K. (2000). E-business essentials: Technology and network requirements for the electronic marketplace. Chicester: John Wiley & Sons Ltd.

Northside United. (2008). *Northside demographics factsheet.* Pittsburgh, PA. Retrieved from http://www.pittsburghunited.org/sites/default/files/attached_files/NSDemographics.pdf

Novak, G., Gavrin, A., Christian, W., & Patterson, E. (1999). Just-in-time teaching: Blending active learning with Web technology. New York: Prentice Hall Series in Educational Innovation.

O'Boyle, S. (2008). IT security: Socially naive or socially aware? *Accountancy Ireland, 40*(2), 65.

O'Dowd, R. (2007). Evaluating the outcomes of online intercultural exchange. *ELT Journal: English Language Teachers Journal, 61*(2), 144–152.

O'Malley, J. M., & Chamot, A. U. (1990). *Learning strategies in second language acquisition.* Cambridge: Cambridge University Press.

O'Neill, G., & McMahon, T. (2007). Student-centred learning: What does it mean for students and lecturers? Retrieved on December 14, 2007, from http//www.aishe.org/readings/2005-1/oneill- Mcmahon-Tues_19th_oct_SCL.pdf

O'Reilly. (2005). *What is Web 2.0: Design patterns and business models for the next generation of software.* O'Reilly Media. Retrieved on September 1, 2008, from http://www.oreillynet.com/pub/a/oreilly/tim/news/2005/09/30/what-is-web-20.html

Oblinger, D., & Oblinger, J. (2005). Is it age or IT: First steps toward understanding the Net generation. In D. Oblinger & J. Oblinger (Eds.), *Educating the Net generation.* Educause (pp. 2.1-2.19). Retrieved on September 1, 2008, from http://www.educause.edu/educatingthenetgen

Ocker, R., & Yaverbaum, G. J. (2002). Collaborative learning environments: Exploring student attitudes and satisfaction in face-to-face and asynchronous computer conferencing settings. Journal of Interactive Learning Research, 12(4), 427–448.

OCW. (2008). MIT OpenCourseWare. Massachusetts Institute of Technology. Retrieved on September 1, 2008, from http://ocw.mit.edu

Oden, R., Temple, D., Cottrell, J., Griggs, R., Turney, G., & Wojcik, F. (2001). Merging library and computing services at Kenyon College: A progress report. *Educause Quarterly, 24*(4), 18-25. Retrieved on August 22, 2008, from http://www.educause.edu/ir/library/pdf/EQM0141.pdf

OECD. (2006). Programme for international student assessment. Paris: Organisation for Economic Cooperation and Development. Retrieved on September 1, 2008, from http://www.pisa.oecd.org/pages/0,2987,en_32252351_32235731_1_1_1_1_1,00.html

Official ITIL Web site. (2008). *ITIL.* Retrieved on October 15, 2008, from http://www.itil-officialsite.com/home/home.asp

Ohmae, K. (1995). *The end of the nation state: The rise of regional economies.* New York: The Free Press.

OLAT. (n.d.) Retrieved on November 21, 2008, from http://www.olat.org/website/en/html/index.html

Oliver, K. (2007). Leveraging Web 2.0 in the redesign of a graduate-level technology integration course. *TechTrends*, *51*(5), 55–61. doi:10.1007/s11528-007-0071-3

Oliver, M., & Trigwell, K. (2005). Can 'blended learning' be redeemed? *E-learning*, *2*(1), 17–26.

Oliver, R., Harper, B., Wills, S., Agostinho, S., & Hedberg, J. G. (2007). Describing ICT based learning designs that promote quality learning outcomes. London: Routledge.

Olt, M. R. (2008). *Ethics and distance education: Strategies for minimizing academic dishonesty in online assessment*. Retrieved on February 2, 2008, from http://www.westga.edu/~distance/ojdla/fall53/olt53.html

Open Text Corporation. (n. d.). *FirstClass*. Retrieved on November 21, 2008, from http://www.firstclass.com/

Opetusministeriö. (2008). Finland: Ministry of Education. Retrieved on September 1, 2008, from http://www.minedu.fi/OPM/Koulutus/koulutusjaerjestelmae/?lang=en

Osguthorpe, R. T., & Graham, C. R. (2003). Blended learning environments: Definitions and directions. *The Quarterly Review of Distance Education*, *4*(3), 227–233.

Osiki, J. O. (1999). The experimental research methodology and randomized controlled trials in psychological investigations: Participants' preference. *Ilorin Journal of Education*, *20*(June), 24–37.

Osiki, J. O. (2007). Empowering distance learners' research prowess through the effective utilization of three psychotherapies. *Lesotho Social Science Review*, *11*, 97–113.

Osiki, J. O. (2008). Enhancing the academic performance through the identification and psychological management of victims of Asperger syndrome. *Ozean Journal of Social Science*, *1*(1), 29–42.

Osiki, J. O. (2008b). Extracurricular activities and teacher attitude to girl-child education and psycho-emotional preparedness. *Indian Journal of Social Science*, *17*(1), 73–82.

Osiki, J. O. (in press). Research empowerment in professional teacher development: The effect of blended learning approach in distance education in Africa. In M. M. Mboya (Ed.), *Open and distance learning*. NEPAD

Osiki, J. O., & Braimoh, D. (in press). Management of learning behaviour in higher education: The outcome of cooperative and collaborative approaches, National University of Lesotho Southern Africa. *South African Journal of Higher Education*.

Otte, G., & Benke, M. (2006). Online learning: New models for leadership and organization in higher education. *Journal of Asynchronous Learning Networks*, *10*(2).

Oxford, R. (1990). *Language learning strategies: What every teacher should know*. New York: Newbury House.

Oxford, R. L., & Anderson, N. J. (1995). A cross-cultural view of learning styles. *Language Teaching*, *28*, 201–215. doi:10.1017/S0261444800000446

Pae, J. K. (2007). Wiki-based English writing: Its effect on English writing proficiency and anxiety and Korean learners' perception. *Multimedia-Assisted Language Learning*, *10*(1), 4.

Palloff, R. M., & Pratt, K. (2003). The virtual student: A profile and guide to working with online learners. San Francisco: Jossey-Bass.

Palloff, R., & Pratt, K. (1999). *Building learning communities in cyberspace: Effective strategies for the online classroom*. San Francisco, CA: Jossey-Bass.

Palloff, R., & Pratt, K. (1999). *Building learning communities in cyberspace*. San Francisco: Josey-Bass Publishers.

Palmer, E., & Devitt, P. (2007). Assessment of higher order cognitive skills in undergraduate education: Modified essay or multiple choice questions? Research paper. *BMC Medical Education*, *7*(1), 49–55. doi:10.1186/1472-6920-7-49

Pang, L., & Penfold, P. (2008). Blending and shaking: Chinese students' perceptions of blended learning in a hospitality and tourism course. Paper presented at the 6th Asia-Pacific (APacCHRIE) Conference and THE-ICE International Panel of Experts Forum, Perth.

Papaefthimiou-Lytra, S. (1987). *Language awareness and foreign language learning*. Athens: The University of Athens Press.

Papaefthimiou-Lytra, S. (1996). Integrating culture in the curriculum. In A. Tsopanoglou (Eds.), The sociolinguistic dimension in the teaching and learning of modern languages. *G.A.L.A.*, 7, 234-252. Thessaloniki: Greece.

Papaefthimiou-Lytra, S. (2004). Multipolar intercultural competence. In E. Joyce & A. Sougari (Eds.), *Challenges in teacher education* (pp. 15-25). Thessaloniki: Aristotle University, Department of English Language & Civilization.

Parker, L., & Lepper, M. (1992). The effects of fantasy contexts on children's learning and motivations: Making learning more fun. Journal of Personality and Social Psychology, 62, 625–633. PubMed doi:10.1037/0022-3514.62.4.625doi:10.1037/0022-3514.62.4.625

Patton, M. Q. (1990). *Qualitative evaluation and research methods*. Newbery Park, CA: SAGE Publications, Inc.

Paulsen, M. (2002). *Online education systems: Discussion and definition of terms*. NKI Distance Education. Retrieved from http://home.nettskolen.com/~morten

Paulsen, M. F. (2003). *On cooperative learning*. Retrieved on April 28, 2008, from http://www.psychegames.com/cooperative-learning.htm

Paulsen, M. P. (1995). Moderating educational computer conferences. In Z. L. Berge & M. P. Collins (Eds.), *Computer-mediated communication and the online classroom in distance education*. Cresskill, NJ: Hampton Press.

Pearson, J. (2006). Investigating ICT using problem-based learning in face-to-face and online learning environments. *Computers & Education*, *47*, 56–73. doi:10.1016/j.compedu.2004.09.001

Pearson, P. H., & Maddi, S. R. (1966). The similes preference inventory: Development of a structured measure of the tendency toward variety. Journal of Consulting Psychology, 30, 301–308. doi:10.1037/h0023540doi:10.1037/h0023540

Pekarik, A. J. (2002). Feeling or learning? *Curator*, *45*(4), 262–264.

Pennington, D. D. (2008). Cross-disciplinary collaboration and learning. *Ecology and Society 13*(2), 8. Retrieved on September 26, 2008, from http://www.ecologyandsociety.org/vol13/iss2/art8/

Pennington, M. C. (2004). Electronic media in second language writing: An overview of tools and research findings. In S. Fotos & C. Browne (Eds.), *New perspectives on CALL for second language classrooms* (pp. 69-92). Mahwah, NJ: Lawrence Erlbaum Associates.

Pennsylvania Department of Education. (2007, August). *Public secondary school dropouts in Pennsylvania in 2005-06*. Harrisburg, PA: J. Bobek.

Perry, G., & Talley, S. (2001). Online video case studies and teacher education: A new tool for preservice teacher education. *International society for technology in education, 17*(4), 26-31.

Peterson, M. (1997). Language teaching and networking. *System*, *25*(1), 29–37. doi:10.1016/S0346-251X(96)00058-9

Phipps, R., & Merisotis, J. (2000). *Quality on the line: Benchmarks for success in Internet-based distance education*. Washington: Institute for Higher Education Policy.

Piaget, J. (1955). *The construction of reality in the child*. London: Routledge.

Pickett, S., Burch, W. R. Jr, & Grove, J. M. (1999). Interdisciplinary research: Maintaining the constructive impulse in a culture of criticism. *Ecosystem*, *2*, 302–307. doi:10.1007/s100219900081

PicoPeta. (2008). PicoPeta Simputers Pvt. Ltd. Retrieved on September 1, 2008, from http://www.picopeta.com

Pinhey, L. A. (1998). *Global education: Internet resources*. ERIC Digest. ED417124.

Pittsburgh, U. N. I. T. E. D. (2007, August). *Racial & economic disparities on Pittsburgh's northside*. Pittsburgh, PA. Retrieved from http://www.pittsburghunited.org/research/08/aug/19/racial-economic-disparities-on-pittsburgh%E2%80%99s-northside

Pope, M., Hare, D., & Howard, E. (2002). Technology integration: Closing the gap between what preservice teachers are taught to do and what they can do. Journal of Technology and Teacher Education, 10(2), 191–203.

Popov, N., & Pironkova, M. (2007). *Образователната система в България* (Educational system in Bulgaria). Sofia.

Powell, E. (2005). Conceptualising and facilitating active learning: Teachers' video-stimulated reflective dialogues. *Reflective Practice*, *6*(3), 407–418. doi:10.1080/14623940500220202

Powers, S. M., & Dallas, L. (2006). Authentic assessment through problem-based learning in the online environment. In V. H. Wright, C. Szymanski Sunal & E. K. Wilson (Eds.), *Research on enhancing the interactivity of online learning* (pp. 65-74). Greenwich, CT: Information Age.

Preece, J. (1999). Empathic communities: Balancing emotional and factual communication. *Interacting with Computers, 12*, 63–77. doi:10.1016/S0953-5438(98)00056-3

Prensky, M. (2001). Digital natives, digital immigrants. *On the Horizon, 9*(5). NCB University Press.

Probst, T. M., & Lawler, J. (2006). Cultural values as moderators of the outcomes of job insecurity: The role of individualism and collectivism. *Applied Psychology: An International Review, 55*, 234–254. doi:10.1111/j.1464-0597.2006.00239.x

Pyvis, D., & Chapman, A. (2007). Why university students choose an international education: A case study in Malaysia. *International Journal of Educational Development, 27*, 235–246. doi:10.1016/j.ijedudev.2006.07.008

RAND Education. (2006, July). *Estimating graduation and dropout rates with longitudinal data: A case study in the Pittsburgh public schools* (WR-372-PPS). Pittsburgh, PA: J. Engberg & B. Gill. Retrieved from http://www.rand.org/pubs/working_papers/WR372/

Read, B. (2007). 'A digitally isolated Africa.' *The Wired Campus of Chronicle of Higher Education*. Retrieved on October 26, 2007, from http://chronicle.com/wiredcampus/article/?id=2447

Reeves, T. (1999). A research agenda for interactive learning in the new millennium. Retrieved on July, 29, 2001, from http://it.coe.uga.edu/~treeves/EM99Key.html

Reeves, T. (2000). *Enhancing the worth of instructional technology research through design experiments and other development research strategies.* Paper presented at the International Perspectives on Instructional Technology Research for the 21st Century, New Orleans, LA.

Reginald, S. (1964). The importance of negative results in psychological research. *Canadian Psychology, 5*(4), 225–232.

Reich, R. (1991). *The work of nations.* New York: Vintage Books.

Rendell, E. (2008, January). *Keynote address at the National Science Foundation: Science education and workforce development: Key challenges for the states workshop.* Washington, D.C.

Report e-Bulgaria. Доклад е-България. (2006). Фондация «Приложни изследвания и комуникации». София. Retrieved on February 15, 2007, from http://www.daits.government.bg/projects.php

Resnick, L. (1987). Learning in school and out. *Educational Research, 16*(1), 1–10.

Rheingold, H. (2002). *Smart mobs: The next social revolution.* Cambridge, MT: Basic Books.

Rhoades-Catanach, S. C. (2003). Dot.com or Dot.bomb? The unpleasant tax surprise of stock options in a volatile market. *Issues in Accounting Education, 18*(4), 385. doi:10.2308/iace.2003.18.4.385

Ridgway, J., McCusker, S., & Pead, D. (2004). *Literature review of e-assessment.* Bristol, UK: Futurelab. Retrieved on March 10, 2009, from http://www.futurelab.org.uk/resources/documents/lit_reviews/Assessment_Review.pdf

Rieber, L. P. (1996). Seriously considering play: Designing interactive learning environments based on the blending of micro-worlds, simulations, and games. *Educational Technology Research and Development, 44*(2), 43–58. doi:10.1007/BF02300540

Ritzer, G. (2000). *The McDonaldization of society.* Thousand Oaks, CA: Pine Forge Press.

Roach, R. (2003). Survey says online learning equal to classroom instruction. *Black Issues in Higher Education, 20*(16), 44.

Roberts, D., Foehr, U., & Rideout, V. (2005). *Generation M: Media in the lives of 8-18 year-olds.* Menlo Park, CA: Kaiser Family Foundation. Retrieved on September 1, 2008, from http://www.kff.org/entmedia/upload/Generation-M-Media-in-the-Lives-of-8-18-Year-olds-Report.pdf

Robertson, R. (1995). Glocalization. In M. Featherstone, et al. (Eds.), *Global modernities.* London: Sage.

Robey, D., & Taggart, W. (2001). Measuring managers' minds: The assessment of style in human information processing. Academy of Management. *Academy of Management Review, 6*(3), 375–383. doi:10.2307/257373

Robson, C. (1993). *Real world research.* Oxford: Blackwell.

Rodgers, W. A. (Ed.). (1997). *Designing for an aging population.* Santa Monica, CA: Human Factors and Ergonomics Society.

Rogers, E. M. (1995). *Diffusion of innovations.* New York: The Free Press.

Rogers, P., Graham, C., & Mayes, C. (2007). Cultural competence and instructional design: Exploration research into the delivery of online instruction cross-culturally. *Educational Technology Research and Development, 55*(2), 197–210. doi:10.1007/s11423-007-9033-x

Romanov, K., & Nevgi, A. (2008). Student activity and learning outcomes in a virtual learning environment. Learning Environments Research, 11(2), 153–162. doi:10.1007/s10984-008-9038-3doi:10.1007/s10984-008-9038-3

Rosas, R., Nussbaum, M., Cumsille, P., Marianov, V., Correa, M., & Flores, P. (2003). Beyond Nintendo: Design and assessment of educational video games for first and second grade students. *Computers & Education, 40*(1), 71–94. doi:10.1016/S0360-1315(02)00099-4

Roth, A., & Fonagy, P. (2005). What works for whom?: A critical review of psychotherapy research, 2nd ed. New York: Guilford Press.

Rothstein, H., Sutton, A., & Borenstein, M. (2005). *Publication bias in meta-analysis: Prevention, assessment, and adjustments.* Chichester: Wiley.

Rourke, L., Anderson, T., Garrison, D. R., & Archer, W. (2001). Methodological issues in the content analysis of computer conference transcripts. *International Journal of Artificial Intelligence in Education*, 12.

Rouse, W. B., & Morris, N. M. (1985). *On looking into the blackbox: Prospects and limits in the search for mental models* (DTIC#AD-A159080). Atlanta, GA: Center for Man-Machine Systems Research, Georgia Institute of Technology.

Rubin, I. B., & Rubin, H. J. (1995). Qualitative interviewing: The art of hearing data. Thousand Oaks: Sage.

Rungtusanatham, N., Ellram, L., Siferd, S., & Salik, S. (2004). Toward a typology of business education in the Internet age. *Decision Sciences Journal of Innovative Education, 2*(2), 101–120. doi:10.1111/j.1540-4609.2004.00040.x

Sadler, D. R. (1998). Formative assessment: Revisiting the territory. *Assessment in Education: Principles . Policy & Practice, 5*(1), 77–84.

Saettler, P. (1990). *The evolution of American educational technology.* Englewood, CO: Libraries Unlimited, Inc.

Sakai Project. (n.d.) Retrieved on November 21, 2008, from http://www.sakaiproject.org/portal

Salili, F. (1994). Age, sex, and cultural differences in the meaning and dimensions of achievement. *Personality and Social Psychology Bulletin, 20*(6), 635–648. doi:10.1177/0146167294206002

Salili, F. (2001). Teacher-student interaction: Attributional implications and effectiveness of teachers' evaluative feedback. In D. A. Watkins, & J. B. Biggs (Eds.), *Teaching the Chinese learner: Psychological and pedagogical perspectives* (pp. 77-98). Hong Kong: Comparative Educational Research Center.

Salmon, G. (2004). *E-moderating: The key to teaching and learning online (2nd ed.).* Abingdon, UK: Taylor & Francis.

Samarawickrema, R. G. (2005). Determinants of student readiness for flexible learning: Some preliminary findings. *Distance Education, 26*(1), 49–66. doi:10.1080/01587910500081277

Sander, L. (2008, March 28). At community colleges, a call to meet new students at the front door. *The Chronicle of Higher Education*, A25.

Santrock, J. W. (1996). *Child development* (7th ed.). Madison, WI: Brown & Benchmark Publishers.

Sapp, D., & Simon, J. (2005). Comparing grades in online and face-to-face writing courses: Interpersonal accountability and institutional commitment. *Computers and Composition, 22*(4), 471–489. doi:10.1016/j.compcom.2005.08.005

Sarter, N., & Woods, D. (1991). Situation awareness: A critical but ill-defined phenomenon. *The International Journal of Aviation Psychology, 1*, 45–47. doi:10.1207/s15327108ijap0101_4

Scardamalia, M. (Ed.). (2002). Collective cognitive responsibility for the advancement of knowledge. Chicago: Open Court.

Schackner, B. (2008, July 6). AGH, CCAC team up to offer pioneering program to train biotech technicians. *Pittsburgh Post Gazette*, B-1. Retrieved from http://www.post-gazette.com/pg/08188/895111-298.stm

Schaffer, S. P., & Richardson, J. (2004). Supporting technology integration within a teacher education System. *Journal of Educational Computing Research, 31*(4), 421–433. doi:10.2190/V1BX-35NW-7AH6-6MME

Schaffer, S. P., Lei, K., Reyes, L., Oakes, W., & Zoltowski, C. (2006). Analyzing cross-disciplinary design teams. Retrieved on September 26, 2008, from http://epics.ecn.purdue.edu/about/papers./ FIE2006_crossdisciplinary.pdf

Schmidt, M. B., Johnston, A. C., Arnett, K. P., Che, J. Q., & Li, S. (2008). A cross-cultural comparison of U.S. and Chinese computer security awareness. *Journal of Global Information Management, 16*(2), 91–103.

SCHOLAR. (2008). *The SCHOLAR programme Web site.* Heriot-Watt University, Edinburgh. Retrieved on September 1, 2008, from http://scholar.hw.ac.uk/

Schön, D. (1983). *The reflective practitioner: How professionals think in action.* New York: Basic Books.

Schön, D. (1987). *Keynote: Educating the reflective practitioner.* Paper presented at the AETA Annual Conference, Washington, D.C.

Schrum, L., & Hong, S. (2002, July). Dimensions and strategies for online success: Voices from experienced educators. *JALN*, 6(1), 57-68. Retrieved on October 26, 2007, from http://www.aln.org/publications/jaln/v6n1/v6n1_schrum.asp

Schrum, L., Burbank, M. D., & Capps, R. (2007, July). Preparing future teachers for diverse schools in an online learning community: Perceptions and practice. *The Internet and Higher Education, 10*(3), 204–211. doi:10.1016/j.iheduc.2007.06.002

Science, I. o. (2003, July 18). *National center for educational statistic.* Retrieved on October 10, 2008, from http://nces.ed.gov/programs/coe/2008/section1/table.asp?tableID=869

Scott, P. (1998). Massification, internationalization, and globalization. In P. Scott (Ed.), *The globalization of higher education* (pp. 108-129). Buckingham: The Society for Research into Higher Education & Open University Press.

Scott, P. (2002). The future of general education in mass higher education systems. *Higher Education Policy, 15*, 61–75. doi:10.1016/S0952-8733(01)00036-8

Seel, N. M. (2001). Epistomology, situated cognition, and mental models: 'Like a bridge over troubled water.' . *Instructional Science, 29*(29), 403–427. doi:10.1023/A:1011952010705

Seligman, M. E. P. (1995). The effectiveness of psychotherapy: The consumer reports study. *The American Psychologist, 50*(12), 965–974. doi:10.1037/0003-066X.50.12.965

Selinger, M. (2001). Learning information and communications technology skills and the subject context of the learning. Journal of information technology for teacher education, 10(1&2), 143-154.

Senn Breivik, P., & Gee, G. (2006). *Higher education in the Internet age: Libraries creating a strategic edge*. Westport, CN: Praeger Publishers.

Shank, G., & Brown, L. (2007). *Exploring educational research literacy.* London: Routledge.

Shank, P. (Ed.). (2007). *The online learning: 95 proven ways to enhance technology-based and blended learning.* San Francisco, CA: John Wiley & Sons.

Sharpe, R., Benfield, G., Roberts, G., & Francis, R. (2006). *The undergraduate experience of blended e-learning: A review of UK literature and practice.* York: The Higher Education Academy.

Shea, P., Fredericksen, E., Pickett, A., Pelz, W., & Swan, K. (2001). Measures of learning effectiveness in the SUNY learning network. In J. Bourne & J. C. Moore (Eds.), Learning effectiveness, faculty satisfaction, and cost effectiveness (Vol. 2, pp. 303-308).

Sherry, L. (1996). Issues in distance learning. *International Journal of Educational Telecommunications, 1*(4), 337–365.

Shetzer, H., & Warschauer, M. (2000). An electronic literacy approach to network-based language teaching. In M. Warschauer & R. Kern (Eds.) *Network-based language teaching: Concepts and practice* (pp. 171-185). Cambridge Applied Linguistics, Cambridge University Press.

Shih, Y., & Cifuentes, L. (2003). Taiwanese intercultural phenomena and issues in a United States-Taiwan telecommunication partnership. *Educational Technology Research and Development, 51*(3), 82–90. doi:10.1007/BF02504555

Shneiderman, B. (2000). Universal usability. *Communications of the ACM, 43*(5), 84–91. doi:10.1145/332833.332843

Shroff, R. H., Vogel, D. R., Coombes, J., & Lee, F. (2007). Student e-learning intrinsic motivation: A qualitative analysis. Communications of the Association for Information Systems, 19(12), 241–260.

Shuayb, M., & O'Donnell, S. (2008). *Aims and values in primary education: England and other countries.* The Primary Review, Research Survey 1/2, National Foundation for Educational Research. Cambridge: University of Cambridge.

Silverman, D. K. (2005). What works in psychotherapy and how do we know?: What evidence-based practice has to offer. *Psychoanalytic Psychology, 22*(2), 306–312. doi:10.1037/0736-9735.22.2.306

Sims, R. (2003). Promises of interactivity: Aligning learner perceptions and expectations with strategies for flexible and online learning. Distance Education, 24(1), 85–103. doi:10.1080/01587910303050doi:10.1080/01587910303050

Singh, H., & Reed, C. (2001). *A white paper: Achieving success with blended learning.* ASTD State of the Industry Report, American Society for Training & Development, Centra Software. Retrieved on November 17, 2008, from http://chriscollieassociates.com/BlendedLearning.pdf

Singh, S. (2006). HCI in South Africa. In C. Ghaoui (Ed.), *Encyclopedia of human computer interaction* (pp. 261-265). UK: Liverpool John Moores University, Idea Group Reference.

Singh, S., & De Ridder, C. (2005, June). *My marriage to cousin Lily.* Paper presented at the 35th Annual SACLA Conference, Kasane, Botswana.

Singh, S., & Engelbrecht, K. (2004, June). *Profiling the learner.* Paper presented at the 34th Annual SACLA Conference, Durban, South Africa.

Singh, S., & Kotze, P. (2003). The socio-political culture of users. In M. Rauterberg, et al. (Eds.), *Human-computer interaction–INTERACT '03* (pp. 900-903). IOS Press.

Slick, T. (2008). *Do learning styles matter?* La Verne: AAT 3301965.

Sluijsmans, D. M. A., Brand-Gruwel, & Van Merrienboer, J. (2002). Peer assessment training in teacher education: Effects on performance and perceptions. *Assessment & Evaluation in Higher Education, 27*(5), 443–454. doi:10.1080/0260293022000009311

Sluijsmans, D., & Prins, F. (2006). A conceptual framework for integrating peer assessment in teacher education. *Studies in Educational Evaluation, 32*(1), 6–22. doi:10.1016/j.stueduc.2006.01.005

Smith, A., Dunckley, L., French, T., Minocha, S., & Chang, Y. (2004). A process model for developing usable cross-cultural Web sites. *Interacting with Computers, 16*(1), 63–91. doi:10.1016/j.intcom.2003.11.005

Smith, G. G., & Kurthen, H. (2007). Front-stage and back-stage in hybrid e-learning face-to-face courses. *International Journal on E-Learning, 6*(3), 455–474.

Smith, H., Cooper, A., & Lancaster, L. (2002). Improving the quality of undergraduate peer assessment: A case for student and staff development. *Innovations in Education and Teaching International, 39*(1), 71–81. doi:10.1080/13558000110102904

Smith, K., & Tillema, H. (2003). Clarifying different types of portfolio use. *Assessment & Evaluation in Higher Education, 28*(6), 625. doi:10.1080/0260293032000130252

Spielberger, C. D., & Starr, L. M. (1994). Curiosity and exploratory behavior. In H. F. O'Neil, Jr. & M. Drillings (Eds.), Motivation: Theory and research. Hillsdale, NJ: Erlbaum.

Spires, H. A., & Estes, T. H. (2002). Reading in Web-based learning environments. In C.C. Block & M. Pressley (Eds.), *Comprehension instruction: Research-based best practices* (pp. 115-125). New York: Guilford.

Sproull, L., & Kiesler, S. B. (1991). *Connections: New ways of working in the networked organization.* Cambridge, MA: MIT Press.

Squire, K. (2005, August). Changing the game: What happens when video games enter the classroom? *Innovate, 1.* Retrieved on August 30, 2006, from http://www.innovateonline.info/index.php?view=article&id=82

Stake, R. E. (1995). *The art of case study research.* Thousand Oaks, CA: SAGE Publications, Inc.

Stansfield, M., McLellan, E., & Connolly, T. (2004). Enhancing student performance in online learning and traditional face-to-face class delivery. *Journal of Information Technology Education, 3*, 173–188.

Steeples, C., Unsworth, C., Bryson, M., Goodyear, P., Riding, P., & Fowell, S. (1996). Technological support for teaching and learning: Computer-mediated communications in higher education. *Computers & Education, 26*(1–3), 71–80. doi:10.1016/0360-1315(95)00082-8

Stephenson, J. (Ed.). (2002). *Teaching & learning online: New pedagogies for new technologies*. London: Kogan Page.

Stewart, K. M. (1997). Beyond entertainment: Using interactive games in Web-based instruction. *Journal of Instruction Delivery System, 11*(2), 18–20.

Stigler, J. W., & Hiebert, J. (1999). *The teaching gap*. New York: Free Press.

Stokes, D. E. (1997). *Pastuer's quadrant: Basic science and technological innovation*. Washington, D.C.: Brookings institution Press.

Strange, S. (1996). *The retreat of the state: The diffusion of power in the world economy*. Cambridge: Cambridge University Press.

Strauss, A. L. (1987). *Qualitative analysis for social scientists*. New York: Cambridge University Press.

Strober, M. H. (2008). *Habits of the mind: Challenges for multi-disciplinary engagement*. Retrieved on September 30, 2008, from http://www.stanford.edu/~myras/challenges.pdf

Stufflebeam, D. L. (2001). Evaluation models. *New Directions for Evaluation, 89*, 7–98. doi:10.1002/ev.3

Sung, Y.-T., Chang, K.-E., Chiou, S.-K., & Hou, H.-T. (2005). The design and application of a Web-based self- and peer-assessment system. *Computers & Education, 45*(2), 187–202. doi:10.1016/j.compedu.2004.07.002

Sutherland-Smith, W. (2002). Weaving the literacy Web: Changes in reading from page to screen. *The Reading Teacher, 55*, 662–669.

Swan, K., & Garrison, R. (2006, May). *Pedagogical principles*. Panel discussion presentation at the Sloan-C Workshop on Blended Learning in Higher Education, Chicago, IL. Retrieved from http://www.uic.edu/depts/oee/blended/workshop/ presentations/Pedagogical%20Principles.pdf

Tan, S. C., Turgeon, A. J., & Johansson, D. H. (2001). Develop critical thinking in group problem solving through computer-supported collaborative argumentation: A case study. Journal of Natural Resources and Life Sciences Education, 30, 97–103.

Tanner, D. (1998). The social consequences of bad research. *Phi Delta Kappan, 79*, 344–349.

Tashakkori, A., & Teddlie, C. (1998). *Mixed methodology: Combining the qualitative and quantitative approaches*. Thousand Oaks, CA: Sage.

Taylor, B. (2007). *Integrity: Academic and political. A letter to my students*. Retrieved on August 23, 2007 from http://www.mcmaster.ca/cll/resources/nifty.notes/david.godden/Integrity.pdf

Teeler, D., & Gray, P. (2000). *How to use the Internet in ELT*. Harlow: Longman.

Tesch, R. (1990). Qualitative research: Analysis types and software tools. New York: Falmer.

Thatcher, A. (2007). Using the World Wide Web to support classroom lectures in a psychology course. *South African Journal of Psychology. Suid-Afrikaanse Tydskrif Vir Sielkunde, 37*(2), 348–353.

The E-Learning Committee. (2002). *E-learning committee survey on Web enhanced and Web based teaching*. St. Cloud State University. E-mail correspondence with R. Kolb, E. Kang & J. Burgeson.

Thelwall, M. (2000). Computer-based assessment: A versatile educational tool. *Computers & Education, 34*, 37–49. doi:10.1016/S0360-1315(99)00037-8

Thomas, C., & McDonald, R. (2006). Disconnects between library culture and millennial generation values. *Educause Quarterly, 26*(4). Retrieved on February 5, 2007, from http://www.educause.edu/apps/eq/eqm06/eqm0640.asp?print=yes

Thorne, K. (2003). Blended learning: How to integrate online and traditional. London: Kogan Page.

Tolmie, A., & Boyle, J. (2000). Factors influencing the success of computer mediated communication (CMC) environments in university teaching: A review and case study. *Computers & Education, 34*(2), 119–140. doi:10.1016/S0360-1315(00)00008-7

Tong, E. T. F., & Hodgson, P. (2007). *Developing higher-order thinking through blended problem-based learning.* Paper presented at the 2007 International Conference on ICT in Teaching and Learning, Hong Kong.

Triandis, H. C. (Ed.). (1991*). Cross-cultural industrial and organizational psychology.* Palo Alto, CA: Consulting Psychologists Press, Inc.

Tryon, C. (2006). Writing and citizenship: Using blogs to teach first-year composition. *Pedagogy, 6*(1), 128–132.

Tsitouridou, M., & Tsolakidis, C. (2001). Teachers and ICTs. In the *Proceedings of the European Symposium on E-Learning and Continuing Education, Thematic Network in University Continuing Education, THENUCE Conference* (pp. 55-65), University of Ioannina.

Tsolakidis, C., & Tsitouridou, M. (2001). The need for primary teachers' training in information and communication technologies. In the *Proceedings of the European Symposium on E-Learning and Continuing Education, European Thematic Network in University Continuing Education, THENUCE Conference* (pp. 67–73), University of Ioannina.

Tulgan, B., & Martin, C. (2001). *Managing generation Y: Global citizens born in the late seventies and early eighties.* Amherst, MA: Human Resource Development Press.

Turban, E., Leidner, D., McLean, E., & Wetherbe, J. (2008). *Information technology for management.* Hoboken, NJ: John Wiley & Sons, Inc.

Twigg, C. (2003). Improving learning and reducing costs: New models for online learning. *EDUCAUSE Review, 38*(5), 28–38.

Tyner, K. (1998). *Literacy in a digital world: Teaching and learning in the age of information.* Mahwah, NJ: Erlbaum.

UKOU. (2008). *LabSpace.* UK: The Open University. Retrieved on September 1, 2008, from http://labspace.open.ac.uk

Underwood, J., & Underwood, G. (1999). Task effects on cooperative and collaborative learning with computers. In K. Littleton & P. Light (Eds.), *Learning with computers: Analysing productive interactions.* London: Routledge.

University of Ibadan. *Nigeria: The vision for the 21st century.* Retrieved on October 2, 2008, from http://www.uiadvancement.org/vision_mission.pdf

University of South Africa. (2007). *Services and procedures 2007.* Pretoria: University of South Africa.

University of South Africa. (2008). *Self-evaluation portfolio for the HECQ institutional audit 2008.* Pretoria: University of South Africa.

Uppsala-Stanford-Karolinska project and the Stanford Alliance for a Global Bioinformatics Curriculum. (2008). *"Cross-Disciplinary Learning: Bioinformatics."* Retrieved on September 26, 2008, from summit.stanford.edu/pdfs/CDLbioinformatics_tearsheet.pdf

Ury, G. (2004). A longitudinal study comparing undergraduate student performance in traditional courses to the performance in online course delivery. *Proc ISECON*, 21, 1-7.

Valiathan, P. (2002). *Blended learning models.* Retrieved on May 26, 2008, from http://www.learningcircuits.com/2002/aug2002/valiathan.html

Van Deven, T. (2008). Access denied: A story of resistance. In J. Zajda, L. Davies & S. Majhanovich (Eds.), *Globalisation, comparative, and global Pedagogies* (Vol. 2, pp. 71-86). The Netherlands: Springer.

Van Ek, J. A. (1977). *The threshold level for modern language teaching in schools.* London: Longman.

van Manen, M. (1990). *Researching lived experience: Human science for an action sensitive pedagogy.* Albany, NY: State University of New York Press.

Van Ryssen, S., & Godar, S. (2000). Going international without going international: Multinational virtual teams. *Journal of International Management, 6,* 49–60. doi:10.1016/S1075-4253(00)00019-3

Vaughan, N. (2007). Perspectives on blended learning in higher education. *International Journal on E-Learning, 6*(1), 81–94.

Veerman, A., & Veldhuis-Diermanse, E. (2001). Collaborative learning through computer mediated communication in academic education. In P. Dillenbourg, A. Eurelings, & K. Hakkarainen (Eds.), *European perspectives on computer-supported collaborative learning* (pp. 625-632). Maastricht, The Netherlands: University of Maastricht.

Vinagre, M. (2008). Politeness strategies in collaborative e-mail exchanges. *Computers & Education, 50*, 1022–1036. doi:10.1016/j.compedu.2006.10.002

Vlachos, K. (2005). Online discourse communities and task based learning in foreign language education. *Annals of the University of Craiova, 4*(9-10), 129–138.

Vlachos, K. (2006a). Online networking and the teaching of English as a foreign language to young learners: A methodological framework. In J. Bardos (Ed.), *HUSSE papers, Proceedings of the Seventh Biennial Conference* (Vol. B, pp. 618-625) Hungary: Veszprem.

Vlachos, K. (2006b). *The use of the Internet and asyncronous online networking for the learning and consolidation of English as a foreign language in European primary schools.* Unpublished doctoral dissertation, University of the Aegean, Rhodes, Greece.

Vlachos, K. (2007). The contribution of online collaboration in the development of learners' intercultural communicative competence and European understanding. In G. Kapsalis & A. Katsikis (Eds.), *Proceedings of the Conference 'Primary Education and the Challenges of Our Times'* (pp. 212-220). Ioannina: University of Ioannina.

Vlachos, K. (2008). Developing intercultural awareness through computer assisted language learning (CALL). In the *Proceedings of the International Conference of the University of Athens: Language in a Changing World.* University of Athens Publications.

Vlachos, K., & Athanasiadis, E. (2005). Online networking and the teaching of second/foreign languages to young learners through project work. *Themes in Education, 6*(1), 29–44.

Vlachos, K., & Athanasiadis, E. (in press). Foreign language development and consolidation through multipolar online networking. In the *Proceedings of the International Conference 42nd Linguistics Colloquium in Rhodes*, September 27-30, 2007. Rhodes: University of the Aegean.

Vlachos, K., & Papaefthymiou-Lytra, S. (2008). Collaboration through asynchronous online networking and the learning of foreign languages. In L. A. Tomei (Eds.), *Encyclopedia of information technology curriculum integration* (Vol. A, pp. 63-70). Hershey, PA: IGI Global.

Vogel, D., Shroff, R. H., Kwok, S., & Coombes, J. (2002, September 2-4). Student e-learning intrinsic motivation: A qualitative analysis. Paper presented at the Pacific Asia Conference on Information Systems, Tokyo, Japan.

Vonderwell, S. (2003). An examination of asynchronous communication experiences and perspectives of students in an online course: A case study. *The Internet and Higher Education, 6*, 77–90. doi:10.1016/S1096-7516(02)00164-1

Vrasidas, C., & Glass, G. V. (Eds.). (2002). *Current perspectives on applied information technologies: Distance education and distributed learning* [electronic version]. Greenwich, CT: Information Age Publishing. Retrieved on December 1, 2002, from http://www.infoagepub.com

Vrasidas, C., & McIsaac, M. (2000). Principles of pedagogy and evaluation for Web-based learning. *Educational Media International, 37*(2), 105–112. doi:10.1080/095239800410405

Vygotsky, L. (1978). *In mind in society.* (Trans. M. Cole). Cambridge, MA: Harvard University Press.

Vygotsky, L. S. (1978). Mind in society. Cambridge, MA: Harvard University Press.

Vygotsky, L. S. (1978). *Mind in society: The development of higher psychological processes* (M. Cole, V. John-Steiner, S. Scribner & E. Souberman, Trans.). Cambridge: MA: Harvard University Press.

Vygotsky, L. S. (1978). *Mind in society: The development of higher psychological processes.* Cambridge, UK: Harvard University Press.

Wade, V. P., & Power, C. (1997). Evaluating the design and delivery of WWW based educational environment and courseware. *SIGCSE Bulletin, 30*(3), 243–248. doi:10.1145/290320.283556

Walker, C. O., Greene, B. A., & Mansell, R. A. (2006). Identification with academics, intrinsic/extrinsic motivation, and self-efficacy as predictors of cognitive engagement. Learning and Individual Differences, 16(1), 1–12. doi:10.1016/j.lindif.2005.06.004doi:10.1016/j.lindif.2005.06.004

Warschauer, M. (1996). Comparing face-to-face and electronic communication in the second language classroom. *CALICO Journal, 13*(2), 7–26.

Warschauer, M. (1997). Computer-mediated collaborative learning: Theory and practice. Modern Language Journal, 81(5), 470–481. doi:10.2307/328890doi:10.2307/328890

Warschauer, M. (1998). Interaction, negotiation, and computer-mediated learning. *Papyrus News: Language Learning & Technology Journal.* Retrieved on July 18, 2006, from http://www.insa-lyon.fr/Departements/CDRL/interaction.html

Warschauer, M. (2001). Online communication. In R. Carter & D. Nunan (Eds.), *The Cambridge guide to teaching English to speakers of other languages* (pp. 207-212). Cambridge: Cambridge University Press.

Warschauer, M. (2005). Sociocultural perspectives on CALL. In J. L. Egbert & G. M. Petrie (Eds.), *CALL research perspectives* (pp. 41-51). New York: Lawrence Erlbaum Associates.

Warschauer, M., & Kern, R. (2000). *Network-based language teaching: Concepts andpractice.* Cambridge Applied Linguistics, Cambridge University Press.

Warschauer, M., & Whittaker, P. F. (1997). The Internet for English teaching: Guidelines for teachers. *The Internet TESL Journal,* 3/10. Retrieved on July 18, 2006, from http://www.aitech.ac.jp/~iteslj/Articles/Warschauer-Internet.html

Watkins, A. (2005). *E-learning activities: Making online learning interactive.* San Francisco, CA: John Wiley & Sons.

Watts, H. (1985). When teachers are researchers, teaching improves. *Journal of Staff Development, 6*(2), 118–127.

Wear, D. N. (1999). Challenges to interdisciplinary discourse. *Ecosystem, 2*, 299–301. doi:10.1007/s100219900080

Webb, N. M., & Palincsar, A. S. (1996). Group processes in the classroom. In D. C. Berliner & R. C. Calfee (Eds.), *Handbook of educational psychology* (pp. 841-873). New York: Macmillan.

Weingart, P. (2000).Interdisciplinarity: The paradoxical discourse. In P. Weingart & N. Stehr (Eds.), *Practicing interdisciplinarity.* Toronto: University of Toronto Press Incorporation.

Weingart, P., & Stehr, N. (2000). *Practicing interdisciplinarity.* Toronto: University of Toronto Press Incorporation.

Wenden, A. (1991). *Learner strategies for learner autonomy.* Cambridge: Prentice Hall International.

Wenger, E. (1998). *Communities of practice: Learning, meaning, and identity.* Cambridge, UK: Cambridge University Press.

Wenger, E., McDermott, R., & Snyder, W. M. (2002). *Cultivating communities of practice.* Boston: Harvard University Press.

West, R., Wright, G., Gabbitas, B., & Graham, C. (2006). Reflections from the introduction of blogs and RSS feeds into a preservice instructional technology course. *TechTrends: Linking Research & Practice to Improve Learning, 50*(4), 54–60.

White, C. (2003). *Language learning in distance education.* Cambridge: Cambridge University Press.

Widdowson, H. (1972). The teaching of English as communication. *English Language Teaching, 27*(1), 15–19.

Widdowson, H. (1979). *Explorations in applied linguistics.* Oxford: Oxford University Press.

Widdowson, H. (1983). New starts and different kinds of failures. In A. Freeman, I. Pringle & J. Yalden (Eds.), *Learning to write: First language/second language.* London: Longman.

Wikibooks: About. (n.d.) Retrieved on February 28, 2008, from http://en.wikibooks.org/wiki/Wikibooks:About

Wikipedia. (2008). *Wikipedia: The free encyclopedia.* Retrieved on September 1, 2008, from http://en.wikipedia.org

Wikipedia: Learning Management System. (n.d.) Retrieved on November 21, 2008, from http://en.wikipedia.org/wiki/Learning_management_system

Wiki–Wikipedia. (n.d.) Retrieved on November 21, 2008, from http://en.wikipedia.org/wiki/Wiki

Williams, P. (2002). The learning Web: The development, implementation, and evaluation of Internet-based undergraduate materials for the teaching of key skills. *Active Learning in Higher Education, 3*, 40–53. doi:10.1177/1469787402003001004

Williams, P. (2005). Lessons from the future: ICT scenarios and the education of teachers. *Journal of Education for Teaching, 31*(4), 319–339. doi:10.1080/02607470500280209

Williams, P. (2007). Valid knowledge: The economy and the academy. *Higher Education, 54*(4), 511–523. doi:10.1007/s10734-007-9051-y

Williams, P. (2008a). Assessing context based learning: Not only rigorous but also relevant. *Assessment & Evaluation in Higher Education, 33*(4), 395–408. doi:10.1080/02602930701562890

Williams, P. (2008b). Leading schools in the digital age: A clash of cultures. *School Leadership & Management, 28*(3), 213–228. doi:10.1080/13632430802145779

Willig, C. (2001). *Introducing qualitative research in psychology adventures in theory and method.* Buckingham: Open University Press.

Willis, B. (1996). Distance education at a glance series from University of Idaho. Retrieved on July 20, 1998, from http://www.uidaho.edu/evo/distglan.html

Willis, J. (1996). *A framework for task-based learning.* Harlow: Longman.

Willis, J. (2001). Making the best of technology: Lessons from the past. In P. Brett (Ed.), *CALL in the 21st century* [CD ROM]. Whitstable: IATEFL.

Wilson, B. G. (1995). Situated instructional design: Blurring the distinctions between theory and practice, design and implementation, curriculum and instruction. In M. Simonson (Ed.), *Proceedings of Selected Research and Development Presentations.* Washington D.C.: Association for Educational Communications and Technology.

Wilson, J. M., & Jennings, W. C. (2000). Studio courses: How information technology is changing the way we teach, on campus and off. *Proceedings of the IEEE, 88*(1), 72–79.

Wilson, M., & Hash, J. (2003). *Building an information technology security awareness and training program.* Gaithersburg, MD: Computer Security Division, Information Technology Laboratory, National Institute of Standards and Technology.

Winiecki, D. J. (1999). Keeping the thread: Adapting conversational practice to help distance students and instructors manage discussions in an asynchronous learning network. *DEOSNEWS, 9*(2).

Winner, T., & Shields, T. (2002). Breaking the island chains: A case study exploring the intricate powers of language shared on the World Wide Web. *Computers and Composition, 19*, 273–284. doi:10.1016/S8755-4615(02)00129-9

Winsor, P. J. T., Butt, R. L., & Reeves, H. (1999). Portraying professional development in preservice teacher education: Can portfolios do the job? *Teachers and Teaching, 5*(1), 9. doi:10.1080/1354060990050102

Woodrow Wilson International Center for Scholars. (2006). *Funding the foundation: Basic science at the crossroads* [brochure]. Washington, D.C.: K. Hughes & L. Sha.

Woodruff, E., Brett, C., MacDonald, R., & Nason, R. (1998). Participation in knowledge-building communities to promote teaching competency in mathematics. Retrieved on March 14, 2002, from http://www.oise.utoronto.ca/~ewoodruff/cp.htm

Wozniak, H., & Silveira, S. (2004). Online discussions: Promoting effective student to student interaction. *Proceedings of ASCILITE Conference 2004.*

Wright, M. C., Taekman, J. M., Barber, L., Hobbs, G., Newman, M. F., & Stafford-Smith, M. (2005). The use of high-fidelity human patient simulation as an evaluative tool in the development of clinical research protocols and procedures. *Contemporary Clinical Trials, 26*(6), 646–659. doi:10.1016/j.cct.2005.09.004

Wright, W. A., Knight, P. T., & Pomerleau, N. (1999). Portfolio people: Teaching and learning dossiers and innovation in higher education. *Innovative Higher Education, 24*(2), 89–103. doi:10.1023/B:IHIE.0000008148.71650.e6

Xie, K., DeBacker, T. K., & Ferguson, C. (2006). Extending the traditional classroom through online discussion: The role of student motivation. *Journal of Educational Computing Research, 34*(1), 67–89. doi:10.2190/7BAK-EGAH-3MH1-K7C6

Yin, R. K. (1994). *Case study research: Design and methods* (2nd ed.). Beverly Hills, CA: Sage.

Yoon, S. W., & Lim, D. (2007). Strategic blending: A conceptual framework to improve learning and performance. *International Journal on E-Learning, 6*(3), 475–489.

You Tube. (2008). Retrieved on September 1, 2008, from http://www.youtube.com

Young, A., & Norgard, C. (2006, April). Assessing the quality of online courses from the students' perspective. *The Internet and Higher Education, 9*(2), 107–115. doi:10.1016/j.iheduc.2006.03.001

Young, J. (2002). 'Hybrid' teaching seeks to end the divide between traditional and online instruction. The *Chronicle of Higher Education*, A33. Retrieved from http://chronicle.com/free/v48/i28/28a03301.htm

Yudko, E., Hirokawa, R., & Chi, R. (2008). Attitudes, beliefs, and attendance in a hybrid course. *Computers & Education, 50*, 1217–1227. doi:10.1016/j.compedu.2006.11.005

Zhang, J. (2002). Teaching statistics online: Our experience and thoughts. *Proceedings of the Sixth International Conference on Teaching Statistics*. The Netherlands: International Statistics Institute.

Zhang, Q. (2006). Immediacy and out-of-class communication: A cross-cultural comparison. *International Journal of Intercultural Relations, 30*, 33–50. doi:10.1016/j.ijintrel.2005.06.006

Zuckerman, M. (1971). Dimensions of sensation seeking. Journal of Consulting and Clinical Psychology, 36, 45–52. doi:10.1037/h0030478doi:10.1037/h0030478

Zuckerman-Parker, M. (2008). Andragogy and technology. In L. A. Tomei (Ed.), *Encyclopedia of information technology curriculum integration* (pp. 30-36). Hershey, PA: Idea Group Publishing.

About the Contributors

Eugenia M. W. Ng is an Associate Professor and IT Division Head in the Department of Mathematics, Science, Social Sciences, and Technology at the Hong Kong Institute of Education. She has extensive teaching experience at tertiary education institute teaching IT subjects. She has published over 70 articles as book chapters, journal articles, conference proceedings and newspaper articles in the area of information systems and IT in education. She is the Co-Editor-in-Chief of *International Journal of Web-based Learning and Teaching Technologies, associate editor of* International Journal of Digital Literacy and Digital Competence *and Advances in Web-based Learning Book Series*, and reviewers for a number of international journals.

* * *

Seta Boghikian-Whitby received B.S. in Computer Science and Computer Engineering, M.E.D. in Computer Education, M.S. in Management of Information Systems, and Ed.D. in Organizational Leadership. Professor Boghikian-Whitby has been the chairperson of the Computer Science and Computer Engineering program at the University of La Verne for the past 21 years. She is the founder of e-commerce major and Information Science concentration. She is very active in the faculty governance structure at the University – being the secretary of the faculty senate, chairing the faculty technology committee, and also being a member of the general education and faculty personnel committees. Professor Boghikian-Whitby is active in consultation in information technology area. Her research interests are the adoption of technology in developing countries and e-learning. She has extensive experience in teaching Online distance learning courses. Dr. Boghikian-Whitby is a sought after speaker and a beloved teacher for 24 years.

Christopher Brook holds the position of Dean Teaching and Learning at the Curtin Business School. Previous roles include Head of School, Postdoctoral Scholar and Instructional Designer. Chris's areas of research interest include learning spaces, flexible learning, blended learning, effective change in teaching practice and community development in online settings. His teaching interests include educational psychology and technology in education.

Charlie C. Chen was educated at Claremont Graduate University and received the degree of Ph.D. in Management Information Systems. Dr. Chen is an Assistant Professor in the Department of Computer Information Systems at Appalachian State University. At present he is engaged in delivering a textbook project on supply chain management. His current research interests are project management and supply chain management. Dr. Chen is also a Project Management Professional (PMP) certified by the Project Management Institute and he has authored more than 30 referred articles and proceedings, presented at many professional conferences and venues. Dr. Chen has published in journals such as Communications of Association for Information Systems, Behaviour and Information Technology, Journal of Knowledge Management Research Practice, and Journal of Information Systems Education. Dr. Chen dedicates himself to be a transnational scholar and is a trip leader for a study abroad program in Asia (Japan and Taiwan).

Christine Compliment, LCSW, is the Student Support Coordinator with the Center for Genomic Sciences, Allegheny Singer Research Institute, West Penn Allegheny Health System. She is currently providing psychosocial support services to students in the Allegheny Women's Biotechnology Workforce Collaborative. She received her B.A. in Social Work from West Chester University in 1980, and earned her master's degree in Social Work from The University of Pittsburgh in 1990. She has participated in national presentations about working with disadvantaged populations in educational settings. Her current work with Community College of Allegheny County students focuses on enhancing disadvantaged student success through social work interventions, including crisis intervention, community networking, and individual and group work.

Garth Ehrlich, PhD, is the founder and Executive Director of Center for Genomic Sciences at Allegheny-Singer Research Institute. He is also Professor of Microbiology and Immunology, and Otolaryngology Head and Neck Surgery at Drexel University College of Medicine, and Adjunct Professor of Biomedical Engineering at Carnegie Mellon University. Dr. Ehrlich is recognized as an expert in molecular diagnostics and wrote the first reference text in this discipline. He is also the developer of the mucosal biofilm paradigm of chronic infectious diseases and the distributed genome hypothesisa and is recognized leader in the field of comparative bacterial genomices. He serves as a reviewer for multiple Federal and international scientific review agencies, and is a member of the editorial boards/reviewer for dozens of scientific journals.

Retta Guy has an Ed.D. in Curriculum and Instruction with emphasis in Instructional Systems Design from the University of Kentucky. She received her masters in Public Administration from Kentucky State University and a Bachelor of Arts degree in Business Education from the University of Kentucky. Currently, she is an Associate Professor in the Department of Business Information Systems at Tennessee State University in Nashville, Tennessee. Online teaching and mobile learning serves as the basis for her current research for which she has presented at conferences and published in refereed journals and book chapters. Her first book entitled "The Evolution of Mobile Teaching and Learning" was published in January, 2009. She has and continues to conduct workshops and training sessions on the use of web-based course management tools as well as mobile learning technologies.

Paula Hodgson is a graduate of the University of South Australia interested in supporting academics who want to integrate learning technologies into learning and teaching in higher education. For almost ten years, she worked in the Educational Development Centre of the Hong Kong Polytechnic University, where her main role was to consult with academics to identify their needs, then to assist them in the design of action plans for integrating technology into their learning and teaching programs. Her research interests lie in the fields of pedagogical applications of learning technologies and their evaluation. Her work involved a number of projects funded by Hong Kong's University Grants Committee, including Action Learning Project (http://www.acad.polyu.edu.hk/~etwalp/index.htm), Megaweb (http://megaweb.polyu.edu.hk/) and e3Learning (http://e3learning.edc.polyu.edu.hk/). Now working in the University of Hong Kong as a Research Assistant Professor, her recent research focuses on the blended mode of learning and assessment experiences in university study.

John Hoover, PhD, served as the Director of the Bureau of Educational Services and Applied Research at the University of North Dakota from 1997 to 2001. He recently accepted an appointment at St. Cloud State University, his alma mater, in Special Education; where he was elected Chair in January of 2003. Hoover's research interests lie in bullying and child-on-child aggression; he has published three books and over 40 research papers, book chapters, reviews, and study guides in the area. Hoover has worked with over 20 school districts in the past five years in violence reduction programs and has evaluated several violence prevention efforts. He is also interested in transition services for students with disabilities, rural special education service delivery, and the application of cognition to interpersonal problem solving in youth with disabilities. He currently serves as the Associate Dean in the College of Education at St. Cloud State University.

Chun Hu (*Ed.D., Columbia, MA, Stanford*) is with Center for Research on Computer Supported Learning and Cognition, which operates within the Faculty of Education and Social Work at the University of Sydney. In addition to engaging research, she teaches ICT in education related courses to undergraduates, postgraduates and in-service teachers. Her current research interests include teacher learning community, blended learning, and cross-cultural web-based collaboration. A list of her selected publications may be found at http://coco.edfac.usyd.edu.au/Members/chu

Yiu Chi Lai is an Assistant Professor in the Department of Mathematics, Science, Social Sciences, and Technology at the Hong Kong Institute of Education. He has extensive teaching experience in Computer subjects and Mathematics. His current teaching and research areas include curriculum and teaching methods of IT subjects, lesson study and learning study, and IT in Mathematics. He is active in educational research and curricular resources development. His publications include school textbooks, workbooks, monographs, journal articles, conference papers, training booklets, newspaper articles, CD-ROMs, computer software, and learning websites. He is also the supervisor of an external funded web site - Friends of Cang Jie (HK). Friends of Cang Jie is a popular portal for teaching and learning Cang Jie Input method.

Hsuan Lorraine Liang is a lecturer in the School of Computing at University of South Africa and a researcher for the FASTAR/Espresso group in the Department of Computer Science at University of Pretoria. She earned her Masters, A Unified Treatment: Spell Checkers and Correctors, in Computer Science at the University of Pretoria (South Africa). She is busy working towards her doctorate. She has broad research interests and her research is primarily concerned with computing education, database design and implementation, informational retrieval, pattern matching, software engineering, text processing. She is members of various international and South African associations such as ACM, IEEE, SAICSIT, and SPIE.

Cher Ping, Lim is the Director of the Asia-Pacific Centre of Excellence for Teacher Education and Innovations and Director of International Partnerships at the School of Education in Edith Cowan University, Australia. He has been the chief investigator of several major research projects that include: (1) Effective Integration of IT in Singapore Schools: Pedagogical and Policy Implications, (2) Supporting E-discussions and e-sharing with New Technologies in Learning Communities, (3) Digital Curricular Literacies, and (4) 3D Multi-User Virtual Environments in Schools. He has also provided consultancy services to the World Bank, World Links, UNESCO, Inter-American Development Bank, World Bank, World Links, Microsoft, ACER Computers, schools and the Government of Barbados and Oman. More details of Professor Lim could be found in the following website http://edresearch.education.ecu.edu.au/chirp/

Graeme Lock is a senior lecturer in the School of Education at Edith Cowan University. He is currently holds the position of Program Director Leadership, having previously been Director of the Primary Program. Graeme's areas of teaching include pedagogical strategies, curriculum and educational policy. Research interests include the use of ICT in school curricula; the learning, cultural and religious needs of international students enrolled in offshore university courses; the experiences of pre-service and graduate teachers in rural educational settings; and curriculum development and implementation.

Chee-Kit Looi is Head of the Centre of Excellence on Learning Innovation at the National Institute of Education (NIE), Nanyang Technological University. He has over two decades of experience with educational technology research in research institutes and universities. His current research interests include studying the different modes of communication in a blended learning environment, interactional analysis, and rapid collaborative knowledge building. He is an editorial member of the International Journal on AI & Education, Journal of Computer-Assisted Learning, the International Journal on CSCL.

B. Dawn Medlin is the Chair and an Associate Professor in the Department of Computer Information Systems, John A. Walker College of Business, and Appalachian State University in Boone, NC. Her teaching and research activities have mainly been in the area of security, health care informatics, and e-commerce. She has published in journals such as The Journal of Information Systems Security, Information Systems Security, International Journal of Electronic Marketing and Retailing, and the International Journal of Healthcare Information Systems and Informatics. Her current research is working on a Security Awareness textbook.

Plamen Miltenoff, PhD, MLIS, is information specialist and Associate Professor at Learning Resources & Technology Services (LR&TS) of St. Cloud State University (SCSU) in St. Cloud, Minnesota. Plamen Miltenoff has graduate degrees from universities in Bulgaria, Austria, and from University of Florida. He holds Ph.D. with Shoumen University in Bulgaria and a separate Ph.D. degree in education with University of North Dakota. His professional interests include new technologies, Web development and multimedia, interactive and Web development in education. Plamen Miltenoff is the liaison of the library (LR&TS) to College of Education at SCSU.

Yehia K. Mortagy received his B.Sc. degree in Aeronautical Engineering for University of Cairo, Cairo, Egypt, MBA from University of California, Los Angeles in 1979, and Ph.D. in Management of Information Systems from the Claremont Graduate School, Claremont, California in 1997. His current research interest includes online education, adoption of technology in developing nations, and quantitative strategic and operational systems. His recent publications include a chapter on the development of strategic information systems (SIS) for the Information Systems Encyclopedia, many papers and conference presentations on online education, and utilization of IT in developing nations. In addition, Dr. Mortagy is interested in quantitative models and their utilization in business.

Jonathan Ohiorenuan Osiki holds the B.Ed, M.Ed and the Doctorate Degrees in Education and Guidance and Counselling (i.e. Educational/Counselling/Clinical Psychology), University of Ibadan, Nigeria. Widely travelled, he has had quite a number of published articles to his credit; and presently, awaits the announcement for his Professorship. He has held various positions, some of which include the Director of the Counselling Unity, and Deputy Dean, both of the Faculty of Education, University of Ibadan Nigeria and a member of the University of Ibadan Senate. He is on a two-year Contract at the National University of Lesotho, Southern Africa where he facilitates the Clinical Pastoral Care and Counselling Programme. The main focus of his research centers on the clinical and overall assessment of the multi-factors affecting learners' (conventional and the distance education programmes) potentials in the achievement of sustainable standard of academic performance with consistent improved school grades.

J. Christopher Post, MD, PhD, FACS, President and Scientific Director of ASRI , Medical Director of CGS, Director of Allegheny Pediatric ENT Associates of Allegheny General Hospital, Professor of Otolaryngology and Microbiology & Immunology at Drexel University College of Medicine. Dr. Post is a nationally renowned pediatric ENT specialist who offers a unique personal and caring approach in providing patient care. Dr. Post has served as the principal investigator for numerous research studies throughout his career and has delivered more than 100 national and international presentations relative to his pediatric otolaryngology specialty and research. He has served as Chairman on the Research Grants and Prizes subcommittee and currently is the Chair of the Infectious Disease Committee for the American Academy of Otolaryngology - Head and Neck Surgery. Dr. Post is also a Colonel in the United States Reserves and was the Commander of the U.S. Army Hospital in Bagram, Afghanastan from June to December, 2002.

Megan Rodella is a Research Assistant for the Director of Educational Research and Workforce Development and Student Support Administrator. Ms Rodella earned her Bachelor's of Arts in psychology from Gettysburg College. During her undergraduate studies she served for three years as a Program Coordinator for the Center for Public Service as part of their Learn and Serve program, organizing a service-learning program for Gettysburg students at a local after-school program. In her current position, Ms. Rodella supports the Director of Educational Research and Workforce Development in the logistics of conducting an educational research project of this scale by helping to collect and maintain data. She also acts as an additional support mechanism for the AWBWC students by providing academic tutoring as well as offering a third point of contact in addition to the Director and Student Support Administrator.

James B. Schreiber, Ph.D. an Associate Professor for the Foundations and Leadership program within Duquesne University's School Education and former Associate Dean for Teacher Education. Dr. Schreiber earned his doctorate at Indiana University in 2000. His research interests include people's beliefs about knowledge, the issues associated with measuring beliefs, and the use of advanced statistical techniques, such as hierarchical linear modeling. He is Senior Researcher and Associate Director, Research at the Center of Advancing the Study of Teaching and Learning and a former Associate Dean for Teacher Education. Dr Schreiber is an Executive Editor for *The Journal of Educational Research* and former Executive Editor for *Genetics, Social and General Psychology Monographs* and *Journal of Experimental Education.*

Ronnie H. Shroff holds a Ph.D. in Information Systems from The City University of Hong Kong. Dr. Shroff's academic background in Information Systems has led to his continuing research in educational technology, by integrating Information and Communications Technology (ICT) in teaching and learning environments. His professional interests include the use of technology to support social constructivist learning, affective learning, collaborative learning and outcomes-based teaching and learning environments. His research is mainly devoted to different pedagogies in terms of approaches, emerging concepts about learners and learning, the use of Information and Communication Technologies (ICT) and the social construction of knowledge through networked learning and e-learning environments. Through his research, Dr. Shroff concentrates on the development of cognitive learning skills and motivational dispositions and how this development can be facilitated through interactive and learner-centered mediated instruction across various teaching and learning settings. Details can be found at: http://www.hkied.edu.hk/kra/te/profile.html

Shawren Singh is a lecturer at the University of South Africa. His research interest include Human Computer Interaction (HCI),Internet Security, Web-based Courseware Tools, Internet Applications, Web-based Education, Blended learning , E-commerce, Accounting Information Systems, HIV&AIDS and ICT.

Lee Yong, Tay is the Head of Department for Research and concurrent Head of Department for Information Communication Technology in Beacon Primary School, one of the Future Schools in Singapore. He has been actively involved in the integration of ICT into the school curriculum since 1997. He obtained his PhD from Edith Cowan University, Western Australia. He also has a degree of Master of Arts in Instructional Design and Technology from the National Institute of Education, Singapore. His current research interest are in the areas of ICT integration into the curriculum, educational use of 3D Multi-User Virtual Environment to re-engage academically at-risk students in academically related tasks and activities, and the use of ICT tools to facilitate the learning of higher-order thinking.

Allysen Todd, PhD, Dean of Academic Affairs at the Community College of Allegheny County. Dr. Todd earned her Bachelor's of Arts Degree in English from Bethany College, her Master's of Arts Degree in English from Duquesne University, and her Ph.D. in Administrative Policies and Studies from the University of Pittsburgh. Dr. Todd has been an educator for thirty-two years, working in both secondary and post-secondary institutions. For the last twenty-seven years, she has been at the Community College of Allegheny County. Dr. Todd has served in various capacities, including professor of English, department chair, academic dean, and interim vice president. Her passion is developmental education by helping students who are struggling to adjust to college in a variety of ways. She enjoys working with faculty to develop curriculum, to write academic policies, and to collaborate with external partners to benefit student learning.

Galin Tzokov, Ph.D., is an Associate Professor of Pedagogy and Educational Management at the Department of Pedagogy of the Plovdiv University in Plovdiv, Bulgaria. Tzokov served as a Vice-President of the Educational Commission Municipal Council and as a Chairman of the Municipal School Board of the city of Shumen. He is a member of the Bulgarian Association of Scientists, the Bulgarian Pedagogical Society and the National Center for Distance Education in Bulgaria. Tzokov's interests include educational management, management of private schools and educational legislation. He works also in the field of information technologies in education and distance education.

Kosmas Vlachos is a tutor in the Hellenic Open University in the MEd program for teachers of the English language. He holds a BA in English Literature and Civilization, a MEd in Applied Linguistics and a PhD in Computer Assisted Language Learning (CALL). His Post Doctoral Research studied the benefits of blended learning in foreign language education. He has published papers in educational journals, encyclopaedias, conference proceedings and edited books. He has presented his work in International Conferences, seminars and workshops. He has participated in international projects organized by the Council of Europe and has been involved as an assessor in many exams. Except for CALL, his interests include content and language integrated learning (CLIL), language learning from an intercultural perspective and teaching foreign languages to young learners.

Lixun Wang obtained his doctoral degree in Applied Linguistics from the University of Birmingham, UK, in 2000. Since 1994, he has been teaching and researching in the areas of Applied Linguistics, Computer-Assisted Language Learning, Corpus Linguistics, and Online Learning. With his colleagues, he has developed a number of computer-assisted language learning applications, including an English-Chinese parallel concordancing software for parallel corpus studies. He has given paper presentations at numerous international conferences, and one of his papers won Best Paper Award at the AAOU conference in 2003. Based on his research, he has published widely in reputable journals such as *System*, *Language Learning and Technology*, *Computer-Assisted Language*, and *Asian Journal of Distance Education*. He is currently working as an Assistant Professor in the English Department at the Hong Kong Institute of Education.

Peter Williams is Lecturer in ICT and eLearning at the Institute for Learning, University of Hull, UK. Previously a deputy headteacher and education authority advisor, he has worked in higher education leading a social and cultural studies degree, a higher education staff development programme, and designing and managing a pioneering online business management course funded by the European Union. His doctoral research examined policy issues for eLearning in universities, and this has been the focus of recent publications which formed part of the University's Research Assessment Exercise 2008 submission. He is a Fellow of the UK Higher Education Academy and chairs a University learning enhancement group. Currently, he contributes to the University of Hull EdD course, leads a teacher education degree specialising in ICT and eLearning, and is conducting evaluation and research studies into the use of Blended Learning and ePortfolios in teacher education.

Craig Wishart has a Ph.D. in Organizational Behavior from Case Western Reserve University. His research and writing has focused upon sustainable community development, education research and reform, as well as change processes in personal and organizational life. Dr. Wishart has fifteen years experience as an organizational consultant in the non-profit and business sectors, including a variety of public, private, educational, community, and international organizations. He has a broad base of experience as a designer and developer of non-profit business and academic programs, researcher and designer of organizational capacity innovations, designer and facilitator of conferences and team building retreats, and is an author of articles and papers for academics and practitioners.

Lung-Hsiang Wong is a Research Scientist of the Learning Sciences Laboratory, National Institute of Education (NIE), Nanyang Technological University, Singapore. He has about two decades of experience with learning technology research in research institutes and universities. His current research interests are computer-supported collaborative learning, knowledge building community, mobile and seamless learning, ICT-supported Chinese Language learning and acquisition, and teachers' professional development. He is the Singapore representative of the Technical Committee 3 (Education), International Federation of Information Processing, UNESCO.

Michelle Zuckerman-Parker, EdD., Director of Educational Research and Workforce Development at Allegheny-Singer Research Institute. She earned a bachelor's degree in Packaging Science from Rochester Institute of Technology's Manufacturing & Mechanical Engineering Technology program. Additionally, she earned both a Master's Degree in Multimedia Technology and Ed.D. in Instructional Technology from Duquesne University. She pioneered the development of technological tools for instruction and distance collaboration learning during her research in China. She is a tenured science educator. Dr. Zuckerman-Parker was also recently awarded the Duquesne University's, "Mind Heart & Spirit Award." The Mind, Heart & Spirit Awards recognize Duquesne alumni who exemplify the pillars of the University's mission—academic excellence; moral and spiritual values; ecumenism and diversity; service; and world concerns.

Index

Symbols

3D environment 243, 244
3D online 238, 241
3D space 238, 239, 241, 243, 245, 246

A

after-school program 231, 232, 235, 237, 238, 239, 240, 241, 242, 243, 244, 245, 246, 247
Allegheny Women's Biotechnology Workforce Collaborative (AWBWC) 204, 205
anthropology 366
anti-government websites 324
architecture of participation 5
authentic assessment 5, 7
awareness-learning program 326
AWBWC model 206, 223
AWBWC program 210, 211, 223
AWBWC program director 210

B

Bachelor of Business Administration (BBA) 133
Ballarat and Clarendon College (BCC) 190
biotechnology workforce 204
Blackboard 70, 72, 74, 75, 76, 77, 83, 84, 278
Blackboard online learning platform 70, 76
Blackboard system 70, 76, 77, 84
blended learning 20, 21, 22, 24, 25, 26, 30, 31, 38, 188, 201, 250, 251, 252, 255, 256, 257, 260, 261, 262, 263, 264, 265, 266, 267, 268, 269, 270, 272
blended learning activities 279, 281, 283, 284, 286, 289, 290, 292, 293, 294, 295, 296, 297, 298
blended learning approach 366, 383
blended learning environment 71, 72, 74, 75, 77, 81, 82, 84
blended learning environments 223
blended learning literature 292
blended learning mode 262
blended learning model 126
blended learning setting 188, 201
blended learning students 261, 262, 263, 264, 265, 266, 267
blended social support 223
bloggers 297
blogs 171, 252, 255
broad-based 237

C

Campus Accelerated Program for Adults (CAPA) 95
Center for Research on Learning and Technology (CRLT) 232, 237
classroom practice 188, 190, 191, 193, 194, 195, 197, 198, 200, 201
Cognitive Ergonomics 71
collaborative learning 208, 209, 227
College of Allegheny College (CCAC) 210
communication science, 366
communication tools 23
community based system 223
computer assisted language learning (CALL) 250, 273
computer-based information systems 131
computer-based learning 233

computer-generated assessment 59
computer-mediated assessment 60, 63
computer-mediated communication 148
computer mediated language learning 251
computer-medicated communication (CMC) 284
computer supported collaborative learning (CSCL) 283, 284
computer usage 213
constructivism 209
constructivist philosophy 1
content and language integrated learning (CLIL) 269
course design 193, 200
course management systems (CMS) 303
course outlines 71
cross-cultural 278, 279, 280, 281, 282, 283, 284, 285, 287, 290, 291, 292, 293, 294, 295, 296, 297, 298, 299, 300
cross-cultural blended learning 278, 279, 281, 282, 284, 285, 290, 292, 293, 294, 295, 296, 297, 298
cross-cultural blended learning 284
cross-cultural communication 290, 295
cross cultural communication activities 266
cross-cultural interactions 295
cross-cultural study 324
cross-cultural web design research 280
cross-disciplinary learning 345, 346, 348, 349, 350, 351, 352, 356, 358
cross-disciplinary learning 346, 347, 348
cultural contexts 280, 283, 284, 286
cultural difference 281
cultural factors 280, 281, 283
cultural variable 281
cultures 323, 324, 326, 327, 335, 336

D

data collection method, 290
demanding learning procedure 253
demographic questionnaire 191
design experiment mode 223
digital divide 40
digital movies 237
digital pioneers 7
digital technologies 2
Distance Education and Training Council (DETC) 22
distance-learning (DL) 72
domain-related problems 232

E

economic hardship 205
e-copy 54
Edith Cowan University (ECU) 190
educational resources 1, 2
EFL blended learning environment 255, 267
EFL lessons 261
egalitarian 82
e-learning 112, 113, 114, 115, 116, 117, 118, 119, 120, 121, 122, 123, 366, 367, 368, 369, 370, 371, 372, 373, 374, 375, 376, 377, 379, 380, 381, 382, 383, 384, 386, 387, 388
e-learning module 72
electronic communication 309
electronic data 213
electronic, multimodal letters 258
electronic texts 257, 258, 262, 264, 266, 268
email 252, 255, 257, 276
e-mentoring 146, 147, 148, 149, 151, 152, 164, 167
European Network and Information Security Agency (ENISA) 324
event-based activities 24

F

face-to-face 50, 51, 52, 57, 58, 63, 64, 89, 90, 92, 93, 94, 95, 96, 97, 98, 99, 100, 101, 102, 103, 104, 105, 106, 107, 108, 109, 110, 250, 251, 252, 255, 256, 257, 258, 260, 261, 262, 263, 264, 265, 266, 267, 268, 269, 273
face-to-face activities 370
face-to-face classroom 90, 94, 95, 110, 127, 134
face-to-face classroom learning 71
face-to-face classroom situations 292
face-to-face communities 285
face-to-face contact 126, 207, 353

face-to-face control 89, 96, 97, 98, 99, 100, 102, 103, 104, 105, 106, 107, 108
face-to-face course 93, 94, 101, 114
face-to-face delivery 126
face-to-face discussions 125, 126, 128, 130, 131, 133, 134, 135, 136, 137, 138, 140, 144, 145
face-to-face environment, 37
face-to-face equivalents 207
face-to-face (F2F) 74
face-to- face group 262
face-to-face group tutorials 50
face-to-face human interaction 279
face-to-face instruction 127, 172, 187, 279
face-to-face instruction mode 331
face-to-face interactions 281, 287, 296
face-to-face interactive 353, 354
face-to-face learning 70, 250, 252, 256, 258, 260, 269
face-to-face learning approach 381
face-to-face lectures 51, 64, 200, 278
face-to-face lessons 252, 268
face-to-face mode 52, 260, 261
face-to-face modules 70
face-to-face project 257, 260, 261
face-to-face settings 126
face-to-face students 207
face-to-face teaching 366, 369, 382, 385
face-to-face tutorials 252, 267
foreign language 250, 251, 252, 253, 254, 255, 256, 257, 268, 269, 272, 273
foreign language education 250, 251, 252, 253, 254, 255, 269, 272

G

General Post and Telecommunications Company (GPTC) 324
globalisation 11, 16, 18
glocalization 13
Google 54
grade point average (GPA) 205

H

hardware 367, 369
healthcare workforce 205
high-quality learning 54
Hong Kong Institute of Education (HKIEd) 70
human resource 22, 25

I

IAOC framework 258, 259
ICT infrastructure 13
ICT Management 174
ICT tools 278, 280
IDI culture 326
idiosyncrasies 351, 352
informal learning 206, 210, 219, 220, 227
information and communications technologies (ICT) 3, 251, 278, 324
information communications and telecommunication (ICT) infrastructure 326
information technology (IT) 171, 365, 371
inquiry-based learning 233
Institute of Systems Science (ISS) 149
institutions of higher learning (IHE) 307
instructor-centered 117, 118, 119, 122
interaction 301, 313, 315
interactive learning style 287
interactive-publishing online platform 257, 258, 263, 264
intercultural 281, 283, 286, 291, 296, 300
intercultural competences 250, 264, 268, 269
Internet medium 11, 12
Internet resources 170, 176

J

just-in-case basis 4
just-in-case learning 4
just-in-time 4
juxtaposing 357

K

knowledge-based economy 5
knowledge economy 1, 4, 12, 13, 15
Knowledge Engineering (KE) 146
Knowledge Portal (KP) 146
knowledge workers 4
Kolb Learning Style Inventory (KSI) 92

L

learning community 206, 209, 210, 211, 212
learning community model 211

Learning. Distributed learning 71
learning environment 127, 140, 278, 281, 283, 290, 291, 297, 298, 299
learning experience 188, 190, 191, 192, 193, 196, 200, 201
learning management system (LMS) 50, 74, 170, 193, 194, 278
learning management system (LMS) platform 170
learning objects 5, 7
learning outcomes 232
learning program 188, 192, 194, 195, 196, 197, 198, 200, 201
Learning resources 52
learning strategies 251, 253, 255, 256, 266, 267, 268, 269, 272
learning theory 189, 200
lecture-by-lecture notes 71
life-long learning 233
lingua franca 6
linguistic knowledge 250, 252, 253, 266, 268
linguistic phenomena 260
linguistics 366
lumins 232, 236, 238, 239, 240, 241, 242, 244, 246

M

management control 131
Management Information Systems 89, 90
Materials tool 28
MCQ testing 59, 63
mental health 213, 214
mental health issues 213, 214
mental health needs 213, 214
mental model 325, 326, 334
methodology 251
microphones 23
Millennials 311
modern life 250
multicultural 281, 283, 285, 291, 298, 299
multi-cultural country 31
multi-device e-learning systems 255
multidimensional learning process 253
multimedia language learning programs 252
multimedia portfolios 285
multimodal electronic texts 257, 262, 264
multimodal output 233, 234, 236
multimodal reports 258, 261
multi-model structure 345, 358
multiplatforms 252, 255
multiple-choice questions (MCQs) 59
multi-user role-playing 232
multi-user virtual environment (MUVE) 231, 248
Myers Briggs Type Inventory (MBTI) 92, 101
myUnisa 23, 24, 25, 26, 27, 28, 30, 31, 32, 34, 36, 38, 40, 41, 42, 43, 44, 45, 46, 47, 48

N

national culture 1, 10, 11, 281, 283, 289
national educational policy 1
network effects 6
Non-ICT activities 231
non-IT academics 365, 370, 373, 376, 379, 382, 383

O

Observations 191, 192
off-line learning modes 251
one-on-one interaction 288
online collaboration 283, 294, 299
online collaborative 268
online collaborative behaviors 283, 288
online communication 252, 257, 258, 263, 264, 265, 266, 267, 269
online communication 267, 273
online delivery 89, 92, 95, 98, 100, 101, 107, 108
online dictionaries 256, 258, 276
online distance learning 95
online education 112, 113, 121, 122
online environments 302
online global environment 336
online instruction 127
online interaction 257, 258, 268
online learning 70, 72, 73, 74, 75, 76, 77, 81, 82, 84, 85, 86
online learning environments 310
online learning management system 70, 72, 74, 76

online learning resources 255
online platform 257, 258, 263, 264
open-distance-learning model 20
open distance learning (ODL) 20
open educational resources 2, 3, 6, 11, 12, 13
oral presentation 59
Osprey 23, 25, 26, 29, 30, 31, 36, 38, 49

P

participatory learning environments (PLEs) 207
PBL strategy 82
PDS 213, 214
pedagogical framework 33
pedagogy 208, 228, 367, 368, 386
peer collaboration 1
Personal Laptops 211
phonology 253, 255
physical resources 366
podcasts 211, 212, 214
podcast usage 213
policy frameworks 13
policy-makers 1, 3, 13, 14
Postmodernist perspective 6
practice-based simulation 50, 51
print-based mode 71
print-bound media 2
problem-based learning (PBL) 80
problem-solving 245
propositional 2, 4, 5, 10, 12, 15
psychosocial issues 221
psychotherapy 213, 345, 355, 356, 357, 359, 361

Q

Q-Packs 239, 241, 244
Quest Atlantis 231, 232, 236, 237, 238, 243, 244, 247
Quest Atlantis (QA) 231, 232
questionnaire 260, 261, 266
quests 232, 234, 236, 238, 239, 240, 241, 242, 243, 244, 245, 246

R

real-life communication 251
real simple syndicate (RSS) 52
reflection-in-action 190
research based educational intervention 204
Restrictive network bandwidth 33
RSS reader 54

S

school context 250
science, technology, engineering, math (STEM) 205
security awareness 323, 324, 325, 326, 327, 328, 330, 331, 332, 333, 334, 335, 336, 337, 338, 339, 341, 342
self-access 252
self-study 252, 256
shareable content objects (SCOs) 7
Skype 23
social bookmarking systems 171
social connection component 210, 220
social educational goals 3
social engagement 2
social interaction 367
social learning environment 251, 256, 261, 265
social network infrastructure 36
social networks 171, 186
social relation 284
social setting 366
social worker 210, 211
socio-constructivist learning 148
socio-cultural 2, 3, 11, 12, 13
socio-cultural theory 283, 284
socio-economics 346, 348
socio-economic status 231
socio-economic sustainability 349, 352
socio-economic transformation 347
sociolinguistic 250, 254, 261, 262, 264, 265, 269, 272
sociolinguistic 264, 268
sociology 366
software 366, 367, 369, 370
software engineering (SE) 146
sole cultural dimension 336

sophisticated software 366
South African context 38
Spanish Without Walls (SWW) 72
spyware 324
student-centered 118, 148
student-centered learning 366
student-centric programs 222
student-facilitated interactions 165
student learning 112, 113, 114, 123
Student OnLine (SOL) 22
symbol system 193, 194, 200, 201
synchronous textual communication 72
synchronous tools 122
syntax control 256, 267, 268
system design 367

T

technological revolution 301, 302
technology-rich collaborative learning environments 208, 227
technology tools 278
telecommunication 283, 285, 300
telecommunication technologies 283
text-based information 73
Text Message 211
theoretical framework 284
traditional didactic methods 9
tutor system 22
typography 33

U

Unisa 20, 21, 22, 23, 24, 25, 26, 27, 28, 29, 30, 31, 32, 33, 34, 36, 37, 38, 39, 40
University of South Africa (UNISA) 39

V

videoconferencing 252, 267
video sharing platforms 171
virtual angle 55
virtual classroom 131, 132, 137, 144
virtual learning, 113
virtual learning environment 232, 238, 239, 240, 241, 245
virtual presentation 170, 171, 173, 174, 176, 177, 178, 180, 181, 182, 183, 184,
virtual retinoscope 55
virus-like propagation 11
vocabulary knowledge 254
Voice-over Internet protocol (VoIP) 72
vSkype 23

W

Web 2.0 1, 2, 3, 5, 6, 7, 8, 11, 12, 13, 14, 17, 50, 51, 52, 54, 63, 170, 171, 172, 173, 177, 178, 184, 186, 187
Web 2.0 applications 1, 2, 3, 7, 11, 12
Web 2.0 technologies 54, 63
Web 2.0 tools 170, 171, 172, 183, 186
web-based cases 55, 58, 63
Web-based courses 112, 113, 114, 122
Web-based delivery 113
web-based exercise 55
Web-based instructional material 33
web-based interactions 63
web-based learning 113
web-based MCQ 63
web-based resources 54
Web-based tool 25
Web-based training 74
Web-based vendors 6
webcams 23
web, computer mediated communication 254
WebCT 278
Web-enhanced 302
Web-mediated learning environment 50
websites 71, 75, 77, 78, 81, 82
web usability 280, 281
Wikibook 70, 80, 81, 82, 83, 84
Wikibook projects 70, 80, 84
Wikipedia 5, 6, 7, 18
wikis 171
wisdom of crowds 5
word processor 255, 256, 257, 258, 263, 266, 267, 268
workplace behaviours 191
work smart 195
World Wide Web (WWW) 51